Frommer's®

San Diego

20th Edition

by Mark Hiss

WILEY
John Wiley & Sons, Inc.

ABOUT THE AUTHOR

Mark Hiss is a third-generation Southern Californian who has spent more than 25 years in San Diego. He was founding editor of both the visitor guide *Where San Diego* and *Performances*, the playbill magazine for the city's leading performing arts venues. He is also author of *Frommer's San Diego Day by Day*, coauthor of *Frommer's California Day by Day*, and a contributor to *Frommer's California*. In a previous life he was a publicist who worked for several of San Diego's top theater companies.

Published by:

JOHN WILEY & SONS, INC.

111 River St.
Hoboken, NJ 07030-5774

ISBN 978-1-118-33764-6 (paper); ISBN 978-1-118-45300-1 (ebk); ISBN 978-1-118-45301-8 (ebk); ISBN 978-1-118-49051-8 (ebk)

Editor: Stephen Bassman
Production Editor: Lindsay Conner
Cartographer: Andrew Dolan
Photo Editor: Richard Fox
Production by Wiley Indianapolis Composition Services

Front cover photo: The shores of Point Loma. © Brett Shoaf / Artistic Visuals
Back cover photo: Fifth Avenue in the Gaslamp Quarter at night. © Brett Shoaf / Artistic Visuals

For information on our other products and services or to obtain technical support, please contact our Customer Care Department within the U.S. at 877/762-2974, outside the U.S. at 317/572-3993 or fax 317/572-4002.

Wiley also publishes its books in a variety of electronic formats. Some content that appears in print may not be available in electronic formats.

Manufactured in the United States of America

5   4   3   2   1

CONTENTS

List of Maps vi

1 THE BEST OF SAN DIEGO 1

The Most Unforgettable San Diego Experiences 2

The Best Food & Drink Experiences 2

The Best Family Experiences 3

The Best Free & Dirt Cheap San Diego 4

The Best Outdoor Activities 5

The Best Historic Experiences 5

The Best San Diego Museums 6

The Best Ways to See San Diego Like a Local 7

2 SAN DIEGO IN DEPTH 9

San Diego Today 9

The Making of San Diego 10

San Diego in Pop Culture 15

Eating & Drinking in San Diego 18

When to Go 19

SAN DIEGO CALENDAR OF EVENTS 21

Responsible Tourism in San Diego 26

IT'S EASY BEING GREEN 27

3 SAN DIEGO NEIGHBORHOODS & SUGGESTED ITINERARIES 28

City Layout 28

NEIGHBORHOODS IN BRIEF 30

THE BEST OF SAN DIEGO IN 1 DAY 31

OFF THE BEATEN PATH: NORTH PARK & BEYOND 32

THE BEST OF SAN DIEGO IN 2 DAYS 34

THE BEST OF SAN DIEGO IN 3 DAYS 35

4 EXPLORING SAN DIEGO 37

San Diego's Top 15 Sites
& Attractions 37

The Three Major Animal Parks 37

San Diego's Beaches 42

Attractions in Balboa Park 46

*ALL ABOUT BALBOA PARK GUIDED
TOURS* 49

More Attractions 54

Free of Charge &
Full of Fun 66

Especially for Kids 68

Special-Interest Sightseeing 70

Organized Tours 73

Outdoor Activities 77

PADDLING WITH THE FISHES 86

THE BEST OF SAN DIEGO ONLINE 88

Sights & Attractions by Theme
Index 89

5 STROLLING AROUND SAN DIEGO 91

WALKING TOUR 1: THE GASLAMP QUARTER 91

WALKING TOUR 2: THE EMBARCADERO 98

WALKING TOUR 3: OLD TOWN 103

WALKING TOUR 4: BALBOA PARK 107

WALKING TOUR 5: LA JOLLA 114

6 WHERE TO EAT 119

Best Bets 119

PRICE CATEGORIES 119

FUN FOR FOODIES IN SAN DIEGO 120

Downtown, Gaslamp Quarter &
Little Italy 121

ATTACK OF THE KILLER BURGERS 126

Hillcrest & Uptown 127

Old Town & Mission Valley 131

Mission Bay & the Beaches 133

BAJA FISH TACOS 134

La Jolla 138

MEAL WITH A VIEW 142

Coronado 143

Bites Off the (Tourist)
Beaten Path 145

Practical Matters: The Restaurant
Scene 146

Restaurants by Cuisine 147

7 SHOPPING 151

Shopping by Area 151

Shopping A to Z 159

8 ENTERTAINMENT & NIGHTLIFE 167

The Performing Arts 168

The Club & Music Scene 170

*SUDS CITY: GRAB A GREAT BREW IN
S.D.* 176

Gay & Lesbian Nightlife 177

Alternative Entertainment 178

FISHY FUN: THE GRUNION RUN 180

Spectator Sports 180

9 WHERE TO STAY 184

Best Bets 184
PRICE CATEGORIES 184
WHAT YOU'LL REALLY PAY 185
Downtown, Gaslamp Quarter &
   Little Italy 186
Hillcrest & Uptown 196
Old Town & Mission Valley 199

Mission Bay & the Beaches 201
La Jolla 206
*THE ROAD TO WELLNESS: HEALTHFUL
   HAVENS* 212
Coronado 213
THE INDELIBLE HOTEL DEL 214
Practical Information 217

10 SIDE TRIPS FROM SAN DIEGO 220

North County Beach Towns 220
THE HAPPIEST SIDE TRIP ON EARTH 236
North County Inland 237
GRAPE ESCAPE: TEMECULA WINERIES 241
Julian: Gold, Fires, Apples &
   More 242

Anza-Borrego Desert
   State Park 248
Tijuana: Going South of the
   Border 253
STAYING SAFE IN TIJUANA 254

11 PLANNING YOUR TRIP TO SAN DIEGO 270

Getting There 270
TRAVELING WITH PETS 274
Special-Interest Trips & Tours 275

Getting Around 276
FAST FACTS: SAN DIEGO 284

Index 299

Accommodations Index 308

Restaurant Index 309

LIST OF MAPS

Suggested Itineraries   29

San Diego Attractions   39

Balboa Park Attractions   47

Downtown & Beyond Attractions   55

Old Town & Mission Valley Attractions   59

La Jolla Attractions   63

Walking Tour 1: The Gaslamp Quarter   93

Walking Tour 2: The Embarcadero   99

Walking Tour 3: Old Town   105

Walking Tour 4: Balboa Park   109

Walking Tour 5: La Jolla   117

Downtown San Diego Restaurants   123

Hillcrest & Uptown Restaurants   129

Old Town & Mission Valley
    Restaurants   133

Mission Bay & the Beaches
    Restaurants   135

La Jolla Restaurants   139

Coronado Restaurants   144

Downtown San Diego Shopping   153

Hillcrest & Uptown Shopping   155

La Jolla Shopping   157

Downtown San Diego Hotels   187

Hillcrest & Uptown Hotels   197

Old Town & Mission Valley Hotels   200

Mission Bay & the Beaches Hotels   203

La Jolla Hotels   207

Coronado Hotels   215

Northern San Diego County   222

Eastern San Diego County   243

Tijuana   255

HOW TO CONTACT US

In researching this book, we discovered many wonderful places—hotels, restaurants, shops, and more. We're sure you'll find others. Please tell us about them, so we can share the information with your fellow travelers in upcoming editions. If you were disappointed with a recommendation, we'd love to know that, too. Please write to:

Frommer's San Diego, 20th Edition
John Wiley & Sons, Inc. • 111 River St. • Hoboken, NJ 07030-5774
frommersfeedback@wiley.com

ADVISORY & DISCLAIMER

Travel information can change quickly and unexpectedly, and we strongly advise you to confirm important details locally before traveling, including information on visas, health and safety, traffic and transport, accommodation, shopping, and eating out. We also encourage you to stay alert while traveling and to remain aware of your surroundings. Avoid civil disturbances, and keep a close eye on cameras, purses, wallets, and other valuables.

While we have endeavored to ensure that the information contained within this guide is accurate and up-to-date at the time of publication, we make no representations or warranties with respect to the accuracy or completeness of the contents of this work and specifically disclaim all warranties, including without limitation warranties of fitness for a particular purpose. We accept no responsibility or liability for any inaccuracy or errors or omissions, or for any inconvenience, loss, damage, costs, or expenses of any nature whatsoever incurred or suffered by anyone as a result of any advice or information contained in this guide.

The inclusion of a company, organization or website in this guide as a service provider and/or potential source of further information does not mean that we endorse them or the information they provide. Be aware that information provided through some websites may be unreliable and can change without notice. Neither the publisher or author shall be liable for any damages arising herefrom.

FROMMER'S STAR RATINGS, ICONS & ABBREVIATIONS

Every hotel, restaurant, and attraction listing in this guide has been ranked for quality, value, service, amenities, and special features using a **star-rating system.** In country, state, and regional guides, we also rate towns and regions to help you narrow down your choices and budget your time accordingly. Hotels and restaurants are rated on a scale of zero (recommended) to three stars (exceptional). Attractions, shopping, nightlife, towns, and regions are rated according to the following scale: zero stars (recommended), one star (highly recommended), two stars (very highly recommended), and three stars (must-see).

In addition to the star-rating system, we also use **seven feature icons** that point you to the great deals, in-the-know advice, and unique experiences that separate travelers from tourists. Throughout the book, look for:

special finds—those places only insiders know about

fun facts—details that make travelers more informed and their trips more fun

kids—best bets for kids and advice for the whole family

special moments—those experiences that memories are made of

overrated—places or experiences not worth your time or money

insider tips—great ways to save time and money

great values—where to get the best deals

The following abbreviations are used for credit cards:

AE   American Express   DISC   Discover   V   Visa

DC   Diners Club   MC   MasterCard

TRAVEL RESOURCES AT FROMMERS.COM

Frommer's travel resources don't end with this guide. Frommer's website, **www.frommers. com** has travel information on more than 4,000 destinations. We update features regularly, giving you access to the most current trip-planning information and the best airfare, lodging, and car-rental bargains. You can also listen to podcasts, connect with other Frommers.com members through our active-reader forums, share your travel photos, read blogs from guidebook editors and fellow travelers, and much more.

THE BEST OF SAN DIEGO

High-end nightclubs. Adventurous dining. Hypermodern architecture. What happened to that nice little Navy town of San Diego? Well, that sleepy burg has woken up and it wants to party. Growth has been fast and furious over the past 2 decades, and this Southern California city now finds itself with a glittering skyline and a fresh attitude. With its beaches and theme parks, it's still one of the most family-friendly destinations in the United States, but the nearly nightly bacchanalia in the Gaslamp Quarter leaves no doubt that this is not your father's San Diego.

THINGS TO DO San Diego's shining jewel is **Balboa Park** (p. 46), a 1,100-acre oasis in the heart of the city. Featuring meticulously maintained gardens, hiking trails, and recreational opportunities, it's also the nation's largest urban cultural park, the setting for 15 museums. And if that's not enough, the park is where you'll also find the world famous **San Diego Zoo** (p. 40). The city's rollicking downtown **Gaslamp Quarter** (p. 91), highlighted by its dazzling Victorian architecture, is where locals and visitors alike go for shopping, dining, and nightclubbing.

ACTIVE PURSUITS With weather that is almost always pleasant, San Diego is a year-round beach town (though water temperatures can be chilly in winter). With some 70 miles of coastline, there's most likely a beach that's just right for you. Looking for a nonstop party? Join the parade along the **Mission Beach** and **Pacific Beach boardwalk.** Family in tow? **Coronado** is just the place. Trying surfing for the first time? **La Jolla Shores** is forgiving. Au naturel sunbathing? Head to **Black's Beach**. See chapter 4.

RESTAURANTS & DINING The locavore movement is in high gear here, with menus featuring generous portions of San Diego–sourced products, from seafood and beef to fruits and vegetables. Mexican food is a high priority, too, with the humble fish taco—an immigrant from Baja California—solidly entrenched as the city's favorite fast food. On the tonier side are the sumptuous restaurants of La Jolla, including two of the area's signature spots (both featuring stupendous views): **The Marine Room** (p. 138) and **George's at the Cove** (p. 140).

NIGHTLIFE & ENTERTAINMENT San Diego is a capital of American theater, having originated numerous award-winning productions, some of which have ended up on Broadway. Leading the pack are the **Old Globe Theatre** (p. 169) and **La Jolla Playhouse** (p. 168), both Tony Award winners for outstanding regional theater. Those who want to break a sweat on the dance floor need look no farther than the city's nightlife nerve center, the **Gaslamp Quarter.** It offers glitzy dance and supper clubs, as well as bars (from dive to swanky) and live music venues.

THE most UNFORGETTABLE SAN DIEGO EXPERIENCES

- **Escaping to Torrey Pines State Reserve:** Poised on a majestic cliff overlooking the Pacific Ocean, this state park is set aside for the rarest pine tree in North America. The reserve has short trails that immerse hikers in a delicate and beautiful coastal environment that includes one of San Diego's finest beaches. See p. 64.

- **Taking in the City's Best Panorama: Cabrillo National Monument** at the tip of Point Loma offers a breathtaking 360-degree view that takes in downtown, the harbor, military bases, Coronado, and, in the distance, Mexico and San Diego's mountainous backcountry. It's also a great vantage point from which to watch migrating Pacific gray whales in the winter. See p. 54.

- **Strolling Through the Gaslamp Quarter:** You'll be convinced you've stepped back in time when you walk through this 16½-block area lined with Victorian commercial buildings. The beautifully restored structures, in the heart of downtown, house some of the city's most popular shops, restaurants, and nightspots. See "Walking Tour 1: The Gaslamp Quarter," on p. 91.

- **Spending an Idyllic Day in Balboa Park:** San Diego's pride and joy, this is the largest urban cultural park in the nation. The buildings that grew out of Balboa Park's two world's fairs (1915–16, 1935–36) create a vision of Spanish Golden Age splendor and provide a home for 15 museums. The park also features gardens, walking trails, theaters, and recreational facilities, and is the home of the San Diego Zoo. See p. 46.

- **Making a Run for the Border:** What a difference a line makes. Once you cross the world's busiest border, you're instantly immersed in the chaotic vibrancy of Mexico's fourth-largest city. Just a 20-minute drive from downtown, **Tijuana** has a raucous tourist zone with plentiful shopping, as well as an array of cultural and culinary delights. See p. 253.

THE best FOOD & DRINK EXPERIENCES

- **Quaffing Local Beer:** Thanks to its more than 40 breweries, San Diego has been named America's number one beer city by *Men's Journal.* San Diego's king of beers is Stone Brewery, which operates a sensational bistro and beer garden that will leave even teetotalers impressed. Rule of thumb: If you're drinking somewhere that doesn't serve local brews, you're in the wrong place. See p. 176.

o **Toasting the Good Life:** Just across the county line in **Temecula** (p. 241), about 60 miles north of downtown San Diego, are more than 2 dozen wineries. They range from mom-and-pop operations with minimal amenities to slick commercial ventures with fancy tasting rooms, retail boutiques, and restaurants. South of the border and within easy reach is the Napa Valley of Mexico: the **Valle de Guadalupe** (p. 267). It's the country's most important winemaking region, with some 20 wineries.

o **Savoring the Appetizing Views:** Given San Diego's privileged coastal location, it's no wonder there are a number of eateries catering to your eyes as well as your palate. From the aerial vistas provided by 12th-floor **Bertrand at Mister A's** to bayside restaurants like **Island Prime** (p. 142), San Diego's view-enhanced dining destinations are guaranteed to please.

o **Enjoying a Fish Taco:** From surfers to CEOs, San Diegans have embraced the fish taco as the go-to fast food. This regional delicacy originated in the fishing towns of Baja California then immigrated north, becoming popular locally in the 1980s. Nothing tastes more like Southern California than a cold beer and a tangy, messy fish taco. See p. 134.

o **Tucking into Your Just Desserts: Extraordinary Desserts** is San Diego's most loved destination for decadent treats. Whether you stop by the way-cool Little Italy location (which also serves light meals and alcohol), or the cozy original spot in Hillcrest, you are in for a sweet time. See p. 125.

o **Feasting on Real Mexican Food:** San Diego is overflowing with Mexican joints, but why not cross the border for the real deal? From street-corner taco stands to high-end, sophisticated fine dining, **Tijuana's food scene** is as diverse as it is delicious. And compared to San Diego prices, it's a real bargain to boot. See p. 260.

THE best FAMILY EXPERIENCES

o **Communing with Seals at the Children's Pool:** This small cove in La Jolla was originally named for the young bathers who could safely frolic behind a man-made sea wall. These days, seals and sea lions sunning themselves on the sand are the main attraction, providing a unique wildlife experience. See p. 44.

o **Letting Children's Imagination Soar: LEGOLAND** is a 128-acre theme park geared toward ages 2 to 12. Besides intricate LEGO creations ranging from Star Wars characters to international landmarks, it features more than 50 family-friendly rides, hands-on attractions, and shows. There's also an aquarium with real fish and a water park. See p. 229.

o **Parking It:** There are so many family attractions in **Balboa Park,** you could spend your whole trip right here. Among Balboa Park's draws are a classic carousel and miniature train ride, a puppet theater, a model train museum, and a science museum filled with interactive exhibits, as well as an IMAX movie theater. See p. 46.

o **Animal Attractions:** With a lineup like the **San Diego Zoo** (p. 40), the **San Diego Zoo Safari Park** (p. 38), and **SeaWorld** (p. 41), it's easy to put together a memorable, animal-centric holiday. Also not to be overlooked is the excellent

Chula Vista Nature Center (p. 66), set in the wetlands south of downtown. It highlights the flora and fauna native to the San Diego area.

o **Getting Wet & Sandy:** San Diego's 70 miles of coastline provide ample opportunity for a surf-and-sand family outing. From **Coronado's** wide, sandy beach (with the Hotel del Coronado providing a picture-perfect backdrop) to the calm waters and parklike setting of **Mission Bay,** you can indulge in everything from swimming and surfing to kayaking and volleyball. See p. 43.

o **Pretending You're Capt. Jack Sparrow:** The **Maritime Museum** features a collection of classic ships, including the 1863 bark *The Star of India* and a Cold War–era submarine. All the boats can be boarded and toured, and there are also permanent and changing exhibitions about seafaring life; bay cruises are also offered aboard a historic pilot boat. See p. 55.

THE best FREE & DIRT CHEAP SAN DIEGO

o **Old Town State Historic Park:** This free park, California's most-visited state park, re-creates life in early San Diego with costumed docents and museum exhibits in some of the town's original adobe structures. After touring the village setting, stop by one of the several restaurants here for happy hour, or browse through the collection of curio shops. See p. 60.

o **Balboa Park:** Besides the obvious pleasures of admiring the lovely gardens, strolling along the shady trails, and gawking at the grand architecture, Balboa Park also has several notable free attractions. The always-gratis **Timken Museum of Art** (p. 53) houses 600 years of art history, including work by Rembrandt and Rubens, while the **Spreckels Organ Pavilion** has been presenting free Sunday concerts since 1915 (p. 53).

o **U.S. Olympic Training Center:** Some of the country's best athletes are living and training at this facility in Chula Vista, one of three Olympic training centers in the United States. You can take a free self-guided tour or join up with a guided tour, available Saturdays and free of charge. See p. 68.

o **Self-Realization Fellowship Retreat and Hermitage:** This compound in Encinitas, with its distinctive lotus-shaped towers, was built by a yogi in 1937. Its cliffside meditation gardens overlook the Pacific and offer incredible vistas. Visitors are welcome free of charge, and no one will give you a spiritual sales pitch. See p. 228.

o **Chicano Park Murals:** More than 70 works of art grace the support structure of the Coronado Bridge in Barrio Logan's Chicano Park. The images celebrate and honor Latino culture and are considered the largest and most important collection of outdoor murals in the country. See p. 66.

o **Mission Beach/Pacific Beach Boardwalk:** A stroll or bike ride along this beachside pathway provides lovely ocean views, but you may not even notice as you watch the nearly nonstop parade of beach denizens that passes by. This is San Diego's coastal culture in all its glory. See p. 44.

o **Hotel del Coronado:** San Diego's most iconic structure, this fanciful Victorian resort is a National Historic Landmark. Whether you are actually staying here or not, take a self-guided tour through this grande dame, which also happens to front one of the area's best beaches. See p. 213.

○ **Renting Bikes, Skates, or Kayaks at Mission Bay:** Landscaped shores, calm waters, and paved paths make Mission Bay Park an unsurpassed aquatic playground. Encompassing 4,200 acres and featuring 27 miles of bayfront beaches and picnic areas, there's plenty to explore on both land and water. See p. 43.

○ **Getting Some Air:** Sunset hot-air-balloon rides carry passengers over the golf courses and luxury homes of North County; they're topped off by a traditional champagne toast. See p. 77. At the **Torrey Pines Gliderport,** you can step off a cliff and soar like a bird on a tandem paraglider flight, no experience necessary. See p. 84. Or for something with a little more oomph, strap into a World War II aircraft for some aerial acrobatics with **Barnstorming Adventures.** The company also offers scenic coastal tours. See p. 78.

○ **Witnessing the Desert's Spring Fling: Anza-Borrego Desert State Park,** California's largest state park, attracts most of its visitors during the spring wildflower season, when a kaleidoscopic carpet of blooms blankets the desert floor. Others come year-round to hike more than 100 miles of trails. See p. 248.

○ **Paddling with the Fishes:** The calm surfaces and clear waters of the **San Diego– La Jolla Underwater Park** are the ultimate spot for kayaking, snorkeling, or scuba diving. This ecological reserve features sea caves and vibrant marine life, including California's state fish, the electric-orange garibaldi. See p. 61.

○ **Teeing Off at Torrey Pines Golf Course:** These two 18-hole championship courses in La Jolla overlook the ocean and provide players with plenty of challenge. In January, the **Farmers Insurance Open** (formerly known as the Buick Invitational) is held here. The rest of the year, these popular municipal courses are open to everybody. See p. 84.

○ **Cruising San Diego Bay:** Whether it's a weekend-brunch sightseeing tour, a chartered sailboat excursion, or just a water-taxi ride to Coronado, don't miss an opportunity to spend some time on San Diego Bay. Spanish conquistador Sebastián Vizcaíno described it in 1602 as a "port which must be the best to be found in all the South Sea." See p. 79.

○ **Catching a Wave:** Whether you are a novice or pink-eyed veteran, San Diego has a surfing spot for you. Beginners can get lessons and rent gear from various surf shops—which can also outfit you in the latest surf style. If you've ever wondered about the allure of surfing, San Diego is a good place to get your feet wet.

○ **Taking a Hike:** It's easy to get out for a vigorous nature walk or hike in San Diego; in fact there are several superb options within a 20-minute drive of downtown. **Cabrillo National Monument** (p. 54) offers incredible city vistas from its easy Bayside Trail; **Balboa Park** (p. 67) has a surprisingly extensive collection of paths; **Torrey Pines State Reserve** (p. 64) is simply sublime; and **Mission Trails Regional Park** (p. 59) is one of the country's biggest urban parks, featuring more than 40 miles worth of trails.

THE best HISTORIC EXPERIENCES

○ **Old Town: Old Town State Historic Park** (p. 60) is the site of San Diego's original pueblo settlement, and it re-creates the small outpost's early days, from 1821 to 1872. Outside of the park proper but in the Old Town neighborhood are other historical attractions such as the **Whaley House** (p. 60), **Junípero Serra Museum** (p. 58), and **El Campo Santo cemetery** (p. 58).

o **Cabrillo National Monument:** This amazing park not only offers some of the city's grandest views but also a handy historical perspective. There are museum installations covering the arrival of conquistador Juan Rodríguez Cabrillo, as well as exhibits dealing with this strategic location's military history. You can also tour the historic lighthouse built here in 1855. See p. 54.

o **The Embarcadero:** Seafaring history is on prominent display along San Diego's waterfront: From the **Maritime Museum** (p. 55) with its flotilla of historic ships to the floating Naval museum that is the **USS _Midway_** (p. 57). You'll also find a handful of monuments and sculptures saluting the city's military history.

o **Missions:** Several of California's 21 missions are located in San Diego County. The two most prominent are **Mission Basilica San Diego de Alcalá** in Mission Valley (p. 58) and **Mission San Luis Rey de Francia** in Oceanside (p. 234). Both are rich in historical and architectural details.

o **Getting in Touch with Your Pioneer Spirit:** The mountain hamlet of **Julian** was founded as a gold-mining town in the 1860s, but it eventually gained fame for a different kind of mother lode: apples. Today, this rustic community has a distinctly Victorian, Old West charm, redolent of hot apple pies. See p. 242.

o **Balboa Park:** With its fine collection of museums, Balboa Park has plenty to offer history aficionados—from the local focus of the **San Diego History Center** (p. 52) and the **San Diego Hall of Champions Sports Museum** (p. 52), to the more far-ranging emphasis of the **San Diego Air & Space Museum** (p. 51) and the **San Diego Natural History Museum** (p. 53).

o **Gaslamp Quarter:** This National Historic District is a living monument to the city's boomtown past. At the **William Heath Davis House Museum** (p. 57), downtown's oldest surviving structure, you can learn about the history of "New Town" San Diego or join up with a neighborhood walking tour on Saturdays.

THE best SAN DIEGO MUSEUMS

o **Museum of Contemporary Art San Diego:** Not only does it have three distinctive locations (including downtown galleries in an annex of historic Santa Fe Depot and the flagship space overlooking the ocean in La Jolla), MCASD also has an internationally renowned collection of art, plus a full roster of special events. Patrons 25 and under are always free, too. See p. 64.

o **Mingei International Museum:** Dedicated to folk art and crafts from around the globe, this museum (the name of which translates as "art of the people" in Japanese) exhibits works that range from ancient to contemporary, created by artisans both celebrated and anonymous. There's also an excellent gift shop. See p. 50.

o **Museum of Photographic Arts:** MoPA's all-inclusive view of the photographic arts makes way for everything from the earliest daguerreotypes to the latest in cutting-edge digital filmmaking. The museum also features a plush cinema and well-stocked bookstore. See p. 50.

o **Maritime Museum:** This fleet of floating museums is a waterfront highlight, particularly the _Star of India,_ the oldest known sailing ship in the world that still goes to sea. The flotilla also includes a reproduction of an 18th-century frigate that appeared in the Russell Crowe film *Master and Commander*. See p. 55.

o **The San Diego Museum of Art:** Housed in one of Balboa Park's most beautiful buildings, this museum often plays host to blockbuster touring exhibitions. It's also permanent home to some 12,000 pieces of art, including an impressive collection of Latin American and South Asian works. See p. 52.

o **Reuben H. Fleet Science Center:** Kids (and probably you too) will love the interactive galleries here, where you can push, pull, twiddle, and thump various mechanisms, all in service of teaching scientific principles. There's also an IMAX theater showing an assortment of giant-screen films and planetarium shows. See p. 51.

o **San Diego Air & Space Museum:** A must-see for anyone with an interest in aviation or military history. The museum pays tribute to aeronautical heroes and heroines, and features more than 60 aircraft on display (everything from World War II fighters to the Apollo 9 command module). See p. 51.

o **Birch Aquarium at Scripps:** The Scripps Institution of Oceanography operates this top-notch facility, which impresses on multiple levels. It has more than 60 marine-life tanks (including a giant kelp forest), informative museum-style exhibits, a well-stocked gift store, a schedule of off-site outdoor adventures, plus a location with jaw-dropping ocean views. See p. 62.

THE best WAYS TO SEE SAN DIEGO LIKE A LOCAL

o **Hit Some Breweries:** Many of San Diego's breweries and tasting rooms are in out-of-the-way neighborhoods, so a trip to one is guaranteed to have you rubbing elbows with the locals. Don't feel like driving? Hop aboard a brew tour. See p. 176.

o **Get in the Water:** Many San Diegans are just flat-out addicted to the ocean and the beach. If you are in, on, or around the water—whether it's for swimming, surfing, kayaking, or diving—you're halfway to becoming a San Diegan. See Outdoor Activities on p. 77.

o **Get Out of Downtown:** Despite the crowds you may encounter in the Gaslamp Quarter, there are plenty of San Diegans who enjoy the downtown scene about as much as a root canal. Check out the bars and restaurants of burgeoning North Park, where local hipsters and foodies find plenty to love. See p. 127.

o **Bike the Boardwalk:** The Mission Beach/Pacific Beach boardwalk is a paved pathway that parallels the sand for almost 3 miles. A bike ride along its length is a quintessential S.D. experience—one of the best shows in town. And if you want to impress people with how local you are, shout "Left!" to get slowpokes to move out of your way as you pass them on the left. See p. 78.

o **Check Out Local Music:** Whether you want to rock out to an indie band at the **Casbah** (p. 171) or groove to some jazz at **Dizzy's** (p. 171), seeking out local music is a great way to get a real taste of San Diego. And a CD from a San Diego band makes an excellent souvenir.

o **See Some Theater:** San Diegans are justly proud of their live theater. From the big boys, such as the Tony Award–winning **Old Globe** and **La Jolla Playhouse,** to smaller companies, such as **Diversionary Theatre** and **Cygnet Theatre,** you're bound to find something to pique your interest. See p. 168.

o **Root, Root, Root for the Home Team:** Despite the heartbreak and disappointment showered upon the city by its professional football and baseball teams, San Diegans love their Chargers and Padres. Buy some peanuts and Cracker Jack and join the faithful at the "Q" or **PETCO Park.** See p. 180.

SAN DIEGO IN DEPTH

by Maya Kroth

L ocals call it the Sunshine Tax: the willingness we all have to make certain concessions for the privilege of living in the place that's been branded "America's Finest City."

Baseball players and corporate executives accept less money for jobs that might pay more handsomely in places such as Boston or Minneapolis, figuring that a minor salary reduction is a reasonable price to pay for never, ever having to shovel another driveway. In fact, a 2010 Harris Poll found that San Diego was the nation's second-most popular place Americans would like to live in or near (New York City came in number one).

The Sunshine Tax hints at the ethos lying at the heart of San Diego. With 70 miles of pristine coastline and plenty of sunny days, this is a place where play comes first, making a buck second.

Sure, there's industry here. In fact, this is one of the country's leading centers for manufacturing, defense, bioscience, and high tech. But it's the fun stuff that really gets us going, and that's not limited to our most famous attractions (the beach, SeaWorld, the Zoo, and Balboa Park).

Due in part to its diverse topography, with canyons and mesas slicing the area into dozens of discrete pockets, San Diego's identity is hard to sum up in a word. It's a city of villages, as civic planners like to say, and each neighborhood has its own style.

There are the coastal enclaves that could only be found in Southern California, from tony La Jolla by the sea to funky, counterculture Ocean Beach to sleepy Encinitas in North County.

Then there's San Diego's urban side. Though they may not have been much 25 years ago, today downtown's Gaslamp Quarter and East Village vibrate with big-city buzz, while hip uptown spots such as Hillcrest and North Park deliver edgier fashion and culture.

Thanks to growing cultural and dining scenes, unparalleled outdoor activities, sports franchises, and other entertainment options, urban San Diego can now go toe-to-toe with any American metropolis.

SAN DIEGO TODAY

San Diego is a place of many identities and perhaps defines itself most strongly in terms of what it isn't: namely, Los Angeles. Home to Hollywood and much of California's industry, Los Angeles casts a long shadow over its kid sister to the south, a city that once hoped to be Southern

California's dominant metropolis. Today, many natives have come to dislike the City of Angels and all that it stands for. Where career-minded Angelenos have a reputation for wheeling and dealing and superficiality, San Diegans are a laid-back lot who seldom ask, "So, what do you do?"

San Diego's redheaded stepchild identity can trace its roots at least as far back as the 1880s, when the city's sudden and dramatic boom hinged on its hope of becoming the West Coast terminus of the Santa Fe Railway's transcontinental railroad. The city's subsequent cataclysmic bust coincided with the Santa Fe's decision to reroute its line through L.A., making San Diego the end of a spur line and squashing dreams of transforming the city's promising port into the seat of commerce and industry in the Southland.

Just as San Diego is defined, in part, by its northern neighbor, so, too, is it shaped by its sibling to the south. With the world's busiest land-border crossing, San Ysidro, located less than 20 miles south of downtown, San Diego is heavily influenced by Tijuana, and vice versa. Despite nearly 600 miles of fencing and concertina wire running along the southwestern border, language, food, and culture fly back and forth. (People, too: Visitors are often surprised by the yellow freeway signs that caution drivers to watch for families running across the highway.) In fact, the Mexican flag flew over Old Town for a few decades before the Mexican-American War, and for nearly a quarter-century, San Diego was the unofficial capital of Upper (Alta) and Lower (Baja) California.

Almost since the beginning, San Diego's climate and natural endowments have been her principal attractions; today the region's nearly 3 million residents partake in outdoor activities with great gusto. Dramatic topography allows for skiing in the morning and surfing in the afternoon, making San Diego a haven for board sports enthusiasts. Skateboarder Tony Hawk and Olympic snowboarder Shaun White are but a few who cut their teeth—and other parts—in San Diego.

And let's not forget about those legendary waves. Always battling other coastal California towns for the title of "Surf City, USA," San Diego wholeheartedly embraces the surfing lifestyle. The sport's local roots go back as far as 1910; some 58 years later, Tom Wolfe famously documented the scene in his essay, *The Pump House Gang,* which chronicled a group of surfers at La Jolla's **Windansea Beach** (p. 44). Windansea remains a coveted—and crowded—surf break, along with the mellow **Swami's** (p. 230), which gets its name from the **Self-Realization Fellowship and Hermitage** (p. 228), an ashram housed on the bluff above the beach.

Today, San Diego's top industries are defense, manufacturing, tourism, and agriculture, which are bolstered by growing biotechnology and telecommunications sectors. While locally based companies, such as Qualcomm, put San Diego's people to work, the city has many other attributes that attract those who love to play. The temperate climate and nearly 100 golf courses have lured retirees; the numerous colleges and universities—more than a dozen—and raucous nightlife are magnets for students; and attractions including **SeaWorld** (p. 41), **LEGOLAND** (p. 229), and the **San Diego Zoo** and **Zoo Safari Park** (p. 38) draw children and families from all over the globe. It all adds up to a quality of life deemed worthy of a little Sunshine Tax.

THE MAKING OF SAN DIEGO

It's been called the Plymouth Rock of the West Coast, the Naples of America, and America's Finest City. San Diego is a city shaped by individuals, from the Spanish explorers who first "discovered" it to the prescient businessmen who envisioned the booming seaside metropolis it was to become, and the many colorful characters who came in between.

FROM NATIVE TIMES TO THE SPANISH CONQUEST In 2009, excavators unearthed a mammoth skull in downtown San Diego estimated to be 500,000 years old, but the human hunters who followed those mammoths over the Bering Straight into North America probably didn't get here until about 20,000 years ago. The area's earliest cultural group, dated to around 7500 B.C., is the San Dieguito Paleo-Indian, followed a millennium later by the La Jollan, Yuman, and Shoshonean tribes.

By A.D. 1500, some 20,000 Indians were living in thatched huts or caves in about 90 settlements, comprising five tribes: the Luiseño, Cahuilla, Cupeño, Ipai, and Kumeyaay, many of which persist today on reservations, some operating **casinos** (p. 179). These are the people the conquistador Juan Rodríguez Cabrillo encountered when he became the first European to set foot on what is now the West Coast of the United States.

In 1542, Cabrillo sailed from Mexico into what he called "a very good enclosed port"; he named it San Miguel and declared it a possession of the king of Spain. Despite this news, Spain didn't send another explorer back to San Miguel until 1602, when Sebastián Vizcaíno led a 200-man expedition from Acapulco, arriving at a port he called "the best to be found in all the South Sea." Not recognizing (perhaps on purpose) that he had stumbled upon Cabrillo's San Miguel, Vizcaíno renamed the spot San Diego, after his flagship and also in honor of a popular 16th-century saint, San Diego de Alcalá de Henares.

Apparently easily impressed, Vizcaíno went on to discover Monterey Bay, declaring *it* "the best port that could be desired," but Spain again failed to act on its explorers' discoveries, leaving California alone for almost another 100 years.

FROM THE MISSION ERA TO THE MEXICAN-AMERICAN WAR Concerned about protecting its New World territories from a potential Russian encroachment from the north, in 1697 the Spanish authorized the construction of Jesuit missions in Baja California, with designs on employing the assimilated Indians as a defense force.

In 1767, the Jesuits were expelled by California's new governor, Gaspar de Portolà, who sent the Franciscans to take over mission building in Alta California. The Franciscans' leader, Father Junípero Serra, arrived in San Diego in 1769 and founded Alta California's first mission, **Mission Basilica San Diego de Alcalá** (p. 58), on July 16 at what is now called **Presidio Hill,** above present-day **Old Town** (p. 60). Five years later, Father Serra moved the mission to an inland site, and despite being damaged in an Indian revolt in 1775, the mission remains there to this day.

Meanwhile, a military presidio at the mission's original site housed a population of soldiers, civilians, and children that numbered 200 by 1790. By 1800, ships from France, America, and Britain had come to trade for cowhide, otter skins, and beef tallow (later they would make the whalers rich by buying tons of whale oil, along with local wool and honey). In 1821, Mexico won independence from Spain, and California swore its allegiance to the newly formed state. The new government began distributing land grants as compensation for its soldiers, who left the presidio to raise cattle on sprawling backcountry ranchos.

Back in town, the presidio went into precipitous decline, while epidemics of smallpox and malaria vanquished much of the remaining Indian population. Mexico, realizing it could no longer afford to support the missions as the Spanish had done, passed the Secularization Act of 1833, which resulted in the closure of Mission San Diego and the sale of its lands.

The **Mexican-American War** arrived on San Diego's doorstep in December 1846, when the Mexican Californios met General Stephen Kearny's Army troops in a valley northeast of San Diego. Historians disagree about which side actually won the bloody Battle of San Pasqual, as both claimed victory, but the end result is the same: California was eventually ceded to the Americans in the 1848 Treaty of Guadalupe Hidalgo, which relinquished the Southwest to the Union for $15 million.

FROM OLD TOWN TO NEW TOWN Having outgrown and then abandoned the presidio in 1835, settlers began building adobe houses at the foot of Presidio Hill. A few of the original adobes remain, including **Casa de Estudillo** and others that have been restored and preserved in **Old Town State Historic Park** (p. 60). By midcentury, Old Town's diverse population of about 650 included Filipinos, Chinese, East Indians, and Afro-Hispanics, and the community showed early signs of modernity: An overland mail route was established; the *San Diego Herald* newspaper began printing; the first public schoolhouse opened; and in 1856, New York–born businessman and sometime brick-maker Thomas Whaley built the first brick structure in Southern California. The still-standing **Whaley House** (p. 60) functioned not only as the Whaley family residence but also variously as a general store, granary, courthouse, school, and the town's first theater. It's also now often described as one of the country's most haunted houses.

But some had a different vision for the city that was developing in Old Town. The British explorer George Vancouver was, in 1793, perhaps the first to wonder why San Diegans had situated their settlement so far away from what most agreed was a rather wonderful port. In 1850, San Francisco merchant William Heath Davis had a similar idea and purchased 160 acres of bayside land in what was then called "New Town" (present-day **downtown**), about 4 miles south of Old Town. In hopes of luring people and businesses, Davis built a wharf, ordered a handful of prefab saltbox houses shipped in from Maine, and oversaw the opening of two hotels. New Town didn't take off, however, and the experiment was dubbed "Davis's Folly."

NEW TOWN BOOM & BUST Less than 2 decades later, another San Francisco businessman, Alonzo Horton, swooped in and picked up 800 acres in New Town for $265. Within 2 years, he rebuilt Davis's previously destroyed wharf and opened a theater; thanks to aggressive promotion, his downtown lots sold like hotcakes.

The decision to move county records from Old Town to New Town in 1871 signaled the direction the city was moving. Old Town's fate was sealed when it was swept by a devastating fire in 1872, followed 2 years later by a massive flood.

San Diego's population had already quadrupled (to about 2,300) by 1870, but that was nothing compared to the boom that was coming. Gold was discovered in the nearby **Julian** hills (p. 242) in 1870, and, in 1873, construction began on an eastward transcontinental railroad line from San Diego. A stock market panic put the kibosh on that project, but by 1885 the first train from the east finally reached the city.

This touched off "the great boom," as speculators realized the commercial potential of combining San Diego's unparalleled port with the railroad's ability to transport goods eastward. A rate war broke out between rival rail lines in 1887, bringing the cost of a westward ticket down from $125 to $1. This brought even more boomers out west, not only to speculate on land but also to partake of the fresh air and whatever it was in the water that was making the local Indians live to 135, as reports of the day claimed.

The 1880s were, by all accounts, a wild time in San Diego. New Town filled with traveling circuses and minstrel shows, with gambling halls and at least 60 saloons, plus more than 100 houses of ill repute, employing hundreds of painted ladies in the **"Stingaree"** district. (The present-day Stingaree nightclub [p. 175] pays homage to the old red-light district.) The boom years brought a variety of notable characters to town, including Wild West lawman Wyatt Earp, who ran three gambling parlors, "Buffalo" Bill Cody, and Ulysses S. Grant, Jr., the president's son.

New Town wasn't the only neighborhood to develop; enclaves such as **La Jolla** (p. 206), **Ocean Beach** (p. 43), and **Pacific Beach** (p. 44) also began to take shape. The northern village of **Carlsbad** (p. 227) boomed, too, when former sea captain John Frazier dug a freshwater well and began touting the healing powers of the mineral water. Midwesterners Elisha S. Babcock and H. L. Story bought and developed the peninsula across the bay from New Town, renaming it Coronado and opening the storybook **Hotel del Coronado** (p. 213) in 1888. The $1.5-million lodge became the world's largest resort hotel, famous for its now-iconic red turrets.

When a San Francisco sugar baron named John D. Spreckels began investing in San Diego—notably in public transit—it became clear that Alonzo Horton's New Town was growing into a full-fledged city.

The population soared to 50,000, but by 1888 the real estate boom had ended, and a nationwide depression sent more than half those fortune seekers back home. The railroads, meanwhile, had quietly moved their operations northward, leaving San Diego merely the end of a spur line from L.A. rather than the transcontinental terminus it had hoped to be. Ironically, in 1919 San Diego would finally get its railroad—just in time for the rising popularity of the automobile to make it nearly obsolete.

EMBRACING TOURISM Perhaps resigned to the notion that it had lost the battle to become California's industrial capital, San Diego turned its attention to tourism. Capitalizing on the completion of the Panama Canal, the city organized the **Panama-California Exposition** of 1915 in its newly flowering crown jewel, **Balboa Park** (p. 46), the 40×40-acre parkland plot designated by Alonzo Horton back in 1868 and later developed by botanist Kate O. Sessions. The iconic **Botanical Building** (p. 48) was constructed, along with a Japanese temple, an outdoor pipe-organ pavilion, and many other buildings. The animals brought in for the exposition remained even after the fair closed, becoming the first residents of the **San Diego Zoo** (p. 38).

A second fair in 1935 showcased curiosities including a nudist colony (now the Zoro Garden butterfly habitat) and "Midget Village," which advertisements described as a display "built on doll-house scale, where more than 100 Lilliputians will work and play." Meanwhile, the fair also showed off the newly built Fine Arts Gallery (now **San Diego Museum of Art,** p. 52), **Natural History Museum** (p. 53), and **Old Globe Theatre** (p. 169).

The park's Spanish Revival architecture seen today was conceived in an effort to present San Diego as a place with a romantic European heritage. Promotional literature dubbed the city the "Naples of America" and exalted its fine Mediterranean climate.

The fairs showed the world that San Diegans were living the good life. Not even Prohibition could dampen spirits in the newly minted Shangri-La, for all the legal drinking one desired could be had just south of the border in Tijuana. With a new racetrack, golf course, resort hotel, casino, and spa, Tijuana became a playground for the Hollywood set—and San Diego its gateway.

By the 1930s, booze was back in vogue and San Diego had its own world-class horse-racing facility in the **Del Mar Racetrack** (p. 182). Founder Bing Crosby himself was there to greet the track's first guests at the gate on opening day in 1937.

THE MILITARY BUILDS A HOME Military defense, a leading industry in San Diego for more than a half-century, began at least as far back as 1796, with the Spaniards' construction of Fort Guijarros (at present-day Point Loma) to defend the port from foreign ships.

In 1911, aviator Glenn Hammond Curtiss established a flight school on Coronado's **North Island** and invited the Army and Navy there to train for free. With the onset of World War I in 1917, the government purchased North Island, which, by then, had already been in use by the Army, Navy, and Marines. The Navy relocated its Pacific Fleet to San Diego in 1919.

North Island's aviation activity continued after the war, too, most notably when a young pilot named **Charles Lindbergh** hired San Diego's Ryan Aeronautical Company to manufacture a special plane of his own design, called the *Spirit of St. Louis*. On May 10, 1927, Lindbergh left North Island for New York on a test flight, setting a transcontinental record in the process. Ten days later, he flew from New York to Paris, becoming the first pilot to make a solo nonstop flight across the Atlantic. San Diego's airport, **Lindbergh Field** (p. 270), pays homage to the flying legend.

San Diego became a key part of U.S. military strategy after the bombing of Pearl Harbor during World War II underscored the Pacific Coast's vulnerability to attack. Giant underwater nets crisscrossed the bay to ward off Japanese subs, while nearly 2,000 Japanese-Americans from San Diego were held at internment camps, such as Manzanar, at the foot of the Sierra Mountains.

Today, military history is honored at the **USS *Midway*** (p. 57), an aircraft carrier museum stationed on the waterfront. Commissioned in 1945 and still active during Desert Storm in 1991, the *Midway* is the world's longest-serving aircraft carrier.

THE RISE OF THE SUBURBS & THE MALL THAT CHANGED EVERYTHING
With suburbanization taking root in America in the wake of the war, neighborhoods with names such as Clairemont Hills flourished outside the center of the city, while San Diego's downtown core was left to decay.

When a few national magazines suggested San Diego had again gone bust, the city renewed its attempts to restore its former glory. The next decade saw several big-city developments, including the construction of new downtown high-rises and the addition of a **symphony** (p. 169), **opera** (p. 170), and major-league sports franchises. By the late '60s, the American Football League's **Chargers** (p. 181) and Major League Baseball's **Padres** (p. 180) were playing at a shiny new stadium in Mission Valley, and **SeaWorld** (p. 41) had opened on Mission Bay.

Trivia: Segregated No More

On January 5, 1931, trustees at Lemon Grove Grammar School instructed Principal Jerome Green to turn Mexican children away at the door, resulting in a lawsuit. The "Lemon Grove Incident" became the first successful school desegregation court decision in U.S. history.

The postwar years also saw the flowering of new education and research institutes, including the public **University of California, San Diego;** the Catholic **University of San Diego;** and the **Salk Institute** (p. 62), founded by polio vaccine developer Jonas Salk. These joined the already-established **Scripps Institution of Oceanography** (p. 62) and San Diego's State Teachers' College (later renamed **San Diego State University**).

Despite civic and cultural improvements, downtown—still overrun with porn theaters, strip clubs, flophouse hotels, and dive bars—was decidedly unbefitting of California's second-largest city. But the 1984 construction of the kaleidoscopic, carnivalesque **Horton Plaza** (p. 152) shopping center, named for founding father Alonzo Horton, kicked off urban renewal in San Diego. Downtown's seedy elements were eradicated, and the quirky, colorful, multilevel mall now anchors the vibrant **Gaslamp Quarter** (p. 54) entertainment district.

The construction of a new baseball stadium east of the Gaslamp Quarter further invigorated downtown. When **PETCO Park** (p. 180) opened in 2004, the surrounding neighborhood (dubbed the **East Village,** p. 54) began to gentrify, with restaurants, galleries, and boutiques replacing industrial warehouses.

Another downtown real estate boom spurred the construction of thousands of apartments and condos, but when the bubble burst a few years ago, developers found themselves with a surplus inventory. Though San Diego was among the economies hit hardest by the crash, it's hard not to sense the opportunity in today's downtown air, and ponder for a moment what someone like Alonzo Horton might do in this situation.

SAN DIEGO IN POP CULTURE

Literature

San Diego's sparkling shores have stirred many a scribe, dating back at least to 19th-century novelist **Helen Hunt Jackson,** whose *Ramona* many agree was inspired by her stay at Rancho Guajome, near Oceanside. It's often cited as the first novel about life in Southern California.

L. Frank Baum, author of *The Wizard of Oz,* began wintering on Coronado in the early 20th century and wrote a few of his *Oz* stories there. Though unnamed, some of the fictional villages in his stories are thought to be thinly veiled depictions of La Jolla.

Later, La Jolla was home to pulp novelist **Raymond Chandler.** His last novel, 1958's *Playback,* finds his hero, Philip Marlowe, tracking Betty Mayfield to the fictional town of Esmeralda, another La Jolla stand-in. (The crime novel continues to be a popular form for San Diegans: Contemporary authors **Don Winslow** and **Joseph Wambaugh** both work in the genre.)

Around the same time Chandler was writing *Playback,* another La Jolla resident, Theodor Seuss Geisel, better known simply as **Dr. Seuss,** published the legendary children's book *The Cat in the Hat.* Geisel later skewered his uppity neighbors in *The Sneetches.*

In the 1960s, **Tom Wolfe** showed a different side of La Jolla in *The Pump House Gang.* Written in Wolfe's "New Journalism" style, the piece offered a portrait of the surf scene centered at Windansea Beach.

Music

San Diego's musical tradition was greatly enriched by the closing of New Orleans's red-light district Storyville in 1917; that brought many Big Easy jazz cats out west, including composer and pianist **Jelly Roll Morton,** who had a regular gig at the US GRANT hotel until he quit upon learning his group was being paid less than the white house-band.

Tom Waits and **Frank Zappa** were two of the bigger artists to come out of San Diego in the '60s and '70s; Waits even spent some time working as a doorman of a Mission Beach nightclub before moving to Los Angeles and releasing *Closing Time* in 1973. During that era, San Diego–based hard rock band **Iron Butterfly** released *In-A-Gadda-Da-Vida,* which was given the industry's first platinum award. Down in Mexico, a young **Carlos Santana** was sharpening his guitar chops in the bars of Tijuana.

In the 1990s, San Diego talents were represented in genres as diverse as folk, grunge, and punk rock. One-named songstress **Jewel** famously lived in a van while gigging at local coffeehouses, while **Eddie Vedder** lived in San Diego before moving to Seattle to front Pearl Jam. Poway's **blink-182** got famous on the back of skate-rock anthems such as "What's My Age Again?" and "All the Small Things."

Contemporary mainstream artists include pop singer **Jason Mraz,** bluegrass trio **Nickel Creek,** soulful surf-rockers **Switchfoot,** and *American Idol* product **Adam Lambert.**

San Diego in Song

When a couple of Russian dignitaries
are on vacation from their land
If they want to live in the style they're
used to, which they claim is very grand
Do they go to Marseille or Arugala Bay
or some far away archipelago?
Nah, they go to San Diego
Dan-dan-dandy San Diego where the
sweet perfume of the waterfront fills
the air

—Mel Tormé, "They Go to San Diego," 1949

Film & Television

San Diego's involvement with the film industry dates back to the earliest days of silent films. Perhaps the most enduring feature to be shot in San Diego, though, was Billy Wilder's 1959 film ***Some Like It Hot,*** which starred Jack Lemmon, Marilyn Monroe, and Tony Curtis, and was filmed at the Hotel del Coronado.

In 1986, ***Top Gun*** told the story of Lt. Pete "Maverick" Mitchell (played by Tom Cruise), a hotshot pilot at the flight school at Miramar. Downtown restaurant Kansas City Barbeque was the backdrop for several scenes; despite suffering a fire in 2008, restaurant owners managed to salvage the piano used by Goose and Maverick to sing "Great Balls of Fire."

Writer/director Cameron Crowe based his rock-'n'-roll coming-of-age picture *Almost Famous* on his own experiences as a 15-year-old rock critic in San Diego. The cross-border drug trade has inspired many set-in-San Diego productions, including *Traffic,* which won an Oscar for director Steven Soderbergh, and the TV series *Weeds,* starring Mary-Louise Parker. Will Ferrell's 1970s-newscaster spoof *Anchorman* remains one of the most often-quoted films among a certain generation of San Diegans. (Demure types are advised to cover their ears should someone start explaining what "San Diego" means in German.)

The list of actors who were born or lived in San Diego includes Annette Bening, Cameron Diaz, Ted Danson, Robert Duvall, Dennis Hopper, Whoopi Goldberg, Gregory Peck, and Raquel Welch, among many others.

Theater

San Diego's theater scene is lively and sophisticated, and it is considered one of the country's major theater scenes. The top regional houses (The Old Globe and La Jolla Playhouse) have originated a number of plays and musicals that went on to success on the Great White Way and beyond. Among these are *Thoroughly Modern Millie, The Who's Tommy, Jersey Boys,* and *Memphis,* which all originated at the La Jolla Playhouse (p. 168). The Old Globe Theatre's (p. 169) contributions include *The Full Monty, Dirty Rotten Scoundrels, Into the Woods,* a 1993 revival of *Damn Yankees,* and holiday favorite *Dr. Seuss' How the Grinch Stole Christmas!* A healthy independent scene is fueled by numerous small companies presenting work for every taste year-round, while the University of California, San Diego has a top professional training program for actors and playwrights alike.

Sports

Legendary baseball player and Hall of Famer **Ted Williams** was a product of San Diego's Hoover High School. Williams played for the minor-league precursor to today's San Diego Padres in 1936 before moving on to the Boston Red Sox and becoming one of the best hitters in history. Hall of Famer **Tony Gwynn** was a Padre throughout his 20-year career. Phillies pitcher and 2008 World Series MVP **Cole Hamels** was also born in San Diego.

Olympic diver **Greg Louganis** hails from here, as does basketball Hall of Famer **Bill Walton** and champion golfer **Phil Mickelson.** Famous footballers include **Marcus Allen, Reggie Bush,** and **Marshall Faulk,** among others. Still, talk to San Diego sports fans for any length of time and you'll quickly notice a certain commonality: pessimism. This is an outgrowth, no doubt, of the sad reality that no local sports team has ever won a major championship (but it must be said the Chargers came out on top in 1963 when they played in the upstart AFL, and the **San Diego Sockers** have won more than 10 indoor soccer titles). In 2009, championship fever gripped the city when the **Park View Little League All-Stars** defeated Chinese Taipei to

---

Trivia: Home-Field Advantage

In October 2007, firestorms swept Southern California. In San Diego, some half-million people were forced to evacuate their homes, part of the largest such order in state history. More than 10,000 took shelter at Qualcomm Stadium where volunteers provided everything from massages to live music.

win the Little League World Series. The team of 12- and 13-year-olds from the South Bay city of Chula Vista became the toast of the town in the process.

EATING & DRINKING IN SAN DIEGO

Some time ago, "San Diego cuisine" meant tacos, burgers, and whatever else could be scarfed at the beach without utensils and washed down with a can of beer. But the city's culinary scene has come a long way in recent years, and modern San Diego boasts fine restaurants and sophisticated food.

Increasing numbers of young, ambitious chefs have set up shop here, attracted by the plentiful, high-quality local produce and fresh seafood. Some find the more laid-back, less cutthroat culinary landscape a great place to experiment with anything from molecular gastronomy to nouvelle French. Throughout the city you'll also find traditional Italian trattorias, old-school steakhouses, lavish Indian buffets, incredible sushi bars, and Spanish tapas restaurants, not to mention spots offering authentic Afghan, Ethiopian, Russian, and, of course, Mexican food. As for homegrown cuisine, here's a look at what you'll find on the menu in San Diego.

> ### Trivia: Fast-Food Fact
>
> In 1951, Robert Oscar Peterson founded the fast-food chain **Jack in the Box** here, opening a drive-through restaurant at 63rd Street and El Cajon Boulevard, near San Diego State University. A hamburger cost 18¢.

Fruits of the Sea

Though much restaurant seafood comes from other places, this town still manages to turn out some of the freshest, whether it be from Alaska or Australia. Local waters produce a variety of fish and shellfish, including **halibut, yellowtail tuna, swordfish, prawns,** and **uni (sea urchin)**. In fall, **spiny lobster** pops up on menus up and down the coast; local lobster differs from its East Coast cousins in that it's smaller and doesn't have claws. The **fish taco,** rumored to have been imported from Mexico by local surfers, is the city's unofficial signature dish; it's practically criminal to leave town without sampling at least one. The fish can be any variety, often mahimahi, which is grilled or deep-fried, topped with shredded cabbage and a creamy sauce, and tucked inside a corn tortilla with a lime wedge. Perfection.

From the Farm to the Table

Don't be surprised to see many restaurant menus crediting farms by name for everything from the pork loin to the baby lettuce. The provenance of produce, meat, and other edibles is taken seriously in this town, especially given the growing "locavore" movement. Eating locally is a pleasure in agriculturally blessed San Diego, whose soil has historically produced excellent **strawberries, grapes, walnuts, corn, tomatoes,** and other crops. Today, we're one of the nation's leading producers of **avocados.** Chefs in the burgeoning farm-to-table movement have taken note, and even California cuisine icons such as Alice Waters and Wolfgang Puck are known to source some ingredients from San Diego. In addition to fruits and veggies, many chefs are also using **pork, beef,** and **dairy** products from local ranches.

Comida De Mexico, Old & New

Without a doubt, what's missed most by those who've left San Diego is the Mexican food. It's hardly an exaggeration to say there's a taco shop on every corner, serving traditional dishes such as **tacos, burritos,** *tortas* (Mexican sandwiches), **tostadas,** and **quesadillas.** Among the regional favorites are *carnitas,* delectable chunks of slow-cooked pork, and the unusual **California burrito,** a giant flour tortilla stuffed with *carne asada* (beef), cheese, guacamole, and french fries. South of the border, chefs are offering an elevated fusion cuisine known as **"Baja Med."** Bearing little resemblance to the familiar food of mainland Mexico, Baja Med, as its name implies, combines Baja ingredients such as tomatoes, olives, and tuna with Mediterranean techniques and flavor profiles.

What to Wash It all Down With

Beer! San Diego is one of the **craft brewing** (p. 176) capitals of the world. The birthplace of "double IPA" (a strong, hoppy India Pale Ale), the region is home to more than 40 boutique breweries that churn out a variety of beers, from no-nonsense, hops-filled brews to delicate fruit-flavored ones. Some San Diego breweries have tasting rooms and offer tours of their facilities; others merely distribute their suds to the many **beer bars** (p. 173) around town. Just across the border, the **Tecate brewery,** in the town of the same name, brews a lighter quaff and also offers tours and tastings, while **Cervecería Tijuana** (p. 265) is a brewery, restaurant, and nightspot.

There are also two **wine regions** within an hour's drive of downtown. The **Temecula Valley** (p. 241) northeast of San Diego grows more than 40 different varietals and is home to more than 30 wineries. South of the border, northern Baja's wine country is tucked into the **Guadalupe Valley** (p. 267) east of Ensenada. Baja produces 90% of Mexico's wine, notably at large-scale producers such as L.A. Cetto, but there are more than 20 smaller wineries that produce anywhere from 500 to 40,000 cases per year. Top varietals in the valley include tempranillo, cabernet franc, nebbiolo, chenin blanc, and more.

Back in central San Diego, a new **wine bar** seems to crop up weekly, each offering convenient and often affordable ways to sample local and international wines by the glass.

WHEN TO GO

San Diego is blessed with a mild climate, low humidity, and good air quality. In fact, Pleasant Weather Rankings, published by Consumer Travel, ranked San Diego's weather number two in the world. It's worth keeping in mind, though, that San Diego County covers more than 4,500 square miles and rises in elevation from sea level to 6,500 feet. It can be a pleasant day on the coast but blisteringly hot on the inland mesas; or it can be a foggy day at the beach but gloriously sunny just minutes away downtown.

With its coastal setting, the city of San Diego maintains a moderate climate. Although the temperature can change 20° to 30°F between day and evening, it rarely reaches a point of extreme heat or cold; daytime highs above 100°F (38°C) are unusual, and the mercury dropping below freezing can be counted in mere hours once or twice each year. San Diego receives very little precipitation (just 10 in. of rainfall in an average year); what rain does fall comes primarily between November and April, and by July, the hillsides start to look brown and parched. It's not unusual for the city to go without measurable precipitation for as long as 6 months in the summer and fall.

Perhaps the best time of year in San Diego is the fall. The days are still warm (even hot), and the cool nights remind you that yes, even in Southern California, there is a change of seasons. February and March are also beautiful periods when the landscapes are greenest and blooming flowers at their peak, although it's still too cold for all but the heartiest people to go into the ocean without a wetsuit. Beachgoers should note that late spring and early summer tanning sessions are often compromised by a local phenomenon called **May Gray** and **June Gloom**—a layer of low-lying clouds or fog along the coast that doesn't burn off until noon (if at all) and returns before sunset. Use days like these to explore inland San Diego, where places such as the Zoo Safari Park are probably warm and clear.

A more unpredictable Southern California phenomenon is the hot, dry winds known as **Santa Anas.** They usually hit a couple times a year, typically between September and December, and can last for several days. These desiccating winds heighten wildfire danger and can be a backcountry firefighter's worst nightmare, but Santa Anas invariably bring warm temperatures and crystal-clear skies. Occurring irregularly every 2 to 7 years, the **El Niño** weather pattern—storms created by a warming of Pacific Ocean waters—can cause unusually heavy winter rains. A 1988 El Niño storm even toppled a research platform off Mission Beach (it can now be explored by divers as part of San Diego's Wreck Alley, p. 86).

San Diego is busiest between Memorial Day and Labor Day. The kids are out of school and *everyone* wants to be by the seashore; if you visit in summer, expect fully booked beachfront hotels and crowded parking lots. The week of the July 4th holiday is a zoo at Mission Beach and Pacific Beach—you'll either love it or hate it. But San Diego's popularity as a convention destination and its temperate year-round weather keep the tourism business steady the rest of the year, as well. The only slow season is from Thanksgiving to early February. Hotels are less full, and the beaches are peaceful and uncrowded; the big family attractions are still busy on weekends, though, with residents taking advantage of holiday breaks. A local secret: Although they're in the coolest, rainiest season (relatively speaking, anyway), November through February are also the sunniest months of the year.

Average Monthly Temperatures (°F & °C) & Rainfall (in.)

	JAN	FEB	MAR	APR	MAY	JUNE	JULY	AUG	SEPT	OCT	NOV	DEC
HIGH (°F)	65	66	66	68	69	72	76	77	77	74	71	66
(°C)	18	18	18	20	20	22	24	25	25	23	21	18
LOW (°F)	48	50	52	55	58	61	65	66	65	60	53	49
(°C)	8	10	11	12	14	16	18	18	18	15	11	9
RAINFALL	2.2	1.6	1.9	0.8	0.2	0.1	0	0.1	0.2	0.4	1.1	1.4

Holidays

Banks, government offices, post offices, and many stores, restaurants, and museums are closed on the following legal national holidays: January 1 (New Year's Day), the third Monday in January (Martin Luther King, Jr., Day), the third Monday in February (Presidents' Day), the last Monday in May (Memorial Day), July 4 (Independence Day), the first Monday in September (Labor Day), the second Monday in October

(Columbus Day), November 11 (Veterans' Day/Armistice Day), the fourth Thursday in November (Thanksgiving Day), and December 25 (Christmas). The Tuesday after the first Monday in November is Election Day, a federal government holiday in presidential-election years (held every 4 years, and next in 2016).

San Diego Calendar of Events

You might want to plan your trip around one of these annual events in the San Diego area (including the destinations covered in chapter 10, "Side Trips from San Diego"). For an exhaustive list of events beyond those listed here, check http://events.frommers.com, where you'll find a searchable, up-to-the-minute roster of what's happening in cities all over the world.

JANUARY

San Diego Restaurant Week encourages diners to check out some of San Diego's best eateries. For 2 weeks, more than 180 restaurants offer special three-course prix-fixe meals. A second Restaurant Week is held in mid-September. For details, go to www.sandiegorestaurantweek.com. Mid- to late January.

The **Carlsbad Marathon & Half Marathon** takes place along a scenic coastal route in San Diego's North County. For more information, call ✆ **760/692-2900**, or visit www.carlsbadmarathon.com. Late January.

Farmers Insurance Open, Torrey Pines Golf Course, La Jolla. This PGA Tour classic, formerly known as the Buick Invitational, draws more than 100,000 spectators each year and features 150 of the finest professional golfers. For information, call ✆ **858/886-4653,** or see www.farmersinsuranceopen.com. Late January.

FEBRUARY

Wildflowers bloom in the desert between late February and the end of March, at Anza-Borrego Desert State Park. Timing varies from year to year, depending on the winter rainfall (see "Anza-Borrego Desert State Park," in chapter 10). For details, call ✆ **760/767-4684,** or go to www.theabf.org.

Mardi Gras in the Gaslamp Quarter is downtown's largest event. This "Fat Tuesday" party features a Mardi Gras parade, live bands and DJs, and plenty of special deals from participating clubs and restaurants. This is a ticketed event for ages 21 and older. For more information, call ✆ **619/233-5227,** or visit www.gaslamp.org. February 12, 2013; March 4, 2014.

MARCH

Kiwanis Ocean Beach Kite Festival. For more than 60 years, the skies over the Ocean Beach Recreation Center have gotten a brilliant shot of color during this kite-flying contest. Festivities include a street fair, live music, and kite making. For more information, see www.oceanbeachkiwanis.org. First Saturday in March.

The **San Diego Latino Film Festival,** one of the largest and most successful Latino film events in the country, features more than 100 movies from throughout Latin America and the United States. Call ✆ **619/230-1938,** or surf to www.sdlatinofilm.com. Mid-March.

St. Patrick's Day Parade, Hillcrest. A tradition since 1980, the parade starts at Sixth Avenue and Juniper Street. An **Irish Festival** follows in Balboa Park. Call ✆ **858/268-9111,** or check www.stpatsparade.org. The Saturday closest to March 17.

Flower fields in bloom at Carlsbad Ranch. One of North County's most spectacular sights is the yearly blossoming of a sea of bright ranunculuses each spring. Visitors are welcome to tour the fields off I-5 (at the Palomar Airport Rd. exit). For more information, call ✆ **760/431-0352,** or go to www.theflowerfields.com. Early March to mid-May.

APRIL

San Diego Crew Classic, Crown Point Shores, Mission Bay. Since its launch in 1973, this has grown into one of the great rowing events in the country, drawing collegiate teams and clubs from throughout the U.S.

Call ✆ **619/225-0300,** or check out www.crewclassic.org. First weekend in April.

Gran Fondo San Diego is a festive, Euro-style biking event through the streets of San Diego. Italian for "big ride," the Gran Fondo starts, appropriately enough, in Little Italy and has courses that cover 105 miles (the Gran Fondo) and 60 miles (the Medio Fondo). There's also an expo, prizes, and post-race party. Check www.granfondosandiego.com for information. Mid-April.

Coronado Flower Show weekend, Spreck-els Park. Organizers claim this is the largest tented flower show in the United States. The weekend-long event includes plant sales, food, and a lineup of entertainment. Go to www.coronadoflowershow.org for more details. Mid-April.

Adams Avenue Unplugged, Normal Heights and Kensington. This 2-day acoustic music festival is held in more than 30 venues and community stages along 2 miles of Adams Avenue. It's free to the public and also fea-tures an open-air market with arts-and-crafts vendors. Call ✆ **619/282-7329,** or stop by www.adamsavenuebusiness.com. Late April.

ArtWalk, Little Italy, along Kettner Boule-vard and India Street. This weekend-long festival is now the largest art event in the San Diego/Tijuana region. For more information, call ✆ **619/615-1090,** or visit www.missionfederalartwalk.org. Late April.

Day at the Docks, Harbor Drive and Scott Street, Point Loma. This sportfishing tourna-ment and festival features food, entertain-ment, fishing contests, seminars, and free boat tours and rides. Call ✆ **619/234-8793,** or see www.sportfishing.org. Mid-April.

Del Mar National Horse Show. This is the first event in the Del Mar racing season and is held at the famous Del Mar Fairgrounds. The field at this show includes Olympic-cali-ber and national championship horse-and-rider teams. Call ✆ **858/792-4252,** or visit www.delmarnational.com. Mid-April to early May.

Lakeside Rodeo. You won't forget you're way out West at this down-home rodeo held in East County. From barrel racing to bull riding, this is the real deal. For information, call ✆ **619/561-4331,** or go to www.lakesiderodeo.com. Late April.

Mainly Mozart Festival, Gaslamp Quarter. Presenting the work of Mozart and his con-temporaries, this acclaimed classical music festival features an all-star orchestra consist-ing of players drawn from around the world. For information, call ✆ **619/239-0100,** or go online at www.mainlymozart.org. Late April through mid-June.

MAY

Fiesta Cinco de Mayo, Old Town. Uni-formed troops march and guns blast to mark the 1862 triumph of Mexican soldiers over the French at the battle of Puebla. Latino culture is celebrated with plentiful food, drink, and entertainment. (**Hint:** Take the trolley and make dining reservations well in advance.) Admission is free. Call ✆ **619/291-4903,** or visit www.oldtownsandiego.org. Weekend closest to May 5.

Gator by the Bay, Harbor Island. Let the good times roll at this annual zydeco and blues music festival. In addition to the music, the festival features Cajun food and cooking demonstrations, dances, and a variety of exhibitors and vendors. Call ✆ **619/234-8612,** or go to www.gatorbythebay.com for more details. Mid-May.

Carlsbad Spring Village Faire, Grand Ave-nue, from Carlsbad Boulevard to Jefferson Street. This event is billed as the biggest and best arts-and-crafts fair in Southern Califor-nia. Call ✆ **760/931-8400** for more details, or go to www.carlsbad.org. Early May (a fall festival is also held in Nov).

JUNE

The **Rock 'n' Roll Marathon and Half Mara-thon** not only offers runners a unique course through Balboa Park, downtown, and around Mission Bay, but it also pumps them (and spectators) up with live bands on 26 stages along the course. There is a prerace fitness expo and post-race concert, featuring big-name talent. Call ✆ **800/311-1255,** or go online at www.san-diego.competitor.com. Early June.

Old Globe Summer Shakespeare Festival, Balboa Park. The Bard takes center stage with several different works staged at the Tony Award–winning Old Globe's open-air theater. Produced in true repertory style, shows alternate each night, performed by the same company of actors. Call ☏ **619/234-5623,** or visit www.theoldglobe. org. Early June through September.

San Diego County Fair. Referred to by locals as the Del Mar Fair, this is the *other* major happening—besides horse racing—at the Del Mar Fairgrounds. In addition to live-stock competitions, thrill rides, flower-and-garden shows, and more, there are also concerts by name performers (some require a separate admission). The fair lasts more than 3 weeks. Call ☏ **858/793-5555,** or visit www.sdfair.com. Early June to early July.

Summer Organ Festival, Balboa Park. These free concerts at the Spreckels Organ Pavilion take place on Monday evenings (year-round there are free concerts on Sun at 2pm). Call ☏ **619/702-8138,** or go to www. sosorgan.com. Mid-June to late August.

San Diego Symphony Summer Pops, downtown. The symphony's summer pops series features lighter classical, jazz, opera, Broadway, and show tunes, all performed under the stars and capped by fireworks. Held most summer weekends at the Embarcadero downtown. For details, call ☏ **619/235-0804,** or visit www.sandiegosymphony.org. Late June to early September.

JULY

World Championship Over-the-Line Tournament, Mission Bay. This popular event is a San Diego original—a beach softball tournament dating from 1953. It's renowned for boisterous, beer-soaked, anything-goes behavior, with a total of 1,200 three-person teams competing and 50,000 fans in attendance. It takes place on 2 consecutive weekends on Fiesta Island in Mission Bay, and admission is free. For more details, call ☏ **619/688-0817,** or visit www.ombac.org. Mid-July.

Thoroughbred Racing Season. The "turf meets the surf" in Del Mar during the thoroughbred racing season at the Del Mar Racetrack. Post time is 2pm most days; the track is dark on Mondays and Tuesdays. For this year's schedule of events, call ☏ **858/755-1141,** or visit www.dmtc.com. Mid-July to early September.

San Diego LGBT Pride Parade, Rally, and Festival. This event is one of San Diego's biggest draws, celebrating the lesbian, gay, bisexual, and transgender community. It begins Friday night with a rally at the Organ Pavilion in Balboa Park, and reconvenes at 11am on Saturday for the parade through Hillcrest, followed by a massive festival—held at the park's Marston Point—that continues Sunday. For more information, call ☏ **619/297-7683,** or visit www.sdpride.org. Late July.

Comic-Con International, downtown. Some 125,000 people attend America's largest comic-book convention each year when it lands at the San Diego Convention Center for 4 days of auctions, dealers, celebrities, film screenings, and seminars focusing on comic books, graphic novels, fantasy, and sci-fi. **Note:** You must preregister online to attend; there are no on-site sales. Single-day tickets do sell out. Call ☏ **619/491-2475,** or check www.comic-con.org. Mid-July.

AUGUST

La Jolla SummerFest is perhaps San Diego's most prestigious annual music event. It features a wide spectrum of classical and contemporary music. SummerFest also offers master classes, open rehearsals, and workshops. It's presented by the La Jolla Music Society; call ☏ **858/459-3728,** or visit www. ljms.org for more information. Early to late August.

Surfing Competitions. Oceanside's pier-side surfing spot attracts several competitions, including the **World Bodysurfing Championships** and the **Longboard Surf Club Competition.** Call the Oceanside Visitors Bureau at ☏ **800/350-7873** or 760/721-1101, or visit www.worldbodysurfing. org and www.oceansidelongboardsurfing club.org. Mid- or late August.

Festival of Sail, Embarcadero. Tall ships from around the world converge on San Diego for this celebration of the golden age of sailing. There are ship tours, mock sea battles, entertainment, and arts-and-crafts vendors. The festivities are hosted by the Maritime Museum, ✆ **619/234-9153** or www.sdmaritime.org. Labor Day weekend.

SEPTEMBER

La Jolla Rough Water Swim, La Jolla Cove. The country's largest rough-water swimming competition began in 1916 and features masters, men's and women's, junior, and amateur heats. Spectators don't need tickets. For information, call ✆ **858/456-2100.** Downloadable entry forms are available at www.ljrws.com. Sunday after Labor Day.

Ocean Beach Music & Art Festival. This daylong outdoor concert features eight seaside stages of jazz, blues, and funk, along with local beer, plenty of food, and exhibiting artists. Check out www.obmusicfest.org. Mid-September.

Julian Fall Apple Harvest. The popular apple harvest season runs for 2 months in early fall; there are plenty of special events to go along with the fresh apple pies. For more information, contact the chamber of commerce at ✆ **760/765-1857;** www.julianca.com. Mid-September to mid-November.

Fleet Week is a bit of a misnomer—it actually lasts a couple of weeks. The nation's largest military appreciation event, it features Navy ship tours, a golf tournament, an auto race of classic speedsters, an air show, and more. Call ✆ **619/858-1545,** or check out www.fleetweeksandiego.org for more information. Mid-September to early October.

Festival of Beer, downtown. San Diego's local breweries (along with guest brewers from around California and beyond) strut their stuff at this outdoor festival. Some 70 different breweries are on tap, along with live music and food at this 21-and-up-only event. For more information go to www.sdbeerfest.org. Mid-September.

San Diego Bayfair. You'll need a good pair of earplugs for this world series of powerboat racing on Mission Bay (they don't call them thunderboats for nothing). This family-friendly event also features a beach festival. For information, call ✆ **760/789-8870,** or go to www.sandiegobayfair.org. Mid-September.

San Diego Film Festival, downtown. Dozens of features, documentaries, shorts, and music videos from around the world are screened over 5 days. There are also educational panels and nightly soirees. Call ✆ **619/582-2368** for more information, or log onto www.sdff.org. Late September.

OCTOBER

California Surf Festival, Oceanside. Surf culture in all its glory is explored via art, music, film, and more at this 4-day event. The film fest features a category of shorts shot by "groms" (kid surfers); proceeds benefit the California Surf Museum. Call ✆ **760/721-6876,** or check out www.californiasurffestival.com. Early October.

Little Italy Festa. One of the largest celebrations of Italian culture in the West, the Festa draws more than 120,000 people to the streets of Little Italy for a day of traditional food, music, and entertainment. Highlights include stickball and chalk-art street-painting competitions. For information, call ✆ **619/233-3898,** or visit www.littleitalysd.com. Mid-October.

NOVEMBER

Carlsbad Fall Village Faire. Billed as the largest 1-day street fair in the United States, this festival features more than 900 vendors on 24 city blocks. The epicenter is the intersection of Grand Avenue and Jefferson Street. Call ✆ **760/931-8400,** or visit www.carlsbad.org. First Sunday in November (a spring festival is held in May as well).

San Diego Beer Week. Brewers, restaurants, and bars throughout the county become even more beer-obsessed than normal for this 10-day celebration of San Diego's thriving craft-brewing culture. The closing-day event, bringing together top chefs and beermeisters, is a highlight. Check www.sdbw.org for information. Early to mid-November.

San Diego Bay Wine & Food Festival. Held at various venues over 5 days, this is Southern California's largest wine and culinary event. More than 200 wineries and restaurants participate. For details, call ✆ **619/312-1212,** or log onto www.worldofwineevents.com. Mid-November.

Dr. Seuss' How the Grinch Stole Christmas! Balboa Park. San Diego was the adopted hometown of Theodor Geisel, aka Dr. Seuss, and, since 1998, the Old Globe Theatre has been transformed into Whoville each holiday season. This musical has become a family tradition, with discounted seats for kids. For more information, call ✆ **619/234-5623,** or check www.theoldglobe.org. Mid-November through December.

Mother Goose Parade, El Cajon. Since 1947, this East County city has celebrated childhood with the largest parade in San Diego. It's classic Americana. Call ✆ **619/444-8712** for info, or go to www.mothergooseparade.org. Late November (the Sun before Thanksgiving).

San Diego Thanksgiving Dixieland Jazz Festival. More than 2 dozen bands perform ragtime, boogie-woogie, blues, and traditional jazz at this annual festival, held over Thanksgiving weekend. There's also an open jam session. Call ✆ **619/297-5277,** or visit www.dixielandjazzfestival.org. Late November.

Encinitas Fall Festival, Encinitas. This street fair takes over quaint downtown Encinitas along Coast Highway and features 450 vendors and live music on two stages. Call ✆ **760/943-1950,** or see www.encinitas101.com. Late November.

DECEMBER

Ocean Beach Holiday Parade. This parade is a family affair (Santa Claus is on hand, of course), but with entries such as the Off-Key Choir and the Geriatric Surf Team, it's definitely quirky. Call ✆ **619/224-4906,** or see www.oceanbeachsandiego.com. First Saturday in December.

Balboa Park December Nights. San Diego's wonderful urban park is decked out in holiday splendor for this 2-night event. The event is free and lasts from 5 to 9pm both days; the park's museums are free during those hours, and special events and ethnic foods add to the good cheer. For more information, call ✆ **619/239-0512,** or visit www.balboapark.org. First Friday and Saturday in December.

Whale-watching season takes place during the winter months along the San Diego County coast. More than 20,000 Pacific gray whales make the annual trek from chilly Alaskan seas to the warm-water breeding lagoons of Baja California, and then back again with their calves in tow. Cabrillo National Monument, on the panoramic Point Loma peninsula, offers a glassed-in observatory from which to spot the whales, examine whale exhibits, and listen to taped narration describing these amazing animals. Various companies offer whale-watching tours throughout the season, as well. For more information, call ✆ **619/557-5450** or 619/236-1212, or visit www.sandiego.org. Mid-December to mid-March.

Mission Bay Boat Parade of Lights, from Quivira Basin in Mission Bay. Held on a Saturday, the best viewing is around Crown Point, on the east side of Vacation Island, or the west side of Fiesta Island; it concludes with the lighting of a 320-foot tower of holiday lights at SeaWorld. Call ✆ **858/488-0501,** or go to www.sandiego.org. For more vessels dressed up like Christmas trees, the **San Diego Boat Parade of Lights** is held in San Diego Bay on two Sundays, with a route starting at Shelter Island and running past Seaport Village and the Coronado Ferry Landing Marketplace. Call ✆ **619/224-2240,** or visit www.sdparadeoflights.org for more information. Mid-December.

College bowl games. San Diego is home to two college football bowl games: the **Holiday Bowl** and the **Poinsettia Bowl,** both held in late December. The Holiday Bowl pits top teams from the Pac 12 and Big 12 conferences, and the Poinsettia Bowl pairs a team from the Mountain West Conference against a Western Athletic Conference opponent. The Poinsettia Bowl (✆ **619/285-5061;** www.poinsettiabowl.com) was inaugurated in 2005; the Holiday Bowl (✆ **619/283-5808;** www.holidaybowl.com) has been around since 1978, and features several special events, including the nation's biggest balloon parade of giant inflatable characters. Late December.

RESPONSIBLE TOURISM IN SAN DIEGO

In San Diego, and throughout the western United States in general, perhaps the biggest environmental concern can be summed up in one word: water. Drought conditions have pushed supply to the limit, and mandatory water conservation efforts are in effect. San Diego has announced proposals that will attempt to curtail water usage by 20% citywide. Golf courses (which lap up some 12 billion gallons annually in San Diego) and resorts with lush landscaping will definitely feel the impact—businesses are being asked to cut water consumption by 45% outside and 3% inside. For more information, go to www.sandiego.gov/water.

Barona Creek Golf Club (p. 82) is leading the way for the county's golf courses in adapting to the water emergency. Barona has reconfigured its course to include less turf and more bunkers, and has also installed a computerized sprinkler system. **Steele Canyon Golf Club** (p. 82) has responded as well, investing in its own weather station that constantly monitors how much water the course requires.

Hotel Indigo (p. 189) is the first hotel in San Diego to be awarded LEED (Leadership in Energy and Environmental Design) certification. The property features a green roof—it's covered completely with drought-resistant plants that insulate the building and filter storm water runoff. Many San Diego restaurants are also doing their part, incorporating local, organic, and sustainable products into their menus. Locavore leaders include **the Linkery** (p. 129), **Zenbu** (p. 140), and **Market** (p. 125).

Although San Diego County sprawls, many of its most popular attractions are in close proximity. For a low-impact visit, consider foregoing a rental car. If you're staying in a downtown hotel, Little Italy, Old Town, Mission Valley, Balboa Park, and even Tijuana are easily accessible via public transportation.

Volunteer travel has become increasingly popular among those who want to venture beyond the standard group-tour experience to learn languages, interact with locals, and make a positive difference while on vacation. Volunteer travel usually doesn't require special skills—just a willingness to work hard—and programs vary in length from a few days to a number of weeks. Some programs provide free housing and food, but many require volunteers to pay for travel expenses, which can add up quickly.

For general information on volunteer travel, visit www.volunteerabroad.org and www.idealist.org. Before you commit to a volunteer program, it's important to make sure any money you're giving is truly going back to the local community, and that the work you'll be doing will be a good fit for you. **Volunteer International** (www.volunteerinternational.org) has a helpful list of questions to ask to determine the intentions and the nature of a volunteer program.

Animal Rights Issues

For information on animal-friendly issues throughout the world, visit Tread Lightly (www.treadlightly.org). For information about the ethics of swimming with dolphins or performing-animal shows at facilities such as SeaWorld, visit the Whale and Dolphin Conservation Society (www.wdcs.org).

IT'S easy BEING GREEN

Here are a few simple ways you can help conserve fuel and energy when you travel:

- Each time you take a flight or drive a car, greenhouse gases release into the atmosphere. You can help neutralize this danger to the planet through "carbon offsetting"—paying someone to invest your money in programs that reduce your greenhouse gas emissions by the same amount you've added. Before buying carbon offset credits, make sure that you're using a reputable company, one with a proven program that invests in renewable energy. Reliable carbon offset companies include **Carbonfund** (www.carbonfund.org), **TerraPass** (www.terrapass.org), and **Carbon Neutral** (www.carbonneutral.com).

- Whenever possible, choose non-stop flights; they generally require less fuel than indirect flights that stop and take off again. Try to fly during the day—some scientists estimate that nighttime flights are twice as harmful to the environment. And pack light—each 15 pounds of luggage on a 5,000-mile flight adds up to 50 pounds of carbon dioxide emitted.

- Where you stay during your travels can have a major environmental impact. The website http://greenhotels.com recommends green-rated member hotels around the world that fulfill the company's stringent environmental requirements. Also consult www.environmentallyfriendlyhotels.com for more green accommodation ratings.

- At hotels, request that your sheets and towels not be changed daily. (Many hotels already have programs like this in place.) Turn off the lights and air conditioner (or heater) when you leave your room.

- Use public transport where possible—trains, buses, and even taxis are more energy-efficient forms of transport than driving. Even better is to walk or cycle; you'll produce zero emissions and stay fit and healthy on your travels.

- If renting a car is necessary, ask the rental agent for a hybrid, or rent the most fuel-efficient car available. You'll use less gas and save money at the pump.

- Eat at locally owned and operated restaurants that use produce grown in the area. Visit **Sustain Lane** (www.sustainlane.com) to find sustainable eating and drinking choices around the U.S.; also check out www.eatwellguide.org for tips on eating sustainably in the U.S. and Canada.

SAN DIEGO NEIGHBORHOODS & SUGGESTED ITINERARIES

3

I f 1 to 3 days is all you have in San Diego, maximize your time with our ready-made itineraries. Hit the beach—at sunset or under the almost-always-shining sun; stroll the vibrant Gaslamp Quarter; head up to La Jolla for upscale shopping and dining; or explore dramatic Torrey Pines State Reserve.

CITY LAYOUT

Tucked into the sunny and parched southwest corner of the United States, San Diego is situated in one of the country's most naturally beautiful metropolitan settings. Learning the lay of the land is neither confusing nor daunting, but it helps to understand a few geographical features. Two major characteristics give San Diego its topographical personality: a superb and varied coastline; and a series of mesas bisected by inland canyons inhabited by coyotes, skunks, and raccoons.

San Diego's downtown—16 miles north of the Mexico border—sits at the edge of a large natural harbor, the San Diego Bay. The harbor is almost enclosed by two fingers of land: flat Coronado "Island" on one side, and peninsular Point Loma on the other. Both of these areas hold important military bases, bordered by classic neighborhoods dating to the 1890s and 1920s, respectively.

Heading north from Point Loma is Mission Bay, a lagoon that was carved out of an estuary in the 1940s and is now a watersports playground. A series of communities is found along the beach-lined coast: Ocean Beach, Mission Beach, Pacific Beach, La Jolla, and, just outside San Diego's city limits, Del Mar. To the south of downtown, you'll find National City, which is distinguished by shipyards on its bay side, then Chula Vista, and San Ysidro, which ends abruptly at the border (and where the huge city of Tijuana begins, equally abruptly).

Inland is Mission Valley, a mile-wide canyon that runs east-west, 2 miles north of downtown. Half a century ago, the valley held little beyond a few dairy farms, California's first mission, and the San Diego River (which is more like a creek most of the year). Then I-8 was built through

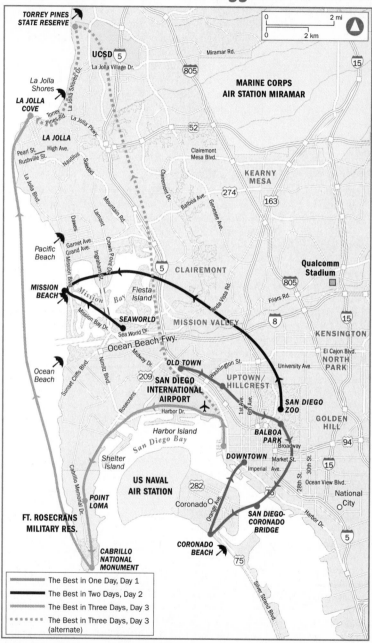

The Best in One Day, Day 1

The Best in Two Days, Day 2

The Best in Three Days, Day 3

The Best in Three Days, Day 3 (alternate)

the valley, followed by a shopping center, a sports stadium, another shopping center, and lots of condos. Today, Mission Valley is the most congested—and least charming—part of the city.

In spite of this, residents all use the valley, and many live along its perimeter: On the southern rim are older neighborhoods such as Mission Hills, Hillcrest, Normal Heights, and Kensington; to the north are Linda Vista and Kearny Mesa (bedroom communities that emerged in the 1950s), and Miramar Naval Air Station. Just outside and to the north of the city limits is Rancho Bernardo, a quiet, clubby suburb.

The city of San Diego possesses one other vital (if man-made) ingredient: Balboa Park. Laid out in a 1,200-acre square between downtown and Mission Valley, the park contains the San Diego Zoo, many of the city's best museums, theaters (including the Tony Award–winning Old Globe), wonderful gardens, recreational facilities, and splendid architecture.

Neighborhoods in Brief

Coronado Locals refer to Coronado as an island, but it's actually on a peninsula connected to the mainland by a long, sandy isthmus known as the **Silver Strand.** It's a wealthy, self-contained community inhabited by lots of retired Navy brass living on quiet, tree-lined streets. The northern portion of the city is home to **Naval Base Coronado** (also referred to as **U.S. Naval Air Station, North Island**), in use since World War I. The southern part of Coronado, with its architecturally rich neighborhoods, features some of the region's priciest real estate, and has a long history as an elite playground for snowbirds. Shops line the main street, Orange Avenue, and you'll find several ritzy resorts, including the landmark **Hotel del Coronado,** referred to locally as "the Del." Coronado has a lovely dune beach (one of the area's finest), plenty of restaurants, and a downtown reminiscent of a small Midwestern town. A stay here ensures plenty of beach time, and quiet evenings.

Downtown After decades of intense development and restoration, downtown San Diego has emerged as a vibrant neighborhood with attractions that have become a magnet for travelers and locals alike. It's the business, shopping, dining, and entertainment heart of the city, encompassing Horton Plaza, the Gaslamp Quarter, the Embarcadero (waterfront), the Convention Center, and Little Italy, all sprawling over eight individual "neighborhoods." The

Gaslamp Quarter is the center of a massive redevelopment, kicked off in the mid-1980s with the opening of the Horton Plaza shopping complex; the area now features renovated historic buildings housing some of the city's top restaurants and clubs. Immediately east of the Gaslamp is the **East Village,** where you'll find **PETCO Park,** home of the San Diego Padres Major League Baseball team since 2004. **Little Italy,** a bustling neighborhood along India Street and Kettner Boulevard, between Cedar and Laurel streets, at the northern edge of downtown, has also undergone a renaissance. It's a great place to find a variety of restaurants (especially Italian) and boutiques. Making downtown your home base means you're right in the middle of the action—but be aware that the party can go late, particularly on weekends.

Hillcrest & Uptown Part of Hillcrest's charm is the number of people out walking, shopping, and just hanging out. As the city's original self-contained suburb, first developed in 1907, it was also the desirable address for bankers and bureaucrats to erect their mansions. Now it's the heart of San Diego's gay and lesbian community, but it's an inclusive neighborhood, charming everyone with an eclectic blend of popular shops and cafes. Despite the cachet of being close to **Balboa Park** (home of the **San Diego Zoo** and numerous **museums**), the area fell into neglect in the 1960s. By the late 1970s, however, legions of preservation-minded residents began restoring Hillcrest. Other old Uptown neighborhoods of interest are **Mission Hills** to the west of Hillcrest, and **University Heights, Normal Heights, North Park, South Park, Golden Hill,** and **Kensington** to the east. These areas lack major hotels—it's more the province of inns and B&Bs—but the city's major attractions are easily accessible from here.

Mission Bay & the Beaches Casual is the word of the day here. Come here when you want to wiggle your toes in the sand, feel the sun warm your skin, exert yourself in recreational activities, and cool off in the blue ocean waters. Mission Bay is a watery playground perfect for waterskiing, sailing, kayaking, and windsurfing. The adjacent communities of **Ocean Beach, Mission Beach,** and **Pacific Beach** are known for their wide stretches of sand, active nightlife, and informal dining. If you've come for the SoCal beach lifestyle, this is where you'll find it. The boardwalk, which runs from South Mission Beach to Pacific Beach, is a popular place for in-line skating, bike riding, people-watching, and sunsets. Accommodations run the gamut from lavish resorts to basic hostels, and like the Gaslamp Quarter, partying is a way of life here.

La Jolla Mediterranean in design and ambience, La Jolla is the Southern California Riviera. This seaside community of about 25,000 is home to an inordinate number of wealthy folks who could probably live anywhere. They choose La Jolla for good reason: It features gorgeous coastline, outstanding restaurants, upscale shops, galleries, and some of the world's best medical facilities, as well as the **University of California, San Diego (UCSD).** The heart of La Jolla is referred to as the **Village,** roughly delineated by Pearl Street to the south, Prospect Street to the north, Torrey Pines Road to the east, and the rugged coast to the west. This is a picturesque neighborhood, which makes it perfect for simply strolling about. It's uncertain whether "La Jolla" (pronounced La-hoy-ya) is misspelled Spanish for "the jewel" or a native people's word for "cave," but once you see it, you'll no doubt go with the first definition. Although nightlife is lacking, there's so much to do and see here, you may not even notice.

Old Town & Mission Valley These two busy areas wrap around the neighborhood of Mission Hills. On one end are the Old Town State Historic Park (where California "began") and several museums that document the city's beginnings. Old Town is said to attract more visitors than any other site in San Diego—it's where you can steep yourself in history while eating and shopping to your stomach and heart's content. Not far from Old Town lies the vast suburban sprawl of Mission Valley, a tribute to the automobile and consumerism with its car dealerships and huge shopping malls. Its main street, aptly named Hotel Circle, is lined with a string of moderately priced hotels as an alternative to the ritzier neighborhoods. In recent years, condo developments have made the valley a residential area and a traffic nightmare. Despite the gridlock, though, these neighborhoods are public transportation hubs, making it easy for visitors to go carless.

THE BEST OF SAN DIEGO IN 1 DAY

To get an overview of San Diego in just 1 day, you'll have to dart around town a bit. Begin with a taste of the area's Hispanic heritage, then embrace San Diego's dazzling beaches, and end the day in the spirited downtown Gaslamp Quarter.

1 Old Town ★

Old Town State Historic Park is the most visited state park in California (and it's free). This is San Diego's original downtown, and history comes to colorful life here, especially at **Fiesta de Reyes,** a once-dilapidated 1930s motel

To the northeast of Balboa Park is **North Park,** one of San Diego's original suburbs. Established in 1911, this mixed-use residential and commercial district was scraped out of a lemon grove, and thrived until the 1970s and '80s. The neighborhood then went into decline, but recent gentrification has brought it roaring back to life. North Park was also the site of the worst aviation disaster in California history. On September 25, 1978, PSA Flight 182 collided in mid-air with a small plane over the community, killing 144 people, including 7 on the ground, and destroying or damaging 22 homes.

North Park's turnaround is best exemplified by the 2005 renovation of the fabulous **Birch North Park Theatre** (p. 167), a 1928 vaudeville house where a variety of performing arts groups strut their stuff. **Eveoke Dance Theatre** (p. 170) has established a permanent home nearby, as well. The area's lively scene gets a monthly showcase with the **Ray at Night Art Walk** (www.northpark arts.org), the second Saturday of the month from 6 to 10pm.

Dining makes a strong showing here, too, with **the Mission** (p. 137), **Spread** (p. 146), **Urban Solace** (p. 130), **Jayne's Gastropub** (p. 146), and **Ranchos Cocina** (p. 146). There are great tacos and more than 250 tequilas and mescals available at **Cantina Mayahuel** (2934 Adams Ave.; www.cantinamayahuel.com; *©* **619/283-6292**), while "gastro-cantina" **El Take It Easy** (3926 30th St.; www.eltakeiteasy.com; *©* **619/291-1859**) ups the ante on Mexican food with its creative menu. Meat lovers will have a field day with the quality sausages at the **Linkery** (p. 129) and the gourmet burgers (more than 30) at **Tioli's Crazee Burger** (p. 126); there's also an ever-changing menu of contemporary American fare at **the Smoking Goat** (3408 30th St.; www.thesmokinggoatrestaurant. com; *©* **619/955-5295**). And don't forget to save room for something sweet from **Heaven Sent Desserts** (3001 University Ave.; www.heavensentdesserts. com; *©* **619/793-4758**). Other eateries making noise on the dining front include **URBN Coal Fired Pizza/Bar** (3085 University Ave.; www.urbnnorthpark.com; *©* **619/255-7300**), **Sea Rocket Bistro** (3382 30th St.; www.searocketbistro.com; *©* **619/255-7049**), and **Farm House**

converted into shopping and dining arcades, replete with mariachi players echoing the sounds of Mexico around an inner courtyard. See p. 199.

2 Hillcrest ★

Hillcrest, San Diego's equivalent of L.A.'s West Hollywood or New York's West Village, is an urban, pedestrian-friendly neighborhood. Its tolerant attitude fosters a large gay community and a hip, eclectic vibe. Pop into trendy boutiques, vintage clothing stores, and an array of restaurants and cafes. Check out the '40s-era Art Deco neighborhood sign dangling above University Avenue (at Fifth Ave.).

3 Breaking Bread 🖳

Bread & Cie., 350 University Ave. (*©* 619/683-9322), is perfect for a quick shot of java and a fresh scone or muffin. Lunch fare features hearty Mediterranean sandwiches served on delectable homemade bread, such as a rosemary and cheese baguette or olive focaccia. Relax at one of the bistro tables or take your bite to go for a picnic at your next stop, Balboa Park. See p. 130.

Café (2121 Adams Ave.; www.farm housecafesd.com; ℰ **619/269-9662**).

By day, there's shopping at independent boutiques and vintage stores; by night, check out a few of the hipster haunts such as **Air Conditioned** (4673 30th St.; www.airconditionedlounge.com; ℰ **619/501-9831**), **Bar Pink** (3829 30th St.; www.barpink.com; ℰ **619/564-7194**), **U-31** (3112 University Ave.; www.u31bar.com; ℰ **619/584-4188**), and **Live Wire** (2103 El Cajon Blvd.; www.livewire bar.com; ℰ **619/291-7450**). The **Toronado** (4026 30th St.; www.toronadosd.com; ℰ **619/282-0456**) has 50 beers on draft, and the **Red Fox Steak House** (2223 El Cajon Blvd.; www.redfox.menu toeat.com; ℰ **619/297-1313**) has an old-school piano bar.

And if you really need your morning edition of *Le Monde*, you can find it at **Paras Newsstand,** the city's best (3911 30th St.; ℰ **619/296-2859**).

In addition to North Park, there's also a neighborhood called South Park (which is actually east of Balboa Park), and it blends into Golden Hill at the park's southeastern corner. Both neighborhoods have architectural gems including meticulously preserved Victorian mansions and Craftsman bungalows. And both areas have a crop of bars and restaurants worth investigating, including the neighborhood bistros **Alchemy** (1503 30th St.; www.alchemysandiego.com; ℰ **619/255-0616**) and **Vagabond** (2310 30th St.; www.vagabondkitchen.com; ℰ **619/255-1035**). There's also the retro **Turf Supper Club** (p. 177), the **Whistle Stop Bar** (2236 Fern St.; www.whistlestopbar.com; ℰ **619/284-6784**), **Hamilton's Tavern** (1521 30th St.; www.hamiltonstavern.com; ℰ **619/238-5460**), and **Influx Cafe** (1948 Broadway; www.influxcafe.com; ℰ **619/255-9470**), with its minimalist-chic decor and home-baked goods. The funky breakfast spot known as the **Big Kitchen** (3003 Grape St.; www.bigkitchencafe.com; ℰ **619/234-5789**) is a local institution—it's where a pre-fame Whoopi Goldberg once worked.

You'll also find creative boutiques, such as **Make Good,** 2207 Fern St. (www.themakegood.com; ℰ **619/563-4600**), which stocks locally made clothing, art, and accessories; and **Progress,** 2225 30th St. (www.progresssouthpark.com; ℰ **619/280-5501**), for modern home decor and gifts.

4 Balboa Park ★★★

Balboa Park, the nation's largest urban cultural park, contains a cluster of diverse museums and theaters, as well as San Diegans lolling about in the grass on any given pristine 70°F (21°C) sunny day (which is pretty much every day). Wander past the Spanish Colonial Revival–style buildings along the pedestrian thoroughfare, El Prado, then take in the sublime beauty of the Botanical Building's lily pond or explore the meandering park trails. See p. 46.

5 The San Diego–Coronado Bay Bridge ★

Drive across the 2-mile-long, curved San Diego–Coronado Bay Bridge with the wind whistling in your ears. If you've rented a convertible, put the top down *now.* In a word: invigorating. See p. 65.

6 Hotel del Coronado & Coronado Beach ★★★

Nicknamed by locals as "the Del," this Victorian landmark, with its spiky red turrets and gingerbread trim, is a San Diego gem. Stroll through the elegant lobby (perhaps you'll meet the resident ghost, Kate Morgan), meander along the sprawling decks facing the Pacific, and take a leisurely walk along Coronado Beach. This is a great place to watch a sunset. See p. 213 and 43.

7 The Gaslamp Quarter ★★

Finish the day in the historic Gaslamp Quarter, which always promises a lively evening street scene. Pick from dozens of restaurants (many housed in restored Victorian commercial buildings), and stick around for live music or dancing after dinner—if you have the energy. See p. 30 and 121.

THE BEST OF SAN DIEGO IN 2 DAYS

Your second full-day tour starts with a famous San Diego theme park, but you'll need to choose which one: SeaWorld or the San Diego Zoo. You could spend the entire day at either one, but if you need a change of scenery halfway through the afternoon, spend a few active hours at the public aquatic park, Mission Bay, or on the Mission Beach boardwalk. If you have no desire to bike or kayak, chill out on the beach and embrace a lazy afternoon under the sun.

1 Pick a Theme Park: SeaWorld ★★ or San Diego Zoo ★★★

You'll get a dose of animals at both places, but do yourself a favor and choose *either* SeaWorld *or* the San Diego Zoo; don't try to do both in 1 day. Get there when the gates open to maximize your touring time, and spend a little more than half of the day exploring. Plan to leave by early afternoon for a late lunch.

At **SeaWorld,** Shamu may be the star, but there's a whole lot more to see and do here. You'll find thrill rides, lovable penguins at the Penguin Encounter, and, of course, animal shows. There's also a passel of *Sesame Street*–related attractions, and a "4-D" interactive movie experience. See p. 41.

More than 3,500 creatures reside at the world-renowned **San Diego Zoo,** known not only for its giant pandas, gorillas, and tigers housed in naturalistic environments, but also for its successful animal preservation efforts. The Children's Zoo petting area is perfect for little ones (and any adult who loves animals). See p. 40.

2 A Post–Theme-Park Break 🍺

If you're coming from SeaWorld and don't mind a little irony, try the fresh-off-the-boat seafood at the Fishery, 5040 Cass St. (📞 858/272-9985)—a casual Pacific Beach fish market. See p. 136. If you spent the morning at the San Diego Zoo, pick up a gourmet taco at colorful Mamá Testa, 1417 University Ave. (📞 619/298-8226), a local favorite. See p. 130.

3 Mission Bay Park ★★ & Mission Beach ★

Outfitters such as **Mission Bay Sportcenter** and **Cheap Rentals** (p. 80 and 78) rent gear including bikes, in-line skates, kayaks, and catamarans to better make your way through and around Mission Bay Park, a 4,200-acre aquatic playground. You can also enjoy unparalleled people-watching along the Mission Beach boardwalk, which hugs the wide swath of sandy beach. Or just grab a blanket, plop down on the sand, catch some rays, and ponder the volleyball players' suntanned muscles. See p. 43.

THE BEST OF SAN DIEGO IN 3 DAYS

After you've followed the previous two itineraries, spend your third day touring the Embarcadero, contemplating the ocean vistas from Point Loma or Torrey Pines, and exploring another spectacular beach (as well as a bevy of outdoor dining venues and high-end boutiques) in La Jolla. If you have kids in tow, consider visiting the theme park you didn't choose on Day 2.

1 The Embarcadero ★

Along the Embarcadero, downtown San Diego's waterfront, you'll find harbor tours, a ferry to Coronado, and historic vessels such as the aircraft carrier USS *Midway* and the *Star of India,* the world's oldest active sailing ship. Both are now floating museums (p. 57 and 55); also close by are the downtown spaces for the **Museum of Contemporary Art San Diego** (p. 56). There are plenty of restaurants and shops at **Seaport Village,** a maritime-themed retail area (p. 152), as well.

2 The Great Outdoors: Cabrillo National Monument ★★★ or Torrey Pines State Reserve ★★★

You don't have to go far to find stunning natural environments in San Diego. The two best and closest are Cabrillo National Monument and Torrey Pines State Reserve. Hours can easily melt away at either of these magical spots, so you'll have to select just one.

Cabrillo National Monument is at the end of Point Loma, a slice of land jutting into the Pacific just southwest of downtown San Diego. This 144-acre park features a statue of Juan Rodríguez Cabrillo, the Portuguese explorer who landed in San Diego in 1542; a restored 1855 lighthouse; museum installations and a bookstore; bayside trails; tide pools; and a 422-foot-high lookout. This is an excellent vantage point to see migrating Pacific gray whales in winter; year-round, you'll enjoy awesome views of San Diego's harbor and skyline, and the rocky Pacific coastline. When skies are clear, you can also see Mexico in the distance. See p. 54.

Just north of La Jolla, **Torrey Pines State Reserve** is one of San Diego's most treasured spots. The 2,000-acre reserve is home to the distinctively gnarled tree that gives the place its name (and which is native only here and on an island off the coast). Trails range from flat and easy to steep and narrow, but all provide breathtaking views of the ocean, lagoon, canyons, sandstone formations, and the famed Torrey Pines Golf Course. Take a hike or just head down to the beach. See p. 64.

3 Fish Tacos & Desserts 🍽

Stop for a snack or lunch at the harborside **Point Loma Seafoods**, 2805 Emerson St. (☎ 619/223-1109), a fish market (with outdoor picnic tables) offering sandwiches, sushi, salads, and tasty fish tacos. See p. 134. In La Jolla, sweet and savory options are available at **Michele Coulon Dessertier,** 7556 Fay Ave., Ste. D (☎ 858/456-5098). If you need something more substantial than sweets, the menu at this small restaurant goes way beyond amazing desserts. Try the onion soup, Belgian endive salad, or a quiche, along with a slice of flourless chocolate cognac cake. See p. 138.

The Best of San Diego in 3 Days

4 La Jolla

End your day in La Jolla, San Diego's swanky neighbor to the north. This town is upscale, exclusive, and home to some of the area's priciest real estate. Take one look at the pristine coastline, and you'll instantly understand the allure. The main shopping and dining venues are clustered along or near Prospect Street, but La Jolla's most spectacular spot is the bluff above La Jolla Cove. Stroll along Coast Boulevard for the most scenic views. With its calm, crystal-clear water, the cove is also great for swimming. In the tide pools at its small, sandy beach, you can glimpse marine life such as starfish, sea anemones, and sea urchins. See p. 61.

EXPLORING SAN DIEGO

Y̶ou won't run out of things to see and do in San Diego, especially if outdoor activities are high on the agenda. The San Diego Zoo, SeaWorld, and the Zoo Safari Park are the city's three top attractions, but there are also Balboa Park's museums, downtown's Gaslamp Quarter, the beaches, and shopping in Old Town. You can catch a performance at one of the city's prized live theaters or a Padres game at downtown PETCO Park, as well. See chapter 3 for itineraries and advice on how to organize your time.

4

SAN DIEGO'S TOP 15 SITES & ATTRACTIONS

- Balboa Park (see p. 46)
- Cabrillo National Monument (see p. 54)
- Torrey Pines State Reserve (see p. 64)
- Old Town State Historic Park (see p. 60)
- San Diego Zoo (see p. 40)
- San Diego Zoo Safari Park (see p. 38)
- SeaWorld (see p. 41)
- LEGOLAND (see p. 229)
- Birch Aquarium at Scripps (see p. 62)
- Mission Basilica San Diego de Alcalá (see p. 58)
- Gaslamp Quarter (see p. 91)
- La Jolla village (see p. 61)
- Mission Bay Park (see p. 43)
- The Children's Pool (see p. 44)
- Museum of Contemporary Art San Diego (see p. 56 and 64)

THE THREE MAJOR ANIMAL PARKS

If you're looking for wild times, San Diego supplies them. The world-famous **San Diego Zoo** is home to more than 650 animal species, many of them rare and exotic. A sister attraction, the **Zoo Safari Park,** showcases some 300 species in an *au naturel* setting. And aquatic animals form a veritable chorus line at **SeaWorld San Diego**—waving their flippers, waddling across an ersatz Antarctica, and blowing dolphin kisses—in various shows throughout the day.

San Diego's "Big Three" family attractions are joined by **LEGOLAND California** (p. 229).

San Diego Zoo Safari Park ★★★ ☺ ZOO   Thirty miles north of San Diego, outside of Escondido, this "zoo of the future" will transport you to the African plains and other faraway landscapes. Originally a breeding facility for the San Diego Zoo, the 1,800-acre Zoo Safari Park (formerly known as the Wild Animal Park) now holds 2,600 animals representing more than 300 different species. What makes the park unique is that many of the animals roam freely in vast enclosures, allowing giraffes to interact with antelopes, much as they would in Africa. You'll find the largest crash of rhinos at any zoological facility in the world, an exhibit for the endangered California condor, and a mature landscape of exotic vegetation from around the globe. Although the San Diego Zoo may be "world famous," it's the Zoo Safari Park that many visitors celebrate as their favorite.

The easiest way to see critters is on the **Africa Tram Safari** (included with admission), aboard an open-air, soft-wheeled tram that runs on biodiesel. Although it visits less park space than the now-retired monorail, the 2½-mile circuit, which takes about 30 minutes, brings guests much nearer to the animals—in some locations up to 300 feet closer. Depending on the crowd size, trams leave every 10 minutes or so. Lines build up by late morning, so make this your first or last attraction of the day (the animals are more active then anyway). The **Cart Safari** is a deluxe, 1-hour experience for up to 10 people. You can choose to visit either the Asian or the African exhibits on this personalized, intimate tour; tickets are $40 (not including admission), and no reservations are necessary. Customized 5- and 8-hour VIP tours with your own guide are also available, starting at $550 per person.

There are several self-guided **walking tours** that take you to various habitats, including **Elephant Overlook** and **Lion Camp;** but why walk when you can tool around the park on Segway personal transporters ($80, minimum age 13)? The commercial hub of the park is **Nairobi Village,** with its souvenir stores and several spots for mediocre dining, but even here animal exhibits are interesting, including the **nursery area,** a **petting station,** the **lowland gorillas,** and the **African Aviary.** There's an amphitheater for bird shows, and other animal encounters are scheduled throughout the park; **Cheetah Run** is a particular highlight, with the world's fastest land mammal chasing after a mechanical lure.

If you want to get really close to the animals, take one of the park's **Safari Caravans,** which shuttle groups in flatbed trucks into the open areas that are inaccessible to the general public. There are a variety of itineraries (some are seasonal with varying age requirements); prices start at $95, and you'll want to make reservations ahead of your visit (📞 **619/718-3000**). You can also get a unique aerial perspective of the park with **Flightline,** a zipline ride that scoots above the African and Asian enclosures ($70, minimum age 10). Visitors should be prepared for sunny, often downright hot weather; it's not unusual for temperatures to be 5° to 10° warmer here than in San Diego.

15500 San Pasqual Valley Rd., Escondido. www.sandiegozoo.org. 📞 **760/747-8702.** Admission $42 adults, $32 children 3–11, free for children 2 and under and active-duty military; discounted 2-day passes can be used for both the zoo and Zoo Safari Park; children 11 and under are free in Oct. AE, DISC, MC, V. Daily 9am–4pm (grounds close at 5pm); extended hours during summer and Festival of Lights (2 weekends in Dec). Parking $10, $15 RVs. Take I-15 to Via Rancho Pkwy.; follow signs for about 3 miles.

San Diego Attractions

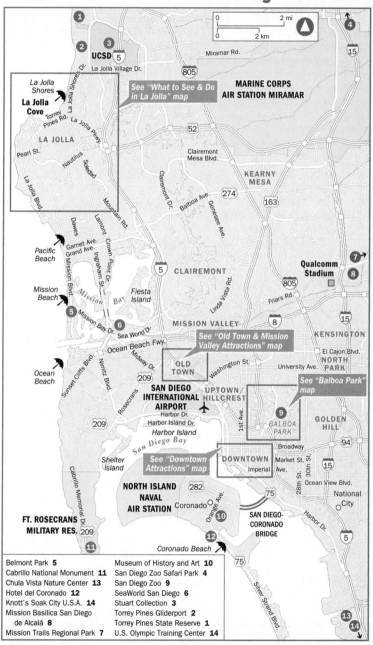

Belmont Park **5**
Cabrillo National Monument **11**
Chula Vista Nature Center **13**
Hotel del Coronado **12**
Knott's Soak City U.S.A. **14**
Mission Basilica San Diego
    de Alcalá **8**
Mission Trails Regional Park **7**

Museum of History and Art **10**
San Diego Zoo Safari Park **4**
San Diego Zoo **9**
SeaWorld San Diego **6**
Stuart Collection **3**
Torrey Pines Gliderport **2**
Torrey Pines State Reserve **1**
U.S. Olympic Training Center **14**

Things That Go Bump in the Night!

The Wild Animal Park's **Roar & Snore sleepover programs,** which are held year-round on most Fridays and Saturdays—except in December and January, and with extended dates in summer—let you camp out next to the animal compound and observe the nocturnal movements of rhinos, lions, and other creatures. There are family and adults-only dates available; prices range from $30 to $262 per person. To request information by mail or to make reservations, call ℂ **619/718-3000.**

San Diego Zoo ★★★ ☺ ZOO   More than 3,700 creatures reside at this influential and justly "world famous" zoo, started in 1916. The zoo's founder, Dr. Harry Wegeforth, traveled the globe and bartered native Southwestern animals such as rattlesnakes and sea lions for more exotic species. "Dr. Harry" also brought home flora, which flourishes in the zoo's botanical gardens; there are now more than 700,000 plants on the zoo's 100 acres.

The zoo is one of only four in the U.S. with giant pandas, and many other rare species are here, including Buerger's tree kangaroos of New Guinea, long-billed kiwis from New Zealand, wild Przewalski's horses from Mongolia, lowland gorillas from Africa, and giant tortoises from the Galapagos. The zoo is also involved with animal preservation efforts around the world and has engineered many firsts in breeding; it was a forerunner in creating sophisticated, naturalistic enclosures, as well.

In the **Lost Forest** zone, you'll find the zoo's largest, most elaborate habitat, re-creating a wooded forest full of endangered species such as the mandrill monkey, clouded leopard, and pygmy hippopotamus; an elevated trail through the treetops allows for close observation of the primate, bird, and plant life that thrives in the forest canopy. Expressive orangutans and siamangs of Indonesia share a lush environment, too, while troops of Western lowland gorillas roam an 8,000-square-foot habitat nearby. The new **Panda Trek** exhibit finds San Diego's celebrity pandas joined by red pandas and goat-antelopes known as takins; pay a visit here first thing in the morning or toward the end of the day when crowds have thinned. Other signature enclosures feature underwater viewing windows, offering fascinating, up-close looks at otters, hippos, and polar bears. **Elephant Odyssey** features a herd of Asian elephants, as well as life-size replicas of prehistoric animals that roamed Southern California; you can also watch handlers interact with the pachyderms at the elephant care center. The **Children's Zoo** features a nursery with baby animals and a petting area where kids can cuddle up to sheep, goats, and the like; there's also a **sea lion show** at the 3,000-seat amphitheater (easy to skip if you're headed to SeaWorld).

A 35-minute, narrated **Guided Bus Tour** covers about 70% of the facility and is included with the price of admission. Because you get only brief glimpses of the enclosures, and animals won't always be visible, you'll want to revisit some areas. Also included with admission is access to the unnarrated **Express Bus,** which allows you to get on and off at one of five different stops along the same route; the free **Skyfari** aerial tram gives you a park overview, as well, though you won't see many creatures. Ideally, take the complete bus tour early in the morning, when the animals are more active (waits for the bus tour can be long on a busy day); after the bus tour, take the Skyfari to the far side of the park and wend your way back on foot or by Express Bus to revisit animals you missed. Other zoo experiences include a new "4-D" movie ($6), sleepovers ($30–$262 per person), and **Backstage Passes** ($99), a 1½-hour, behind-the-scenes tour (ages 5 and up) that includes interacting with animals and trainers; call ✆ **619/718-3000** for more information and reservations.

In addition to several fast-food options, **Albert's** restaurant is a beautiful oasis at the lip of a canyon and a lovely place to take a break.

2920 Zoo Dr., Balboa Park. www.sandiegozoo.org. ✆ **619/234-3153** (recorded info) or 619/231-1515. Admission $42 adults, $32 children 3–11, free for children 2 and under and active-duty military; discounted 2-day passes can be used for both the zoo and Zoo Safari Park; children 11 and under are free in Oct. AE, DISC, MC, V. Sept to mid-Dec and mid-Jan to mid-June daily 9am–4pm (grounds close at 5 or 6pm); mid-June through Aug and mid-Dec to mid-Jan daily 9am–8pm (grounds close at 9pm). Bus: 7. I-5 S. to Pershing Dr., follow signs.

SeaWorld San Diego ★★ ☺ ZOO Opened in 1964, this aquatic theme park is perhaps the country's premier showplace for marine life, made politically correct with a nominally informative atmosphere. At its heart, SeaWorld is a shoreside family entertainment center where the performers are whales, dolphins, otters, sea lions, walruses, and seals. The 20-minute shows run several times daily, with visitors cycling through the various open-air amphitheaters.

Several successive 4-ton, black-and-white killer whales have taken turns as the park's mascot, Shamu, who stars in **One Ocean,** SeaWorld's latest show. Performed in a 5,500-seat stadium, the stage is a 7-million-gallon pool lined with Plexiglas walls with magnified views of the huge performers. But think twice before you sit in the seats down front—multiple drenchings of the first 16 or so rows of spectators are a highlight of the act. A seasonal nighttime show (spring and summer), **Shamu Rocks,** features concert lighting, animation, and a rock soundtrack; **Blue Horizons** is a theatrical presentation mixing dolphins, whales, birds, and human performers. The slapstick **Sea Lions Live** and **Pets Rule***!* are other performing-animal routines, all in venues seating more than 2,000; during the summer, human acrobats are added to the mix with **Cirque de la Mer.** A collection of rides is led by **Journey to Atlantis,** a roller coaster and log flume; **Shipwreck Rapids** is a splashy adventure on raftlike inner tubes, and **Wild Arctic** is a simulated helicopter trip to the frozen north. **Manta** is a brand-new coaster ride that immerses guests in the world of rays. There's

 Now *That's* **a Deal!**

If you plan to visit both the zoo and the Zoo Safari Park, a 2-Visit Pass is $76 for adults, $56 for children ages 3 to 11; passes are valid for 1 year (and can be used twice at the same attraction, if you choose). A 3-for-1 pass gives you 1-day passes to the zoo and Zoo Safari Park, and unlimited entry to SeaWorld for 7 days from first use. The cost is $135 adults, $105 children ages 3 to 9.

Other value options include the **Southern California CityPass** (✆ **888/330-5008;** www.citypass.com), which covers

the zoo or Zoo Safari Park, plus SeaWorld, Disneyland Resorts, and Universal Studios in Los Angeles; passes are $279 for adults, or $239 for kids age 3 to 9 (a savings of about 25%), and are valid for 14 days. The **Go San Diego Card** (✆ **866/628-9032;** www.gosandiegocard.com) offers unlimited general admission to more than 50 attractions, including the zoo and LEGOLAND, as well as deals on tours, shopping, and dining. One-day packages start at $74 for adults and $58 for children (ages 3–12).

also a passel of *Sesame Street*–related attractions, including rides and a "4-D" interactive movie experience. **Quick Queue** passes (an additional $25–$35) provide front-of-line access to some rides and shows.

SeaWorld's real specialties are simulated marine environments, though, including an arctic enclosure featuring beluga whales and polar bears; other animal highlights are the **Shark Encounter** and **Penguin Encounter.**

Visitors can also sign up for various guided tours and interactive offerings. The **Dolphin** and **Beluga Interaction Programs** allow you to wade waist-deep with dolphins and beluga whales; there is some classroom time involved before participants wriggle into a wetsuit and climb into the water for 20 minutes. It costs $190 per person (not including park admission); participants must be age 10 or older. Advance reservations required (© **800/257-4268**).

Although SeaWorld is best known as the home to pirouetting dolphins and fluke-flinging killer whales, it also plays a role in rescuing and rehabilitating beached animals found along the West Coast. Still, there is a troubling aspect to this kind of facility—for another point of view, check out the **Whale and Dolphin Conservation Society** at www.wdcs.org.

500 SeaWorld Dr., Mission Bay. www.seaworld.com. © **800/257-4268** or 619/226-3901. Admission $73 adults, $65 children 3–9, free for children 2 and under; tickets are good for 7 consecutive days of unlimited admission. AE, DISC, MC, V. Hours vary seasonally, but always at least daily 10am–5pm; most weekends and during summer 9am–11pm. Parking $14, $19 RVs. Bus: 9. From I-5, take SeaWorld Dr. exit; from I-8, take W. Mission Bay Dr. exit to SeaWorld Dr.

SAN DIEGO'S BEACHES

San Diego County is blessed with 70 miles of sandy coastline and more than 30 individual beaches. When it comes to enjoying the San Diego shores, though, a word (or four actually) to the wise: **May Gray** and **June Gloom.** They're both names for a local weather pattern that can be counted on to foil sunbathing most mornings (and sometimes all day) from mid-May to mid-July. Overcast skies appear as the desert heats up at the end of spring, sucking the marine layer—a thick bank of fog—inland for a few miles each night. Be prepared for moist mornings and evenings (and sometimes afternoons) at the beaches this time of year. *But remember:* The sun may not be shining brightly, but that doesn't mean you're not being exposed to harmful UV rays; always wear sunscreen during prolonged outdoor exposure. Another beach precaution worth remembering is the "stingray shuffle." At beaches where the water is calm, such as Mission Bay and La Jolla Shores, it's a good idea to shuffle your feet as you walk through the surf—it rousts any stingrays that might be in your path.

Another sting to beware of is the pain you might feel if you're caught drinking alcohol or smoking on any San Diego beach, bay shore, or at coastal parks. In 2008, voters approved a **ban on alcohol** at the beach; first offense has a maximum fine of $250. Smoking is also illegal at all city beaches, boardwalks, piers, and parks.

Exploring **tide pools**—potholed, rocky shores that retain ponds of water after the tide has gone out, providing homes for a plethora of sea creatures—is a time-honored coastal pleasure. You can get a tide chart free or for a nominal charge from many surf and diving shops. Among the best places for tide-pooling are Cabrillo National Monument, at the oceanside base of Point Loma; Sunset Cliffs in Ocean Beach; and along the rocky coast immediately south of the cove in La Jolla.

Here's a list of San Diego's most noteworthy beaches, each with its own personality and devotees. They're listed geographically from south to north. All California beaches are open to the public to the mean high-tide line (essentially the hard-packed sand), and you can check www.sandiego.gov/lifeguards/beaches for descriptions and water quality. Beach closures due to bacterial contamination are a modern-day fact of life, especially following storms when runoff from city streets makes its way to the ocean—check for posted warnings, or call the county's Beach and Bay Status hot line (© 619/338-2073) for the latest info. For the daily beach, tide, dive, and surf report, call © 619/221-8824. *Note:* All beaches are good for swimming except as indicated. For a map of San Diego's beaches, see the color map at the beginning of this book.

Imperial Beach

Imperial Beach is just a half-hour south of downtown San Diego by car or trolley, and only a few minutes from the Mexican border. It's popular with surfers and "I.B." locals, who can be somewhat territorial about "their" beach in summer. There are 3 miles of surf breaks plus a guarded "swimmers only" stretch; check with lifeguards before getting wet, though, since sewage runoff from nearby Mexico can sometimes foul the water.

Coronado Beach ★★

Lovely, wide, and sparkling, this beach is conducive to strolling and lingering, especially in the late afternoon. At the north end, you can watch fighter jets in formation flying from the Naval Air Station, while just south is the pretty section fronting Ocean Boulevard and the Hotel del Coronado. Waves are gentle here, so the beach draws many Coronado families—and their dogs, which are allowed off-leash at the most northwesterly end. South of the Hotel Del, the beach becomes the beautiful, often deserted **Silver Strand.**

Ocean Beach ★

The northern end of Ocean Beach Park, officially known as **Dog Beach,** is one of only a few in the county where your pooch can roam freely on the sand (and frolic with several dozen other people's pets). Surfers generally congregate around the O.B. Pier, mostly in the water but often at the snack shack on the end. Rip currents can be strong here and sometimes discourage swimmers from venturing beyond waist depth (check with the lifeguard stations). Facilities at the beach include restrooms, showers, picnic tables, volleyball courts, and plenty of metered parking lots. To reach the beach, take West Point Loma Boulevard all the way to the end.

Mission Bay Park ★★

This 4,200-acre aquatic playground contains 27 miles of bayfront, picnic areas, children's playgrounds, and paths for biking, in-line skating, and jogging. This man-made bay lends itself to windsurfing, sailing, water-skiing, and fishing. There are dozens of access points; one of the most popular is off I-5 at Clairemont Drive. Also accessed from this spot is **Fiesta Island,** where the annual **World Championship Over-the-Line Tournament** is held to raucous enthusiasm in July (see "Calendar of Events," in chapter 2). A 4-mile road loops around the island. Parts of the bay have been subject to closure over the years due to high levels of bacteria, so check for posted warnings.

Bonita Cove/Mariner's Point & Mission Point ★★

Also enclosed in Mission Bay Park, near the mouth of the Mission Bay Channel, this pretty and protected cove's calm waters, grassy picnic areas, and playground equipment make it perfect for families—or as a paddling destination, if you've rented kayaks elsewhere in the bay. The water is also cleaner for swimming than in the northeastern reaches of Mission Bay. Get to Bonita Cove from Mission Boulevard in south Mission Beach; reach Mariner's Point via Mariner's Way, off West Mission Bay Drive.

Mission Beach ★

While Mission Bay Park is a body of saltwater surrounded by land and bridges, Mission Beach is actually a beach on the Pacific Ocean, anchored by the **Giant Dipper** roller coaster. Always popular, the sands and wide cement "boardwalk" sizzle with activity and people-watching in summer (or anytime the weather is nice); at the southern end, a volleyball game is almost always underway. The long beach and path extend from the jetty north to Belmont Park and Pacific Beach Drive. Parking is often tough, with your best bets being the public lots at Belmont Park or at the south end of West Mission Bay Drive; this street intersects with Mission Boulevard, the center-line of a 2-block-wide isthmus that leads a mile north to Pacific Beach.

Pacific Beach ★

There's always action here, particularly along **Ocean Front Walk,** a paved promenade featuring a human parade akin to L.A.'s Venice Beach boardwalk. It runs along Ocean Boulevard (just west of Mission Blvd.) to the pier. Surfing is popular year-round here, in marked sections; and the beach is well staffed with lifeguards. You're on your own to find street parking. Pacific Beach is also the home of **Tourmaline Surfing Park,** a half-mile north of the pier, where the sport's old guard gathers to surf waters where swimmers are prohibited; reach it via Tourmaline Street, off Mission Boulevard.

Windansea Beach ★★

The fabled locale of Tom Wolfe's *Pump House Gang,* Windansea is legendary to this day among California's surf elite and remains one of San Diego's prettiest strands. Reached by way of Bonair Street (at Neptune Place), Windansea has no facilities, and street parking is first-come, first-served. It's not ideal for swimming, so come to surf (no novices, please), watch surfers, or soak in the camaraderie and party atmosphere.

Children's Pool ★★★

Think clothing-optional Black's Beach is the city's most controversial sun-sea-sand situation? Think again—the Children's Pool is currently home to the biggest man-vs.-beast struggle since *Moby-Dick.* A sea wall protects this pocket of sand, originally intended as a calm swimming bay for children. Since 1994, when a rock outcrop off the shore was designated as a protected mammal reserve, the beach has been colonized by a **harbor seal** population. On an average day (usually fall to spring) you'll spot dozens lolling in the sun. Some humans did not take kindly to their beach banishment, and the fight was on. After much heated debate (and even acts of civil disobedience), swimming was reinstated—to the displeasure of many. So while it is possible to now swim at the Children's Pool, keep in mind those are federally protected *wild* animals and it is illegal to approach them or harass them in any way. Volunteers, with speed dials set to "lifeguard," keep watch to make sure bathers don't interfere with the colony—scofflaws will get arrested. The dispute rages on—for the latest info check www.lajollafriendsoftheseals.org. The beach is at Coast Boulevard and Jenner Street; there's limited free street parking.

La Jolla Cove ★★★

The cove's protected, calm waters—celebrated as the clearest along the coast—attract snorkelers and scuba divers, along with a fair share of families. The stunning setting offers a small sandy beach, with **Ellen Browning Scripps Park** located on the cliffs above. The cove's "look but don't touch" policy protects the colorful garibaldi, California's state fish, plus other marine life, including abalone, octopus, and lobster. The unique Underwater Park stretches from here to the northern end of Torrey Pines State Reserve and incorporates kelp forests, artificial reefs, two deep canyons, and tidal pools. The cove is terrific for swimming, cramped for sunbathing, and accessible from Coast Boulevard; parking is scarce.

La Jolla Shores ★★★

The wide, flat mile of sand at La Jolla Shores is popular with joggers, swimmers, families, kayakers, novice scuba divers, and beginning body- and board-surfers. It looks like a picture postcard, with fine sand under blue skies, kissed by gentle waves. Weekend crowds can be enormous, though, quickly claiming fire rings and occupying both the sand and the metered parking spaces in the lot. There are restrooms and showers, as well as picnic areas at grassy, palm-lined Kellogg Park.

Black's Beach ★★★

The area's unofficial nude beach (though technically nude sunbathing is illegal), 2-mile-long Black's lies between La Jolla Shores and Torrey Pines State Beach, at the base of steep, 300-foot-high cliffs. The beach is out-of-the-way and not easy to reach, but it draws scores with its secluded beauty and good swimming and surfing—the graceful spectacle of paragliders launching from the cliffs above adds to the show. To get here, take North Torrey Pines Road, watch for signs for the Gliderport (where you can park), and clamber down the makeshift path, staying alert to avoid veering off a false trail. To bypass the cliff descent, you can walk to Black's from beaches north (Torrey Pines) or south (La Jolla Shores). **Note:** There are no restroom facilities and no permanent lifeguard station, though lifeguards are usually present from spring holidays to October. The beach's notoriety came about when, from 1974 to 1977, swimsuits *were* optional—the only such beach in the U.S. to be so designated at the time. Rich neighbors on the cliffs above complained enough to the city about their property being denigrated that the clothing-optional status was reversed. Still, citations for nude sunbathing are rarely issued—lifeguards will either ignore it or just ask you to cover up. Tickets *will* be written if you disregard their request.

Torrey Pines Beach ★★★

Past the north end of Black's Beach, at the foot of Torrey Pines State Park, is this fabulous, underused strand, accessed by a pay parking lot at the entrance to the park. Combining a visit to the park with a day at the beach makes for the quintessential San Diego outdoor experience. It's rarely crowded, though you need to be aware of high tide (when most of the sand gets a bath). In almost any weather, it's a great beach for walking. **Note:** At this and any other bluffside beach, never sit at the bottom of the cliffs; they are unstable and could collapse.

Del Mar Beach ★★

The Del Mar Thoroughbred Club's slogan, as famously sung by DMTC founder Bing Crosby, is "where the turf meets the surf." This town beach represents the "surf" portion of that phrase. It's a long stretch of sand backed by grassy cliffs and a playground area. This area is not too heavily trafficked, and you can dine right alongside the beach at **Jake's** (p. 224) or **Poseidon** (p. 223). Del Mar is about 15 miles from downtown San Diego; see "North County Beach Towns," in chapter 10, on p. 220.

Northern San Diego County Beaches

Those inclined to venture farther north in San Diego County won't be disappointed—Pacific Coast Highway leads to a string of inviting beaches. In Encinitas, there are peaceful **Boneyards Beach, Swami's Beach** for surfing, and **Moonlight Beach,** popular with families and volleyball buffs. Farthest north is **Oceanside,** which has one of the West Coast's longest wooden piers, wide sandy beaches, and several popular surfing areas. See "North County Beach Towns," in chapter 10, on p. 220, for more information.

ATTRACTIONS IN BALBOA PARK

San Diego's crown jewel is Balboa Park, a 1,174-acre playground and the nation's largest urban cultural park. It's also the country's second-oldest city park (after New York's Central Park), established in 1868 in the heart of the city, bordered by downtown to the southwest and fringed by the early communities of Hillcrest and Golden Hill to the north and east. Originally called City Park, the name was eventually changed to commemorate the Spanish explorer Balboa. Tree plantings started in the late 19th century, while the initial buildings were created to host the 1915–16 Panama-California Exposition; another expo in 1935–36 brought additional developments.

The park's most distinctive features are its mature landscaping, the architectural beauty of the Spanish Colonial Revival–style buildings lining El Prado (the park's east-west pedestrian thoroughfare), and the engaging and diverse museums contained within it. You'll also find eight different gardens, walkways, 4.5 miles of hiking trails in Florida Canyon, an ornate pavilion with one of the world's largest outdoor organs, an IMAX domed theater, the acclaimed **Old Globe Theatre** (p. 169), and the **San Diego Zoo** (p. 40).

The park is divided into three distinct sections, separated by Hwy. 163 and Florida Canyon. The narrow western wing of the park consists of largely grassy open areas that parallel Sixth Avenue—it's a good place for picnics, strolling, sunning, and dog-walking; the only museum in this section is the **Marston House** (p. 50). The eastern section is devoid of cultural attractions, but has the **Balboa Park Municipal Golf Course** (p. 82). The central portion of the park, between Hwy. 163 and Florida Drive, contains the zoo and all of the museums.

If you really want to visit the zoo and a few of the park's museums, don't try to tackle it all in the same day. Allow at least 3 hours to tour the zoo; the amount of time you spend in the 15 major museums will vary depending on your personal interests. Check out the **walking tour** that takes in most of the park's highlights (p. 107). There are informal restaurants serving sandwiches and snacks throughout the park—for breakfast, **Tobey's 19th Hole** at the municipal golf course is a find (p. 82); try lunch at the Japanese Friendship Garden's **Tea Pavilion** (p. 50) or in the **San Diego**

Balboa Park Attractions

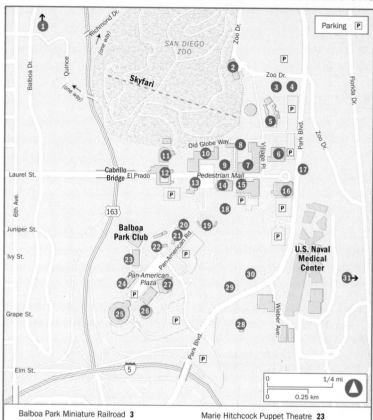

Balboa Park Miniature Railroad **3**
Balboa Park Municipal Golf Course **31**
Botanical Building and Lily Pond **8**
Carousel **4**
Casa de Balboa **15**
   Museum of Photographic Arts
   San Diego History Center
   San Diego Model Railroad Museum
Casa del Prado **7**
Centro Cultural de la Raza **30**
Hall of Nations **20**
House of Charm **13**
   Mingei International Museum
   SDAI Museum of the Living Artist
House of Hospitality **14**
   Balboa Park Visitors Center
   Prado Restaurant
House of Pacific Relations
   International Cottages **22**
Japanese Friendship Garden **18**

Marie Hitchcock Puppet Theatre **23**
Marston House **1**
Old Globe Theatre **11**
Reuben H. Fleet Science Center **16**
Rose and Desert Gardens **17**
San Diego Air & Space Museum **25**
San Diego Automotive Museum **24**
San Diego Hall of Champions
   Sports Museum **27**
San Diego Museum of Art **10**
San Diego Museum of Man **12**
San Diego Natural History Museum **6**
San Diego Zoo entrance **2**
Spanish Village Art Center **5**
Spreckels Organ Pavilion **19**
Starlight Bowl **26**
Timken Museum of Art **9**
United Nations Building **21**
Veterans Museum & Memorial Center **28**
WorldBeat Center **29**

Museum of Art's sculpture garden (p. 52). The **Prado Restaurant** is also a San Diego favorite for lunch or dinner.

There are two primary **road entrances** into the heart of the park. The most distinctive is from Sixth Avenue and Laurel Street: Laurel turns into El Prado as it traverses the beautiful **Cabrillo Bridge** ★ across Highway 163. You can also enter via Presidents Way from Park Boulevard. Major **parking areas** are at Inspiration Point just east of Park Boulevard at Presidents Way; in front of the zoo; and along Presidents Way between the Aerospace Museum and Spreckels Organ Pavilion. Other lots, though more centrally located, are small and in high demand, especially on weekends.

Public **bus** no. 7 runs along Park Boulevard; for the west side of the park, nos. 1, 3, and 120 run along Fourth and Fifth avenues (except for the Marston House, all museums are closer to Park Blvd.). Free **tram** transportation within the park runs daily from 8:15am to 5:15pm, with extended hours in summer months. The red trolley trams originate at the Inspiration Point parking lot to circuit the park, arriving every 8 to 10 minutes and stopping at designated pickup areas. Stop by the **Balboa Park Visitors Center,** in the House of Hospitality (© 619/239-0512; www.balboapark.org), to learn about walking and museum **tours,** or to pick up a brochure about the **gardens** of the park; the visitor center is open daily, 9:30am to 4:30pm. *Note:* Some museums are closed on Mondays.

Balboa Park Miniature Railroad and Carousel ☺ AMUSEMENT PARK

Just east of the zoo entrance, these antiquated enticements never fail to delight the preteen set. The open-air railroad takes a 3-minute journey through a grove of eucalyptus trees, while the charming carousel is one of the last in the world to still offer a ring grab (free ride if you seize the brass one). The carousel, built in 1910, is a classic, with hand-carved wood frogs, horses, and pigs.

Zoo Dr., next to San Diego Zoo entrance. www.sandiegozoo.org. Railroad © **619-231-1515.** Admission $3 Railroad (free for children 11 months and under). Summer daily 11am–6:30pm; Sept–May weekends and holidays only 11am–4:30pm. Carousel © **619/239-0512.** www.balboapark.org. Admission $3 Carousel. Summer daily 11am–5pm; Sept–May weekends and holidays only 11am–5pm. Bus: 7.

Botanical Building and Lily Pond ★ PARK/GARDEN

This serene park within the park features ferns, orchids, impatiens, begonias, and other plants—about 2,100 tropical and flowering varieties, plus rotating exhibits. The graceful,

Balboa Park Money-Savers

If you plan to visit more than three of the park's museums, buy the **Passport to Balboa Park**—it allows entrance to 14 museums and attractions, and is valid for 1 week. It's $49 for adults, $27 for children 3 to 12. If you plan to spend a day at the zoo and return for the museums another day, buy the **Passport/Zoo Combo,** which provides one ticket to the zoo and admission to the museums for $83 adults, $47 children. The **Stay-for-the-Day** pass gives you 1-day access to five museums for $39 (ages 13 and above only). Passports can be purchased at any participating attraction (but not the zoo), at the visitor center, or online at www.balboapark.org. *Note:* Passports may not cover admission to special exhibitions.

ALL ABOUT BALBOA PARK guided TOURS

Guided tours of the park cater to a wide variety of interests, from historical to horticultural (most tours start from the **visitor center**, ℂ 619/239-0512; www. balboapark.org). There are free rotating tours on Saturdays at 10am that highlight either the palm trees and vegetation or park history; park rangers lead free 1-hour tours focusing on the park's history, architecture, and botanical resources every Tuesday and Sunday at 11am. Rangers also conduct trail walks through the park on the second Wednesday of the month. The **Committee of 100** (ℂ **619/795-9362;** www.c100.org), an organization dedicated to preserving the park's Spanish Colonial architecture, offers a free exploration of the historic structures on the first Wednesday of the month. A self-guided audio tour is also available at the visitor center

costing $5 for adults; $4 for seniors, students, and military; and $3 for children 3 to 11.

The 90-minute **Old Globe Theatre Tour** visits the three performance venues and backstage areas on most Saturdays and Sundays at 10:30am; the tour costs $5 for adults and $3 for seniors and students (ℂ **619/231-1941;** www.theold globe.org). **Plant Day** at the San Diego Zoo is held the third Friday of each month and features self-guided and guided horticultural tours and activities. The orchid house is open to the public 10am to 2pm on Plant Day, as well as for **Orchid Odyssey** on the first Sundays of March, June, September, and December (zoo admission required; call ℂ **619/231-1515** for more details, or go to www. sandiegozoo.org).

250-foot-long domed building, part of the 1915 Panama-California Exposition, is one of the world's largest wood lath structures. Kids love the "touch and smell" garden and the smelly bog of carnivorous plants. The lily pond out front attracts sun worshipers, painters, and buskers.

El Prado. www.balboapark.org. ℂ **619/235-1100.** Free admission. Fri–Wed 10am–4pm; closed Thurs and major holidays. Bus: 7.

Centro Cultural de la Raza 🏛 CULTURAL INSTITUTION   This building has a less glamorous provenance than most other park facilities—it's an old water storage tank built during World War II. The circular structure is now festooned with colorful murals and hosts performances, art exhibits, and classes in support and celebration of Mexican, Chicano, and indigenous art and culture.

2125 Park Blvd. www.centroculturaldelaraza.org. ℂ **619/235-6135.** Gallery admission $3–$5 donation suggested. Tues–Sun noon–4pm. Bus: 7.

House of Pacific Relations International Cottages CULTURAL INSTITUTION   This cluster of 17 charming one- and two-room cottages disseminates information about the culture, traditions, and history of more than 30 countries. Open houses are scheduled every Sunday from noon to 4pm; ethnic foods are served and outdoor lawn programs are presented by one of the nations every Sunday, from 2 to 3pm, March through October. The adjacent **United Nations Building** houses an international gift shop where you can buy jewelry, toys, books, and UNICEF greeting cards (ℂ **619/233-5044;** www.unasd.org); it's open daily from 10am to 4:30pm.

Adjacent to Pan American Plaza. www.sdhpr.org. ℂ **619/234-0739.** Free admission (donations welcome). Sun noon–4pm; 2nd and 4th Tues of each month 11am–3pm. Bus: 7.

Japanese Friendship Garden 🏛 PARK/GARDEN Of the 12 acres designated for the garden, only 2 acres have been developed. Still to come are herb and tea gardens, a cherry tree grove, a lily pond, and an amphitheater. What is here, though, is beautifully serene and is referred to as *San-Kei-En,* or "three-scene garden." It represents ties to San Diego's sister city of Yokohama, which has a similarly named garden. From the main gate, a crooked path (to confound evil spirits, who move only in a straight line) threads its way to the information center in a traditional Japanese-style house. Here you can view the most ancient kind of garden, the *sekitei,* made only of sand and stone (a self-guided tour is available). Tea, sushi, noodles, and more are served on a deck to the left of the entrance; imported gifts are also for sale. Japanese holidays are celebrated here, and the public is invited.

2125 Park Blvd., adjacent to the Organ Pavilion. www.niwa.org. ⓒ **619/232-2721.** Admission $4 adults; $3 seniors, students, and military; free for children 6 and under. Daily 10am–4pm (closed every 5th Mon of the month). Bus: 7.

Marston House Museum & Gardens ★ HISTORIC HOME Noted San Diego architects Irving Gill and William Hebbard designed this Craftsman house in 1905 for George Marston, a local businessman and philanthropist. The architecture shows the Asian influence of the Arts and Crafts movement as well as elements of Frank Lloyd Wright's Prairie School; the home is also furnished with Roycroft, Stickley, and Limbert pieces, and a lovely collection of art pottery. The home and gardens, which are listed on the National Register of Historic Places, are complemented by a gift shop in the carriage house; you'll find books, decorative items, and more. Tours take about 45 minutes and depart every half-hour.

3525 Seventh Ave. (northwest corner of Balboa Park at Balboa Dr. and Upas St.). www.sohosan diego.org. ⓒ **619/297-9327** or 619/298-3142. $10 adults, $7 seniors, $4 children 6–12, free for children 5 and under. Fri–Mon 10am–5pm (Thurs–Mon in summer). Bus: 3 or 120.

Mingei International Museum ★★ MUSEUM This captivating museum (pronounced "*min*-gay," meaning "art of the people" in Japanese) offers changing exhibitions generally describable as folk art. The exhibits—usually four at a time—encompass artists from countries across the globe; displays include textiles, costumes, jewelry, toys, pottery, paintings, and sculpture. The permanent collection features whimsical contemporary sculptures by French artist Niki de Saint Phalle, who made San Diego her home from 1993 until her death in 2002. Martha Longenecker, a potter and professor emeritus of art at San Diego State University, opened the museum in 1978. It is one of only a few major museums in the United States devoted to folk crafts on a worldwide scale and well worth a look. Allow up to an hour to view the exhibits; there's also a wonderful gift store that's worth a visit on its own.

1439 El Prado, in the House of Charm. www.mingei.org. ⓒ **619/239-0003.** Admission $8 adults; $5 seniors; children 6–17, students, and military with ID; free for children 5 and under. Tues–Sun 10am–4pm. Bus: 7.

Museum of Photographic Arts ★★★ MUSEUM If the names Ansel Adams and Edward Weston stimulate your fingers to do the shutterbug, then don't miss a taste of the 7,000-plus collection of images housed here. This is one of the few museums in the country devoted exclusively to the photographic arts (which, at MoPA, encompasses cinema, video, and digital photography). A 1999 expansion allowed the museum to display even more of the permanent collection, while leaving room for provocative traveling exhibits that change every few months. Photos by Alfred

Stieglitz, Margaret Bourke-White, Imogen Cunningham, and Manuel Alvarez Bravo are all in the permanent collection, and the plush cinema illuminates classic films on an ongoing basis. Allow 30 to 60 minutes to see the collection.

1649 El Prado. www.mopa.org. ✆ **619/238-7559.** Admission $8 adults, $6 seniors and retired military (and their dependents), $5 students, free for active-duty military (and their dependents) and children 12 and under with adult. Tues–Sun 10am–5pm. Bus: 7.

Reuben H. Fleet Science Center ★ ☺ MUSEUM   A must-see for kids of any age, this tantalizing collection of more than 100 interactive exhibits and experiences is designed to stimulate the imagination and teach scientific principles. The Fleet also houses an IMAX Dome Theater (the world's first) showing films on such a grand scale that ocean footage can actually give you motion sickness; every Friday evening, three or four different IMAX films are shown in succession at discounted prices. The Fleet also has a spiffy planetarium simulator powered by computer graphics; planetarium shows are presented daily ($12–$16 adults, $10–$13 seniors and kids 3–12). With all the interactive attractions, you'll need at least 90 minutes here. If it's during the school year, plan to visit after 1pm when school groups have departed.

1875 El Prado. www.rhfleet.org. ✆ **619/238-1233.** Admission plus an IMAX film $16 adults, $13 seniors and children 3–12 (exhibit gallery can be purchased individually, $12 adults, $10 seniors and children). Mon–Thurs 10am–5pm; Fri 10am–8pm; Sat 10am–7pm; Sun 10am–6pm. Bus: 7.

San Diego Air & Space Museum ★★ ☺ MUSEUM   The other big kid-pleaser of the museums (along with the Reuben H. Fleet Science Center, above), this popular facility has more than 60 aircraft on display, providing an overview of aeronautical history from hot-air balloons to spacecraft. It emphasizes local aviation history, particularly the construction here of the *Spirit of St. Louis*; you'll also find flight simulator rides and a theater screening 3-D films (with added "4-D" special effects built into the seats). The museum is housed in a cylindrical hall built by the Ford Motor Company in 1935 for the park's second international expo. The imaginative gift shop stocks items such as old-fashioned leather flight hoods and new-fashioned freeze-dried astronaut ice cream. Allow at least an hour for your visit.

2001 Pan American Plaza. www.sandiegoairandspace.org. ✆ **619/234-8291.** Admission $18 adults; $15 seniors, retired military, and students with ID; $7 children 3–11; free for active military with ID and children 2 and under. Sept–May daily 10am–4:30pm; June–Aug daily 10am–5:30pm. Bus: 7.

SDAI Museum of the Living Artist ART MUSEUM   Established in 1941, the San Diego Art Institute exhibits new pieces by local artists. The 10,000-square-foot municipal gallery rotates juried shows in and out every 4 to 6 weeks, ensuring a variety of mediums and styles. It's a good place to see what the San Diego art community is up to; young artists from area schools exhibit here, too. Local artisans sell their wares in the gift store. Plan to spend about half an hour here.

1439 El Prado. www.sandiego-art.org. ✆ **619/236-0011.** Admission $3 adults; $2 seniors, students, and military; free for children 12 and under. Tues–Sat 10am–4pm; Sun noon–4pm. Bus: 7.

San Diego Automotive Museum ★ MUSEUM   Even if you don't know a distributor from a dipstick, you're bound to *ooh* and *aah* over the more than 80 classic, antique, and exotic cars here. Each one is so pristine you'd swear it just rolled off the line, from an 1886 Benz to a 1931 Rolls-Royce Phaeton to the 1981 DeLorean. Most of the time, temporary shows take over the facility, so check ahead to see if it's one you're interested in. Some days you can take a peek at the ongoing restoration program, and the museum sponsors many car rallies and other special events. Allow 30 to 45 minutes for your visit.

2080 Pan American Plaza. www.sdautomuseum.org. ⓒ **619/231-2886.** Admission $8 adults, $6 seniors and active military, $5 students, $4 children 6–15, free for children 5 and under. Daily 10am–5pm (last admission 4:30pm). Bus: 7.

San Diego Hall of Champions Sports Museum MUSEUM   From Padres great Tony Gwynn and skateboard icon Tony Hawk to Olympic gold medalist Shaun White and Hall of Fame quarterback Dan Fouts, this slick museum celebrates San Diego's best-ever athletes and the sports they played. This three-level, 68,000-square-foot facility features more than 25 exhibits, including memorabilia from around the world of sports (the biggies and the niche ones), rotating art shows, and interactive stations where you can try out your play-by-play skills. One particularly interesting exhibit is devoted to athletes with disabilities. You can see it all in under an hour.

2131 Pan American Plaza. www.sdhoc.com. ⓒ **619/234-2544.** Admission $8 adults; $6 seniors 65 and older, students, and military; $4 children 7–17; free for children 6 and under. Daily 10am–4:30pm. Bus: 7.

San Diego History Center MUSEUM   Operated by the San Diego Historical Society, this museum offers permanent and changing exhibits on topics related to the history of the region. Past shows have examined subjects ranging from San Diego's role as a Hollywood film location to the city's architectural heritage; many of the museum's photographs depict Balboa Park and the growth of the city. Plan to spend about 30 to 45 minutes here. Books about San Diego's history are available in the gift shop, and the research library downstairs is open Wednesday through Saturday (9:30am–1pm).

1649 El Prado, in Casa del Balboa. www.sandiegohistory.org. ⓒ **619/232-6203.** Admission $6 adults; $4 students, seniors, and military with ID; $3 children 6–17; free for children 5 and under. Tues–Sun 10am–5pm. Bus: 7.

San Diego Model Railroad Museum ★ ☺ MUSEUM   So it's not exactly high culture, but this museum is worth your time, especially if you have kids in tow. Five permanent, scale-model railroads depict Southern California's transportation history and terrain with an astounding attention to miniature details. The exhibits occupy a 27,000-square-foot space, making it the world's largest indoor model railroad display. Children will enjoy the hands-on Lionel trains, and train buffs of all ages will appreciate the interactive multimedia displays. Allow a half-hour to an hour for your visit.

1649 El Prado (Casa de Balboa), under the Museum of Photographic Arts. www.sdmrm.org. ⓒ **619/696-0199.** Admission $8 adults, $6 seniors, $3 students, $4 military, free for children 14 and under. Tues–Fri 11am–4pm; Sat–Sun 11am–5pm. Bus: 7.

The San Diego Museum of Art ★ ART MUSEUM   Opened in 1926, this is the oldest and largest art museum in San Diego. It's known for its collection of Spanish baroque painting and possibly the most extensive horde of South Asian paintings outside India; the museum's holdings of Latin American work have grown significantly in recent years, as well. The American collection, which features paintings and decorative arts, includes works by Georgia O'Keeffe, Mary Cassatt, and Thomas Eakins. Only a small percentage of the 12,000-piece permanent collection is on display at any given time, though, in favor of varied—often prestigious—touring shows. SDMA also has an ongoing schedule of concerts, films, cocktail parties, and lectures, usually tied thematically to a current exhibition. The museum's **Sculpture Court Café** (11am–3pm) is a casually elegant outdoor dining spot, highlighted by works of art by Henry Moore and others.

1450 El Prado. www.sdmart.org. © **619/232-7931.** Admission $12 adults, $9 seniors and military, $8 students, $4.50 children 7–17, free for children 6 and under; family 4-pack $28. Admission to traveling exhibits varies. Tues–Sat 10am–5pm; Sun noon–5pm; Thurs 10am–9pm in summer. Bus: 7.

San Diego Museum of Man ★ MUSEUM The iconic California Building, with its amazing tiled dome and signature bell tower, is where you will find this museum devoted to anthropology. Exhibits emphasize the peoples of North and South America, and also include life-size replicas of a dozen types of *Homo sapiens* (from Cro-Magnon to Neanderthal) as well as Egyptian mummies and artifacts. Don't overlook the annex across the street, which houses more displays; the museum store, with its selection of books, clothing, and folk art, is worth a peek, too. Several times a year the museum celebrates a different international culture with its Tower After Hours soiree ($20 adults, $15 students), featuring music, food, and special exhibits. Allow at least an hour for your visit.

1350 El Prado. www.museumofman.org. © **619/239-2001.** Admission $13 adults; $10 seniors and active-duty military, $8 students, $5 children 3–12; free for children 2 and under. Daily 10am–4:30pm. Bus: 3, 7, or 120.

San Diego Natural History Museum ☺ MUSEUM Founded in 1874, the Nat is one of the oldest scientific institutions in the western United States. It focuses on the flora, fauna, and mineralogy of Southern California, including Baja; as a binational museum, research is done on both sides of the border and most exhibits are bilingual. You can see them all in about an hour. There's a 300-seat large-format movie theater that boasts the latest in 3-D technology, and two or three films are screened throughout the day (included with admission). The interactive installation *Fossil Mysteries* explores the region's prehistory and includes life-size models of primeval animals such as the Megalodon shark, the largest predator the world has ever known. The Nat also leads free nature hikes and has a full schedule of classes, lectures, and overnight expeditions for both children and adults.

1788 El Prado. www.sdnhm.org. © **619/232-3821.** Admission $17 adults; $15 seniors; $12 students, children age 13–17, and active-duty military; $11 children 3–12; free for children 2 and under. Daily 10am–5pm. Bus: 7.

Spreckels Organ Pavilion PERFORMING ARTS VENUE Presented to the citizens of San Diego in 1914 by brothers John D. and Adolph Spreckels, the ornate, curved pavilion houses a magnificent organ with 4,518 individual pipes. They range in length from the size of a pencil to 32 feet, making it one of the largest outdoor organs in the world. Visitors can enjoy free hour-long concerts on Sundays at 2pm, given by civic organist Carol Williams; free concerts are also held in the evening during the summer months. There's seating for 2,400 but little shade, so bring some sunscreen.

South of El Prado. www.sosorgan.com. © **619/702-8138.** Free 1-hr. organ concerts Sun 2pm year-round; free organ concerts late June–Aug Mon 7:30pm (see website for a schedule); free Twilight in the Park concerts Tues–Thurs, mid-June to Aug, 6:15–7:15pm (© 619/239-0512 for schedule). Bus: 7.

Timken Museum of Art ★ 📷 ART MUSEUM How many art museums invite you to see great works of art for free? The Timken houses the Putnam Foundation's collection of 19th-century American paintings and works by European old masters, as well as a worthy display of Russian icons. Yes, it's a small collection, but the marquee attractions include Peter Paul Rubens's *Portrait of a Young Man in Armor;* San Diego's only Rembrandt, *St. Bartholomew;* and a masterpiece by Eastman Johnson, *The Cranberry Harvest.* Because you can tour all of the museum in well under an hour, the Timken also makes for an easy introduction to fine art for younger travelers; free docent tours are available daily.

1500 El Prado. www.timkenmuseum.org. (C) **619/239-5548.** Free admission. Tues–Sat 10am–4:30pm; Sun 1:30–4:30pm. Bus: 7.

WorldBeat Center ★ 🏛 CULTURAL INSTITUTION   In a former water storage tank on Park Boulevard, the WorldBeat Center is on a mission to "heal the world through music, dance, art, technology, and culture." They start by bringing in some of the biggest names in reggae and African music, and follow up by holding nearly daily drum and dance classes (drop-ins welcome). Special events, lectures, and roots-conscious celebrations are all part of the mix, too. Musical instruments, textiles, decorative accessories, and other fair-trade items made by indigenous cultures from around the globe are on sale at the gift store. Are you feeling *irie?*

2100 Park Blvd. www.worldbeatcenter.org. (C) **619/230-1190.** Admission price to events and classes varies. Mon–Fri 10am–7pm; Sat–Sun noon–6pm. Bus: 7.

MORE ATTRACTIONS
Downtown & Beyond

Wander through the turn-of-the-20th-century **Gaslamp Quarter ★★** to the joyful, modern architecture of the **Horton Plaza ★** shopping center. (See "Walking Tour 1: The Gaslamp Quarter," in chapter 5.) Adjacent to the Gaslamp is the East Village, which, thanks to the opening of **PETCO Park ★** (p. 180) in 2004, has extended downtown a few blocks farther east.

   Seaport Village (p. 152) is a shopping and dining complex on the waterfront offering stellar views; while another way to experience San Diego's waterfront is with one of several harbor tours (see "Organized Tours," later in this chapter).

Cabrillo National Monument ★★★ 📷 HISTORIC SITE   Breathtaking views mingle with the history of San Diego, starting with the arrival of Juan Rodríguez Cabrillo in 1542. His statue dominates the tip of Point Loma, 422 feet above sea level; this is also a vantage point for watching migrating Pacific gray whales en route from the Arctic Ocean to Baja California (and back again) December through March. A self-guided tour of the restored lighthouse, built in 1855, illuminates what life was like here more than a century ago. National Park Service rangers lead walks at the monument, and there are tide pools to explore at the base of the peninsula. On the other side of the point is the Bayside Trail, a 3-mile round-trip down to a lookout over the bay. Free 25-minute videos and slide shows on Cabrillo, tide pools, and the whales are shown on the hour daily from 10am to 4pm. *Tip:* Even on a sunny day, temperatures here can be cool, so bring a jacket; and pack a lunch—the site has great picnicking spots but no food facilities. You should plan on a minimum of 90 minutes here.

1800 Cabrillo Memorial Dr., Point Loma. www.nps.gov/cabr. (C) **619/557-5450.** Admission $5 per vehicle, $3 for walk-ins (valid for 7 days from purchase). Daily 9am–5pm (last entrance 4:30pm). Bus: 84. By car, take I-8 W. to Rosecrans St., turn right on Canon St., left on Catalina, and follow signs.

Downtown & Beyond Attractions

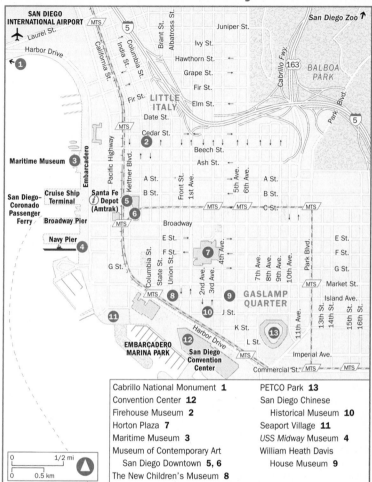

Cabrillo National Monument **1**
Convention Center **12**
Firehouse Museum **2**
Horton Plaza **7**
Maritime Museum **3**
Museum of Contemporary Art
San Diego Downtown **5, 6**
The New Children's Museum **8**

PETCO Park **13**
San Diego Chinese
Historical Museum **10**
Seaport Village **11**
USS Midway Museum **4**
William Heath Davis
House Museum **9**

Firehouse Museum ☺ MUSEUM   Housed in San Diego's oldest firehouse, the museum features shiny fire engines, including hand-drawn and horse-drawn models, a 1903 steam pumper, and memorabilia such as antique alarms, fire hats, and foundry molds for fire hydrants. There's also a small gift shop. Allow about half an hour for your visit.

1572 Columbia St. (at Cedar St.). www.sandiegofirehousemuseum.com. ✆ **619/232-3473.** Admission $3 adults; $2 seniors, military in uniform, and ages 13–17; free for children 12 and under. Thurs–Fri 10am–2pm; Sat–Sun 10am–4pm. Bus: 83. Trolley: County Center/Little Italy.

Maritime Museum ★★ ☺ MUSEUM   This flotilla of classic ships is led by the full-rigged merchant vessel *Star of India* (1863), a National Historic Landmark and the world's oldest sailing ship that still goes to sea. The gleaming white San Francisco–Oakland steam-powered ferry *Berkeley* (1898) worked round-the-clock to carry people to safety following the 1906 San Francisco earthquake; it now pulls duty as a museum with fine ship models on display. The elegant *Medea* (1904) is one of the world's few remaining large steam yachts, and the *Pilot* (1914) was San Diego Bay's official pilot boat for 82 years. Among the more recent additions are a 300-foot-long Cold War–era Soviet attack submarine and the HMS *Surprise*. This painstakingly accurate reproduction of an 18th-century Royal Navy frigate played a supporting role to Russell Crowe in the film *Master and Commander*. You can board and tour each vessel; give yourself 90 minutes.

1492 N. Harbor Dr. www.sdmaritime.org. © **619/234-9153.** Admission $14 adults; $11 seniors 62 and over, students 13–17, and active military with ID; $8 children 6–12; free for children 5 and under. Daily 9am–8pm (till 9pm in summer). Bus: 810, 820, 850, 860, 923, or 992. Trolley: County Center/Little Italy or America Plaza.

Museum of Contemporary Art San Diego Downtown ★★★ ART

MUSEUM   In 2007, the Museum of Contemporary Art opened a new downtown space known as the Jacobs Building. The annex is boldly grafted onto the end of the historic Santa Fe Depot, built in 1915, and transforms what had been the train station's baggage building into a state-of-the-art museum and educational facility. Designed by the architect responsible for the Warhol museum in Pittsburgh and the Museo Picasso in Málaga, Spain, the new wing provides an additional 30,000 feet of programming space; the expansion also features permanent, site-specific work by artists Richard Serra, Jenny Holzer, and others. Across the street at America Plaza are MCASD's original downtown galleries (MCASD's flagship museum is in La Jolla, p. 64). Lectures and special events for adults and children are presented, and free tours are given every third Thursday at 5 and 6pm and weekends at 2pm. Depending on the exhibits, allow yourself an hour.

1100 and 1001 Kettner Blvd. (btw. B St. and Broadway). www.mcasd.org. © **858/454-3541.** Admission $10 adults; $5 seniors, students age 26 and over, and military; free for anyone 25 and under; free admission every 3rd Thurs 5–7pm; paid ticket valid for 7 days at all MCASD locations. Thurs–Tues 11am–5pm; 3rd Thurs 11am–7pm; closed Wed. Bus: 83 and numerous Broadway routes. Trolley: America Plaza.

The New Children's Museum ★ ☺ MUSEUM   Have some restless kids on

your hands? Turn them loose in this high-style, $25-million facility that opened in 2008. Industrial and angular, the museum features ever-changing artworks by local artists that can be climbed on, touched, or interacted with in some way (and which just might intrigue the adults in tow as well). There are also lots of arts-based classes, and good old-fashioned play areas. Designed for kids from toddlers to teens, the New Children's Museum will appeal mostly to the under-13 set.

200 W. Island Ave. (at Front St.). www.thinkplaycreate.org. © **619/233-8792.** Admission $10 adults, $5 seniors and military; free for children 11 months and under; free admission the 2nd Sun of the month. Mon–Tues and Fri–Sat 10am–4pm; Thurs 10am–6pm; Sun noon–4pm (2nd Sun of the month 10am–4pm); closed Wed. Parking $10. Bus: 11. Trolley: Convention Center.

San Diego Chinese Historical Museum MUSEUM   In the former Chinese

Mission, where Chinese immigrants learned English and adapted to their new environment, this small museum contains antique Chinese lottery equipment, a series of panels documenting the gold rush, and artifacts unearthed from San Diego's old Chinatown (south of Market, btw. Third and Fifth aves.). A nice gift shop and a pleasant garden in back with a bronze statue of Confucius complete the experience. Allow about half an hour for your visit. Walking tours of the Asian Pacific Historic District start here on the second Saturday of the month at 11am; the cost is $4.

404 Third Ave. (at J St.). www.sdchm.org. ℭ **619/338-9888.** Admission $2 adults, free for children 11 and under. Tues–Sat 10:30am–4pm; Sun noon–4pm. Bus: 3, 11, or 120. Trolley: Convention Center.

USS _Midway_ Museum HISTORIC SITE   This aircraft carrier had a 47-year military history that began a week after the Japanese surrender of World War II in 1945. By the time the _Midway_ was decommissioned in 1991, the warship had patrolled the Taiwan Straits in 1955, operated in the Tonkin Gulf, served as the flagship from which Desert Storm was conducted, and evacuated 1,800 people from volcano-threatened Subic Bay Naval Base in the Philippines. In all, more than 225,000 men served aboard the _Midway._ The carrier is now moored at the Embarcadero and in 2004 became a floating naval-aviation museum. Self-guided audio tours take visitors to several levels of the ship while recounting the story of life on board; the highlight is climbing up the superstructure to the bridge and gazing down on the 1,001-foot-long flight deck, with various aircraft poised for duty. _Note:_ Be prepared for stairs and ladders (about 60% of the exhibits are wheelchair accessible); allow 90 minutes for your visit.

910 Harbor Dr. (at Navy Pier). www.midway.org. ℭ **619/544-9600.** Admission $18 adults, $15 seniors and students, $10 retired military and children 6–17, free for children 5 and under and active-duty military. Daily 10am–5pm. Limited parking on Navy Pier, $7 for 4 hr.; metered parking available nearby. Bus: 992. Trolley: Santa Fe Depot.

William Heath Davis House Museum HISTORIC HOME   Shipped by boat to San Diego in 1850 from Portland, Maine, this is the oldest structure in the Gaslamp Quarter. It is a well-preserved example of a prefabricated "saltbox" family home and has remained structurally unchanged for more than 150 years (although it originally stood at another location). A museum on the first and second floors documents life in New Town and profiles some of the city's early movers and shakers; you can tour the house in 30 minutes. The Gaslamp Quarter Historical Foundation also makes its home here, and it sponsors walking tours of the neighborhood for $10 ($8 for seniors, students, and military) every Saturday at 11am. The foundation has a nice gift store here, too, located in the basement; there's also a small, shady park adjacent to the house.

410 Island Ave. (at Fourth Ave.). www.gaslampquarter.org.ℭ **619/233-4692.** Admission $5 adults and children; $4 seniors, military, and students. Tues–Sat 10am–5pm; Sun 9am–4pm. Bus: 3, 11, or 120. Trolley: Gaslamp Quarter or Convention Center.

Old Town & Mission Valley

The birthplace of San Diego—indeed, of California—Old Town takes you back to the Mexican California of the mid-1800s. "Walking Tour 3: Old Town," in chapter 5, covers Old Town's historic sights.

Mission Valley, which starts just north of Presidio Park and heads straight east, is decidedly more modern; until I-8 was built in the 1950s, it was little more than cow pastures with a couple of dirt roads. Shopping malls, motels, a golf course, condos, car dealerships, and a massive sports stadium fill the expanse today. Farther upstream along the San Diego River is the **Mission Basilica San Diego,** and just a few miles beyond lies an outstanding park with walking trails. Few visitors make it this far, but

Mission Trails Regional Park reveals what San Diego looked like before the Spanish (and the car dealers) arrived.

El Campo Santo CEMETERY Behind an adobe wall along San Diego Avenue is San Diego's first cemetery, established in 1850. This small plot is the final resting place for Yankee Jim Robinson, a local troublemaker who was hanged for stealing a rowboat in 1852. Some say he still hangs around at the **Whaley House** (p. 60). Of more historical note is the grave of Antonio Garra, chief of the Cupeño Indians, who led an uprising of dispossessed tribes after a tax was levied against their livestock; it seems the Mission-educated Garra had learned that taxation without representation is tyranny. He was executed by a firing squad at his graveside in 1852. His final words: "Gentlemen, I ask your pardon for all my offenses; I expect yours in return." **Note:** The small brass markers on the sidewalk and in the street indicate the still-buried remains of some of the city's earliest residents, paved over by the tide of progress.

2410 San Diego Ave. (btw. Conde and Arista sts.). Free admission. Open daily 24 hr. Bus: Numerous Old Town routes including 8, 9, 10, 28, or 30. Trolley: Old Town.

Heritage Park ARCHITECTURE This 7.8-acre park is home to seven original 19th-century structures moved here from other parts of the city and given new leases on life, including San Diego's first synagogue, Temple Beth Israel, built in 1889. Big plans to turn this park into a kind of B&B village have stalled, but it still provides a wonderful opportunity to bask in the beauty of ornate Victorian architecture. Allow 20 minutes for your visit.

2450 Heritage Park Row (corner of Juan and Harney sts.). www.heritageparksd.com. Free admission. Daily sunrise to sunset. Bus: Numerous Old Town routes including 8, 9, 10, 28, or 30. Trolley: Old Town.

Junípero Serra Museum ★ MUSEUM On the hill above Old Town, this iconic Spanish mission–style building built in 1929 overlooks the slopes where, in 1769, the first mission, first presidio (fort), and first nonnative settlement on the west coast of the United States and Canada were founded. The museum's exhibits introduce visitors to the Native American, Spanish, and Mexican people who first called this place home. On display are their belongings, from cannons to cookware. From the 70-foot tower, visitors can compare the spectacular view with historic photos to see how this land has changed over time.

2727 Presidio Dr., Presidio Park. www.sandiegohistory.org. © **619/232-6203.** Admission $6 adults; $4 seniors, students, and military; $3 children 6–17; free for children 5 and under. Sat–Sun 10am–5pm (Apr–Oct), Sat–Sun 10am–4pm (Nov–Mar). Bus: Numerous Old Town routes including 8, 9, 10, 28, 30, or 83. Trolley: Old Town. Take I-8 to the Taylor St. exit. Turn right on Taylor, and then left on Presidio Dr.

Mission Basilica San Diego de Alcalá CHURCH Established in 1769 above Old Town, this was the first link in a chain of 21 California missions founded by Spanish missionary Junípero Serra. In 1774, the mission was moved from Old Town to its present site for agricultural reasons—and to separate the indigenous converts from the fortress that included the original building. The mission was sacked by the local tribe a year after it was built, leading Father Serra to reconstruct it using 5- to 7-foot-thick adobe walls and clay tile roofs, rendering it harder to burn. In the process, he inspired a bevy of 20th-century California architects. A few bricks belonging to the original mission can be seen in Presidio Park in Old Town. Mass is said daily in this active Catholic parish. Other missions in San Diego County include **Mission San Luis Rey de Francia** in Oceanside, **Mission San Antonio de Pala** near

Old Town & Mission Valley Attractions

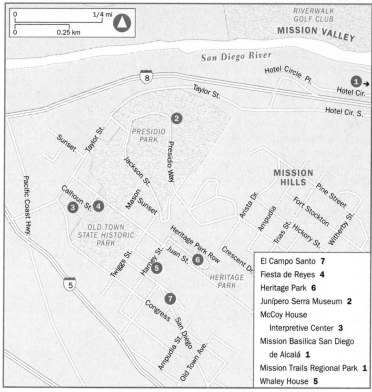

0 ___ 1/4 mi
0 ___ 0.25 km

RIVERWALK GOLF CLUB
MISSION VALLEY

San Diego River

Hotel Circle Pl.

Hotel Cir.

Hotel Cir. S.

8

Taylor St.

2

PRESIDIO PARK

Sunset

Taylor St.

Jackson St.

Presidio Way

Mason

Sunset

MISSION HILLS

Pine Street

Arista Dr.

Ampudia

Fort Stockton

Trias St.

Hickory St.

Witherby St.

Pacific Coast Hwy.

Calhoun St.

3

4

OLD TOWN STATE HISTORIC PARK

Heritage Park Row

Crescent Dr.

Twiggs St.

Harney St.

Juan St.

6

HERITAGE PARK

5

Congress

San Diego St.

Ampudia

Old Town Ave.

7

El Campo Santo **7**
Fiesta de Reyes **4**
Heritage Park **6**
Junípero Serra Museum **2**
McCoy House
　Interpretive Center **3**
Mission Basilica San Diego
　de Alcalá **1**
Mission Trails Regional Park **1**
Whaley House **5**

Mount Palomar, and **Mission Santa Ysabel** near Julian. Known as "the King of Missions," the San Luis Rey is the largest of California's missions and one of its most beautiful (see "North County Beach Towns," in chapter 10). You can tour the church and grounds in about 45 minutes.

10818 San Diego Mission Rd., Mission Valley. www.missionsandiego.com. © **619/281-8449.** Admission $3 adults, $2 seniors and students, $1 children 11 and under. Free Sun and for daily Masses. Museum and gift shop daily 9am–4:45pm; Mass daily 7am (except Sat) and 5:30pm, with additional Sun Mass at 8am, 10am, 11am, and noon. Trolley: Mission San Diego. Take I-8 to Mission Gorge Rd. to Twain Ave., which turns into San Diego Mission Rd.

Mission Trails Regional Park ★ 🎋 PARK/GARDEN   Well off the beaten track for tourists, but only 8 miles from downtown San Diego, this is one of the nation's largest urban parks. Encompassing some 5,800 acres, it includes abundant bird life, two lakes, a picturesque stretch of the San Diego River, the Old Mission Dam (probably the first irrigation project in the West), and 1,592-foot Cowles Mountain, the summit of which reveals outstanding views over much of the county. The park boasts more than 40 miles of trails, including a 1.5-mile interpretive trail; some paths are designated for mountain bike use. There's also a 46-space campground (© **619/668-2748**). Mission Trails was founded in 1974, after the area surrounding Cowles

Mountain began to experience a housing boom. In 1989, the first park ranger was hired; in 1995, the slick visitor center opened.

1 Father Junípero Serra Trail, Mission Gorge. www.mtrp.org. © **619/668-3281.** Free admission. Daily sunrise–sundown (visitor center 9am–5pm). Take I-8 to Mission Gorge Rd.; follow for 4 miles to entrance.

Old Town State Historic Park ★ HISTORIC SITE   Dedicated to re-creating the early life of the city from 1821 to 1872, this is where San Diego's Mexican heritage shines brightest. The community was briefly Mexico's informal capital of the California territory; the Stars and Stripes were eventually raised over Old Town in 1846. Of the park's 20 structures, 7 are original, including homes made of adobe; the rest are reconstructed. The park's headquarters is at the Robinson-Rose House, 4002 Wallace St., where you can pick up a map and peruse a model of Old Town as it looked in 1872. Among the park's attractions is La Casa de Estudillo, which depicts the living conditions of a wealthy family in 1872, and Seeley Stables, named after A. L. Seeley, who ran the stagecoach and mail service here from 1867 to 1871. The stables have two floors of wagons, carriages, stagecoaches, and other memorabilia, including washboards, slot machines, and hand-worked saddles. On Wednesdays and Saturdays, from 10am to 4pm, costumed park volunteers reenact life in the 1800s with cooking and crafts demonstrations, a working blacksmith, and parlor singing; there's storytelling on the green Tuesdays and Thursdays, noon to 2pm, and Friday from 1 to 3pm. Free 1-hour walking tours leave daily at 11am and 2pm from the Robinson-Rose House. Plan on 90 minutes here; more if you want to dine or seriously shop.

4002 Wallace St., Old Town. www.parks.ca.gov. © **619/220-5422.** Free admission (donations welcome). Museums daily 10am–5pm (till 4pm Oct–Apr); most restaurants till 9pm. Bus: Numerous Old Town routes including 8, 9, 10, 28, or 30. Trolley: Old Town. Take I-5 to the Old Town exit and follow signs.

Whaley House HISTORIC HOME   In 1856, this striking two-story house (the first in these parts to be constructed with brick) was built for Thomas Whaley and his family. It's an urban legend that this house is "officially" designated as haunted, but 100,000 people visit each year to see for themselves. Up to four spirits are said to haunt the grounds, including the ghost of Yankee Jim Robinson, who was hanged in 1852 on the site where the house now stands. Exhibits include a life mask of Abraham Lincoln, one of only six made, and the spinet piano used in the movie *Gone With the Wind*. The Whaley complex includes several other historic structures, including the Verna House and two false-front buildings, both dating from the 1870s. The Verna House is now an excellent little gift shop run by the Save Our Heritage Organization, selling beautiful Arts and Crafts pottery, architecture-themed books, and crafts, as well as your admission tickets; you can tour the house in about 30 minutes. With 2 weeks' notice, you can also arrange a private, after-hours visit ($75 per person for 1 hour, minimum 2 people).

2476 San Diego Ave. www.whaleyhouse.org. © **619/297-7511.** Admission before 5pm $6 adults, $5 seniors 65 and older, $4 children 3–12; admission after 5pm $10 adults, $5 children 3–12. Free for children 2 and under. June–Aug daily 10am–9:30pm; Sept–May Sun–Tues 10am–5pm, Thurs–Sat 10am–9:30pm, closed Wed. Bus: Numerous Old Town routes including 8, 9, 10, 28, or 30. Trolley: Old Town.

Mission Bay & the Beaches

Opened to the public in 1949, **Mission Bay Park** is a man-made, 4,200-acre aquatic playground created by dredging tidal mud flats and opening them to seawater.

Today, this is a great area for walking, jogging, in-line skating, biking, and boating. For all of these activities, see the appropriate headings in "Outdoor Activities," later in this chapter. For **SeaWorld San Diego,** see p. 41.

For a **spectacular view,** drive north on Mission Boulevard, past Turquoise Street, where it turns into La Jolla Mesa Drive. Proceed up the hill ¾ mile and turn around. From here, you'll see the beaches and Point Loma in front of you, Mission Bay and San Diego Bay, downtown, the Hillcrest/Uptown area, and (on a clear day) the hills of Tijuana, and to the east, San Diego's backcountry.

Belmont Park ☺ AMUSEMENT PARK This seaside amusement park was opened in 1925 by business tycoon John D. Spreckels. No, it wasn't quite the magnanimous gesture it seems; it was actually a real estate scheme to lure people to what was then a scarcely populated area. Today, Belmont Park's star attraction is the **Giant Dipper roller coaster ★**, one of two surviving fixtures from the original park and a registered National Historic Landmark. There are a variety of carny-style rides at Belmont Park, but something more unique awaits next door at the **Wave House ★** (✆ **858/228-9304;** www.wavehousesandiego.com). This self-described "royal palace of youth culture" features **FlowBarrel ★**, a wave machine designed to create stand-up rides on a 10-foot wave, and **FlowRider,** which provides a less gnarly wave-riding experience for novices. *Note:* As of this writing Belmont Park is in bankruptcy receivership. It's unknown how this will affect future operations, but **the Plunge** indoor swimming pool, the park's other 1925 holdover, has been shuttered.

3146 Mission Blvd., corner of W. Mission Bay Dr. www.giantdipper.com. ✆ **858/488-1549.** Ride on the Giant Dipper $6; unlimited rides $27; FlowRider $20 for 1 hr. (plus $10 registration fee), Flow-Barrel $40 for 1 hr. Belmont Park daily 11am–8pm (extended weekend and summer hours; closed Mon–Thurs Jan–Feb); FlowRider/FlowBarrel Mon–Fri noon–5pm, Sat–Sun 11am–7pm. Bus: 8. Take I-5 to the SeaWorld exit, and follow W. Mission Bay Dr. to Belmont Park.

La Jolla

One of San Diego's most scenic spots—the star of postcards for more than 100 years—is **La Jolla Cove ★★★** and **Ellen Browning Scripps Park ★★** on the bluff above it. The walk through the park, along Coast Boulevard (start from the north at Prospect St.), offers some of California's finest coastal scenery. Just south is the **Children's Pool ★★★**, a beach where dozens of harbor seals can be spotted lazing in the sun. The 6,000-acre **San Diego–La Jolla Underwater Park ★★★**, established in 1970, stretches for 10 miles from La Jolla Cove to the northern end of Torrey Pines State Reserve, and extends from the shoreline to a depth of 900 feet. The park is a boat-free zone. Its undersea life draws scuba divers and snorkelers, many of them hoping for a glimpse of the brilliant orange garibaldi, California's state fish.

La Jolla has architectural treasures as well; highlights include **Mary Star of the Sea,** 7727 Girard Ave., a small Roman Catholic church with some stylish art; and **La Valencia Hotel** (p. 208), a fine Spanish Colonial–style structure. The **La Jolla Woman's Club,** 7791 Draper Ave.; the adjacent **Museum of Contemporary Art San Diego La Jolla ★★★**; the **La Jolla Recreation Center;** and the **Bishop's School** are all the handiwork of famed architect Irving Gill.

At La Jolla's north end, you'll find the 1,200-acre, 22,000-student **University of California, San Diego (UCSD),** which was established in 1960 and represents the county's largest single employer. The campus features the **Geisel Library ★★**, a striking and distinguished contemporary structure, as well as the **Stuart Collection ★** of public sculpture and the **Birch Aquarium at Scripps ★★** (see individual listings, to follow). One of celebrated architect Louis I. Kahn's masterpieces is the **Salk Institute for Biological Studies ★★★**, 10010 N. Torrey Pines Rd., a research facility named for the creator of the polio vaccine. (For tours, see "For Architecture Buffs," later in this chapter.) Farther north is an ersatz jewel, the **Lodge at Torrey Pines** (p. 208), a modern, 175-room luxury resort in the guise of an early-20th-century Craftsman-style manse. It overlooks the revered **Torrey Pines Golf Course** (p. 84).

For a fine scenic drive, follow La Jolla Boulevard to Nautilus Street and turn east to get to 823-foot-high **Mount Soledad ★**, which offers a 360-degree view of the area. The appropriateness of the 43-foot-tall cross on top, erected in 1954 in this public park, has been the subject of more than 20 years of legal jousting (religious symbols are prohibited on public land). In 2008, a federal judge ruled the cross could stay; in 2011, another judge ruled it was unconstitutional. Stay tuned—this could be heading to the United States Supreme Court.

Athenaeum Music & Arts Library ★★ 🏛 CULTURAL INSTITUTION

Founded in 1899, this is 1 of only 16 nonprofit membership libraries in the United States. Year-round, it hosts exceptional art exhibits, intimate concerts (from jazz and classical to more experimental new music), lectures, special events, and classes that are open to the general public. An incredible collection of books, music, and more makes for fascinating browsing, but only members can check something out. The Athenaeum has been located at this site from the very beginning and over the years has expanded into adjacent buildings, including the beautiful Spanish Renaissance–style rotunda, designed by renowned architect William Templeton Johnson and dating to 1921. Free tours are conducted every third Saturday at 11am.

1008 Wall St. (at Girard Ave.) www.ljathenaeum.org. ✆ **858/454-5872.** Gallery and library admission free; various prices for concerts, classes, and lectures. Tues and Thurs–Sat 10am–5:30pm; Wed 10am–8:30pm; closed Sun–Mon. Bus: 30. Take Torrey Pines Rd. to Prospect Place and turn right. Prospect Place becomes Prospect St.; turn left on Girard Ave.

Birch Aquarium at Scripps ★★ ☺ AQUARIUM

This beautiful facility is both an aquarium and a museum, operated as the interpretive arm of the world-famous Scripps Institution of Oceanography. With more than 60 marine-life tanks, the aquarium affords close-up views of sea creatures from the Pacific Northwest, the California coast, Mexico's Sea of Cortés, and the tropical seas. The giant kelp forest is particularly impressive; other highlights include a variety of sharks and ethereal moon jellies. The outdoor demonstration tide pool not only displays marine coastal life but also offers an amazing view of Scripps Pier, La Jolla Shores Beach, the village of La Jolla, and the ocean. The museum section has numerous interpretive exhibits on current and past research at the Scripps Institution, which was established in 1903 and became part of the University of California system in 1912. The bookstore is well stocked with textbooks, science books, educational toys, gifts, and T-shirts. Off-site adventures, such as tide-pooling, scouting for grunion runs (p. 180), and whale-watching, are also conducted year-round (call for more details). Give yourself at least 90 minutes here.

2300 Expedition Way. www.aquarium.ucsd.edu. ✆ **858/534-3474.** Admission $14 adults, $10 seniors and college students with ID, $9.50 children 3–17, free for children 2 and under. Daily 9am–5pm. Free 3-hr. parking. Bus: 30. Take I-5 to La Jolla Village Dr. exit, go west 1 mile, and turn left at Expedition Way.

EXPLORING SAN DIEGO | More Attractions

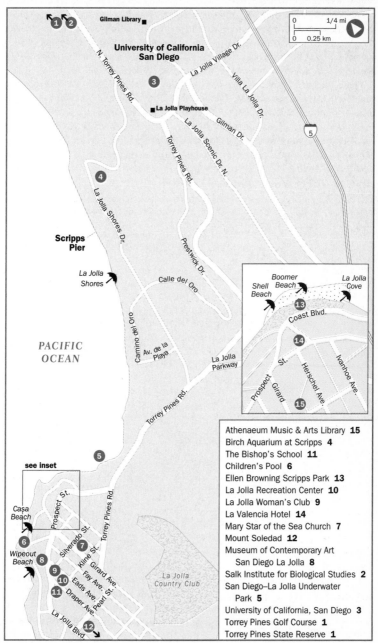

La Jolla Attractions

Gilman Library ■

University of California
San Diego

N. Torrey Pines Rd.

La Jolla Village Dr.

Villa La Jolla Dr.

La Jolla Scenic Dr. N.

La Jolla Playhouse ■

Gilman Dr.

Torrey Pines Rd.

5

La Jolla Shores Dr.

Scripps
Pier

Prestwick Dr.

La Jolla
Shores

Calle del Oro

Camino de Oro

Av. de la
Playa

PACIFIC
OCEAN

La Jolla
Parkway

Torrey Pines Rd.

Boomer
Beach
La Jolla
Cove
Shell
Beach

13

Coast Blvd.

14

Prospect St.

Girard

Herschel Ave.

Ivanhoe Ave.

15

see inset

5

Casa
Beach

Prospect St.

St.

Torrey Pines Rd.

6

Wipeout
Beach

8

Silverado St.

Girard Ave.

Kline St.

7

9

Fay Ave.

Pearl St.

10

Eads Ave.

11

Draper Ave.

La Jolla Blvd.

12

La Jolla
Country Club

0   1/4 mi
0   0.25 km

Athenaeum Music & Arts Library 15
Birch Aquarium at Scripps 4
The Bishop's School 11
Children's Pool 6
Ellen Browning Scripps Park 13
La Jolla Recreation Center 10
La Jolla Woman's Club 9
La Valencia Hotel 14
Mary Star of the Sea Church 7
Mount Soledad 12
Museum of Contemporary Art
   San Diego La Jolla 8
Salk Institute for Biological Studies 2
San Diego–La Jolla Underwater
   Park 5
University of California, San Diego 3
Torrey Pines Golf Course 1
Torrey Pines State Reserve 1

Museum of Contemporary Art San Diego La Jolla ★★★ ART MUSEUM
Focusing on work produced since 1950, this museum is internationally recognized for its permanent collection and thought-provoking exhibitions. MCASD's holdings include more than 4,000 paintings, sculptures, photographs, videos, and multimedia and installation pieces, with a strong showing by California artists. The museum itself is perched on a cliff overlooking the Pacific Ocean; the views from the galleries are gorgeous. The original building was the residence of legendary philanthropist Ellen Browning Scripps and was designed by Irving Gill in 1916; the outdoor sculptures are site specific. It became an art museum in 1941, and the Gill building facade was uncovered and restored in 1996. More than a dozen exhibitions are scheduled each year, and MCASD also offers lectures, cutting-edge films, and special events on an ongoing basis; depending on the show, you should plan on at least an hour here. The bookstore is also a great place for contemporary gifts, and the cafe is a pleasant stop before or after your visit. Free docent tours are available the third Thursday of the month at 5 and 6pm and weekends at 2pm.

700 Prospect St. www.mcasd.org. *©* **858/454-3541.** Admission $10 adults; $5 seniors, students 26 and over, and military; free for anyone 25 and under; free admission every 3rd Thurs 5–7pm; paid ticket valid for 7 days at all MCASD locations (there are 2 downtown galleries; p. 56). Thurs–Tues 11am–5pm; 3rd Thurs 11am–7pm; closed Wed. Bus: 30. Take I-5 N to La Jolla Pkwy. or take I-5 S to La Jolla Village Dr. W. Take Torrey Pines Rd. to Prospect Place and turn right; Prospect Place becomes Prospect St.

Stuart Collection ★ CULTURAL INSTITUTION Through a 1982 agreement between the Stuart Foundation and UCSD, this still-growing collection consists of site-related sculptures by leading contemporary artists, from Robert Irwin to John Baldessari. Start by picking up a map from the information booth, and wend your way through the 1,200-acre campus to discover the 18 highly diverse artworks. Among them is Niki de Saint Phalle's *Sun God,* a jubilant 14-foot-high fiberglass bird on a 15-foot concrete base. It's been made an unofficial mascot by the students, who use it as the centerpiece of their annual Sun God Festival. Alexis Smith's *Snake Path* is a 560-foot-long slate-tile pathway that winds up the hill from the Engineering Mall to the east terrace of the spectacular Geisel Library (breathtaking architecture that's a fabulous sculpture itself). Tim Hawkinson's *Bear* is a massive teddy bear abstraction comprised of eight seemingly precariously perched granite boulders. Allow at least 2 hours to tour the entire collection.

University of California, San Diego. http://stuartcollection.ucsd.edu. *©* **858/534-2117.** Free admission. Bus: 30, 41, 101, 150, or 921. From La Jolla, take Torrey Pines Rd. to La Jolla Village Dr., turn right, go 2 blocks to Gilman Dr. and turn left into the campus; in about 1 block the information booth will be visible on the right.

Torrey Pines State Reserve ★★★ 📷 PARK/GARDEN The rare Torrey pine tree is native to only two places in the world: Santa Rosa Island, 175 miles northwest of San Diego, and here, at the north end of La Jolla. Even if the twisted shape of these awkwardly beautiful trees doesn't lure you to this spot, the equally scarce undeveloped coastal scenery should; this 2,000-acre reserve is one of San Diego's unique treasures, a taste of what Southern California's coast looked like a couple hundred years ago. The reserve encompasses the beach below, as well as a lagoon immediately north, but the focus is the 300-foot-high, water-carved sandstone bluffs that provide a precarious footing for the trees. In spring, the wildflower show includes blooming bush poppies, Cleveland sage, agave, and yucca. A half-dozen trails, all under 1.5 miles in length, travel from the road to the cliff edge or down to the beach; watch for migrating gray whales in winter or dolphins that patrol these shores year-round. Interpretive nature walks are held weekends and holidays at 10am and 2pm, departing from the small visitor center, built in the traditional adobe style of the Hopi Indians. *Note:* No facilities for food or drinks are available in the park. You can bring a picnic lunch, but you have to eat it on the beach; food and drink (other than water) are not allowed in the upper portion of the reserve. You could spend your whole day here, 90 minutes at least.

12600 N. Torrey Pines Rd., btw. La Jolla and Del Mar. www.torreypine.org. © **858/755-2063.** Admission $10 per car; hourly rates available at the North Beach lot ($4 for 1 hr.). Daily 8am–sunset. Bus: 101. From I-5, take Carmel Valley Rd. west; turn left at Hwy. 101.

Coronado

It's hard to miss San Diego Bay's most noteworthy landmark: the **San Diego–Coronado Bay Bridge** ★. Completed in 1969, this graceful five-lane bridge spans 2¼ miles and links the city and the "island" of Coronado. At 246 feet in height, the bridge was designed to be tall enough for the Navy's aircraft carriers to pass beneath. Heading to Coronado by car is a thrill because you can see Mexico and the shipyards of National City to the left, the San Diego skyline to the right, and Coronado, the naval station, and Point Loma in front of you (designated drivers have to promise to keep their eyes on the road). When the bridge opened, it put the antiquated commuter ferries out of business, though, in 1986, passenger-only ferry service restarted (see "By Water," in the "Getting Around" section, in chapter 11). Bus no. 901 from downtown will also take you across the bridge.

Hotel del Coronado ★★★ ICON   Built in 1888, this turreted Victorian seaside resort (p. 213) remains an enduring, endearing national treasure. Whether you are staying here, dining here, or simply touring the grounds and photo gallery, prepare to be enchanted.

1500 Orange Ave., Coronado. www.hoteldel.com.© **800/468-3533** or 619/435-6611. Free admission. Parking $15 first 2 hr., $10 for each additional hr.; 3 hr. free parking if you spend $50 on property. Bus: 901 or 904. Ferry: Broadway Pier, and then a half-hour walk, or take the bus, or rent a bike. From I-5 take the Coronado Bridge and make a left on Orange Ave.

Museum of History and Art MUSEUM   This museum features archival materials about the development of Coronado, as well as tourist information. Exhibits include photographs of the Hotel Del in its infancy, the old ferries, Tent City (a seaside campground for middle-income vacationers from 1900–39), and notable residents and visitors. You'll also learn about the island's military aviation history during World Wars I and II. Plan to spend up to half an hour here. The museum has a gift store with Coronado-themed items and offers guided and self-guided walking tours of the area. Guided tours of the Hotel Del are scheduled for Tuesdays and Fridays at 10:30am, and weekends at 2pm ($15); a neighborhood tour departs from the museum on Wednesdays at 10:30am ($10). Reservations are required for both.

1100 Orange Ave. www.coronadohistory.org.© **866/599-7242** or 619/435-7242. Suggested donation $4 adults, $3 seniors and military, $2 youths 9–18, free for children 8 and under. Mon–Fri 10am–6pm; Sat–Sun 10am–5pm. Bus: 901 or 904. From I-5 take the Coronado Bridge and make a left on Orange Ave.

Farther Afield

Chula Vista Nature Center ★ 🎁 ☺ NATURE RESERVE   Overshadowed by SeaWorld and the zoo, this wonderful interactive nature center highlights the plants and animals native to San Diego Bay and the surrounding wetlands. Featuring exhibits of stingrays and small sharks in kid-level open tanks, the center's most recent addition is its $3-million Discovery Center, which is home to **Turtle Lagoon,** a habitat for endangered green sea turtles. There are also large tanks with moon jellyfish, eels, and rainbow trout. CVNC is in Sweetwater Marsh, one of San Diego's top bird-watching spots. The nature center has walking trails and a facility for experiencing the bird life (including aviaries with shorebirds and raptors). The parking lot is located away from the center, and a shuttle bus ferries guests between the two points every 10 to 15 minutes.

1000 Gunpowder Point Dr., Chula Vista. www.chulavistanaturecenter.org. 🕐 **619/409-5900.** $14 adults; $9 seniors, students, and ages 4–17; free for children 3 and under. Daily 10am–5pm (last shuttle at 4pm). Free parking. Trolley: Bayfront/E St. (Request shuttle at trolley info center.) From I-5 S., take the E St. exit.

Knott's Soak City U.S.A. ☺ WATER PARK   Themed to replicate Southern California's surfer towns of the 1950s and 1960s, this 32-acre water park has more than 20 slides of all shapes and sizes, a 500,000-gallon wave pool, a quarter-mile lazy river, and assorted snack facilities. The park is about 25 minutes south of downtown, just north of the border.

2052 Entertainment Circle, Chula Vista. www.knotts.com. 🕐 **619/661-7373.** Admission $33 adults, $23 seniors and children ages 3–11; discounted tickets available online. Late May–Aug daily 10am–6pm or later; weekends-only in Sept. Parking $14, $20 RVs. Take I-5 or I-805 to Main St.; turn right on Entertainment Circle.

FREE OF CHARGE & FULL OF FUN

Here's a helpful summary of free San Diego activities, most of which are described in detail earlier in this chapter. In addition, scan the lists of "Special-Interest Sightseeing," below; "Outdoor Activities" and "Spectator Sports" on p. 180; and the "San Diego Calendar of Events," in chapter 2. Many events listed in these sections are no-charge affairs. Also note that the walking tours outlined in chapter 5 are free to anyone.

Downtown & Beyond

It doesn't cost a penny to stroll around the **Gaslamp Quarter,** which brims with restaurants, shops, and historic buildings, along the Embarcadero (waterfront), or around the shops at Seaport Village or Horton Plaza. And don't forget: **Walkabout International** offers free guided walking tours (described in "Organized Tours," later in this chapter), and Centre City Redevelopment Corporation's **Downtown Information Center** (p. 71) gives bus tours one Saturday a month.

If you'd rather drive around, ask for the map of the **52-mile San Diego Scenic Drive** when you're at the International Visitor Information Center on the Embarcadero (near Broadway).

The **murals** in **Chicano Park** (🕐 **619/563-4661;** www.chicano-park.org), painted on the support system of the San Diego–Coronado Bay Bridge, are a colorful road map through Mexican and Chicano history. South of downtown (exit Cesar Chavez Pkwy. from I-5), the 70-plus murals represent some of San Diego's most important pieces of public art. For visibility and safety's sake, plan your visit during the day. The **Museum of Contemporary Art San Diego**'s two downtown spaces are free to everyone 25 and under; for those who have to pay, your ticket will get you into MCA's La Jolla museum for free, if you visit within 7 days. Both the La Jolla and downtown museums are also free every third Thursday from 5 to 7pm.

You can fish free of charge from any municipal pier (that is, if you bring your own pole). A fishing license is not required.

Balboa Park

Promenading along the park's architecturally rich pedestrian thoroughfare (which is often lined with street entertainers), lingering in the meticulously maintained gardens, or hiking the park's trails are all free to do. Balboa Park also offers a handful of free attractions and activities, including the **Botanical Building and Lily Pond, House of Pacific Relations International Cottages,** the **Timken Museum of Art,** and the **San Diego Museum of Art's Sculpture Garden.** The **Spreckels Organ Pavilion** hosts free 1-hour Sunday afternoon organ concerts at 2pm year-round, and free concerts Monday evenings in summer. Several free **tours** of the park are available; they leave from in front of the visitor center. The **San Diego Zoo** is free to all on the first Monday of October (Founders Day), and children 11 and under enter free every day during October.

Old Town & Mission Valley

Explore **Heritage Park, Presidio Park, Old Town State Historic Park,** or **El Campo Santo.** A 1-hour walking tour of the state park is conducted twice daily, and frontier reenactments are staged Wednesdays and Saturdays from 10am to 4pm; actors from Cygnet Theatre provide a little drama on Tuesdays and Thursdays, from noon to 2pm, and Fridays from 1 to 3pm. There's free nightly and weekend entertainment (mariachis and folk dancers) at **Fiesta de Reyes** (p. 155), and the **Old Town Market,** 4010 Twiggs St. (© **619/260-1078**), has costumed storytellers and a small museum. The free **William B. Kolender San Diego County Sheriff's Museum,** 2384 San Diego Ave. (© **619/260-1850;** www.sheriffmuseum.org), traces the evolution of the department and its equipment since the first San Diego officer pinned on a badge in 1850. Renovated in 2010, the **Mormon Battalion Historic Site** museum, 2510 Juan St. (© **619/298-3317**), is slick, high-tech, and free. It relates the story of the more than 500 men and women, members of the Church of Latter-day Saints, recruited by the U.S. Army in 1846 to help fight the Mexican-American War. The battalion marched from Iowa to San Diego (nearly 2,000 miles), and its resulting maps and trailblazing helped open the way for westward expansion. And yes, you'll get a dose of religion along with the tour. **Mission Trails Regional Park** (p. 59), offers hiking trails and an interpretive center.

Mission Bay, Pacific Beach & Beyond

Walk along the **beach,** the boardwalk, or around the bay—it's good exercise and there's a nonstop parade of colorful characters. Bring a picnic lunch to enjoy on the **Ocean Beach Pier** or the **Crystal Pier** in Pacific Beach.

La Jolla

The half-mile **Coast Walk** between the La Jolla Cove and Children's Pool is San Diego at its most beautiful. Dabble in the tide pools along the way and enjoy the harbor seal colony at Seal Rock and the Children's Pool.

It's also fun to meander around the campus of the University of California, San Diego, and view the **Stuart Collection** (bring a pocketful of quarters for the hungry parking meters). The main branch of the **Museum of Contemporary Art San Diego** is always free to those 25 and under; a paid ticket will get you into the downtown spaces for free (within 7 days). MCASD's museums are also free every third Thursday from 5 to 7pm. The **Athenaeum Music & Arts Library** (p. 62) is also free to browse through.

Watching the hang gliders and paragliders launching from the **Gliderport** near Torrey Pines is always a blast (p. 84). For another **great vista,** follow the SCENIC DRIVE signs from La Jolla Boulevard to Nautilus Street, leading up to Mount Soledad and its 360-degree view of the area.

4 Coronado

Drive across the toll-free San Diego–Coronado Bay Bridge and take a self-guided tour of the **Hotel del Coronado**'s grounds and photo gallery. A walk on beautiful Coronado **beach** costs nothing—nor does a lookie-loo tour of the neighborhood's restored Victorian and Craftsman homes.

Farther Afield

At the **U.S. Olympic Training Center** in Chula Vista, 2800 Olympic Pkwy. (www.teamusa.org; ✆ **619/656-1500** or 619/482-6222), you'll find some of the world's top amateur athletes honing their skills in a variety of sports, including soccer, volleyball, swimming, BMX, and track and field. On the western shore of Lower Otay Reservoir in Chula Vista, this is one of three United States Olympic training centers. It's open year-round and self-guided tours are available daily, 9am to 4pm; guided tours are offered Saturday at 11am. Visitors can watch a short film about the Olympic movement then check out the highlights of the 155-acre center. To get there, take I-805 S. to the Olympic Parkway exit, and then go east about 8 miles until you reach a sign directing you to the Copley Visitor Center.

ESPECIALLY FOR KIDS

Dozens of public parks, 70 miles of beaches, and numerous museums are just part of what awaits kids and families. For current information about activities for children, pick up a free copy of the monthly *San Diego Family Magazine,* or check it out online at www.sandiegofamily.com; its calendar of events is geared toward family activities and kids' interests. The **International Visitor Information Center,** 1140 N. Harbor Dr. (www.sandiego.org; ✆ **619/236-1212**), is also a great resource.

The Top Five Attractions for Kids

○ **Balboa Park** (p. 46) has street entertainers and clowns that always rate high with kids. They can usually be found around El Prado on weekends. The **Natural History Museum,** the **Model Railroad Museum,** the **Air & Space Museum,** and the **Reuben H. Fleet Science Center** (with its hands-on exhibits and IMAX theater) draw kids like magnets.

- The **San Diego Zoo** (p. 40) appeals to children of all ages, and the double-decker bus tours bring all the animals into easy view of even the smallest visitors. There's a Children's Zoo within the zoo, and kids adore the performing sea lion show.
- **SeaWorld San Diego** (p. 41), on Mission Bay, entertains everyone with killer whales, dolphins to pet, and plenty of penguins. There are also wet and wild thrill rides and a collection of *Sesame Street*–related attractions, including rides and a "4-D" interactive movie experience.
- The **Zoo Safari Park** (p. 38) delivers a memorable wildlife experience, re-creating the savannas of Africa with free-roaming animals. For visitors age 3 and up, the Roar & Snore sleepover program—held year-round on weekends (except Dec and Jan)—is immensely popular.
- **LEGOLAND California** (p. 229), in Carlsbad, features impressive models built entirely with LEGO blocks. There are also rides, special events, and contests; a sea-life aquarium (with real fish) and a water park have been added, as well. The park advertises itself as a "country just for kids"—need you say more?

Other Top Kid-Friendly Attractions

- **Birch Aquarium at Scripps** (p. 62), in La Jolla, is an aquarium that lets kids explore the realms of the deep and learn about life in the sea.
- **The New Children's Museum** (p. 56), downtown, is a $25-million, modern space where kids can indulge in educational and cultural playtime, including hands-on art projects and storytelling.
- **Maritime Museum** (p. 55), along the Embarcadero, will have kids unleashing their inner Capt. Jack Sparrow, as they swashbuckle their way through this collection of classic sailing vessels.
- **Seaport Village** (p. 152) has an old-fashioned carousel for kids, lots of kid-friendly shops and outdoor eateries, and harbor views of some very impressive ships.
- **Whale-Watching Tours** (p. 76) offer a chance to spot 40-foot gray whales that migrate past San Diego each winter.
- **Old Town State Historic Park** (p. 60) has a one-room schoolhouse that rates high with kids. They'll also enjoy the freedom of running around the safe, parklike compound to discover their own fun.
- **The Gliderport** (p. 84) will transfix kids as they watch aerial acrobats swoop through the skies of La Jolla.
- **Chula Vista Nature Center** (p. 66) is a small facility near the southern end of San Diego Bay that has open tanks for getting up close to turtles, stingrays, and small sharks; there's also a walk-through aviary.

That's Entertainment!

The **Old Globe Theatre** (www.theoldglobe.org; ✆ 619/234-5623) in Balboa Park showcases *Dr. Seuss' How the Grinch Stole Christmas!* each year during the holidays. Performances are scheduled late November through December. Tickets start at $39 for adults, $24 for kids 17 and under. The **San Diego Junior Theatre** (www.junior theatre.com; ✆ 619/239-8355) is the oldest continuing children's theater program in the country, operating since 1948. The productions (shows such as *Willy Wonka* and *Beauty and the Beast*) are acted and crewed by kids 8 to 18 and are staged at two different theaters: Balboa Park's Casa del Prado Theatre and the YMCA Firehouse in La Jolla, 7877 Herschel Ave. Nearly a dozen shows are staged each season, with performances held on Friday evenings and Saturday and Sunday afternoons; ticket prices are $8 to $14.

Sunday afternoon is a great time for kids in **Balboa Park.** They can visit both the outdoor Spreckels Organ Pavilion for a free concert (the mix of music isn't too high-brow for a young audience) and the House of Pacific Relations to watch folk dancing on the lawn and taste food from many nations. Or try the **Marie Hitchcock Puppet Theater,** in Balboa Park's Palisades Building (www.balboaparkpuppets.com; ℂ **619/544-9203**). Individual shows might feature marionettes, hand puppets, or ventriloquism; the stories range from classic *Grimm's Fairy Tales* and *Aesop's Fables* to more obscure yarns. Performances are Wednesday through Friday at 10 and 11:30am, and Saturday and Sunday at 11am, 1, and 2:30pm (additional showtimes are added in summer). The cost is $6 for adults, $5 for seniors, and $4 for children 2 and older; free for children 1 and under.

SPECIAL-INTEREST SIGHTSEEING

4 For Architecture Buffs

San Diego's historical architecture often features the Spanish mission style introduced to California by Father Junípero Serra at the **Mission Basilica San Diego de Alcalá.** Ostensibly, the adobe walls and tile roofs made it harder for Native Americans to burn down his churches. Spanish Colonial style was revived gloriously for the 1915–16 **Panama-California Exposition** in Balboa Park by New York architect Bertram Goodhue, who oversaw the creation of a fantastically romantic landscape abounding with Mediterranean flourishes.

But San Diego's first important architect was Irving Gill, who arrived in the city in 1893 and soon made his mark by designing buildings to integrate into the desertlike landscape. Gill's structures include numerous homes in Uptown and La Jolla. Gill's **First Church of Christ Scientist** building, 2444 Second Ave. (at Laurel) in Hillcrest, is on the National Historic Landmark list. Following the Expo, prolific local architects such as William Templeton Johnson and Richard Requa integrated the Spanish/Mediterranean concept into their structures around the city—most famously the **Serra Museum** at Presidio Park, the Embarcadero's **County Administration Center**, **Fiesta de Reyes** in Old Town (formerly the Casa de Pico Motel), and the **Torrey Pines Visitors Center.**

Modernism swept through the city after World War II, championed by Lloyd Ruocco; his office, built in 1949, can be found at 3611 Fifth Ave. (it still operates as a design center). The city's steady growth after the war allowed many inspired architects to leave their handprint on San Diego; more recently, though, unchecked development has led to more than a few blunders along the way. The expansion of the **San Diego Convention Center,** for instance, proves most effective as a ludicrous barrier to any view of the waterfront from downtown.

Historic buildings of particular interest include houses such as the Craftsman-style **Marston House** (p. 50) and Victorian **Villa Montezuma.** Located southeast of downtown, the fantastical Villa Montezuma was operated as a museum by the San Diego History Center, but it has been closed in recent years; check www.villamontezuma museum.org for current information. The **Gaslamp Quarter** walking tour (see chapter 5) will lead you past the area's restored Victorian commercial buildings; a stroll along Balboa Park's **El Prado** (also described in chapter 5) is a must, while turn-of-the-20th-century neighborhoods such as **Bankers Hill** (just west of Balboa Park) and **Mission**

Hills (west of Hillcrest) are feasts of Victorian mansions and Craftsman abodes. **Jolla,** you'll find the classic buildings created by Irving Gill (see "More Attraction earlier in this chapter).

Downtown blends old and new with mixed results, though no one can deny the value of saving the **Gaslamp Quarter** from probable demolition in the 1970s. **Little Italy,** the hot business and residential district along India Street (btw. Ash and Laurel sts.), has been completely transformed by the building craze in recent years; it's thriving amid some of the city's most progressive architecture. While you're in the central business district, take a look at the sprawling scale model of the city at the Centre City Development Corporation's **Downtown Information Center** in Horton Plaza (www.ccdc.com; ✆ **619/235-2222**); it gives a taste of where the city is headed. It's open Monday through Friday, 9am to 5pm.

A splendid corridor of contemporary architecture has sprouted around the University of California, San Diego, including the campus's spacecraft-like **Geisel Library,** by William Pereira. Nearby are the Louis I. Kahn–designed **Salk Institute** and the **Neurosciences Institute,** a 1996 creation by Tod Williams Billie Tsien Architects. A free tour of the Salk Institute, one of Kahn's masterpieces, is held Monday through Friday at noon; reservations are required at least 2 days in advance and can be made online (www.salk.edu; ✆ **858/453-4100,** ext. 1287).

For more information on San Diego architecture, call the local branch of the **American Institute of Architects** (✆ **619/232-0109;** www.aiasandiego.org). And for a self-guided tour of the city's highlights, Dirk Sutro's *San Diego Architecture* (San Diego Architectural Foundation, 2002; $25) is indispensable, with maps, addresses, and descriptions of hundreds of important structures throughout the city and county. Midcentury fans should check out the **Modern San Diego** website, www.modern sandiego.com; it offers a neighborhood-by-neighborhood breakdown of the architectural highlights.

For Gardeners

Although most years San Diego struggles with too little rain, nevertheless this is a gardener's paradise. A big inspiration for San Diego gardeners is Kate Sessions, who planted the initial trees that led to today's mature landscapes in **Balboa Park** (p. 46). While in the park, be sure to visit the **Japanese Friendship Garden,** the **Botanical Building and Lily Pond,** and the **rose and desert gardens** (across Park Blvd. from Plaza de Balboa). And you'll notice both the **San Diego Zoo** (p. 40) and **Zoo Safari Park** (p. 38) are outstanding botanical facilities. Many visitors who admire the landscaping at the zoo don't realize the plantings have been carefully developed over the years. The 100 acres were once scrub-covered hillsides with few trees. Today, towering eucalyptus and graceful palms, birds of paradise, and hibiscus are just a few of the 6,500 botanical species from all over the world that flourish here.

Garden enthusiasts will also want to stop by the 35-acre **San Diego Botanic Garden** (formerly known as the Quail Botanical Gardens) in Encinitas (see "North County Beach Towns," in chapter 10). If you'd like to take plants home with you, visit some of the area's nurseries. Start with the charming neighborhood one founded in 1910 by Kate Sessions herself, the **Mission Hills Nursery,** 1525 Fort Stockton Dr. (www.missionhillsnursery.com; ✆ **619/295-2808**). **Walter Andersen Nursery,** 3642 Enterprise St. (www.walterandersen.com; ✆ **619/224-8271**), is also a local favorite, located not far from Old Town. See chapter 10 for information on nurseries in North County; flower growing is big business in this area, and plant enthusiasts

...eek just visiting the retail and wholesale purveyors of everything from ...trees.

...907 by Kate Sessions, the **San Diego Floral Association** is the ...ub in Southern California. It's based in the Casa del Prado in Balboa ...ral.org; © **619/232-5762**) and offers workshops and exhibits, as ...ll as day tours to places of horticultural interest; the website features a roundup of all the gardening-related activities happening in the county.

For Military Buffs

San Diego's military history dates to the U.S. Navy's aviation achievements at Coronado in the 1910s. Today, one-third of the Navy's Pacific Fleet is home-ported in the city's natural harbor. San Diego salutes its armed forces during **Fleet Week,** which takes place from mid-September to early October; it's headlined by the popular Miramar Air Show, with aerial performances by the Blue Angels. For more information, see www.fleetweeksandiego.org or www.miramarairshow.com.

The city's flagship (pardon the pun) military attraction is the aircraft carrier **USS Midway** (p. 57), making its final tour of duty as a floating museum. The *Midway* served from the end of World War II until the first Gulf War, and it's now docked along the Embarcadero. The **San Diego Air & Space Museum** (p. 51) in Balboa Park celebrates the history of flight, and has a strong focus on aviation's military heroes and heroines. The park is also the location of the **Veterans Museum & Memorial Center,** 2115 Park Blvd. (www.veteranmuseum.org; © **619/239-2300**), a resource center with a small museum that has holdings dating back to the Civil War.

Both **Flagship** and **Hornblower Cruises** (p. 74) tour San Diego Bay, providing a glimpse of naval activities; and **Old Town Trolley Tours** offers an amphibious Sea and Land (SEAL) tour of the bay (p. 75). At **Cabrillo National Monument** in Point Loma, visitors gain an excellent view of the harbor, including the nuclear submarine base; a museum installation tells about the gun batteries established on the peninsula during World War II.

Just before you reach the gates of Cabrillo National Monument, you can pay your respects at **Fort Rosecrans National Cemetery** (www.cem.va.gov; © **619/553-2084**). It didn't officially become a National Cemetery until 1934, but remains interred here date back to 1846 and the Battle of San Pasqual. With its row upon row of gleaming white headstones and sweeping ocean views, this is a very moving and inspirational spot. It's open Monday through Friday 8am to 4:30pm, Saturday and Sunday 9:30am to 5pm.

The public is invited to the **recruit graduation** at the Marine Corps Recruit Depot, off Pacific Coast Highway (near Barnett St.), held most Fridays at 10am (www.mccsmcrd.com; © **619/725-6400**). The **Command Museum** on the base (www.mcrdmuseumhistoricalsociety.org; © **619/524-6719**) has a huge collection of Marine memorabilia; it was updated and expanded in 2007 and includes a gallery devoted to the Vietnam experience. Hours are Monday through Saturday, 8am to 4pm; it's free, but admittance to the base requires a photo ID.

For Wine Lovers

Visit **Orfila Vineyards,** 13455 San Pasqual Rd., Escondido (www.orfila.com; © **800/868-9463** or 760/738-6500), on the way to or from the San Diego Zoo Safari Park (p. 38). Besides producing excellent chardonnay and merlot, the winery also makes several Rhône and Italian varietals. The tasting room is open daily from 10am

Special-Interest Sightseeing

EXPLORING SAN DIEGO

to 6pm; guided tours are offered at noon. The property also features a parklike picnic area and a gift shop. Another tasting room and gift shop is located about 2 miles outside the mountain town of Julian, 4470 Hwy. 78, near Wynola Road (© **760/765-0102**); hours are Friday through Tuesday, 10am to 5pm.

Surrounded by suburbia, **Bernardo Winery,** 13330 Paseo del Verano N., Escondido (www.bernardowinery.com; © **858/487-1866**), has an assortment of shopping and dining options on site. Founded in 1889, it's Southern California's oldest continuously operating winery, surviving Prohibition by making grape juice and sacramental wine. The tasting room is open daily 9am to 5pm (later on weekends in spring and summer); the shops and bistro are closed on Mondays. **Fallbrook Winery,** 2554 Via Rancheros, Fallbrook (www.fallbrookwinery.com; © **760/728-0156**), produces award-winning sauvignon blancs and syrahs; a tasting room is set up in the aging cellar, but you need to call ahead to make a reservation.

In **Temecula,** just across the San Diego County line in Riverside, there are more than 30 wineries that are open for tours and tastings; see p. 241. Mexico's wineries in the **Valle de Guadalupe** are also within reach; they are east of Ensenada, about a 90-minute drive from downtown (p. 267).

ORGANIZED TOURS

Centre City Development Corporation's **Downtown Information Center** in Horton Plaza (www.ccdc.com; © **619/235-2222**) offers free downtown bus tours the first Saturday of the month at 10am and noon. Reservations are required for the 90-minute tour, which is aimed at prospective home-buyers in the downtown area, as well as curious locals trying to stay abreast of developments. Go inside the information center to see an enormous scale model of the downtown area. The office is open Monday through Friday from 9am to 5pm.

Water Excursions

Flagship TOUR   This company (formerly known as San Diego Harbor Excursion) offers daily 1- and 2-hour narrated tours of the bay. There are two 1-hour itineraries, each covering about 12 miles. The south bay tour includes the San Diego–Coronado Bridge and Navy shipyards; the north bay route motors past Naval Air Station North Island and Cabrillo National Monument. The 25-mile, 2-hour tour encompasses the entire bay. Two-hour Sunday (and Sat in summer) brunch and nightly 2½-hour dinner cruises are also available. In winter, whale-watching excursions feature onboard naturalists from the Birch Aquarium.

1050 N. Harbor Dr. (foot of Broadway). www.flagshipsd.com. © **800/442-7847** or 619/234-4111. Harbor tours $22–$27, $2 off for seniors and military, half-price for children 4–12. Dinner cruises start at $67 adults, $38 children; brunch cruise $55 adults, $38 children; whale-watching trips $35–$40 adults, $30–$35 seniors and military, $18–$20 children. Bus: 992. Trolley: America Plaza or Santa Fe Depot.

The Gondola Company TOUR   This unique business operates from Loews Coronado Bay Resort, plying the canals and marinas of a nearby luxury waterside community. The gondolas are crafted according to centuries-old designs from Venice and feature all the trimmings, right down to the striped-shirt gondolier with ribbons waving from his or her straw hat. Mediterranean music plays while you and up to five friends recline with snuggly blankets. The company will even provide antipasti or chocolate-covered strawberries, along with chilled wineglasses and ice for the

If you can't decide between a bus tour or a bay cruise, opt for both—an amphibious tour on Old Town Trolley Tour's **Sea and Land Adventures.** The 90-minute SEAL tour departs from Seaport Village and motors along the Embarcadero until splashing into San Diego Bay. This specially built craft holds 46 passengers, and the narrated tour gives you the maritime and military history of San Diego from the right perspective. Reservations are required for the trips which are usually scheduled daily, April through October from 10am to 5pm, and Thursday through Monday 10am to 4pm the rest of the year. The cost is $34 for adults and $19 for kids 4 to 12. Free for children 3 and under. For information and tickets, visit www.historictours.com.call or call © **888/910-8687** or 619/298-8687.

Another novel way to see the sights is via **GoCar Tours** (www.gocartours. com; © **800/914-6227**), small, three-wheeled vehicles that zip around town at about 35 mph (56kmph). These two-person open-air minicars are equipped with GPS technology that not only gives directions, but also indicates points of interest and narrates San Diego history (in five languages). Don't feel like listening to a talking car? Just pop a disc into the CD player. GoCar Tours is at 2100 Kettner Blvd. in Little Italy and is open daily from 8:30am to 5pm. Rates start at $49 for the first hour, and you must be 18 to rent; it's suggested you reserve 24 hours in advance.

beverage of your choice (BYOB). You can even arrange for an onboard mandolin or violin player; there are also massage and wine-tasting packages.

4000 Coronado Bay Rd., Coronado. www.gondolacompany.com. © **619/429-6317.** 50-min. cruise $85 per couple, $20 for each additional passenger (up to 6 total), free for children 2 and under. Reservations required. Mon–Fri 3pm–midnight; Sat–Sun 11am–midnight. Bus: 901.

Hornblower Cruises TOUR   These 1- or 2-hour narrated tours lead passengers through San Diego harbor on tours that highlight dozens of San Diego landmarks. You'll see the *Star of India*, cruise under the San Diego–Coronado Bridge, and swing by a submarine base and an aircraft carrier or two. Guests can visit the captain's wheelhouse for a photo op, and harbor seals and sea lions on buoys are a regular sighting. Whale-watching trips (mid-Dec to late Mar) are a blast; a 2-hour Sunday champagne-brunch cruise departs at 11am, and there are 3-hour dinner/dance cruises nightly.

1066 N. Harbor Dr. www.hornblower.com. © **888/467-6256** or 619/686-8715. Harbor tours $22–$27 adults, $2 off for seniors and military, half-price for children 4–12. Dinner cruises start at $70; brunch cruise $56; whale-watching trips $35–$40 ($2 off for seniors and military), $18–$20 children. Bus: 992. Trolley: America Plaza or Santa Fe Depot.

Xplore Offshore ★★ 👕 TOUR   There are only two small boats in this fleet, and the one to ride is the tricked-out RIB (rigid-inflatable boat), similar to the crafts used by the U.S. Navy SEALS. Capable of cruising at up to 45 mph, the RIB is built for speed and comfort; there's lots of padding and straddle seating up front, and even a surprisingly roomy head—not bad for a 24-foot vessel. Other special features include hot water for showering after a swim and an underwater camera for those who want to look but not get wet. Trips are unscripted; you can do what you want to do and go wherever you want to go. You can do some rip-roaring wave riding or serene pleasure boating, go whale-watching or night diving, take a booze cruise to bayside restaurants and concerts, or camp on a remote Catalina beach—it's your call.

Pickup points are flexible, but usually Dana Landing in Mission Bay. www.xploreoffshore.com. ✆ **858/456-1636.** 3-hr. rates start at $49–$79 per person. Bus: 9 (for Dana Landing).

Bus Tours

Gray Line (www.sandiegograyline.com; ✆ **800/331-5077** or 619/266-7365) has a plethora of outings, including a daylong Grand Tour that covers San Diego, Tijuana, and a 1-hour harbor cruise. There are also trips to the San Diego Zoo, Zoo Safari Park, LEGOLAND, SeaWorld, Disneyland, Universal Studios, Tijuana, Rosarito Beach, and Ensenada. Prices range from $36 for the 4-hour City Tour to $65 for the Grand Tour (prices range $20–$36 for children 3–11). Multiple tours can be combined for discounted rates, and passengers can be picked up at most area hotels.

Not to be confused with the public transit trolley, the narrated **Old Town Trolley Tours** (www.historictours.com; ✆ **888/910-8687** or 619/298-8687) offer an easy way to get an overview of the city. You can tie together visits to several major attractions without driving or resorting to pricey cabs. These vehicles, gussied up like old-time trolleys, do a 30-mile circular route; you can hop off at any one of 11 stops, explore at leisure, and reboard when you please (the trolleys run every half-hour). Stops include Old Town, the Gaslamp Quarter, Coronado, the San Diego Zoo, and Balboa Park. You can begin wherever you want, but you must purchase tickets before boarding (most stops have a ticket kiosk, or you can get discounted tickets online). The tour costs $34 for adults ($17 for kids 4–12, free for children 3 and under) for one complete circuit; the route by itself takes about 2 hours. The trolleys operate daily from 9am to 5pm November to February, with extended hours the rest of the year.

Vizit Tours (www.vizitsandiegotours.com; ✆ **619/727-4007**) features narrated tours aboard open-top double-decker buses along several routes, including loops along the harbor (which includes Old Town and downtown) and through Balboa Park. There are on-and-off privileges, and each tour is about an hour; you can also combine the routes into city tours that include admission to the zoo or a harbor cruise (all loop tickets are valid for 48 hours). Tours start in Seaport Village and most run daily from 10am to 5pm; prices range from $15 to $52 for adults, and $12 to $39 for children (you can save some cash by buying tickets online ahead of time).

Walking Tours

Walkabout International, 2650 Truxton Rd., Ste. 110, Point Loma (www.walkabout-int.org; ✆ **619/231-7463**), sponsors more than 100 free walking tours every month that are led by local volunteers, listed in a monthly newsletter and on the website. Walking tours hit all parts of the county, including the Gaslamp Quarter, La Jolla, and the beaches. A wilderness hike takes place most Wednesdays and Saturdays.

Urban Safaris (www.walkingtoursofsandiego.com; ✆ **619/944-9255**) provides walking tours of various San Diego neighborhoods, including Ocean Beach and Hillcrest. Tours depart from designated meeting places in the neighborhood where the walk takes place. All tours are $10.

Where You Want to Be Tours (www.wheretours.com; ✆ **619/917-6037**) puts a lighthearted touch on its offerings, which include walking, biking, and Segway tours. For your own personal guide, check out the company's "Rent a Local" offering ($210 for 3 hours).

For those who want to combine some socializing and nightlife with a guided outing, both **So Diego Tours** (www.sodiegotours.com; ✆ 619/233-8687) and **Bite San Diego** (www.bitesandiego.com; ✆ 619/634-8476) offer neighborhood walking tours that combine history with restaurant and bar crawls. Prices start at $45.

The **Gaslamp Quarter Historical Foundation** offers 2-hour tours that focus on the Gaslamp's 19th-century history, every Saturday at 11am. Tours depart from the William Heath Davis House museum, 410 Island Ave., and cost $10 for adults; $8 for seniors (ages 55 and above), students, and military (museum admission is included); free for children ages 12 and under. For more information, contact the foundation at www.gaslampquarter.org or ✆ 619/233-4692.

Take a walk on the supernatural side with **Old Town's Most Haunted** (www.oldtownsmosthaunted.com; ✆ 619/972-3900). These 90-minute walking tours through Old Town State Historic Park and environs go in search of real paranormal activity, Thursday through Sunday at 9pm (private tours are available at 11pm). The cost is $19 adults, $10 ages 6 to 12, and free for children 5 and under; cash only.

Volunteers from the Canyoneer group of the **San Diego Natural History Museum** (www.sdnhm.org; ✆ 619/232-3821) lead free, guided nature walks throughout San Diego County. The walks are held every Saturday and Sunday (except July–Aug), and usually focus on the flora and fauna of a particular area, which might be a city park or as far away as Anza-Borrego Desert.

At **Cabrillo National Monument** (p. 54) on the tip of Point Loma, rangers often lead free walking tours. Docents at **Torrey Pines State Reserve** (p. 64) in La Jolla lead interpretive nature walks at 10am and 2pm on weekends and holidays; guided walks are often scheduled at **Mission Trails Regional Park** (p. 59), as well.

Also see "Hiking & Walking," later in this chapter, for unguided trail options.

Whale-Watching

Along the California coast, whale-watching is an eagerly anticipated wintertime activity, particularly in San Diego where Pacific gray whales pass close by Point Loma on their annual migratory trek. Local whaling in the 1870s greatly reduced their numbers, but federal protection has allowed the species to repopulate; current estimates put the number of grays at about 20,000. When they approach San Diego, the 40- to 50-foot gray whales are more than three-quarters of the way along their nearly 6,000-mile journey from Alaska to breeding lagoons in the Sea of Cortés, around the southern tip of Baja California. After mating and calving they will pass by again, calves in tow, heading back to the rich Alaskan feeding grounds. From mid-December to mid-March is the best time to see the migration, and there are several ways to view the procession.

The easiest (and cheapest) is to grab a pair of binoculars and head to a good landbound vantage point. The best is **Cabrillo National Monument,** at the tip of Point Loma, where you'll find a glassed-in observatory and educational whale exhibits 400 feet above sea level. When the weather cooperates, you can often spot the whales as they surface for breathing—as many as eight grays per hour at peak commute (mid-Jan). Each January, the rangers conduct a special "Whale Watch Weekend," featuring presentations by whale experts, children's programs, and entertainment. For more information on Cabrillo National Monument, see p. 54.

If you want to get a closer look, head out to sea on one of the excursions that locate and follow gray whales, taking care not to disturb their journey. **Whakapono Sailing Charters** (www.whakapono.us; ✆ **800/659-0141** or 619/988-9644) offers two trips per day (8:30am and 1pm); each lasts 3 hours and carries a maximum of six passengers. Sailboats are less distracting to the whales than motorized yachts, but more expensive; the cruises are $75 per person (minimum two passengers), including beverages and snacks. **OEX Dive & Kayak Centers** (www.oexcalifornia.com; ✆ **858/454-6195**) leads guided kayak tours in search of passing whales. It's about a 4-mile paddle that departs from La Jolla Shores and lasts 4 hours; the cost is $55 for a single kayak, $85 for a double (no experience needed).

Companies that offer traditional, engine-driven expeditions include **Hornblower Cruises** and **Flagship** (see "Water Excursions," above). Excursions are 3 or 3½ hours, and fares run $35 to $40 for adults, with discounts for kids. **H&M Landing,** 2803 Emerson St., Point Loma (www.hmlanding.com; ✆ **619/222-1144**), has 3- and 6-hour trips, starting at $33 for ages 13 and up, $18 for ages 2 to 12. Naturalist-led trips to the Mexican calving grounds, lasting 9 to 11 days, are also scheduled.

In La Jolla, the **Birch Aquarium at Scripps** celebrates gray whale season with classes, educational activities, and exhibits, and the outdoor terrace offers another vantage point for spotting the mammals from shore. Multiday trips to San Ignacio in Baja California, where the whales mate and calve, are offered in February and March, and Birch provides naturalists to accompany the whale-watching done by Flagship (see "Water Excursions," above). Call ✆ **858/534-3474,** or go to www.aquarium. ucsd.edu for more information. The **San Diego Natural History Museum** also offers multiday, naturalist-guided whale-watching trips to Baja. For a schedule and preregistration information, call ✆ **619/232-3821,** or check www.sdnhm.org.

OUTDOOR ACTIVITIES

See the section titled "San Diego's Beaches" earlier in this chapter for a complete rundown.

Ballooning & Scenic Flights

A peaceful balloon ride reveals sweeping vistas of the Southern California coast, the wine country surrounding Temecula (70 min. north of downtown), or rambling estates and golf courses around Del Mar and Rancho Santa Fe (25 min. north of downtown). For a sunrise (Temecula) or sunset (Del Mar) flight, followed by a traditional champagne toast, contact **Skysurfer Balloon Company** (www.sandiego hotairballoons.com; ✆ **800/660-6809** or 858/481-6800). The cost is $175 for sunrise ballooning, $210 for sunset trips. **California Dreamin'** (www.california dreamin.com; ✆ **800/373-3359** or 951/699-0601) has sunrise Temecula flights with rates ranging from $138 to $158, Del Mar rides for $198, and biplane excursions over Temecula's wine country starting at $248 for two people. Check both companies' websites for special offers. Also of interest to balloonatics is the **Temecula Balloon & Wine Festival** held in early June; call ✆ **951/676-6713,** or visit www.tvbwf.com for information.

For more nonmotorized flight, you can soar like an eagle on thermal winds with **Sky Sailing** (www.skysailing.com; ✆ **760/782-0404**), 31930 Hwy. 79 in Warner Springs, about a 90-minute drive from downtown San Diego. A 20-minute flight aboard a glider, for one or two people, starts at $125.

Barnstorming Adventures (🅒 **800/759-5667** or 760/930-0903; www.barn storming.com) offers just about everything but wing-walking. Vintage biplane flights leave from Montgomery Field, 3750 John J. Montgomery Dr., in Kearny Mesa, taking passengers on scenic flights along the coast; rates start at $199 for one- or two-person, 20-minute rides. Air Combat flights ($596), with you at the controls (under the guidance of active-duty fighter pilots), offer simulated dogfights; reserve space 1 to 2 weeks in advance. You can also opt for a flight—with or without aerial acrobatics—in a 1941 SNJ-4 warbird ($345 and up), or a 30-minute you-fly-it experience (no pilot's license necessary; $177).

Biking

With its impeccable weather and varied terrain, San Diego is one of the nation's preeminent bicycling destinations—the city is often lauded by *Bicycling* magazine. Many major thoroughfares offer bike lanes, but downtown is definitely a challenge; to download a detailed map of San Diego County's bike lanes and routes go to www.511sd.com and click on the "Bicycling" link. You might also want to talk to the **San Diego County Bicycle Coalition** (www.sdcbc.org; 🅒 **858/487-6063**). For information on taking your bike onto public transportation, see "By Bicycle," in the "Getting Around" section, on p. 276, in chapter 11. Bicycle helmets are legally required for those 17 and under.

The paths around Mission Bay, in particular, are great for leisurely rides; the oceanfront boardwalk between Pacific Beach and Mission Beach can get very crowded, especially on weekends (but that's half the fun). The **Bayshore Bikeway** around San Diego Bay is one of the region's most popular rides. This 16-mile round-trip bike trail starts at the Ferry Landing Marketplace in Coronado and follows a well-marked route down to Imperial Beach, along the Silver Strand. The road out to Point Loma (Catalina Dr.) offers moderate hills and wonderful scenery. Traveling old State Route 101 (aka the Pacific Coast Hwy.) from La Jolla north to Oceanside offers terrific coastal views, along with plenty of places to refuel with coffee, a snack, or a swim. The 13-mile climb up steep switchbacks to the summit of 6,140-foot Mt. Palomar is perhaps the county's most invigorating challenge and offers its most gleeful descent. *Cycling San Diego* by Nelson Copp and Jerry Schad is a good resource for bicyclists and is available at many local bike shops.

RENTALS, ORGANIZED BIKE TOURS & OTHER TWO-WHEEL ADVENTURES

Downtown, call **the Bike Revolution,** 522 Sixth Ave. (www.thebikerevolution.com; 🅒 **619/564-4843**), where city/hybrid bike rentals start at $25 for the day; guided tours are $65 to $89. Other downtown spots include **San Diego Bike Shop,** 619 C St. (🅒 www.sdbikeshop.com; **619/237-1245**), which rents hybrid bikes for $30 per day; and across the street, **Pennyfarthing's Bicycle Store,** 630 C St. (www. pennyfarthingsbicycles.com; 🅒 **619/233-7696**). Rates here start at $10 for the first hour and $5 for each additional hour. If you don't feel like huffing and puffing against a headwind, you can get an electric bike in Little Italy at **Ivan Stewart's Electric Bike Center,** 2021 India St. (www.iselectricbikecenter.com; 🅒 **619/564-7028**); rates start at $40 for 2 hours.

In Mission Beach, there's **Cheap Rentals,** 3689 Mission Blvd. (www.cheaprentals.com; 🅒 **800/941-7761** or 858/488-9070), which rents everything from beach cruisers ($12 per day) to tandems ($24 per day) and baby trailers ($12 per day), as well as skates, surfboards, and even chairs, umbrellas, and coolers. Or try **Mission**

Beach Surf & Skate, 704 Ventura Place, off Mission Boulevard at Ocean Front Walk (② **858/488-5050**), for classic beach cruisers and more. In Coronado, there are two great places for rentals (both owned by the same folks), **Holland's Bicycles,** 977 Orange Ave. (www.hollandsbicycles.com; ② **619/435-3153**), and **Bikes and Beyond,** 1201 First St., at the Ferry Landing Marketplace (② **619/435-7180**). They've got beach cruisers and hybrids, mountain bikes, pedal surreys, and skate rentals; expect to pay $7 per hour for a basic cruiser, $30 for 24 hours.

For organized bike tours, **Hike Bike Kayak San Diego,** 2246 Av. de la Playa, La Jolla (www.hikebikekayak.com; ② **866/425-2925** or 858/551-9510), has a variety of offerings, including a La Jolla coastal ride and a family excursion around Mission Bay, but the big draw is the plunge down La Jolla's Mount Soledad. It's a 3.5-mile descent through luxury neighborhoods with scintillating vistas (ages 14 and up; $50). There's also a Mission Beach location at 819 San Fernando Place (② **858/488-5599**).

Bird-Watching

The birding scene is huge: More than 500 species have been observed in San Diego County, more than in any other county in the continental United States. The area is a haven along the Pacific Flyway—the migratory route along the Pacific Coast—and the diverse range of ecosystems also helps to lure a wide range of winged creatures. It's possible for birders to enjoy four distinct bird habitats in a single day.

Among the best places for bird-watching is the **Chula Vista Nature Center** at Sweetwater Marsh National Wildlife Refuge (www.chulavistanaturecenter.org; ② **619/409-5900**). You may spot rare residents such as the light-footed clapper rail and the western snowy plover, as well as predatory species including the American peregrine falcon and northern harrier. In addition, the nature center has aquariums for turtles, sharks, and rays; aviaries featuring raptors and shorebirds; and a garden with native plants (p. 66). Also worth visiting is the **Kendall-Frost Reserve** in Mission Bay. Most of this 30-acre area is off-limits to the public, but you can get close to it via the pathway that extends north from Crown Point or by kayak. The reserve draws skimmers, shorebirds, brants, and, in winter, the large-billed savannah sparrow. **Torrey Pines State Reserve** (p. 64), north of La Jolla, is a protected habitat for swifts, thrashers, woodpeckers, and wren tits. Inland, **Mission Trails Regional Park** (p. 59) is a 5,800-acre urban park that is visited by orange-crowned warblers, swallows, raptors, and numerous riparian species; and the **Anza-Borrego Desert State Park** (see chapter 10) makes an excellent day trip from San Diego—268 species of birds have been recorded here.

Birders coming to the area can obtain a copy of the free brochure *Birding Hot Spots of San Diego,* available at the Port Administration Building, 3165 Pacific Hwy., and at the San Diego Zoo, Zoo Safari Park, San Diego Natural History Museum, and Birch Aquarium. It's also posted online at www.portofsandiego.org/environment; click on "Birds of San Diego Bay." The **San Diego Audubon Society** is another great source of birding information (www.sandiegoaudubon.org; ② **858/273-7800**). The group also operates two wildlife sanctuaries that are open to the public on weekends.

Boating

There are some 55,000 registered watercraft docked at more than 25 marinas throughout San Diego County. Sailors have a choice of the calm waters of 4,200-acre **Mission Bay,** with its 27 miles of shoreline; **San Diego Bay,** one of the most beautiful natural harbors in the world; or the **Pacific Ocean,** where you can sail south to the Islas los Coronados (the trio of uninhabited islets on the Mexico side of the border). Joining a chartered sailing trip is easy.

The **Maritime Museum of San Diego** (www.sdmaritime.org; ☎ **619/234-9153**) offers half-day and 4- to 7-day sailing adventures aboard the *Californian*, the official tall ship of the state. This ship is a replica of an 1847 cutter that sailed the coast during the gold rush. Half-day sails depart select Saturdays and Sundays at 12:30pm from the Maritime Museum downtown and are priced $42 for adults; $34 for seniors 62 and older, active military, and ages 13 to 17; and $31 for kids 12 and under. Reservations are required for multiday trips that make for Catalina Island; fares start at $675. One-hour bay cruises are also available most days aboard *Pilot,* the bay's official pilot boat for 82 years. Tickets are $3 plus regular museum admission price.

Sail Jada Charters (www.sailjada.com; ☎ 619/572-3443) offers sunset champagne cruises on a gorgeous wooden (and truly yare) sailing yacht. Constructed of oak, cedar, and teak in 1938, *Jada* plies the bay Thursday to Sunday ($110 per person); it's also available for whale-watching and private charters.

You can pretend you're racing for your country's honor with **Next Level Sailing** (www.nextlevelsailing.com; ☎ 800/644-3454), which offers bay sails aboard one of two 80-foot International America's Cup Class racing yachts. The 2½-hour excursions, either on *Stars and Stripes* or *Abracadabra,* are $99 adults and $50 ages 4 to 12; trips depart from the Maritime Museum (p. 55). Whale-watching excursions are offered in winter as well, aboard the 139-foot schooner *America,* a replica of the yacht that brought home what came to be known as the America's Cup in 1851.

If you have sailing or boating experience, go for a nonchartered rental. **Seaforth Boat Rental** (www.seaforthboatrental.com; ☎ 888/834-2628) has a wide variety of boats for bay and ocean, from kayaks ($12–$18 for 1 hr.) to 240-horsepower cabin cruisers ($385; 2-hr. minimum). Sailboats start at $35 to $38 for 1 hour; jet skis begin at $90 to $99 for 1 hour. Half- and full-day rates are available. Stand-up paddle boards, catamarans, and pedal boats are also available, as well as fishing boats and equipment. Seaforth has several locations including: Mission Bay, 1641 Quivira Rd. (☎ 619/223-1681); downtown at the Marriott San Diego Hotel & Marina, 333 W. Harbor Dr. (☎ 619/239-2628); and in Coronado at 1715 Strand Way (☎ 619/437-1514).

Mission Bay Sportcenter, 1010 Santa Clara Place (www.missionbaysportcenter.com; ☎ 858/488-1004), is located on an isthmus extending into the bay and is adjacent to basketball courts, a baseball field, and picnic areas. It rents sailboats (from $24 per hr.), catamarans (from $30 per hr.), sailboards ($18 per hr.), kayaks (from $13 per hr.), jet skis ($95 per hr.), pedal boats ($17 per hr.), and powerboats (from $175 per hr.). There are discounts for 4-hour and full-day rentals. In summer, a variety of youth programs (ages 4–16) teach watersports such as surfing and sailing.

Fishing

The sportfishing fleet consists of more than 75 large commercial vessels and several dozen private charter yachts; a variety of half-, full-, and multiday trips are available. The saltwater fishing season kicks off each spring with the traditional **Port of San Diego Day at the Docks,** held in April at Sportfishing Landing, near Shelter Island; for more information, call ☎ 619/234-8793, or see www.sportfishing.org. Anglers of any age can fish free of charge without a license off any municipal pier in California.

Public fishing piers are on Shelter Island (where there's a statue dedicated to anglers), Ocean Beach, and Imperial Beach.

An ideal time for fishing is summer or fall, when the waters around Point Loma are brimming with bass, bonito, and barracuda. The Islas los Coronados, which belong to Mexico but are only about 18 miles from San Diego, are popular for yellowtail, yellowfin, and big-eyed tuna. Some outfitters will take you farther into Baja California waters on multiday trips (a world-record tuna—405.2 pounds—was caught on a long-range trip out of San Diego in 2010). Fishing charters depart from Harbor and Shelter Islands, Point Loma, the Imperial Beach pier, and Quivira Basin in Mission Bay (near the Hyatt Islandia Hotel). Participants 17 and over need a California fishing license.

Rates for trips on a large boat average $45 for a half-day trip or $95 for a three-quarter-day trip, or you can spring about $195 for a 20-hour overnight trip to the Coronados—call around and compare prices. Discounts are offered for kids and for twilight sailings; charters or "limited load" rates are also available. The following outfitters offer short or extended outings with daily departures: **H&M Landing,** 2803 Emerson St. (www.hmlanding.com; *C* **619/222-1144**); **Point Loma Sportfishing,** 1403 Scott St. (www.pointlomasportfishing.com; *C* **619/223-1627**); and **Seaforth Sportfishing**, 1717 Quivira Rd. (www.seaforthlanding.com; *C* **619/224-3383**). Check in with **Lee Palm Sportfishers,** 2801 Emerson St. (www.redrooster3.com; *C* **619/224-3857**), if you want to hit the high seas for a 3- to 16-day outing. All of these shops rent tackle.

For freshwater fishing, San Diego's lakes and rivers are home to bass, channel and bullhead catfish, bluegill, trout, crappie, and sunfish. Most lakes have rental facilities for boats, tackle, and bait, and they also provide picnic and (usually) camping areas. A 1-day California State Fishing License costs $14, a 2-day is $22, and a 10-day, nonresident license is $45. For information on lake fishing, call the city's **Lakes Line** *C* **619/465-3474.**

For information on fishing at **Lake Cuyamaca,** 1 hour from San Diego near Julian, see "Julian: Gold, Fires, Apples & More," in chapter 10. For more information on fishing in California, contact the **California Department of Fish and Game** (www.dfg.ca.gov; *C* **858/467-4201**). For fishing in Mexican waters, including the area off the Coronado Islands, angling permits are required. Most charter companies will take care of the details, but if not, contact the **Mexican Department of Fisheries,** 2550 Fifth Ave., Ste. 15, San Diego, CA 92103-6622 (www.conapesca sandiego.org; *C* **619/233-4324**).

Note: California has rolled out its Automated License Data System, an ATM-like console that issues fishing licenses. Many small outfitters and shops are not furnished with these machines, so call ahead. Licenses can also be purchased online; call *C* **858/467-4201,** or go to www.dfg.ca.gov for information.

Golf

With 90-plus courses, more than 50 of them open to the public, San Diego County offers golf enthusiasts innumerable opportunities to play their game. Courses are diverse: Some have vistas of the Pacific, others views of country hillsides or desert landscapes. For a full listing of area courses, including fees, stats, and complete score cards, visit www.golfsd.com, or request the *Golf Guide* from the **San Diego Convention and Visitors Bureau** (*C* **619/236-1212**); it's also available online at www. sandiego.org.

In addition to the well-established courses listed below, other acclaimed links include **Maderas Golf Club** (www.maderasgolf.com; ✆ 858/451-8100), **Barona Creek Golf Club** (www.barona.com; ✆ 619/387-7018), **Steele Canyon Golf Club** (www.steelecanyon.com; ✆ 619/441-6900), **Salt Creek Golf Club** (www. saltcreekgc.com; ✆ 619/482-4666), the **Grand Del Mar Golf Club** (p. 225), and **La Costa Resort and Spa** (p. 232).

San Diego Golf (www.sandiegogolf.com; ✆ 866/717-6552 or 858/964-1110) can arrange tee times for you at San Diego's premier golf courses. There's no charge for the service, except for Torrey Pines reservations (up to 90 days in advance; $25 per person). And when you just want to practice your swing, head to **Stadium Golf Center & Batting Cages,** 2990 Murphy Canyon Rd., in Mission Valley (www. stadiumgolfcenter.com; ✆ 858/277-6667). It's open daily from 7am to 10pm, with 72 artificial turf and natural grass hitting stations, plus greens and bunkers to practice your short game. A complete pro shop offers club rentals; a bucket of balls costs $8 to $19. Golf instruction and clinics are also available.

Aviara Golf Club ★★★　Designed by Arnold Palmer, this uniquely landscaped course incorporates natural elements that blend in neatly with the protected Batiquitos Lagoon nearby. The course is 7,007 yards from the championship tees, laid out over rolling hillsides with plenty of bunker and water challenges; casual duffers may be frustrated here. Greens fees are $215 (including mandatory cart) Monday through Thursday, and $235 Friday through Sunday; afternoon rates start at 1:30pm in winter, 3pm in summer ($140 weekday, $145 weekend). There are practice areas for putting, chipping, sand play, and driving, and the pro shop and clubhouse are fully equipped. Golf packages are available for guests of the hotel.

7447 Batiquitos Dr., Carlsbad. www.golfaviara.com. ✆ **760/603-6900.** From I-5 N., take the Aviara Pkwy. exit east to Batiquitos Dr. Turn right and continue 2 miles to the clubhouse.

Balboa Park Municipal Golf Course　Everybody has a humble municipal course like this at home, with a bare-bones 1920s clubhouse where old guys hold down lunch-counter stools for hours after the game and players take a few more mulligans than they would elsewhere. Surrounded by the beauty of Balboa Park, this 18-hole course features fairways sprinkled with eucalyptus leaves and distractingly nice views of the San Diego skyline. It's so convenient and affordable that it's the perfect choice for visitors who want to work some golf into their vacation rather than the other way around. The course even rents clubs ($25). Nonresident greens fees are $40 weekdays ($18 for 9 holes), $50 weekends ($23 for 9 holes); the 18-hole twilight rate is $24 weekdays, $30 weekends. Cart rental is $28. Reservations are suggested at least a week in advance; first-come, first-served tee times are offered from 6:30 to 7am.

You don't have to be a golfer to enjoy **Tobey's 19th Hole,** the clubhouse's simple cafe, offering splendid views from its deck of Point Loma, downtown, and the park. The food is cheap and diner-esque—omelets, biscuits and gravy, corned beef hash for breakfast; chili burgers and sandwiches for lunch—but this local hangout is a nice find for visitors.

2600 Golf Course Dr. (off Pershing Dr. or 26th St. in the southeast corner of the park), San Diego. www.sandiego.gov/golf. ✆ **619/570-1234** (automated reservation system), 619/235-1184 (info), or 619/239-1660 (pro shop).

Coronado Municipal Golf Course　Opened in 1957, this course is mostly for the locals—and visitors—who just can't bear to leave the "island" of Coronado. It's an

18-hole, par-72 course with distractingly beautiful views of San Diego Bay, the Coronado Bridge, and the downtown skyline beyond; there are also a coffee shop, pro shop, and driving range. Half of the daily tee times are awarded via a day-of-play lottery (6–8:59am); the rest can be obtained by calling ℃ 619/435-3122 up to 2 days out, or ℃ 619/435-3121, ext. 1, 3 to 14 days prior ($30 fee). If you don't win the lottery, you can still add your name to a standby list and step in for no-shows. Greens fees are $30 for 18 holes ($35 on weekends); cart fees are $16 per person. For twilight play (1pm winter, 4pm summer), greens fees are $15; cart rates are $11 per person. Club rental is $50, $30 twilight rate.

2000 Visalia Row, Coronado. www.golfcoronado.com. ℃ 619/435-3121. From Coronado Bridge, turn left on Orange Ave., left on Fourth St., right on Glorietta Blvd., and left on Visalia Row.

Mt. Woodson Golf Club ★ One of San Diego County's most dramatic golf courses, Mt. Woodson is a par-70, 6,180-yard course on 150 beautiful acres. The award-winning 18-hole course meanders up and down hills, across bridges, and around granite boulders. Elevated tees provide striking views of Ramona and Mount Palomar, and, on a clear day, you can see for almost 100 miles. It's easy to combine a game of golf with a weekend getaway to Julian (see chapter 10). Greens fees for 18 holes are $55 Monday through Friday, $65 Saturday and Sunday. Twilight rates are available, and seniors and golfers age 16 and under get a discount. Mt. Woodson is about 40 minutes north of San Diego.

16422 N. Woodson Dr., Ramona. www.mtwoodsongc.com. ℃ 760/788-3555. Take I-15 N. to Poway Rd. exit; at the end of Poway Rd., turn left (north) onto Rte. 67 and drive 3¾ miles to Archie Moore Rd.; turn left. Entrance is on the left.

Rancho Bernardo Inn ★ Rancho Bernardo has a mature 18-hole, 72-par championship course with different terrains, water hazards, sand traps, lakes, and waterfalls. It was recently renovated and now plays to more than 6,600 yards; there are also four sets of tees for all level of play. Stay-and-play golf packages are available. Greens fees are $100 Monday through Thursday, $115 Friday, and $135 weekends, including a cart. Twilight rates (after 1pm winter, 2pm summer) are available.

17550 Bernardo Oaks Dr., Rancho Bernardo. www.ranchobernardoinn.com or www.jcgolf.com. ℃ 858/385-8733 or 858/675-8470. From I-15 N., exit at Rancho Bernardo Rd. Head east to Bernardo Oaks Dr., turn left, and continue to the resort entrance.

Riverwalk Golf Club ★ These links wander along the Mission Valley floor and are the most convenient courses for anyone staying downtown or near the beaches. Replacing the private Stardust Golf Club, which hosted PGA tournaments in the 1950s and '60s, the course reopened in 1998 sporting a slick, upscale new clubhouse. There are also four lakes with waterfalls (water features are in play on 13 of the 27 holes); open, undulating fairways; and one peculiar feature: trolley tracks. The bright red trolley speeds through now and then but doesn't prove too distracting. Nonresident greens fees, including cart, are $99 Monday through Thursday, $125 Friday through Sunday; senior, twilight, and early-bird rates are available.

1150 Fashion Valley Rd., Mission Valley. www.riverwalkgc.com. ℃ 619/296-4653. Take I-8 to Hotel Circle south, and turn on Fashion Valley Rd.

Sycuan Resort & Casino ★ Offering 54 holes of golf (two championship courses and a 2,500-yd., par-54 executive course), Sycuan takes advantage of the area's natural terrain. Mountains, natural rock outcroppings, and aged oaks and sycamores add character to individual holes. The course also has a golf school for women taught by women. Greens fees are $57 Monday through Thursday, $62 Friday, $79 weekends for the two par-72 courses, and $19 to $26 on the shorter course; carts are $15 per person. Twilight rates are available. The course, formerly known as Singing Hills, is part of an Indian gaming resort (p. 180), which offers a variety of good-value packages; it's about 30 minutes from downtown San Diego.

3007 Dehesa Rd., El Cajon. www.sycuanresort.com. © **800/457-5568** or 619/442-3425. Take Calif. 94 to the Willow Glen exit. Turn right and continue to the entrance.

Torrey Pines Golf Course ★★★ These two gorgeous municipal 18-hole championship courses are on the coast between La Jolla and Del Mar, only 20 minutes from downtown San Diego. Home of the Farmers Insurance Open (formerly known as the Buick Invitational), and the setting of a memorable U.S. Open in 2008, Torrey Pines is second only to Pebble Beach as California's top golf destination. Situated on a bluff overlooking the ocean, the north course has the postcard-perfect signature hole (no. 6), but the south course is more challenging, has more sea-facing play, and benefits from a $3.5-million overhaul in 2002. In summer, course conditions can be less than ideal due to the sheer number of people lined up to play, and "tee scalpers" aren't uncommon. Tee times are taken 8 to 90 days in advance by automated telephone system ($43 booking fee). Golf professionals are available for lessons (which assure you a spot on the course), and the pro shop rents clubs. Greens fees on the south course are $183 weekdays, $229 weekends; the north course is $100 weekdays and $125 weekends. Cart rentals are $40, and twilight and senior rates are available. *Tip:* First-come, first-served tee times are available Monday through Thursday from 6:30am to 7:20am, and Friday to Sunday from sunup to 7:20am. Single golfers also stand a good chance of getting on the course if they just turn up and get on the waiting list for a threesome.

11480 Torrey Pines Rd., La Jolla. www.sandiego.gov/torreypines or www.torreypinesgolfcourse. com. © **877/581-7171** or 858/581-7171 (option 3 for automated reservations 8–90 days in advance); 800/985-4653 or 858/452-3226 for the pro shop and lessons. From I-5, take Genesee Ave. exit west, and go left on N. Torrey Pines Rd. Bus: 101.

Hang Gliding & Paragliding

Since 1928, the **Torrey Pines Gliderport** ★★★, 2800 Torrey Pines Scenic Dr., La Jolla (© **858/452-9858;** www.flytorrey.com), has been one of the world's top spots for nonmotorized flight. Set on a windy clifftop above Black's Beach, it draws legions of hang-gliding and paragliding enthusiasts, as well as hobbyists with radio-control aircraft. A 20- to 25-minute tandem flight with a qualified instructor costs $150 for paragliding and $200 for hang gliding (no age limit; $10 discount for paying cash). The difference between the two sports? Hang gliders are suspended from a fixed wing, while paragliders are secured to a parachute-like nylon wing. If you've ever dreamed of flying like a bird, this is your opportunity. Even if you don't muster the courage to try a tandem flight—and there is something rather nerve-racking about stepping off a 300-foot cliff—sitting at the cafe here and watching the graceful acrobatics is a treat in itself.

If you already have experience, you can rent or buy equipment from the shop at the Gliderport—note that the conditions here are considered "P3"—or take lessons from the crew of able instructors. A 5- to 7-day beginning paragliding package is $1,095; advanced hang-gliding lessons run $195 per day and must be scheduled ahead of time. Winds in December and January are slightest (that is, least conducive for the activities here), while March through June is best. Peak flying time is in the early afternoon, so call in the morning to check on conditions; reservations are not accepted. The Gliderport is open daily from 9am to sunset.

Hiking & Walking

Walking along the water is particularly rewarding. The best **beaches** for walking are Coronado, Mission Beach, La Jolla Shores, and Torrey Pines, but pretty much any shore is a good choice. You can also walk around most of Mission Bay on a series of connected footpaths. If a four-legged friend is your walking companion, head for Dog Beach in Ocean Beach or Fiesta Island in Mission Bay; they're two of the few areas where dogs can legally go unleashed. The **Coast Walk** in La Jolla offers supreme surf-line views.

The **Sierra Club** sponsors regular hikes in the San Diego area, and nonmembers are welcome to participate. A Wednesday mountain hike usually treks in the Cuyamaca Mountains, sometimes in the Lagunas; there are also outings for singles, families, and gays and lesbians. Call the office at ℭ **858/569-6005** weekdays from 9am to 5pm, or consult the website, www.sandiego.sierraclub.org. Volunteers from the **Natural History Museum** (www.sdnhm.org; ℭ **619/232-3821**) also lead free nature walks throughout San Diego County.

Marian Bear Memorial Park (www.sandiego.gov/park-and-recreation; ℭ **858/581-9961** for park ranger) in San Clemente Canyon has a 7-mile round-trip trail that runs directly underneath Highway 52. Most of the trail is flat, hard-packed dirt, but some areas are rocky. Benches and places to sit allow you to have a quiet picnic. From Highway 52 West, take the Genesee South exit; at the stoplight, make a U-turn and an immediate right into the parking lot. From Highway 52 East, exit at Genesee and make a right at the light, and then an immediate right into the parking lot.

Lake Miramar Reservoir has a 4.9-mile paved trail with a wonderful view of the lake and mountains. Take I-15 North and exit on Mira Mesa Boulevard. Turn right on Scripps Ranch Boulevard, then left on Scripps Lake Drive, and make a left at the Lake Miramar sign. Hours are sunrise to sunset, 7 days a week; parking is free. There's also a pleasant path around **Lake Murray.** Take the Lake Murray Boulevard exit off I-8 and follow the signs. See www.sandiego.gov/water/recreation for information on both locations.

Other places for scenic hikes listed earlier in this chapter include **Torrey Pines State Reserve** (p. 64), **Cabrillo National Monument** (p. 54), and **Mission Trails Regional Park** (p. 59). Guided walks are also offered at each of these parks.

Jogging

An invigorating route downtown is along the wide sidewalks of the Embarcadero, stretching around the bay. A locals' favorite place to jog is the pathway that follows the east side of Mission Bay; start at the old (shuttered) Visitor Information Center and head south past the Hilton to Fiesta Island. A good spot for a short run is La Jolla Shores Beach, where there's hard-packed sand even when it isn't low tide. The beach at Coronado is also a good place for jogging, as is the shore at Pacific Beach and Mission Beach.

Safety note: When jogging alone, be wary of secluded trails in Balboa Park, even during daylight hours.

4

EXPLORING SAN DIEGO

Outdoor Activities

paddling WITH THE FISHES

With no experience and a little arm strength, you can enjoy one of San Diego's best marine adventures—and it's not at any theme park. Explore the protected waters of La Jolla, from its legendary cove to its seven sea caves, in a kayak. You can go solo or in a tandem kayak, self-guided, or on a tour, and it's almost guaranteed that you'll spot frolicking seals or California's neon-bright state fish, the garibaldi. In summer, you may spy harmless leopard sharks circling beneath you; in winter you can head out for whale watching. For rentals or tours, check in with **La Jolla Kayak,** 2199 Avenida de la Playa (www.lajollakayak.com; ✆ **858/459-1114**).

Scuba Diving & Snorkeling

San Diego's underwater scene ranges from the magnificent giant kelp forests of Point Loma to the nautical graveyard off Mission Beach called **Wreck Alley.** At the aquatic Ecological Reserve off La Jolla Cove, fishing and boating activity has been banned since 1929. Diving and snorkeling, though, are welcome in the 533-acre reserve; it's a reliable place to spot garibaldi, California's state fish, as well as endangered giant black sea bass. Shore diving here or at nearby La Jolla Shores is common, and there are dive shops to help you get set up.

But boat dives are the rule. Check out the Islas los Coronados, a trio of uninhabited islets off Mexico (a 90-min. boat ride from San Diego), where seals, sea lions, eels, and more cavort against a landscape of boulders (watch for swift currents). There's also the *Yukon,* a 366-foot Canadian destroyer that was intentionally sunk in 2000. It's part of Wreck Alley, an artificial reef less than 1 mile out from Mission Beach that includes several other vessels and the remains of a research platform toppled by a storm in 1988. Water visibility is best in the fall; water temperatures are cold year-round.

The **San Diego Oceans Foundation** (www.sdoceans.org; ✆ 619/523-1903) is a nonprofit organization devoted to the stewardship of local marine waters; the website features good information about the diving scene. Notable dive outfits include **Ocean Enterprises,** 7710 Balboa Ave. (www.oceanenterprises.com; ✆ 858/565-6054); **Lois Ann Dive Charters,** 1717 Quivira Way (www.loisann.com; ✆ 800/201-4381 or 858/780-0130); and **Scuba San Diego** (www.scubasandiego.com; ✆ 619/260-1880). **OEX Dive & Kayak Centers** (www.oexcalifornia.com) has locations in La Jolla, 2243 Av. de la Playa (✆ 858/454-6195), and Mission Bay, 1010 Santa Clara Place (✆ 619/866-6129).

Skating

Gliding around San Diego, especially the Mission Bay area, on in-line skates is the quintessential Southern California experience. In Mission Beach, rent a pair of in-line skates or a skateboard ($5 per hr.) from **Cheap Rentals,** 3689 Mission Blvd. (www.cheap-rentals.com; ✆ 800/941-7761 or 858/488-9070). In Coronado, go to **Bikes and Beyond,** 1201 First St. at the Ferry Landing (✆ 619/435-7180; www.hollandsbicycles.com); rates are $6 per hour.

If you'd rather ice-skate, try **Ice Town** at University Towne Center, 4545 La Jolla Village Dr., at Genesee Avenue (www.lajollaicetown.com; ✆ 858/452-9110).

During the winter holidays, outdoor skating rinks open at the Hotel del Coronado (p. 213) and downtown at Horton Square.

Surfing

Some of the best surf spots include Windansea, La Jolla Shores, Pacific Beach, Mission Beach, Ocean Beach, and Imperial Beach. In North County, you might consider Swami's in Encinitas, Carlsbad State Beach, and Oceanside. The best waves are in late summer and early fall, but winter storms bring big surf, too; even in summer, you'll probably need a wetsuit. For surf reports, check out www.surfingsandiego.com or www.surfline.com (click on "cams and reports" and scroll down to "Southern California"). *A **word of advice:*** Don't get in over your head; hazards include strong riptides and territorial locals.

Soft boards are available for rent from stands at many popular beaches. Many local surf shops also rent equipment and provide lessons, including **La Jolla Surf Systems,** 2132 Av. de la Playa, La Jolla Shores (www.lajollasurfsystems.com; © **858/456-2777**); **Pacific Beach Surf Shop,** 4150 Mission Blvd. (www.pacificbeachsurfshop.com; © **858/373-1138**); and **Ocean Beach Surf & Skate,** 4976 Newport Ave. (www.obsurfandskate.com or www.oceanexperience.net; © **619/225-0674**). In Coronado, you can rent boards at **Emerald City: The Boarding Source,** 1118 Orange Ave. (www.emeraldcitysurf.com; © 619/435-6677).

For surfing lessons in the North County, check with **Kahuna Bob's Surf School** (www.kahunabob.com; © **800/524-8627** or 760/721-7700), based in Encinitas; **San Diego Surfing Academy** (www.surfsdsa.com; © **800/447-7873** or 760/230-1474), which offers lessons at South Carlsbad State Beach; and **Surf Diva,** 2160 Av. de la Playa (www.surfdiva.com; © **858/454-8273**), a surfing school for women and girls, based in La Jolla. Surf Diva has become so popular it now does lessons for guys, as well as co-ed group instruction; in summer there are co-ed surf camps for ages 5 to 17.

Swimming

Most San Diego hotels have pools, but there are plenty of other swimming options for visitors. The centrally located Mission Valley **YMCA,** 5505 Friars Rd. (www.missionvalley.ymca.org; © **619/298-3576**), has two pools available daily (and nightly), including an outdoor facility—call for schedule information. The nonmember fee is $5 for adults, $1.50 for seniors (62 and over) and children 15 and under. In Balboa Park, you can swim in the **Kearns Memorial Swimming Pool,** 2229 Morley Field Dr. (www.sandiego.gov/park-and-recreation/aquatics; © **619/692-4920**). The fee for using the public pool is $4 for adults, $2 for seniors (62 and up) and children 15 and under; call for seasonal hours and laps-only restrictions.

In La Jolla, you can swim at the **Lawrence Family Jewish Community Center,** 4126 Executive Dr. (www.lfjcc.org; © **858/457-3030**). This heated Olympic outdoor pool (with an ozone filter; no chlorine) is open to the public Monday through Thursday from 6am to 7:30pm, Friday from 6am to 5pm, and weekends from 8:30am to 5pm. Admission is $10 adults, $5 for ages 14 and under.

Tennis

At the **La Jolla Tennis Club,** 7632 Draper Ave., at Prospect Street (www.ljtc.org; © **858/454-4434**), there are nine public courts, the oldest of which have been here

THE best OF SAN DIEGO ONLINE

- **www.sandiego.org** is maintained by the San Diego Convention & Visitors Bureau and includes up-to-date weather data, a calendar of events, and a hotel booking engine.

- **www.sandiegoartandsol.com** is the link for cultural tourism. You'll find a list of art shows and music events, plus intriguing touring itineraries that delve into the city's culture.

- **www.sandiegomagazine.com** is the online site for *San Diego Magazine,* offering feature stories and dining and events listings.

- **www.sandiegoreader.com,** the site of the free weekly *San Diego Reader,* is a great resource for club and show listings. It also offers discounts for dining and other services, plus opinionated arts, eats, and entertainment critiques.

- **www.utsandiego.com** is the site for the city's last major daily newspaper, the *U-T San Diego.* It has headline news, plus reviews and information on restaurants, music, movies, performing arts, museums, outdoor recreation, beaches, and sports.

- **www.wheresd.com** provides information on arts, culture, special events, shopping, and dining for San Diego, Orange County, and Los Angeles. You can also make hotel reservations through the site.

- **www.voiceofsandiego.org** is an excellent online news source that offers information on what's happening in the city politically and culturally.

- **www.sezio.org** is a hip spot where you can check in with the local art and music scene and learn about the latest openings and shows.

- **www.sdartstix.com** is where you can purchase discounted tickets to theater, music, and dance performances.

- **www.sandiego.com** is another great source for San Diego news, reviews, and more—it has content for both locals and visitors.

- **www.travelzoo.com** and **www. yipit.com** are aggregators that compile discounts in cities around the country, including San Diego; you'll find deals on everything from massages to hot-air balloon rides.

since 1915, a gift from the ubiquitous Ellen Browning Scripps. It costs $10 for adults and is free for those 18 and under; it's open daily from dawn until the lights go off around 9pm. The **Balboa Tennis Club,** 2221 Morley Field Dr., in Balboa Park (www.balboatennis.com; ✆ **619/295-9278**), has more than 2 dozen courts, including a stadium court. Day passes are $6 adults, $4 seniors 65 and above, $2 for children 17 and under; reservations are for members only. The courts are open weekdays from 8am to 9pm, weekends from 8am to 8pm. The ultramodern **Barnes Tennis Center,** 4490 W. Point Loma Blvd., near Ocean Beach and SeaWorld (www.tennis sandiego.com; ✆ **619/221-9000**), has 20 lighted hard courts and 4 clay courts. They're open Monday through Thursday from 8am to 9pm, Friday through Sunday 8am to 7pm. Court rental is $6 to $10 per person for all-day usage (upon availability); a $4 light fee may apply for night play. Those 17 and under play for free during the day, $2 in the evening.

SIGHTS & ATTRACTIONS BY THEME INDEX

AMUSEMENT PARK
Balboa Park Miniature Railroad and Carousel (p. 48)
Belmont Park (p. 61)

AQUARIUM
Birch Aquarium at Scripps ★★ (p. 62)

ARCHITECTURE
Heritage Park (p. 58)

ART MUSEUM
Museum of Contemporary Art San Diego ★★★ (p. 56 and 64)
The San Diego Museum of Art ★ (p. 52)
SDAI Museum of the Living Artist (p. 51)
Timken Museum of Art ★ (p. 53)

CEMETERY
El Campo Santo (p. 58)

CHURCH
Mission Basilica San Diego de Alcalá (p. 58)

CULTURAL INSTITUTION
Athenaeum Music & Arts Library ★★ (p. 62)
Centro Cultural de la Raza (p. 49)
House of Pacific Relations International Cottages (p. 49)
Stuart Collection ★ (p. 64)
WorldBeat Center ★ (p. 54)

HISTORIC HOME
Marston House Museum & Gardens ★ (p. 50)
Whaley House (p. 60)
William Heath Davis House Museum (p. 57)

HISTORIC SITE
Cabrillo National Monument ★★★ (p. 54)
USS *Midway* Museum (p. 57)
Old Town State Historic Park ★ (p. 60)

ICON
Hotel del Coronado ★★★ (p. 65)

MUSEUM
Firehouse Museum (p. 55)
Junípero Serra Museum ★ (p. 58)
Maritime Museum ★★ (p. 55)
Mingei International Museum ★★ (p. 50)
Museum of History and Art (p. 65)
Museum of Photographic Arts ★★★ (p. 50)
The New Children's Museum ★ (p. 56)
Reuben H. Fleet Science Center ★ (p. 51)
San Diego Air & Space Museum ★★ (p. 51)
San Diego Automotive Museum ★ (p. 51)
San Diego Chinese Historical Museum (p. 56)
San Diego Hall of Champions Sports Museum (p. 52)
San Diego History Center (p. 52)
San Diego Model Railroad Museum ★ (p. 52)
San Diego Museum of Man ★ (p. 53)
San Diego Natural History Museum (p. 53)

NATURE RESERVE
Chula Vista Nature Center ★ (p. 66)

PARK/GARDEN
Botanical Building and Lily Pond ★ (p. 48)
Japanese Friendship Garden (p. 50)
Mission Trails Regional Park ★ (p. 59)
Torrey Pines State Reserve ★★★ (p. 64)

PERFORMING ARTS VENUE
Spreckels Organ Pavilion (p. 53)

TOUR
Flagship (p. 73)
The Gondola Company (p. 73)

Hornblower Cruises (p. 74)
Xplore Offshore ★★ (p. 74)

WATER PARK
Knott's Soak City U.S.A. (p. 66)

ZOO
San Diego Zoo ★★★ (p. 40)
San Diego Zoo Safari Park ★★★ (p. 38)
SeaWorld San Diego ★★ (p. 41)

STROLLING
AROUND
SAN DIEGO

From the history-heavy Gaslamp Quarter to idyllic Balboa Park, San Diego easily lends itself to the long, leisurely stroll. The four walking tours in this chapter will give you a special sense of the city, as well as a look at some of its most appealing sights and structures.

WALKING TOUR 1: THE GASLAMP QUARTER

START:	**Fourth Avenue and E Street, at Horton Plaza.**
FINISH:	**Fourth Avenue and F Street.**
TIME:	**Approximately 1½ hours, not including shopping and dining.**
BEST TIMES:	**During the day.**
WORST TIMES:	**Evenings, when the area's popular restaurants and nightspots attract big crowds.**

A National Historic District covering 16½ city blocks, the Gaslamp Quarter contains many Victorian and Edwardian commercial buildings built between the Civil War and World War I. The quarter—featuring electric versions of old gas lamps—lies between Fourth Avenue to the west, Sixth Avenue to the east, Broadway to the north, and L Street and the waterfront to the south. The blocks are not large; developer Alonzo Horton knew corner lots were desirable to buyers, so he created more of them. This tour hits some highlights along Fourth and Fifth avenues; Fifth Avenue, in fact, was named one of "America's Great Streets" by the nonprofit educational group the American Planning Association. If this whets your appetite for more, the **Gaslamp Quarter Historical Foundation,** 410 Island Ave. (www.gaslampquarter.org; ✆ **619/233-4692**), offers guided walking tours every Saturday at 11am ($10, including museum admission, or $8 for seniors, students, and military; free for children 11 and under). The book *San Diego's Gaslamp Quarter,* jointly produced by the GQHF, the San Diego Historical Society, and the Gaslamp Quarter Association, makes an excellent, lightweight walking companion; it has then-and-now photos and historical background.

1 Horton Plaza

It's a colorful conglomeration of shops, eateries, and architectural flourishes—and a tourist attraction. Ernest W. Hahn, who planned and implemented the redevelopment and revitalization of downtown San Diego, built the plaza in 1985. This core project, which covers 12 acres and 6½ blocks in the heart of downtown, represents the successful integration of public and private funding.

The ground floor at Horton Plaza is home to the **Jessop Street Clock.** The timepiece has 20 dials, 12 of which tell the time in places throughout the world. Designed by Joseph Jessop, Sr., and built primarily by Claude D. Ledger, the clock stood outside Jessop's Jewelry Store on Fifth Avenue from 1907 until being moved to Horton Plaza in 1985. Until recently, it had reportedly stopped only three times in its history: once after being hit by a team of horses, once after an earthquake, and again on the day in 1935 when Mr. Ledger died.

Exit Horton Plaza on the north side, street level. At the corner of Fourth and Broadway is:

2 Horton Plaza Park

Its centerpiece is a **fountain** designed by well-known local architect Irving Gill and modeled after the monument of Lysicrates in Athens. Dedicated Oct. 15, 1910, it was the first successful attempt in the United States to combine electric lights with flowing water. On the fountain's base are bronze medallions of San Diego's "founding fathers": Juan Rodríguez Cabrillo, Father Junípero Serra, and Alonzo Horton.

Walk south along Fourth Avenue to the:

3 Balboa Theatre

Constructed in 1924, the Spanish Renaissance–style building, at the southwest corner of Fourth Avenue and E Street, has a distinctive tile dome, striking tile work in the entry, and two 20-foot-high ornamental waterfalls inside. In the theater's heyday, plays and vaudeville took top billing. After years of sitting dormant and decrepit, the renovated Balboa (www.sandiegotheatres.org) is hosting live performances of dance, theater, music, and spoken word once again.

Cross Fourth Avenue and proceed along E Street to Fifth Avenue. The tall, striking building to your left at the northeast corner of Fifth and E is the:

4 Watts-Robinson Building

Built in 1913, this was one of San Diego's first skyscrapers. It once housed 70 jewelers and is now a boutique hotel (see the review for **Gaslamp Plaza Suites** on p. 193). Take a minute to look inside at the marble wainscoting, tile floors, ornate ceiling, and brass ornamentation.

Return to the southwest corner of Fifth Avenue and E Street. On the opposite side of the street, at 837 Fifth Ave., is the unmistakable "grand old lady of the Gaslamp," the twin-towered baroque revival:

5 Louis Bank of Commerce

You can admire the next few buildings from the west side of the street and then continue south from here. Built in 1888, this proud building was the first in San Diego made of granite. It once housed the city's first ice-cream parlor; an oyster bar frequented by legendary lawman Wyatt Earp (of O.K. Corral shootout

Walking Tour 1: The Gaslamp Quarter

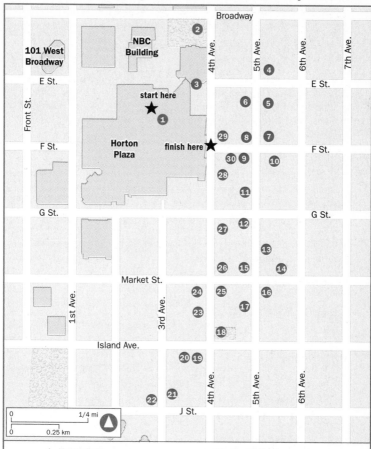

1 Horton Plaza
2 Horton Plaza Park
3 Balboa Theatre
4 Watts-Robinson Building
5 Louis Bank of Commerce
6 F.W. Woolworth Building
7 Marston Building
8 Keating Building
9 Spencer-Ogden Building
10 William Penn Hotel
11 Llewelyn Building
12 Old City Hall
13 Yuma Building
14 I.O.O.F. Building
15 Backesto Building
16 Metropolitan Hotel

17 Lincoln Hotel
18 William Heath Davis House
19 Horton Grand Hotel
20 Cheese Shop/Palace Bar
21 Former Home of Ah Quin
22 Chinese Mission
23 Royal Pie Bakery Building
24 Frey Block Building
25 Hotel Lester
26 Brokers Building
27 Carriage Works
28 Labor Temple Building
29 Ingle Building
30 Café Lulu

fame); and the Golden Poppy Hotel, a brothel run by a fortuneteller, Madame Coara. After a fire in 1904, the original towers of the building were removed, and the iron eagles perched atop them disappeared. A 2002 renovation installed a new pair of eagles, cast at the same English foundry as the originals.

On the west side of Fifth Avenue, at no. 840, near E Street, you'll find the:

6 F. W. Woolworth Building

Built in 1910, this building had been the site of San Diego Hardware since 1922; sadly, the store relocated to friendlier confines in 2006. The amazing hammered-tin ceiling is still a highlight, though, of the current occupant, **Cremolose.** This stylish Italian cafe is the first U.S. location of a European chain.

Across the street, at 801 Fifth Ave., stands the two-story:

7 Marston Building

This Italianate Victorian–style building dates from 1881 and housed business-man and philanthropist George W. Marston's department store for 15 years. In 1885, San Diego Federal Savings' first office was here, and the Prohibition Temperance Union held its meetings here in the late 1880s. Ironically, the site was later occupied by a series of bars and strip clubs. After a fire in 1903, the building was remodeled extensively. The current restaurant/bar in residence, retro-themed **Analog,** features odes to albums, cassettes, and tall-boy beers.

The redbrick Romanesque revival on the northwest corner of Fifth Avenue and F Street is the:

8 Keating Building

A San Diego landmark dating from 1890, this structure was nicknamed the "marriage building." It was developed by businessman George Keating, who died halfway through construction; his wife, Fannie, finished the project, changing some of the design along the way. She had her husband's name engraved in the top cornice as a tribute to him. Originally heralded as one of the city's most prestigious office buildings, it featured conveniences such as steam heat and a wire-cage elevator. A boutique hotel, the **Keating Hotel,** is now ensconced here (p. 190).

Continuing south on Fifth Avenue, cross F Street, and stand in front of the:

9 Spencer-Ogden Building

It's on the southwest corner at 770 Fifth Ave. Built in 1874, this is one of the oldest buildings in the Gaslamp Quarter—and it's lucky to still be standing. It escaped major damage after an explosion in 1887 caused by a druggist who was making fireworks. Other tenants over the years included realtors, an import business, a home-furnishings business, and a "Painless Parker" dental office. Edgar Parker owned a chain of dental offices and legally changed his name to "Painless" in order to avoid claims of false advertising.

Directly across the street stands the:

10 William Penn Hotel

Built in 1913, it started out as the elegant Oxford Hotel; a double room with private bathroom and toilet cost $1.50. Note the restored glasswork that wraps around the building.

11 Llewelyn Building

Built in 1887 by William Llewelyn, this building housed his family shoe store until 1906. Of architectural note are its arched windows, molding, and cornices. Through the decades, it has been home to a series of hotels, none of which had a particularly high standing among those in proper society; in 1917 charges were brought against the proprietor for operating a "cat house." Today the Llewelyn is a colorful hostel.

On the southwest corner of Fifth Avenue and G Street is the:

12 Old City Hall

Dating from 1874, when it was a bank, this Florentine Italianate building features 16-foot ceilings, 12-foot windows framed with brick arches, antique columns, and a wrought-iron cage elevator. Notice the windows on each floor are different. (The top two stories were added in 1887, when it became the city's public library.) Incredibly, in a 1950s attempt at modernization, this beauty was completely encased in stucco. It was restored in the 1980s.

Across the street in the middle of the block, at 631–633 Fifth Ave., is the:

13 Yuma Building

This striking edifice was built in 1888 and was one of the first brick buildings downtown. The brothel at the Yuma was the first to be closed during the infamous 1912 cleanup of the area. In the end, 138 women (and no men) were arrested. They were given a choice: Join the Door of Hope charity and reform or take a one-way train ride to Los Angeles. One hundred thirty-six went to L.A. (many were back within days), one woman was pronounced insane, and the last became San Diego's first telephone operator.

Go left on Market Street; at no. 526 is the:

14 I.O.O.F. Building

Finally finished in 1882 after 9 years of construction, this handsome building served as a joint lodge for the Masons and Odd Fellows. Gaslamp lore has it that while watching a parade from the balcony, Kalakaua, Hawaii's last reigning king, caught cold and died shortly thereafter in San Francisco in 1891.

Head back toward Fifth Avenue. On the northwest corner of Fifth Avenue and Market Street is the:

15 Backesto Building

Built in 1873, this classical revival and Victorian-style building fills most of the block. Originally a one-story structure on the corner, it expanded to its present size and height over its first 15 years. At the turn of the 20th century, this part of the Gaslamp was known as the **Stingaree,** the city's notorious red-light district. Gambling, opium dens, and wild saloons were all part of the mix.

Across Market Street, on the east side of the street, is the former:

16 The Metropolitan

This building had bay windows and a cupola when it was built in 1886; now it looks decidedly contemporary—until you spot the rugged 19th-century columns still visible on the street level. The Metropolitan also features arrestingly realistic *trompe l'oeil* effects painted on the facade. When the building was being renovated in the '80s, it was determined a faithful restoration would be too costly, so the owner was permitted to do the faux finish. Today the Metropolitan is another of San Diego's well-located hostels.

In the middle of the block, at 536 Fifth Ave., is the small but distinctive:

17 Lincoln Hotel

It dates from 1913—the date is cast in a grand concrete pediment two stories up. An equally grand stone lion's head once reigned atop the parapet, but tumbled to the street during an earthquake in 1986 and was quickly snatched by a passerby. The building's unusual green-and-white ceramic tile facade is thankfully intact. At one time, the block was comprised of primarily Japanese-owned businesses; Japanese residents ended up being held in the hotel during World War II before being sent to internment camps.

Proceed to Island Avenue and turn right. The saltbox house at the corner of Fourth Avenue is the:

18 William Heath Davis House

Downtown's oldest surviving structure, this prefabricated lumber home was shipped to San Diego around Cape Horn from New England in 1850. Alonzo Horton lived in the house in 1867, at its original location at the corner of Market and State streets. Around 1873, it was moved to 11th Avenue and K Street, where it served as the county hospital. It was relocated to this site in 1984 and completely refurbished. The entire house, now a **museum** and gift shop, and the small park next to it are open to the public (p. 57). The Gaslamp Quarter Historical Foundation is also headquartered here.

At the southwest corner of Island and Fourth avenues you'll see the bay windows of the winsome:

19 Horton Grand Hotel

Two 1886 hotels were moved here—very gently—from other sites, and then renovated and connected by an atrium; the original Grand Horton is to your left, the Brooklyn Hotel to your right. Now it's all one: the **Horton Grand Hotel** (p. 189). The reception desk is a recycled pew from a choir loft, and old post-office boxes now hold guests' keys; there's also a life-size papier-mâché horse named Sunshine (it stood in front of the Brooklyn Hotel when the ground floor was a saddlery). In the Palace Bar, look for the portrait of Ida Bailey, a local madam whose establishment, the Canary Cottage, once stood nearby. Wyatt Earp was also a regular; he lived upstairs at the Brooklyn for most of his 7 years in San Diego.

20 Take a Break 🍺

The Cheese Shop (📞 619/232-2303) is open for breakfast or lunch with house-made corned beef hash, blueberry pancakes, fresh soups, and tasty pork sandwiches; after 4pm, try the Palace Bar (📞 619/544-1886). Both are located in the Horton Grand Hotel, which is a good place to relax while surrounded by a bit of history. The bar is part of the same choir-loft pew that has been turned into the reception desk.

21 Former Home of Ah Quin

One of the first Chinese merchants in San Diego, Ah Quin arrived in the 1880s and became known as the "Mayor of Chinatown" (an area bound by Market and J sts., and Third and Fifth aves.). He helped hundreds of Chinese immigrants find work on the railroad and owned a general merchandise store on Fifth Avenue. He was a respected father (of 12 children), and a leader and spokesperson for the city's Chinese population.

The Ah Quin home is not open to the public, but across the street at 404 Third Ave. is the:

22 Chinese Mission

Originally located on First Avenue, this charming brick building, built in 1927, was a place where Chinese immigrants (primarily men) could learn English and find employment. Religious instruction and living quarters were also provided. The building was rescued from demolition and moved to its present location, where it now contains the **San Diego Chinese Historical Museum** (p. 56). There's a gift shop with Chinese wares, a small Asian garden with a memorial to the father of modern China, Sun Yat-sen, and a statue of Confucius. Admission is $2.

When you leave the museum, retrace your steps back to Fourth and Island and walk north; in the middle of the block on the west side you will come to the:

23 Royal Pie Bakery Building

Erected in 1911, this building was a bakery for most of its existence. Something else was cooking upstairs, though—the second floor housed the Anchor Hotel, which was eventually closed because of "rampant immorality."

At the southwest corner of Fourth Avenue and Market Street stands the:

24 Frey Block Building

Built in 1911, this was first a secondhand store, then a series of Chinese restaurants. But real fame arrived in the 1950s when it became the Crossroads, one of San Diego's most important jazz clubs. It was a venue for local and touring African-American artists.

Across the street on the southeast corner, at 401–417 Market St., is the:

25 Hotel Lester

This hotel dates from 1906. It housed a saloon, pool hall, and hotel of ill repute when this was a red-light district. It's still a hotel (cheap but not tawdry) upstairs, while the ground level supports retail businesses, including a boutique from a *Project Runway* reality TV contestant.

On the northeast corner of Fourth Avenue and Market Street, at 402 Market St., stands the:

26 Brokers Building

Constructed in 1889, this building has 16-foot wood-beam ceilings and cast-iron columns. In recent years, it was converted to artists' lofts, with the ground floor dedicated to the downtown branch of the Hooters chain. Due to the failure

5

STROLLING AROUND SAN DIEGO

The Gaslamp Quarter

of many previous ventures here, as well as a fire and a structural collapse, this was thought of as a cursed corner.

At the north end of this block, you will find the:

27 Carriage Works

Established in 1890, it once served as storage for wagons and carriages. It then segued to horseless carriages, serving as a Studebaker showroom and repair shop. The building now features restaurants and clubs.

Cross G Street and walk to the middle of the block to the:

28 Labor Temple Building

Dating from 1907, it has striking arched windows on the second floor. The inside was once used as a meeting hall for unions representing everyone from cigar makers to theatrical employees. Le Travel Store is now located here.

Continue north; at 801 Fourth Ave. is the:

29 Ingle Building

It dates from 1906 and now houses the **Hard Rock Cafe.** The mural on the F Street side of the building depicts a group of deceased rock stars (Janis Joplin, Jimi Hendrix, John Lennon, Jim Morrison, and Elvis) lounging at sidewalk tables. Original stained-glass windows from the old Golden Lion Tavern (1907–32) front Fourth Avenue. Inside, the colorful stained-glass ceiling was taken from an Elks Club in Stockton, California, and much of the floor is original.

30 Winding Down ☕

Walk to bohemian Café Lulu, 419 F St. (✆ 619/238-0114), near Fourth Avenue, for coffee and sweets; or head back into Horton Plaza, where you can choose from many kinds of cuisine, from Chinese to Indian, along with good old American fast food.

WALKING TOUR 2: **THE EMBARCADERO**

START:	**The Maritime Museum, at Harbor Drive and Ash Street.**
FINISH:	**The Convention Center, at Harbor Drive and Fifth Avenue.**
TIME:	**1½ hours, not including museum and shopping stops.**
BEST TIMES:	**Weekday mornings (when it's less crowded and easier to park).**
WORST TIMES:	**Weekends, especially in the afternoon, when the Maritime Museum and Seaport Village are crowded; also when cruise ships are in port (days vary).**

San Diego's colorful Embarcadero, or waterfront, cradles a bevy of seagoing vessels—frigates, ferries, yachts, cruise ships, a merchant vessel, an aircraft carrier, and even a Soviet submarine. You'll also find the equally colorful Seaport Village, a shopping and dining center with a nautical theme. It's not all about the water, though—you'll also find the two downtown wings of the Museum of Contemporary Art San Diego, including a spectacular annex that opened in 2007. **Note:** This area will be undergoing a massive face-lift over the next several years. The North Embarcadero Visionary Plan, which broke ground in 2012, includes an esplanade, with groves of jacarandas and formal gardens, and a new public square at the foot of Broadway, with a cafe, information center, restrooms, and public art.

Walking Tour 2: The Embarcadero

0   1/4 mi
0   0.25 km

Information ⓘ
Trolley Line

Harbor Dr.

❷

County Administration
Center

Beech St.

India St.

start here ★
❶
Ash St.
❸

A St.

Pacific Highway

B St.

B Street Pier

ⓘ

❽ C St.
America
❹ ❼ Plaza

❻
Broadway Pier ❺
Broadway

SAN DIEGO BAY

E St.

Navy Pier

Harbor Dr.

Kettner Blvd.

PANTOJA
PARK

❾

G Street Pier
❿

G St.

❶❷
G St.
❶❶

W Harbor Dr.

❶❸

❶❼ₐ

❶❹

finish here ★

❶❻→
❶❼ᵦ→

❶❺

EMBARCADERO
MARINA PARK

1 Maritime Museum
2 County Administration Center
3 Anthony's Fishette ☕
4 Harbor Cruises
5 Coronado Ferry
6 Port Pavilion
7 Santa Fe Depot
8 Museum of Contemporary Art San Diego
9 USS *Midway*
10 The Greatest Generation Art Collection
11 Tuna Harbor
12 Fish Market/Top of the Market ☕
13 Ruocco Park
14 Seaport Village
15 Embarcadero Marina Park North
16 Convention Center/Embarcadero
     Marina Park South
17a Top of the Hyatt ☕
17b Roy's ☕

5

STROLLING AROUND SAN DIEGO

The Embarcadero

1 Maritime Museum

Not a building, but a collection of ships, the **Maritime Museum** is at Harbor Drive at Ash Street (see the review on p. 55). The main attraction is the magnificent *Star of India*—the world's oldest sailing ship that still goes to sea—built in 1863 as the *Euterpe*. The ship, whose billowing sails are a familiar sight along Harbor Drive, once carried cargo to India and immigrants to New Zealand, and it braved the arctic ice in Alaska to work in the salmon industry. Another component of the museum is the 1898 ferry *Berkeley*, built to operate between San Francisco and Oakland. In service through 1958, it carried survivors to safety 24 hours a day for 4 days after the 1906 San Francisco earthquake. You can also check out the HMS *Surprise*, which had a star turn in the film *Master and Commander*; a Soviet-era B-39 attack submarine; the *Californian*, a replica of a 19th-century revenue cutter; the *Medea*, a 1904 steam yacht; and the *Pilot*, which served as San Diego Bay's official pilot boat for 82 years.

From this vantage point, you get a fine view of the:

2 County Administration Center

This complex was built in 1936 with funds from the Works Progress Administration, and was dedicated in 1938 by President Franklin D. Roosevelt. The 23-foot-high granite sculpture in front, *Guardian of Water*, was completed by Donal Hord—San Diego's most notable sculptor—in 1939; it depicts a stoic woman shouldering a water jug. On weekdays, the building is open from 8am to 5pm; there are restrooms and a cafeteria inside (you will need to pass through security, though).

3 Take a Break ☕

The cafeteria on the fourth floor of the County Administration Center, 1600 Pacific Coast Hwy. (𝒞 619/515-4258), isn't exactly posh, but it has lovely harbor views; it serves breakfast and lunch weekdays from 7am to 2:30pm. The salads, panini, and burgers are all modestly priced. If you can't pass up the chance to have some seafood, return to the waterfront to Anthony's Fishette, 1360 N. Harbor Dr. (𝒞 619/232-5105), a simple eatery with a simply marvelous location. You can dine alfresco to enjoy your fish and chips and clam chowder.

Continue south past the B St. Pier cruise ship terminal to the:

4 Harbor Cruises

They depart from the Embarcadero all day; there are evening dinner cruises, too. Ticket booths are right on the water. See "Organized Tours" in chapter 4 for more details.

A little farther south, near the Broadway Pier, is the:

5 Coronado Ferry

It makes hourly trips between San Diego and Coronado. Buy tickets from the Flagship booth—a one-way trip is 15 minutes. See "By Ferry" within the "Getting Around" section in chapter 11 for more information.

Head out onto the Broadway Pier for a better look at the:

6 Port Pavilion

Unveiled in 2010, this 52,000-square-foot, $28-million facility is a cruise ship terminal and event space; it's also a LEED-certified green building. The most notable feature of this aqua-shaded, steel and glass building with the saw-toothed roof is the soaring, sculptured exterior wall designed by artist Leni Schwendinger. Described by its creator as a "monumental sea creature," the piece is called *Tidal Radiance,* and it's at its shimmering best after dark. There are also restrooms here.

Head straight back to Broadway, you'll see the two gold mission-style towers of the:

7 Santa Fe Depot

This mosaic-draped railroad station was built in 1915 and provides one of the city's best examples of Spanish Colonial Revival style. It's only 1½ blocks away, so walk over and look inside at the vaulted ceiling, wooden benches, and walls covered in striking green-and-gold tiles.

Continue to the north end of the station where you will find the:

8 Museum of Contemporary Art San Diego

What was once the station's baggage building is now the Museum of Contemporary Art San Diego's dynamic **Jacobs Building** (p. 56). Designed by the architect responsible for the Warhol museum in Pittsburgh and the Picasso museum in Spain, this is one of the city's cultural flagships. The original downtown annex is across the street.

Return to Harbor Drive and head south; you'll stroll through a small tree- and bench-lined park and to the:

9 USS *Midway*

This aircraft carrier had a 47-year military history that started 1 week after the Japanese surrender of World War II in 1945. By the time the *Midway* was decommissioned in 1991, more than 225,000 men had served aboard. The carrier is now a naval museum, telling the story of life on board the ship, of the wars it fought, and of the records it set (the *Midway* was tasked with setting new standards throughout much of its career). For more information, see p. 57.

South of the *Midway,* at Pier 11, is the:

10 The Greatest Generation Art Collection

This collection of patriotic art at Tuna Harbor Park is dedicated to the heroes of World War II. Pieces include the 7-foot bronze sculpture *Homecoming,* depicting a sailor in loving embrace with his reunited family, and the USS *San Diego* memorial, a massive granite installation that chronicles the ship's exploits during the war. *A National Salute to Bob Hope and the Military* features a cast of 16 bronze statues, including the legendary comedian who, for more than 50 years, devoted himself to entertaining the troops.

Continue along the walkway to:

11 Tuna Harbor

This is where the commercial fishing boats congregate. San Diego's tuna fleet is based here but is a shadow of its former self—it was once the world's largest.

12 Take a Break 🍴

The red building on the peninsula to your right houses the Fish Market, 750 N. Harbor Dr. (✆ 619/232-3474), a market and casual restaurant, and its upscale counterpart, Top of the Market, just upstairs. A meal here is fresh off the boat. Both serve lunch and dinner, and the Fish Market has a children's menu and an oyster and sushi bar. It's fine to drop in just for a drink and to savor the mighty view. Prices are moderate downstairs, expensive upstairs. For dessert or coffee, go inside Seaport Village, 849 W. Harbor Dr., to Upstart Crow (✆ 619/232-4855), a bookstore and coffeehouse.

Keep walking south to:

13 Ruocco Park

This brand-new 3¼-acre park is dedicated to Lloyd Ruocco, San Diego's most important modernist architect, and his wife Ilse, an interior designer, artist, and educator. The park's trellis sculpture is by one of the city's most prominent artists, Roman De Salvo.

The walkway continues to:

14 Seaport Village

This outdoor shopping center contains myriad boutiques and restaurants. The **carousel** is pure nostalgia—Charles Looff, who built the first carousel at Coney Island, carved the animals out of poplar in 1895. You will no doubt also notice the official symbol of Seaport Village: a 45-foot-high detailed replica of the famous Mukilteo Lighthouse in Washington State.

From Seaport Village, continue your waterfront walk southeast to the:

15 Embarcadero Marina Park North

Jutting out into the bay, Embarcadero Marina Park North is a lovely patch of green, well used by San Diegans for strolling and jogging. It features expansive views and is often fairly deserted. The four hotel towers here that wall you off from the rest of the city belong to the Manchester Grand Hyatt and the Marriott San Diego Hotel & Marina. A concession at the marina rents boats by the hour, and arranges diving, water-skiing, and fishing outings.

The waterfront walkway continues to the:

16 Convention Center/Embarcadero Marina Park South

This building is another striking piece of architecture hugging the city's waterfront. When it was first completed in late 1989, its presence on the Embarcadero was a major factor in the revitalization of downtown San Diego. It was later enlarged to an even more imposing size, to less acclaim. Embarcadero Marina Park South stretches out into the bay from here; you'll find a restaurant, basketball courts, a concession stand, and a fishing pier. You can also catch a ferry to Coronado.

To access the Gaslamp Quarter or San Diego Trolley, you'll need to head back to Seaport Village or cut through the lobbies of the Hyatt or Marriott hotels.

17 Winding Down 🍺

There's no better place in San Diego to catch a sunset than the Top of the Hyatt, 1 Market Place (✆ 619/232-1234), a 40th-floor lounge with sweeping views of the city and harbor. It's located in the eastern tower of the Manchester Grand Hyatt and opens at 3pm daily. For those afraid of heights, there's a branch of the popular Pacific Rim–fusion eatery Roy's, 333 W. Harbor Dr. (✆ 619/239-7697), on the marina side of the Marriott, perched right above the action along the pedestrian pathway.

WALKING TOUR 3: OLD TOWN

START:	**The McCoy House, overlooking the San Diego Trolley's Old Town station.**
FINISH:	**Heritage Park.**
TIME:	**2 hours, not including shopping or dining.**
BEST TIMES:	**Weekdays; there are daily 1-hour free tours at 11am and 2pm; on Wednesdays and Saturdays, from 10am to 4pm, costumed park volunteers reenact life in the 1800s. There's storytelling on the green Tuesdays and Thursdays, noon to 2pm, and Fridays from 1 to 3pm. Be prepared to be joined by lots of school groups.**
WORST TIMES:	**Weekends, especially if you want to dine at one of the restaurants, where waits can be long. Of special note is Cinco de Mayo weekend (the first weekend in May)—Old Town is a madhouse, so plan accordingly. The holiday celebrates Mexico's defeat of the French on May 5, 1862, in the Battle of Puebla, and there are a number of special events held.**

When you visit Old Town, you go back to a time of one-room schoolhouses and village greens, when many of the people who lived, worked, and played here spoke Spanish. Inside the state park the buildings are old or built to look that way, making it easy to let the modern world slip away—you don't have to look hard or very far to see yesterday. The time warp is especially palpable at night, when you can stroll along the unpaved streets and look up at the stars. Begin your tour at the McCoy House, at the northwestern end of this historic district, which preserves the essence of the small Mexican and fledgling American communities that existed here from 1821 to 1872. The core of Old Town State Historic Park is a 6-block area with no vehicular traffic and a collection of restaurants and retail shops; the commercial district of Old Town continues for several blocks, with San Diego Avenue as the main drag.

Start at the intersection of Wallace and Calhoun, the location of the:

1 McCoy House

This is the interpretive center for the park and is a historically accurate replication of the home of James McCoy, a lawman/legislator who lived on this site until the devastating fire of 1872. With exhibits, artifacts, and visitor information, the house gives a great overview of life in San Diego in the 19th century.

After checking in here and getting your bearings, head to the neighboring:

2 Robinson-Rose House

Built in 1853 as a family home, it also served as a newspaper and railroad office; now, it's the visitor center for the park. Here you'll see a large model of Old Town the way it looked prior to 1872, the year a large fire broke out (or was set). The blaze destroyed much of the town and initiated the population exodus to New Town, now downtown San Diego. Old Town State Historic Park contains seven original buildings, including the Robinson-Rose House, and replicas of other buildings that once stood here.

From here, turn left and stroll into the colorful world of Mexican California called:

3 Fiesta de Reyes

Located at 2754 Calhoun St., this is where colorful shops and restaurants spill into a flower-filled courtyard. Costumed employees and nightly entertainment create an early California atmosphere throughout what was once a 1930s motel (albeit one designed by acclaimed architect Richard Requa). See p. 155 for additional information.

4 Take a Break ☕

This is a good opportunity to sample the Mexican food in and around Fiesta de Reyes. In addition to Casa Guadalajara (located outside the plaza and reviewed on p. 132), there are other restaurants in the immediate area—Barra Barra Old Town Saloon (✆ 619/291-3200), Casa de Reyes (✆ 619/220-5040), and the Cosmopolitan Hotel and Restaurant (✆ 619/297-1874). All offer indoor/outdoor dining and a lively ambience, but the Cosmo offers the most sophisticated, accomplished food and drink. If the wait for a table is long at one, put your name on the list at another. The restaurants are open from 10 or 11am to 9 or 10pm, and Fiesta de Reyes shops are open from 10am to 9pm, with shorter winter hours.

From Fiesta de Reyes, stroll into the grassy plaza, where you'll see a:

5 Large Rock Monument

This monument commemorates the first U.S. flag raised in Southern California. After Northern California had been wrested from Mexico by invading U.S. forces in July 1846, the USS *Cyane* sailed into San Diego Bay to lay claim to the southern portion of the state. Aboard ship were John C. Frémont (who would go on to become one of California's first senators and the first Republican candidate for president) and legendary frontiersman and scout Kit Carson. On July 29, 1846, a detail raised the Stars and Stripes on this spot. When Frémont rode off with his battalion 10 days later, though, the town was left to its own devices and loyal *Californios* hoisted the Mexican flag again. A sailmaker, Albert B. Smith, eventually nailed Old Glory permanently in place to the flagpole.

Straight ahead, at the plaza's eastern edge, is:

6 La Casa de Estudillo

An original adobe building dating from 1827, the U-shaped house has covered walkways and an open central patio. The patio covering is made of *corraza* cane, the seeds for which were brought by Father Junípero Serra in 1769. The walls are 3 to 5 feet thick, holding up the heavy beams and tiles, and they work as terrific insulators against summer heat. In those days, the thicker the walls, the wealthier the family. The furnishings in this "upper-class" house are representative of the 19th century (note the beautiful four-poster beds); the original furniture came from as far away as Asia. The Estudillo family, which then numbered 12, lived in the house until 1887; today family members still live in San Diego.

After you exit La Casa de Estudillo, turn right. Here you'll find the:

7 Casa de Bandini/Cosmopolitan Hotel

Now a beautifully renovated restaurant and hotel, the Casa de Bandini was completed in 1829. It was the home of Peruvian-born Juan Bandini, who arrived in California in 1818 and became one of early San Diego's most prominent citizens. The 14-room home was the hub of the small town's social and political life. When U.S. troops invaded in 1846, Bandini welcomed them and appealed to

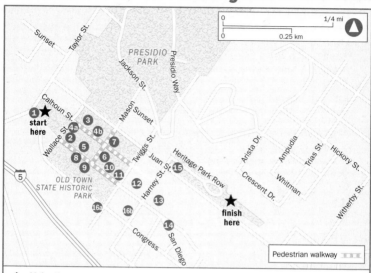

1	McCoy House	**9**	Mason Street School
2	Robinson-Rose House	**10**	Pedroreña House
3	Fiesta de Reyes	**11**	San Diego Union Printing Office
4a	Barra Barra Old Town Saloon	**12**	Immaculate Conception Catholic Church
4b	Casa de Reyes	**13**	Whaley House
5	Large Rock Monument	**14**	El Campo Santo
6	La Casa de Estudillo	**15**	Heritage Park
7	Cosmopolitan Hotel & Restaurant	**16a**	Berta's Latin American Restaurant
8	Colorado House	**16b**	Harney Sushi

others to do the same. In fact, the commander of the U.S. force, Samuel Du Pont, was a guest in the Bandini home, where there was music and dancing every night during his stay. In 1869, the building, with a second story added, became the Cosmopolitan Hotel.

Walk back across the plaza to the:

8 Colorado House

Built in 1851, it was destroyed by fire in 1872—as were most buildings on this side of the park. Today it's the home of the Wells Fargo Historical Museum, but the original housed San Diego's first two-story hotel. The museum features an original Wells Fargo stagecoach, numerous displays of the overland-express business, and a video presentation (as well as ATMs if you need some cash). Next door to the Wells Fargo museum, and kitty-corner to La Casa de Estudillo, is the small, redbrick San Diego Court House and City Hall.

From here, continue along the pedestrian walkway, turn right, and walk down to a reddish-brown building. This is the one-room:

9 Mason Street School

This is an original building dating from 1865 and is California's first public school. You'll notice that the boards that make up the walls don't match; they were leftovers from the construction of San Diego homes. The school was commissioned by San Diego's first mayor, Joshua Bean, whose brother was the notorious Roy Bean, who would go on to become an eccentric judge in Texas. Before Roy Bean became known as "the law west of the Pecos," though, he had to escape a San Diego jail by digging his way through the adobe walls with a knife that, legend has it, was hidden in a tamale (he had been jailed for wounding a man in a duel).

When you leave the schoolhouse, retrace your steps to the walkway (which is the extension of San Diego Ave.) and turn right. On your left, you'll see two buildings with brown shingle roofs. The first is the:

10 Pedroreña House

No. 2616 is an original Old Town house built in 1869, with stained glass over the doorway. The shop inside now sells fossils, minerals, and gems. The original owner was Miguel Pedroreña, a Spanish-born merchant and local bigwig. He also owned the house next door, which became the:

11 San Diego *Union* Printing Office

The newspaper was first published here in 1868. This house arrived in Old Town after being prefabricated in Maine in 1851 and shipped around the Horn (it has a distinctly New England appearance). Inside you'll see the original hand press used to print the paper, which merged with the *San Diego Tribune* in 1992. The publication is now known as the *U-T San Diego,* and is located in Mission Valley, about 3 miles away.

At the end of the pedestrian part of San Diego Avenue stands a railing; beyond it is Twiggs Street, dividing the historic park from the rest of Old Town, which is more commercial, with shops, galleries, and restaurants.

At the corner of Twiggs Street and San Diego Avenue stands the Spanish mission–style:

12 Immaculate Conception Catholic Church

The cornerstone was laid in 1868, making it the first church built in California that was not part of the mission system. With the movement of the community to New Town in 1872, though, it lost its parishioners and was not dedicated until 1919. Today the church serves about 300 families in the Old Town area.

Continue along San Diego Avenue 1 block to Harney Street. On your left is the restored:

13 Whaley House

The first two-story brick structure in Southern California, it was built between 1856 and 1857. The house is said to be haunted by several ghosts, including that of Yankee Jim Robinson, who was hanged on the site in 1852—for stealing a rowboat. The house is beautifully furnished with period pieces and features a life mask of Abraham Lincoln, the spinet piano used in the film *Gone With the Wind,* and the concert piano that accompanied Swedish soprano Jenny Lind on her final U.S. concert tour in 1852. See p. 60.

Continue down San Diego Avenue 2 short blocks to:

14 El Campo Santo

This is San Diego's first cemetery, established in 1850. The small plot is home to the mortal remains of several notable characters, including the hanged boat thief Yankee Jim Robinson and Antonio Garra, who led the Southland's last Native American uprising. The small brass plaques you see on the sidewalk and in the street indicate where the remains of some of San Diego's earliest citizens are still interred. Stories float through Old Town about cars that are unable to start after parking over these markers, or whose alarms go off for no reason. See p. 58.

Return down Old Town Avenue and make a right on Harney Street. Head up the hill 1½ blocks to the collection of Victorian jewels known as:

15 Heritage Park

There are seven original 19th-century buildings in this 7¾-acre park; each was saved from destruction and moved here from other parts of the city. Among the highlights are the Sherman-Gilbert House (1887), with its distinctive widow's walk, and the classic revival Temple Beth Israel, dating from 1889. Plans to develop this parcel into a bed-and-breakfast village have stalled, but the park remains open.

16 Winding Down 🍵

You've been immersed in California's Mexican culture, but two of Old Town's best restaurants don't follow suit, serving sushi and South American fare. At the end of your walk, make your way back down Harney Street, past San Diego Avenue to **Harney Sushi**, 3964 Harney St. (© 619/295-3272). If this hip and lively sushi joint isn't your style, continue to Congress Street, make a right, and head 1 block to **Berta's Latin American Restaurant**, 3928 Twiggs St. (© 619/295-2343). This unassuming eatery offers a travelogue of dishes that roams from El Salvador to Argentina (see p. 131 and 132).

5

WALKING TOUR 4: **BALBOA PARK**

START:	**Sefton Plaza, at Laurel Street and Sixth Avenue.**
FINISH:	**San Diego Zoo.**
TIME:	**2½ hours, not including museum or zoo stops. If you get tired, hop on the free park tram.**
BEST TIMES:	**Anytime. If you want to get especially good photographs, come in the afternoon, when the sun lends a glow to the already photogenic buildings. Most museums are open until 4 or 5pm (many are closed on Mon).**
WORST TIMES:	**More people (especially families) visit the park on weekends. But there is a festive—rather than overcrowded—spirit even then, particularly on Sunday afternoons when you can catch a free organ concert at the outdoor Spreckels Organ Pavilion at 2pm.**

Established in 1868, Balboa Park is the second-oldest city park in the United States, after New York's Central Park. Much of its striking architecture was the product of the 1915–16 Panama-California Exposition and the 1935–36 California-Pacific

STROLLING AROUND SAN DIEGO

Balboa Park

International Exposition. The structures, which now house a variety of museums, contribute to the overall beauty of the park. But what makes Balboa Park truly unique is the extensive botanical collection, thanks largely to Kate Sessions, a horticulturist who devoted her life to transforming the barren mesas and scrub-filled canyons into the oases they are today. Originally called "City Park," it was renamed in 1910 when Mrs. Harriet Phillips won a contest, naming it in honor of the Spanish conquistador Vasco Núñez de Balboa, who in 1513 was the first European to see the Pacific Ocean.

Take bus no. 3 or 120 along Fifth Avenue to Laurel Street, and head east into the park to:

1 Sefton Plaza

Introduce yourself to the folks who made everything you're about to see possible. On the north side of the street, at what's known as Founder's Plaza, are the bronze statues of the "fathers" of Balboa Park: Alonzo Horton, George Marston, and Ephraim Morse. Across the street, pay your respects to the "mother" of Balboa Park, Kate Sessions. There's also a kiosk here with touch-screen information about the park and an ATM; it's a Wi-Fi hotspot as well.

Cross the street to the park's most dramatic entrance:

2 Cabrillo Bridge

It has expansive views of downtown San Diego and straddles scenic, sycamore-lined Hwy. 163 (which John F. Kennedy allegedly proclaimed as "the most beautiful highway I've ever seen," during his 1963 visit to San Diego). Built in 1915 for the Panama-California Exposition and patterned after a bridge in Ronda, Spain, the dramatic cantilever-style bridge has seven pseudo-arches. As you cross the bridge, to your left you'll see the yellow cars of the zoo's aerial tram and, directly ahead, the distinctive California Tower of the Museum of Man. The delightful sounds of the 100-bell **Symphonic Carillon** can be heard every quarter-hour. Sitting atop this San Diego landmark is a weather vane shaped like the ship in which Cabrillo sailed to California in 1542. The city skyline lies to your right.

Once you've crossed the bridge, go through the:

3 West Gate

The heart of Balboa Park is accessed through this ceremonial arch. Built for the 1915 Exposition, the gateway's two reclining figures hold flowing water jugs and represent the Atlantic and Pacific oceans. The park's cornucopia of attractions lies just beyond. For now, just view the museums from the outside. (Read more about them, and all the park's museums, in chapter 4.)

You have entered the park's major thoroughfare, El Prado—if you're driving a car, you'll want to find a parking space (the map on p. 109 shows all public lots) and go to the:

4 San Diego Museum of Man

Architect Bertram Goodhue designed this structure, originally known as the California Building, in 1915—it now houses an anthropological museum. Goodhue, considered the world's foremost authority on Spanish Colonial architecture, was the master architect for the 1915–16 exposition. The exterior doubled

Walking Tour 4: Balboa Park

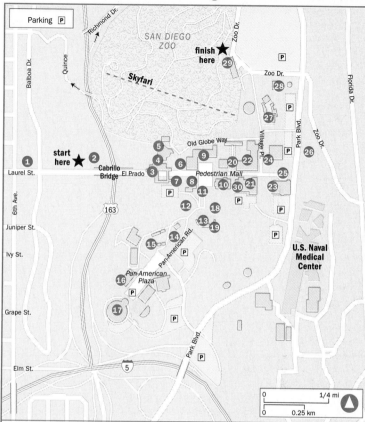

1. Sefton Plaza
2. Cabrillo Bridge
3. West Gate
4. San Diego Museum of Man
5. Old Globe Theatre
6. Sculpture Garden of the Museum of Art
7. Alcazar Garden
8. House of Charm
9. San Diego Museum of Art
10. Visitor Center
11. El Cid Campeador
12. Palm Canyon
13. Spreckels Organ Pavilion
14. United Nations Building
15. House of Pacific Relations
    International Cottages
16. San Diego Automotive Museum
17. San Diego Air & Space Museum
18. Japanese Friendship Garden
19. Tea Pavilion ☕
20. Botanical Building & Lily Pond
21. Casa de Balboa
22. Casa del Prado
23. Reuben H. Fleet Science Center
24. San Diego Natural History Museum
25. Bea Evenson Fountain
26. Gardens
27. Spanish Village Art Center
28. Miniature Railroad and Carousel
29. San Diego Zoo entrance
30. Prado Restaurant ☕

as part of Kane's mansion in the 1941 Orson Welles classic *Citizen Kane;* historical figures carved on the facade include conquistador Juan Rodríguez Cabrillo, Spanish kings Charles I and Phillip III, and, at the very top, Father Junípero Serra. See p. 53.

Just beyond and up the steps to the left is the nationally acclaimed:

5 Old Globe Theatre

This is actually a three-theater complex that includes the Old Globe, an outdoor stage, and a small theater-in-the-round. The Old Globe was built for the 1935 exposition as a replica of Shakespeare's Globe Theatre; it was meant to be demolished at the conclusion of the expo but was saved by a group of dedicated citizens. In 1978, an arsonist destroyed the theater, which was rebuilt into what you see today; if you have the opportunity to go inside, you can see the bronze bust of Shakespeare that miraculously survived the fire, battered but unbowed. In 2010, the Globe completed sweeping renovations in honor of its 75th anniversary. See p. 69 and 169 for more information.

Beside the theater is the:

6 Sculpture Garden of the Museum of Art

The San Diego Museum of Art Sculpture Garden features works by Joan Miró and Alexander Calder, as well as a signature piece, *Reclining Figure: Arch Leg,* by Henry Moore. *Reclining Figure* was damaged by a falling tree branch several years ago, but it was seamlessly repaired and reclaimed its spot in the garden. Admission is free.

Across the street, to your right as you stroll along the Prado, is the:

7 Alcazar Garden

It was designed in 1935 by Richard Requa and W. Allen Perry. They patterned it after the gardens surrounding the Alcazar Castle in Sevilla, Spain. The garden is formally laid out and trimmed with low clipped hedges; in the center walkway are two star-shaped yellow-and-blue tile fountains. The large tree at the rear is an Indian laurel fig, planted by Kate Sessions when the park was first landscaped.

Exit to your left at the opposite end of the garden, and you'll be back on El Prado.
Proceed east to the corner; on your right is the:

8 House of Charm

This is the site of the **San Diego Art Institute** gallery (p. 51) and the **Mingei International Museum** (p. 50). The Art Institute is a nonprofit space that primarily exhibits works by local artists; the Mingei offers changing exhibitions that celebrate human creativity expressed in textiles, costumes, jewelry, toys, pottery, paintings, and sculpture.

To your left is the imposing:

9 San Diego Museum of Art

This exquisite facade was patterned after the famous university building in Salamanca, Spain. The three life-size figures over the scalloped entryway are the Spanish painters Bartolomé Murillo, Francisco de Zurbarán, and Diego Velázquez. The museum holds San Diego's most extensive collection of fine art; major touring shows are presented, as well. There's also an ongoing schedule of concerts, films, and lectures, usually themed with a current exhibition. See p. 52 for more information.

Across the street are the House of Hospitality and the park's:

10 Visitor Center

Pick up maps, souvenirs, and discount tickets to the museums here; the park's guided tours also depart from this location. In the central courtyard behind the visitor center is the beautiful *Woman of Tehuantepec* fountain sculpture by Donal Hord, as well as the attractive **Prado** restaurant.

Head back toward the House of Charm, passing the statue of the mounted:

11 El Cid Campeador

Created by Anna Hyatt Huntington and dedicated in 1930, this sculpture of the 11th-century Spanish hero was made from a mold of the original statue in the court of the Hispanic Society of America in New York. A third version is in Sevilla, Spain. A decidedly more modern sculpture is found outside the entrance to the Mingei Museum. Created by Niki de Saint Phalle, a French artist who made San Diego her home until her death in 2002, the colorful mosaic alligator is a favorite with kids, who love to clamber over it.

Continue to your left toward the ornamental outdoor Organ Pavilion. Before reaching the pavilion, the wooden bridge above the ravine on your right will take you into:

12 Palm Canyon

Fifty species of palm, plus magnolia trees and a Moreton Bay fig tree provide a tropical canopy here. It's secluded, so care should be exercised if you're walking solo, but you can get a good sense of its beauty by venturing only a short distance along the path. The walkway dead-ends, so you must exit from where you entered.

From the top of Palm Canyon, continue to the ornate:

13 Spreckels Organ Pavilion

Donated to San Diego by brothers John D. and Adolph B. Spreckels, the pavilion was dedicated on December 31, 1914. Famed contralto Ernestine Schumann-Heink sang at the ceremony; a brass plaque honors her charity and patriotism. Free, lively recitals featuring one of the largest outdoor organs in the world (its vast structure contains 4,518 pipes) are given Sundays at 2pm, with additional concerts and events scheduled in the summer. See p. 53.

As you continue on, you'll see the Hall of Nations on your right, and beside it, the:

14 United Nations Building

This building also houses the United Nations International Gift Shop, a favorite for its diverse merchandise, much of it handmade around the world. You'll recognize the shop by the United States and United Nations flags out front. Check the bulletin board, or ask inside, for the park's calendar of events. If you need to rest, there's a pleasant spot with a few benches opposite the gift shop.

You will notice a cluster of small houses with red-tile roofs. They are the:

15 House of Pacific Relations International Cottages

These charming dollhouse cottages promote ethnic and cultural awareness and are open to the public on Sunday afternoons and on the fourth Tuesday of the month year-round. From March to October, there are lawn programs with folk dancing. See p. 49.

Take a quick peek into some of the cottages, and then keep heading south to see more of the park's museums; to your right is the notable:

16 San Diego Automotive Museum

Whether you're a gearhead into muscle cars or someone who appreciates the sculptural beauty of fine design, this museum has something for everyone. It features a changing roster of exhibits, as well as a permanent collection of fabulous wheels. See p. 51 for more information.

And the cylindrical:

17 San Diego Air & Space Museum

The museums in this part of the park operate in structures built for the 1935–36 Exposition. It is not necessary to walk all the way to the Air & Space Museum (located appropriately enough under the flight path to San Diego's airport), but it's one of San Diego's finest examples of Art Deco architecture. Across the parking lot on the left is the Hall of Champions Sports Museum, with another fun Niki de Saint Phalle sculpture in front. See p. 51 and 52.

Go back past the parking lot and the Organ Pavilion. Take a shortcut through the pavilion, exit directly opposite the stage, and follow the sidewalk to your right. Almost immediately, you'll come to the:

18 Japanese Friendship Garden

Only a small portion of this 12-acre canyon has been developed, but the part that has been incorporates beautifully serene, traditional Japanese elements. At the entrance is an attractive teahouse whose deck overlooks the entire ravine; there is a small meditation garden beside it. See p. 71.

19 Take a Break 🍵

Now is your chance to have a bite to eat, sip a cool drink, and review the tourist literature you picked up at the visitor center. The Tea Pavilion (② 619/231-0048) at the Japanese Friendship Garden serves fresh sushi, noodle soups, and Asian salads—it also carries imported Japanese candies and beverages as well as more familiar snacks.

Return to El Prado, which becomes a pedestrian mall to the east of the El Cid sculpture. Set your sights on the fountain at the end of the broad walkway and head toward it. Stroll down the middle of El Prado to get the full benefit of the lovely buildings on either side. On weekends, you'll pass street musicians, artists, and clowns—one of their favorite haunts is around the fountain.

The latticework building you see to the left is the:

20 Botanical Building & Lily Pond

An open-air conservatory, this delicate wood lath structure dates to the 1915–16 Exposition, and is filled with 2,100 permanent plants, plus seasonal displays. Particularly noteworthy is the collection of cycads and ferns. Admission is free, and the gardens are a cool retreat on a hot day. Directly in front is the Lily Pond. See p. 48.

Back on El Prado, left of the Lily Pond, you'll see the:

21 Casa de Balboa

Inside, you'll find the **Museum of Photographic Arts** (p. 50), the **Model Railroad Museum** (p. 52), and the **San Diego History Center** (p. 52). Note the realistic-looking bare-breasted figures atop the Casa de Balboa. These shameless caryatids were the perfect complement to the nudist colony that temporarily sprouted as an attraction in Zoro Garden—the canyon immediately east of the building—during the 1935–36 Exposition.

On the other side of El Prado, on your left, note the ornate work on the:

22 Casa del Prado

While it doesn't house a museum, it's one of the best—and most ornate—of the El Prado buildings, featuring baroque Spanish Golden Age ornamentation.

At the end of El Prado, on either side of the fountain, are two museums particularly appealing to children; the first, on the right, is the:

23 Reuben H. Fleet Science Center

This science fun house has plenty of hands-on attractions, as well as a giant-screen IMAX theater. See p. 51 for a complete review of this popular attraction.

To the left is the:

24 San Diego Natural History Museum

The original building that stood on this spot burned to the ground in 1925—hours before local firefighters were to gather there for their annual gala. A new structure, funded by the ever-generous Ellen Browning Scripps, rose in 1933. In 2001, the museum more than doubled in size with the completion of an ultramodern wing that springs from the building's north side. See p. 53.

In the center of the Plaza de Balboa is the high-spouting:

25 Bea Evenson Fountain

This fountain was added to the park in 1972, and was later named in honor of the woman who formed the "Committee of 100," a group dedicated to preserving the park's architecture. It spouts water almost 60 feet into the air, but what makes it truly unique is a wind regulator on top of the Natural History Museum—as the wind increases, the fountain's water pressure is lowered so the water doesn't spray over the edges. The 200-foot-wide fountain is especially beautiful at night when it's illuminated by colored lights.

From here, use the pedestrian bridge to cross the road and visit the nearly secret:

26 Gardens

They are tucked away on the other side of the boulevard: to your left, a Desert Garden for plants at home in an arid landscape; to your right, the Inez Grant Parker Memorial Rose Gardens, home to 2,400 roses. The World Rose Society voted the latter as one of the top 16 rose gardens in the world. Blooms peak March through May, but there are almost always some flowers visible, except in January and February when they are pruned. After you've enjoyed the flowers and plants, return to El Prado.

Just past the Natural History Museum, take a right. Behind the museum is another voluptuous Moreton Bay fig tree, planted in 1915 for the exposition; it's now more than 62 feet tall, with a canopy 100 feet in diameter.

Straight ahead is the quiet:

27 Spanish Village Art Center

Artists work here daily from 11am to 4pm. They create jewelry, paintings, and sculptures in tile-roofed studios around a courtyard. There are restrooms here, too.

Exit at the back of the Spanish Village Art Center and take the paved, palm-lined sidewalk that will take you past the:

28 Miniature Railroad and Carousel

The tiny train makes a 3-minute loop through the eucalyptus trees, while the charming 1910 carousel offers a ride atop hand-carved wood frogs, horses, and pigs. The train and carousel are open daily in summer, weekends the rest of the year.

To the left is the entrance to the world-famous:

29 San Diego Zoo

You can also retrace your steps and visit some of the tempting museums you just passed, saving the zoo for another day.

Bus tip: From here, you can walk out past the zoo parking lot to Park Boulevard; the bus stop (a brown-shingled kiosk) is on your right. The no. 7 bus will take you back to downtown San Diego.

30 Winding Down 🍴

Back on El Prado (in the House of Hospitality), the Prado Restaurant (📞 619/557-9441) has a handsome view of the park from oversize windows and a great patio for outdoor dining. Far from your average park concession, the Prado boasts a zesty menu with colorful ethnic influences—plus inventive margaritas and Latin cocktails. Lunch starts daily at 11:30am (Sat–Sun at 11am), and a festive (expensive) dinner menu takes over at 5pm (daily except Mon; reservations advisable). In between, a long list of tapas will satisfy any hunger pangs.

WALKING TOUR 5: **LA JOLLA**

START:	**Silverado Street and Girard Avenue.**
FINISH:	**Prepkitchen, 7556 Fay Ave.**
TIME:	**2 to 4 hours, depending on how long you linger in the museums, parks, and boutiques.**
BEST TIMES:	**Thursday to Tuesday, if you want to see the Museum of Contemporary Art (free admission third Thurs 5–7pm). The Athenaeum is also open Tuesday to Saturday; on Sunday, Wednesday, and Fridays, bridge is played at Ellen Browning Scripps Park.**
WORST TIMES:	**This is a parking-challenged neighborhood, particularly on weekends.**

La Jolla is Southern California's Riviera. This seaside community of about 25,000 is home to an inordinate number of wealthy folk who could probably live anywhere. They choose La Jolla for good reason—it's surrounded by the beach, the University of California, San Diego, outstanding restaurants, boutiques, galleries, and some of the world's best medical facilities. The heart of La Jolla is referred to as the Village, roughly delineated by Pearl Street to the south, Prospect Street to the north, Torrey Pines Road to the east, and the rugged coast to the west; this picturesque neighborhood is an ideal place to simply stroll about. It's undetermined whether "La Jolla" (pronounced La-*hoy*-ya) is misspelled Spanish for "the jewel" or an indigenous word for "cave," but once you see it, you'll likely go with the first definition.

Take bus route 30 to Silverado St. and Girard Ave. Walk south (away from the ocean) on Girard Ave. until you reach:

1 Mary, Star of the Sea

Dedicated in 1937, this beautiful little mission-style Catholic church (7669 Girard Ave.; www.marystarlajolla.org; © **858/454-2631**; Mon–Fri 6am–noon and daily services) was designed by noted San Diego architect Carleton Winslow, Sr. Above the entrance, a striking mosaic re-creates the original fresco painted there by Mexican artist Alfredo Ramos Martínez. An influential art instructor in Mexico, Martínez once taught Rufino Tamayo and David Alfaro Siqueiros. Inside the church, the unique mural above the altar was painted by accomplished Polish artist John De Rosen. It depicts the Virgin Mary on a crescent moon, presiding over a storm-tossed sea.

From the church, walk north on Girard Ave. (toward the ocean) for 2 blocks, then turn left at Silverado St. Walk down Silverado until you reach the:

2 Museum of Contemporary Art San Diego

The works collected here, produced since 1950, include noteworthy examples of minimalism, light and space work, conceptualism, installation, and site-specific art (the outside sculptures were designed specifically for this location). MCASD also offers lectures, cutting-edge films, and special events on an ongoing basis; the bookstore is a great place for contemporary gifts, and the cafe is a pleasant stop before or after your visit. The museum is on a cliff overlooking the Pacific Ocean, and the views from the galleries are gorgeous. The original building on the site, designed by Irving Gill in 1916, was the residence of philanthropist Ellen Browning Scripps. For more information, see p. 56.

From here, head northeast on Prospect St. (with the ocean on your left), then turn left at Jenner St., which becomes Coast Blvd. to:

3 Children's Pool

A sea wall protects this pocket of sand—originally intended as a calm swimming bay for children, but currently serving, since 1994, as a sanctuary for a colony of harbor seals; on an average day you'll spot dozens lolling in the sun. After much heated debate (and even acts of civil disobedience), people were allowed to swim here again—to the displeasure of many. While it is possible to now go in the water at the Children's Pool, keep in mind those are federally protected wild animals, and it is illegal to approach them or harass them in any way. Volunteers, with speed dials set to "lifeguard," keep watch to make sure bathers don't bother the colony. For more information, see p. 44.

From the beach, follow Coast Blvd. northeast (with the ocean on your left) to:

4 Ellen Browning Scripps Park

This park and the bluffside walkway that courses through it afford some of California's finest coastal scenery. There's plenty of soft grass where you can toss a Frisbee, have a picnic, or just laze. A series of rustic wooden shelters—popular with seagulls, pigeons, and pedestrians—overlooks La Jolla's shapely curves.

The **La Jolla Cove Bridge Club** (www.lajollacovebridgeclub.org; games Sun, Wed, and Thurs, noon–3:30pm; $3 for nonmembers) is a Works Project Administration structure dating to 1939. This is undoubtedly one of the world's most view-enhanced card rooms.

Follow the bluffside walkway to:

5 La Jolla Cove

These protected calm waters, celebrated as the clearest along the coast, attract snorkelers, scuba divers, and families. The small sandy beach gets a bit cramped during the summer, but the cove's "look but don't touch" policy safeguards the colorful garibaldi, California's state fish, plus other marine life, including abalone, octopus, and lobster. The unique Underwater Park stretches from here to the northern end of Torrey Pines State Reserve and incorporates kelp forests, artificial reefs, two deep canyons, and tidal pools.

Leave the park via Coast Blvd., and follow it along the coast until you get to Prospect Street, where you'll find the:

6 Sunny Jim Cave

The only one of La Jolla's seven sea caves accessible by land, the Sunny Jim Cave (1325 Cave St., just off Prospect St.; www.cavestore.com; ℂ **858/459-0746**; $4 adults, $3 kids 3–16, free for 2 and under) is reached by a narrow, often slippery, staircase in the Cave Store. Sunny Jim was a cartoon character created in 1902 for a cereal advertising campaign, and the cave opening resembles his profile; the passageway with 145 steps was dug through the rock that same year. Part art gallery, part antiques store, this cliff-top shop also rents snorkel equipment.

From the Cave Store, as you face the ocean, you'll find two paths:

7 Coast Walk

One leads to a fabulous wood-platform overlook, the other continues along the bluffs. It's a cool little trail, affording expansive views of the coast. You can exit at a stairway that leads back to Prospect Street (before you come to the white wooden bridge) and circle back into town. If you continue along the trail, it will put you on Torrey Pines Road, an extra 10- to 15-minute walk back to the village.

Head back to Coast Blvd., taking it south (away from the ocean), until you get to Prospect St., take a sharp left and proceed to:

8 La Valencia

Within its bougainvillea-draped walls and wrought-iron garden gates, this bastion of gentility resurrects a golden age, when such celebrities as Greta Garbo and Charlie Chaplin vacationed here. The bluff-top hotel, which looks much like a Mediterranean villa, has been the centerpiece of La Jolla since opening in 1926. There are several lounges and restaurants, some with incredible vistas, which can also be enjoyed by nonguests; the **Whaling Bar** is a classic, old-school haunt. (See p. 208 for hotel review.)

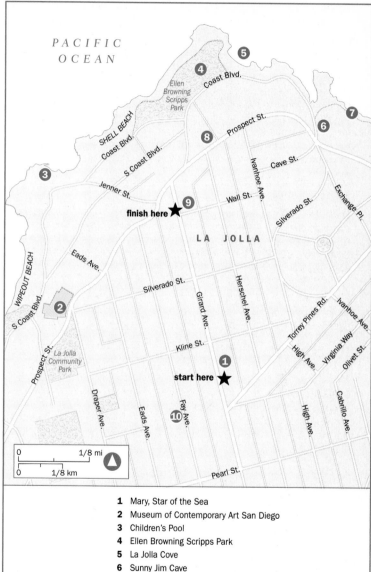

PACIFIC OCEAN

Ellen Browning Scripts Park

Coast Blvd.

SHELL BEACH

Coast Blvd.

S Coast Blvd.

Jenner St.

Prospect St.

Cave St.

Ivanhoe Ave.

Wall St.

Silverado St.

Exchange Pl.

finish here ★ 9

LA JOLLA

Eads Ave.

WIPEOUT BEACH

S Coast Blvd.

Silverado St.

Girard Ave.

Herschel Ave.

Torrey Pines Rd.

Ivanhoe Ave.

Prospect St.

La Jolla Community Park

Kline St.

High Ave.

Virginia Way

Olivet St.

start here ★ 1

Draper Ave.

Eads Ave.

Fay Ave.

High Ave.

Cabrillo Ave.

0 — 1/8 mi
0 — 1/8 km

Pearl St.

1 Mary, Star of the Sea
2 Museum of Contemporary Art San Diego
3 Children's Pool
4 Ellen Browning Scripps Park
5 La Jolla Cove
6 Sunny Jim Cave
7 Coast Walk
8 La Valencia
9 Athenaeum Music and Arts Library
10 Prepkitchen

From La Valencia, head south on Prospect St., and make a left at Herschel Ave. and go 1 block, then turn right at Wall St. and go 1½ blocks, where you will see the:

9 Athenaeum Music & Arts Library

One of only 17 nonprofit, membership libraries in the U.S., the Athenaeum hosts art exhibits, jazz and classical concerts, lectures, and special events open to the general public. Visitors can browse through the vast collection of books, music, and more, but only members can take something out. Founded in 1899, the library has expanded into adjacent buildings, including one built by Balboa Park architect William Templeton Johnson. It's open Tuesday, Thursday, Friday, and Saturday 10am to 5:30pm, and Wednesday 10am to 8:30pm. See p. 62 for more information.

After you finish at the Athenaeum, turn right and head back to Girard Ave. and go left. You can browse the shops along this street, then turn right on Kline St. and left on Fay Ave. to:

10 Take a Break 💂

Prepkitchen (7556 Fay Ave.; www.prepkitchen.com; ℭ 858/875-7737), is a great spot to grab some goodies to go for a picnic by the shore; there's also limited indoor and outdoor seating at this small restaurant. The seasonal menu offers creative takes on such basics as soups, salads, and sandwiches, but also features more elaborate fare like local grouper or duck leg confit; brunch is served on weekends as well. A family takeout deal, feeding 4 to 5 people for $79 is available daily (evenings only Sat and Sun). It's open daily 11am–9pm.

WHERE TO EAT

Thanks to an influx of creative young chefs, San Diego's fine-dining scene is flourishing like never before. And the bounty from San Diego's farms, ranches, and open waters is playing a starring role—the locavore movement is in full swing.

What remains unchanged is the city's obsession with simple Mexican fare, including the beloved fish taco. **Note:** Some of San Diego's best dining venues lie 30 to 40 minutes to the north, in the communities of Del Mar, Carlsbad, and Rancho Santa Fe. These are found in chapter 10, as are dining options for south of the border.

BEST BETS

- **Best Splurge: Addison** is San Diego County's one and only AAA 5 Diamond restaurant. This sumptuous dining destination is grandly European, offering daily tasting menus of modern French cuisine and featuring a jaw-dropping wine list that's more like a wine book. See p. 223.

- **Best View:** Many restaurants overlook the ocean, but only from **Brockton Villa** (p. 141), a restored beach bungalow dating from 1894, can you see stunning La Jolla Cove. At the **Marine Room** (p. 138) in La Jolla, beachside dining is elevated to a fine art; while 12th-floor **Bertrand at Mister A's** (p. 127), one of the city's finest restaurants, also offers unparalleled cityscape views.

- **Most Romantic:** At **George's at the Cove** in La Jolla you can choose from alfresco dining featuring sublime ocean views or opt for a meal indoors in a sophisticated, contemporary space. It's long been a favorite spot for first dates, marriage proposals, and wedding receptions. And it's all overseen by one of the city's most respected chefs. See p. 140.

- **Best Service:** The Park Hyatt Aviara Resort's high level of service definitely makes its presence known at its fine dining destination, stylish **Vivace.** Servers are knowledgeable, without being pretentious, and just generally seem to care about your experience. See p. 232.

price CATEGORIES

Restaurants are categorized by price, which includes the average cost of one entree, an appetizer (if the entree does not come with a side dish or appetizer), one *nonalcoholic* drink, tax, and tip.		
Very Expensive	$50 per person	
Expensive	$30–$50	
Moderate	$15–$30	
Inexpensive	Less than $15	

FUN FOR foodies IN SAN DIEGO

San Diego's dining scene is cooking on all burners these days, serving up a wide range of cuisine, often highlighted by the region's local bounty. A great way to experience the city's best eateries is timing your visit with the biannual **San Diego Restaurant Week,** held mid-September and mid-January. More than 180 restaurants participate—everything from casual bistros to high-end steakhouses—offering prix fixe, two-course lunches ($10–$20) and three-course dinners ($20–$40). You don't need tickets or passes, just check the list of dining spots at www.sandiegorestaurantweek.com and head on in (making reservations with the establishment itself is recommended, though).

You might also consider the 5-day **San Diego Bay Wine & Food Festival,** held in mid-November. Southern California's largest food and wine event, it features a cornucopia of celebrity chefs, classes, auctions, parties, and dinners. And of course there are plenty of food, wine, spirits, and craft beers on hand for sampling. For more information call ✆ **619/312-1212,** or go to www.worldofwineevents.com.

Year-round, **Bite San Diego** (www.bitesandiego.com; ✆ **619/634-8476**) and **So Diego Tours** (www.sodiegotours.com; ✆ **619/233-8687**) offer evening walking tours that will take you to some of the city's most popular restaurants and bars.

○ **Best Value:** The word "huge" barely begins to describe the portions at **Filippi's Pizza Grotto,** where a salad for one is enough for three, and an order of lasagna must weigh a pound. There's a kids' menu as well. Filippi's has locations all over, including Pacific Beach, Mission Valley, and Escondido. See p. 126.

○ **Best for Families:** With its sassy waitresses, game room, and oldies rock 'n' roll, **Corvette Diner** (p. 137) will put a smile on the entire family's face. Looking for a fine-dining option that makes room for the kids too? Try **Baleen** (p. 134) at the Paradise Point Resort.

○ **Best Local Cuisine:** Many San Diego restaurants are highlighting their menus with quality product harvested from local farms and ranches, or caught in local waters. The locavore movement is being led by eateries like **Zenbu** (p. 140), **the Linkery** (p. 129), and **Market Restaurant + Bar** (p. 224).

○ **Best Mexican Cuisine:** Rather than the typical "combination plate" fare, **El Agave Tequileria** (p. 131) offers memorable recipes from Veracruz, Chiapas, Puebla, and Mexico City—along with a massive selection of boutique and artisan tequilas and mescals. **Candelas** (p. 122), which has two locations (including a view-enhanced bayside perch in Coronado), adds a dash of European sophistication to its menu.

○ **Best Late-Night Dining:** When nothing will satisfy your dance-weary bones like a 3am helping of chicken and waffles, **Brian's 24 Restaurant Bar & Grill** has you covered. This is the Gaslamp Quarter's only 24/7 restaurant, and it's surprisingly nice. See p. 124.

○ **Best Fast Food:** A fish taco may sound strange to the uninitiated, but once you taste one, you'll know why locals line up for them. See p. 134 for suggestions on the best places to become a believer.

DOWNTOWN, GASLAMP QUARTER & LITTLE ITALY

You can grab breakfast at a quirky stalwart such as **Cafe 222** ★, 222 Island Ave. (www.cafe222.com; ✆ **619/236-9902**), or sit down to some gourmet pancakes at **Richard Walker's Pancake House** ★, 520 Front St. (www.richardwalkers.com; ✆ **619/231-7777**); then have lunch with the artists and musicians at **Pokez Mexican Restaurant,** 947 E St. (www.pokezsd.com; ✆ **619/702-7160**), where they offer more than 30 vegetarian dishes. Come evening, you can dine with the party crowd at the sexy supper club **Stingaree** ★, 454 Sixth Ave. (✆ **619/544-9500;** www.stingsandiego.com). International choices include Thai at **Rama** ★, 327 Fourth Ave. (www.ramarestaurant.com; ✆ **619/501-8424**), and Persian cuisine at **Bandar** ★, 845 Fourth Ave. (www.bandarrestaurant.com; ✆ **619/238-0101**).

Downtown encompasses many more options beyond the 16½-block Gaslamp Quarter, and hotel restaurants in the area make an especially strong showing. Highlights include the Manchester Grand Hyatt's (p. 190) bayside **Sally's** ★★ (www. sallyssandiego.com; ✆ **619/358-6740**), the US GRANT's (p. 192) reinvented **Grant Grill** ★★ (www.grantgrill.com; ✆ **619/744-2077**), the Westgate Hotel's (p. 192) **Westgate Room** ★ (www.westgatehotel.com; ✆ **619/238-1818**), and **the Restaurant at the W** ★ (www.whotels.com/sandiego; ✆ **619/398-3082**) at the W Hotel (p. 193).

Little Italy is home to a variety of eateries including, of course, fine Italian at **Bencotto Italian Kitchen** ★★, located in a stylish glass-box setting at 750 W. Fir St. (www.lovebencotto.com; ✆ **619/450-4786**), **Po Pazzo** ★, 1917 India St. (www. popazzo.com; ✆ **619/238-1917**), and **Buon Appetito** ★★, 1609 India St. (www. buonappetito.signonsandiego.com; ✆ **619/238-9880**). The owners of Buon Appetito also operate a sister property next door, the wine bar **Sogno DiVino** ★, 1607 India St. (www.sognodivino.signonsandiego.com; ✆ **619/531-8887**), and a gourmet Italian market adjacent to that.

Very Expensive

Nobu ★★ SUSHI/PACIFIC RIM/ASIAN FUSION   Celebrity chef Nobu Matsuhisa has earned a devoted worldwide following for his creative sushi and Asian fusion cuisine. Following a 3-year stint in Peru (hence the ceviche and Pisco sours on the Nobu menu), Matsuhisa found himself in Los Angeles, where he became friends with actor Robert De Niro, now one of his partners for the Nobu franchise installed at the **Hard Rock Hotel** (p. 188). You may hear complaints about the restaurant's pricey fare, lean portions, and full-volume ambience, but you'll be hard-pressed to argue with the textures, flavors, and beautiful presentations. House specialties include the broiled black cod with miso and the Sino-Latino scallops *tiradito;* when in doubt, entrust yourself to the chef with the *omakase* tasting menu.

207 Fifth Ave. (at L St.), Gaslamp Quarter. www.noburestaurants.com. ✆ **619/814-4124.** Reservations recommended. Main courses $24–$120, sushi $2–$125. AE, DC, DISC, MC, V. Sun–Thurs 5:30–10:15pm; Fri–Sat 5:30–11:15pm. Lounge/bar Sun–Thurs 5:30–10:15pm; Fri–Sat 5:30–11:15pm. Valet parking $20–$30 with validation. Trolley: Gaslamp Quarter.

Expensive

Anthology ★★ CALIFORNIAN   It's difficult to categorize Anthology: Is it a fine-dining establishment or a world-class live music venue? The answer to both is a resounding "yes." Featuring a menu with Mediterranean flair (octopus carpaccio, baked rigatoni) and highlighted by local ingredients, Anthology is also a sophisticated, acoustically excellent concert hall. The music is eclectic, from jazz and world music, to rock and blues, but it won't drown out the food—in fact, you'll know the band onstage is really jamming when you're able to tear your attention away from your meal.

1337 India St. (btw. A and Ash sts.), downtown. www.anthologysd.com. *©* **619/595-0300.** Reservations recommended. Main courses $22–$32. AE, DISC, MC, V. Tues–Sat 5–11pm; open selected Sun. Bus: 83.

Candelas ★★ MEXICAN   If you're in the mood for a sophisticated, romantic fine-dining experience, look no farther than Candelas. Owner Alberto Mestre and Executive Chef Eduardo Baeza are both natives of Mexico City and brought with them that city's culinary influences, which often blend Mexican and European elements. The chef's signature creation is *langosta Baeza:* fresh lobster in its shell, stuffed with mushrooms, chilies, onions, bacon, and tequila. Candelas, which also has a sexy lounge next door, may forever alter your notion of Mexican food. The restaurant has a second location in Coronado at the Ferry Landing, 1201 First St. (*©* **619/435-4900**), offering panoramic views of downtown from across the bay, a more extensive menu, and lower price points; they serve dinner nightly, weekday lunch, and Sunday brunch.

416 Third Ave. (at J St.), Gaslamp Quarter. www.candelas-sd.com. *©* **619/702-4455.** Reservations recommended. Main courses $7–$18 brunch, $17–$62 dinner. AE, DC, DISC, MC, V. Brunch Sun 8am–4pm; lunch Mon–Fri 11am–4pm; dinner daily 5–10:30pm (Sun–Thurs) or 11pm (Fri–Sat). Bus: 11 or 120. Trolley: Convention Center.

Cowboy Star ★★ AMERICAN   This restaurant and butcher shop celebrates the Old West as seen through the squint of a celluloid cowboy. It's an unabashed homage to the Hollywood westerns of the 1930s and 1940s, combined with an unstinting commitment to the finest products available. Specializing in dry-aged meats and game fowl, all products come from sustainable sources; everything is organic, hormone-free, grass-fed, or free-range. The adjacent butcher shop stocks the same cuts you get at the restaurant, and sells house-made sauces and rubs, too. The decor features exposed wood beams and cow skulls, but never dips into kitsch; you can definitely picture Gary Cooper in one of the deep booths, sipping on one of the many specialty cocktails, unwinding after a day on the set.

650 10th Ave. (btw. G and Market sts.), East Village. www.thecowboystar.com. *©* **619/450-5880**. Reservations recommended. Main courses $8–$82 lunch, $22–$82 dinner. AE, DISC, MC, V. Lunch Tues–Fri 11:30am–2:30pm; dinner Tues–Thurs 5–10pm, Fri–Sat 5–10:30pm, Sun 5–9pm; bar menu Tues–Sat 4–10pm (10:30pm Fri–Sat). Butcher shop Tues–Sat noon–7pm. Bus: 3, 5, 11, 901, or 929. Trolley: Park and Market.

Island Prime ★★ SEAFOOD   With its over-the-water dining, patio with fireplace, plentiful free parking, and spectacular bay and skyline views, it would be easy to understand if Island Prime didn't bother to make its food interesting. Executive Chef Deborah Scott isn't just going through the motions here, though. With such dishes as shaved corn with black truffle and fresh herbs, hazelnut-crusted diver

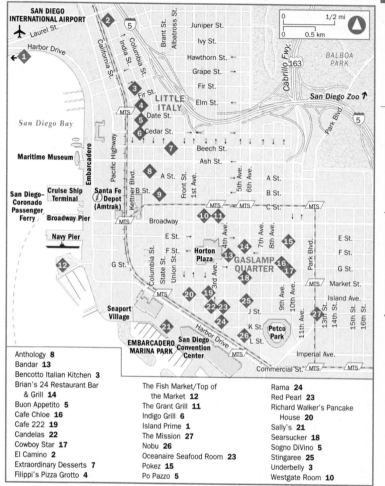

Anthology **8**
Bandar **13**
Bencotto Italian Kitchen **3**
Brian's 24 Restaurant Bar
& Grill **14**
Buon Appetito **5**
Cafe Chloe **16**
Cafe 222 **19**
Candelas **22**
Cowboy Star **17**
El Camino **2**
Extraordinary Desserts **7**
Filippi's Pizza Grotto **4**

The Fish Market/Top of
the Market **12**
The Grant Grill **11**
Indigo Grill **6**
Island Prime **1**
The Mission **27**
Nobu **26**
Oceanaire Seafood Room **23**
Pokez **15**
Po Pazzo **5**

Rama **24**
Red Pearl **23**
Richard Walker's Pancake
House **20**
Sally's **21**
Searsucker **18**
Sogno DiVino **5**
Stingaree **25**
Underbelly **3**
Westgate Room **10**

scallops, and porcini-dusted rack of Colorado lamb with Moroccan-spiced tomato jam, the views actually have some competition. The restaurant's **C Level Lounge** serves lunch and has a bar menu of both food and specialty cocktails. *Tip:* If you're stuck at Lindbergh Field, Island Prime is only a short distance from Terminal 1. Scott is also the mastermind behind the successful Little Italy eatery **Indigo Grill ★**, 1536 India St. (© **619-234-6802**), serving a culinary mishmash of Pacific Coast and Mexican/Southwestern cuisines to good effect.

880 Harbor Island Dr., Harbor Island. www.cohnrestaurants.com. © **619/298-6802.** Reservations recommended. Main courses $15–$29 lunch, $25–$52 dinner. AE, DC, DISC, MC, V. Lunch and dinner daily 11:30am–11pm. Free parking. Bus: 923 or 992.

The Oceanaire Seafood Room ★★ SEAFOOD   As you sweep up the dramatic staircase of the Oceanaire, the retro-nautical decor may evoke the grand elegance of a *Titanic*-style luxury liner. Don't worry, though—the only iceberg ahead is of the lettuce variety. A Minneapolis-based chain that opened here in 2004, the popular Oceanaire features top local products as well as fish brought in daily from around the globe. Preparations incorporate elements of Pacific Rim, Italian, classic French, and Asian cuisine; or you can have your catch-of-the-day simply grilled or broiled. Those who don't eat fish can enjoy top-quality prime beef, chicken, and pork.

400 J St. (at Fourth Ave.), Gaslamp Quarter. www.theoceanaire.com. © **619/858-2277.** Reservations recommended. Main courses $23–$43. AE, DISC, MC, V. Sun–Thurs 5–10pm; Fri–Sat 5–11pm. Valet parking from 5pm $15–$20. Bus: 3, 11, or 120. Trolley: Convention Center.

Searsucker ★★ AMERICAN   Sitting on a prime corner in the heart of the Gaslamp Quarter, this rustically chic restaurant and bar aims to appeal to a wide demographic—from local business types in search of a casual lunch, to couples craving a special night out, to conventioneers looking for a lively taste of San Diego, to downtown revelers seeking the next it-lounge. Searsucker, helmed by a *Top Chef* reality TV finalist, manages to not only keep all comers happy, but to do it with panache. Serving an ever-evolving menu of contemporary American food (both small plates and traditional entrees) such as short ribs braised in local beer, bacon-infused grits, or pork belly, the menu also makes room for plenty of seafood, like the scallops with foie gras and figs. It can get loud in this large, open space, but with its creative-yet-approachable fare, Searsucker is a perfect fit for the Gaslamp.

611 Fifth Ave. (at Market St.), Gaslamp Quarter. www.searsucker.com. © **619/233-7327.** Dinner reservations recommended. Main courses $9–$18 brunch, $9–$14 lunch, $16–$75 dinner. AE, DISC, MC, V. Mon–Fri 11:30am–2pm; Sun–Thurs 5:30–10pm; Fri–Sat 5:30–11pm; bar 5pm–close; brunch Sun 10am–2pm. Valet parking from 5pm $15. Bus: 3, 11, or 120. Trolley: Gaslamp Quarter.

Moderate

Brian's 24 Restaurant Bar & Grill AMERICAN   If you've been partying all night in the Gaslamp Quarter and have a hankering for chicken and waffles at 3am, Brian's 24 has got you covered. It's surprisingly nice for a 24/7 restaurant (the only one in the neighborhood) with touches of class like hammered copper vents in the exposed kitchen and the gorgeous centerpiece bar, purportedly once owned by actress Joan Crawford. The eclectic menu features American comfort food, such as meatloaf and fried chicken, as well as such curiosities as fried pickles and the Elvis-approved burger topped with peanut butter and bacon; there are also Mexican and Italian dishes, as well as a full bar (till 2am). The Gaslamp offers better places to spend your dinner dollars, but for a late-night nosh or an anytime breakfast, Brian's can't be beat.

828 Sixth Ave. (at F St.), Gaslamp Quarter. www.brians24.com. © **619/702-8410.** Main courses $11–$17. AE, DISC, MC, V. Open 24 hr. Bus: 3, 120, or 992.

Cafe Chloe ★★ FRENCH   Creative, whimsical touches (such as a patio built for two) abound at this bistro infused with the refined tastes and *joie de vivre* of its proprietors. Cafe Chloe is small, it's loud when at capacity, and its tiny kitchen can get backed up. But the neighborly conviviality—combined with a short-but-sweet French-inspired menu covering breakfast, lunch, dinner, and weekend brunch—makes for a winning dining experience, and one unique enough to sustain a buzz in ever-morphing San Diego.

721 Ninth Ave. (at G St.), East Village. www.cafechloe.com. © **619/232-3242.** Reservations for parties of 5 or more only, or for afternoon tea (3–5pm). Main courses $9–$16 breakfast, $7–$18 lunch, $17–$27 dinner. AE, MC, V. Mon–Fri 7:30am–10:30pm; Sat 8:30am–10:30pm; Sun 8:30am–9:30pm. Bus: 3, 5, 11, 901, or 929.

El Camino ★ MEXICAN   Combining a lively south-of-the-border cantina ambience with a hipster aesthetic, this *"super cocina mexicana"* serves simple, traditional fare like open-face street-style tacos, enchiladas, and burritos created from local, organic products (vegetarian offerings are available too). Adorned with bold and kitschy graphics, including a graffiti-inspired *Day of the Dead* mural that bursts from the restaurant's back wall, El Camino segues into a casual nightspot with DJs and live music (Weds feature local jazz mainstay Gilbert Castellanos). The open-air back patio, where jets scream overhead on approach to Lindbergh Field, is a cool hangout with vintage Atari games and air hockey.

2400 India St. (at W. Kalmia St.), Little Italy. www.elcaminosd.com. ©**619/685-3881.** Main courses $9–$14. AE, MC, V. Mon 5–10pm; Tues–Sat 5–11pm; Sun 10am–10pm. Bar open Tues–Sun till 1 or 2am. Bus: 83.

The Fish Market/Top of the Market ★ SEAFOOD/SUSHI   The bustling Fish Market at the end of the G Street Pier on the Embarcadero is a San Diego institution; touristy, but an institution. Chalkboards announce the day's catches, which are sold in the retail market by the pound, or available in a number of classic, simple preparations in the casual, always-packed restaurant. Upstairs, the fancy offshoot **Top of the Market** offers sea fare with souped-up presentations (and jacked-up prices). Have a cocktail in Top's plush, clubby atmosphere to enjoy the panoramic bay views, and then head downstairs for more affordable fare or treats from the sushi and oyster bars. There's another Fish Market in Del Mar at 640 Via de la Valle (© **858/755-2277**).

750 N. Harbor Dr., Embarcadero. www.thefishmarket.com. © **619/232-3474.** Reservations for parties of 8 or more only. Main courses $10–$43 lunch, $10–$48 dinner. Top of the Market main courses $13–$40 lunch, $23–$49 dinner. AE, DC, DISC, MC, V. Daily 11am–9:30pm (Fri–Sat till 10pm). Valet parking $8. Trolley: Seaport Village.

Red Pearl Kitchen ★★ CHINESE/PACIFIC RIM/ASIAN FUSION   Specializing in dim sum dishes with a contemporary, Pan-Asian flair, this sexy Gaslamp Quarter restaurant is decorated in hues of deep red and features stone and tile accents, a cool pebbled floor, some nice deep booths, and two private dining areas. At Red Pearl, you may see a kung fu flick on one of the flatscreens over the bar while dining on your strawberry-cinnamon short ribs, duck lettuce wraps, or wok-fired Kobe beef with papaya and mint. For dessert, don't miss the airy *andagi*, the Japanese version of a doughnut hole. Get a glimpse of professionals in action—Red Pearl has an in-kitchen chef's table seating for up to 12 people. Like any Chinese restaurant worth its noodles, Red Pearl also has takeout.

440 J St. (btw. Fourth and Fifth aves.), Gaslamp Quarter. www.redpearlkitchen.com/sandiego. ©**619/231-1100.** Reservations recommended. Main courses $12–$24. AE, MC, V. Daily 5–10pm (Thurs–Sat till 11pm). Valet parking $15. Bus: 3, 11, or 120. Trolley: Convention Center or Gaslamp Quarter.

Inexpensive

Extraordinary Desserts ★★★ DESSERTS/LIGHT FARE   Dozens of divine creations are available daily at this architecturally striking space, including a passion fruit ricotta torte bursting with kiwis, strawberries, and bananas, or a *gianduia* of

ATTACK OF THE KILLER burgers

Burgers, it seems, are the new black. Upscale hamburger spots are popping up all around town, putting fast-food joints to shame with their chic surroundings, grass-fed organic beef, and snazzy beer and wine menus.

Sleekly industrial **Burger Lounge ★** (www.burgerlounge.com) has six locations: La Jolla, 1101 Wall St. (© **858/ 456-0196**); Coronado, 922 Orange Ave. (© **619/435-6835**); Little Italy, 1608 India St. (© **619/237-7878**); Hillcrest, 406 University Ave. (© **619/487-1183**); Kensington, 4116 Adams Ave. (© **619/ 584-2929**); and the Gaslamp, 528 Fifth Ave. (© **619/955-5727**). The 10-item menu cuts right to the chase, featuring natural beef (as well as turkey and veggie) burgers, salads, milkshakes, and wine and beer. The amazing skyline mosaic on the back wall is reason enough to pay a visit to **Neighborhood ★★**, 777 G St., downtown (www.neighborhoodsd.com; © **619/446-0002**). The 30 beers on tap (including plenty of local brews), sophisticated wine list, gourmet takes on burgers and classic bar food (kosher hot dogs with chipotle purée), and creative salads will give you all the incentive you need to stay.

The don't-miss spot for burger aficionados is **Tioli's Crazee Burger ★** (www. tioliscrazeeburger.com), with two locations: 4201 30th St., North Park (© **619/ 282-6044**), and 2415 San Diego Ave., Old Town (© **619/269-3333**). This eatery isn't hip or modern, but it takes a truly fine-dining approach toward its more than 30 burger offerings. Go crazy and order an ostrich, buffalo, or alligator burger; the German owners also take justifiable pride in the bratwurst. **Hodad's ★** (www.hodadies.com), 5010 Newport Ave., Ocean Beach (© **619/ 224-4623**), and 945 Broadway (© **619/ 234-6323**), isn't new or urbane, either, but many locals insist it has the city's best burgers. The original Ocean Beach location is classic. Dive bar connoisseurs can get their burger on at **Rocky's Crown Pub,** 3786 Ingraham St., Pacific Beach (www.rockyscrownpub.com; © **858/273-9140**), and **Danny's Palm Bar & Grill,** 965 Orange Ave., Coronado (© **619/435-3171**). Rocky's is another longtime contender for the best-burger-in-town title; Danny's, which dates to 1908, also has a legion of fans. Kids are welcome at Danny's while the grill is open.

chocolate cake lathered with hazelnut butter cream, chocolate mousse, boysenberry preserves, and sprinkled with shards of praline. Chef and founder Karen Krasne's menu also includes panini, salads, and artisan cheeses, as well as organic wines, boutique beers, and more than 50 different loose-leaf teas; a light breakfast featuring pastries, granola, and smoked salmon is offered Sundays from 11am to 2pm ($17). Krasne also sells her own line of jams, chutneys, syrups, spices, and confections. The original location in Hillcrest, 2929 Fifth Ave. (© **619/294-2132**), is more cozy and intimate but serves only desserts and does not have alcohol.

1430 Union St. (at Ash St.), Little Italy. www.extraordinarydesserts.com. © **619/294-7001.** Desserts $2–$9, salads and sandwiches $8–$18. AE, MC, V. Mon–Thurs 8:30am–11pm; Fri 8:30am–midnight; Sat 10am–midnight; Sun 10am–11pm. Bus: 30.

Filippi's Pizza Grotto ◢ ITALIAN   When longtime locals think "Little Italy," Filippi's often comes to mind. To get to the dining area decorated with chianti bottles and red-checked tablecloths, you walk through a "cash and carry" Italian grocery store and deli stocked with cheeses, pastas, wines, bottles of olive oil, and salamis. The intoxicating smell of pizza wafts into the street; Filippi's has more than 15 varieties (including vegetarian). They also offer huge portions of spaghetti, lasagna, and other pasta; children's portions are available, too. On Friday and Saturday night the lines to get in can look intimidating, but they move quickly. The original of a dozen branches throughout the county, this Filippi's has free parking. Other locations include one in Pacific Beach at 962 Garnet Ave. (✆ **858/483-6222**).

1747 India St. (btw. Date and Fir sts.), Little Italy. www.realcheesepizza.com. ✆**619/232-5094.** Reservations Mon–Thurs for groups of 8 or more. Main courses $6–$13. AE, DC, DISC, MC, V. Sun–Mon 11am–10pm; Tues–Thurs 11am–10:30pm; Fri–Sat 11am–11:30pm; deli open daily at 8am. Free parking. Bus: 83. Trolley: Little Italy.

Underbelly ★★ JAPANESE   This gleaming, modernist noodle house added a new wrinkle to the Little Italy dining scene when it opened in 2011. The short menu features small plates like shrimp pot stickers, teriyaki chicken salad, and oysters, but the main event is the ramen. The Belly of the Beast ramen includes an oxtail dumpling, smoked brisket, and a hoisin-glazed short rib; the Underbelly has pork belly, bacon, and Kurobuta sausage. Vegetarian and vegan options, like the charred kimchi ramen, are also available. One thing you won't find here are spoons, so feel free to pick up your bowl and slurp away—it's encouraged. There's only space for about 50 people around the U-shaped bar (with its 27 handles of draft beer) and at the indoor/outdoor window seats, but as of this writing, plans are underway for the opening of an upstairs whiskey and raw bar.

750 W. Fir St. (at Kettner Blvd.), Little Italy. www.godblessunderbelly.com. ✆**619/269-4626.** Reservations not accepted. Main courses $8–$12. AE, DISC, MC, V. Daily 11:30am–midnight. Bus: 83. Trolley: County Center/Little Italy.

HILLCREST & UPTOWN

Whether it's ethnic food, bistro fare, retro comfort food, or specialty cafes and bakeries, Hillcrest and the other gentrified uptown neighborhoods to its west and east are jam-packed with great eateries catering to any palate and any wallet.

Hash House a Go Go ★, 3628 Fifth Ave. (www.hashhouseagogo.com; ✆ **619/298-4646**), offers a menu of upscale comfort food; it serves three meals a day, but breakfast is the most popular. *Tip:* Portions are mountainous. Get one meal and pay $5 for a split order—you'll probably still leave with leftovers. If you're looking for a classic American diner where waitresses in uniforms call you "honey," then check out **Hob Nob Hill** ★, 2272 First Ave. (www.hobnobhill.com; ✆ **619/239-8176**); it's been going strong since 1944. Another spot favored by locals is **Saffron** ★, 3731 and 3737 India St. (www.saffronsandiego.com; ✆ **619/574-0177** or 574-7737) two low-key storefront spaces on the west side of Mission Hills. One spot serves noodles and satay; the other specializes in Thai-style grilled chicken. Also note that the popular **Whole Foods** supermarket, 711 University Ave. (www.wholefoodsmarket.com; ✆ **619/294-2800**), has a mouthwatering deli and a robust salad bar—you can pack for a picnic or eat at the tables up front.

Very Expensive

Bertrand at Mister A's ★★★ 📷 AMERICAN/MEDITERRANEAN   Since 1965, San Diegans have come to high-rise Mister A's for proms, anniversaries, power meals, and other special occasions. A reported $1-million makeover turned the original Mister A's into Bertrand at Mister A's—an elegant, bright, sophisticated space with an array of modern art. The seasonal menu is modern American with a French/Mediterranean twist (think veal medallions, bouillabaisse, and Maine lobster strudel). A bar/patio menu gives diners on a budget access to the unsurpassed vistas. Bertrand at Mister A's has an equally impressive sister restaurant in the North County neighborhood of Rancho Santa Fe, romantic **Mille Fleurs,** 6009 Paseo Delicias (🕿 **858/756-3085;** www.millefleurs.com).

2550 Fifth Ave. (at Laurel St.), Hillcrest. www.bertrandatmisteras.com. 🕿 **619/239-1377.** Reservations recommended. Main courses $19–$24 lunch, $26–$45 dinner. AE, DC, MC, V. Mon–Fri 11:30am–2:30pm and 5:30–9:30pm; Sat–Sun 5–9:30pm. Valet parking $7.50. Bus: 3 or 120.

Expensive

The Tractor Room ★★ AMERICAN   Dark and woody, with a touch of industrial design, this self-described "hunting lodge" is a carnivore's delight and a haven for those who like their spirits amber and peaty. Prominently featuring game meats such as bison, rabbit, venison, and boar, as well as manly cuts of steak, the Tractor Room also has a massive selection of scotch, whiskey, bourbon, and rye. Vegetarians? Well, this place even throws a stick of jerky into its Bloody Mary, so not so much. Non–meat eaters will do best contenting themselves at the bar with cocktails both classic and inventive (many of which have no meat products in them), or the weekend brunch, where you'll find flapjacks, French toast, and granola on the menu, along with the elk hash.

3687 Fifth Ave. (at Pennsylvania Ave.), Hillcrest. www.thetractorroom.com. 🕿 **619/543-1007.** Main courses $15–$36. AE, DISC, MC, V. Mon–Thurs 5pm–midnight; Fri 5pm–2am (kitchen till midnight); Sat 9am–2pm and 5pm–2am (kitchen till midnight); Sun 9am–2pm and 5–11pm. Bus: 3 or 120.

Moderate

Bankers Hill Bar + Restaurant ★★ 🎁 AMERICAN   A once-inconspicuous corridor between downtown and Hillcrest has begun to sizzle with new restaurants, and this modern American bistro is a major link in the burgeoning foodie chain. Named for the neighborhood it's located in, Bankers Hill exudes a masculine, 19th-century charm with its exposed timber bones, brick floors, Edison bulbs, and glass and steel accents; the series of large, pivoting front doors with their valve-wheel handles sets the industrial tone. The food is anything but mechanical, though. Opened by the creators of Del Mar's celebrated **Market Restaurant + Bar** (p. 224), the menu is refreshed about every 2 weeks to take advantage of seasonal ingredients. Past highlights have included pumpkin soup; artichoke and Marcona almond tart with goat cheese; spice-rubbed local sea bass; crispy pork tacos; and braised boneless lamb shank. There's also an extensive beer list, craft cocktails, house-made desserts, and patio seating.

2202 Fourth Ave. (at Ivy St.), Bankers Hill. www.bankershillsd.com. 🕿 **619/231-0222.** Reservations recommended. Main courses $15–$20. AE, DISC, MC, V. Mon–Thurs 4:30–10pm; Fri 4:30–11pm; Sat 5–11pm; Sun 5–10pm. Bus: 3 or 120.

Cucina Urbana ★★★ ITALIAN   Casually cool and visually striking, Cucina Urbana has been a resounding smash, becoming one of the city's food-scene darlings since opening in 2009. Featuring rustic Italian fare that is often sourced from local and organic producers, it keeps one's pocketbook in mind while at no time sacrificing quality or creativity. No dish is more than $24 and there's a small-but-thoughtful wine-shop component that allows you to browse for a bottle and enjoy it at retail cost

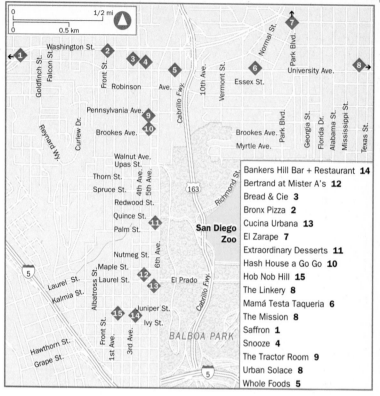

Bankers Hill Bar + Restaurant **14**
Bertrand at Mister A's **12**
Bread & Cie **3**
Bronx Pizza **2**
Cucina Urbana **13**
El Zarape **7**
Extraordinary Desserts **11**
Hash House a Go Go **10**
Hob Nob Hill **15**
The Linkery **8**
Mamá Testa Taqueria **6**
The Mission **8**
Saffron **1**
Snooze **4**
The Tractor Room **9**
Urban Solace **8**
Whole Foods **5**

plus $8 corkage. There are both family-style plates to share and traditional entrees, with highlights including the Gorgonzola-walnut mousse with sun-dried tomato on crostini, gourmet wood-fired pizzas, the daily salami and cheese boards, and artisanal cocktails.

505 Laurel St. (at Fifth Ave.), Balboa Park. www.cucinaurbana.com. © **619/239-2222.** Reservations recommended. Main courses $10–$17 lunch, $13–$24 dinner. AE, DISC, MC, V. Sun 4:30–9pm; Mon 5–9pm; Tues–Thurs 5–10pm; Fri–Sat 5–10:30pm (limited menu till midnight); lunch Tues–Fri 11:30am–2pm. Valet parking $7 (Fri–Sat evenings only). Bus: 3 or 120.

The Linkery ★★ AMERICAN   You'll hear yelps of indignity about the 18% tip built into the check or the seemingly high prices for small portions. But after dining at this farm-to-table hot spot that made a name for itself with its homemade sausages, you'll probably want to tell the naysayers to . . . well, stuff it. The Linkery is one of the leaders in the city's locavore, sustainable food movement, and meticulously identifies the family-owned farms and artisan producers where the product on its menu originated; the restaurant also makes everything from bread to ketchup in-house. Besides charcuterie, the changing fare includes pastas, a local catch of the day, and lamb stew. Non–meat eaters have nothing to fear—there are always vegetarian and vegan options available. This rustically industrial spot also has a fabulous beer list, serving a host of local brews, as well as cider, mead, and sophisticated wines.

3794 30th St. (at North Park Way), North Park. www.thelinkery.com. © **619/255-8778.** Main courses $11–$22. AE, DC, DISC, MC, V. Mon–Fri 11:30am–11pm (Thurs–Fri till midnight); Sat–Sun 11am–midnight. Bus: 2, 6, 7, or 10.

Urban Solace ★★ AMERICAN   One of the bright lights along North Park's burgeoning restaurant row, this loud and cheerful spot will definitely take you to a happy place. With its New Orleans–style facade, outdoor patio, and menu of American comfort food, Urban Solace offers just that. Look for creative, contemporary takes on old standards like the lamb meatloaf with figs, pine nuts, and feta cheese; or mac 'n' cheese with duck confit and blue cheese. The bacon-wrapped trout stuffed with spinach and mushrooms is also a winner. A selection of local beer, West Coast wines, and specialty cocktails—as well as Sunday brunch served with a side of live bluegrass music—ensure that the good times keep rolling.

3823 30th St. (at University Ave.), North Park. www.urbansolace.net. © **619/295-6465.** Main courses $10–$20 lunch, $10–$25 dinner. AE, DISC, MC, V. Mon–Thurs 11:30am–10pm; Fri 11:30am–11pm; Sat 10:30am–11pm; Sun 10am–2:30pm and 5–9pm. Bus: 2, 6, 7, or 10.

Inexpensive

Bread & Cie. ★★ LIGHT FARE/MEDITERRANEAN   The traditions of European artisan bread making and attention to the fine points of texture and crust quickly catapulted Bread & Cie. to local stardom—they now supply bread to dozens of local restaurants. Some favorites are available daily, including anise and fig, black olive, and jalapeño and cheese; others are available just 1 or 2 days a week. Ask for a free sample or order one of the many Mediterranean-inspired sandwiches. A specialty coffee drink perfectly accompanies a light breakfast of fresh scones, muffins, and homemade granola with yogurt. Seating is at bistro-style tables in full view of the busy ovens.

350 University Ave. (at Fourth St.), Hillcrest. www.breadandcie.com. © **619/683-9322.** Reservations not accepted. Sandwiches and light meals $4–$11. DISC, MC, V. Mon–Fri 7am–7pm; Sat 7am–6pm; Sun 8am–6pm. Free 1-hr. parking. Bus: 1, 3, 10, 11, or 120.

Bronx Pizza ★ 🍴 ITALIAN   With its red vinyl booths, checkered curtains, and pictures of boxers on the walls, the interior dining room of this pizzeria looks as if it were airlifted straight out of the boroughs of New York. Bronx Pizza makes only pizzas and calzones—no salads, no chicken wings. And if there's a line out the door (a frequent occurrence), don't hesitate to order when you get to the counter: These guys will definitely drop a little New York attitude on you, and you may find yourself living out the *Seinfeld* Soup Nazi episode. Choices are simple, though. It's all thin-crust, 18-inch pies, or by the slice, with straightforward toppings—although Bronx Pizza has made concessions to the locals by including such ingredients as marinated artichokes and pesto.

111 Washington St. (at First Ave.), Hillcrest. www.bronxpizza.com. © **619/291-3341.** Phone orders accepted for full pies. Pies $14–$20, $2.50 by the slice ($2 for cheese). Cash only. Sun–Thurs 11am–10pm; Fri–Sat 11am–11pm. Street parking. Bus: 3, 10, or 83.

Mamá Testa Taqueria ★★ MEXICAN   The subject of who makes San Diego's best fish taco can spark a lively debate, but this colorful and casual spot can make a strong claim for top honors. The proof came in a televised throwdown with celeb chef Bobby Flay, who came up short against Mamá's fish tacos. Besides a few sides, such as rice and beans, and such desserts as churros and flan, tacos are all this friendly eatery offers, and you'd be hard-pressed to find a better *taquería* on either side of the border. And if you think that means there's a limited menu, you'll actually be fairly overwhelmed by choices that span the various regions of Mexico. There are steamed, rolled, and crunchy variations, some spicy or vegetarian, stuffed with anything from scallops to mashed potatoes; there's also a veritable smorgasbord of fresh salsas available. Add in $2.50 *cerveza* specials and patio seating in the liveliest section of Hillcrest, and you have one of San Diego's best Mexican experiences.

1417A University Ave. (at Richmond St.), Hillcrest. www.mamatestataqueria.com. © **619/298-8226.** Taco plates $7–$13. AE, DISC, MC, V. Mon–Thurs 11:30am–9pm; Fri–Sat 11:30am–11pm; Sun noon–8pm. Bus: 1, 10, or 11.

Snooze ★★ BREAKFAST   The jolt of happiness delivered by this "a.m. eatery" isn't just a side effect of the organic Guatemalan coffee it has flown in weekly. With it's bold and bright midcentury style—that never devolves into kitsch—and its superlative architecture (soaring ceiling and skylights), this minichain from Colorado delights before you've even taken your first bite. Morning staples get creative takes (breakfast pot pie, apple and mascarpone-stuffed French toast, sweet potato pancakes), and are joined by such lunch items as corned beef and sauerkraut stacked on a pretzel roll and fresh-catch fish tacos. Want to try a flight of different pancakes? Create your own custom dish? That's A-Okay with the Snooze crew, too. Plenty of eye-openers are on hand, as well, including the Brewmosa (Belgian-style ale and OJ) and the A.M. Manhattan (bourbon, Irish cream, and espresso, served warm).

3940 Fifth Ave. (btw. University Ave. and Washington St.), Hillcrest. www.snoozeeatery.com. © **619/500-3344.** Reservations not accepted. Main courses $7–$12. AE, DISC, MC, V. Mon–Fri 6:30am–2:30pm; Sat–Sun 7am–2:30pm. Bus: 1, 3, 10, 11, 83, or 120.

OLD TOWN & MISSION VALLEY

Visitors often have at least one meal in Old Town. Although this area is San Diego at its most touristy, you can't argue with the appeal of dining in California's charming original European settlement. Mexican food and bathtub-size margaritas are the big draws, and **Old Town Mexican Cafe,** 2489 San Diego Ave. (www.oldtownmexcafe. com; © **619/297-4330**), in particular, has become so popular it's practically a tourist attraction in its own right. The food is rarely worth braving the long wait to get in, though. For a change of pace, stop by the hip sushi joint **Harney Sushi** ★, 3964 Harney St. (www.harneysushi.com; © **619/295-3272**), which serves a menu of all-sustainable seafood.

Old Town is the gateway to the decidedly less historic Mission Valley where there are plenty of chain eateries, both good and bad. In the busy Fashion Valley Center complex (p. 164), you'll find the **Cheesecake Factory, California Pizza Kitchen,** and **P.F. Chang's China Bistro.**

Expensive

El Agave Tequileria ★★ MEXICAN   Don't be misled by this restaurant's less-than-impressive location above a liquor store. The regional Mexican cuisine here leaves Old Town's touristy fajitas and *cerveza* joints far behind. El Agave is named for the plant from which tequila and its smoky cousin mescal are derived, and the restaurant boasts more than 850 different brands. Needless to say, El Agave serves some of the best margaritas in town. Even teetotalers, though, will enjoy the restaurant's authentically flavored mole sauces—from Taxco, rich with walnuts; tangy tomatillo from Oaxaca; and the more familiar dark mole flavored with chocolate and sesame.

2304 San Diego Ave., Old Town. www.elagave.com. © **619/220-0692.** Reservations recommended. Main courses $10–$20 lunch, $16–$32 dinner. AE, MC, V. Daily 11am–10pm. Street parking. Bus: Numerous Old Town routes, including 8, 9, 10, 28, and 30. Trolley: Old Town.

Moderate

Berta's Latin American Restaurant ★ LATIN AMERICAN Housed in a charming cottage tucked away on a side street, Berta's faithfully re-creates the sunny flavors of Central and South America, where slow cooking mellows the heat of chilies and other spices. Everyone starts with a basket of fresh flour tortillas and mild salsa verde. Mouthwatering dishes include Guatemalan *chilemal,* a rich pork-and-vegetable casserole with chilies, cornmeal *masa,* coriander, and cloves; or try the Salvadoran *pupusas* (at lunch only)—dense corn-mash turnovers with melted cheese and black beans, their texture perfectly offset with crunchy cabbage salad and one of Berta's special salsas. You can also opt for a table full of Spanish-style tapas, grazing alternately on crispy *empanadas* (filled turnovers), strong Spanish olives, or *pincho moruno* (skewered lamb and onion redolent of spices and red saffron).

3928 Twiggs St. (at Congress St.), Old Town. www.bertasinoldtown.com. © **619/295-2343.** Main courses $7–$12 lunch, $13–$19 dinner. AE, DISC, MC, V. Tues–Sun 11am–10pm (lunch menu till 3pm). Free parking. Bus: Numerous Old Town routes, including 8, 9, 10, 28, and 30. Trolley: Old Town.

Casa Guadalajara ☺ MEXICAN Bazaar Del Mundo Shops, a warren of mostly Latin-themed gift stores, operates this Mexican restaurant a block away from Old Town State Historic Park. Casa Guadalajara is both better and less crowded than most Old Town options, although waits of 30 minutes or more are not unusual on Friday and Saturday. Mariachi tunes played by strolling musicians enliven the room nightly, and you can dine alfresco in a picturesque courtyard occupied by a 200-year-old pepper tree. Birdbath-size margaritas start most meals, and dining ranges from simple south-of-the-border fare to more gourmet items such as tequila-lime shrimp and mango-chipotle chicken. Of course the extensive menu features all the usual fajita and combo plates, too; breakfast items are served till 2pm. This place is touristy, but out-of-towners looking for old California ambience and reliable Mexican food will find it here.

4105 Taylor St. (at Juan St.), Old Town. www.bazaardelmundo.com. © **619/295-5111.** Reservations recommended. Main courses $8–$12 breakfast, $9–$18 lunch and dinner. AE, DC, DISC, MC, V. Mon–Thurs 11am–10pm; Fri 11am–11pm; Sat 8am–11pm; Sun 8am–10pm. Free parking. Bus: Numerous Old Town routes, including 8, 9, 10, 28, and 30. Trolley: Old Town.

25 Forty Bistro & Bakehouse ★ 🎁 AMERICAN/ITALIAN This charming bistro is an oasis of calm in Old Town. The cottage setting—updated with a modern design sensibility—offers a pleasurable antidote to the blaring mariachi music and army of tortilla ladies patting their hearts out a block away. Featuring indoor and outdoor seating, the patio is especially inviting with its fire pit and communal table mounted upon a handsome flagstone base. The fare is mostly contemporary Italian, including such house-made pastas as pumpkin gnocchi and vegan fettuccine, but the menu also makes room for more wide-ranging fare like bratwurst, a duck and white bean casserole, and rib-eye steak with chimichurri sauce. Weekend brunch (10am–4pm) sees the addition of items like Nutella French toast, omelets, and sandwiches.

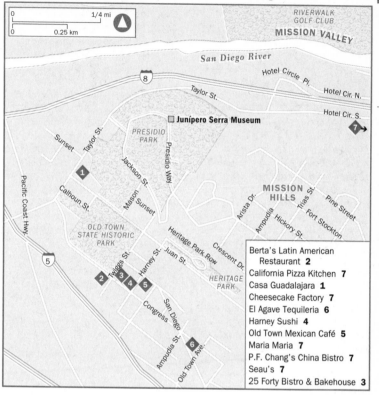

Berta's Latin American Restaurant **2**
California Pizza Kitchen **7**
Casa Guadalajara **1**
Cheesecake Factory **7**
El Agave Tequileria **6**
Harney Sushi **4**
Old Town Mexican Café **5**
Maria Maria **7**
P.F. Chang's China Bistro **7**
Seau's **7**
25 Forty Bistro & Bakehouse **3**

2540 Congress St. (btw. Twiggs and Harney sts.), Old Town. www.25fortybistro.com. ✆ **619/294-2540.** Main courses $8–$10 lunch, $7–$16 brunch, $14–$22 dinner. AE, DISC, MC, V. Tues–Fri 11:30am–2:30pm (lunch Thurs–Fri only in winter); Tues–Thurs 5–9:30pm; Fri 5–10pm; Sat 10am–9:30pm; Sun 10am–9pm. Bus: Numerous Old Town routes including 8, 9, 10, 28, and 30. Trolley: Old Town.

MISSION BAY & THE BEACHES

Restaurants at the beach exist primarily to provide an excuse for sitting and gazing at the water. Because this activity is most commonly accompanied by steady drinking, it stands to reason the food often isn't remarkable. Happily, the past few years have seen an influx of places bucking the trend.

The beautiful party people get their groove and their feed bag on in Pacific Beach at **JRDN** ★ (pronounced "Jordan") in the swank Tower 23 hotel (p. 203), 723 Felspar St. (www.jrdn.com; ✆ 858/270-5736). The creator of **the Mission** (p. 137) is proprietor of hip **Isabel's Cantina** ★, 966 Felspar St. (✆ 858/272-8400; www.isabelscantina.com), an Asian-Latino fusion cafe serving breakfast, lunch, and dinner in the remnants of an old bakery. Or start your day at the beach at **Kono's Surf Club**

BAJA FISH tacos

One of San Diego's culinary ironies is that despite its rich Hispanic heritage and proximity to the Mexican border, it's hard to find anything other than gringo-ized combo plates in many local Mexican restaurants. But one item you'll see on plenty of menus here is the fish taco—a native of Baja California. Consisting of batter-dipped, deep-fried filets wrapped in a corn tortilla with shredded cabbage, salsa, and a tangy sauce, fish tacos were popularized in San Diego by **Rubio's Fresh Mexican Grill** in the early 1980s. Rubio's has since grown into a sizable chain, and it's a good option if you're on the go—the original stand is still operating at the east end of Pacific Beach, 4504 E. Mission Bay Dr., at Bunker Hill Street (www.rubios.com; ✆ **858/272-2801**).

Fish tacos are a casual food, served in casual settings. Here are some of the best places to taste one: **Bay Park Fish Co.** ★, 4121 Ashton St., Bay Park (www.baayparkfishco.com; ✆ **619/276-3474**);

Blue Water Seafood Market and Grill ★, 3667 India St., Mission Hills (www.bluewaterseafoodsandiego.com; ✆ **619/497-0914**); **Lucha Libre Gourmet Taco Shop** ★, 1810 W. Washington St., Mission Hills (www.tacosmackdown.com; ✆ **619/296-8226**); **the Brigantine** (p. 143); **the Fishery** ★ (below); **Mamá Testa** ★★ (see above); **Point Loma Seafoods** ★, 2805 Emerson St., Point Loma (www.pointlomaseafoods.com; ✆ **619/223-1109**); **South Beach Bar & Grill**, 5059 Newport Ave., Ocean Beach (www.southbeachob.com; ✆ **619/226-4577**); and **El Zarape** ★, 4642 Park Blvd., University Heights (✆ **619/692-1652**). Another worthy chain is **Wahoo's Fish Taco** (www.wahoos.com), with locations including La Jolla (637 Pearl St.; ✆ **858/459-0027**), Encinitas (1006 N. El Camino Real; ✆ **760/753-5060**), Mission Valley (2195 Station Village Way; ✆ **619/299-4550**), and the Sports Arena area (3944 W. Point Loma Blvd.; ✆ **619/222-0020**).

Cafe, 704 Garnet Ave., Pacific Beach (✆ 858/483-1669), a Hawaiian-themed boardwalk breakfast shack that's cheap and delicious. A plump Kono's breakfast burrito provides enough fuel for a day of surfing or sightseeing; a side order of savory "Kono Potatoes" is a meal in itself. For lunch or dinner, **Costa Brava** ★★, 1653 Garnet Ave. (www.costabravasd.com; ✆ 858/273-1218), is a real find, serving traditional Spanish tapas.

Very Expensive

Baleen ★★ ☺ SEAFOOD/CALIFORNIAN   This attractive waterfront eatery is located right in the middle of Mission Bay at the Paradise Point Resort (p. 202)—the patio dining is sublime here. With its lush bayfront view, it's easy to miss the design details indoors—from a monkey motif that includes simians hanging off chandeliers to specialized serving platters for many of Baleen's artistically arranged dishes. Ocean fare takes precedence, and local fish and shellfish are featured in a chef's tasting menu. There's also classic surf and turf or a selection of simply wood-roasted meats and seafood. **Note:** This is a family-oriented resort, so knee-high types may be sharing the space; a children's menu goes beyond the usual burgers-and-fries option and includes items such as shrimp scampi and petit filet.

1404 Vacation Rd. (Paradise Point Resort), Mission Bay. www.paradisepoint.com. ✆ **858/490-6363.** Reservations recommended. Main courses $22–$78. AE, DC, DISC, MC, V. Daily 5–10pm. Free parking. Bus: 9.

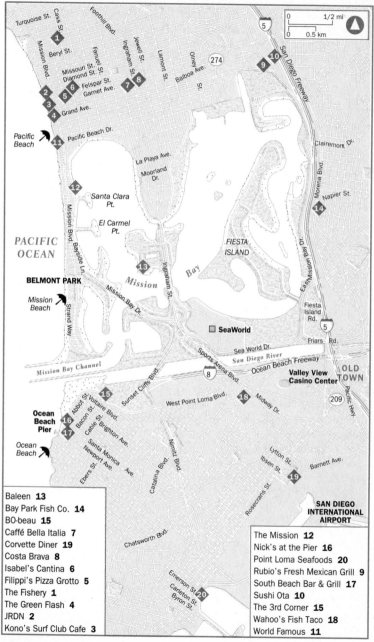

Baleen **13**
Bay Park Fish Co. **14**
BO-beau **15**
Caffé Bella Italia **7**
Corvette Diner **19**
Costa Brava **8**
Isabel's Cantina **6**
Filippi's Pizza Grotto **5**
The Fishery **1**
The Green Flash **4**
JRDN **2**
Kono's Surf Club Cafe **3**

The Mission **12**
Nick's at the Pier **16**
Point Loma Seafoods **20**
Rubio's Fresh Mexican Grill **9**
South Beach Bar & Grill **17**
Sushi Ota **10**
The 3rd Corner **15**
Wahoo's Fish Taco **18**
World Famous **11**

Moderate

BO-beau ★ FRENCH/MEDITERRANEAN For a generation, the Bungalow served the most grown-up food in ultra-casual Ocean Beach. With its metamorphosis into BO-beau in late 2010, everything has changed for this once-creaky cottage, except it's still one of the best places in the beach area for those who crave something more than tacos and burritos. The menu has been dialed down from Euro-formal to a winning bistro style, with only the Bungalow's boeuf bourguignon surviving the changeover. The physical improvements are impressive, too, with a complete renovation that evokes a rustic French abode (albeit one with a full bar and patio with outdoor oven). It's all theme-park faux, but it doesn't take much in the way of crispy Brussels sprouts, mussels in red curry broth, or a charcuterie plate to get you to play along.

4996 W. Point Loma Blvd. (at Bacon St.), Ocean Beach. www.bobeaukitchen.com. ℂ **619/224-2884.** Reservations not accepted. Main courses $14–$20. AE, DC, DISC, MC, V. Sun–Wed 4:30–11pm; Thurs–Sat 4:30–midnight. Free parking. Bus: 35 or 923.

Caffé Bella Italia ★★ ITALIAN It's well away from the surf, has a rather odd-looking exterior, and is in a less-than-inspiring section of P.B., but this place is lovely inside—and the food can knock your socks off. It's the best spot in the area for shellfish-laden pasta, wood-fired pizzas (a selection of more than 30), and management that welcomes guests like family. Romantic lighting, sheer draperies, and warm earth tones create a Mediterranean ambience, assisted by the lilting Milanese accents of the staff (when the din of a few dozen happy diners doesn't drown them out, that is). A sister restaurant, the stylish **Solare,** is at Liberty Station in Point Loma, 2820 Roosevelt Rd. (ℂ **619/270-9670;** www.solarelounge.com).

1525 Garnet Ave. (btw. Ingraham and Haines sts.), Pacific Beach. www.caffebellaitalia.com. ℂ **858/273-1224.** Reservations suggested. Main courses $15–$27. AE, DC, DISC, MC, V. Daily 4:30–10pm. Free (small) parking lot. Bus: 9 or 27.

The Fishery ★ 🍴 SEAFOOD You're pretty well guaranteed to get fresh-off-the-boat seafood at this off-the-beaten-track establishment—it's really a wholesale warehouse and retail fish market with a casual restaurant attached. The owners work with local, national, and global suppliers, and the wide range of bounty is reflected in an eclectic menu that ranges from sushi rolls and clam chowder to Scottish salmon and Mexican lobster. The Fishery makes an effort to offer sustainable product, so look for owner-caught harpooned swordfish in season. In spite of its informal air, there's a surprisingly impressive wine list, including some 35 vinos served by the glass; belly up to the restaurant's **Fish Bar** for some Prosecco and mussels.

5040 Cass St. (at Opal St., ¾-mile north of Garnet Ave.), Pacific Beach. www.thefishery.com. ℂ **858/272-9985.** Reservations recommended for dinner. Main courses $9–$18 lunch, $14–$34 dinner. AE, DC, DISC, MC, V. Daily 11am–10pm. Street parking usually available. Bus: 30.

Sushi Ota ★★★ 🍴 SUSHI Masterful chef-owner Yukito Ota creates San Diego's finest sushi. This sophisticated, traditional restaurant is a minimalist bento box with stark white walls and black furniture, softened by indirect lighting. The sushi menu is short, because discerning regulars look first to the daily specials posted behind the counter. The city's most experienced chefs, armed with nimble fingers and seriously sharp knives, turn the day's fresh catch into artful little bundles accented with mounds of wasabi and ginger. The rest of the varied menu features seafood, teriyaki-glazed meats, feather-light tempura, and a variety of small appetizers perfect to accompany a large sushi order. This restaurant is difficult to find, mainly because it's hard to believe that such outstanding dining would hide next to a Laundromat and convenience store in the rear of a mini-mall.

4529 Mission Bay Dr. (at Bunker Hill), Pacific Beach. www.sushiota.com. © **858/270-5670.** Reservations strongly recommended on weekends. Main courses $6–$14 lunch, $9–$22 dinner, sushi $4–$13. AE, MC, V. Mon 5:30–10:30pm; Tues–Fri 11:30am–2pm and 5:30–10:30pm; Sat–Sun 5–10:30pm. Free parking (additional lot behind the mall). Bus: 30.

The 3rd Corner ★★ 🛍 FRENCH   Set in an old beach bungalow on the outskirts of Ocean Beach, the 3rd Corner is part wine shop, part bistro, part neighborhood bar. Intimate, convivial, and unique, you can wander through racks of wine (about 1,000 bottles are available at any given time), pick the one you like, and find yourself a spot to enjoy a menu of small plates and entrees with a French-Mediterranean flair ($5 corkage). Seating for dining is limited, but there's a full bar, lounge, and patio. Look for wine-friendly fare such as charcuterie plates, an array of cheeses, and pâté, as well as black truffle risotto and duck confit; Sunday brunch is served 11am to 3pm. Best of all, 3rd Corner serves food and drinks late—until 1am (except Mon). There's also an outpost in Encinitas at the Lumberyard shopping center, 897 S. Coast Hwy. (© 760/942-2104).

2265 Bacon St. (at W. Point Loma Blvd.), Ocean Beach. www.the3rdcorner.com. © **619/223-2700.** Main courses $6–$21. AE, DISC, MC, V. Kitchen Tues–Sat 11:30am–1am, Sun 10am–1am (brunch until 3). Wine shop Tues–Sun 10am–1:30am. Free parking. Bus: 35 or 923.

Inexpensive

Corvette Diner ☺ AMERICAN   This family-friendly time warp serves burgers, sandwiches, appetizer munchies, blue-plate specials, and salads, along with a *very* full page of fountain favorites; beer, wine, and cocktails are also available. In 2009, after 22 years in Hillcrest, Corvette Diner relocated to Liberty Station, the massive redevelopment project that was once the U.S. Naval Training Center in Point Loma. The new spot is twice the size of the original and is set in what was once the NTC officers' club. There are themed rooms (the Corvette Room, the '70s Blacklight Room, and the Diner Car); an arcade with everything from air hockey to Guitar Hero; and a huge parking lot (a big improvement over parking-challenged Hillcrest). What hasn't changed are the sassy, dancing waitstaff and the loud, vintage rock 'n' roll.

2965 Historic Decatur Rd. (in Liberty Station, off Rosecrans St.), Point Loma. www.cohnrestaurants. com. © **619/542-1476.** Reservations not accepted. Main courses $9–$14, kids' plates $7. AE, DC, DISC, MC, V. Sun 11am–9pm; Mon–Thurs 11:30am–9pm; Fri 11:30am–11pm; Sat 11am–11pm. Free parking. Bus: 28 or 923.

The Mission ★ 🍴 BREAKFAST/LIGHT FARE   Located alongside the funky surf shops and bikini boutiques of bohemian Mission Beach, the Mission is the neighborhood's central meeting place. The menu features all-day breakfasts, from traditional pancakes and nouvelle egg dishes to burritos and quesadillas. Standouts include chicken-apple sausage with eggs and a mound of rosemary potatoes, and cinnamon French toast with blackberry purée. At lunch, the menu expands to include sandwiches, salads, and a few Chino-Latino items such as ginger-sesame chicken tacos. Seating is casual, comfy, and conducive to lingering, if only with a soup bowl–size latte. Expect waits of half an hour or more on weekends. Other locations: 2801 University Ave., in North Park (© 619/220-8992), and 1250 J St., downtown (© 619/232-7662); both have similar menus and hours.

3795 Mission Blvd. (at San Jose), Mission Beach. www.themissionsd.com. © **858/488-9060.** All items $6–$13. AE, MC, V. Daily 7am–3pm. Bus: 8.

LA JOLLA

As befits an upscale community with time (and money) on its hands, La Jolla has more than its fair share of good restaurants, and thankfully, not all of them are expensive. While many dining spots are clustered in the village (on Prospect Street and the few blocks directly east), you can also cruise down La Jolla Boulevard or up by the La Jolla Beach & Tennis Club for additional choices.

There are old-school favorites that still impress, such as the recently renovated, utterly romantic **Sky Room** ★★ at the La Valencia Hotel (p. 208), 1132 Prospect St. (www.lavalencia.com; ⓒ 858/454-0771), which features fabulous views and French-inspired cuisine. There are more Gallic goings-on at **Michele Coulon Dessertier** ★★, 7556D Fay Ave. (www.dessertier.com; ⓒ 858/456-5098). This small cafe and bakery specializes in decadent desserts, but also serves very good light lunches (quiches, salads, sandwiches). For lunch or breakfast, the **Coffee Cup** ★, 1109 Wall St. (www.isabelscantina.com; ⓒ 858/551-8514), is a spot popular with locals; for traditional Mexican, head down La Jolla Boulevard to **Su Casa,** 6738 La Jolla Blvd. (www.sucasarestaurant.com; ⓒ 858/454-0369), a family-friendly place that's been here forever (well, since 1967 anyway).

Very Expensive

The Marine Room ★★★ 📷 FRENCH/CALIFORNIAN   Since 1941, San Diego's most celebrated dining room has been this shorefront institution. Executive Chef Bernard Guillas, of Brittany, works with local produce, but never hesitates to pursue unusual flavors from other corners of the globe—pomegranate-and-macadamia-coated Scottish salmon with red quinoa, bok choy, and lemon verbena essence; or nectarine-glazed pompano with crab risotto and a sake emulsion. The Marine Room ranks as one of San Diego's most expensive venues, but it's usually filled to the gills on weekends; weekdays it's much easier to score a table. Ideally, schedule your reservation a half-hour or so before sunset; if you can't get in at that magic hour, experience sundown by the bar—a more wallet-friendly lounge and happy-hour menu are available. In fall and winter, special high-tide breakfasts are served, as waves crash against the picture windows.

2000 Spindrift Dr., La Jolla. www.marineroom.com. ⓒ **866/644-2351.** Reservations recommended, especially weekends. Main courses $26–$43. AE, DC, DISC, MC, V. Daily 6–9:30pm (till 10pm Fri–Sat). Lounge daily 4pm–closing. Valet parking $5. Bus: 30.

Nine-Ten ★★★ CALIFORNIAN   This warmly stylish space is the place for market-fresh cuisine, prepared by Jason Knibb, another member of San Diego's cadre of skilled chefs. Knibb, who was mentored by such culinary figures as Wolfgang Puck, Roy Yamaguchi, and Hans Rockenwagner, presides over a shifting, seasonal menu that's best enjoyed via small-plate grazing. Past offerings have included espresso- and chocolate-braised boneless short ribs, Maine scallops with apple risotto, and harissa-marinated shrimp. Or better yet, turn yourself over to the "Mercy of the Chef," a five-course tasting menu for $80, or $120 with wine pairings (your whole table has to participate, though), served till 9pm. When you're looking for a classy fine-dining experience without the old-guard attitude, Nine-Ten, located at the Grande Colonial hotel (p. 210), fits the bill very nicely. Breakfast and lunch are served, too.

910 Prospect St. (btw. Fay and Girard aves.), La Jolla. www.nine-ten.com. ⓒ858/964-5400. Reservations recommended. Main courses $8–$14 breakfast, $12–$16 lunch, $29–$37 dinner. AE, DC, DISC, MC, V. Mon–Sat 6:30am–2:30pm; Tues–Sat 6–10pm; Sun–Mon 6–9:30pm. Valet parking $5. Bus: 30.

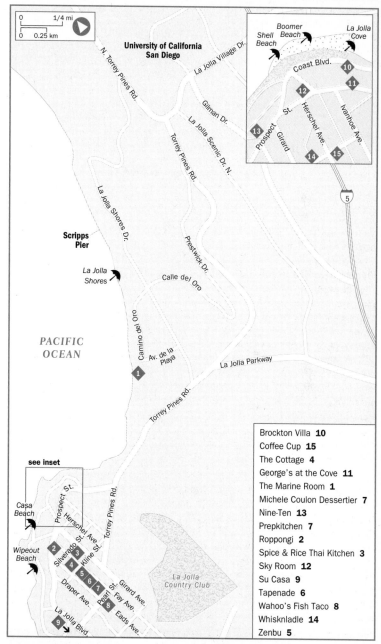

Brockton Villa **10**
Coffee Cup **15**
The Cottage **4**
George's at the Cove **11**
The Marine Room **1**
Michele Coulon Dessertier **7**
Nine-Ten **13**
Prepkitchen **7**
Roppongi **2**
Spice & Rice Thai Kitchen **3**
Sky Room **12**
Su Casa **9**
Tapenade **6**
Wahoo's Fish Taco **8**
Whisknladle **14**
Zenbu **5**

Expensive

George's at the Cove ★★★ 📷 CALIFORNIAN

This is perhaps La Jolla's signature restaurant. It has it all: stunning ocean views, style, impeccable service, and above all, a world-class chef. The George's moniker actually refers to three distinct on-site options: **George's California Modern, George's Bar,** and **Ocean Terrace.** California Modern is the upscale, design-forward dinner spot where Chef Trey Foshee, named one of America's top 10 chefs by *Food & Wine,* is at his most innovative; the indoor/outdoor George's Bar and the glorious rooftop Ocean Terrace serve less-pricey bistro fare for both lunch and dinner. All the food comes out of the same award-winning kitchen, though, which is noted for its intensely seasonal—and often local—fare (even the artisan cocktails change with the time of year). Vegan and vegetarian items are always available, too, as is the signature black bean soup with smoked chicken and broccoli.

1250 Prospect St., La Jolla. www.georgesatthecove.com. ✆ **858/454-4244.** Reservations strongly recommended. California Modern main courses $28–$48. AE, DC, DISC, MC, V. Mon–Thurs 5:30–10pm; Fri–Sat 5–11pm; Sun 5–10pm. Ocean Terrace/George's Bar main courses $11–$18 lunch, $17–$26 dinner. AE, MC, V. Daily 11am–9pm (Fri–Sat till 10:30pm). Valet parking $8. Bus: 30.

Roppongi ★ PACIFIC RIM/ASIAN FUSION

At Roppongi, the cuisines of Japan, Thailand, China, Vietnam, Korea, and India collide, sometimes gracefully, in a vibrant explosion of flavors. You might not get past the first menu page, a long list of tapas designed for sharing; each table is preset with a tall stack of plates that quietly encourages a communal meal of successive appetizers. You can jump from Thai satay and Chinese potstickers to a Mongolian duck quesadilla and Indonesian spicy shrimp without missing a beat. When you order right, it works. Options increase exponentially when you start considering the sushi bar menu. There are also traditionally sized main courses featuring seafood, meat, and game, all colorfully prepared; at lunch there's a selection of wraps, sandwiches, and entree salads.

875 Prospect St. (at Fay Ave.), La Jolla. www.roppongiusa.com. ✆ **858/551-5252.** Reservations recommended. Tapas $8–$19; sushi $6–$18; main courses $10–$14 lunch, $17–$30 dinner. AE, DC, DISC, MC, V. Daily 11:30am–9:30pm. Valet parking $5–$8; garage parking available for dinner. Bus: 30.

Tapenade ★★★ FRENCH

This elegant and distinguished restaurant is the poster child for the giant leap forward the local dining scene has taken over the last decade. A labor-of-love endeavor operated by husband-and-wife team Sylvie and Jean Michel Diot, Tapenade is a showcase for Jean Michel's light, creative touch in the kitchen—a talent he honed at a series of Michelin two- and three-star restaurants in his native France. He moved to San Diego in 1998 after establishing a series of successful bistros in New York. The Big Apple's loss has been San Diego's gain; Tapenade's fresh, sunny fare has helped redefine French cuisine here. Lunch and early-bird prix-fixe menus, as well as selections for vegetarians and children, are served.

7612 Fay Ave. (btw. Kline and Pearls sts.), La Jolla. www.tapenaderestaurant.com. ✆ **858/551-7500.** Dinner reservations recommended. Main courses $14–$22 lunch, $24–$42 dinner. AE, MC, V. Tues–Fri 11:30am–2:30pm; Sun–Thurs 5:30–9:30pm; Fri–Sat 5:30–10pm. Parking in lot behind the building. Bus: 30.

Zenbu ★★ SUSHI/SEAFOOD

La Jolla native Matt Rimel loved fishing so much he bought a commercial fishing boat. He now operates four restaurants and still owns that local boat—not to mention an international fleet that trawls for his eateries as well as select clients. You can order something from the sushi bar, like creamy uni or one of the specialty rolls; you can also try an entree such as steak of locally harpooned swordfish or grilled local fish of the day. The fabulous lobster dynamite, a half lobster (local, naturally) and crab baked in a special sauce, is given a dramatic, flaming presentation. Next door, intimate **Zenbu Lounge** (Thurs–Sat) has a sushi bar and DJs. If you're in North County and craving sushi there's a second Zenbu location in Cardiff-by-the-Sea, 2003 San Elijo Ave. (✆ **760/633-2233**).

7660 Fay Ave. (at Kline St.), La Jolla. www.zenbusushi.com. ✆ **858/454-4540.** Reservations not accepted. Main courses $22–$30. AE, DC, DISC, MC, V. Sun and Tues–Wed 5–10:30pm; Thurs–Sat 5–11pm. Happy hour nightly 5–7pm. Free parking. Bus: 30.

Moderate

Brockton Villa ★ BREAKFAST/CALIFORNIAN   A restored 1894 beach bungalow, this charming cafe is named for an early resident's hometown (Brockton, MA) and occupies a breathtaking perch overlooking La Jolla Cove. The biggest buzz is at breakfast, when you can enjoy such inventive dishes as soufflé-like "Coast Toast" and Greek "steamers" (eggs scrambled with an espresso steamer, and then mixed with feta cheese, tomato, and basil). Breakfasts are served until noon weekdays, until 3pm weekends. Lunch highlights include house-made soups, salads, and sandwiches including the grilled organic salmon BLT. The supper menu includes seafood and steak dishes, plus pastas and grilled meats. **Note:** Steep stairs from the street limit wheelchair access.

1235 Coast Blvd. (across from La Jolla Cove), La Jolla. www.brocktonvilla.com. ✆ **858/454-7393.** Reservations recommended. Main courses $9–$15 breakfast, $9–$16 lunch, $15–$29 dinner. AE, DISC, MC, V. Daily 8am–9pm. Bus: 30.

Spice & Rice Thai Kitchen ★ THAI   The lunch crowd at this attractive Thai restaurant consists of shoppers and tourists, while dinner is quieter. The covered front patio has a secluded garden feel, perfect for a romantic evening. The food is excellent, with polished presentations and expert renditions of classics such as pad Thai, curry, and glazed duck. Consider making a meal of appetizer specialties including "gold bags" (minced pork, vegetables, glass noodles, and herbs wrapped in crispy rice paper and served with earthy plum sauce) or prawns with yellow curry lobster sauce. Despite the passage of time, this all-around satisfier remains something of an insider's secret.

7734 Girard Ave., La Jolla. www.spiceandricethaikitchen.com. ✆ **858/456-0466.** Reservations recommended. Main courses $9–$12 lunch, $12–$15 dinner. AE, DC, DISC, MC, V. Mon–Fri 11am–3pm and 5–10pm (Fri until 11pm); Sat 11:30am–3:30pm and 5–11pm; Sun 5–10pm. Bus: 30.

Whisknladle ★★ AMERICAN   Serving a menu of farm-to-table goodness, you'll find gourmet comfort food created from top-quality products (many of them local). There are items meant for sharing, like charcuterie, flatbreads, charred bone marrow, and Carlsbad mussels, as well as main courses like pastas, pan-roasted flat iron steak, and a pork belly sandwich. Chef Ryan Johnston, a protégé of French Laundry's Thomas Keller, is fanatical about making things from scratch, doing everything from curing and smoking meats to baking the bread and churning the ice cream in-house. The Whisknladle folks are also behind **Prepkitchen** ★★, 7556 Fay Ave. (✆ **858/875-7737;** www.prepkitchen.com), a great little spot where you can pick up soups, salads, and sandwiches to go; there are also Prepkitchens in Del Mar, 1201 Camino del Mar (✆ **858/792-7737**), and Little Italy, 1660 India St. (✆ **619/398-8383**).

MEAL WITH A view

Incredible ocean vistas, a glittering skyline, and sailboats slicing through the water offshore—it's the classic backdrop for a memorable meal. So where can you find the best views?

Downtown, the **Fish Market** and its pricier cousin **Top of the Market** (p. 125) overlook San Diego Bay, and offer a good look at aircraft carriers and other vessels docked at the naval station in Coronado. With its over-the-water setting on Harbor Island, near the airport, **Island Prime** (p. 122) is another visual overachiever (with plenty of outdoor seating). Mai tais and tikis come along with the bay perspective at 1950s holdover **Bali Hai** on Shelter Island, 2230 Shelter Island Dr. (www.balihairestaurant. com; ℂ **619/222-1181**). Across the harbor in Coronado, **Il Fornaio,** 1333 First St. (www.ilfornaio.com; ℂ **619/437-4911**); **Peohe's,** 1201 First St. (www. peohes.com; ℂ **619/437-4474**); and **Candelas** (p. 122) offer gorgeous views of the San Diego skyline; tony **Mistral ★★** (below), at Loews Coronado Bay Resort, provides a unique north-facing look across the bay.

In Ocean Beach, **Nick's at the Pier,** 5083 Santa Monica Ave. (www.nicksat thepier.com; ℂ **619/222-7437**), sits on a second-floor perch right across the street from the beach. In Pacific Beach, **Green Flash,** 701 Thomas Ave., (www.green flashrestaurant.com; ℂ **858/270-7715**); **World Famous,** 711 Pacific Beach Dr. (www.worldfamouspb.com; ℂ **858/272-3100**); and **JRDN** (p. 133) are just an arm's length from the sand (although the year-round parade of bodies may prove a distraction from your food). In La Jolla, the **Sky Room** (p. 138) and **George's at the Cove** (above) offer sweeping, elevated views of the coast, but **Brockton Villa** (above) actually offers the La Jolla Cove perspective as advertised on every postcard stand in town. If you want to get up close and personal with the oceanic scene, head to the **Marine Room** (above). Located right on La Jolla Shores beach, the restaurant's windows utilize SeaWorld technology to withstand the seasonal tides that crash into the glass.

Uptown, **Bertrand at Mister A's** (p. 127) sits on the 12th floor at Fifth and Laurel, and the panorama here encompasses Balboa Park (as well as the living rooms of some ritzy condo towers) to the east, downtown to the south, and San Diego Harbor and Point Loma to the west. The vistas here are unsurpassed.

1044 Wall St. (at Herschel), La Jolla. www.whisknladle.com. ℂ **858/551-7575.** Reservations recommended. Main courses $14–$28. AE, DISC, MC, V. Mon–Thurs 11:30am–9pm; Fri 11:30am–10pm; Sat 10am–10pm; Sun 10am–9pm (brunch till 3pm). Free 2-hr. validated parking at Hotel Parisi. Bus: 30.

Inexpensive

The Cottage ★ BREAKFAST/LIGHT FARE   La Jolla's best—and friendliest—breakfast is served at this turn-of-the-20th-century bungalow. The cottage is light and airy, but most diners opt for tables outside, where a charming white picket fence encloses the trellis-shaded brick patio. Omelets and egg dishes feature Mediterranean, Cal-Latino, and classic American touches. Homemade granola is a favorite, as well (it's even packaged and sold to take home). The Cottage also bakes its own muffins, rolls, and coffeecakes. While breakfast dishes are served all day, toward lunchtime the kitchen begins turning out freshly made healthful soups, light meals, and sandwiches. Dinners (served in summer only) are a delight, particularly when you're seated before dark on a balmy night.

7702 Fay Ave. (at Kline St.), La Jolla. www.cottagelajolla.com. © **858/454-8409.** Reservations accepted for dinner only. Main courses $9–$14 breakfast, $9–$15 lunch, $13–$22 dinner. AE, DISC, MC, V. Daily 7:30am–3pm; dinner (May–Sept only) Tues–Sat 5–9:30pm. Bus: 30.

CORONADO

Rather like the conservative aura that pervades the entire "island," Coronado's dining options are reliable, but the restaurants aren't exactly breaking new culinary ground. A couple of exceptions are the dining rooms at **Loews Coronado Bay Resort** (p. 215) and the **Hotel del Coronado** (p. 213). If you're in the mood for a special-occasion meal that'll knock your socks off, consider Loews' **Mistral ★★** (www. loewshotels.com; © **619/424-4000**). With its plushly upholstered, gilded, and view-endowed setting, this stylish dining room wins continual raves from deep-pocketed San Diego foodies willing to cross the bay for inventive and artistic California-Mediterranean creations. Read on for information about the Del's signature restaurant, **1500 Ocean.** If you can manage to tear your attention away from the view, you'll notice there's excellent Mexican food at **Candelas** (p. 122), as well as more gringo-style fare at popular **Miguel's Cocina,** 1351 Orange Ave. (www.brigantine.com; © **619/437-4237**).

Very Expensive

1500 Ocean ★★ CALIFORNIAN   The Hotel del Coronado's longtime fine dining option, the **Prince of Wales,** was dethroned by 1500 Ocean, which opened to enthusiastic reviews in 2006. This smart, contemporary space eschews the Del's ever-present Victoriana for a stylish California Craftsman look. The menu is California-oriented as well, featuring a Southland coastal cuisine that draws inspiration—and top-quality product—from Baja to Santa Barbara. A four-course tasting menu ($75) is offered, as well as entrees like lamb porterhouse with stewed fennel and pan-seared scallops in a black truffle vinaigrette. For dessert, don't miss the spicy chipotle chocolate cake, if it's available. There's also fabulous patio dining with views of the ocean and Point Loma.

1500 Orange Ave., Coronado. www.hoteldel.com. © **619/522-8490.** Reservations recommended. Main courses $31–$48. AE, DC, DISC, MC, V. Tues–Sat 5:30–10pm. Bar Tues–Sat 5–11pm. Bus: 901 or 904.

Expensive

The Brigantine AMERICAN/SEAFOOD   The Brigantine is best known for its oyster-bar happy hour (Mon 3–6pm, Tues–Fri 3–6pm, Sun 4:30–10pm); beer, margaritas, and food are heavily discounted, and you can expect standing room only. Prix fixe specials include a seafood, steak, or chicken entree served with soup or salad, a side of veggies, and bread for $19 to $25 (Mon 5–10pm, Tues–Thurs 5–6:30pm, Sun 4:30–6:30pm). The food is good, not great, but the congenial atmosphere is a certifiable draw. Inside, the decor is upscale and resolutely nautical; outside, there's a pleasant patio with heaters to take the chill off the night air. At lunch, you can get everything from crab cakes or fish and chips to fresh fish or pasta. There are several other Brig locations, including Point Loma (the original), 2725 Shelter Island Dr. (© **619/224-2871**), and Del Mar, 3263 Camino del Mar (© **858/481-1166**).

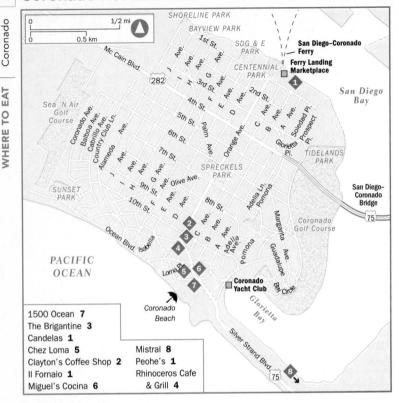

1500 Ocean 7
The Brigantine 3
Candelas 1
Chez Loma 5
Clayton's Coffee Shop 2
Il Fornaio 1
Miguel's Cocina 6

Mistral 8
Peohe's 1
Rhinoceros Cafe & Grill 4

1333 Orange Ave., Coronado. www.brigantine.com. ℂ **619/435-4166.** Reservations recommended on weekends. Main courses $9–$18 lunch, $16–$48 dinner. AE, DC, MC, V. Mon–Thurs 11:30am–9pm; Fri–Sat 11:30am–9:30pm; Sun 4:30–9pm. Small parking lot. Bus: 901 or 904.

Chez Loma ★ FRENCH   This intimate Victorian cottage filled with antiques and subdued candlelight makes for romantic dining. The building dates from 1889, the French restaurant from 1975. Tables are scattered throughout the house and on the enclosed garden terrace; an upstairs wine salon, reminiscent of a Victorian parlor, is a cozy spot. Among the entrees are roasted salmon in a horseradish crust with smoked-tomato vinaigrette, and roast duck with lingonberry, port, and burnt orange sauce. Follow dinner with a cheese platter with berries and port sauce, or a dessert sampler. California wines and American microbrews are available, in addition to a full bar. Early birds enjoy specially priced meals: $25 for a three-course dinner until 5:45pm and all night on Tuesday.

1132 Loma (off Orange Ave.), Coronado. www.chezloma.com. ℂ **619/435-0661.** Reservations recommended. Main courses $24–$37. AE, DC, DISC, MC, V. Tues–Sun 5–9pm. Bus: 901 or 904.

Moderate

Rhinoceros Cafe & Grille ★ AMERICAN   This light, bright bistro is more casual than it looks from the street and offers large portions, though the kitchen can be a little heavy-handed with sauces and spices. At lunch, try the popular penne à la vodka in creamy tomato sauce; favorite dinner specials include Italian cioppino, Southwestern-style meatloaf, and salmon poached and crusted with herb sauce. Plenty of crispy fresh salads balance out the menu; *vino* drinkers will find a fair wine list.

1166 Orange Ave., Coronado. www.rhinocafe.com. ✆ **619/435-2121.** Reservations recommended. Main courses $6–$12 lunch, $12–$28 dinner. AE, DC, DISC, MC, V. Daily 11am–10pm. Street parking usually available. Bus: 901 or 904.

Inexpensive

Clayton's Coffee Shop 🍴 AMERICAN/BREAKFAST   The Hotel Del isn't the only relic of a bygone era in Coronado—just wait until you see this humble neighborhood favorite. Clayton's has occupied this corner spot forever, and it still serves up plain American good eatin' for under $10. The horseshoe counter, chrome bar stools, and well-worn pleather-lined booths are "retro," but the burgers, fries, and turkey noodle soup are timeless and quite tasty—plus you can still play three oldies for a quarter on the table-side jukebox. Behind the coffee shop is Clayton's *hermana* restaurant, **Mexican Take Out,** 1107 10th St. (✆ **619/437-8811**). This closet-size, no-frills spot does a brisk business in tamales and other Mexican staples. As the straightforward name implies, it's takeout only.

979 Orange Ave., Coronado. ✆ **619/435-5425.** Main courses $7–$10. DISC, MC, V. Mon–Sat 6am–9pm; Sun 6am–8pm. Bus: 901 or 904.

BITES OFF THE (TOURIST) BEATEN PATH

Don't limit your dining experience in San Diego to the main tourist zones outlined above. Five minutes north of Mission Valley is the mostly business neighborhood of Kearny Mesa, home to San Diego's best Asian venues. **Jasmine Seafood Restaurant** ★, 4609 Convoy St. (www.jasmineseafood.com; ✆ **858/268-0888**), is the city's premier dim sum lunch spot; dinner is highlighted by the Cantonese-style roast duck (service here can range from gruff to incomprehensible, though). Other notable Chinese restaurants include **China Max** ★, 4698 Convoy St. (www.chinamaxsandiego.com; ✆ **858/650-3333**); **Spicy City** ★, 4690 Convoy St. (www.spicycity.menutoeat.com; ✆ **858/278-1818**); and **Dumpling Inn** ★, 4619 Convoy St. (http://dumplinginn.menutoeat.com; ✆ **858/268-9638**).

For a dining experience that will transport you straight to Japan, seek out tiny **Wa Dining Okan** ★★, 3860 Convoy St. (www.okanus.com; ✆ **858/279-0941**). This friendly, hard-to-find spot has become a sensation (you'll need reservations); it serves traditional, home-style delicacies just like your mother would make, if she were Japanese ("okan" translates as "mom"). It's tucked into a shopping mall next to a Japanese market and has little signage.

East of Hillcrest in Kensington you'll find the **Kensington Grill** ★★, 4055 Adams Ave. (www.kensingtongrill.com; ✆ **619/281-4014**), next to the Ken Cinema.

It's owned by the same crew in charge of the dining hot spot **Cucina Urbana** (p. 128) and features contemporary American cuisine in a chic setting that draws lots of neighborhood types. Across the street is the lively, authentically rustic **Bleu Bohème ★★**, 4090 Adams Ave. (www.bleuboheme.com; ✆ **619/255-4167**). This boisterous bistro is known for its mussels, meat and cheese platters, and French onion soup. In nearby Normal Heights, **Jyoti Bihanga ★**, 3351 Adams Ave. (www.jyotibihanga.com; ✆ **619/282-4116**), delivers a vegetarian menu of Indian-influenced salads, wraps, and curries; the "neatloaf," made with grains and tofu, is a winner. Entrees are priced under $13.

South of Adams Avenue, University Avenue runs through North Park (p. 32). This working-class neighborhood has been infused with new life and new development, most notably the resurrected North Park Theatre. Next door to the theater is **Spread ★**, 2879 University Ave. (www.spreadtherestaurant.com; ✆ **619/543-0406**), where the "nouveau comfort food" menu is vegetarian/vegan, relying on a daily influx of seasonal, organic products. Excellent health-conscious Mexican food (yes, it does exist) is found at **Ranchos Cocina ★**, 3910 30th St. (www.ranchoscocinanorthpark.com; ✆ **619/574-1288**), just off University Avenue. This popular eatery will even prepare you something vegan—try asking for *that* in Old Town. There is also an outlet in Ocean Beach at 1830 Sunset Cliffs Blvd. (www.ranchosnaturalfoods.com; ✆ **619/226-7619**). **Jayne's Gastropub ★**, 4677 30th St. (www.jaynesgastropub.com; ✆ **619/563-1011**), reflects the neighborhood's casual cool, featuring a sophisticated beer and wine list, and a menu that runs from mussels with chorizo to a stupendous burger.

Out in the far-flung 'burb of Rancho Bernardo awaits one of San Diego's most memorable dining experiences. **El Bizcocho ★★★** is the fine-dining restaurant at the golf and tennis resort Rancho Bernardo Inn, 17550 Bernardo Oaks Dr. (www.ranchobernardoinn.com; ✆ **858/675-8550**). It's one of the last of San Diego's formal, gourmet experiences, serving contemporary American fare, as well as Sunday brunch. No tennis shoes or denim are allowed; jackets and ties are suggested (but not required) for men.

PRACTICAL MATTERS: THE RESTAURANT SCENE

While San Diego hasn't quite achieved top-tier foodie status, its culinary profile is at an all-time high. The city still clings to conservative tastes and service can sometimes be casual to the point of indifference, but the pieces are in place and San Diego's dining renaissance is well underway.

Number one on most visitors' list of culinary priorities is Mexican food—a logical choice given the city's history and location. You'll find lots of Americanized, fairly satisfying interpretations of Mexican fare (that is, combo plates heaped with melted cheddar cheese) along with a few hidden gems.

Plan on making reservations a day or two in advance for dining on a Friday or Saturday night, particularly downtown or in La Jolla. You can either call restaurants directly or go to www.opentable.com to make online reservations. And in keeping with the prevalent beach culture, even in the more pricey places, dress tends to be relaxed.

For diners on a budget, the more expensive San Diego restaurants are usually accommodating if you prefer to order a few appetizers instead of a main course, and many offer reasonably priced lunch menus. Some also feature modestly priced bar and lounge menus; and just about every bar will offer food and/or drink bargains at happy hour (usually Mon–Fri, 5–7pm). Worthwhile discount coupons are found in the *San Diego Reader,* available free on Thursdays, and quite a few restaurants offer "early bird" specials—discounted dining for those who don't mind being seated by 6pm or so.

Drivers can expect to park within 2 or 3 blocks of a restaurant. If you can't find a free or metered space on the street, you can seek out a garage or lot; many restaurants also offer valet parking. On evenings when the Padres are playing (Apr–Sept) or when a big convention fills area hotels, you'll compete for parking downtown. Fortunately, pedicabs—three-wheeled bikes that carry two or three passengers each—are easy to hire. But if you take a taxi or the trolley downtown on game nights, you'll find most restaurants easy to get into once the baseball crowd has made its way into the ballpark and the first pitch is thrown.

RESTAURANTS BY CUISINE

AMERICAN

Bankers Hill Bar + Restaurant ★★ (Bankers Hill, $$, p. 128)

Bertrand at Mister A's ★★★ (Hillcrest/Uptown, $$$, p. 127)

Brian's 24 Restaurant Bar & Grill (Downtown, $$, p. 124)

The Brigantine (Coronado and other locations, $$$, p. 143)

Burger Lounge ★ (Coronado, Gaslamp Quarter, Hillcrest, Kensington, Little Italy, La Jolla, $, p. 126)

Clayton's Coffee Shop (Coronado, $, p. 145)

Corvette Diner (Point Loma, $, p. 137)

Cowboy Star ★★ (Downtown, $$$, p. 122)

Danny's Palm Bar & Grill (Coronado, $, p. 126)

El Bizcocho ★★★ (Rancho Bernardo, $$$$, p. 146)

The Green Flash (Pacific Beach, $$, p. 142)

Hash House a Go Go ★ (Hillcrest/Uptown, $$, p. 127)

Hob Nob Hill ★ (Hillcrest/Uptown, $$, p. 127)

Hodad's ★ (Downtown, Ocean Beach, $, p. 126)

Jayne's Gastropub ★ (North Park, $$, p. 146)

Kensington Grill ★★ (Kensington, $$$, p. 145)

The Linkery ★★ (North Park, $$, p. 129)

Neighborhood ★★ (Downtown, $, p. 126)

Nick's at the Pier (Coronado, $$, p. 142)

Rhinoceros Cafe & Grille ★ (Coronado, $$, p. 145)

Rocky's Crown Pub (Pacific Beach, $, p. 126)

Searsucker ★★ (Downtown, $$$, p. 124)

South Beach Bar & Grill (Ocean Beach, $, p. 134)

Tioli's Crazee Burger ★ (North Park, Old Town, $, p. 126)

The Tractor Room ★★ (Hillcrest/Uptown, $$, p. 128)

25 Forty Bistro & Bakehouse ★ (Old Town, $$, p. 132)

Urban Solace ★★ (North Park, $$, p. 130)

Whisknladle ★★ (La Jolla, $$, p. 141)

World Famous ★ (Pacific Beach, $$, p. 142)

BREAKFAST

Brockton Villa ★ (La Jolla, $$, p. 141)

Cafe 222 ★ (Downtown, $$, p. 121)

Clayton's Coffee Shop (Coronado, $, p. 145)

Coffee Cup ★ (La Jolla, $, p. 138)

The Cottage ★ (La Jolla, $, p. 142)

Hash House a Go Go ★ (Hillcrest/Uptown, $$, p. 127)

Hob Nob Hill ★ (Hillcrest/Uptown, $$, p. 127)

Isabel's Cantina ★ (Pacific Beach, $$, p. 133)

Kono's Surf Club Cafe (Pacific Beach, $, p. 133)

The Mission ★ (Downtown, Mission Beach, North Park, $, p. 137)

Richard Walker's Pancake House ★ (Downtown, $, p. 121)

Snooze ★★ (Hillcrest, $, p. 131)

CALIFORNIAN

Baleen ★★ (Mission Bay, $$$$, p. 134)

Brockton Villa ★ (La Jolla, $$, p. 141)

1500 Ocean ★★ (Coronado, $$$$, p. 143)

George's at the Cove ★★★ (La Jolla, $$$, p. 140)

Grant Grill ★★ (Downtown, $$$, p. 121)

Indigo Grill ★ (Little Italy, $$$, p. 123)

The Marine Room ★★★ (La Jolla, $$$$, p. 138)

Mistral ★★ (Coronado, $$$, p. 143)

Nine-Ten ★★★ (La Jolla, $$$$, p. 138)

Stingaree ★ (Downtown, $$$, p. 121)

The Westgate Room ★ (Downtown, $$$, p. 121)

CHINESE

China Max ★ (Kearny Mesa, $$, p. 145)

Dumpling Inn ★ (Kearny Mesa, $, p. 145)

Jasmine Seafood Restaurant ★ (Kearny Mesa, $$, p. 145)

Red Pearl Kitchen ★★ (Downtown, $$, p. 125)

Spicy City ★ (Kearny Mesa, $$, p. 145)

DESSERTS

Extraordinary Desserts ★★★ (Hillcrest/Uptown, Little Italy, $, p. 125)

Michele Coulon Dessertier ★★ (La Jolla, $, p. 138)

FRENCH

Bleu Bohème ★★ (Kensington, $$, p. 146)

BO-beau ★ (Ocean Beach, $$, p. 136)

Cafe Chloe ★★ (Downtown, $$, p. 124)

Chez Loma ★ (Coronado, $$$, p. 144)

The Marine Room ★★★ (La Jolla, $$$$, p. 138)

Sky Room ★★ (La Jolla, $$$$, p. 138)

Tapenade ★★★ (La Jolla, $$$, p. 140)

The 3rd Corner ★★ (Ocean Beach, Encinitas, $$, p. 137)

INTERNATIONAL

Bandar ★ (Downtown, $$, p. 121)

Costa Brava ★★ (Pacific Beach, $$, p. 134)

Isabel's Cantina ★ (Pacific Beach, $$, p. 133)

The Restaurant at the W ★★ (Downtown, $$$, p. 121)

ITALIAN

Bencotto Italian Kitchen ★★ (Little Italy, $$, p. 121)

Bronx Pizza ★ (Hillcrest/Uptown, $, p. 130)

Buon Appetito ★★ (Little Italy, $$, p. 121)

Caffé Bella Italia ★★ (Pacific Beach, $$, p. 136)

Cucina Urbana ★★★ (Hillcrest/Uptown, $$, p. 128)

Filippi's Pizza Grotto (Downtown, Pacific Beach, and other locations, $, p. 126)

Il Fornaio (Coronado, $$, p. 142)

Po Pazzo ★ (Little Italy, $$$, p. 121)

Sogno DiVino ★ (Little Italy, $, p. 121)

Solare (Point Loma, $$, p. 136)

25 Forty Bistro & Bakehouse ★ (Old Town, $$, p. 132)

LATIN AMERICAN

Berta's Latin American Restaurant ★ (Old Town, $$, p. 132)

LIGHT FARE

Bread & Cie. ★★ (Hillcrest/Uptown, $, p. 130)

The Cottage ★ (La Jolla, $, p. 142)

Extraordinary Desserts ★★★ (Little Italy, $, p. 125)

Michele Coulon Dessertier ★★ (La Jolla, $, p. 138)

The Mission ★ (Downtown, Mission Beach, North Park, $, p. 137)

Prepkitchen ★★ (Del Mar, La Jolla, Little Italy, $, p. 141)

MEDITERRANEAN

Anthology ★★★ (Downtown, $$$, p. 122)

Bertrand at Mister A's ★★★ (Hillcrest/Uptown, $$$, p. 127)

BO-beau ★ (Ocean Beach, $$, p. 136)

Bread & Cie. ★★ (Hillcrest/Uptown, $, p. 130)

Mistral ★★ (Coronado, $$$, p. 143)

Sally's ★★ (Downtown, $$$, p. 121)

MEXICAN

Candelas ★★ (Downtown, Coronado, $$$, p. 122)

Casa Guadalajara (Old Town, $$, p. 132)

El Agave Tequileria ★★ (Old Town, $$$, p. 131)

El Camino ★ (Little Italy, $$, p. 125)

El Zarape ★ (Hillcrest/Uptown, $, p. 134)

Lucha Libre Gourmet Taco Shop ★ (Mission Hills, $, p. 134)

Mamá Testa ★★ (Hillcrest/Uptown, $, p. 130)

Miguel's Cocina (Coronado, $$, p. 143)

Old Town Mexican Cafe (Old Town, $, p. 131)

Pokez Mexican Restaurant (Downtown, $, p. 121)

Ranchos Cocina ★ (North Park, Ocean Beach, $$, p. 146)

Rubio's Fresh Mexican Grill (throughout the city, $, p. 134)

Su Casa (La Jolla, $$, p. 138)

Wahoo's Fish Taco (La Jolla, Mission Valley, and other locations $, p. 134)

PACIFIC RIM/ASIAN FUSION

Bali Hai (Shelter Island, $$, p. 142)

Nobu ★★ (Downtown, $$$$, p. 121)

Red Pearl Kitchen ★★ (Downtown, $$, p. 125)

Roppongi ✋ (La Jolla, $$$, p. 140)

Underbelly ★★ (Little Italy, $, p. 127)

Wa Dining Okan ★★ (Kearny Mesa, $$, p. 145)

SEAFOOD

Baleen ★★ (Mission Bay, $$$$, p. 134)

Bay Park Fish Co. ★ (Bay Park, $$, p. 134)

Blue Water Seafood Market and Grill ★ (Mission Hills, $$, p. 134)

The Brigantine (Coronado and other locations, $$$, p. 143)

The Fishery ★ (Pacific Beach, $$, p. 136)

The Fish Market/Top of the Market ★ (Downtown, Del Mar, $$, p. 125)

Island Prime ★★ (Harbor Island, $$$, p. 122)

JRDN ★ (Pacific Beach, $$$, p. 133)

The Oceanaire Seafood Room ★★★ (Downtown, $$$, p. 124)

Peohe's (Coronado, $$, p. 142)

Point Loma Seafoods ★ (Point Loma, $, p. 134)

World Famous ★ (Pacific Beach, $$, p. 142)

Zenbu ★★ (La Jolla, Cardiff-by-the-Sea, $$$, p. 140)

SUSHI

The Fish Market/Top of the Market ★ (Downtown, Del Mar, $$, p. 125)

Harney Sushi ★ (Old Town, Oceanside, $$, p. 131)

Nobu ★★ (Downtown, $$$$, p. 121)

Sushi Ota ★★★ (Pacific Beach, $$, p. 136)

Zenbu ★★ (La Jolla, Cardiff-by-the-Sea, $$$, p. 140)

THAI

Rama ★ (Downtown, $$, p. 121)
Saffron ★ (Mission Hills, $$, p. 127)
Spice & Rice Thai Kitchen ★ (La Jolla, $$, p. 141)

VEGETARIAN

Jyoti Bihanga ★ (Normal Heights, $, p. 146)
Pokez Mexican Restaurant (Downtown, $, p. 121)
Ranchos Cocina ★ (North Park, Ocean Beach, $$, p. 146)
Spread ★ (North Park, $$, p. 146)

SHOPPING

W hether you're looking for a souvenir, a gift, or a quick replacement for an item inadvertently left at home, you'll find no shortage of stores in San Diego. This is, after all, Southern California, where looking good is a high priority and shopping in sunny outdoor malls is a way of life.

SHOPPING BY AREA

Downtown, the Gaslamp Quarter & Little Italy

In the Gaslamp Quarter, high rents have led to the influx of deep-pocketed chains and brand names, such as **Urban Outfitters,** 665 Fifth Ave. (www. urbanoutfitters.com; ☎ **619/231-0102**); **Quiksilver,** 402 Fifth Ave. (www. quiksilver.com; ☎ **619/234-3125**); and **G-Star,** 470 Fifth Ave. (www.g-star.com; ☎ **619/238-7088**). A few intrepid boutiques can still be found among the big retailers and the area's multitudinous eateries, though.

For hip and glamorous women's clothing, *Project Runway* contestant Gordana Gehlhausen offers her designs at **GOGA by Gordana,** 401 Market St. (www.shopgoga.com; ☎ **619/564-7660**); or check out the new vintage-style fashions at **Bettie Page,** 430 Fifth Ave. (www.bettie pageclothing.com; ☎ **619/544-1950**); **Kita Ceramics & Glassware,** 517 Fourth Ave. (www.kitaceramicsglass.com; ☎ **619/239-2600**), stocks fine Japanese pottery and colorful Italian glass products. **HatWorks,** 433 E St. (☎ **619/234-0457**), has had a presence in downtown since 1922; if you've got a head, they have something to fit your style, from Stetson to Kangol. Animation fans will want to duck into **Chuck Jones Gallery,** 232 Fifth Ave. (www.chuckjones.com; ☎ **619/294-9880**); it features animation cels by the likes of Dr. Seuss and Jones himself, who was creator of Bugs Bunny, Daffy Duck, and others. There's also high-end and contemporary art at two sister galleries downtown: **Alexander Salazar Fine Art,** 640 Broadway (www.alexandersalazarfineart.com; ☎ **619/531-8996**), and **White Box Contemporary,** 1040 Seventh Ave. (www.white boxcontemporary.com; ☎ **619/531-8996**).

You never can tell what might pop up at **Industry Showroom,** 345 Sixth Ave. (☎ **619/701-2162;** www.industryshowroom.com), a "retail experiment" featuring art, design, and fashion in a DIY collective environment. Once a month, Industry Showroom also hosts its indie **Bohemian Market,** bringing in even more crafty vendors and entertainment.

You can continue your search for serious art, design, and home furnishings in Little Italy. The conglomeration of stores and galleries along Kettner Boulevard and India Street, from Laurel to Date streets, has become known as the **Kettner Art & Design District.** Throughout the year, Friday evening open-house events known as Kettner Nights are scheduled; for information, check www.littleitalysd.com. Among the district's highlights for modern furnishings and accessories are **Boomerang for Modern,** 2475 Kettner Blvd. (www.boomerang formodern.com; ✆ **619/239-2040**); **Mixture,** 2210 Kettner Blvd. (www.mixture home.com; ✆ **619/239-4788**); and **DNA European Design Studio,** 750 W. Fir St. (www.dnaeuropeandesign.com; ✆ **619/235-6882**). Look for fine art at **Noel-Baza Fine Art,** 2165 India St. (www.noel-bazafineart.com; ✆ **619/876-4160**), and ocean- and San Diego-themed work at **Pecoff Gallery,** 1825 India St. (www.pecoff. com; ✆ **619/231-1991**). **Subtext Gallery,** 2479 Kettner Blvd. (www.subtextgallery. com; ✆ **619/546-8800**), is a way-cool art-and-design gallery and bookstore. And if you don't have a chance to make it to Mexico, drop by **Casa Artelexia,** 2419 Kettner Blvd. (www.artelexia.com; ✆ **619/544-1011**)—it brings Mexico to you.

The nearby Fir Street Cottages are a quaint cluster of festively painted stores where the highlights include **Carol Gardyne,** 1840 Columbia St. (www.carol gardyne.com; ✆ **619/233-8066**), which has hand-painted, one-of-a-kind silk scarves and wall hangings; **Vitreum,** 619 W. Fir St. (www.vitreum-us.com; ✆ **619/ 237-9810**), an artfully Zen shop that sells glassware, as well home decor, tea sets, tableware, and jewelry; and **Rosamariposa,** 611 W. Fir St. (www.rosamariposasd. com; ✆ **619/237-8064**), stocking exotic (but responsibly crafted) baubles and bangles from Indonesia and India.

Downtown's two destination shopping centers are:

Horton Plaza ★ The Disneyland of shopping malls, Horton Plaza is the heart of the revitalized city center, bounded by Broadway, First and Fourth avenues, and G Street. Covering 6½ city blocks, the multilevel shopping center has more than 130 specialty shops and kiosks—there are clothing and shoe stores, fun shops for kids, and a bookstore. There's a performing arts venue (the Lyceum Theatre, home to the San Diego Repertory Theatre, p. 169), a 14-screen cinema, two major department stores, and a variety of restaurants and short-order eateries. Horton Plaza opened in 1985 to rave reviews and provided an initial catalyst for the Gaslamp Quarter's redevelopment. It's almost as much an attraction as SeaWorld or the San Diego Zoo, transcending its genre with a conglomeration of crisscrossing paths, bridges, towers, and piazzas.

Anchor stores are Macy's and Nordstrom, while name outlets such as Abercrombie & Fitch, Victoria's Secret, and Louis Vuitton are also in the mix; the top-level food court has a good variety of meal options, too. Three hours of free parking are available from 7am to 9pm; there are machines scattered throughout the mall where you can self-validate. The lot is open 24 hours and costs $8 per hour. The parking levels are confusing, and temporarily losing your car is part of the Horton Plaza experience; if you need help or information, you can find a plaza concierge on the first level (daily 10am–6pm). There's also a Downtown Information Center (✆ **619/235-2222**), open Monday through Friday, 9am to 5pm. 324 Horton Plaza. www.westfield.com/horton-plaza. ✆ **619/239-8180.** Bus: 2, 3, 7, 11, 15, 30, 50, 120, 150, 210, 810, 820, 850, 860, 901, 923, or 992. Trolley: Civic Center.

Seaport Village ☺ Designed as an ersatz seaside community, this choice, 14-acre bayfront outdoor mall provides an idyllic setting that visitors love. Many of the more than 50 shops are of the Southern California cutesy variety, but the atmosphere is

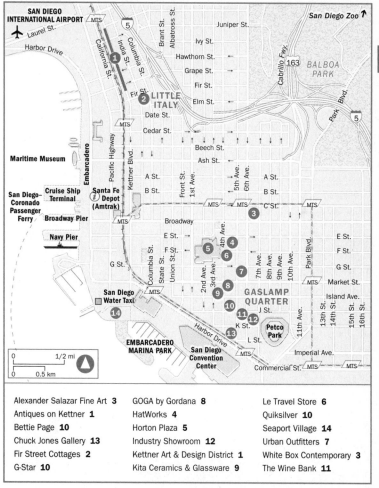

Alexander Salazar Fine Art **3**	GOGA by Gordana **8**	Le Travel Store **6**
Antiques on Kettner **1**	HatWorks **4**	Quiksilver **10**
Bettie Page **10**	Horton Plaza **5**	Seaport Village **14**
Chuck Jones Gallery **13**	Industry Showroom **12**	Urban Outfitters **7**
Fir Street Cottages **2**	Kettner Art & Design District **1**	White Box Contemporary **3**
G-Star **10**	Kita Ceramics & Glassware **9**	The Wine Bank **11**

pleasant, and there are a few gems. Favorites include the **Tile Shop,** featuring hand-painted tiles from Mexico and beyond; **Best of San Diego,** where you can stock up on all your city-themed souvenir needs; and the **Upstart Crow** bookshop and cof-feehouse, with the Crow's Nest children's bookstore inside. Other stores specialize in kites, hammocks, travel accessories, and more. There are four sit-down restaurants and a variety of sidewalk eateries, and live music is often scheduled for weekend afternoons; the carousel, with its hand-carved menagerie dating from 1895, is a popu-lar draw with families. Two hours of parking are $1 with purchase ($4 per hr. thereaf-ter). Open daily 10am to 9pm; restaurants have extended hours. 849 W. Harbor Dr. (at Kettner Blvd.). www.seaportvillage.com. © **619/235-4014.** Trolley: Seaport Village.

Hillcrest & Uptown

Compact Hillcrest is an ideal shopping destination. As the hub of San Diego's gay and lesbian community, hip fashion and chic housewares are the order of the day here. There are plenty of establishments selling cool trinkets, used books, vintage clothing, and memorabilia; you'll also find a plethora of modestly priced globe-hopping dining options, too.

Street parking is available; most meters run 2 hours and devour quarters at a rate of one every 12 minutes. Some blocks have just one meter; use cash or credit card to get a receipt to place on your dashboard. You can also park in a lot—rates vary, but you'll come out ahead if you're planning to stroll for several hours. There's no defined zone in which shops are found, so you may as well start at the neighborhood's axis, the busy intersection of University and Fifth avenues. From this corner the greatest concentration of boutiques spreads for 1 or 2 blocks in each direction, but farther east on University—between 10th Avenue and Vermont Street—you'll find another aggregation of good options, especially in the home furnishing category. **Co-Habitat,** 1433 University Ave. (www.cohabitathome.com; ✆ **619/688-1390**), has colorful decor and textiles from India; **Nativa,** 1003 University Ave. (www.nativafurniture. com; ✆ **619/299-4664**), has a huge showroom with sumptuous furniture made mostly from plantation-grown South American wood; while **Furniture and Treasures,** 1251 University Ave. (www.furnitureandtreasures.com; ✆ **619/294-4228**), offers just that.

If you're looking for postcards or provocative gifts, step into wacky **Babette Schwartz,** 421 University Ave. (www.babette.com; ✆ **619/220-7048**), a pop-culture emporium named for a local drag queen and located under the can't-miss HILLCREST street sign. You'll find books, clothing, and kitsch accessories. A couple of doors away, **Cathedral,** 435 University Ave. (www.shopcathedral.com; ✆ **619/296-4046**), is stocked with candles of all scents and shapes, plus unusual holders.

If all this walking is wearing a hole in your shoes, you can get a pair of urban-fabulous sneakers at **Mint,** 525 University Ave. (www.mintshoes.com; ✆ **619/291-6468**); nearby are **Urban Outfitters,** 3946 Fifth Ave. (www.urbanoutfitters.com; ✆ **619/209-5279**), and **American Apparel,** 3867 Fourth Ave. (www.american apparel.net; ✆ **619/291-1845**). Headgear—from straw hats to knit caps to classy fedoras—fills the **Village Hat Shop,** 3821 Fourth Ave. (www.villagehatshop.com; ✆ **619/683-5533**); there's also a minimuseum of stylishly displayed vintage hats.

Lovers of rare and used books will want to poke around the **used bookstores** on Fifth Avenue, between University and Robinson avenues. Though their number has decreased with the advent of online shopping, you can always find something to pique your interest. This block is also home to a couple of vintage clothing/secondhand style outposts: **Flashbacks Recycled Fashions,** 3849 Fifth Ave. (www.flash backintime.com; ✆ **619/291-4200**), and **Buffalo Exchange,** 3862 Fifth Ave. (www.buffaloexchange.com; ✆ **619/298-4411**).

To the north and east of Hillcrest are University Heights and North Park, which are brimming with interesting shops. You'll find independent-minded boutiques such as **Mimi & Red,** 3032 University Ave. (www.mimiandred.com; ✆ **619/298-7933**), and **Pigment,** 3827 30th St. (www.shoppigment.com; ✆ **619/501-6318**), which offers everything from pet accessories to home decor; there are also unusual gift stores such as **Vintage Religion,** 3821 32nd St. (www.vintagereligion.com; ✆ **619/280-8408**), selling jewelry, apparel, and collectibles inspired by global religions and cultures.

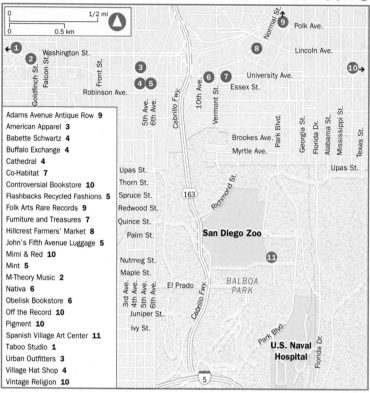

Adams Avenue Antique Row **9**
American Apparel **3**
Babette Schwartz **4**
Buffalo Exchange **4**
Cathedral **4**
Co-Habitat **7**
Controversial Bookstore **10**
Flashbacks Recycled Fashions **5**
Folk Arts Rare Records **9**
Furniture and Treasures **7**
Hillcrest Farmers' Market **8**
John's Fifth Avenue Luggage **5**
Mimi & Red **10**
Mint **5**
M-Theory Music **2**
Nativa **6**
Obelisk Bookstore **6**
Off the Record **10**
Pigment **10**
Spanish Village Art Center **11**
Taboo Studio **1**
Urban Outfitters **3**
Village Hat Shop **4**
Vintage Religion **10**

Running east from where Park Boulevard T-bones Adams Avenue is the area once known as **Adams Avenue Antique Row.** It doesn't have the concentration of antiques stores it once had, but along with vintage-clothing boutiques and used book and record shops, there are plenty of coffeehouses, pubs, and small restaurants to enliven the excursion. The district stretches a couple miles from Arizona Street to Normal Heights, so it's best tackled by car. For more information, contact the **Adams Avenue Business Association** (www.adamsavenuebusiness.com; ✆ **619/282-7329**).

Old Town & Mission Valley

Old Town State Historic Park features restored historic sites and adobe structures, a number of which now house shops that cater to tourists. Many have a "general-store" theme and carry gourmet treats and inexpensive Mexican crafts alongside the obligatory T-shirts, baseball caps, and other San Diego–emblazoned souvenirs. **Fiesta de Reyes,** Juan Street, between Wallace and Mason streets (www.fiestade reyes.com; ✆ **619/297-3100**), maintains the park's old *Californio* theme, and features more than a dozen specialty shops, and three restaurants. Costumed employees, special events and activities, and strolling musicians add to the festive flavor at this quaint courtyard surrounded by shady arcades.

There's also plenty of shopping outside the park, too. **Bazaar del Mundo,** 4133 Taylor St. (www.bazaardelmundo.com; ℂ **619/296-3161**), has a gaggle of stores featuring Mexican and Latin American folk art, accessories, and clothing; Old Town's best spot for Mexican collectibles, though, is **Miranda's Courtyard,** 2548 Congress St. (ℂ **619/296-6611**). For museum-quality nautical antiques—from sextants to diving suits—check out **West Sea Company,** 2495 Congress St. (www.westsea.com; ℂ **619/296-5356**); or, for a fine collection of Native American art and jewelry, breeze into **Four Winds Trading,** 2448 San Diego Ave. (www.4windsarts.com; ℂ **619/692-0466**). You can also watch as one-of-a-kind glass art is created at **Lowery's Hot Glass,** 3985 Harney St. (www.loweryshotglass.com; ℂ **619/297-3473**), an Old Town staple since 1995.

Mission Valley is home to two giant malls, **Fashion Valley Center** (p. 164) and **Mission Valley Center** (p. 164), with more than enough stores to satisfy any shopper, and free parking—both can be reached via the San Diego Trolley from downtown.

Mission Bay & the Beaches

The beach communities offer laid-back shopping, with plenty of surf shops, recreational gear, and casual garb. If you're looking for something more distinctive than T-shirts and shorts, you'd best head east to Mission Valley or north to La Jolla.

For women in need of a new bikini, the best selection is at **Pilar's,** 3745 Mission Blvd., Mission Beach (www.pilarsbeachwear.com; ℂ **858/488-3056**), where choices range from stylish designer numbers to suits inspired by surf- and skate-wear. Across the street is **Liquid Foundation Surf Shop,** 3731 Mission Blvd. (www.liquidfoundationsurfshop.com; ℂ **858/488-3260**), which specializes in board shorts for guys. For affordable shoes, check out the **Skechers USA,** 4475 Mission Blvd. (www.skechers.com; ℂ **858/581-6010**), at the corner of Garnet Avenue; **Chillers Showroom,** 4667 Cass St. (www.chillersshowroom.com; ℂ **858/274-3112**), has his and hers clothing and accessories, and you can even design your own custom screen-printed T-shirt.

In Pacific Beach, **Pangaea Outpost,** 909 Garnet Ave. (www.pangaeaoutpost.com; ℂ **858/581-0555**), gathers more than 70 diverse artists and merchants under one roof; while San Diego's greatest concentration of antiques stores is found in the **Ocean Beach Antique District** (www.antiquesinsandiego.com), along the 4800 block of Newport Avenue, the community's main drag. Several of the stores are mall-style, featuring dozens of dealers under one roof, and although you won't find a horde of pricey, centuries-old European antiques, the overall quality is high enough to make it interesting for any collector. Most of the O.B. antiques stores are open daily from 10am to 6pm, with somewhat shorter hours Sunday.

If you've come to O.B. for that hippie vibe, you can find it alive and well at **the Black,** 5017 Newport Ave. (ℂ **619/222-5498**), an old-fashioned head shop that's a local institution, and **Falling Sky Pottery,** 1951 Abbott St. (ℂ **619/226-6820**), a collective of potters that's been around since the late 1960s.

La Jolla

It's clear from the look of La Jolla's village that shopping is a major pastime in this upscale community. Precious gems and pearl necklaces sparkle in their cases, luxurious Persian rugs await your caress, crystal goblets prism the light—even if you're not in the market for any of it, it makes for great window-shopping. (For a less touristy La Jolla shopping excursion, head about 2 miles south of the village to the Bird Rock

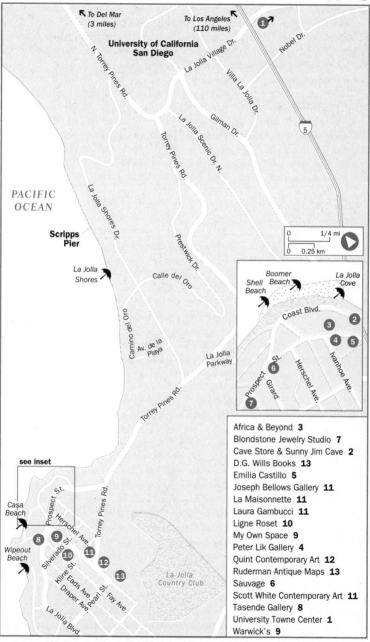

Africa & Beyond **3**
Blondstone Jewelry Studio **7**
Cave Store & Sunny Jim Cave **2**
D.G. Wills Books **13**
Emilia Castillo **5**
Joseph Bellows Gallery **11**
La Maisonnette **11**
Laura Gambucci **11**
Ligne Roset **10**
My Own Space **9**
Peter Lik Gallery **4**
Quint Contemporary Art **12**
Ruderman Antique Maps **13**
Sauvage **6**
Scott White Contemporary Art **11**
Tasende Gallery **8**
University Towne Center **1**
Warwick's **9**

neighborhood. You'll find several blocks of boutiques and dining options between Camino de la Costa and Midway Street; check www.birdrock.org for more information.)

The village clothing boutiques tend to be conservative and costly (and mostly geared toward women), like those lining Girard Avenue and Prospect Street, such as **Armani Exchange, Polo Ralph Lauren,** and **Sigi's Boutique.** But you'll also find less pricey venues like **Banana Republic.**

Laura Gambucci, 7629 Girard Ave., Ste. C3 (✆ **858/551-0214**), bucks the staid trend with contemporary apparel for women; and a sexy, glamorous local line of bathing suits (for her and him) is at **Sauvage,** 1025 Prospect St. (www.sauvagewear. com; ✆ **858/729-0015**). **Blondstone Jewelry Studio,** 925 Prospect St. (www. blondstone.com; ✆ **858/456-1994**), has locally made designs as well, producing adornments that incorporate seashells and tumbled sea-glass "mermaid tears." **Emilia Castillo,** 1273 Prospect St. (✆ **858/551-9600;** www.emiliacastillolajolla. com), features one-of-a-kind jewelry and home decor from a silversmith based in Taxco, Mexico.

You'll find modern and minimalist home furnishings at **My Own Space,** 7840 Girard Ave. (www.mosmyownspace.com; ✆ **866/607-7223** or 858/459-0099), and **Ligne Roset,** 7726 Girard Ave. (www.ligneroset-lajolla.com; ✆ **858/454-3366**); the Ligne Roset showroom is ensconced in what had previously been one of the last single-screen theaters in San Diego. For something a little more traditional, look for the French-country style at **La Maisonnette,** 7631 Girard Ave. (www.lamaisonnette france.com; ✆ **858/551-1222**). History buffs should not miss **Ruderman Antique Maps,** 7463 Girard Ave. (www.raremaps.com; ✆ **858/551-8500**), which sells maps, atlases, and books that date from the 15th through 19th centuries.

There are also more than 20 art galleries in La Jolla village, including two of the city's best for contemporary art: **Quint Contemporary Art,** 7547 Girard Ave. (www. quintgallery.com; ✆ **858/454-3409**), and **Scott White Contemporary Art,** 7655 Girard Ave. (www.scottwhiteart.com; ✆ **858/255-8574**). Although most of the others won't appeal to serious collectors, there are crowd-pleasers such as the sensuous landscape photography at **Peter Lik Gallery,** 1205 Prospect St. (www.peterlik.com; ✆ **858/200-0990**); and **Africa & Beyond,** 1250 Prospect St. (www.africaand beyond.com; ✆ **800/422-3742** or 858/454-9983), with its contemporary and traditional African sculpture, textiles, jewelry, and furnishings. Serene, museumlike **Tasende Gallery,** 820 Prospect St. (✆ **858/454-3691;** www.tasendegallery.com), has sculptural work; **Joseph Bellows Gallery,** 7661 Girard Ave. (www.joseph bellows.com; ✆ **858/456-5620**), exhibits vintage and contemporary photography.

A unique experience awaits at the **Cave Store,** 1325 Coast Blvd., just off Prospect Street (www.cavestore.com; ✆ **858/459-0746**). The shop is equal parts boutique and curio store (that also rents snorkel gear), but the main attraction is the **Sunny Jim Cave,** a large sea cave reached by a steep, narrow staircase that was tunneled through the rock more than 100 years ago; admission is $4 for adults, $3 for kids 3 to 16, free for 2 and under.

Coronado

This rather insular, conservative Navy community doesn't have many stellar shopping opportunities; the best of the lot line Orange Avenue at the southwestern end of the town. You'll find some scattered housewares and home-decor boutiques, several women's boutiques, and resort gift shops.

There is an excellent independent bookshop, **Bay Books,** 1029 Orange Ave. (www. baybookscoronado.com; ✆ **619/435-0070**), which carries a selection in many categories, plus volumes of local historical interest, audio books, and Mexican and European magazines. **In Good Taste,** 1146 Orange Ave. (✆ **619/435-8356**), has a small but choice selection of gourmet gift items—in addition to a tempting display of luscious truffles and sweets. **Zazen,** 1110 First Ave. (✆ **619/435-4780**), is a women's boutique with fine jewelry and accessories; and, if you're in pursuit of swimwear, poke your head into **Dale's Swim Shop,** 1150 Orange Ave. (✆ **619/435-7301**), a tiny shop jam-packed with suits to fit all bodies, including styles from European makers seldom available in this country. You'll find artful cards and stationery at **Seaside Papery,** 1162 Orange Ave. (www.seasidepapery.com; ✆ **619/435-5565**).

Ferry Landing Marketplace Approached by ferry, the entrance is impressive— turreted red rooftops with jaunty blue flags fluttering in the wind. As you stroll up the pier, you'll find yourself in the midst of more than 20 souvenir shops and galleries filled with gifts, jewelry, and crafts. You can get a quick bite to eat or have a leisurely dinner with a view, wander along landscaped walkways, or laze on a beach or grassy bank. Open daily 10am to 7pm or later. There's also a farmers' market every Tuesday from 2:30 to 6pm. 1201 First St. (at B Ave.), Coronado. www.coronadoferrylandingshops.com. ✆ **619/435-8895.** Bus: 904. Ferry: From Broadway Pier or Fifth Ave. Landing. Take I-5 to Coronado Bay Bridge, to B Ave., and turn right.

Elsewhere in San Diego County

The **Cedros Design District ★★**, along the 100 and 200 blocks of South Cedros Avenue in Solana Beach, is an outstanding place for designer interior decorating goods. Many of the shops are housed in a row of Quonset huts that were once used by a company that made photographic equipment for spy planes. Today, you can find more than two dozen chic shops selling furniture, original art, imported goods, home decor, antiques, and clothing, plus a couple of good cafes—there's even a wine-tasting room. The strip is located just north of the Del Mar Racetrack; reach it by taking the Via de la Valle exit off I-5 and going right on Cedros Avenue. The Coaster commuter train stops at the Solana Beach station next to the district. For more information, go to www.cedrosavenue.com.

Garden fanciers will find North County the best hunting grounds for bulbs, seeds, and starter cuttings. **North County nurseries** are known throughout the state for rare and hard-to-find plants—notably begonias, orchids, bromeliads, succulents, and ranunculuses. For more information on the area's largest growers, the **Flower Fields at Carlsbad Ranch,** and **Weidners' Gardens,** see chapter 10.

SHOPPING A TO Z

Large stores and shops in malls tend to stay open until about 9pm on weekdays, 6pm on weekends. Smaller businesses usually close at 5 or 6pm or may keep odd hours. When in doubt, call ahead.

Antiques & Collectibles

See also the "Hillcrest & Uptown" and "Mission Bay & the Beaches" sections in "Shopping by Area," earlier in this chapter.

Antiques on Kettner ★ Nearly 30 individual dealers share this 10,000-square-foot space, offering a wide selection of antiques and collectibles, including artwork, pottery, and glassware. Open daily 10am to 6pm. 2400 Kettner Blvd., Ste. 106, Little Italy. www.antiquesonkettner.com. ℂ **619/234-3332.** Bus: 83.

Newport Avenue Antique Center & Coffee House ★   With 18,000 square feet of retail, this is the big daddy of the Ocean Beach Antique District malls—it even has a small espresso bar. One corner is a haven for collectors of 1940s and 1950s kitchenware; there's also a fine selection of vintage linens and chinoiserie. Open daily 10am to 6pm; reduced hours on Sunday. 4864 Newport Ave., Ocean Beach. www.antiquesinsandiego.com. ℂ **619/222-8686.** Bus: 35 or 923.

Art & Crafts

While San Diego is not known as a powerhouse art city, you'll find some 25 galleries in La Jolla village alone; downtown, Little Italy, and North Park also offer a concentration of galleries. To get an overview of North Park's alternative art spaces, consider the **Ray at Night** gallery crawl (www.northparkarts.org), scheduled the second Saturday of every month from 6 to 10pm; more than 30 galleries, boutiques, and cafes participate.

Four Winds Trading Company ★   In the heart of Old Town, this shop has a bevy of authentic Native American and Mexican crafts and jewelry. Browse among pottery (including the sought-after Mata Ortiz), oil and watercolor paintings (originals and prints), silversmith products (Zuni, Kumeyaay, Navajo, Isleta Pueblo), rugs, kachinas, and baskets. Open daily 10am to 9pm. 2448 San Diego Ave., Old Town. www.4windsarts.com. ℂ **619/692-0466.** Bus: Numerous Old Town routes, including 8, 9, 10, 28, or 30. Trolley: Old Town.

Joseph Bellows Gallery ★★   Devotees of photography will want to check out this gallery showcasing both contemporary and vintage work. Solo and group shows are presented on an ongoing basis. Open Tuesday to Saturday 10am to 5pm. 7661 Girard Ave., La Jolla. www.josephbellows.com. ℂ **858/456-5620.** Bus: 30.

Spanish Village Art Center ★   Spanish Village is a collection of 37 charming and historic casitas set around a colorful courtyard in Balboa Park. Dating from the 1935–36 California-Pacific Exposition, the structures today are home to more than 250 artists specializing in various media, including painting, pottery, jewelry, metal art, origami, fused and blown glass, woodcarving, and wearable art. Many of the artists work on site, allowing you to see their products in the making. Open daily 11am to 4pm. 1770 Village Place, Balboa Park. www.spanishvillageart.com. ℂ **619/233-9050.** Bus: 7.

Taboo Studio ★★★   This impressive gallery exhibits and sells the work of jewelry designers from throughout the United States. Focusing on jewelry as wearable art, these are one-of-a-kind pieces and limited editions, made from a variety of materials. Four major exhibitions are usually held each year. Open Tuesday through Friday, 11am to 6pm, Saturday 10am to 5pm. 1615½ W. Lewis St., Mission Hills. www.taboostudio.com. ℂ **619/692-0099.** Bus: 83.

Tasende Gallery ★★   You probably won't walk away with a newly purchased Louise Nevelson or Fernando Botero, but a detour into this museumlike sculpture gallery is well worth your time. The calm and serenity, coupled with the modern architecture, provide a great respite from the commercial hubbub nearby. Open Tuesday to Friday 10am to 6pm, Saturday 11am to 5pm. 820 Prospect St., La Jolla. www.tasendegallery.com. ℂ **858/454-3691.** Bus: 30.

Books

For travel-related books, also note the shops listed under "Travel Accessories," later.

Barnes & Noble ★ The main San Diego branch of this book discounter sits amid one of Mission Valley's smaller malls, Hazard Center, just off Friar's Road (east of Hwy. 163). Besides a wide selection of paperback and hardcover titles, it offers a comprehensive periodicals rack and free Wi-Fi. Open daily 10am to 9pm. 7610 Hazard Center Dr., Mission Valley. www.barnesandnoble.com. ✆ **619/220-0175.** Trolley: Hazard Center.

Controversial Bookstore ★ San Diego's oldest metaphysical and spiritual bookstore started out in 1963, originally heavy on conspiracy and political tomes, as far right and far left as possible—hence the moniker. The store has evolved to embrace books on healing and alternative medicine, magic and witchcraft, astrology, UFO studies, women's issues, and spiritual pathways. It also stocks crystals, New Age music, incense, and jewelry. Open Monday to Friday 10am to 7pm, Saturday 10am to 6pm, Sunday 11am to 5pm. 3063 University Ave., North Park. www.controversialbookstore.com. ✆ **619/296-1560.** Bus: 2, 7, or 10.

D.G. Wills Books ★★ This bookstore has tomes stacked to its wood rafters—if you're looking for something scholarly, offbeat, or esoteric, this place is for you. Over the years this charmingly musty La Jolla treasure has hosted readings by such power-houses as Norman Mailer, Gore Vidal, Allen Ginsberg, and Maureen Dowd. Open Monday to Saturday 10am to 7pm, Sunday 11am to 6pm. 7461 Girard Ave., La Jolla. www.dgwillsbooks.com. ✆ **858/456-1800.** Bus: 30.

Obelisk Bookstore ★ This is San Diego's main gay and lesbian gift shop/bookstore. You'll find just about every gay magazine there is, and gay-themed movies for sale or rent, novelties, and cards, as well as everything from skin-care products to watches. It's also a clearinghouse for info on local LGBT events. Open Monday to Thursday 10am to 9pm, Friday and Saturday 10am to 10pm, Sunday 11am to 9pm. 1029 University Ave., Hillcrest. www.obeliskshoppe.com. ✆ **619/297-4171.** Bus: 1, 10, or 11.

Warwick's ★★★ This popular family-run bookstore is a browser's delight, with more than 40,000 titles, a large travel section, gifts, cards, and stationery. The Warwick family has been in the book and stationery business since 1896. The La Jolla store was established in the mid-1930s, and the fourth generation is now involved with the store's day-to-day operation. Authors come in for readings several times a week at this pet-friendly spot. Open Monday to Saturday 9am to 6pm, Sunday 10am to 5:30pm. 7812 Girard Ave., La Jolla. www.warwicks.com. ✆ **858/454-0347.** Bus: 30.

Department Stores

You'll find plenty of major retailers in large shopping centers that provide ample opportunity to browse for gifts, mementos, or necessities.

Bloomingdale's ★ This venerable department store, founded in 1872, made its way to San Diego and the upscale Fashion Valley mall in 2006. Designers such as Tommy Hilfiger, Donna Karan, and Ralph Lauren got their first big exposure through the chain, which operates more than 40 stores around the country. The store's cafe, **59th & Lex,** offers a full menu. Hours vary, but are generally Monday to Saturday 10am to 9pm, Sunday 11am to 7pm. Fashion Valley Center, Mission Valley. www.bloomingdales.com. ✆ **619/610-6400.** Bus: 6, 20, 25, 41, 88, 120, or 928. Trolley: Fashion Valley.

Macy's ★ This comprehensive store has a number of local branches, carrying clothing for women, men, and children, as well as housewares, electronics, and luggage. Besides downtown at Horton Plaza, Macy's also has stores in Mission Valley Center (including a housewares-only store), University Towne Center La Jolla, Carlsbad, and North County Fair (Escondido). Open Monday to Friday 10am to 9pm, Saturday 10am to 8pm, Sunday 11am to 6pm. Horton Plaza, downtown. www.macys.com. © **619/231-4747.** Bus: 2, 3, 7, 11, 15, 30, 50, 120, 150, 210, 850, 860, 901, 923, or 992. Trolley: Civic Center.

Nordstrom ★★ A San Diego favorite, Nordstrom is best known for its outstanding customer service and fine selection of shoes. It features a variety of stylish fashions and accessories for women, men, and children. Tailoring is done on the premises, and there's a full-service restaurant on the top floor. Nordstrom also has stores at Fashion Valley Center, University Towne Center La Jolla, and North County Fair (Escondido), and there's an outlet store—Nordstrom Rack—in the Mission Valley Shopping Center. Open Monday to Friday 10am to 9pm, Saturday 10am to 8pm, Sunday 11am to 6pm. Horton Plaza, downtown. www.nordstrom.com. © **619/239-1700.** Bus/Trolley: Same as Macy's above.

Discount Shopping

Carlsbad Premium Outlets ★★★ With some 90 stores, this mall includes favorites such as **Barneys New York, Crate & Barrel, Converse, Juicy Couture,** and **Swarovski.** This handsome outdoor shopping center also has a fine-dining restaurant on site. These outlets are located 32 miles north of downtown San Diego, close to LEGOLAND. Open Monday to Saturday 10am to 9pm, Sunday 10am to 7pm. 5600 Paseo del Norte. www.premiumoutlets.com. © **888/790-7467** or 760/804-9000. I-5 N. to Palomar Rd. exit; the mall is next to the freeway. Bus: 321.

Kobey's Swap Meet ✦ Since 1976, this gigantic open-air market positioned at the west end of the Valley View Casino Center (formerly the San Diego Sports Arena) parking lot has been a bargain-hunter's dream come true. Some 1,000 vendors fill row after row with new and used clothing, jewelry, electronics, hardware, appliances, furniture, collectibles, crafts, antiques, auto accessories, toys, and books. There's produce, too, along with food stalls and restrooms. Although Kobey's is open Friday, the weekend is when the good stuff is out—and it goes quickly, so arrive early. Open Friday to Sunday 7am to 3pm. Valley View Casino Center, 3500 Sports Arena Blvd. www.kobeyswap.com. © **619/226-0650.** Admission Fri 50¢; Sat–Sun $1; free for children 11 and under. Take I-8 W. to Sports Arena Blvd. turnoff, or I-5 to Rosecrans St. and turn right on Sports Arena Blvd. Bus: 8 or 9.

Las Americas Premium Outlets ★ This outlet mall, San Diego's largest, is in San Ysidro, immediately north of the Tijuana border crossing. Currently home to some 125 stores, including **Nike, Banana Republic, Guess, Kenneth Cole,** and the **Disney Store,** it's located 16 miles south of downtown. Open Monday to Saturday 10am to 9pm and Sunday 10am to 7pm. 4211 Camino de la Plaza. www.lasamericas.com. © **619/934-8400.** Take I-5 S. to Camino de la Plaza, then the last U.S. exit; go right at the light. Bus: 929. Trolley: San Ysidro.

Viejas Outlet Center ★★ More discount name-brand shopping is found at the Viejas Casino, east of El Cajon. Here you'll find **Vans, Eddie Bauer, Gap, Levi's,** and **Polo Ralph Lauren**—30-plus stores in all. Tuesdays are Senior Citizen Days, with additional discounts at some stores. There is also nightly entertainment at the Showcourt, with pyrotechnics, music, and an interactive fountain—and if that's not enough, there's also a casino, bowling alley, and seasonal ice-skating. Viejas is about 30 miles east of downtown. Open Monday to Saturday 10am to 8pm and Sunday 11am to 7pm. 5005 Willows Rd., Alpine. www.shopviejas.com. © **619/659-2070.** Take I-8 E. to Willows Rd. exit; turn left and follow the signs to Viejas Casino. Bus: 864.

Farmers' Markets

We love our open-air markets. Throughout the county, nearly 50 regularly scheduled street fests are stocked with the freshest fruits and vegetables from Southern California farms, augmented by crafts, fresh-cooked ethnic foods, flower stands, and other surprises. San Diego County produces more than $1-billion worth of fruits, flowers, and other crops each year. Avocados, known locally as "green gold," are the most profitable crop and have been grown here for more than 100 years. Citrus fruit follows close behind, and flowers are the area's third most important crop; ranunculus bulbs from here are sent all over the world, as are the famous Ecke poinsettias.

Here's a schedule of noteworthy farmers' markets—you can also check with the San Diego Farm Bureau (www.sdfarmbureau.org; © 760/745-3023).

There are several farmers' markets **downtown.** One is a seasonal affair, held in the square just north of Horton Plaza, running March through October on Thursdays from 11am to 3pm; call © **760/741-3763** for information. The Third Avenue market, specializing in Asian goods, takes place between Island Avenue and J Street. It runs throughout the year on Sundays from 9am to 1pm; call © **619/279-0032** for details. The very popular Little Italy Mercato (www.littleitalymercato.com; © **619/ 233-3769**) is on Saturdays, 9am to 1:30pm, along Date Street, between India and Columbia streets.

In **Hillcrest,** the market runs Sundays from 9am to 2pm at the corner of Normal Street and Lincoln Avenue, 1 block north of University Avenue. The atmosphere is festive, and exotic culinary delights reflect the eclectic neighborhood. For more information, go to www.hillcrestfarmersmarket.com or call © **619/237-1632.**

La **Jolla** also has a Sunday market; it's held on the playground at La Jolla Elementary School, 7335 Girard Ave., from 9am to 1pm. Go to www.lajollamarket.com or call © **858/454-1699** for more information.

Point **Loma's** open-air market is held on Sunday along the 2900 block of Canon Street, between Rosecrans and Shafter streets, from 9:30am to 2:30pm. Call © **619/795-3363** for information.

In **Ocean Beach,** a fun-filled market is held Wednesday evenings between 5 and 8pm (4–7pm Jan–Mar) along the 4900 block of Newport Avenue. In addition to fresh-cut flowers, produce, and exotic fruits and foods laid out for sampling, the market features art and entertainment. For more information, check www.ocean beachsandiego.com or call © **619/279-0032.**

Head to **Pacific Beach** on Saturday from 8am to noon, when Mission Boulevard between Reed Avenue and Pacific Beach Drive is transformed into a bustling marketplace. Call © **760/741-3763** for more information.

In **Coronado,** every Tuesday afternoon the Ferry Landing hosts a produce and crafts market from 2:30 to 6pm; call © **760/741-3763** for more details.

Food & Drink

The 3rd Corner ★★ Relaxed and sophisticated, this old beach bungalow is now part wine store, part casual eatery (p. 137). You can browse for a bottle of wine, and then settle into a leather couch to enjoy your purchase ($5 corkage) with a platter of cheese. It serves late and is popular with local bar and restaurant workers. There's also an outpost in Encinitas at the Lumberyard shopping center, 897 S. Coast Hwy. (© 760/942-2104). Open Tuesday to Sunday 10am to 1:30am. 2265 Bacon St., Ocean Beach. www.the3rdcorner.com. © 619/223-2700. Bus: 35 or 923.

The Wine Bank ★★★   This wonderful wine shop features a great selection from around the world, as well as spirits and liqueurs. You'll find rare wines from France, Italy, and Spain, and bottles from seemingly every winery in California, plus a small trove of Mexican wines. Wine tastings ($20 per person) are held Fridays (6–8pm) and Saturdays (3–5pm). Open Monday to Saturday 10am to 10pm, Sunday noon to 10pm. 363 Fifth Ave. (at J St.), downtown. www.sdwinebank.com. © 619/234-7487. Bus: 3, 11, or 120. Trolley: Gaslamp Quarter.

WineSellar & Brasserie ★★★   You'll feel like you've really accomplished something when you finally locate this place in its odd business-park setting, about 15 miles north of downtown. Starting out as a wine storage facility, it has grown into one of the area's best wine stores—and there's also an excellent French-inspired restaurant upstairs; pick a bottle and head on up (reservations definitely recommended). Casual wine-tastings are scheduled every Wednesday from 5 to 7pm, and Saturdays from 11:30am to 2pm. Store hours are Monday 9am to 6pm, Tuesday to Saturday 9am to 9pm; the restaurant is open Tuesday to Saturday, 11:30am to 2pm for lunch, and 5:30 to 8:30pm for dinner. 9550 Waples St., Ste. 115, Sorrento Mesa. www.winesellar.com. © 858/450-9557. Bus: 921. From I-805, take Mira Mesa Blvd. east; turn right on Huennekens St., left on Waples St., and take the second driveway on the left. Turn left where the parking lot Ts.

Malls

See p. 152 for details on **Horton Plaza;** also see "Discount Shopping," above.

Fashion Valley Center ★★   The Mission Valley corridor, running east-west about 2 miles north of downtown along I-8, is where you'll find San Diego's major shopping centers. Fashion Valley is the most attractive and most upscale, with five anchor stores: **Neiman Marcus, Nordstrom, Bloomingdale's, Macy's,** and **JCPenney** (most of which keep extended hours). There are also some 200 specialty shops and eateries, and an 18-screen AMC movie theater. Other noteworthy shops include **H&M, Jimmy Choo, M.A.C, Louis Vuitton, Michael Kors, Tiffany & Co.,** and **Bose.** Open Monday to Saturday 10am to 9pm and Sunday 11am to 7pm. 7007 Friars Rd. www.simon.com. © 619/688-9113. Bus: 6, 20, 25, 41, 88, 120, or 928. Hwy. 163 to Friars Rd. W. Trolley: Fashion Valley.

Mission Valley Center   This old-fashioned outdoor mall predates sleek Fashion Valley and has found a niche with budget-minded stores such as **Loehmann's, Nordstrom Rack,** and **Target;** you'll also find **Macy's Home Furniture, West Elm, Sport Chalet,** and **Bed Bath & Beyond.** There's a 20-screen AMC movie theater and 150 other stores and places to eat. Across from the center to the north and west are separate complexes that feature Saks Fifth Avenue's **Off Fifth** (an outlet store) and more. Open Monday to Saturday 10am to 9pm and Sunday 11am to 6pm. 1640 Camino del Rio N. www.westfield.com/missionvalley. © 619/296-6375. I-8 to Mission Center Rd. Bus: 6. Trolley: Mission Valley Center.

University Towne Center (UTC) ★★   This outdoor shopping complex is in La Jolla, east of the university, and underwent a $150-million upgrade in 2012. Improvements include a new, upscale 14-screen movie theater, an expanded fitness center with pool and basketball court, and public Wi-Fi. There are more than 150 stores and dining spots, including some big ones such as **Nordstrom, Sears,** and **Macy's.** It is also home to an **Apple Store;** a year-round ice-skating rink, **Ice Town;** and an outlet of Encinitas-based **Chuao Chocolatier,** a fabulous artisan chocolate shop. The center is open Monday through Friday 10am to 9pm, Saturday 10am to 8pm, and Sunday 11am to 7pm. 4545 La Jolla Village Dr. www.westfield.com/utc. © **858/546-8858.** I-5 to La Jolla Village Dr. and go east, or I-805 to La Jolla Village Dr. and go west. Bus: 30, 31, 50, 101, 105, 150, 201, 202, 880, or 960.

Music

Folk Arts Rare Records ★★★   Tom Waits-approved nirvana for serious jazz, folk, blues, and country collectors. Operated since 1967 by local legend Lou Curtiss, it offers a huge selection of 78s and first-edition rarities on vinyl, most of them fairly priced. If you're not a collector or don't have a turntable, the store specializes in creating custom recordings of the vintage music on CD or cassette. Monday to Friday 9am to 5pm, Saturday and Sunday 10am to 6pm. 2881 Adams Ave., Normal Heights. www.folkartsrarerecords.com. © **619/282-7833.** Bus: 11.

Lou's Records ★   Sadly diminished from its glory days but still a worthwhile stop, this longtime local favorite is located in Encinitas, about 30 minutes north of downtown. You'll find new, import, and used CDs, as well as vinyl and DVDs (even VHS). You can buy turntables and styluses too. Open Monday to Thursday 10am to 7pm, Friday and Saturday 10am to 9pm, Sunday 11am to 7pm. 434 Hwy. 101, Encinitas. www.lousrecords.com. © **888/568-7732** or 760/753-1382. Bus: 101.

M-Theory Music ★   Offers CDs and vinyl (as well as DVDs) in an eclectic range of genres, from indie rock to old-school R&B. M-Theory also hosts lots of in-store band appearances. Open Monday to Saturday 10am to 8pm, Sunday 11am to 7pm. 915 W. Washington St., Mission Hills. www.mtheorymusic.com. © **619/220-0485.** Bus: 10 or 83.

Off the Record   A San Diego fixture, this small independent shop has relocated several times over the years, and now finds itself in the up-and-coming neighborhood of North Park. You'll find a good selection of new and used CDs and vinyl; plus there's lots of other fun stuff in the surrounding blocks. It's open daily, 11am to 8pm. 2912 University Ave., North Park. www.offtherecordmusic.com. © **619/298-4755.** Bus: 2, 6, 7, or 10.

Toys & Games

Apple Box Toys ★   Batteries are not included here. Apple Box, one of the original stores at downtown's Seaport Village, specializes in wooden toys. You'll find everything from puzzles and pull toys to rocking horses and toy chests. The items can be personalized with names, slogans, whatever you want (they can even do it in Hebrew). Open daily 10am to 9pm. 837 W. Harbor Dr., Ste. C, Embarcadero. www.appleboxtoys.com. © **800/676-7529.** Trolley: Seaport Village.

Travel Accessories

John's Fifth Avenue Luggage ★★   This San Diego institution carries just about everything you can imagine in the way of luggage, travel accessories, computer cases, handbags, and wallets; there's on-premises luggage repair, too. Open Monday to Friday 10am to 5:30pm, and Saturday 10am to 4pm. There is also a location in the Fashion Valley shopping center (© **619/574-0086**) that has extended hours. 3833 Fourth Ave., Hillcrest. www.johnsluggage.com. © **619/298-0993.** Bus: 1, 3, or 120.

Le Travel Store ★★ In business since 1976, Le Travel Store has a good selection of soft-sided luggage (particularly the Eagle Creek brand), travel books, language tapes, maps, and lots of travel accessories. The Gaslamp Quarter location makes this spot extra handy. Open Monday to Saturday 11am to 5pm, Sunday noon to 6pm. 745 Fourth Ave. (btw. F and G sts.). www.letravelstore.com. © **800/713-4260** or 619/544-0005. Bus: 3, 120, or numerous Broadway routes. Trolley: Civic Center.

Traveler's Depot ★★ Around since 1983, this family-run shop offers an extensive selection of travel books and maps, plus a great array of travel gear and accessories, backpacks, and luggage. Open Monday to Saturday 10am to 6pm, and Sunday 11am to 5pm. 1655 Garnet Ave., Pacific Beach. www.travelersdepot.com. © **858/483-1421.** Bus: 9 or 27.

ENTERTAINMENT & NIGHTLIFE

H istorically, San Diego's cultural scene has languished in the shadows cast by those of Los Angeles and San Francisco. The go-go '90s, though, brought new blood and money into the city, and arts organizations felt the impact. The biggest

winner was the San Diego Symphony, which, in 2002, received the largest single donation to a symphony anywhere, ever—$120 million. More recently, individual donors have lavished big bucks on other groups: The Old Globe Theatre received $20-million and $10-million gifts, while the Museum of Contemporary Art San Diego was bestowed with a $3-million donation. But don't think "after dark" in this city is limited to highfalutin' affairs—rock and pop concerts, bars (both swank and dive), and nightclubs crank up the volume on a nightly basis.

Thankfully, San Diego's orgy of development over the past 2 decades has included more than just luxury condos and hotels. The **NTC at Liberty Station** in Point Loma (www.ntclibertystation.com; ✆ **619/573-9260**) consists of 26 historic buildings on 28 bayfront acres. It's the remnants of a huge Navy base transformed into a flagship hub of creative activity, housing museums and galleries, educational facilities, and arts groups. The **Birch North Park Theatre,** 2891 University Ave. (www.birchnorth parktheatre.net; ✆ **619/239-8836** or 231-5714), is a 1928 vaudeville and movie house resurrected to its original glory. It's now the home base for Lyric Opera San Diego, and plays host to numerous other groups throughout the year. The **Balboa Theatre,** 868 Fourth Ave. (www.san diegotheatres.org; ✆ **619/570-1100** or 619/615-4000), is another gilded beauty given a new lease on life. Built in 1924, the Balboa sat empty and decaying for years, barely avoiding the wrecking ball several times. This Gaslamp Quarter icon reopened in 2008 and is once again presenting music, dance, theater, and films.

Finding Out What's On

For a rundown of the week's performances, gallery openings, and other events, check the listings in the free, weekly alternative publications **San Diego CityBeat** (www.sdcitybeat.com), published on Wednesday, and the **San Diego Reader** (www.sandiegoreader.com), which comes out on Thursday. The **U-T San Diego** entertainment section, "Night and Day," also appears on Thursday (www.utsandiego.com). The local convention and visitors bureau's *Art + Sol* campaign provides a calendar of events covering the performing and visual arts, and more; see www.sandiegoartandsol.com.

Getting Tickets

Deeply discounted tickets to theater, music, and dance events are available at the **ARTS TIX** booth in Horton Plaza Park, at Broadway and Third Avenue. It's open Tuesday through Thursday 9:30am to 5pm, Friday and Saturday 9:30am to 6pm, and some Sundays (call ahead). Some discount tickets are available only for same-day shows, others can be bought in advance; for a daily listing of offerings, call ✆ **858/381-5595,** or check www.sdartstix.com (you can also make purchases online).

For full-price advance tickets, the Horton Plaza kiosk doubles as a Ticketmaster outlet (www.ticketmaster.com; ✆ **800/745-3000**), selling seats to concerts throughout California. Although Ticketmaster sells seats for a majority of local events, you'll avoid bruising "convenience" fees by purchasing directly from the venue's box office.

THE PERFORMING ARTS
Theater

These listings focus on the best known of San Diego's many talented theater companies, but don't hesitate to try a less prominent troupe if the show appeals to you. Smaller/independent companies doing notable work include **Cygnet Theatre** (www.cygnettheatre.com; ✆ 619/337-1525), **North Coast Repertory Theatre** (www.northcoastrep.org; ✆ 858/481-1055), and **Moxie Theatre** (www.moxietheatre.com; ✆ 858/598-7620). **Broadway San Diego** (www.broadwaysd.com; ✆ 619/564-3000 for information, or 619/570-1100 for tickets) presents touring megamusicals at the Civic Theatre downtown; the **California Center for the Performing Arts** in Escondido also books major productions of all types (see "North County Inland," in chapter 10). For shows oriented toward kids, see "That's Entertainment!," in chapter 4.

Diversionary Theatre ★ Diversionary was founded in 1986 and focuses on plays with LGBT themes. The 104-seat theater is in the charming neighborhood of University Heights, 2 blocks north of El Cajon Boulevard. Box office hours vary, but are usually Wednesday through Saturday from noon to 8pm (when shows are playing); discounts are available for students, seniors, and military. It's a parking-challenged area, so it's a good idea to come early and have dinner at one of the neighborhood eateries. 4545 Park Blvd. www.diversionary.org. ✆ **619/220-0097.** Tickets $20–$33, $12 student rush 1 hr. prior to curtain. Bus: 11.

La Jolla Playhouse ★★★ The Playhouse boasts a Hollywood pedigree (it was founded in 1947 by Gregory Peck, Dorothy McGuire, and Mel Ferrer) and a 1993 Tony Award for outstanding regional theater. The Playhouse is known for its contemporary takes on classics and commitment to *commedia dell'arte* style, as well as producing Broadway-bound blockbusters such as *Jersey Boys*. This three-theater complex is also the site of Wolfgang Puck's Asian-fusion restaurant, **Jai.** Subject to availability, half-priced tickets are available for students, seniors (62 and over), and active-duty military in a "public rush" sale 1 hour before curtain (1 ticket per person). Box office hours are Monday to Saturday from noon to 6pm on nonperformance days, noon to curtain when shows are playing. 2910 La Jolla Village Dr. (at Torrey Pines Rd.). www.lajollaplayhouse.org. ✆ **858/550-1010.** Tickets $35–$80. Parking $2, free on weekends. Bus: 30, 41, 101, 150, or 921.

Lamb's Players Theatre ★ One of the few professional companies in the country with a true resident ensemble, Lamb's was established in 1971. It features five shows annually at its 350-seat main stage in Coronado's historic **Spreckels Building** (where no seat is more than seven rows from the stage), plus a show at the Horton Grand Theatre (444 Fourth Ave.) in the Gaslamp Quarter. Additionally, Lamb's produces two Christmas productions, one of which is a dinner theater extravaganza at the Hotel del Coronado. You'll see well-acted, well-designed plays, both premieres and classics. The box office is open Tuesday through Saturday from noon to 7pm, Sunday from noon to 2pm; senior, military, and student discounts available. 1142 Orange Ave., Coronado. www.lambsplayers.org. © **619/437-6000.** Tickets $26–$60. Street parking or pay parking garage nearby. Bus: 901 or 904.

The Old Globe Theatre ★★★   This Tony Award–winning, three-theater complex is in Balboa Park, behind the Museum of Man. Though best known for the 580-seat Old Globe—fashioned after Shakespeare's wooden-O theater—there's also a 612-seat open-air theater and a 250-seat arena stage. More than a dozen plays are scheduled here year-round, from world premieres (and subsequent Broadway hits like *The Full Monty*) to the excellent summer Shakespeare festival; *Dr. Seuss' How the Grinch Stole Christmas!* has been a popular family draw during the holidays since 1997. Just in time for its 75th anniversary in 2010, the Globe underwent a massive face-lift, adding new educational facilities and patron amenities; backstage tours are offered most weekends at 10:30am and cost $5 for adults, $3 for students, seniors, and military. The box office is open Tuesday through Sunday, noon to 6pm, and noon until curtain on performance days. Balboa Park. www.theoldglobe.org. © **619/234-5623.** Tickets $29–$94. Senior, student, and military discounts available. Free parking in the park's public lots; valet parking located at the Prado restaurant. Bus: 3, 7, or 120.

San Diego Repertory Theatre ★   Founded in 1976, the Rep mounts plays and musicals at the Lyceum Theatre in Horton Plaza, which consists of the 545-seat Lyceum Stage and the 260-seat Lyceum Space. The theater acts as a "cultural town hall," hosting nearly daily events, exhibits, and shows, in addition to the Rep's work. The Rep has a strong multicultural bent—it has had a long association with Chicano playwright Luis Valdez, and produces the annual African-American Kuumba Fest and the Jewish Arts Festival. A tiled obelisk rising from a sunken courtyard marks the spot where you'll find the theater, situated at the entrance to Horton Plaza. The box office is open Tuesday through Sunday from noon to 6pm (or curtain time). 79 Broadway Circle, in Horton Plaza. www.sdrep.org. © **619/544-1000.** Tickets $29–$53; $18 for students (senior and military discounts available as well). Free validated parking at Horton Plaza Shopping Center. Bus: All Broadway routes. Trolley: Civic Center.

Classical Music

La Jolla Music Society ★★   This well-respected organization has been bringing marquee names to San Diego since 1968. About half of the 40-plus annual shows are held October through May in the 500-seat Sherwood Auditorium at the Museum of Contemporary Art in La Jolla; others are presented at venues around town, including the acoustically excellent Neurosciences Institute, Copley Symphony Hall, and the restored Birch North Park Theatre. The annual highlight is **SummerFest**, a 3-week series of concerts, forums, open rehearsals, talks, and artist encounters—it's held in August and is perhaps San Diego's most prestigious musical event. Box office: 7946 Ivanhoe Ave., Ste. 103, La Jolla. www.ljms.org. © **858/459-3728.** Tickets $25–$95. Bus: 30.

San Diego Symphony ★   The symphony's home, Copley Symphony Hall, is a baroque jewel dating from 1929, swallowed whole by a downtown financial tower;

the building's modern exterior gives no hint of the plush theater inside. The season runs October through May; a Summer Pops series, with programs devoted to big band, Broadway, and Tchaikovsky, is held weekends from July to early September on the Embarcadero—always bring a sweater for these pleasantly brisk evenings on the water. The box office is open Monday through Friday from 10am to 6pm, till intermission on performance days; concert Saturdays from noon to intermission; and Sunday from noon to 4pm (phone only). There is a $10 student rush 1 hour prior to curtain for most Symphony Hall concerts. 750 B St., at Seventh Ave. www.sandiegosymphony.org. ℂ **619/235-0804.** Tickets $20–$100. Bus: Numerous Broadway routes. Trolley: Fifth Ave.

Opera

San Diego Opera ★★★   One of the community's most successful arts organizations, San Diego Opera has been presenting work here since 1965. The annual season runs from late January to mid-May, with five offerings at downtown's 3,000-seat Civic Theatre, as well as occasional recitals at smaller venues. The productions range from such well-trod warhorses as *Carmen* to edgier works such as Alban Berg's *Wozzeck*, all performed by name talent from around the world, as well as local singers. To purchase tickets in person, visit patron services at the opera offices (Civic Center Plaza, 18th floor, directly across from the theater), Monday through Friday 8:30am to 4:30pm; rush tickets ($20–$50, cash only) become available 2 hours before curtain at the theater. Civic Theatre, 1200 Third Ave. www.sdopera.com. ℂ **619/533-7000** (box office) or 232-7636 (admin.). Tickets $50–$275. Bus: Numerous Broadway routes. Trolley: Civic Center.

Dance

Dance Place at NTC Promenade has become the heart of the city's dance scene, providing studio, performance, and educational space for several of San Diego's leading companies, including **San Diego Ballet** (www.sandiegoballet.org; ℂ **619/294-7311** or 619/294-7378), **Malashock Dance** (www.malashockdance.org; ℂ **619/260-1622**), and **Jean Isaacs San Diego Dance Theater** (www.sandiegodancetheater.org; ℂ **619/225-1803**).

Other major dance companies include **California Ballet** (www.californiaballet.org; ℂ **858/560-5676**), a classical company that produces four shows annually at the Civic Theatre downtown and elsewhere (*The Nutcracker* is a Christmas tradition); and **City Ballet** (www.cityballet.org; ℂ **858/272-8663**), which is officially sanctioned by the George Balanchine Foundation to perform that choreographer's work. Turning hearts and minds (but hopefully not ankles) is the socially conscious modern-dance troupe **Eveoke Dance Theatre** (ℂ **619/238-1153;** www.eveoke.org). Their studio space is in the heart of North Park at 2811 University Ave., where they offer a full lineup of drop-in classes.

THE CLUB & MUSIC SCENE

Live Music

Maddeningly, some artists bypass San Diego, but on the plus side—especially when it comes to acts that haven't pushed through to the mainstream—if they do play locally, chances are it's in a venue smaller than what you'd find them in up in L.A. ***Note:*** Many of the city's nightspots are for ages 21 and up.

SMALL & MEDIUM-SIZE VENUES

AMSDconcerts ★ 🎒 One of San Diego's most unique venues is a nearly 100-year-old church in Normal Heights, which hosts shows presented by AMSDconcerts (formerly known as Acoustic Music San Diego). Programming is entirely non-religious and ranges from Americana and blues to bluegrass and Celtic. Many artists sign autographs and hawk merchandise between sets in the church's adjacent auditorium. 4650 Mansfield St., Normal Heights (south of Adams Ave.). www.amsdconcerts.com. ✆ **619/303-8176.** $20–$25 (cash only if purchasing at the door); dinner packages with seats in first several rows $47–$52. Bus: 11.

Anthology ★★★ This is a fine-dining establishment masquerading as a top-notch music venue. Or is it the other way around? However you want to describe it, this acoustically excellent and architecturally alluring supper club books big-name jazz, blues, world music, and rock musicians, as well as local talent. You don't have to eat here to see a show, but diners get the best seats—and the **food** is almost as much of an attraction as the artists (see review p. 122). 1337 India St. (btw. A and Ash sts.), downtown. www.anthologysd.com. ✆ **619/595-0300.** $10–$99. Bus: 83.

The Belly Up Tavern ★ This club in Solana Beach, a 30-minute drive from downtown, has played host to critically acclaimed and international artists of all genres. The eclectic mix ranges from Lucinda Williams and Toots and the Maytals to Frank Black and the Roots; a funky setting in recycled Quonset huts underscores the venue's uniqueness. Look into advance tickets, if possible, though you can avoid excessive Ticketmaster fees by purchasing your tickets at the box office. You can also dine before the show at the **BUT's Wild Note Cafe.** 143 S. Cedros Ave., Solana Beach (1½ blocks from the Coaster stop). www.bellyup.com. ✆ **858/481-9022** (recorded info) or 481-8140 (box office). $8–$28. Bus: 101.

The Casbah ★ It may have a total dive ambience, and passing jets overhead sometimes drown out ballads, but this rockin' Little Italy club has a well-earned rep for showcasing indie and punk bands that either are, were, or will be famous (Arcade Fire, the Damned, Gogol Bordello). Look into advance tickets if possible (✆ **888/512-7469;** www.casbahtickets.com)—capacity is only about 200. Live music can be counted on at least 6 nights a week. Doors open 8:30pm. 2501 Kettner Blvd., at Laurel St., near the airport. www.casbahmusic.com. ✆ **619/232-4355.** $8–$20. Bus: 83.

Croce's Restaurant & Jazz Bar ★ Croce's is a cornerstone of Gaslamp Quarter nightlife: a loud, crowded, and mainstream gathering place where you'll find a variety of jazz and rhythm 'n' blues stylings 7 nights a week (Sun–Thurs starting at 7:30pm; Fri–Sat at 8:30pm); there's also a jazz brunch on weekends from 10am to 2:30pm (music begins at 11:30am). The venue is named for the late singer/songwriter Jim Croce and is owned by his widow, Ingrid, who was a vital component of the Gaslamp's revitalization. The cover charge is waived if you eat at the pricey restaurant (from where you can see and hear the music from most tables). 802 Fifth Ave. (at F St.). www.croces.com. ✆ **619/233-4355.** $5–$10. Bus: 3, 120, or 992.

Dizzy's ★ As of this writing, this excellent jazz club is homeless, but still presenting shows at a variety of venues around town. Fans of serious jazz should check the website to see where its concerts might be popping up or if it has found a new permanent location. ✆ **858/270-7467.** www.dizzysjazz.com. $10–$15 (tickets available at the door; cash only).

4th & B   In a former bank building downtown, 4th & B received a $4.5-million sprucing up in 2006, giving this formerly no-frills venue a bit more panache. The back of the room, which had previously been bleacher-type seating, now features VIP boxes and lounges. The genre is barrier-free, including live music, DJs, and comedy shows. The box office is open Monday to Friday, 10am to 5pm, and 1 hour prior to showtime. 345 B St., downtown. www.4thandbevents.com. ✆ **619/231-4343.** $10–$50. Bus: 3, 120, or numerous Broadway routes. Trolley: Civic Center or Fifth Avenue.

House of Blues ★★   Whatever your feelings about corporate music entities, there's no denying House of Blues knows how to do things right. A visual feast of amazing outsider art fills this multiroom venue, which features a restaurant serving multicultural cuisine; there's also a swag store, a bar, and two stages (including a 1,100-person capacity concert space). HOB's booking power brings in an eclectic range of music, from world beat to punk (and yes, blues, too). VIP dinner packages are available. 1055 Fifth Ave., downtown. (btw. Broadway and C St.). www.hob.com/sandiego. ✆ **619/299-2583.** $20–$40. Bus: 3, 120, or numerous Broadway routes. Trolley: Fifth Ave.

Humphrey's ★   This locally beloved 1,400-seat outdoor venue is set alongside the bay, next to bobbing yachts. The annual lineup covers the spectrum of entertainment—rock, jazz, blues, folk, and comedy. You can snag a seat in the first seven rows by buying the dinner/concert package ($67 extra); there are also packages with the adjacent hotel that can get you in the first four rows. Concerts are held from mid-April to October only, and most shows go on sale in March (seats are also available through Ticketmaster). The hotel's indoor lounge, **Humphrey's Backstage,** also has music nightly. 2241 Shelter Island Dr., Point Loma. www.humphreysconcerts.com. ✆ **800/745-3000** or 619/224-3577 and 619/224-3411 for package reservations. $28–$92. Bus: 28.

LARGE VENUES

Built in 1967, the **Valley View Casino Center** (formerly known as the San Diego Sports Arena), 3500 Sports Arena Blvd. (www.valleyviewcasinocenter.com; ✆ **619/224-4171**), is a 15,000- to 18,000-seat indoor venue with middling acoustics. Located west of Old Town, it hosts a handful of big-name concerts every year because of the seating capacity and availability of paid parking. **Qualcomm Stadium,** 9449 Friars Rd., in Mission Valley (www.sandiego.gov/qualcomm; ✆ **619/641-3100**), is a 71,000-seat outdoor stadium mainly occupied by football (Chargers and San Diego State University).

The **Open Air Theatre** (www.as.sdsu.edu; ✆ **619/594-6947** or 619/594-0429), on the San Diego State University campus, northeast of downtown along I-8, is a 4,000-seat outdoor amphitheater. It has great acoustics—if you can't get a ticket, you can sit outside and hear the entire show. Also located at SDSU is **Viejas Arena** (same contact info as the Open Air); it has equally superb acoustics in an indoor, 12,000-seat facility that is used for bigger draws. Both these venues are easily accessed by the San Diego Trolley. **Cricket Wireless Amphitheatre,** 2050 Entertainment Circle (www.livenation.com; ✆ **619/671-3608** or 619/671-3500), is a slick facility in Chula Vista, a stone's throw north of the Mexican border. Built in 1999, the venue has a capacity of 20,000 (10,000 in festival seating in a grassy outfield) and boasts excellent acoustics and good sightlines; many of the big summer tours play here. The drawbacks: overpriced snacks and drinks, and a location 25 to 45 minutes south of downtown (depending on traffic).

The **Spreckels Theatre,** 121 Broadway (www.spreckels.net; ✆ **619/235-950**), and **Copley Symphony Hall,** 750 B St. (www.sandiegosymphony.org; ✆ **619/235-0804**), are wonderful old vaudeville houses located downtown, used by touring acts throughout the year.

Comedy Clubs

The American Comedy Co. ★ This "A-list" comedy club debuted in the Gaslamp Quarter in 2012. It presents nationally touring comics, Tuesday through Sunday nights at 8pm, with additional 10pm shows on Friday and Saturday; the last Tuesday of the month is open-mic night. The 200-seat venue is for ages 21 and over; appetizers and full meals are served. 818 Sixth Ave. (btw. E and F sts.), Gaslamp Quarter. www.americancomedyco.com. © **619/795-3858.** Cover $5–$22 (plus 2-drink minimum). Bus: 3, 120, or numerous Broadway routes.

The Comedy Store ★ Yes, it's a branch of the famous Sunset Strip club in Los Angeles, and yes, plenty of L.A. comics make the trek to headline Friday and Saturday shows here. Comedians from around the region perform Wednesday, Thursday, and Sunday. Monday is open-mic night; it can be hilarious, horrendous—or both. Shows start at 8pm, with later shows on weekends; ages 21 and over only. 916 Pearl St., La Jolla. www.thecomedystore.com. © **858/454-9176.** Cover none–$20 (plus 2-drink minimum). Bus: 30.

National Comedy Theatre ★ Two teams of professional comedians square off in a 90-minute, family-friendly improv competition to see which can make you laugh hardest. The action is all based on your suggestions—you call it out, they make it funny. Showtimes are Friday and Saturday at 7:30pm and 9:45pm, Sunday at 8pm. Thursdays are collegiate night (7:30pm), when teams from schools around the state go at it; midnight shows are scheduled the last Saturday of the month (ages 16 and over only). 3717 India St. (at W. Washington St.), Mission Hills. www.nationalcomedy.com. © **619/295-4999.** Cover $10–$15. Bus: 10 or 30. Trolley: Washington Street.

Bars, Cocktail Lounges & Dance Clubs
DOWNTOWN
Downtown is the busiest place for nightlife—you'll find something going on nightly. The best nights (or worst, depending on your tolerance for crowds) are Thursday through Saturday, when the 20-somethings pour in and dance clubs spring into action. Cover charges range from about $10 to $20 these nights, but some bars and lounges, particularly those in restaurants and hotels, are usually free. Most clubs discount or waive cover charges if you go before 10pm; dining at nightspots that offer food service is another way to avoid lines and covers. Keep in mind that many clubs have "city style" dress codes—no tank tops, sports jerseys, tennis shoes, and the like.

Altitude Sky Lounge ★★ Twenty-two stories up in the Gaslamp Quarter Marriott (p. 191), this long, narrow open-air space looks down on PETCO Park and the Convention Center. The best view of downtown is curiously walled off by a water sculpture that backs the bar. No worries—there's still lots to look at, as well as fire pits and DJ-spun grooves. And in a Gaslamp rarity, there's no cover charge. Open daily 5pm to 1:30am. 660 K St. (btw. Sixth and Seventh aves.), Gaslamp Quarter. www.altitudeskylounge.com. © **619/696-0234.** Bus: 3, 11, or 120. Trolley: Gaslamp Quarter.

Boudoir ★ At this three-floor, fetish-inspired club you can take a walk on the wild side—or at least take a spin on the bondage wheel (don't forget to tip your dominatrix!). There's magic, burlesque, or just plain old dancing, if you're into that sort of thing. Open Thursday through Saturday. 701 C St. (btw. Seventh and Eighth aves.), downtown. www.boudoirsd.com. © **619/237-0529.** Cover: $20. Bus: Numerous Broadway routes. Trolley: Fifth Ave.

Craft & Commerce ★★★ 🏛

The rough-hewn timber beams with philosophical entreaties hand-scrawled on them; the books and torn pages used as interior design; the servers with their flat caps, suspenders, and tattoos—it all lends a steam punk vibe to this smashingly successful gastropub. C&C takes a serious, artisanal approach to cocktails, beer, and food. Open Monday through Friday 11:30am to 1am, weekends 10am to 1am; kitchen till 11pm. 675 W. Beech (at Kettner Blvd.). Little Italy. www. craft-commerce.com. © **619/269-2202.** Bus: 83. Trolley: County Center/Little Italy.

East Village Tavern & Bowl

Whether you bowl passionately or ironically, this raucous spot has you covered. Featuring 12 colorfully lighted bowling lanes, as well as a separate bar area with outdoor seating, there's classic bar food (limited menu served until 1am), a good selection of beer on tap, and billiards. Open daily 11:30am to 2am; kids are allowed in until 9pm. 930 Market St. (btw. Ninth and 10th aves.), East Village. www.bowlevt.com. © **619/677-2695.** Bus: 3, 5, 11, 901, or 929. Trolley: Park and Market.

Ivy Nightclub/Ivy Rooftop ★★

These are the hip and very happening spots located in the ultra-stylish Andaz Hotel (p. 186). Multilevel Ivy Nightclub is chic and sexy, with a definite scenester vibe; Ivy Rooftop is an open-air bar where beautiful people prove a distraction to the beautiful views. There's also an on-site wine bar featuring 88 automatically dispensed pours. The nightclub is open Thursday to Saturday 9pm to 2am; rooftop hours are Sunday to Wednesday 11am to midnight, Thursday to Saturday 11am to 2am; the wine bar is open Sunday to Wednesday 5pm to midnight, Thursday to Saturday 5pm to 2am. 600 F St. (btw. Sixth and Seventh aves.), Gaslamp Quarter. www.envysandiego.com. © **619/814-2055.** Nightclub cover $20. Bus: 3 or 120.

LOUNGEsix ★

Considerably more earthbound than Altitude (see above), LOUNGEsix is on the fourth-floor pool deck of the Hotel Solamar. Let's see: fire pits, check. Cabanas, check. Comfy lounges, check. A menu of small-plate edibles from the first-floor restaurant, check. Cool music playing overhead, check. Excellent views of the Gaslamp Quarter action, check. Yup, everything you need for a great afternoon or evening. Open daily 11:30am to midnight; no cover. 616 J St. (at Sixth Ave.), Gaslamp Quarter. www.hotelsolamar.com. © **619/531-8744.** Bus: 3, 11, or 120. Trolley: Gaslamp Quarter.

Noble Experiment ★★★ 🏛

With its wall of skulls and high ceiling adorned with tragically romantic images, this speak-easy is vaguely spooky. But never fear—San Diego's top mixologists are here to enlighten, not frighten. It's tiny (35-person capacity), and you have to text ahead for availability; when you get the OK, head over to **Neighborhood** (p. 126), go to the back of the restaurant, and push on the wall of kegs. Behind it, you'll find an experiment that's not just noble, it's triumphant. 777 G St. (btw. Seventh and Eighth aves.). East Village. www.nobleexperimentsd.com. © **619/888-4713** (text only). No cover. Bus: 3 or 11.

The Onyx Room/Thin ★★

This upstairs/downstairs combo makes for a nightlife twofer that can't be beat. At street level is hypermodern Thin, where specialty cocktails mix with a variety of DJ-spun grooves; subterranean Onyx is more classic lounge, where you can catch a diverse range of performances, including spoken word and live R&B/Neo Soul. It's open Tuesday and Friday from 9pm to 2am, and Saturday 9pm to 4am; the cover charge gets you into both. 852 Fifth Ave. (btw. E and F sts.), Gaslamp Quarter. www.onyxroom.com. © **619/235-6699.** Cover $5–$20. Bus: 3, 120, or numerous Broadway routes. Trolley: Fifth Ave.

Stingaree ★★   This $6-million, three-level club has been a hot destination in the Gaslamp Quarter since 2005. It has more than 22,000 square feet of space, a fine-dining component, a handful of bars and private nooks, and a rooftop deck with cabanas and a fire pit. The decor is a chic combination of mod and retro; the name is a throwback to San Diego's Wild West days when this area was known as the Stingaree. Open Tuesday through Thursday 6pm to midnight, and Friday and Saturday 6pm to 2am (restaurant till 10pm). 454 Sixth Ave. (btw. Island Ave. and J St.), Gaslamp Quarter. www.stingsandiego.com. ✆ **619/544-9500.** Cover $20. Trolley: Gaslamp Quarter.

The Tipsy Crow ★   With three floors, this Gaslamp Quarter spot—formerly known as the Bitter End—manages to be a concert venue, comedy club, neighborhood bar (with shuffleboard and Wii), and dance club rolled all into one. The top-floor "Nest" is the bar's standout space, reflecting the building's classic 1874 pedigree. Open Monday to Friday 3pm to 2am, and weekends from noon to 2am. 770 Fifth Ave. (at F St.), Gaslamp Quarter. www.thetipsycrow.com. ✆ **619/338-9300.** Cover Fri–Sat $5 after 9pm. Bus: 3, 120, or numerous Broadway routes. Trolley: Fifth Ave.

Top of the Hyatt ★★★ 📷   This is San Diego's ultimate bar with a view, the 40th floor of the West Coast's tallest waterfront building, the Manchester Grand Hyatt (p. 190). You'll get a wide view of the city, harbor, and Coronado; the bar is open 3pm to 1:30am daily and is an unparalleled spot from which to watch the sunset. No cover charge. 1 Market Place (at Harbor Dr.), Embarcadero. www.manchestergrand.hyatt.com. ✆ **619/232-1234.** Trolley: Seaport Village.

Vin de Syrah Spirit & Wine Parlor ★★ 🎁   Go down the rabbit hole to this underground space with an oddball *Alice in Wonderland* setting. Far from your typically sedate wine bar, you can find tastings, cocktails, and people dancing away to DJs. *Note:* The front door is camouflaged by AstroTurf—and the folks inside are amusedly watching you on closed-circuit TV as you fumble to find your way in. It's open Tuesday, Wednesday, and Sunday, 4pm to midnight, and Thursday through Saturday 4pm to 2am. No cover. 901 Fifth Ave. (at the corner of E St.), Gaslamp Quarter. www.syrahwineparlor.com. ✆ **619/234-4166.** Bus: 3, 120, or numerous Broadway routes. Trolley: Fifth Ave.

Voyeur ★★   This club has established itself as a Gaslamp Quarter darling, but sweetness isn't the vibe it's going for. The Goth fun-house decor includes AK-47–shaped lamps, skull motifs, and go-go dancers embedded in a floor-to-ceiling wall of pulsing LED lights. The club pulls top talent to man the decks; and depending on what time you arrive, cover can range from zip to $30. Voyeur is open Thursday to Saturday, 10am to 2am. 755 Fifth Ave. (btw. F and G sts.), Gaslamp Quarter. www.voyeursd.com. ✆ **619/756-7678.** Bus: 3, 120, or numerous Broadway routes. Trolley: Fifth Ave.

ELSEWHERE IN SAN DIEGO

The BeachWood   You can get a total Pacific Beach experience at this tri-level space. You can go for the ground-floor rock-'n'-roll bar (Reds Saloon); a midlevel dance club; a casual dining experience; or an ocean-view, open-air rooftop party. It's open Monday through Friday 11am to 2am, weekends from 10am; food is served till 10pm. 4190 Mission Blvd. (btw. Pacific Beach Dr. and Reed Ave.), Pacific Beach. www.the beachwood.com. ✆ **858/750-2512.** Bus: 8.

Lips ★   This drag revue supper club has a different show nightly, such as Bitchy Bingo on Wednesday and celebrity impersonations on Thursday. Dinner seating is at 7pm Sunday through Thursday; Friday and Saturday it's at 6pm, with an additional seating at 9pm. Sunday gospel brunch begins at 11am. Weekend late shows are ages

suds city: GRAB A GREAT BREW IN S.D.

With more than 40 breweries in town, it's no wonder *Men's Journal* declared San Diego to be America's number one beer city. Here is just a small sampling of the places a serious beer drinker is guaranteed to love.

San Diego's most acclaimed brewery is headquartered in far-flung Escondido, but elegant **Stone Brewing World Bistro & Gardens** (p. 240) is worth the drive. **Pizza Port Brewing Company** (www.pizzaport.com) has three locations: 1956 Bacon St., Ocean Beach (© **619/224-4700**); 135 N. Hwy. 101, Solana Beach (© **858/481-7332**); and 571 Carlsbad Village Dr., in Carlsbad (© **760/720-7007**). Kids can get in on the action with Pizza Port's house-made root beer. At **Pacific Beach AleHouse,** 721 Grand Ave. (www.pbalehouse.com; © **858/581-2337**), you can watch a Pacific sunset from the rooftop deck while you sip on a Pacific Sunset IPA. In Normal Heights, one of the city's great beer bars, **Blind Lady Ale House,** 3416 Adams Ave. (www.blindladyalehouse.com; © **619/255-2491**), makes occasional forays into brewing (one of the owners was a master brewer at Stone once upon a time).

Set in an old factory building constructed in 1894, the East Village's **Mission Brewery,** 1441 L St. (www.missionbrewery.com; © **619/544-0555**), has a cavernous tasting room heady with the smell of hops. There's more brewing going on downtown at the **Beer Company,** 602 Broadway (www.thebeerco.net; © **619/398-0707**) and **Karl Strauss Brewery & Grill,** 1157 Columbia St. (www.karlstrauss.com; © **619/234-2739**). Karl Strauss, which launched San Diego's brewpub scene in the late 1980s, also has locations in La Jolla (1044 Wall St., © **858/551-2739**), Carlsbad (5801 Armada Dr., © **760/431-2739**), and Sorrento Mesa (9675 Scranton Rd., © **858/587-2739**), where the setting is a lovely, incongruous Japanese garden.

For an overview of what San Diego (and the world) has to offer in the way of beer, head over to **Bottlecraft,** 2161 India St., Little Italy (www.bottlecraftbeer.com; © **619/487-9493**), a beer shop and tasting room. If you'd like to do some tours and sampling without the driving, check out **Brewery Tours of San Diego** (www.brewerytoursofsandiego.com; © **619/961-7999**) or **Brew Hop** (www.brewhop.com; © **858/361-8457**).

21 and over only; reservations are recommended. 3036 El Cajon Blvd. (at 30th St.), North Park. www.lipssd.com. © **619/295-7900.** Cover $3–$7, food minimum $15. Bus: 1, 2, or 15.

Nunu's Cocktail Lounge 🍸 You'll find lots of 1960s Naugahyde-style, cheap drinks, and an eclectic crowd at this classic Hillcrest dive, plus a kitchen that whips up specialties such as the Jack Daniel's burger with breaded artichoke hearts. It's open daily from 6am to 2am; kitchen is closed on Mondays. 3537 Fifth Ave. (at Ivy Lane), Hillcrest. www.nunuscocktails.com. © **619/295-2878.** Bus: 3 or 120.

Shakespeare Pub & Grille ★ When you want to tuck into a shepherd's pie while watching some Premier League footie, this is your place. You won't find a more authentic U.K. experience in San Diego; adjacent to the pub is Shakespeare's **Corner Shoppe** (© 619/683-2748; Mon–Fri 10am–8pm, weekends from 9am) selling packaged foods and souvenirs from across the pond. Open Monday to Thursday 10:30am to midnight, Friday 10:30am to 1am, Saturday 8am to 1am, and Sunday 8am to midnight. 3701 India St. (south of Washington St.), Mission Hills. www.shakespearepub.com. © **619/299-0230.** Bus: 10. Trolley: Washington St.

Starlite ★★ 🍴 Local musician Steve Poltz and the mastermind behind the Casbah (p. 171) joined forces to create this great little drinking and dining spot. It has sophisticated design sense, a lounge vibe with cool tunes, and fine food; there's also a sweet outdoor patio. Open daily 5pm to 2am, with Sunday brunch served 10:30am–2pm; food is served till midnight. Reservations accepted. 3175 India St. (at Spruce St.), Mission Hills. www.starlitesandiego.com. *©* **619/358-9766.** Bus: 83. Trolley: Middletown.

Turf Supper Club ★ 🍴 The gimmick at this retro steakhouse is all about cheap, "grill your own" dinners. Steaks and hamburgers ($7–$16) are delivered raw, but seasoned, on a paper plate with sides—you do the rest. If red meat isn't your thing, there are seafood, veggie, and chicken options. The decor is pure 1950s and approved by the cocktail crowd; the volume level is not always conducive to intimate dining, though. Monday to Thursday 5pm to 2am, Friday to Sunday 1pm to 2am. 1116 25th Ave. (at C St.), Golden Hill. www.turfsupperclub.com. *©* **619/234-6363.** Bus: 2.

Coffeehouses with Performances

Claire de Lune Coffee Lounge ★ 🍴 Housed in a handsome building dating from 1929, this coffeehouse has helped create a happening little scene in the neighborhood. There's usually entertainment Friday and Saturday, ranging from world-beat music to belly dancing. Open Monday to Thursday 6:30am to 10pm, Friday and Saturday 6:30am to midnight, Sunday 6:30am to 9pm. 2906 University Ave. (at Kansas St.), North Park. www.clairedelune.com. *©* **619/688-9845.** Bus: 7 or 10.

Lestat's Coffee House ★ 🍴 This local's favorite is open 24/7. There's entertainment nightly, everything from guitar-strumming troubadours (some of the city's best) and rock bands to comics and open-mic hopefuls (Mon). 3343 Adams Ave. (at Felton St.), Normal Heights. www.lestats.com. *©* **619/282-0437.** Bus: 11.

GAY & LESBIAN NIGHTLIFE

Despite it's historically conservative reputation, San Diego is actually a very gay-friendly destination. Hillcrest is the heart of the community; it has a number of queer bars and clubs, and is party central for the annual **Pride Parade, Rally, and Festival** (see p. 23), one of the country's biggest LGBT events. For what's happening at the gay clubs, get the weekly *San Diego Gay & Lesbian Times*, or check out the events online at www.gaylesbiantimes.com. Beyond the clubs, you'll also find a lively scene at several Hillcrest restaurants that are popular with gay patrons: **Urban Mo's Bar & Grill,** 308 University Ave. (www.urbanmos.com; *©* **619/491-0400**); **Baja Betty's,** 1421 University Ave. (www.bettyssd.com; *©* **619/269-8510**); and **Gossip Grill,** 1440 University Ave. (www.thegossipgrill.com; *©* **619/260-8023**).

Bourbon Street Bar & Grill ★ This longtime favorite has several spaces, including an outdoor patio meant to evoke jazzy New Orleans; a performance area for open-mic nights, karaoke, and drag shows; and a lounge where DJs spin dance music. Open daily from 4pm to 2am; the restaurant serves Tuesday through Saturday till 10pm, and Sunday brunch from 11am to 4pm. Sunday nights are all about the girls. 4612 Park Blvd. (near Adams Ave.), University Heights. www.bourbonstreetsd.com. *©* **619/291-4043.** Bus: 11.

The Brass Rail San Diego's oldest gay bar (open since 1960) has been remodeled, refreshed, and given a jolt of new energy. It now features VIP rooms, bottle service, upgraded sound and lighting, and food (tacos, burgers). The popular Manic Monday features '80s music; Thursday is karaoke night; Saturday features Latin grooves; and every 2nd, 3rd, and 4th Friday is ladies' night. Open daily 2pm to 2am. 3796 Fifth Ave. (at Robinson St.), Hillcrest. www.thebrassrailsd.com. ✆ **619/298-2233.** Cover none–$15. Bus: 1, 3, or 120.

The Flame ★   Across the street from Numbers (see review below), the Flame has two rooms (including a VIP section), three bars, and some very cool neon out front. Every 2nd, 4th, and 5th Saturday, the Goth Club Sabbat takes over; Fridays are Soul Kiss for women. Open Thursday 9pm to 2am, and Friday through Sunday 1pm to 2am. 3780 Park Blvd. (at Robinson Ave.), Hillcrest. www.flamesandiego.com. ✆ **619/795-8578.** Cover none–$10. Bus: 1, 7, 10, or 11.

Flicks ★   Since 1983, this video bar has featured VJs drawing from a database of 15,000 music and comedy clips. There are also various weekly special events, contests, and games, as well as karaoke on Sunday and Monday. Open Monday to Thursday 4pm to 2am, Friday to Sunday 2pm to 2am. 1017 University Ave., Hillcrest. www.sdflicks.com. ✆ **619/297-2056.** Bus: 1, 10, or 11.

Numbers ★   It's a predominantly male crowd at this busy dance emporium, with three bars, two dance floors, and go-go boy dancers. Open Tuesday to Friday 4pm to 2am, weekends 1pm to 2am. Saturday is Femme Fatale night for the girls. 3811 Park Blvd. (at University Ave.), Hillcrest. www.numberssd.com. ✆ **619/294-7583.** Cover none–$10. Bus: 1, 7, 10, or 11.

Rich's ★   This mega–dance club in the heart of Hillcrest has been an institution for years. A variety of special events are scheduled, including ladies' nights on Thursdays and a "bear" dance party the third Saturday of every month. A renovation has opened the space up with windows and a sidewalk patio. Hours are Wednesday to Sunday 9pm to 2am. 1051 University Ave. (btw. Vermont St. and 10th Ave.), Hillcrest. www.richssandiego.com. ✆ **619/295-2195.** Cover $5–$15. Bus: 1, 10, or 11.

Top of the Park ★★   The penthouse bar of the Inn at the Park (see p. 197), offering spectacular views of Balboa Park and beyond, is a very popular social scene on Friday evenings from 5 to 10pm. The weekend party scene officially begins here. 525 Spruce St. (at Fifth Ave.), Hillcrest. www.shellhospitality.com. ✆ **619/291-0999.** Bus: 3 or 120.

ALTERNATIVE ENTERTAINMENT

Evening Bay Cruises

Flagship   This company (formerly known as San Diego Harbor Excursion) offers nightly dinner packages, with choice of meat or vegetarian entree, dessert, and cocktails; prime rib is offered on Sundays. For an additional $50 per couple, you can guarantee yourself a private table with window, plus a bottle of champagne, wine, or cider. A DJ plays dance music during the 2½-hour outing. Boarding is at 6pm, and the cruise lasts from 6:30 to 9pm. 1050 N. Harbor Dr. (at Broadway Pier). www.flagshipsd.com. ✆ **800/442-7847** or 619/234-4111. Tickets $67 adults ($89 with fully hosted bar), $38 children ages 4–12, free for children 3 and under; all prices $10 higher on Sat. Bus: 992. Trolley: America Plaza.

Hornblower Cruises   Aboard the 151-foot antique-style yacht *Lord Hornblower*, you'll be entertained—and encouraged to dance—by a DJ playing a variety of music. The three-course meal is standard-issue banquet style (vegetarian options are available), but the scenery is marvelous. Boarding is at 6:30pm, and the cruise runs from 7 to 10pm. 1800 N. Harbor Dr. (at Grape St. Pier). www.hornblower.com. ✆ **888/467-6256** or

619/686-8700. Tickets Sun–Fri $70, Sat $80 adults, $68–$78 seniors (55 and above) and military, $42–$48 children ages 4–12, free for children 3 and under; drinks cost extra. Bus: 923 or 992. Trolley: County Center/Little Italy.

Cinema

Current independent and foreign films play at Landmark Theatre's five-screen **Hillcrest Cinema,** 3965 Fifth Ave., Hillcrest, which offers 3 hours of free parking; the **Ken Cinema,** 4061 Adams Ave., Kensington, San Diego's last single-screen theater (built in 1946); and the four-screen **La Jolla Village,** 8879 Villa La Jolla Dr., La Jolla, also with free parking. For info on any of them, call ✆ **619/819-0236,** or go to www.landmarktheatres.com.

The **Museum of Photographic Arts,** in Balboa Park (www.mopa.org; ✆ 619/238-7559), and the **Museum of Contemporary Art San Diego,** in La Jolla (www.mcasd.org; ✆ 858/454-3541), both have ongoing film programs that are worth investigating. The **IMAX Dome Theater** at the Reuben H. Fleet Science Center (www.rhfleet.org; ✆ 619/238-1233), also in Balboa Park, features movies projected onto an enormous dome screen (films are shown in the early evening, with later screenings on weekends).

Another unique venue is located behind a hair salon in Mission Hills. **Cinema Under the Stars,** 4040 Goldfinch St. (www.topspresents.com; ✆ **619/295-4221**), is an intimate, outdoor movie-going experience that usually runs from spring through fall (Thurs–Sun), featuring both classic and new releases. Patrons can lounge in zero-gravity chairs or sit at cafe tables; get your tickets early—these shows sell out.

San Diego also hosts several prominent film festivals: the **San Diego Film Festival** in late September (www.sdff.org; ✆ **619/582-2368**); the **San Diego Latino Film Festival,** mid-March (www.sdlatinofilm.com; ✆ 619/230-1938); the **San Diego Black Film Festival,** late January (www.sdbff.com; ✆ 619/685-7215); the **San Diego Jewish Film Festival** in mid-February (www.sdjff.org; ✆ 858/362-1330); and, in early November, the **San Diego Asian Film Festival** (www.sdaff.org; ✆ **619/400-5911**).

Casinos

San Diego County has 18 Native American tribes—more than any other county in the nation. More than half of them operate casinos in east and north San Diego County; **Valley View Casino,** 16300 Nyemii Pass Rd, Valley Center (www.valleyviewcasino.com; ✆ 866/843-9946), is the most recent to unveil a stylish hotel to go along with its gaming. The **Convention & Visitors Bureau** (www.sandiego.org; ✆ **619/232-3101**) has comprehensive listings and discounts on its website. Casino locations are shown on the "Eastern San Diego County" map on p. 243.

The most easily accessible casino from the downtown area is **Viejas Casino,** 5000 Willows Rd., in Alpine (www.viejas.com; ✆ **800/847-6537** or 619/445-5400)—it's a straight shot out I-8 (exit Willows Rd.), less than a half-hour drive away. Besides the usual table games, slots, bingo, and satellite wagering, Viejas presents live music in its 700-seat showroom; there is also an outlet center with more than 30 brand-name retailers, a 12-lane bowling alley, and a seasonal ice rink. In 2006, the casino added 48,000 square feet of new space, encompassing a VIP lounge and high-end bar, the V Lounge.

The **Barona Resort & Casino** is at 1932 Wildcat Canyon Rd., Lakeside (www.barona.com; ✆ **888/722-7662** or 619/443-2300). Take I-8 East to Route 67 North; at Willows Road, turn right and continue to Wildcat Canyon Road; turn left and

FISHY FUN: the grunion run

The **Grunion Run ★** is a local tradition—so if someone invites you down to the beach for a late-night fishing expedition, armed only with a sack and flashlight, don't be afraid. Grunion are 5- to 6-inch silvery fish that wriggle out of the water to lay their eggs in the sand. Found only in Southern and Baja California, they make for decent eating, coated in flour and cornmeal, and then fried. April to early June is peak spawning season, but they may only be caught—**by hand**—during the months of March and then June through August; a fishing license is required for those 16 and older. Grunion runs happen twice a month after the highest tides, about 2 to 5 nights after a full or new moon. Anywhere from a few dozen to thousands of grunion can appear during a run. They prefer wide, flat, sandy beaches (such as the Coronado Strand, Mission Beach, and La Jolla Shores); you'll spot more grunion if you go to a less-populated stretch of beach, with a minimum amount of light. For details, go to the little critters' website, www.grunion. pepperdine.edu, or check with the Department of Fish and Game at www. dfg.ca.gov.

continue 6 miles to the 7,500-acre Barona Reservation (allow 40 min. from downtown). The casino features 2,000 Vegas-style slots, 80 table games, and an off-track betting area. The resort, which includes 400 guest rooms, a spa, and an 18-hole championship golf course, restricts alcohol consumption (limited to the hotel, 4 of the 11 restaurants, and golf course), but allows smoking (the Indian reservations are exempt from California's nonsmoking laws).

Sycuan Resort & Casino is outside El Cajon, at 5469 Casino Way (www.sycuan. com; 𝄐 **800/279-2826** or 619/445-6002). Follow I-8 East for 10 miles to the El Cajon Boulevard exit. Take El Cajon 3 blocks to Washington Avenue, turning right and continuing on Washington as it turns into Dehesa Road. Stay on Dehesa for 5 miles, and follow the signs (allow 30 min. from downtown). Sycuan features 2,000 slots, 60 gaming tables, a 24-table poker room, a 1,200-seat bingo palace, and a 450-seat theater that books name touring acts. The property was refreshed with a $27-million renovation in 2012, and a nonsmoking boutique casino, complete with separate entrance, opened in 2008. The nearby resort offers 100 rooms and 54 holes of golf.

SPECTATOR SPORTS

Baseball & Softball

The **San Diego Padres** of the National League play April through September at downtown's $474-million **PETCO Park ★**, 100 Park Blvd. Mired in litigation and controversy, the 42,000-seat ballpark finally opened in 2004 to enthusiastic acclaim from baseball fans and civic boosters.

A total of seven historic buildings were incorporated into the stadium, most prominently the Western Metal Supply building, a four-story brick structure dating to 1909 that now sprouts left field bleachers. The restaurant and bar here are hot spots during the game. Another unique feature is the Park at the Park, a grassy area beyond center field where kids can romp and watch the game at the same time; the area has its own playground and concession stands, as well as a heroic bronze statue of Padres Hall of Famer Tony Gwynn.

This ballpark isn't the first to offer sushi alongside the usual franks and fries, but you'll find plenty of dining options. Several Mexican-themed eateries serve south-of-the-border fare, there's a barbecue stand run by former Padres pitcher Randy Jones, and one stand sells nothing but gluten-free items. PETCO parking is limited and can be costly; expect to pay anywhere from $8 to $20, depending on how close to the stadium you get. Less expensive lots are found around Santa Fe depot at Kettner Boulevard and Broadway—a 15- to 20-minute walk from the ballpark. Better yet, take the San Diego Trolley, which has three stops near the park. For Padres information and tickets (ranging in price from $5–$98), visit www.padres.com or call © **877/374-2784** or 619/795-5000.

The highlight of many San Diegans' summer is the racy softball event known as the **World Championship Over-the-Line Tournament,** held on Fiesta Island in Mission Bay on the second and third weekends of July. For more information, see the "San Diego Calendar of Events," on p. 21.

Boating Events

Nearly two dozen tall ships from around the world make for San Diego during the **Festival of Sail,** held over the long Labor Day weekend (Labor Day is always the first Mon in Sept). Canons roar, sea chanteys are sung, racing yachts offer bay cruises, and arts and crafts vendors ply their wares along the Embarcadero. Your ticket ($15 adults, $10 seniors and children 12 and under) allows you to tour the ships, including the collection at the **Maritime Museum** (p. 55), which hosts the event. The annual **San Diego Crew Classic,** held on Mission Bay the first weekend in April (www.crewclassic.org; © **619/225-0300**), is one of the country's premier regattas, drawing rowing teams from throughout the United States. The **Wooden Boat Festival** is held on Shelter Island every June over Father's Day weekend (www.koehlerkraft.com; © **619/222-9051**). More than 80 boats—from rowboats to schooners—participate in the festival, which features nautical displays, seminars, food, music, and crafts. Admission is $5 adults, $3 children 6 to 12, free for children 5 and under.

Football

San Diego's National Football League team, the **Chargers,** has been shopping for another city (including others within the county) since failing to generate interest—and lots of public funding—for an audacious plan to create a huge urban village around a new stadium in Mission Valley. For now, the **Chargers** (www.chargers.com; © **800/745-3000** for single tickets, 877/242-7437, or 619/280-2121) play at **Qualcomm Stadium** ("the Q"), 9449 Friars Rd., Mission Valley. The season runs from August to December; single tickets are $54 to $98. The **Sports Fan Shuttle** (www.sportsfanexpress.com; © **866/766-4937**) costs $20 to $25 round trip and picks up passengers at five different locations throughout the city; the stadium is also easily reached via the San Diego Trolley. General parking is $25; the tailgate zone is $75. The parking hot line is © **619/281-7275.**

Golf Tournaments

When General Motors collapsed in 2009, one of the country's biggest golf tournaments was left with an identity crisis and no sponsor. The former **Buick Invitational,** which takes place in late January at Torrey Pines Golf Course in La Jolla, was hastily rechristened as the **San Diego Open;** then, just days before the event, it got another name: the **Farmers Insurance Open** (www.farmersinsuranceopen.com; ✆ **858/535-4500** or 858/886-4653). The insurance giant has now signed on to the tournament until 2014. The weeklong tourney draws the PGA Tour's top golfers and features a number of special events, including clinics and pro-ams. Single-day tickets are $21 to $32, and $21 for seniors; tournament passes are $120 (discount tickets are available in advance online). Monday, when the PGA players do their practice rounds, is free. General parking is offered at several locations including the Torrey Pines Glider Port, just south of the main entrance, and the Del Mar Show Park, located off I-5 at Via de la Valle; the cost is $20 including round-trip shuttle service.

Horse Racing & Equestrian Events

Live thoroughbred racing takes place at the **Del Mar Racetrack** (www.dmtc.com; ✆ **858/755-1141** for information and racing schedules) from mid-July to early September. Post time for the 8- to 10-race program is 2pm (except for Fri, when it's 4pm; 3:30pm on the final three Fri); there's no racing on Monday (except Labor Day) or Tuesday. Admission to the clubhouse is $10, including program. Stretch-run admission is $6 with program and infield access; reserved seats are $5 to $15. Free for children 17 and under. Tables for four with food service run $60 to $125 (excluding admission). The infield area has a jungle gym where kids can play or watch shows put on by BMX riders and skateboarders; there's also a day camp offered for kids ages 5 to 12 ($24 per child). Party crowds are lured by post-race concerts by major artists and other special events. General parking is $10; valet parking is $20. Double-decker buses also transport race goers for free from the Solana Beach train station. Year-round, satellite wagering is available at the fairgrounds' race book, **Surfside Race Place** (www.surfsideraceplace.com; ✆ **858/755-1167**). It operates Wednesday through Monday, opening at 9am (closing time varies); $5 admission.

Since 1946, the **Del Mar National Horse Show** has taken place at the Del Mar Fairgrounds. From mid-April to early May, Olympic-caliber and national championship riders participate in Western, hunter/jumper, and dressage competitions; the "Night of the Horse" is a popular evening event that changes themes annually. Tickets are $10 to $18; for information, check www.delmarnational.com or call ✆ **858/792-4252** or 858/792-4288.

The **San Diego Polo Club,** in Del Mar, 14555 El Camino Real (www.sandiego polo.com; ✆ **858/481-9217**), has Sunday matches from June to October (with a summer break mid-July to mid-Aug), beginning at 1pm. The scene is casual and convivial, with a touch of class; and even if you don't know a chukker from a ride-off, watching these skilled horsemen is plenty exciting. Tickets are $10 (free for children 12 and under), or $30 for reserved VIP seating ($15 children). Parking is $5, or you can tailgate alongside the field for $25. And FYI: A chukker is a period of play, and a ride-off is the polo equivalent of a hockey body-check.

Roller Derby

Revived locally in recent years by the **San Diego Derby Dolls,** the spectacle of roller derby has deep roots in California, dating back to the mid-1950s. Racing around banked and flat-track ovals on roller skates—elbowing their way past blockers, scoring points by lapping their opponents—the Derby Dolls sport names like Bo Toxic, Heidi Evidence, and Slamurai. Scheduled year-round, there's plenty of fast, family-friendly action (and a full bar). The "Dollhouse" is located at the Del Mar Fairgrounds, 2260 Jimmy Durante Blvd.; tickets are $15 to $20, $13 for seniors, military, and children 6 to 12, free for kids 5 and under. For information go to www.sd.derbydolls.com or call ✆ **619/228-6060.**

Soccer

San Diego's most successful sports franchise, the **Sockers,** won 10 indoor soccer championships—and still managed to fold twice in less than 10 years. In 2009, the Sockers were resurrected for a third time, this time as part of the Professional Arena Soccer League, playing in the Del Mar Arena at the fairgrounds, 2260 Jimmy Durante Blvd. Sure enough, the team has picked up right where it left off, earning back-to-back championships in the 2010 and 2011 seasons. Matches are scheduled from November to February and tickets are $10 to $20; for information, call ✆ **866/799-4625,** or go to www.sdsockers.com.

South of the border, Tijuanenses are mad for their **Club Tijuana Xoloitzcuintles de Caliente** (www.xolos.com.mx; ✆ **664/647-4786**), a team that belongs to Mexico's top-level professional division, playing in a 33,000-seat stadium inaugurated in 2007. See p. 266.

WHERE TO STAY

San Diego accommodations are as varied as the county's diverse topography. From beaches, to mountains, to desert, you'll find hip high-rises, spa- and golf-blessed resorts, and properties rife with history, as well as backpacker hostels and out-of-the-ordinary B&Bs. *Note:* This chapter explores all the options within the city proper. Lodging for Del Mar, Encinitas, and Carlsbad (all beautifully situated along the coast and within 40 min. of the city) are found in chapter 10, as are hotels for south-of-the-border and inland regions.

BEST BETS

- **Best Splurge:** Resembling an ornate Tuscan villa, the **Grand Del Mar,** is an aptly named resort tucked into the foothills of Del Mar. Opened in 2007, it features exquisite terraces, fountains, gardens, and amenities galore. Its stand-alone restaurant, **Addison,** is the first San Diego dining establishment to receive an AAA Five Diamond Award. See p. 225.

- **Best for Families:** The **Paradise Point Resort & Spa** (p. 202) is a tropical playground offering enough activities to keep family members of all ages happy. In addition to a virtual Disneyland of on-site options, the aquatic playground of Mission Bay surrounds the hotel's private peninsula. **Loews Coronado Bay Resort** (p. 215) also provides plenty of diversions for adults and children alike. It's located on its own 15-acre peninsula and has a private marina, access to miles of beach, and lots of supervised activities for the kids.

- **Most Romantic:** At the **Lodge at Torrey Pines** (p. 208)—one of only three AAA Five-Diamond hotels in the county—you can enjoy a fireplace in your room, sunset ocean views from your balcony, a couple's massage at the fabulous spa, and superb meals at the hotel's A.R. Valentien restaurant. In the Gaslamp Quarter, the **Andaz Hotel** (p. 186) has seriously sexy accommodations, where see-through showers separate the bed and bathroom areas; one room even has a stripper pole.

- **Best Service:** The Zen-inspired boutique **Hotel Parisi** (p. 210) is small enough to provide personalized service and upscale enough to offer in-room treatments ranging from acupuncture to ear coning. In

PRICE CATEGORIES

Very Expensive	$300 and up	Moderate	$100–$200
Expensive	$200–$300	Inexpensive	Under $100

WHAT YOU'LL really pay

A hotel's "rack rate" is the official published rate, and the prices quoted here are all high-season rack rates. The truth is, though, *hardly anybody pays rack rates*, and with the exception of smaller B&Bs, you can usually pay quite a bit less by using online discounters such as **Hotels.com** or **Expedia** (see "Getting the Best Deal," on p. 218, for more tips). Also keep in mind that the rates given in this chapter do not include the hotel tax, which is an additional 10.5%, or 12.5% for lodgings with 70 or more rooms. But *always* peruse the category above your target price—you might just find the perfect match.

I called several downtown hotels one Tuesday morning to see what their best rate on a room for that same night would be. In all instances the rate I was quoted was 25% to 40% lower than the rack rate. When I called the Grand Hyatt, I was first quoted $240—a third off the rack rate. The price fell to $220 when I mentioned my AAA membership. I said, "Thanks, I'll get back to you." The very helpful reservations agent countered, "Let me check to see if there are any packages available." Within a few seconds she found a rate of $139 that included breakfast for two, free parking, and a 15% discount off dinner at the hotel. I started to end the call again, and she cut me off to say, "Oh, here's a $99 promotional rate you might want to consider . . ."

Note: Quoted discount rates almost never include breakfast, hotel tax, or any applicable resort fees.

Carlsbad, the **Park Hyatt Aviara Resort** (p. 232) has maintained the AAA Five-Diamond rating the property earned when it was a Four Seasons, and top-notch service is one of the reasons why.

- **Best Value:** In Little Italy, **La Pensione Hotel** (p. 195) feels like a small European hotel and offers tidy lodgings at bargain prices. There's an abundance of great dining in the surrounding blocks, and you'll be perfectly situated to explore the area by trolley. At the **Gaslamp Plaza Suites** (p. 193) you can be right in the heart of the downtown action, surrounded by Edwardian architectural flourishes, while paying considerably less than you would at trendier properties nearby.
- **Best Historic Hotel:** The **Hotel del Coronado** positively oozes history. Opened in 1888, this Victorian masterpiece had some of the first electric lights in existence, and over the years has hosted kings, presidents, and movie stars. Meticulous restoration has enhanced this glorious landmark, whose early days are well chronicled in displays throughout the hotel. See p. 213.
- **Best Place to Stay on the Beach:** Although the Hotel Del is the grande dame of West Coast seaside resorts, if you really want to be in the heart of San Diego's beach culture, no place is better than **Tower 23.** This sleek, modernist hotel—which takes its name from an old lifeguard station—sits right on the Pacific Beach boardwalk. See p. 203.
- **Best Bed-and-Breakfast:** The **Britt Scripps Inn** is set in a glorious Victorian mansion, once home to one of the city's most prominent families. It offers incredible architectural details, top-of-the-line amenities, and a great location near Balboa Park. See p. 196.
- **Best Eco-Friendly Hotel:** The **Hotel Indigo** is not only one of downtown's more stylish properties, it's also the greenest. It is San Diego's first hotel to be

awarded LEED (Leadership in Energy and Environmental Design) certification, incorporating everything from composting to in-room natural lighting. See p. 189.

○ **Best Hotel Pool:** The top-floor pool, sun deck, and lounge at the **Andaz Hotel** (p. 186) collectively make up downtown's largest rooftop space. Although the pool is shallow, the video-enhanced cabanas, Gaslamp Quarter vistas, and clubby vibe attract the beautiful people (some of whom are also shallow). For a more private, guests-only experience, the pool at **La Valencia Hotel** (p. 208) is oh-so-special, with its spectacular setting overlooking Scripps Park and the Pacific.

DOWNTOWN, GASLAMP QUARTER & LITTLE ITALY

San Diego's downtown is an excellent place for travelers to stay. The nightlife and dining in the Gaslamp Quarter and shopping at Horton Plaza are close at hand; Balboa Park, Hillcrest, Old Town, and Coronado are less than 10 minutes away by car; and beaches aren't much farther. It's also the city's public transportation hub, and thus very convenient for car-free visitors.

Best For: Just about everything. There are museums, bars and nightclubs, fine dining, and shopping opportunities galore.

Drawbacks: The action goes on late and loud here, particularly on weekends, and some of the most popular nightspots are in hotels.

Very Expensive

Omni San Diego Hotel ★★   This downtown property has a fourth-floor skybridge that connects it with PETCO Park—it's the only hotel in the United States that's directly linked to a major-league ballpark. Twelve rooms even have (limited) views of the field, and the hotel's common areas are adorned with baseball memorabilia, such as Babe Ruth's 1932 contract with the Yankees and Joe DiMaggio's cleats from his record-setting 1941 season. Packages that include tickets to a Padres game are available. Outside of baseball season, this 32-story high-rise caters to the business crowd, luring conventioneers with more than 27,000 square feet of meeting space and an up-to-the-minute business center. The airy, contemporary rooms feature floor-to-ceiling windows (that open)—some have balconies—and provide awesome vistas. The hotel's street-level function space is fronted by a surprisingly adventurous art gallery that focuses on the work of California artists, while **McCormick & Schmick's Seafood Restaurant** adds name recognition to the on-site dining offerings.

675 L St. (at Sixth Ave.), San Diego, CA 92101. www.omnihotels.com. ℂ **888/444-6664** or 619/231-6664. Fax 619/231-8060. 511 units. $309–$329 double; from $500 suite. Children 12 and under stay free in parent's room. Packages available. AE, DC, DISC, MC, V. Valet parking $35. Trolley: Gaslamp Quarter. Pets under 40 lb. accepted with $50 nonrefundable fee. **Amenities:** Restaurant; 2 bars; concierge; exercise room; Jacuzzi; outdoor pool; room service. *In room:* A/C, TV/DVD, hair dryer, minibar, MP3 docking station, Wi-Fi ($10/day or free with loyalty program sign-up).

Expensive

Andaz Hotel ★★   Built in 1914, this property has been transformed into a world-class, high-style luxury destination (formerly known as the Ivy). Its unbeatable Gaslamp Quarter address assures a steady stream of beautiful people making their way into **Ivy,** the hotel's multilevel nightclub; Andaz also boasts downtown's largest rooftop pool and entertainment area, a 17,000-square-foot playground known as **Ivy**

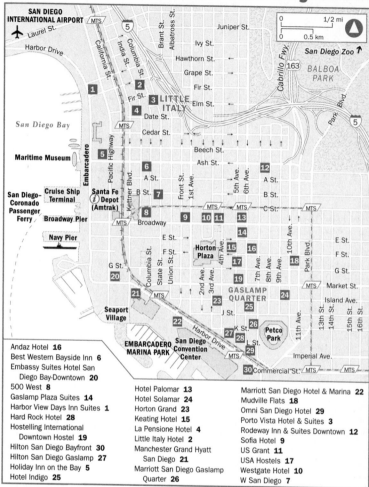

SAN DIEGO INTERNATIONAL AIRPORT
Laurel St.
Harbor Drive
Juniper St.
Ivy St.
Hawthorn St.
Grape St.
Fir St.
San Diego Zoo ↑
BALBOA PARK
LITTLE ITALY
Elm St.
Date St.
Cedar St.
San Diego Bay
Beech St.
Maritime Museum
Ash St.
A St.
A St.
B St.
B St.
San Diego–Coronado Passenger Ferry
Cruise Ship Terminal
Santa Fe Depot (Amtrak)
Broadway Pier
Broadway
C St.
Navy Pier
E St.
E St.
Horton Plaza
F St.
F St.
G St.
G St.
Market St.
Seaport Village
GASLAMP QUARTER
Island Ave.
J St.
Harbor Drive
EMBARCADERO MARINA PARK
San Diego Convention Center
K St.
L St.
Petco Park
Imperial Ave.
Commercial St.

Andaz Hotel 16
Best Western Bayside Inn 6
Embassy Suites Hotel San Diego Bay-Downtown 20
500 West 8
Gaslamp Plaza Suites 14
Harbor View Days Inn Suites 1
Hard Rock Hotel 28
Hostelling International Downtown Hostel 19
Hilton San Diego Bayfront 30
Hilton San Diego Gaslamp 27
Holiday Inn on the Bay 5
Hotel Indigo 25

Hotel Palomar 13
Hotel Solamar 24
Horton Grand 23
Keating Hotel 15
La Pensione Hotel 4
Little Italy Hotel 2
Manchester Grand Hyatt San Diego 21
Marriott San Diego Gaslamp Quarter 26

Marriott San Diego Hotel & Marina 22
Mudville Flats 18
Omni San Diego Hotel 29
Porto Vista Hotel & Suites 3
Rodeway Inn & Suites Downtown 12
Sofia Hotel 9
US Grant 11
USA Hostels 17
Westgate Hotel 10
W San Diego 7

Rooftop. Design-forward sushi resto **Katsuya by Starck** joined the party in 2012 and occupies the hotel's cavernous dining room. **Note:** These are popular weekend nightspots; if you don't care to play along, you may want to look elsewhere. The fashionable rooms are modern but warm, but demure types should note that most feature a sexy, see-through cocoon of a shower/tub combination. You'll find a selection of freebie drinks and snacks in your digs; there's also complimentary wine available every evening in the lobby. The signature suite at this nonsmoking property is a split-level affair with a spiral staircase that leads to a private poolside cabana.

600 F St. (btw. Sixth and Seventh aves.), San Diego, CA 92101. www.andaz.com. ℂ **800/492-8804** or 619/849-1234. Fax 619/531-7955. 159 units. From $239 double; from $329 suite. Children 12 and under stay free in parent's room. Packages available. AE, DC, DISC, MC, V. Valet parking $35. Bus:

3 or 120. Pets less than 40 lb. accepted for $45/night. **Amenities:** Restaurant; 2 bars; nightclub; 24-hr. concierge; fitness center; outdoor pool; room service; spa services. *In room:* A/C, TV/DVD, CD player, full bar, hair dryer, MP3 docking station, free Wi-Fi.

Embassy Suites Hotel San Diego Bay-Downtown ★★

If you can snag a room when a big convention isn't forcing up downtown rates, this business hotel can be a good deal for families. This spot provides modern accommodations with lots of room for families or claustrophobes. Built in 1988, the neoclassical high-rise is topped with a distinctive neon bull's-eye that's visible from far away. Every room is a suite, with a king or two doubles in the bedroom, plus a sofa bed in the living/dining area; each has convenient features such as a kitchenette and a dining table that converts into a work area. All rooms open onto a 12-story atrium filled with palm trees, koi ponds, and a bubbling fountain; each also has a city or bay view. It's 1 block from Seaport Village and 8 blocks from the Gaslamp Quarter.

601 Pacific Hwy. (at N. Harbor Dr.), San Diego, CA 92101. www.embassysuites.com. ⓒ **800/362-2779** or 619/239-2400. Fax 619/239-1520. 337 units. $199–$259 suite. Extra person $20. Rates include full breakfast and cocktail hour. Children 18 and under stay free in parent's room. AE, DC, DISC, MC, V. Valet parking $29. Trolley: Seaport Village. Pets up to 75 lb. accepted with $75 fee. **Amenities:** 3 restaurants; bar; children's programs; concierge; exercise room; Jacuzzi; indoor pool. *In room:* A/C, TV, fridge, hair dryer, Internet ($13), kitchenette.

Hard Rock Hotel San Diego ★★

A far cry from the tired burger-and-memorabilia joint over on Fourth Avenue, this 12-story condo-hotel has a sweet location—at the gateway to the Gaslamp Quarter—and plenty of star power. The Black Eyed Peas weigh in with a million-dollar "doped-out" suite specially designed by the group. It's one of 17 "Rock Star" suites, some of which include private decks, fire pits, outdoor hot tubs, and 270-degree city views. Standard rooms are hip and modern, with sophisticated furnishings and 42-inch TVs; accommodations are also well soundproofed from the Gaslamp hubbub. Master Chef Nobuyuki Matsuhisa, who has partnered with actor Robert De Niro on restaurants around the world, adds San Diego to the list with **Nobu,** the hotel's signature eatery (p. 121). The Hard Rock also features a full-service **spa,** retail boutique, a happening lounge, and an outdoor party space adjacent to the fourth-floor pool.

207 Fifth Ave. (btw. K and L sts.), San Diego, CA 92101. www.hardrockhotelsd.com. ⓒ **866/751-7625** or 619/702-3000. Fax 619/702-3007. 420 units. From $249 double; from $289 suite. AE, DC, DISC, MC, V. Valet parking $37. Trolley: Gaslamp Quarter. **Amenities:** 2 restaurants, 2 bars; music venue; concierge; exercise room; outdoor pool; room service; spa. *In room:* A/C, TV, hair dryer, minibar, MP3 docking station, free Wi-Fi.

Hilton San Diego Bayfront ★★

Just steps from the bay, this sleek hotel towers above its closest neighbors, the convention center and PETCO Park. Separated from the Gaslamp Quarter by busy Harbor Drive, this nonsmoking property, opened in late 2008, is downtown's most isolated. It's built on the grounds of a former shipyard, and views into an adjacent, still-working shipyard add a gritty counterpoint to the pristine hotel grounds. A Calatrava-esque pedestrian bridge connects the hotel to the ballpark and provides direct access to the East Village and Gaslamp action. The comfortable rooms, which offer marvelous, unimpeded views in all directions, play to the business-class base, featuring pullout workstation tables, supportive Herman Miller chairs, and easy access outlets. An on-site sports bar, lounge, spa, and upscale restaurant help soften the hotel's meeting-facility feel; now if they'd only dim the lights in the cavernous, office-bright lobby.

1 Park Blvd. (at Harbor Dr.), San Diego, CA 92101. www.hiltonsandiegobayfront.com. © **800/774-1500** or 619/564-3333. Fax 619/564-3344. 1,189 units (most with shower-only bathrooms). From $205 double; from $255 suite (discounts for advance payment online). AE, DC, DISC, MC, V. Valet parking $36; self-parking $27. Pets up to 75 lb. accepted with $50 fee. From airport head south on Harbor Dr., turn right on Park Blvd. **Amenities:** 3 restaurants; 2 bars; concierge; exercise room; Jacuzzi; outdoor pool; room service; spa. *In room:* A/C, TV, hair dryer, Wi-Fi ($14/day).

Hilton San Diego Gaslamp Quarter ★★★

At the foot of the Gaslamp Quarter and across the street from the convention center, this hotel is ideally situated for both business and leisure travelers. It's a great place for guests who want to be close to the action (which includes loads of restaurants, nightlife, and the ballpark within a few blocks), but not get lost in the shuffle. This nonsmoking hotel opened in 2001 on the site of the old Bridgeworks building—part of San Diego's original wharf a century ago; much of the brick facade was incorporated into the hotel's polished design. Standard rooms boast upmarket furniture. There are also suites and an executive floor, but the really snazzy picks are rooms in the **Lofts on Fifth Avenue,** a hotel within the hotel that features 30 oversize guest rooms with towering ceilings, custom furnishings, and lavish tubs. These are some of the handsomest hotel rooms downtown.

401 K St. (at Fourth Ave.), San Diego, CA 92101. www.hilton.com. © **800/445-8667** or 619/231-4040. Fax 619/231-6439. 283 units. $239 double; from $309 suite. Children 11 and under stay free in parent's room. AE, DC, DISC, MC, V. Valet parking $40. Trolley: Gaslamp Quarter or Convention Center. Pets less than 75 lb. accepted with $75 fee. **Amenities:** 2 restaurants; bar; babysitting; concierge; health club; Jacuzzi; outdoor pool; room service; full-service spa. *In room:* A/C, TV, hair dryer, Internet, minibar.

Horton Grand ★ 🎁

A cross between an elegant hotel and a charming inn, the Horton Grand combines two hotels that date from 1886—one of which was the residence of lawman Wyatt Earp during his San Diego days. Both properties were saved from demolition, moved to this spot, and connected by an airy atrium lobby filled with white wicker. The facade, with its graceful bay windows, is original. Each room at this nonsmoking property is unique, with vintage furnishings and gas fireplaces; bathrooms are lush, with reproduction floor tiles, fine brass fixtures, and genteel appointments. Rooms overlook either the city or the fig tree–filled courtyard; the suites (really just large studio-style rooms) are in a newer wing—choosing one means sacrificing historic character for a sitting area/sofa bed and minibar with microwave. If you're lonely, request room 309, where Roger the ghost hangs out.

311 Island Ave. (at Fourth Ave.), San Diego, CA 92101. www.hortongrand.com. © **800/542-1886** or 619/544-1886. Fax 619/544-0058. 132 units. From $209 double; from $309 suite. Extra person $20. Children 17 and under stay free in parent's room. AE, DC, MC, V. Valet parking $25. Bus: 3, 11, or 120. Trolley: Convention Center. **Amenities:** Restaurant (breakfast and lunch only); bar. *In room:* A/C, TV, hair dryer, Wi-Fi ($10).

Hotel Indigo ★★

Opened in 2009, this is San Diego's first LEED-certified hotel, meaning it was designed and built—and continues to operate—under the highest standards of sustainability. It has eco-friendly features like a 4,000-square-foot rooftop garden for insulation, energy-efficient lighting (and floor-to-ceiling windows to maximize natural light), and in-room recycling receptacles. Best of all, this nonsmoking, pet-friendly property sees to it you don't sacrifice one little bit of style or comfort. Liberal doses of nature-inspired original art, including colorful in-room wall murals, stylish hardwood floors, and plenty of easily accessible outlets for plugging in electronics, give the accommodations a livable, residential feel. The ninth-floor **Level 9 Rooftop Bar** is a great spot for a cocktail, affording tantalizing views right into PETCO Park.

509 Ninth Ave. (at Island Ave.), San Diego, CA 92101. www.hotelindigo.com/sandiego. © **877/270-1392** or 619/727-4000. Fax 619/727-4010. 210 units (most bathrooms have showers only). From $248 double; from $440 suite. Children 17 and under stay free in parent's room. AE, DC, DISC, MC, V. Valet parking $38. Bus: 3, 11, 901, or 929. Hwy. 163 S. becomes 10th Ave.; make a right on Island Ave. Pets accepted (no fees). **Amenities:** Restaurant; 2 bars; concierge; exercise room; room service. *In room:* A/C, TV, hair dryer, MP3 docking station, free Wi-Fi.

Hotel Palomar ★★★

What happens when hotel developers pull out all the stops to create sanctuaries of sophistication and luxury like this property? Sometimes they go broke. Luckily for travelers, though, this hotel—formerly known as Sè San Diego—has been rescued by the Kimpton Hotel group, which has overseen its triumphant turnaround. Opened in 2008, this 23-story steel-and-glass tower is one of the city's sexiest hotels, with such elaborate touches as a massive 9,000-pound pivoting front door, stingray skin–clad check-in stations, and accommodations featuring 10-foot ceilings, hardwood floors, and picture windows that open; there are also suites with lavish kitchens. The raucous pool-deck nightlife scene of old has been chilled out, the dining component has been heated up, and serious mixologists are killing it in the bar. There's also a full-service spa.

1047 Fifth Ave. (at Broadway), San Diego, CA 92101. www.hotelpalomar-sandiego.com. © **888/288-6601** or 619/515-3000. Fax 619/515-3006. 184 units (shower-only bathrooms). From $219 double; from $339 suite. AE, DISC, MC, V. Valet parking $36. Bus: 3, 120, or numerous Broadway routes. Trolley: Fifth Ave. Pets accepted. **Amenities:** Restaurant; 2 bars; concierge; exercise room; pool; room service; spa. *In room:* A/C, TV, CD player, hair dryer, minibar, MP3 docking station, Wi-Fi ($10/day).

Keating Hotel ★

Pininfarina, the Italian design group behind Ferrari and Maserati, made its first foray into hotel design right here in San Diego. The Keating Hotel is located in the heart of the Gaslamp Quarter in a gorgeous Romanesque-style structure built in 1890. Boutique in size with 35 rooms, this nonsmoking property features ultramodern interiors and luxury amenities, such as Frette linens, Bang & Olufsen electronics, and even in-room espresso machines. The rooms are highly contemporary—some may find them cold—and feature an interior design that does away with walls between the bed and bathroom areas. The hotel's club **Sway** is a Gaslamp hot spot (the late-night cover charge is waived for guests), while the **Merk Bistro** restaurant keeps the style quotient high. Hotel packages are available that include the use of a Ferrari. *Note:* If you're not interested in partaking of the Gaslamp's loud and late revelry, you might want to look for quieter accommodations.

432 F St. (btw. Fourth and Fifth aves.), San Diego, CA 92101. www.keatinghotel.com. © **619/814-5700.** Fax 619/814-5750. 35 units. From $275 double; from $548 suite. Children 17 and under stay free in parent's room. Packages available. AE, DC, DISC, MC, V. Valet parking $32. Bus: 3 or 120. Pets accepted with $25 fee. **Amenities:** Restaurant; bar; babysitting; 24-hr. concierge; room service; spa services. *In room:* A/C, TV/DVD, CD player, hair dryer, minibar, MP3 docking station, free Wi-Fi.

Manchester Grand Hyatt San Diego ★★

If you're looking for a room with a view (and windows that allow some fresh air in), you can't do better than this twin-towered behemoth. The shorter structure, a 33-story expansion completed in 2003, stands alongside the original 40-story hotel, built in 1992. The tallest waterfront building on the West Coast, it's crowned by the **Top of the Hyatt** lounge—worth a visit whether you are staying here or not. The hotel is adjacent to the convention center and Seaport Village shopping complex. The facilities and attractions in Seaport Village create a neatly insular, if touristy, little world, complete with bayside parks, restaurants, a marina, and a walking path. In the other direction, busy Harbor Drive separates the hotel from the rollicking Gaslamp Quarter.

1 Market Place (Market St. at Harbor Dr.), San Diego, CA 92101. www.manchestergrand.hyatt.com. © **800/233-1234** or 619/232-1234. Fax 619/233-6464. 1,625 units (95 suites). $239–$314 double; from $465 suite. Children 17 and under stay free in parent's room. Packages available. AE, DC, DISC, MC, V. Valet parking $36; self-parking $26. Trolley: Seaport Village. Pets accepted. **Amenities:** 3 restaurants; 4 bars; basketball court; concierge; exercise room; 2 Jacuzzis; 2 outdoor pools; room service, spa; 2 tennis courts; volleyball court. In room: A/C, TV, hair dryer, minibar, Wi-Fi ($13/day).

Marriott San Diego Gaslamp Quarter ★

The Marriott chain took control of a 22-story eyesore hotel and in 2004 turned it into something worthy of this happening Gaslamp Quarter location. A massive renovation transformed the property into a stylish, nonsmoking destination with a boutique feel, despite its 300-plus rooms. A sleek, street-level restaurant and bar, **Soleil@K,** complements an even hipper outdoor bar on the top floor. With its fire pits and direct views into PETCO Park, **Altitude** is worth a visit even if you're staying elsewhere. The hotel has no pool, though, so if that's important to you, stay elsewhere (although guests here do have access to the pool a few blocks away at the Marriott San Diego Hotel & Marina, below).

660 K St. (btw. Sixth and Seventh aves.), San Diego, CA 92101. www.sandiegogaslamphotel.com. © **800/228-9290** or 619/696-0234. Fax 619/231-8199. 306 units. $249–$309 double; from $995 suite. AE, DC, DISC, MC, V. Valet parking $36. Trolley: Gaslamp Quarter. **Amenities:** Restaurant; 2 bars; concierge; concierge-level rooms; exercise room; access to pool at Marriott San Diego Hotel & Marina; room service. In room: A/C, TV, CD player, hair dryer, Wi-Fi ($10/day).

Marriott San Diego Hotel & Marina ★★

Well before the San Diego Convention Center was even a blueprint, the Marriott's stylish, mirrored towers, with their banquet rooms and ballrooms, *were* a convention center. Today they merely stand next door, garnering a large share of convention attendees who are drawn to the scenic 446-slip marina, lush grounds, waterfall pool, and breathtaking views. This nonsmoking property competes with the newer Grand Hyatt next door, so guests benefit from constantly improved facilities. Leisure travelers can also take advantage of greatly reduced weekend rates and enjoy a free-form tropical pool area. Note that all rooms in the north tower have a small balcony, but only the suites in the south tower do. Because the Marriott tends to focus on public features and business services, guest quarters are well maintained but plain, and standard rooms are on the small side. **Roy's Hawaiian Fusion Cuisine** restaurant operates on site, perched alongside the marina.

333 W. Harbor Dr. (at Front St.), San Diego, CA 92101. www.marriott.com. © **800/228-9290** or 619/234-1500. Fax 619/234-8678. 1,360 units. $249–$324 double; from $729 suite. Children 17 and under stay free in parent's room. AE, DC, DISC, MC, V. Valet parking $36; self-parking $26. Trolley: Convention Center. Pets accepted with $75 fee. **Amenities:** 3 restaurants; bar; bike rentals; concierge; concierge-level rooms; exercise room; Jacuzzi; 2 lagoonlike outdoor pools; room service; sauna; 6 lighted tennis courts; watersports equipment/rentals. In room: A/C, TV, hair dryer, Internet ($13), minibar.

The Sofia Hotel ★

Built in 1926 and originally known as the Pickwick, this gorgeous Gothic Revival brick structure was once one of the city's luxury properties, offering the city's first "en suite" bathrooms. Following an 18-month, $16-million renovation, the Sofia Hotel opened with renewed charm and sparkle in 2007. Centrally located on the edge of the Gaslamp Quarter and a short distance from the

Embarcadero and Little Italy, the Sofia has a comfortably chic design scheme and features modern amenities. This nonsmoking property keeps things humming 24/7: A concierge is available day and night, a 24-hour yoga studio features audio and video programming and an on-call instructor, and the complimentary business center is open round-the-clock. Worth a visit is the Sofia's restaurant, **Currant.** This American-style bistro has a romantically baroque design and serves breakfast, lunch, and dinner.

150 W. Broadway (btw. Front St. and First Ave.), San Diego, CA 92101. www.thesofiahotel.com. ✆ **800/826-0009** or 619/234-9200. Fax 619/544-9879. 211 units. $229–$259 double; from $339 suite. Children 17 and under stay free in parent's room. Packages available. AE, DC, DISC, MC, V. Valet parking $30. Bus: Numerous downtown routes including 2, 7, 15, 30, 150, 923, or 992. Trolley: Civic Center. Small pets accepted with $25/night fee per pet. **Amenities:** Restaurant; bar; 24-hr. concierge; exercise room; spa services. In room: A/C, TV, fridge, hair dryer, Internet, microwave, MP3 docking station, Wi-Fi.

THE US GRANT ★★★ Originally built in 1910 by the son of Ulysses S. Grant, this grandiose 11-story property reopened in the fall of 2006 following a 20-month, $56-million renovation. Perched at the northern edge of the Gaslamp Quarter, this impressive Beaux Arts beauty is owned by the Sycuan Band of the Kumeyaay Nation—a nice touch of irony, as the tribe was given its sovereignty in 1875 by President Grant. Guest rooms all have 9-foot ceilings, plush wool carpets, ornate moldings, custom furniture, Italian linens, and Native American artwork. The **Grant Grill,** long a clubby spot for power lunches and dinners, has been given a modern Art Deco makeover, with plenty of curves, creamy white leather booths, rich mahogany, and iron filigrees—and a sophisticated menu and artisan cocktails to go along with it.

326 Broadway (btw. Third and Fourth aves., main entrance on Fourth Ave.), San Diego, CA 92101. www.usgrant.net. ✆ **866/837-4270.** Fax 619/232-3626. 317 units. From $284 double; from $355 suite. Children 17 and under stay free in parent's room. Packages available. AE, DC, DISC, MC, V. Valet parking $35. Bus: Numerous downtown routes, including 2, 3, 7, 120, 923, or 992. Trolley: Civic Center. Dogs less than 40 lb. accepted for $150. **Amenities:** Restaurant; bar; babysitting; 24-hr. concierge; exercise room; room service. In room: A/C, TV, CD player, hair dryer, minibar (upon request), Wi-Fi ($12).

The Westgate Hotel ★★ It may look like a 1970s office building from the outside, but the interior of the Westgate Hotel is positively Palace of Versailles. With its lavish decor, which includes baroque furnishings, antiques, chandeliers, and a sweeping grand staircase, this is about as "Old World" as San Diego gets. This nonsmoking property is a hub of cultural and culinary activities, including afternoon teas (Fri–Sun), wine dinners, and special events. It has a great downtown location across the street from the Horton Plaza shopping center and the beginning of the Gaslamp Quarter. Behind the hotel is the San Diego Concourse, featuring convention spaces, the Civic Theatre, and the seat of city government. There's even a trolley stop right on the corner. International foods, including wine, cheese, and chocolates, are available at the **Gourmet Wine Shop and Delicatessen,** and there's fine dining and a sumptuous Sunday brunch (10am–2pm), as well.

1055 Second Ave. (btw. Broadway and C St.), San Diego, CA 92101. www.westgatehotel.com. ✆ **800/522-1564** or 619/238-1818. Fax 619/557-3737. 223 units. From $204 double; from $465 suite. $15/day facility fee. Children 13 and under stay free in parent's room. Packages available. AE, DC, DISC, MC, V. Valet parking $32. Bus: Numerous downtown routes, including 2, 3, 7, 120, 923, or 992. Trolley: Civic Center. **Amenities:** 2 restaurants; bar; babysitting; 24-hr. concierge; exercise room; room service; spa services. In room: A/C, TV/DVD, hair dryer, minibar, MP3 docking station, free Wi-Fi.

W San Diego ★★ The W took San Diego by storm in 2003, delivering swanky nightlife beyond the Gaslamp Quarter. Rooms are bright and cheery—like mod beach cabanas beamed into downtown, replete with beach ball–shaped pillows, cozy window seats, and sexy showers. For those who want to go all out, the **Extreme Wow Suite** on the 19th floor is a 1,250-square-foot luxury accommodation with a host of state-of-the-art features and killer views. The **Restaurant at the W** has an adventurous menu featuring contemporary global cuisine; the adjoining lounge, **Access,** has a menu of creative cocktails; and the airy lobby bar, **Living Room,** has turntables and board games. **Beach,** on the second floor, is where the developers let it rip: The open-air bar has a sand floor (heated at night), a fire pit, and cabanas. Pets feel the love here, too—the hotel offers "peticure" nail and paw treatments and doggie happy hours.

421 W. B St. (at State St.), San Diego, CA 92101. www.thewsandiegohotel.com. ✆ **877/946-8357** or 619/398-3100. Fax 619/231-5779. 258 units. From $265 double; from $600 suite. Children 12 and under stay free in parent's room. AE, DC, DISC, MC, V. Valet parking $35. Bus: All Broadway routes. Trolley: America Plaza. Dogs accepted, usually under 40 lb., with $100 cleaning fee plus $25 extra per night. **Amenities:** Restaurant; 3 bars; 24-hr. concierge; exercise room; pool; room service; spa. *In room:* A/C, TV/DVD, CD player, hair dryer, minibar, Wi-Fi ($15/day).

Moderate

Best Western Bayside Inn This high-rise representative of reliable Best Western offers quiet lodgings, even though this corner of downtown has been a hotbed of redevelopment. Although calling it "bayview" would be more accurate than "bayside," rooms in the 14-story hotel reveal nice city and harbor views. Rooms and bathrooms are basic chain-hotel issue, but they are well maintained and have balconies—ask for the higher floors for the best vistas. The accommodating staff makes this a mecca for budget-minded business travelers (if you've forgotten anything, from razor to toothbrush, they'll fix you up), and this Best Western is also close to downtown's tourist sites. It's an easy walk to the Embarcadero, a bit farther to Horton Plaza, and just 3 blocks to the train station.

555 W. Ash St. (at Columbia St.), San Diego, CA 92101. www.baysideinn.com. ✆ **800/341-1818** or 619/233-7500. Fax 619/239-8060. 122 units. $160–$170 double. Extra person $10. Children 12 and under stay free in parent's room. Rates include continental breakfast. AE, DC, DISC, MC, V. Parking $14. Bus: 83. Trolley: America Plaza. **Amenities:** Restaurant (breakfast daily, dinner Mon–Fri 5–9pm, no lunch); bar; free airport transfers (7am–11pm); Jacuzzi; outdoor pool; room service. *In room:* A/C, TV, fridge, hair dryer, microwave, MP3 docking station, free Wi-Fi.

Gaslamp Plaza Suites ★★ 🍴 This restored Edwardian beauty in the center of the Gaslamp Quarter was San Diego's first skyscraper. Crafted of Australian gumwood, marble, brass, and exquisite etched glass, the splendid building originally housed San Diego Trust & Savings. Various other businesses set up shop here until 1988, when the elegant structure was placed on the National Register of Historic Places and reopened as a boutique hotel. Timeless elegance abounds at this nonsmoking property. Most rooms are spacious and offer luxuries such as pillow-top mattresses and premium toiletries; microwaves and dinnerware; and impressive luxury bathrooms. Beware of the cheapest rooms on the back side—they are uncomfortably small (although they do have regular-size bathrooms) and have no view. The higher floors boast splendid city and bay views, as do the rooftop patio and breakfast room. And despite noise-muffling windows, don't be surprised to hear a hum from the street below on the weekends.

520 E St. (corner of Fifth Ave.), San Diego, CA 92101. www.gaslampplaza.com. ✆ **800/874-8770** or 619/232-9500. Fax 619/238-9945. 64 units. From $129 double; from $189 suite. Extra person $15.

Rates include continental breakfast. AE, DC, DISC, MC, V. Valet parking $28. Bus: 3 or 120, plus numerous downtown routes. Trolley: Fifth Ave. **Amenities:** 2 restaurants, concierge. *In room:* A/C, TV, fridge, hair dryer, microwave, Wi-Fi ($10/day).

Holiday Inn on the Bay ★★ ☺ This better-than-average Holiday Inn is reliable and nearly always offers great deals. The three-building complex is on the Embarcadero across from the harbor and the Maritime Museum. This scenic spot is only 1½ miles from the airport (you can watch planes landing and taking off) and 2 blocks from the train station and trolley. Rooms, while basic and identical, always have clean new furnishings and plenty of thoughtful comforts; most have balconies. The only choice you have to make is whether you want marvelous bay views or a look at the San Diego skyline. In either case, request the highest floor possible.

1355 N. Harbor Dr. (at Ash St.), San Diego, CA 92101. www.holiday-inn.com/san-onthebay. © **800/315-2621** or 619/232-3861. Fax 619/232-4924. 600 units. From $149 double; from $276 suite. Children 17 and under stay free in parent's room. AE, DC, DISC, MC, V. Valet parking $28; self-parking $22. Bus: 810, 820, 850, 860, 923, or 992. Trolley: America Plaza. Pets accepted for $25/day. **Amenities:** 3 restaurants; bar; babysitting; bikes; concierge; exercise room; outdoor heated pool; room service. *In room:* A/C, TV, hair dryer, free Wi-Fi.

Mudville Flats ★★ 💼 Make yourself right at home in these classy, comfy Edwardian digs, set in an East Village neighborhood that still has a bit of an edge to it, but is easy walking distance to the Convention Center, PETCO Park, and the Gaslamp Quarter. Originally built in 1905 as apartments, the rooms feature rich wood floors and built-ins, claw-foot tubs, full kitchens, and modern amenities like hi-def TVs and air-conditioning; there's also a communal courtyard, where you can barbecue a meal or play a game of chess. Congenial on-site owners also add a level of personal service at this nonsmoking boutique hotel. The property's name is derived from the famous baseball poem *Casey at the Bat*, a nod to its ballpark-district locale, and you will find some baseball memorabilia here; but this place is more an ode to Craftsman architecture than to America's favorite pastime.

747 10th Ave. (btw. F and G sts.), San Diego, CA 92101. www.mudvilleflats.com. © **619/232-4045.** 3 units. $179 (units sleep up to 4; no children under 12; 2-night minimum may be required). AE, DISC, MC, V. Free parking in secured garage. From Hwy. 163 S., continue on 10th Ave. Bus: 3, 11, 120, or numerous Broadway routes. **Amenities:** Barbecue grill. *In room:* A/C, TV/DVD, CD player, full kitchen, hair dryer, MP3 docking station, free Wi-Fi.

Porto Vista Hotel & Suites ★ 💼 At first glance Porto Vista has plenty of style, with its mod, glass-fronted lobby and romantic fourth-floor restaurant and bar, the **Glass Door** (which yields swoon-inducing views of Little Italy and the bay). It's all the more impressive because until Porto Vista's opening in 2008, the core of this hotel used to be a standard-issue budget motel. Once past the contemporary facade, though, the hotel stumbles a bit with accommodations that still feel motelish, despite such additions as bold in-room murals featuring images that could have been torn from the pages of a 1960s European fashion magazine. Given Porto Vista's excellent location and extras like free yoga sessions, cooking classes, and pet-friendly happy hours on the rooftop deck, a stay here will still feel like *la dolce vita*.

1835 Columbia St. (at Fir St.), San Diego, CA 92101. www.portovistasd.com. © **800/537-9902** or 619/544-0164. Fax 619/237-9940. 189 units (all rooms are nonsmoking; most have shower-only bathrooms). $171–$209 double; from $246 suite. Children 17 and under stay free in parent's room. Extra person $10. AE, DC, DISC, MC, V. Valet parking $22. Bus: 83. From Laurel St., head south on Kettner Blvd., go left on Grape St., then right on Columbia St. Pets up to 40 lb. accepted with $75 fee. **Amenities:** Restaurant; bar; free airport shuttle. *In room:* A/C, TV, CD player, fridge (some rooms), hair dryer, microwave (some rooms), MP3 docking station (some rooms), free Wi-Fi.

Rodeway Inn & Suites Downtown   Set in the northern corner of downtown, this place is good for business travelers without expense accounts and vacationers who just need reliable, safe accommodations. This humble chain motel must be surprised to find itself in a quickly gentrifying part of town: The El Cortez Hotel across the street has been transformed into upscale condos and shops, and new residential construction has blossomed nearby. The Rodeway is designed so rooms open onto exterior walkways surrounding the drive-in entry courtyard, lending an insular feel in this once-dicey part of town. *Note:* The hilltop location gives thighs a workout on the walk to and from the Gaslamp Quarter, but third-floor rooms offer the best chance of a view.

719 Ash St. (at Seventh Ave.), San Diego, CA 92101. www.rodewayinn.com. © **877/424-6423** or 619/232-2525. Fax 619/687-3024. 67 units. From $124 double; from $134 suite. Extra person $15. Children 17 and under stay free in parent's room. Rates include continental breakfast. AE, DISC, MC, V. Parking $16. Bus: 3 or 120. Pets less than 35 lb. accepted, one-time $75 fee. *In room:* A/C, TV, fridge (in some), hair dryer, microwave (in some), free Wi-Fi.

Inexpensive

La Pensione Hotel ★★ ✦   Made even better following a major renovation in 2011, this place has much going for it: up-to-date amenities, remarkable value, a central location in the heart of Little Italy, a friendly staff, and free parking (a rare perk in San Diego). The four-story structure, erected in 1926 then modernized in 1991 by one of the city's most acclaimed architects, is built around a courtyard and feels like a small European hotel. The moderately sized but comfortable rooms offer contemporary design, private bathrooms, and some have killer views; ask for room 422, which has floor-to-ceiling windows, or room 320, which has its own balcony. La Pensione is within walking distance of eateries (two restaurants are directly downstairs), nightspots, and a trolley station. Noise-sensitive travelers should note this is a very active neighborhood where the cafes stay busy until midnight on weekends and trains rumble by a block away.

606 W. Date St. (at India St.), San Diego, CA 92101. www.lapensionehotel.com. © **800/232-4683** or 619/236-8000. Fax 619/236-8088. 68 units. $100 double. AE, DC, DISC, MC, V. Limited free underground parking. Bus: 83. Trolley: Little Italy. **Amenities:** 2 restaurants; exercise room. *In room:* A/C, TV, fridge, hair dryer, free Wi-Fi.

Little Italy Hotel ★ ✦   Originally a boardinghouse for Italian fishermen, this renovated 1910 property is a boutique bed-and-breakfast just steps from the galleries, delightful eateries, and hip boutiques of Little Italy. It's also just a short distance from the Gaslamp Quarter and Balboa Park. While preserving the building's historic architecture, the owner has added the latest in guest comforts, such as wireless Internet and a healthful, filling continental breakfast. The accommodations are cozy, romantic, and tastefully appointed with antiques, but are not fussy or precious; every room is unique and smoke free (smoking is allowed on the outdoor patio only). Some feature bay views, in-room Jacuzzi tubs, or kitchenettes (one has a full kitchen), as well as oversize closets, wood floors, and spacious bathrooms with plush bathrobes; some rooms have shared bathrooms. And though the inn is located at an intersection of planes, trains, and automobiles, the rooms are well insulated from the sound.

505 W. Grape St. (at India St.), San Diego, CA 92101. www.littleitalyhotel.com. © **800/518-9930** or 619/230-1600. Fax 619/230-0322. 23 units. From $99 double; from $149 suite. Extra person $15. Rates include continental breakfast. AE, DISC, MC, V. Street parking only. Bus: 83. *In room:* A/C, TV/DVD, fridge, hair dryer, free Wi-Fi.

HILLCREST & UPTOWN

The gentrified historic neighborhoods north of downtown are something of a bargain; they're convenient to Balboa Park and offer easy access to the rest of town. Filled with casual and upscale restaurants, eclectic shops, and percolating nightlife, the area is also easy to navigate. All of the following accommodations cater to the mainstream market and attract a gay and lesbian clientele, as well. *Note:* All these properties can be reached via I-5.

Best For: Those who want to log time at the zoo and Balboa Park, yet still want to be within striking distance of the downtown action.

Drawbacks: It lacks the glitzy wattage of downtown's Gaslamp Quarter (which is also one of the neighborhood's strengths).

Expensive

Britt Scripps Inn ★★★ Built around 1887, this property was home to one of San Diego's most prominent families, the Scripps. Today the house and its grounds function as a nine-room "estate hotel"—part B&B, part luxury hotel. With first-class amenities, such as 1,000-thread-count sheets, flatscreen TVs (most hidden in antique armoires), free Wi-Fi, and heated towel racks, this gracious lady lays on the personal charm as well, with gourmet breakfasts including homemade pastries and breads, late-afternoon wine and cheese, and a vintage Steinway piano in the music alcove. Staff is always on site but usually out of sight. Striking architectural elements include seven gables, a dramatic turret, a wraparound porch, a twisting oak staircase, and a two-story, three-paneled stained-glass window. And it's all just a block away from Balboa Park.

406 Maple St. (at Fourth Ave.), San Diego, CA 92103. www.brittscripps.com. ✆ **888/881-1991** or 619/230-1991. Fax 619/230-1188. 9 units. From $269 double. Rates include full breakfast and after-noon wine and hors d'oeuvres. AE, DC, MC, V. Bus: 3 or 120. Take the Laurel St. exit off I-5; then make a left on Laurel, a left on Fifth Ave., and a left on Maple St. *In room:* A/C, TV/DVD, CD player, hair dryer, MP3 docking station, free Wi-Fi.

Moderate

The Cottage This romantic hideaway is tucked behind a homestead-style house at the end of a residential cul-de-sac. Built in 1913, the Cottage is surrounded by gardens growing herbs and climbing roses, and has its own private entry. More of a vacation rental than a B&B (breakfast is not included), the Cottage is filled with wal-nut and oak antique furnishings—the proprietor used to run an antiques store, and it shows. There's a wood-burning stove in the living room as well as a queen-size sofa bed; the bedroom has a king-size bed. This charming space also has a fully equipped kitchen and a full bathroom. The Cottage is 5 blocks from the cafes of Mission Hills and Hillcrest and a short drive from Balboa Park. Book early for this find.

3829 Albatross St. (off Robinson Ave.), San Diego, CA 92103. www.cottagevacation.us. ✆ **619/299-1564.** Fax 619/299-6213. 1 unit. $125–$175 double. Extra person $10. 4-night minimum stay. AE, MC, V. Bus: 10. Take Washington St. exit off I-5, exit at University Ave., right on First Ave., right on Robinson Ave. *In room:* TV, hair dryer, kitchen.

Crone's Cobblestone Cottage Bed & Breakfast ★ 📷 Artist and book-maker Joan Crone lives in the architectural award-winning addition to her 1913 Craftsman bungalow, a designated historical landmark. Her warmly welcomed guests have the run of the entire house, including a book-filled, wood-paneled den and

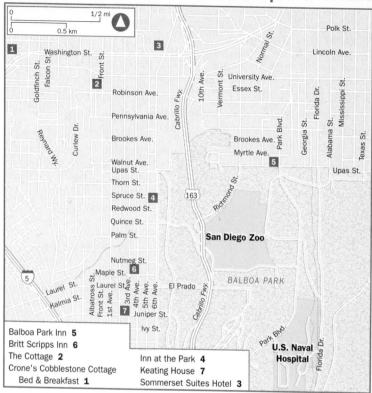

Map legend:
- Balboa Park Inn **5**
- Britt Scripps Inn **6**
- The Cottage **2**
- Crone's Cobblestone Cottage Bed & Breakfast **1**
- Inn at the Park **4**
- Keating House **7**
- Sommerset Suites Hotel **3**

Map labels: Polk St., Lincoln Ave., Washington St., Goldfinch St., Falcon St., Front St., Robinson Ave., University Ave., Essex St., Normal St., 10th Ave., Vermont St., Pennsylvania Ave., Cabrillo Fwy., Brookes Ave., Brookes Ave., Myrtle Ave., Park Blvd., Georgia St., Florida Dr., Alabama St., Mississippi St., Texas St., Reynard Wy., Curlew Dr., Walnut Ave., Upas St., Upas St., Thorn St., Spruce St. **4**, Richmond St., 163, Redwood St., Quince St., Palm St., San Diego Zoo, Nutmeg St., Maple St. **6**, BALBOA PARK, Laurel St., Laurel St., El Prado, Albatross St., Front St., 1st Ave., 3rd Ave., 4th Ave., 5th Ave., 6th Ave., Kalmia St., Juniper St. **7**, Cabrillo Fwy., Ivy St., U.S. Naval Hospital, Park Blvd., Florida Dr.

antiques-filled living room. Both cozy guest rooms are nonsmoking and have antique beds, goose-down pillows and comforters, and eclectic bedside reading. They share a full bathroom; the Eaton Room also has a private half bathroom. You can rent the entire house (two bedrooms plus the den), to sleep five or six. Mission Hills, the neighborhood a half-mile west of Hillcrest, is one of San Diego's treasures, and lots of other historic homes can be explored along quiet streets; shopping and dining are just blocks away.

1302 Washington Place (4 blocks west of Goldfinch St. at Ingalls St.), San Diego, CA 92103. www.cronescobblestonebandb.com. © **619/295-4765.** 2 units. $165 double. Rates include continental breakfast. 3-night minimum stay. No credit cards (checks accepted). Bus: 10. From I-5, take the Washington St. exit east uphill. Make a U-turn at Goldfinch, and then keep right at the Y-intersection onto Washington Place. *In room:* No phone.

Inn at the Park ★ 🐾 This eight-story property, formerly known as Park Manor Suites, was built as a full-service luxury hotel in 1926 and sits on a prime corner overlooking Balboa Park. Guest rooms are huge (ranging from 400 to 1,100 sq. ft.) and comfortable, featuring full kitchens (except in the smallest suites), dining rooms, living rooms, and bedrooms with separate dressing areas; as of this writing, the property is also being renovated. No two rooms are alike, and some feature period-perfect chinoiserie; some have balconies with seating areas (request one when you book). The overall feeling is that of a prewar East Coast apartment building, complete with steam heat and lavish moldings. There's a **restaurant** on the ground floor (with piano bar) that serves dinner nightly, and lunch is served weekdays in the Top of the Park penthouse (the view is spectacular).

525 Spruce St. (btw. Fifth and Sixth aves.), San Diego, CA 92103. www.shellhospitality.com. ⓒ **800/874-2649** or 619/291-0999. Fax 619/291-8844. 75 units. From $160 studio; from $219 1-bedroom suite; from $269 2-bedroom suite. Extra person $15. Children 11 and under stay free in parent's room. Rates include continental breakfast. AE, DC, DISC, MC, V. Valet $15; free street parking. Bus: 3 or 120. Take Washington St. exit off I-5, right on Fourth Ave., left on Spruce. **Amenities:** 2 restaurants; bar; room service. *In room:* TV, hair dryer, kitchen, free Wi-Fi.

Keating House ★ 🛅 This grand 1880s Bankers Hill mansion, between downtown and Hillcrest and 4 blocks from Balboa Park, has been meticulously restored by two energetic innkeepers. Even the overflowing gardens that bloom on four sides of this local landmark are authentically period. The house contains a comfortable hodgepodge of antique furnishings, and the downstairs entry, parlor, and dining room all have cozy fireplaces. Bathrooms—all private—are gorgeously restored with updated period fixtures. There are six rooms in the main house, with three additional rooms in the restored carriage house, which opens onto an exotic garden patio (all rooms are nonsmoking). Breakfast is served in a sunny, friendly setting; special dietary needs are cheerfully considered. In contrast to many B&Bs in Victorian-era homes, this one eschews dollhouse frills for a classy, sophisticated approach.

2331 Second Ave. (btw. Juniper and Kalmia sts.), San Diego, CA 92101. www.keatinghouse.com. ⓒ **800/995-8644** or 619/239-8585. Fax 619/239-5774. 9 units. From $119 double. Rates include full breakfast. AE, MC, V. Bus: 11. From the airport, take Harbor Dr. toward downtown, turn left on Laurel St., and then right on Second Ave. *In room:* A/C, hair dryer, no phone, free Wi-Fi.

Sommerset Suites Hotel ★ This all-suites hotel on a busy street was originally built as apartment housing for interns at the nearby hospital. This nonsmoking property retains a welcoming, residential ambience and features unexpected amenities such as huge closets, medicine cabinets, and fully equipped kitchens in all rooms (even dishwashers). Rooms are oversize and comfortably furnished, and each has a private balcony; be prepared for noise from the busy thoroughfare below, though. Poolside barbecue facilities encourage warm-weather mingling, while just across the street you'll find several blocks' worth of restaurants and shops, plus a multiplex cinema. Package deals and extended stays add bang to your buck here, making it a good choice for families and business travelers.

606 Washington St. (at Sixth Ave.), San Diego, CA 92103. www.sommersetsuites.com. ⓒ **800/962-9665** or 619/692-5200. Fax 619/692-5299. 80 units. From $189. Extra person $10. Children 15 and under stay free in parent's room. Rates include continental breakfast. AE, DC, DISC, MC, V. Parking $7. Bus: 3, 10, or 83. Take the Washington St. exit off I-5. Pets less than 35 lb. accepted with $50 nonrefundable fee. **Amenities:** Jacuzzi; outdoor pool. *In room:* A/C, TV, hair dryer, kitchen, free Wi-Fi.

Inexpensive

Balboa Park Inn ★ Insiders looking for unusual accommodations head for this small inn at the northern edge of Balboa Park. This cluster of four Spanish Colonial–style former apartment buildings lies in a mostly residential neighborhood a half-mile east from the heart of Hillcrest; the hotel has long been popular with gay travelers drawn to the area's restaurants and clubs. All the rooms and standard suites are themed (and nonsmoking), some evoking Victorian or Art Deco sensibilities, others reaching for a more elaborate fantasy, such as the "Orient Express" room with its red hues and Chinese wedding bed. Seven of the rooms have Jacuzzi tubs, and most have kitchens—all have private entrances, though the front desk operates 24 hours. From here, you can walk to the San Diego Zoo and other Balboa Park attractions.

3402 Park Blvd. (at Upas St.), San Diego, CA 92103. www.balboaparkinn.com. © **800/938-8181** or 619/298-0823. Fax 619/294-8070. 26 units. $99 double; from $149 suites. Extra person $10. Children 11 and under stay free in parent's room. Rates include continental breakfast. AE, DC, DISC, MC, V. Parking available on street. Bus: 7. From I-5, take Washington St. east, follow signs to University Ave. E., and turn right at Park Blvd. *In room:* TV, fridge, microwave, free Wi-Fi.

OLD TOWN & MISSION VALLEY

Old Town is a popular area for families because of its proximity to Old Town State Historic Park and other attractions that are within walking distance; SeaWorld and the San Diego Zoo are within a 10-minute drive. Around the corner is Mission Valley, where you'll find the city's largest collection of hotels offering rooms under $100 a night. Mission Valley lacks much personality—this is the spot for chain restaurants and shopping malls, not gardens or water views. But it caters to convention groups, families visiting the University of San Diego or San Diego State University, and leisure travelers drawn by the lower prices and competitive facilities. **Note:** All Old Town and Mission Valley hotels are reached from either I-5 or I-8.

Best For: Families looking for less expensive digs close by major attractions; the area is also a transportation hub.

Drawbacks: The style quotient drops considerably in the commuter corridor of Mission Valley.

Moderate

Cosmopolitan Hotel and Restaurant ★
Uniquely situated in the heart of pedestrian-only Old Town State Historic Park, the Cosmo allows you to fully immerse yourself in the park's frontier fantasy. Originally completed as a single-story adobe home for one of fledgling San Diego's most prominent citizens in 1829, a wood-frame second story was added in 1869. A 3-year, $7-million restoration completed in 2010 has now beautifully recaptured the structure's glory days. Upstairs, rooms are nonsmoking and tastefully furnished with antiques, and in keeping with the Victorian atmosphere amenities are basic (no phone, no TV). Downstairs you'll find a saloon and one of Old Town's more serious **restaurants,** with a lovely patio and servers in period costume. The Cosmo isn't very appropriate for small children; once the day-trippers and diners clear out, things get mighty quiet here. And with the park and its environs a popular site for ghost-hunting tours, it's a tad spooky, too.

2660 Calhoun St., San Diego, CA 92110. www.oldtowncosmopolitan.com. © **619/297-1874.** Fax 619/692-1869. 10 units. $175–$290 double. Rates include continental breakfast. AE, DISC, MC, V. Free parking. Bus: 8, 9, 10, 28, 30, 35, 44, 88, 105, or 150. Trolley: Old Town. **Amenities:** Restaurant; 2 bars; room service. *In room:* A/C, fridge (upon request), hair dryer, no phone, free Wi-Fi.

Crowne Plaza San Diego ★
Formerly known as the Red Lion Hanalei, this Mission Valley hotel has a Polynesian theme and comfort-conscious sophistication. Most rooms are split between two eight-story towers and set back from the freeway so that the balconies open onto the tropically landscaped pool courtyard or the attractive

Old Town & Mission Valley Hotels

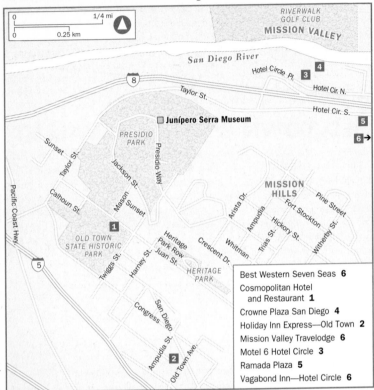

0   1/4 mi
0   0.25 km

RIVERWALK GOLF CLUB
MISSION VALLEY

San Diego River

Hotel Circle Pl.
Hotel Cir. N.
Hotel Cir. S.

Taylor St.

□ Junípero Serra Museum

PRESIDIO PARK

Sunset
Taylor St.
Jackson St.
Presidio Way
Calhoun St.
Mason
Sunset
Pacific Coast Hwy.

MISSION HILLS
Arista Dr.
Ampudia
Fort Stockton
Pine Street
Hickory St.
Whitman
Trias St.
Witherby St.

OLD TOWN STATE HISTORIC PARK

Heritage Park Row
Juan St.
Crescent Dr.
Harney St.
Twiggs St.

HERITAGE PARK

Congress
San Diego
Ampudia St.
Old Town Ave.

Best Western Seven Seas **6**
Cosmopolitan Hotel and Restaurant **1**
Crowne Plaza San Diego **4**
Holiday Inn Express—Old Town **2**
Mission Valley Travelodge **6**
Motel 6 Hotel Circle **3**
Ramada Plaza **5**
Vagabond Inn—Hotel Circle **6**

links of an adjacent golf club. The few rooms in a third structure are a little too close to the freeway. The heated outdoor pool and oversize Jacuzzi are large enough for any luau, and there's even a waterfall in an open-air atrium. The **Islands** restaurant serves a breakfast buffet, lunch, and dinner, bringing out the sushi and pupu platters in the evening to go along with the specialty tropical cocktails. Hotel services include a free shuttle to Old Town and the Fashion Valley Shopping Center.

2270 Hotel Circle N., San Diego, CA 92108. www.cp-sandiego.com. ✆ **800/227-6963** or 619/297-1101. Fax 619/297-6049. 417 units. From $171 double; from $275 suite. AE, DC, DISC, MC, V. Pets accepted with $75 fee. Parking $12. Bus: 88. From I-8, take Hotel Circle exit, follow signs for Hotel Circle N. **Amenities:** 2 restaurants; bar; exercise room; nearby golf course (packages available); Jacuzzi; outdoor pool; room service; spa. *In room:* A/C, TV, hair dryer, Internet ($10).

Holiday Inn Express–Old Town ★   Just a couple of easy walking blocks from the heart of Old Town, this Holiday Inn has a Spanish Colonial exterior that suits the neighborhood's theme. Inside you'll find better-than-they-have-to-be contemporary furnishings and surprising small touches that make this hotel an affordable option favored by business travelers and families alike. Renovated in 2011, the hotel is smartly oriented toward the inside; request a room that has a patio or balcony opening onto the pleasant courtyard. Rooms are thoughtfully and practically appointed, with extras such as microwaves and writing tables. The lobby, surrounded by French doors, features a large fireplace, several sitting areas, and a TV. Although the address is listed as Old Town Avenue, the hotel entrance is on Jefferson Street, which runs perpendicular to Old Town Avenue.

3900 Old Town Ave., San Diego, CA 92110. www.hioldtownhotel.com ℭ **855/212-0196** or 619/299-7400. Fax 619/299-1619. 125 units. From $159 double; from $189 suite. Extra person $10. Children 17 and under stay free in parent's room. Rates include continental breakfast. AE, DC, DISC, MC, V. Parking $14. Bus: Numerous Old Town routes, including 10 or 30. Trolley: Old Town. Take I-5 to Old Town Ave. exit. **Amenities:** Jacuzzi; outdoor pool. *In room:* A/C, TV, fridge, microwave, free Wi-Fi.

Inexpensive

Motel 6 Hotel Circle   Yes, it's a Motel 6, so you know the drill: no mint on the pillow and you have to trundle down to the front desk to retrieve a cup of coffee in the morning. On the other hand, these budget hotels—part of the mammoth Accor chain, one of the world's largest hotel companies—know how to provide a consistent product at dependably inexpensive rates, and this one is very central to San Diego's sightseeing. The modern, four-story motel sits at the western end of Hotel Circle. Rooms are sparingly but adequately outfitted, with standard motel furnishings; bathrooms are perfunctory. Stay away from the loud freeway side—rooms in the four-story structure in back overlook a scenic 18-hole golf course and river.

2424 Hotel Circle N., San Diego, CA 92108. www.motel6.com ℭ **800/466-8356** or 619/296-1612. Fax 619/543-9305. 204 units. $99 double. Children 17 and under stay free in parent's room. AE, DC, DISC, MC, V. Free parking. Bus: 88. From I-8, take Taylor St. exit. Pets accepted for a $10–$50 daily fee. **Amenities:** Outdoor pool. *In room:* A/C, TV, Wi-Fi ($3/day).

MISSION BAY & THE BEACHES

If the beach and aquatic activities are front-and-center on your San Diego agenda, this part of town may be just the ticket. Although the beach communities don't offer much in the way of cultural or upscale attractions, downtown and Balboa Park are only a 15-minute drive away. Some hotels are right on Mission Bay, San Diego's water playground; they're usually good choices for families. Ocean Beach is more neighborhood-oriented and easygoing, while Mission Beach and Pacific Beach provide a total immersion in the beach lifestyle—they can be raucous at times, especially in summer. If you're looking for a more refined landing, head to La Jolla or Coronado. **Note:** All directions are provided from I-5.

Best For: Families looking for fun in the sun, or anyone with a penchant for outdoor recreation.

Drawbacks: The party almost never stops (or maybe that's a good thing).

Very Expensive

Catamaran Resort Hotel ★★ ☺   Right on Mission Bay, the Catamaran has its own beach, complete with watersports facilities. Built in the 1950s, the hotel has been fully renovated to modern standards without losing its trademark Polynesian theme, highlighted by a lobby waterfall and koi-filled lagoons. Guest rooms—in either a 13-story building or one of the six two-story buildings—have subdued South Pacific decor, and each has a balcony or patio. Tower rooms on higher floors have commanding views, and studios and suites have kitchenettes; the 9,300-square-foot spa features a menu of South Pacific and Asian-inspired treatments. The Catamaran is also within a few blocks of Pacific Beach's restaurant-and-nightlife scene, or you can visit the resort's resident eel at **Moray's Lounge.** During the summer, *The Bahia Belle,* a Mississippi River–style stern-wheeler boat, plies Mission Bay nightly (weekends only the rest of the year); guests board free of charge. Luaus are also a part of the summer fun.

3999 Mission Blvd. (4 blocks south of Grand Ave.), San Diego, CA 92109. www.catamaranresort. com. © **800/422-8386** or 858/488-1081. Fax 858/488-1619. 313 units. From $309 double; from $529 suite. Children 11 and under stay free in parent's room. AE, DC, DISC, MC, V. Valet parking $17; self-parking $13. Bus: 8. Take Grand/Garnet exit off I-5 and go west on Grand Ave., and then south on Mission Blvd. **Amenities:** Restaurant; 2 bars; bikes; children's programs; concierge; exercise room; Jacuzzi; outdoor pool; room service; full-service spa; watersports equipment/rentals. *In room:* A/C, TV, fridge (in most), hair dryer, MP3 docking station, free Wi-Fi.

Pacific Terrace Hotel ★　Located at the north end of the Pacific Beach boardwalk, this modern hotel swaggers with a heavy-handed South Seas–meets–Spanish Colonial ambience. More upscale than most of the casual places nearby, it features large, comfortable guest rooms, each with balconies or terraces and fancy wall safes; bathrooms, designed with warm-toned marble and natural woods, have a separate sink/vanity area. About half the rooms have kitchenettes, and top-floor rooms in this three-story hotel enjoy particularly nice views. The lushly landscaped pool and hot tub are 15 feet from the boardwalk, overlooking a relatively quiet stretch of beach. Four nearby restaurants allow meals to be billed to the hotel, but there's no restaurant on the premises.

610 Diamond St., San Diego, CA 92109. www.pacificterrace.com. © **800/344-3370** or 858/581-3500. Fax 858/274-2534. 73 units. From $381 double; from $486 suite. Children 12 and under stay free in parent's room. Extra person $15. 2- to 4-night minimums apply in summer. AE, DC, DISC, MC, V. Parking $22. Bus: 30. Take I-5 to Grand/Garnet exit and follow Grand or Garnet west to Mission Blvd., turn right (north), and then left (west) onto Diamond. **Amenities:** Concierge; exercise room; Jacuzzi; pool; room service; spa services. *In room:* A/C, TV/DVD, fridge, hair dryer, microwave (in some), minibar, Wi-Fi ($10/day).

Paradise Point Resort & Spa ★★ ☺　Smack in the middle of Mission Bay, this hotel complex is almost as much a theme park as its closest neighbor, SeaWorld (you can even take a water taxi to a private SeaWorld entrance). Single-story accommodations are spread across 44 tropically landscaped acres of duck-filled lagoons, lush gardens, and swim-friendly beaches; all have private verandas and plenty of thoughtful conveniences. The resort completed a $20-million renovation in 2010 and features refreshingly colorful beach-cottage decor, while still retaining its low-tech 1960s charm. Standard "lanai" rooms range considerably in price, based solely on view; despite daunting high-season rack rates, though, you can usually get a deal here. An upscale waterfront restaurant, **Baleen** (p. 134), offers fine dining in a contemporary, fun space. A stunning Indonesian-inspired spa offers cool serenity and aromatic Asian treatments; this spa is a vacation in itself.

1404 Vacation Rd. (off Ingraham St.), San Diego, CA 92109. www.paradisepoint.com. © **800/344-2626** or 858/274-4630. Fax 858/581-5924. 462 units. From $350 double; from $670 suite. Extra person $20. Children 17 and under stay free in parent's room. AE, DC, DISC, MC, V. Parking $32. Bus: 9. Follow I-8 west to Mission Bay Dr. exit; take Ingraham St. north to Vacation Rd. Pets less than 15 lb. accepted with $100 fee. **Amenities:** 2 restaurants; 2 bars; bikes; concierge; exercise room; 18-hole miniature golf course; Jacuzzi; 5 outdoor pools; room service; full-service spa; tennis/basketball courts; marina w/watersports equipment/rentals. *In room:* A/C, TV, fridge, hair dryer, Internet.

Mission Bay & the Beaches Hotels

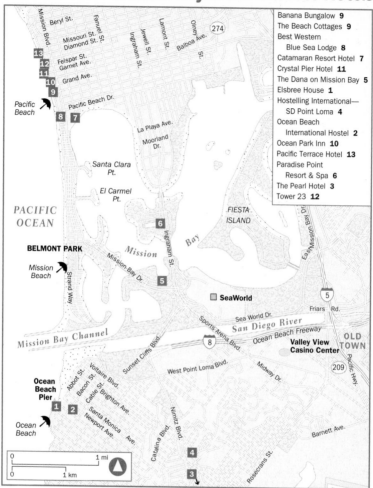

Banana Bungalow **9**
The Beach Cottages **9**
Best Western
Blue Sea Lodge **8**
Catamaran Resort Hotel **7**
Crystal Pier Hotel **11**
The Dana on Mission Bay **5**
Elsbree House **1**
Hostelling International—
SD Point Loma **4**
Ocean Beach
International Hostel **2**
Ocean Park Inn **10**
Pacific Terrace Hotel **13**
Paradise Point
Resort & Spa **6**
The Pearl Hotel **3**
Tower 23 **12**

Tower 23 ★★ Named for a lifeguard station that once pulled duty nearby, Tower 23 is a modernist beach resort that opened in 2005. Sitting on the Pacific Beach (aka P.B.) boardwalk, the hotel enjoys a sky-high people-watching quotient matched only by its first-class contemporary amenities, including wireless Internet access right on the beach. Featuring clean lines and glass-box architecture, Tower 23's rooms all have private balconies or patios (though not all with ocean views); a guest-only second-story deck with industrial fire pit overlooks the beach. The hotel's **Tower Bar,** which has indoor/outdoor seating along the boardwalk, and **JRDN** restaurant, serving contemporary steak and seafood (there's also an eight-seat sushi bar), are worth checking out whether you're staying here or not. Although it's the most chic bar/restaurant in the area, the P.B. party atmosphere still pervades.

723 Felspar St., San Diego, CA 92109. www.t23hotel.com. © **866/869-3723** or 858/270-2323. Fax 858/274-2333. 44 units. From $389 double; from $689 suite. Children 17 and under stay free in parent's room. AE, DC, MC, V. Valet parking $20. Bus: 8, 9, 27, or 30. Take I-5 to Grand/Garnet exit, left on Grand Ave., right on Mission Blvd., left on Felspar St. Pets less than 25 lb. accepted with $150 fee. **Amenities:** Restaurant; bar; room service; spa services. *In room:* A/C, TV/DVD, CD player, hair dryer, minibar, MP3 docking station, free Wi-Fi.

Expensive

Best Western Blue Sea Lodge   Looking like a Mediterranean resort designed by a Soviet architect, the squat, three-story Blue Sea Lodge is a reliable choice in a prime location. Despite the rates listed, this nonsmoking property can be a bargain; ask about possible discounts. Aesthetically, the original rooms are a snore, but nevertheless boast a balcony or patio and a handful of necessary comforts. Rooms with full ocean views overlook the sand and have more privacy than those on the street, but the Pacific Beach boardwalk has never been known for quiet or solitude. If an ocean view is not important, save a few bucks and book one of the units in an expansion building that opened in 2003; the decor is brighter and more enticing. The lobby has basic breakfast fare available for guests in the morning, and there's a heated pool and Jacuzzi just steps from the beach.

707 Pacific Beach Dr., San Diego, CA 92109. www.bestwestern-bluesea.com. © **800/258-3732** or 858/488-4700. Fax 858/488-7276. 136 units. $278–$368 double; from $409 suite. Children 17 and under stay free in parent's room. AE, DC, DISC, MC, V. Parking $17. Bus: 8. Take I-5 to Grand/ Garnet exit, follow Grand Ave. to Mission Blvd. and turn left; then turn right onto Pacific Beach Dr. **Amenities:** Bike rental; Jacuzzi; outdoor pool. *In room:* A/C, TV, fridge, hair dryer, microwave, free Wi-Fi.

The Dana on Mission Bay ★   A 2004 renovation added 74 contemporary rooms to this 1960s Mission Bay stalwart, set right on the water's edge. Some rooms on this 10-acre property overlook bobbing sailboats in the recreational marina; others face onto the original kidney-shaped pool whose surrounding tiki torch–lit gardens offer shuffleboard and table tennis. You'll pay a little extra for bay and marina views; every one of the old rooms is the same size, with plain but well-maintained furnishings. The new rooms are bigger and feature water views and reclaimed redwood beam ceilings. Beaches and SeaWorld are a 15-minute walk away; there's also a complimentary shuttle that can take you to the theme park.

1710 W. Mission Bay Dr., San Diego, CA 92109. www.thedana.com. © **888/809-4914** or 888/325-1981. Fax 619/222-5916. 271 units. From $224 double; from $324 suites. AE, DC, DISC, MC, V. Parking $18. Bus: 8. Follow I-8 west to Mission Bay Dr. exit; take W. Mission Bay Dr. **Amenities:** 2 restaurants; bike rentals; concierge; exercise room; 2 Jacuzzis; 2 outdoor heated pools; room service; spa services; marina w/watersports equipment/rentals. *In room:* A/C, TV, fridge, hair dryer, microwave (in some), wet bar (in some), free Wi-Fi.

Ocean Park Inn ★   This oceanfront motor hotel offers simple, attractive, spacious rooms with contemporary furnishings. The nonsmoking property has a bit of sophistication uncommon in this surfer-populated area, but you won't find much solitude with the boisterous scene outside. You can't beat the sand access and the view—both are directly onto the beach. Rates vary according to the view, but most rooms have at least a partial ocean view; all have a private balcony or patio. Units in front are most desirable; but take note, it can get noisy directly above the boardwalk. Go for the second or third floor, or pick one of the junior suites, which have huge bathrooms and pool views.

710 Grand Ave., San Diego, CA 92109. www.oceanparkinn.com. © **800/231-7735** or 858/483-5858. Fax 858/274-0823. 72 units. From $239 double; from $349 suite. Rates include continental breakfast. AE, DC, DISC, MC, V. Parking $10. Bus: 8, 9, or 30. Take Grand/Garnet exit off I-5; follow Grand Ave. to ocean. **Amenities:** Jacuzzi; outdoor pool; room service; spa services. *In room:* A/C, TV, fridge, hair dryer, microwave, free Wi-Fi.

Moderate

The Beach Cottages   This family-owned operation has been around since 1948 and offers a variety of guest quarters, most of them geared to the long-term visitor. Most appealing are the 17 cute little detached cottages just steps from the sand, though some of them lack a view; each has a patio with tables and chairs. Adjoining apartments are perfectly adequate, especially for budget-minded families who want to log major hours on the beach—all cottages and apartments sleep four or more and have full kitchens. There are also standard motel rooms that are worn but cheap (most of these sleep two). The property features shared barbecue grills, shuffleboard courts, and table tennis, and is also within walking distance of shops and restaurants. The cottages themselves aren't pristine, but they have a rustic charm—reserve one well in advance.

4255 Ocean Blvd. (1 block south of Grand Ave.), San Diego, CA 92109. www.beachcottages.com. © **858/483-7440.** Fax 858/273-9365. 61 units, 17 cottages. From $140 double; from $285 cottages and apts. for 4–6. Extra person $10. 2-night minimum on weekends. AE, DC, DISC, MC, V. Free parking. Bus: 8 or 30. Take I-5 to Grand/Garnet exit, go west on Grand Ave. and left on Mission Blvd. *In room:* TV, fridge, kitchen (in some), free Wi-Fi.

Crystal Pier Hotel ★★ 🏨 ☺   If historical charm is higher on your wish list than hotel-style service, head to this unique cluster of cottages sitting over the surf on the vintage Crystal Pier in Pacific Beach. You'll get a separate living room and bedroom, a fully equipped kitchenette, and a private deck with breathtaking ocean views—all within the whitewashed walls of carefully renovated cottages from 1930. Each of the Cape Cod–style cottages has a deck; the more expensive units farthest out have more privacy. Six less expensive units are not actually on the pier, but still offer sunset-facing sea views. Guests park beside their cottages, a real boon on crowded weekends. This nonsmoking operation is strictly BYOBT (bring your own beach towels), and the office is open only from 8am to 8pm. These accommodations book up fast; reserve at least 4 to 6 months in advance.

4500 Ocean Blvd. (at Garnet Ave.), San Diego, CA 92109. www.crystalpier.com. © **800/748-5894** or 858/483-6983. Fax 858/483-6811. 29 units. From $165 double; $500 for larger unit sleeping 6. 3-night minimum in summer, 2-night minimum in winter. DISC, MC, V. Free parking. Bus: 8, 9, 27, or 30. Take I-5 to Grand/Garnet exit; follow Garnet to the pier. **Amenities:** Beach equipment rental. *In room:* TV, kitchen.

Elsbree House ★   Katie and Phil Elsbree turned this modern Cape Cod–style building into an immaculate, comfortable B&B, half a block from the water's edge in Ocean Beach. Each of the five guest rooms has a patio or balcony, as well as a private entryway and full, private bathroom. Guests at this smoke-free property share the cozy living room (with a fireplace and TV), breakfast room, and kitchen. There is also a fully furnished condo unit with private entrance; it rents for a 4-day minimum (breakfast not included in condo rental—it has a full kitchen) and sleeps up to six people. This Ocean Beach neighborhood is eclectic, occupied by ocean-loving couples, dedicated surf bums, and the occasional contingent of punk skater kids who congregate near the pier.

Its strengths are proximity to the beach, a casual-but-pleasing selection of eateries and bars that attract mostly locals, and San Diego's best antiquing (along Newport Ave.).

5054 Narragansett Ave. (at Bacon St.), San Diego, CA 92107. www.bbinob.com. © **800/607-4133** or 619/226-4133. Fax 619/223-4133. 6 units. From $150 double; $1,800 per week or $350 per night 3-bedroom condo (lower rates if only 1 or 2 rooms used). 3-night minimum for advance guest room reservations in summer; 4-night minimum for condo. Rates include continental breakfast (except condo). MC, V. Bus: 35 or 923. From airport, take Harbor Dr. west to Nimitz Blvd. to Lowell St., which becomes Narragansett Ave. No children under 12 allowed. *In room:* Hair dryer, no phone, free Wi-Fi.

The Pearl Hotel ★ 🧳 The designers of this midcentury modernist gem took a run-down motel dating from 1959 and let fly with the vintage cool—the lounge area features high-style furniture and light fixtures, exposed stone, and shag carpet and throw pillows that encourage guests to relax on the floor and play a board game. Accommodations at this nonsmoking property are modest in size but have been refreshed with amenities such as Internet radios and contemporary chrome bathroom fixtures; thoughtful design touches include custom mosaic artwork and a pet fish in each room. The Pearl's restaurant and lounge area is snug and features outdoor dining spaces alongside the saltwater pool (where "dive-in" movies are screened weekly). Although there are no beaches in the immediate area, this is a nautical neighborhood, with the marinas, bars, and restaurants of Shelter Island nearby; the airport and Cabrillo National Monument are also just minutes away.

1410 Rosecrans St. (at Fenelon St.), San Diego, CA 92106. www.thepearlsd.com. © **877/732-7573** or 619/226-6100. Fax 619/226-6161. 23 units. From $169 double. "Play & Stay" rate $79 after midnight (must be booked on site, subject to availability). AE, DISC, MC, V. Parking $10. Bus: 28. Take I-5 S. to Rosecrans St. exit. **Amenities:** Restaurant; bar; bike rentals; outdoor saltwater pool; spa services. *In room:* A/C, TV, hair dryer, MP3 docking station, free Wi-Fi.

LA JOLLA

"La Jolla" is thought by many to be misspelled Spanish for "the jewel," while others believe the name is derived from an indigenous word meaning "cave." One look at La Jolla's beautiful coastline and upscale downtown village, and you'll be firmly in the Spanish camp. *Note:* From **I-5 North,** use the La Jolla Parkway exit or from **I-5 South,** take the La Jolla Village Drive West exit, both of which merge with Torrey Pines Road.

Best For: Those who want it all—style, luxury, fine dining, excellent shopping, sophisticated cultural attractions, and outdoor activities.

Drawbacks: All that good stuff is going to cost you; there's also not much in the way of nightlife here.

Very Expensive

La Jolla Shores Hotel ★ ☺ Formerly known as the Sea Lodge, this three-story 1960s hotel in a residential enclave is under the same management as the **La Jolla Beach & Tennis Club** (p. 211). It has an identical on-the-sand location, minus the country-club ambience. About half the rooms at this nonsmoking property have some view of the ocean, and the rest look out on the pool or a tiled courtyard. Priced by view and size, the rooms are pretty basic but were upgraded in 2008. Bathrooms feature separate dressing areas with large closets; balconies or patios are standard, and some rooms have fully equipped kitchenettes. From the beach, you can gaze

La Jolla Hotels

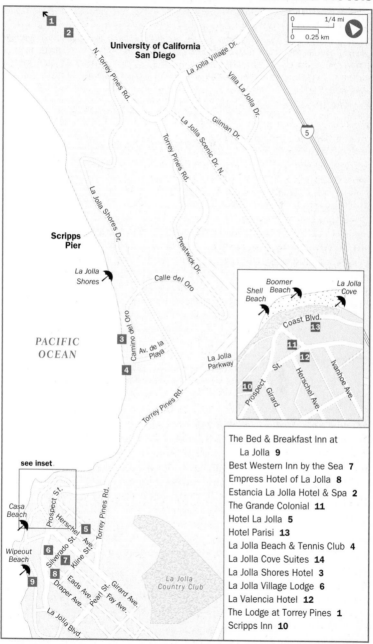

University of California
San Diego

N. Torrey Pines Rd.

La Jolla Village Dr.

Villa La Jolla Dr.

Gilman Dr.

La Jolla Scenic Dr. N.

Torrey Pines Rd.

5

La Jolla Shores Dr.

Scripps
Pier

Prestwick Dr.

La Jolla
Shores

Calle del Oro

PACIFIC
OCEAN

Camino del Oro

Av. de la
Playa

La Jolla
Parkway

Torrey Pines Rd.

Boomer
Beach

La Jolla
Cove

Shell
Beach

Coast Blvd.

La Jolla
Parkway

Prospect
St.

Girard

Herschel Ave.

Ivanhoe Ave.

see inset

Prospect St.

Herschel St.

Casa
Beach

Wipeout
Beach

Silverado St.

Kline St.

Torrey Pines Rd.

Eads Ave.

Pearl St.

Girard Ave.

Fay Ave.

Draper Ave.

La Jolla Blvd.

La Jolla
Country Club

The Bed & Breakfast Inn at
  La Jolla **9**
Best Western Inn by the Sea **7**
Empress Hotel of La Jolla **8**
Estancia La Jolla Hotel & Spa **2**
The Grande Colonial **11**
Hotel La Jolla **5**
Hotel Parisi **13**
La Jolla Beach & Tennis Club **4**
La Jolla Cove Suites **14**
La Jolla Shores Hotel **3**
La Jolla Village Lodge **6**
La Valencia Hotel **12**
The Lodge at Torrey Pines **1**
Scripps Inn **10**

toward the top of the cliffs, where La Jolla's village hums with activity (and relentless traffic). Like the Beach & Tennis Club, this property is popular with families but also attracts business travelers looking to balance meetings with time on the beach or the tennis court.

8110 Camino del Oro (at Av. de la Playa), La Jolla, CA 92037. www.ljshoreshotel.com. © **877/346-6714** or 858/459-8271. Fax 858/456-9346. 128 units. From $369 double; from $799 suite. Extra person $20. Children 11 and under stay free in parent's room. AE, DC, DISC, MC, V. Parking $16. Bus: 30. Take La Jolla Shores Dr., turn left onto Av. de la Playa, turn right on Camino del Oro. **Amenities:** 2 restaurants; babysitting; beach chairs/umbrellas; concierge; exercise room; Jacuzzi; 2 outdoor pools (including a wading pool for kids); room service; sauna; spa services; 2 tennis courts. *In room:* A/C, TV/DVD, fridge, hair dryer, kitchenette (in some), MP3 docking station, free Wi-Fi.

La Valencia Hotel ★★★   Looking much like a Mediterranean villa, "La V" has been the centerpiece of La Jolla since it opened in 1926. Brides still pose in front of the lobby's picture window against a backdrop of the Pacific Ocean, well-coiffed ladies lunch in the dappled shade of the garden patio, and neighborhood cronies quaff libations in the clubby **Whaling Bar.** La Valencia is famous for its history and scenic location, but you won't be disappointed by the old-world standards of service and style. Most rooms are quite comfortable, each boasting lavish appointments and all-marble bathrooms. Because rates vary wildly according to the view (from sweeping to *nada*), get a cheaper room and enjoy the scene from one of the many lounges, serene garden terraces, or the amazing pool that fronts the Pacific and nearby Scripps Park. Room decor, layouts, and size (starting at a snug 250 sq. ft.) are all over the map, too; if you've got the bucks, spring for one of the newer villas featuring fireplaces and butler service. And—budget permitting—don't miss the hotel's romantic **Sky Room.**

1132 Prospect St. (at Herschel Ave.), La Jolla, CA 92037. www.lavalencia.com. © **800/451-0772** or 858/454-0771. Fax 858/456-3921. 112 units. From $299 double; from $595 suites and villas. Minimum stays may be required in summer and on weekends. AE, DC, DISC, MC, V. Valet parking $29. Bus: 30. Take Torrey Pines Rd. to Prospect Place and turn right. Prospect Place becomes Prospect St. Pets less than 75 lb. accepted with $25 nightly fee. **Amenities:** 3 restaurants; 2 bars; babysitting; concierge; exercise room; Jacuzzi; outdoor pool; room service; sauna; spa services. *In room:* A/C, TV/DVD, hair dryer, minibar, free Wi-Fi.

The Lodge at Torrey Pines ★★★   Ten minutes north of La Jolla proper, you'll find this triumphant Craftsman-style creation at the edge of the Torrey Pines Golf Course. This AAA Five-Diamond property brims with clinker-brick masonry, art glass windows and doors, and Stickley furniture. Even the least expensive rooms are an unstinting 520 square feet and lavished with Tiffany-style lamps, period wallpaper, framed Hiroshige prints, and lots of wood accents; views face a courtyard carefully landscaped to mimic the rare seaside environment just beyond the hotel grounds. More expensive rooms overlook the golf course and the ocean in the distance; most of these have balconies, fireplaces, and giant bathrooms. The 9,500-square-foot spa specializes in treatments utilizing coastal sage and other local plants, and there's an elegant pool area with an elevated Jacuzzi sheltered under a gazebo. An excellent **restaurant** named after painter A. R. Valentien features top-quality seasonal offerings.

11480 N. Torrey Pines Rd., La Jolla, CA 92037. www.lodgetorreypines.com. © **800/656-0087** or 858/453-4420. Fax 858/453-7464. 170 units. From $412 double; from $659 suite. Children 17 and under stay free in parent's room. AE, DC, DISC, MC, V. Valet parking $27; self-parking $23. Bus: 101. From I-5 take La Jolla Village Dr. west, bear right (north) onto N. Torrey Pines Rd. **Amenities:** 2 restaurants; bar; concierge; exercise room; preferential tee times at the golf course; Jacuzzi; outdoor pool; room service; spa. *In room:* A/C, TV, CD player, hair dryer, minibar, free Wi-Fi.

Scripps Inn ★★ 🍴   This meticulously maintained inn is hidden away behind the Museum of Contemporary Art, offering seclusion even though the attractions of La Jolla are just a short walk away. Only a small, grassy park comes between the inn and the beach, cliffs, and tide pools; the view from the second-story deck can hypnotize guests, who gaze out to sea indefinitely. Rates vary depending on ocean view (all have one, but some are better than others). Rooms have a pleasant pale cream/sand palette with new bathroom fixtures and appointments. All rooms have sofa beds; two have wood-burning fireplaces, and four have kitchenettes. The inn supplies beach towels, firewood, and pastries each morning. Repeat guests return for their favorite rooms, so book early for the best choice.

555 Coast Blvd. S. (at Cuvier), La Jolla, CA 92037. www.scrippsinn.com. ✆ **866/860-6318** or 858/454-3391. Fax 858/456-0389. 14 units. From $320 double; from $350 suite. Extra person $10. Children 4 and under stay free in parent's room. Rates include continental breakfast. AE, DC, DISC, MC, V. Parking $10. Bus: 30. Take Torrey Pines Rd., turn right on Prospect Place; past the museum, turn right onto Cuvier. Pets accepted with $50 fee. *In room:* Ceiling fans, TV, fridge, hair dryer, free Wi-Fi.

Expensive

The Bed & Breakfast Inn at La Jolla ★★ 🍴   This 1913 house designed by San Diego's first important architect, Irving Gill, is the setting for this cultured and elegant B&B. Reconfigured as lodgings, the house—which was the family home of composer/conductor John Philip Sousa in the 1920s—has lost none of its charm. This nonsmoking inn features lovely enclosed gardens and a cozy library and sitting room (featuring a TV and guest computer). Some rooms have a fireplace or ocean view; each room has a private bathroom, most of which are on the compact side. The period furnishings are tasteful and cottage-style, with plenty of old photos of La Jolla adding to the sense of history. A gourmet breakfast with mimosas is served wherever you desire—dining room, patio, sun deck, or in your room; there's also afternoon wine and cheese offered.

7753 Draper Ave. (near Prospect), La Jolla, CA 92037. www.innlajolla.com. ✆ **888/988-8481** or 858/456-2066. Fax 858/456-1510. 15 units. From $199 double; from $300 suite. 2-night minimum on weekends. Children under 12 not allowed. Rates include full breakfast. AE, DISC, MC, V. Limited free parking. Bus: 30. Take Torrey Pines Rd. to Prospect Place and turn right. Prospect Place becomes Prospect St.; proceed to Draper Ave. and turn left. One dog less than 35 lb. accepted with $200 deposit and $50 nightly fee. **Amenities:** Beach chairs/umbrellas; CD players; picnic-basket lunches; free Wi-Fi. *In room:* A/C, TV (in some), hair dryer, MP3 docking station (in some).

Empress Hotel of La Jolla ★   The Empress Hotel offers spacious, nonsmoking quarters just a block or two from La Jolla's main drag and the ocean. It's quieter here than at the premium cliff-top properties, and you'll sacrifice little other than direct ocean views (many rooms on the top floors afford a partial view). If you're planning to explore La Jolla on foot, the Empress is a good base; it also exudes a class many comparably priced chains lack, with warm service to boot. Rooms are tastefully decorated and well equipped; four "Empress" rooms have sitting areas with full-size sleeper sofas. Breakfast is set up next to a serene sun deck; you can grab dinner at the hotel's **Manhattan** restaurant, a loungey, old-school Italian spot.

7766 Fay Ave. (at Silverado), La Jolla, CA 92037. www.empress-hotel.com. ✆ **888/369-9900** or 858/454-3001. Fax 858/454-6387. 73 units. From $239 double; from $409 suite. Rates include continental breakfast. AE, DC, DISC, MC, V. Valet parking $18. Bus: 30. Take Torrey Pines Rd. to Girard Ave., turn right, and then left on Silverado St. **Amenities:** Restaurant; bar; exercise room; room service; spa services. *In room:* A/C, TV, fridge, hair dryer, free Wi-Fi.

Estancia La Jolla Hotel & Spa ★★★   This California rancho-style property was built in 2004, and shortly thereafter was named one of the world's hottest new hotels by *Condé Nast Traveler.* The 9½-acre spread has some pretty cool neighbors: the Louis I. Kahn–designed Salk Institute, UC San Diego, the Torrey Pines Gliderport, and Blacks Beach. You won't see any of those things from this self-contained retreat, but the romance created by the hacienda flavor and the meticulously maintained gardens with their native flora and bubbling fountains is diversion enough. Guest rooms face a central courtyard, and many rooms have balconies or patios. All rooms are tastefully appointed with comfy furnishings that would be at home in an upscale residence. With its old *Californio* exterior and live Spanish guitar music, the **Mustangs & Burros** lounge and bar is a great place to chill out. There's also an award-winning restaurant on the premises and a full-service spa.

9700 N. Torrey Pines Rd., La Jolla, CA 92037. www.estancialajolla.com. © **877/437-8262** or 858/550-1000. Fax 858/550-1001. 210 units. From $229 double; from $279 suite. Bed-and-breakfast packages available for an additional $20. AE, DC, DISC, MC, V. Valet parking $25; self-parking $20. Bus: 101. From I-5 take the Genesee Ave. exit westbound, go left on N. Torrey Pines Rd. **Amenities:** 2 restaurants; 2 bars; babysitting; concierge; exercise room w/yoga and personal training; Jacuzzi; outdoor pool; room service; full-service spa. *In room:* A/C, TV, hair dryer, minibar, Wi-Fi ($12/day).

The Grande Colonial ★★★ 🏨   Possessed of an old-world European flair that's more London or Georgetown than seaside La Jolla, the Grande Colonial has earned accolades for its meticulous restorations. A 2007 renovation of two adjacent properties, the **Little Hotel by the Sea** and the **Garden Terrace,** added 18 more suites to the Grande Colonial fold. Some of theses feature ocean views, fireplaces, and full kitchens. The Little Hotel is also crowned with a way-cool rooftop loft and deck area from which you can watch the seals at play at the nearby Children's Pool. In the main hotel lounge, guests gather in front of the fireplace for drinks—often before enjoying dinner at the hotel's excellent **Nine-Ten** restaurant (p. 138). Guest rooms at this nonsmoking property are quiet and elegantly appointed, with beautiful draperies and traditional furnishings; many rooms in the original building have sea views, as well.

910 Prospect St. (btw. Fay and Girard aves.), La Jolla, CA 92037. www.thegrandecolonial.com. © **888/828-5498** or 858/454-2181. Fax 858/454-5679. 93 units. From $259 double; from $425 suite. Children 11 and under stay free in parent's room. AE, DC, MC, V. Valet parking $22. Bus: 30. Take Torrey Pines Rd. to Prospect Place and turn right. Prospect Place becomes Prospect St. **Amenities:** Restaurant; bar; concierge; access to nearby health club; outdoor pool; room service. *In room:* A/C, TV, hair dryer, kitchen (in some), MP3 docking station, free Wi-Fi.

Hotel Parisi ★★★ 🏨   This intimate hotel is on the second floor overlooking one of La Jolla's main intersections (street-facing rooms are well insulated from the modest din). Parisi's nurturing, wellness-inspired vibe first becomes evident in the lobby, where elements of earth, wind, fire, water, and metal blend according to feng shui principles. The Italy-meets-Zen composition is carried into the guest rooms, where custom furnishings are modern yet comfy. Parisi calls the spacious accommodations "suites" (some are more like junior suites), and each has an ergonomic desk, dimmable lighting, goose-down super-luxe bedding, and creamy, calming neutral decor. Less expensive rooms at this nonsmoking property are smaller with little or no view; across the street from the hotel is **Parisi Apart**—seven luxury one-bedroom units available for extended stays. The personal service stops at nothing—there's even a menu of 24-hour in-room holistic health services (from yoga to psychotherapy).

1111 Prospect St. (at Herschel Ave.), La Jolla, CA 92037. www.hotelparisi.com. © **877/472-7474** or 858/454-1511. Fax 858/454-1531. 29 units. From $238 double; from $358 suite; extended stay from $265. Rates include continental breakfast. AE, DC, DISC, MC, V. Parking $15. Bus: 30. Take Torrey Pines Rd. to Prospect Place and turn right; Prospect Place becomes Prospect St., turn left on Herschel Ave. **Amenities:** Room service; spa services. *In room:* A/C, TV/DVD, CD player, hair dryer, minibar, free Wi-Fi.

La Jolla Beach & Tennis Club ★ ☺ ✋

The location is unbeatable—right on La Jolla Shores beach—but standard accommodations at this family-oriented resort, first opened in 1935, are uninspired. Beachfront rooms are tiny, but the wide ocean panorama at the foot of your bed is undeniably splendid; many rooms also feature full kitchens. A variety of suites are available, ranging from one-bedroom street-side digs to deluxe two- and three-bedroom spaces facing the ocean. The beach is popular and the staff stays busy shooing away nonguests—in California, all beaches are public only up to the median high-tide line and the LJBTC defends its turf. Watersports equipment can be rented, there are lighted tennis courts, and a pitch-and-putt golf course; you can also make arrangements for your own private beach barbecue. The hotel's distinctive **Marine Room** restaurant (p. 138) is one of San Diego's best. All told, though, you get better room value for your money at the club's sister hotel, the **La Jolla Shores Hotel** (p. 206).

2000 Spindrift Dr., La Jolla, CA 92037. www.ljbtc.com. © **888/828-0948** or 858/454-7126. Fax 858/456-3805. 98 units. From $269 double; from $419 suite. 3-night minimum in summer. Extra person $20. Children 11 and under stay free in parent's room. AE, DC, MC, V. Free parking. Bus: 30. Take La Jolla Shores Dr., turn left on Paseo Dorado, and follow to Spindrift Dr. **Amenities:** 2 restaurants; seasonal beach snack bar; babysitting; children's programs; exercise room; 9-hole pitch-and-putt golf course; 75-ft. heated outdoor pool; room service; 12 lighted tennis courts; spa services; watersports equipment/rentals. *In room:* A/C, TV/DVD, movie library, CD player, hair dryer, free Internet, kitchenette (in some), MP3 docking station.

La Jolla Cove Suites

Tucked beside high-end condos across from Ellen Browning Scripps Park, this family-run 1950s-era catbird seat is actually closer to the ocean than its pricey uphill neighbor, La Valencia. The to-die-for ocean view is completely unobstructed, and La Jolla Cove—one of California's prettiest swimming spots—is steps away. The property is peaceful at night, but village dining and shopping are only a short walk away. You'll pay according to the quality of your view; about 80% of guest quarters gaze upon the ocean. Most rooms are wonderfully spacious, each featuring a fully equipped kitchen, plus a private balcony or patio; they have functional, almost institutional furnishings. A rooftop deck offers lounge chairs, cafe tables, and coastal vistas; breakfast is served there each morning.

1155 Coast Blvd. (across from the Cove), La Jolla, CA 92037. www.lajollacove.com. © **888/525-6552** or 858/459-2621. Fax 858/551-3405. 113 units. From $275 double; from $335 suite. Extra person $25. Children 12 and under stay free in parent's room. Rates include continental breakfast. AE, DC, DISC, MC, V. Parking $15. Bus: 30. Take Torrey Pines Rd. to Prospect Place and turn right. When the road forks, veer right (downhill) onto Coast Blvd. Pets up to 30 lb. accepted with $25 nightly fee. **Amenities:** BBQ grills; access to nearby health club; Jacuzzi; heated outdoor pool. *In room:* A/C (in some), TV, kitchen.

Moderate

Best Western Plus Inn by the Sea ★

The Best Western (like the more formal Empress, a block away; p. 209) offers a terrific alternative to pricier digs nearby. Occupying an enviable location at the heart of La Jolla's charming village, this

THE ROAD TO WELLNESS: healthful havens

Health-conscious San Diego is home to a collection of some of the finest fitness spas in the country. These aren't pedicure-and-a-sauna resort spas, but places where you will engage in regimented mind-and-body workouts that just might change your life.

The Golden Door ★★★, 777 Deer Springs Rd., Escondido (www.golden door.com; © **800/424-0777** or 760/744-5777), is a Zen-influenced sanctuary in North County where a maximum of 40 people engage in a weeklong program of massage, beauty treatments, and fitness activities like yoga, tennis, and hiking. Most weeks are same-sex, but co-ed stays are also available; a 4-to-1 ratio of staff (including a fitness guide, dietician, and esthetician) to guest helps explain the $7,749 price tag (some 3- and 4-day programs are also available). Accommodations and gourmet spa-cuisine meals, featuring products grown on-site, are included.

Rancho La Puerta ★★★, Carretera A Km 5, Tecate, Mexico (www.rancho lapuerta.com; © **800/443-7565** or 858/764-5500), is located about an hour from San Diego, just across the border in Baja California. Opened in 1940, it lays claim to being the world's first fitness spa. This elegant, beautifully landscaped resort is set on some 3,000 acres and encompasses part of a mountain held sacred by the indigenous Kumeyaay people. Weeklong residences are encouraged, but a limited number of partial stays are available. More than 70 classes and activities are held each week. Rates start at $2,835 and include transportation from San Diego International Airport.

Cal-a-Vie ★★★, 29402 Spa Havens Way, Vista (www.cal-a-vie.com; © **866/772-4283** or 760/842-6831), sits on 200-plus acres in San Diego's North County, offering 3-, 4-, and 7-night packages. A maximum of 30 guests enjoy exceptional spa cuisine, fitness classes, hiking, lectures, and spa treatments; Cal-a-Vie also has its own 18-hole golf course. Three-night plans start at $4,195.

Chopra Center for Wellbeing ★★, 2013 Costa del Mar Rd., Carlsbad (www. chopra.com; © **888/736-6895** or 760/494-1639), is located on the grounds of the La Costa Resort and Spa (p. 232). Founded by holistic guru Deepak Chopra, the center has yoga and meditation classes daily (including a free group meditation held every day), spa treatments based on 5,000-year-old Ayurvedic principles, multiday healing programs, and a gift store with books, jewelry, and more. An overnight stay is not required, but a special rate is offered.

independently managed, nonsmoking property puts guests just a short walk from the cliffs and beach. The low-rise tops out at five stories, with the upper floors enjoying ocean views (and the highest room rates). Renovated rooms here are Best Western standard issue—freshly maintained, but nothing special. All rooms do have balconies, though, and refrigerators are available at no extra charge; in addition, the hotel offers plenty of welcome amenities.

7830 Fay Ave. (btw. Prospect and Silverado sts.), La Jolla, CA 92037. www.lajollainnbythesea.com. © **800/526-4545** or 858/459-4461. Fax 858/456-2578. 129 units. From $199 double; from $239 suite. Children 17 and under stay free in parent's room. Rates include continental breakfast. AE, DC, DISC, MC, V. Parking $12. Bus: 30. Take Torrey Pines Rd. to Prospect Place and turn right. Prospect Place becomes Prospect St.; proceed to Fay Ave. and turn left. **Amenities:** Access to nearby health club; outdoor heated pool. *In room:* A/C, TV, hair dryer, MP3 docking station, free Wi-Fi.

CORONADO

The "island" (really a peninsula) of Coronado is a great escape. It has quiet, architecturally rich streets; a small-town, Navy-oriented atmosphere; and one of the state's most beautiful and welcoming beaches. Coronado's resorts are especially popular with Southern California and Arizona families for weekend escapes. Although downtown San Diego is just a 10-minute drive or 15-minute ferry ride away, you may feel pleasantly isolated in Coronado, but it isn't your best choice if you're planning to spend lots of time in central parts of the city. *Note:* To reach the places listed here, take I-5 to the Coronado Bridge, and then follow individual directions.

Best For: Families and those who want some quality beach time without the raucous partying.

Drawbacks: Things get mighty quiet here after dark.

Very Expensive

Hotel del Coronado ★★★   Opened in 1888 and designated a National Historic Landmark in 1977, the "Hotel Del" is the last of California's stately old seaside hotels. This monument to Victorian grandeur boasts tall cupolas, red turrets, and gingerbread trim, all spread out over 28 acres. Even if you don't stay here, be sure to stroll through the sumptuous, wood-paneled lobby and along the pristine, wide beach. Rooms run the gamut from compact to extravagant, and all are packed with antique charm. The least expensive rooms are snug and don't have views; the best are junior suites with large windows and balconies fronting one of the state's finest white-sand beaches. Almost half the hotel's rooms are in the renovated, seven-story tower—it has more living space, but none of the historical ambience. The Del's signature restaurant, the distinctive and contemporary **1500 Ocean** (p. 143), serves a sophisticated "Southland Coastal" cuisine; and don't miss the Sunday brunch in the amazing **Crown Room.** Recent additions to the Del include a state-of-the-art spa and **Beach Village,** a collection of 78 "coastal cottages." These privately owned two- and three-bedroom condos feature fireplaces and oceanview balconies, and are available for rent.

1500 Orange Ave., Coronado, CA 92118. www.hoteldel.com. ℂ **800/468-3533** or 619/435-6611. Fax 619/522-8238. 757 rooms. From $325 double; from $560 suite; from $1,200 cottage. Extra person $25. Children 17 and under stay free in parent's room. Minimum stay requirements apply most weekends. $25/day resort fee. Packages available. AE, DC, DISC, MC, V. Valet parking $40; self-parking $30. Bus: 901 or 904. From Coronado Bridge, turn left onto Orange Ave. **Amenities:** 5 restaurants; 4 bars; airport transfers; babysitting; bike rentals; children's programs; concierge; health club; 2 Jacuzzis; 2 outdoor pools; room service; full-service spa. *In room:* A/C, TV, hair dryer, Internet ($10/day), minibar, free Wi-Fi (some rooms).

Expensive

El Cordova Hotel ★   This Spanish hacienda across the street from the Hotel del Coronado began life as a private mansion in 1902. By the 1930s, it had become a hotel. Shaped like a baseball diamond and surrounding a courtyard with meandering tiled pathways, flowering shrubs, a swimming pool, boutique shops, and patio seating for **Miguel's Cocina Mexican** restaurant, El Cordova hums pleasantly with activity. Renovated in 2011, Each room is a little different—some sport a Mexican Colonial ambience, while others evoke a comfy beach cottage. Most rooms in this nonsmoking hotel have kitchenettes with gas stoves; all feature ceiling fans and brightly tiled bathrooms, but lack much in the way of frills. El Cordova's prime location makes it a

THE indelible HOTEL DEL

San Diego's romantic **Hotel del Coronado** is an unmistakable landmark with a colorful past. When it opened in 1888, it was among the first buildings with Thomas Edison's new invention, electric light; the hotel's own electrical power plant supplied the entire city of Coronado until 1922. Author L. Frank Baum, a frequent guest, designed the Crown Room's original crown-shaped chandeliers. He wrote several of the books in his beloved *Wizard of Oz* series in Coronado, and some believe he modeled elements of the Emerald City after the Del.

The hotel has played host to royalty and celebrities as well. The first visiting monarch was Kalakaua, Hawaii's last king, who spent Christmas here in 1890. But the best-known royal guest was Edward, Prince of Wales (later King Edward VIII, and then Duke of Windsor). He came to the hotel in April 1920, the first British royal to visit California. Of the many lavish social affairs held during his stay, at least two were attended by Wallis Simpson (then Navy wife Wallis Warfield). Though some like to speculate their love affair, which culminated in his abdication of the throne, might have begun right here, it's very unlikely it did. Her official introduction to him came 15 years later in London.

Author Henry James wrote in 1905 of "the charming sweetness and comfort of this spot"; and, in 1927, Charles Lindbergh was honored here following his historic 33½-hour solo flight across the Atlantic in his San Diego-built *Spirit of St. Louis*. Hollywood Golden Age stars including Mary Pickford, Greta Garbo, Charlie Chaplin, and Esther Williams flocked to the Del; and the hotel has also hosted 11 U.S. presidents.

Perhaps most famously, director Billy Wilder filmed *Some Like It Hot* at the hotel with Marilyn Monroe, Tony Curtis, and Jack Lemmon. *The Stunt Man*, starring Peter O'Toole, was also filmed here in 1980. And some guests have never left: The ghost of Kate Morgan, whose body was found in 1892, supposedly still roams the halls—room 3327 has a reputation for being haunted. Visitors and guests intrigued by the Hotel Del's past can stroll through the lower-level History Gallery, a minimuseum of hotel memorabilia.

popular option; reserve several months in advance for summer visits. Facilities include a barbecue area with picnic table.

1351 Orange Ave. (at Adella Ave.), Coronado, CA 92118. www.elcordovahotel.com. ☏ **800/229-2032** or 619/435-4131. Fax 619/435-0632. 40 units. From $249 double; from $329 suite. Children 11 and under stay free in parent's room. Extra person $10. AE, DC, DISC, MC, V. Parking in neighboring structure $8. Bus: 901 or 904. From Coronado Bridge, turn left onto Orange Ave. **Amenities:** 4 restaurants; BBQ grill; bike rentals; Jacuzzi; outdoor pool; watersports equipment/rentals. *In room:* A/C, TV, free Wi-Fi.

Glorietta Bay Inn ★★   Right across the street from the Hotel Del, this pretty white hotel consists of the charmingly historic John D. Spreckels mansion and several younger—and less charming—motel-style buildings. Only 11 rooms in this nonsmoking hotel are in the mansion, which dates from 1908, and it boasts original fixtures, a grand staircase, and music room. The guest rooms are decked out in antiques and have a romantic and nostalgic ambience. Rooms and suites in the 1950s annexes are much less expensive but were upgraded from motel-plain to better match the main house's classy vibe; some have kitchenettes and marina views. The least expensive units are small and have parking-lot views. Wherever your room is, you'll enjoy the

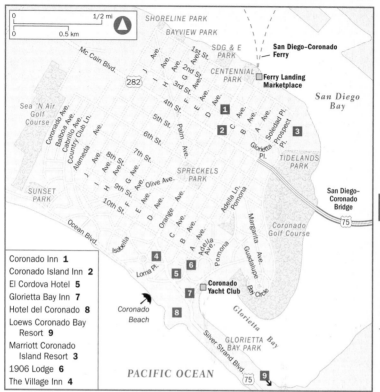

Coronado Inn **1**
Coronado Island Inn **2**
El Cordova Hotel **5**
Glorietta Bay Inn **7**
Hotel del Coronado **8**
Loews Coronado Bay
   Resort **9**
Marriott Coronado
   Island Resort **3**
1906 Lodge **6**
The Village Inn **4**

inn's excellent customer service. Glorietta Bay, with its boat rentals and excursions, is right outside your door, and the hotel is within easy walking distance of the beach, golf, tennis, watersports, shopping, and dining.

1630 Glorietta Blvd. (near Orange Ave.), Coronado, CA 92118. www.gloriettabayinn.com. ✆ **800/283-9383** or 619/435-3101. Fax 619/435-6182. 100 units. 3- or 4-night minimum some summer weekends. From $199 double; from $279 suite. Extra person $10. Children 17 and under stay free in parent's room. Rates include continental breakfast and afternoon refreshment. AE, DC, DISC, MC, V. Self-parking $10. Bus: 901 or 904. From Coronado Bridge, turn left on Orange Ave. After 2 miles, turn left onto Glorietta Blvd.; the inn is across the street from the Hotel del Coronado. **Amenities:** Babysitting; concierge; access to nearby health club; Jacuzzi; outdoor pool; spa services. *In room:* A/C, TV/DVD, CD player, fridge, hair dryer, free Wi-Fi.

Loews Coronado Bay Resort ★★ ☺   On its own private 15-acre peninsula 4 miles south of downtown Coronado and across the highway from the Silver Strand State Beach, the Loews is an all-inclusive resort destination. It offers a plethora of water-related activities such as sailing and Jet Ski-ing from its private 80-slip marina; it also has direct, private access to the beach. It's a family-friendly place with special (healthy) kids' menus, supervised children's activities, and teen-themed DVDs and Gameboys to borrow; pets are always welcome—and catered to—at Loews, as well. Adult pleasures include romantic gondola rides through the canals of the adjacent

Coronado Cays, an exclusive waterside community; fine dining at the excellent **Mistral** restaurant (ask for table 61 or 64 for the best vistas); and a full-service spa, one of the few in Southern California to offer Watsu, the shiatsu-influenced massage that is given as you float in a pool heated to body temperature.

4000 Coronado Bay Rd., Coronado, CA 92118. www.loewshotels.com. © **800/815-6397** or 619/424-4000. Fax 619/424-4400. 439 units. From $279 double; from $499 suite. Up to 2 children 17 and under stay free in parent's room. Extra person $25. Packages available. AE, DC, DISC, MC, V. Valet parking $30; self-parking $25. Bus: 901. From Coronado Bridge, turn left on Orange Ave., left on Coronado Bay Rd. Pets accepted with $25 fee. **Amenities:** 2 restaurants; 2 bars; babysitting and pet-sitting; children's programs; concierge; exercise room and classes; 2 Jacuzzis; 3 outdoor pools; room service; spa; 3 lighted tennis courts; marina w/watersports equipment/rentals. *In room:* A/C, TV/DVD, CD player, hair dryer, minibar, Wi-Fi ($13/day).

Marriott Coronado Island Resort ★★
Elegance and luxury here are understated. Although the physical property is generic, the staff goes out of its way to provide upbeat attention; guests just seem to get whatever they need, be it a lift downtown (by water taxi from the private dock), a tee time at the neighboring golf course, or a prime appointment at the spa. Despite its mostly business clientele, this nonsmoking hotel offers much for the leisure traveler: a prime waterfront setting with a sweeping view of the San Diego skyline, a location within a mile of Coronado shopping and dining, walking distance from the ferry landing, and a wealth of sporting and recreational activities. Guest rooms are generously sized and attractively, comfortably furnished, and all feature balconies or patios. In terms of room size and amenities, your dollar goes farther here than at the Hotel Del.

2000 Second St. (at Glorietta Blvd.), Coronado, CA 92118. www.marriotthotels.com/sanci. © **800/228-9290** or 619/435-3000. Fax 619/435-4183. 300 units. From $289 double; from $389 suite. Children 11 and under stay free in parent's room. AE, DC, MC, V. Valet parking $28; self-parking $22. Bus: 901 or 904. Ferry: From Broadway Pier. From Coronado Bridge, turn right onto Glorietta Blvd., take 1st right to hotel. **Amenities:** 2 restaurants; bar; babysitting; bike rentals; concierge; exercise room; 2 Jacuzzis; 3 outdoor pools; room service; spa; 6 lighted tennis courts; watersports equipment/rentals. *In room:* A/C, TV, hair dryer, minibar, MP3 docking station, Wi-Fi ($13/day).

Moderate

Coronado Inn ★
Centrally located and terrifically priced, this renovated 1940s courtyard motel has such a friendly ambience, it's like staying with old friends. A continental breakfast is served poolside in the morning; iced tea, lemonade, and fresh fruit are provided in the lobby each afternoon. It's still a motel, though, so rooms are pretty basic. There are six rooms with small kitchens at this nonsmoking hotel; microwaves are available in the rest. Rooms close to the street are noisiest, so ask for one toward the back. The Coronado shuttle stops a block away; it serves the shopping areas and Hotel Del. The Coronado Inn's sister property, the **Coronado Island Inn,** 301 Orange Ave. (© **800/598-6624** or 619/435-0935), is a block away and offers some of the cheapest digs on the island.

266 Orange Ave. (corner of Third St.), Coronado, CA 92118. www.coronadoinn.com. © **800/598-6624** or 619/435-4121. Fax 619/435-6296. 30 units. From $159 double; from $199 suite. Children 16 and under stay free in parent's room. Extra person $15. Rates include continental breakfast. AE, DISC, MC, V. Limited free parking. Bus: 901 or 904. From Coronado Bridge, stay on Third St. Pets accepted for $15/night. **Amenities:** BBQ grills; outdoor pool. *In room:* A/C, TV, fridge, hair dryer, kitchen (in some), microwave, free Wi-Fi.

1906 Lodge ★★★
Unpretentious luxury, gracious hospitality, and generous servings of local history make this an unbeatable B&B experience in Coronado. Located in a residential neighborhood a short walk from shops, restaurants, the Hotel

del Coronado, and the beach, this nonsmoking property features two wings. One is the original 1906 boarding house, designed by San Diego's legendary architecture team of Irving Gill and William Hebbard, featuring six guest rooms; the second building was constructed from the ground up and completed in 2009. Nicely complementing the historic building, it offers the more spacious accommodations (11 suites and junior suites), as well as plusses like spa tubs, fireplaces, private entrances, and balconies or patios. Each room is named and tastefully themed after a Coronado-related person or place, and is adorned with vintage postcards, photos, and newspaper articles. The buffet breakfast includes a scrumptious entree, and afternoon wine and cheese are served in the homey parlor.

1060 Adella Ave., Coronado, CA 92118. www.1906lodge.com. © **866/435-1906** or 619/437-1900. Fax 619/319-5828. 17 units. $189–$499 double. Children 17 and under stay free in parent's room. Rates include full breakfast. AE, DC, DISC, MC, V. Free parking. Bus: 901 or 904. *In room:* A/C, TV/DVD, CD player, fridge (new building only), hair dryer, MP3 docking station, free Wi-Fi.

Inexpensive

The Village Inn ⚑   Its location a block or two from Coronado's main sights is this inn's most appealing feature. Historical charm runs a close second; a plaque outside identifies the three-story brick-and-stucco hotel as the once-chic Blue Lantern Inn, built in 1928. The vintage lobby sets the mood in this European-style hostelry; each simple but well-maintained room holds a four-poster bed and antique dressers and armoires, plus lovely Battenberg lace bedcovers and shams. Front rooms enjoy the best view, and the communal full kitchen is available day and night for guest use. The inn's only Achilles' heel is tiny (but private) bathrooms, though some have been updated with Jacuzzi tubs.

1017 Park Place (at Orange Ave.), Coronado, CA 92118. www.coronadovillageinn.com. ©**619/435-9318.** 15 units. $85–$95 double. Rates include continental breakfast. AE, MC, V. Parking available on street. Bus: 901 or 904. From Coronado Bridge, turn left onto Orange Ave., and then right on Park Place. **Amenities:** Kitchen. *In room:* TV.

PRACTICAL INFORMATION

The Big Picture

Whatever you are looking for in an accommodation, whatever your price range, you will find it in San Diego. Historical ambience? Sleek modernism? Plush luxury? A dorm bed? It's all here.

By law, public spaces need to be accessible to all, so travelers with disabilities should have few problems finding a place to stay. Also note San Diego has a hotel tax that will not be included in published rates; it's an additional 10.5%, or 12.5% for lodgings with 70 or more rooms.

High season is vaguely defined as the summer period between Memorial Day and Labor Day—some hotels push rates higher still in July and August, when Comic-Con and the Del Mar racing season are in full swing. Beach accommodations tend to book up solid on summer weekends and even some weekdays (with luck you can sometimes nab a day-of reservation, filling in for a no-show).

Because San Diego is a very popular convention destination, you'll find that rates for the larger downtown hotels and a few of the Mission Valley hotels are largely determined by the ebb and flow of conventions in town—which means that weekend and winter holiday rates can be good bargains. Leisure-oriented hotels along the coast and in Mission Valley are generally busier on weekends, especially in summer, so midweek deals are easier to snag. Here's an idea to maximize your discounts: Spend the weekend at a downtown high-rise and duck into a beach bungalow on Monday. And remember, in the current economic conditions, *everybody* is making deals. You might be able to wrangle a room in one of the city's finest hotels for a pittance.

Getting the Best Deal

While the rack rates at San Diego's most desirable hotels may deliver something in the way of sticker shock (remember, this book quotes high-season prices), there are ways to score a deal.

- Dial direct; or better yet, book online at the hotel's website.
- Ask about special rates or other discounts.
- Look into group or long-stay discounts.
- Avoid excess charges and hidden costs (such as minibar charges).
- Book an efficiency.
- Investigate reservations services such as **Quikbook** (www.quikbook.com; ✆ 800/789-9887, or 212/779-7666 outside the U.S.) and **Hotel Discounts** (www. hoteldiscount.com; ✆ 800/715-7666 in the U.S. and Canada, 00800/1066-1066 in Europe, or 1214/369-1264 elsewhere). You can also look for deals with online booking sites like **Expedia, Hotels.com, Kayak.com, Priceline,** and **Travelocity.**

Room rates at properties on Hotel Circle are significantly cheaper than those in many other parts of the city. You'll find a cluster of inexpensive chain hotels and motels, including **Best Western Seven Seas** (www.bw7seas.com; ✆ 800/328-1618 or 619/291-1300), **Mission Valley Travelodge** (www.travelodge.com; ✆ 800/525-4055 or 619/297-2271), **Ramada Plaza** (www.ramada.com; ✆ 800/854-9517 or 619/291-6500), and **Vagabond Inn—Hotel Circle** (www.vagabondhc.com; ✆ 800/571-2933 or 619/297-1691).

Many downtown hotels seem designed for the expense-account crowd, but in the budget category, you can't beat the 259-room **500 West,** 500 W. Broadway (www.500westhotel.com; ✆ 866/500-7533 or 619/234-5252). It offers small but comfortable rooms starting around $70 a night in a seven-story building dating to 1924. It has contemporary style, history, and a good location, but bathrooms are down the hall. Cheaper still are downtown's hostels; see p. 219.

Inexpensive motels like the **Harbor View Days Inn Suites,** 1919 Pacific Hwy. (www.daysinn.com; ✆ 800/329-7466 or 619/232-1077), also line Pacific Highway between the airport and downtown.

Wealthy, image-conscious La Jolla is really *not* the best place for deep bargains, but if you're determined to stay there as cheaply as possible, you won't do better than the **La Jolla Village Lodge,** 1141 Silverado St., at Herschel Ave. (www.lajollavillage lodge.com; ✆ 877/551-2001 or 858/551-2001). This 30-room motel is standard Americana, arranged around a small parking lot with cinder-block construction and small, basic rooms. Rates vary wildly by season and day of the week—a room that costs $100 midweek in February doubles in price for a summer weekend.

Alternative Accommodations

BED & BREAKFASTS Travelers who seek bed-and-breakfast accommodations will be pleasantly surprised by the variety and affordability of San Diego B&Bs. Many B&Bs are traditional, reflecting the personality of an on-site innkeeper and offering as few as two guest rooms; others accommodate more guests in a slickly professional way. A handful of B&Bs are part of the close-knit **San Diego Bed & Breakfast Guild** (www.bandbguildsandiego.org; ✆ **619/523-1300**), whose members work actively at keeping prices reasonable; many good B&Bs average $100 to $125 a night.

HOSTELS Those in search of rock-bottom prices should check into San Diego's collection of hostels. You should be prepared for shared dorm-style rooms, although private rooms are also found at most. Communal kitchens are also available at most hostels, and some offer inexpensive breakfasts or other meals. Reservations are a good idea any time of year, and overbooking is not uncommon. Hostel rates will also fluctuate according to the season and what local events are taking place.

USAHostels (www.usahostels.com; ✆ **800/438-8622** or 619/232-3100) is in the heart of the Gaslamp Quarter at 726 Fifth Ave., in a historic building; private rooms start at $72, four-bed rooms are $32, and six-bed rooms run $30 per person (online reservations receive a discount). Also in the Gaslamp is **Hostelling International—SD Downtown** (www.sandiegohostels.org; ✆ **888/464-4872**, ext. 156, or 619/525-1531), at 521 Market St. This facility has 4-, 6-, and 10-person rooms, with or without en suite bathrooms; and double, twin, and family-size private rooms, with or without bathroom. Reception is open 24 hours. Private rooms start at $120 and dorm rooms start at $39.

Hostelling International—SD Point Loma is a 55-bed hostel (✆ **888/464-4872**, ext. 157, or 619/223-4778), at 3790 Udall St., which is about 2 miles inland from Ocean Beach; rates start at $26 per person, and private rooms that sleep two start at $56. The **Ocean Beach International Hostel,** 4961 Newport Ave. (www.california hostel.com; ✆ **800/339-7263** or 619/223-7873), has more than 60 beds and is just 2 blocks from the beach. Bunk rates start at $35 per person, and they offer free pickup from the airport, train, or bus station. There's an extensive collection of DVDs for guests, complimentary breakfast, free Wi-Fi, and barbecues are held Tuesday and Friday. U.S. residents must show current student ID, proof of international travel within the last 6 months, or be a member of a hostelling organization in order to stay.

You can also embrace your inner beach bum at **Banana Bungalow,** 707 Reed Ave. (www.bananabungalowsandiego.com; ✆ **858/273-3060**). You won't get any closer to the beach than this—it's right on the raucous Pacific Beach boardwalk. In summer, dorm rooms are $35 and private rooms are $150 for two people (add $15 for each additional person).

PRIVATE HOMES/ROOMS House-swapping is becoming a more popular and viable means of travel: you stay in their place, they stay in yours, and you both get an authentic and personal view of the area, the opposite of the escapist retreat that many hotels offer. Try **HomeLink International** (www.homelink.org), the largest and oldest home-swapping organization, founded in 1953, with more than 13,000 listings worldwide ($119 for a yearly membership). **HomeExchange.com** ($48 for a 3-month membership) and **InterVac.com** ($119 for an annual membership) are also reliable. Many travelers find great housing swaps on **Craigslist** (www.craigslist.org), too, though the offerings cannot be vetted or vouched for; proceed at your own risk.

Even without a house to swap, you can find private accommodations ranging from an entire home to a shared room. With **Airbnb** (www.airbnb.com; ✆ **855/424-7262** or 415/800-5959, in the U.K. ✆ **44-203-318-1111**), you'll find San Diego listings for everything from hip downtown condos to a cabin on a sailboat. **VRBO,** "Vacation Rentals by Owner" (www.vrbo.com), specializes in upscale properties.

9

SIDE TRIPS FROM SAN DIEGO

Popular day trips include the beaches and inland towns of "North County" (as locals call the part of San Diego County north of the I-5/I-805 junction), as well as our south-of-the-border neighbor, Tijuana. All are less than an hour away. If you have time for a longer trip, you can explore some distinct areas (all within 2 hr. of the city), such as the wine country of **Temecula;** the gold-mining town of **Julian,** known for its apple pies; and the vast **Anza-Borrego Desert.** Whichever excursion you choose, you're in for a treat.

NORTH COUNTY BEACH TOWNS

10

The string of picturesque beach towns that dot the coast of San Diego County from Del Mar to Oceanside make great day-trip destinations for sun worshipers and surfers. *Be forewarned:* You'll be tempted to spend the night.

Essentials

GETTING THERE   **Del Mar** is only 18 miles north of downtown San Diego, **Carlsbad** about 33 miles, and **Oceanside** approximately 36 miles. If you're driving, follow I-5 North; Del Mar, Solana Beach, Encinitas, Carlsbad, and Oceanside all have freeway exits. The northernmost point, Oceanside, will take about 45 minutes. The other choice by car is to wander up the old coast road, known as Camino del Mar, "PCH" (Pacific Coast Hwy.), Old Highway 101, and County Highway S21.

From San Diego, the **Coaster** commuter train provides service to Solana Beach, Encinitas, Carlsbad, and Oceanside; and **Amtrak** stops in Solana Beach—just a few minutes north of Del Mar—and Oceanside. The Coaster makes the trip a number of times (6:30am–7pm) on weekdays and four times on weekends; Amtrak passes through a dozen times daily each way. For the Coaster, call ✆ 800/262-7837 or 511, or visit www.transit.511sd.com; check with Amtrak at ✆ 800/872-7245 or www.amtrak.com. United Express departs from Los Angeles and flies into the **McClellan Palomar Airport** (www.sdcounty.ca.gov; ✆ 760/431-4646), 3 miles east of I-5 in Carlsbad.

Del Mar ★★

A small community, Del Mar is home to about 4,500 inhabitants in a 2-square-mile municipality. The town has adamantly maintained its independence, eschewing incorporation into the city of San Diego. It's one of the most upscale communities in the greater San Diego area, yet Del Mar somehow manages to maintain a casual, small-town ambience that radiates personality and charm. Come summer, the town swells as visitors flock in for the thoroughbred horse-racing season and the San Diego County Fair.

VISITOR INFORMATION

For more information about Del Mar, check out the Del Mar Village Association website at www.delmarmainstreet.com; there's also a helpful city-run website, www.delmar.ca.us.

EXPLORING DEL MAR

The history and popularity of Del Mar are linked to the **Del Mar Racetrack & Fairgrounds,** 2260 Jimmy Durante Blvd. (www.sdfair.com; ℂ 858/755-1161 or 858/793-5555). In 1933, actor/crooner Bing Crosby developed the Del Mar Thoroughbred Club, enlisting the help of Hollywood celebrity friends including Lucille Ball, Desi Arnaz, Betty Grable, and Bob Hope. Soon the good times were off and running around Del Mar; racing season is mid-July through early September. The expansive complex also hosts San Diego's largest annual event, the **San Diego County Fair** (early June to early July), still referred to by most locals as the Del Mar Fair.

Two excellent beaches flank Del Mar: **Torrey Pines State Beach** and **Del Mar State Beach.** Both are wide, well-patrolled strands popular for sunbathing, swimming, and surfing (in marked areas). The sand stretches north to the mouth of the **San Dieguito Lagoon,** where people bring their dogs for a romp in the sea. Torrey Pines State Beach is accessed from I-5 via Carmel Valley Road; take a left on McGonigle Road to a large parking area to the south. For Del Mar State Beach, take 15th Street west to **Seagrove Park,** where you can usually find volleyballs and Frisbees in flight. Just past this cliffside park is the sand; be aware that parking spaces here are in short supply on weekends and any day in summer. There are free concerts at adjacent **Powerhouse Park** during the summer; for information, call ℂ **858/635-1366,** or go to www.delmarfoundation.org. This grassy expanse extends right to the shore and gets its name from the distinctive building at its north end—a power plant built in 1928. It's now a community center with restrooms, showers, meeting space, and lovely verandas. *Note:* Del Mar's beaches and parks are smoke-free.

Beyond the surf and the turf is the **Del Mar Plaza,** 1555 Camino del Mar (www.delmarplaza.com), an open-air shopping center with fountains, sculptures, and palazzo-style terraces. This is one stylish shopping center; its collection of restaurants and shops, coupled with the ocean views, make it a great place to while away an afternoon. Also check out the **Del Mar Library,** 1309 Camino del Mar (www.sdcl.org; ℂ **858/755-1666**), built in 1914 as St. James Catholic Church and restored by the city in the 1990s.

Most evenings near dusk, brightly colored **hot-air balloons** punctuate the skies just east of the racetrack; they're easily enjoyed from the racetrack area (and by traffic-jammed drivers on I-5). See "Outdoor Activities," in chapter 4, for more details.

WHERE TO EAT

At the upper level of the centrally located Del Mar Plaza, at Camino del Mar and 15th Street, you'll find **Il Fornaio Cucina Italiana** ★ (www.ilfornaio.com; ℂ **858/755-8876**), for moderately priced and pleasing Italian cuisine and an *enoteca*

North County Beach Towns

Northern San Diego County

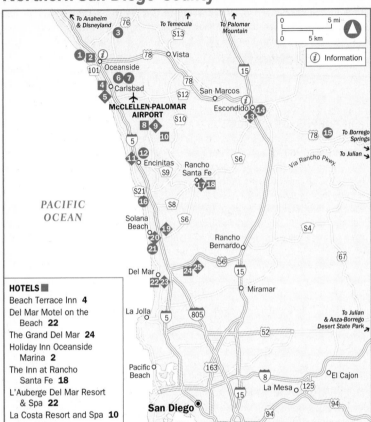

HOTELS ■

Beach Terrace Inn **4**
Del Mar Motel on the
Beach **22**
The Grand Del Mar **24**
Holiday Inn Oceanside
Marina **2**
The Inn at Rancho
Santa Fe **18**
L'Auberge Del Mar Resort
& Spa **22**
La Costa Resort and Spa **10**
Les Artistes **22**
Oceanside Marina Suites **2**
Park Hyatt Aviara Resort **8**
Pelican Cove Inn **4**
Rancho Valencia Resort
& Spa **18**
Tamarack Beach Resort **4**
Wave Crest **22**
West Inn & Suites **4**
Wyndham Oceanside Pier
Resort **2**

RESTAURANTS ◆

Addison **25**
Bellefleur Restaurant **5**
Burlap **23**
Delicias **17**
Hacienda de Vega **13**
Jake's Del Mar **23**

Market Restaurant + Bar **19**
Mille Fleurs **17**
Pamplemousse Grille **20**
Q'ero **11**
Shimbashi Izakaya **23**
Solace & The Moonlight
Lounge **11**
Stone Brewing World Bistro **13**
Vivace **9**

ATTRACTIONS ●

California Center for
the Arts **14**
California Surf Museum **1**
Carlsbad Premium Outlets **6**
Cedros Design District **21**
Del Mar Racetrack
& Fairgrounds **21**

Flower Fields **6**
LEGOLAND California **7**
Lux Art Institute **12**
Mission San Luis Rey **3**
Museum of Making Music **7**
Oceanside Museum of Art **1**
Orfila Vineyards **14**
Queen Califia's Magical
Circle **14**
San Diego Botanic Garden **12**
San Diego Zoo Safari Park **15**
San Elijo Lagoon Ecological
Reserve **16**
San Pasqual Battlefield State
Historic Park **15**
Self-Realization Fellowship
Retreat and Hermitage **12**

(wine bar) with great ocean views; **Pacifica Del Mar ★★** (*C* 858/792-0476; www.pacificadelmar.com), which serves outstanding seafood; and airy, modern **Flavor Del Mar ★★** (www.flavordelmar.com; *C* 858/755-3663), featuring new American cuisine, a lively bar scene, and more ocean vistas. Head west from the plaza on 15th Street, and you'll run into neighborhood favorite **Sbicca ★★**, 215 15th St. (www.sbiccabistro.com; *C* 858/481-1001), serving modern American cuisine sweetened with great wine deals; right on the beach is **Poseidon on the Beach,** 1670 Coast Blvd. (www.theposeidonrestaurant.com; *C* 858/755-9345), good for California cuisine and fabulous sunsets.

Join the locals for happy hour at **Zel's Del Mar ★★**, 1247 Camino del Mar (www.zelsdelmar.com; *C* 858/755-0076), or grab some high-quality, Mediterranean-inspired fare for lunch, dinner, or weekend brunch (or takeout) from **Prep-kitchen ★★**, 1201 Camino del Mar (www.prepkitchen.com; *C* 858/792-7737).

The racetrack contingent congregates at **Bully's Restaurant,** 1404 Camino del Mar (www.bullysdelmar.com; *C* 858/755-1660), for burgers, prime rib, and crab legs. Also near the track, located in the Flower Hill Mall, is **Paradise Grille ★**, 2690 Via de la Valle (www.paradisegrille.com; *C* 858/350-0808), a casual-but-sophisticated spot for seasonal California cuisine and a "Wall of Scotch" (40 different single malts). And if you're looking for fresh seafood—and lots of it—make a beeline to the Del Mar branch of San Diego's popular **Fish Market ★**, 640 Via de la Valle (www.thefishmarket.com; *C* 858/755-2277), near the racetrack (reviewed on p. 125).

Addison ★★★ ◙ FRENCH   On a hillside overlooking a golf course, this stand-alone restaurant at the Grand Del Mar hotel is San Diego County's one and only AAA Five-Diamond dining establishment. Although it is named for Addison Mizner—the early-20th-century architect noted for his work in Florida—with its gaping fireplaces, plush draperies, carved stone columns, and wrought-iron fixtures, this sumptuous dining destination is grandly European. There's even a private banquet space that resembles a great room in a Spanish castle. Featuring daily 3-, 4-, 7-, and 10(!)-course tasting menus of modern French cuisine, Chef William Bradley incorporates the best local and seasonal ingredients. There's also a jaw-dropping wine list that's more like a wine book, with a knowledgeable staff to keep you from getting too overwhelmed.

5200 Grand Del Mar Way (from I-5, merge onto Hwy. 56 E., exit Carmel Country Rd. and turn right, and then left at Grand Del Mar Way). www.addisondelmar.com. *C* **858/314-1900.** Reservations recommended. 3-course menu $90; 4-course menu $98; 7-course menu $140; 10-course menu $225. AE, DC, DISC, MC, V. Tues–Sat 5:30–9pm. Free valet parking.

Burlap ★ ASIAN FUSION   Restaurateur Brian Malarkey, a veteran of TV's *Top Chef* competition, just seems to know how to give San Diego what it wants. His expanding empire includes the Gaslamp Quarter hit **Searsucker** (p. 124) and this wildly popular "Asian Cowboy" spot in the Del Mar Highlands shopping center. Part fusion eatery, part happening nightspot (DJs lay grooves Thurs–Sat), this loud, large, and lively restaurant and bar has a brash swagger about it, to go along with the industrial, pan-Asian decor (everything from rising suns to Chinese parade dragons to carved Indonesian reliefs). The food covers plenty of ground as well and includes raw appetizers (oyster-uni shooter), prime steak cuts, rotisserie choices (even whole pig with advance notice), and lots of options designed for sharing.

12995 El Camino Real (at Del Mar Heights Rd.), Del Mar. www.burlapeats.com. *C* **858/369-5700.** Main courses $10–$25 lunch and brunch, $22–$80 dinner. AE, DISC, MC, V. Mon–Sat 11:30am–2pm; Sun brunch 10am–2pm; Sun–Thurs 5–10pm; Fri–Sat 5–11pm. Valet parking from 5pm $4; free parking in shopping center.

North County Beach Towns

Jake's Del Mar ★ SEAFOOD/CALIFORNIAN   Occupying a building originally constructed in 1910, Jake's has a perfect seat next to the sand so that diners get straight-on views of the beach scene—sunbathers, surfers, and the occasional school of dolphins pass by. The predictable menu can't live up to the panorama, but it's prepared competently and service is swift (sometimes too swift, actually—don't let them rush you). At lunch you'll find a mixed seafood grill and pecan-crusted sea bass; sandwiches and salads round out the offerings. Dinner brings in the big boys: Maine lobster tails, giant scampi, and rib-eye steak, for example. To enjoy the scene without the wallet wallop, come for happy hour (Mon–Fri 4–6pm and Sat 2:30–4:30pm), when a shorter bar/bistro menu is up to half-off; mai tais are $4 on Wednesday.

1660 Coast Blvd. (at 15th St.), Del Mar. www.jakesdelmar.com. ✆ **858/755-2002.** Reservations recommended. Main courses $11–$17 lunch and brunch, $14–$52 dinner. AE, DISC, MC, V. Tues–Sat 11:30am–2:30pm; Sun brunch 10am–2pm; dinner Mon–Thurs 5–9pm, Fri 5–9:30pm, Sat 4:30–9:30pm, Sun 4:30–9pm. Bar bistro Mon 4–9pm, Tues–Thurs 11:30am–9pm, Fri–Sat 11:30am–9:30pm, Sun 10am–9pm. Valet parking $4. Bus: 101.

Market Restaurant + Bar ★★★ 🎎 CALIFORNIAN   Native San Diegan Carl Schroeder has made a major splash with this comfortably elegant restaurant in an off-the-beaten path location. Schroeder specializes in a regional San Diego cuisine, showcasing the best ingredients from the area's top farms, ranches, and fishmongers. The menu is printed daily, depending on what he finds at the produce stands; the weekly wine list is no less quality-obsessed, focusing on small and nontraditional wineries. Past Market menu items have included blue cheese soufflé with roasted pears, candied pecans, and fig-port reduction; tempura black sea bass; and a tasting of game hen served three ways. Market also has four-course tasting menus ($68) and sushi offerings. This is truly fine dining in a relaxed atmosphere.

3702 Via de la Valle (at El Camino Real), Del Mar. www.marketdelmar.com. ✆ **858/523-0007.** Reservations recommended. Main courses $25–$35, sushi $12–$22. AE, DISC, MC, V. Daily 5:30–10pm. Free valet parking. Bus: 308.

Pamplemousse Grille ★★★ FRENCH   The whimsical interior murals of pigs on parade and a slouched chef with a cigarette dangling from his lips might lead one to believe this isn't a serious restaurant. Even the name, which is French for "grapefruit," is a bit silly. But make no mistake—this is one of the county's upper-echelon dining destinations. The internationally inspired menu also has room for personal input: You can create your own entree of grilled meats (prime rib-eye, lamb chops, and so on) with a choice of sauce (wild mushroom, peppercorn, and others), along with a selection of veggies and potatoes (truffled Parmesan fries!); a vegetarian entree is always available, too. Happy hour, Monday to Friday 4:30 to 6:30pm, features more casual fare (including a great burger) and drink specials.

514 Via de la Valle (across from the Del Mar Fairgrounds), Solana Beach. www.pgrille.com. ✆ **858/792-9090.** Dinner reservations recommended (and a necessity during race season). Main courses $20–$25 lunch (served Fri only), $24–$49 dinner. AE, MC, V. Daily 5–9pm; also Fri 11:30am–2pm. Bus: 308.

Shimbashi Izakaya ★★ 🎎 JAPANESE   Re-creating the Japanese pub (*izakaya*) experience, this oceanview spot cooks up traditional fare. Incorporating seasonal products, it serves small plates designed for grazing; the menu includes authentic staples such as yakitori skewers of barbecued meats and vegetables, green-tea soba noodles, and shabu-shabu hot pots of thinly sliced beef in broth. You'll also find sushi and sashimi, and plenty of vegetarian offerings. Of course, you'll also find Japanese beer on tap and sake choices to keep both newbies and aficionados happy; the drink list also includes specialty cocktails, plum wine, and shochu, the bracing spirit distilled from barley, wheat, or potato that has gained popularity despite its use in feudal Japan as a disinfectant. *Kampai!*

1555 Camino del Mar, Ste. 201 (at 15th St.). www.shimbashiizakaya.com. © **858/523-0479.** Reservations recommended for weekends. Small plates $4–$16, sushi $4–$22, bento box lunch $16. AE, DISC, MC, V. Mon–Fri noon–2:30pm and 4–10pm; Sat–Sun noon–10pm; happy hour Mon–Fri 4–6pm and Sat–Sun noon–6pm. Free 2-hr. parking in garage with validation. Bus: 101.

WHERE TO STAY
Very Expensive
The Grand Del Mar ★★★ ☺ 📷   Resembling a Tuscan villa transported to the foothills of Del Mar, this luxury resort boasts a Las Vegas–like opulence, from its marbled lobby to its manicured croquet lawn. Paying homage to the Spanish Revival creations of architect Addison Mizner, the Grand Del Mar features fragrant landscaping, Mediterranean-style courtyards, terraces and walkways with sweeping views of the Tom Fazio–designed golf course, as well as outdoor fireplaces and fountains. Other amenities include tennis courts, four swimming pools, a kids' activity center, and a 21,000-square-foot spa. It also operates an equestrian center offering trail outings and riding lessons. The signature restaurant, **Addison** (p. 223), is one of San Diego's most refined dining rooms, and is the county's only AAA Five-Diamond restaurant. The resort's name is truly no idle boast; this is one grand hotel.

5300 Grand Del Mar Court, San Diego, CA 92130. www.thegranddelmar.com. © **855/314-2030** or 858/314-2000. Fax 858/314-2001. 249 units. From $445 double; from $795 suites. Children 17 and under stay free in parent's room. Packages available. AE, DC, DISC, MC, V. Valet parking $25; free self-parking. From I-5 merge onto Hwy. 56 E., exit Carmel Country Rd. and turn right, left at Grand Del Mar Way. **Amenities:** 4 restaurants; 5 bars; live entertainment; kids' activity center; concierge; 18-hole championship golf course; equestrian center; exercise room; Jacuzzi; 4 swimming pools; room service; spa; 2 tennis courts; free transportation (14-mile radius). *In room:* A/C, TV/DVD, CD player, hair dryer, minibar, free Wi-Fi.

L'Auberge Del Mar Resort & Spa ★★★   Sporting a French beach-château look, this classy property received a top-to-bottom, $25-million renovation in 2009. Changes include a stand-alone spa (with indoor/outdoor relaxation spaces) and a handsome pool area with lattice deck, chill-out fire pit lounge, and dramatic one-story water-wall feature. Guest rooms are given a homey touch by fireplaces and bureaus topped with shelves stocked with coffee-table books and decorative seashells. Not all are rooms-with-a-view, but many have balconies or patios. Unchanged, of course, is the hotel's prime location—the beach is a 3-minute walk away down a private pathway, and Del Mar's main shopping and dining scene is just across the street. Fine dining has always been one of the resort's priorities, and the signature eatery **Kitchen 1540** doesn't miss a beat. Serving a seasonal California cuisine that utilizes organic, sustainable products, it offers a "White Flag" option: a chef's-choice tasting menu that doesn't stop until you cry uncle.

1540 Camino del Mar (at 15th St.), Del Mar, CA 92014. www.laubergedelmar.com. © **800/245-9757** or 858/259-1515. Fax 858/755-4940. 120 units. From $350 double; from $600 suite. AE, DC, MC, V. Valet parking $25. Take I-5 to Del Mar Heights Rd. west, and then turn right onto Camino del Mar Rd. **Amenities:** Restaurant; 2 bars; concierge; access to nearby health club; Jacuzzi; 2 outdoor pools; room service; full-service spa; 2 tennis courts. *In room:* A/C, TV, CD player, hair dryer, minibar, MP3 docking station, free Wi-Fi.

North County Beach Towns

Expensive

Del Mar Motel on the Beach ☺ 🛍 The only property in Del Mar right on the beach, this simply furnished, aggressively stuccoed motel has been here since 1946. All of the well-kept rooms are of good size; upstairs units have one king-size bed, and downstairs rooms have two double beds. Most of them don't have much in the way of a view, but two oceanfront rooms sit right over the sand and feature larger bathrooms. This place is a good choice for beach lovers because you can walk along the shore for miles; there's also a glass-fronted patio that provides a front-row seat for the beach action. Families can be comfortable knowing a lifeguard station is right next door, as are the popular seaside restaurants **Poseidon** and **Jake's** (p. 223 and 224). The motel has a renovated deck with barbecue and picnic table for guests' use as well.

1702 Coast Blvd. (at 17th St.), Del Mar, CA 92014. www.delmarmotelonthebeach.com. © **800/223-8449** for reservations or 858/755-1534. 44 units (upper units with shower only). $259–$334 double; check for reduced Oct–May rates. AE, DISC, MC, V. Free parking. Take I-5 to Via de la Valle exit. Go west, and then south on Hwy. 101 (Pacific Coast Hwy.); veer west onto Coast Blvd. **Amenities:** Picnic and barbecue area; free use of boogie boards, beach chairs, and sand toys. *In room:* A/C, TV, fridge, hair dryer, free Wi-Fi.

Wave Crest ★★ On a bluff overlooking the Pacific, these gray-shingled bungalow condominiums are beautifully maintained and wonderfully private—from the street it looks nothing like a hotel. The studios and suites surround a lovingly landscaped courtyard; each has a queen-size bed, sofa bed, reproduced artwork, stereo, full bathroom, and fully equipped kitchen with dishwasher. The studios sleep two people; the one-bedroom accommodates up to four; two-bedroom units can sleep six. Some units face the garden or shady street; rooms with ocean views are about $30 extra. In racing season (mid-July to early Sept), 90% of the guests are track-bound. It's a 5-minute walk to the beach, and shopping and dining spots are a few blocks away. There is an extra fee for maid service.

1400 Ocean Ave., Del Mar, CA 92014. www.wavecrestresort.com. © **858/755-0100.** 31 units. $210–$235 studio; $320–$380 1 bedroom; $495 2 bedroom. Weekly rates available. MC, V. Free parking. Take I-5 to Del Mar Heights Rd. west, turn right onto Camino del Mar, and drive to 15th St. Turn left and drive to Ocean Ave., and turn left. **Amenities:** Jacuzzi; outdoor pool. *In room:* TV/DVD, kitchen, free Wi-Fi.

Moderate

Les Artistes ★★ 🛍 What do you get when you take a 1940s motel and put it in the hands of an owner with an artistic flair? In the case of this property, just off Del Mar's main drag, you get an Indo-Latino mash-up that is intriguingly funky, and feels like a rustic, jungle hotel in Mexico. The upstairs rooms at this nonsmoking property have partial ocean views, and charming touches abound, such as a lily and koi pond, communal fireplaces, and lush landscaping (downstairs rooms have tiny private garden decks). Ten rooms are tributes to artists; two more were given a Japanese makeover. The Diego Rivera room feels like a warm Mexican painting come to life; the Japanese Furo room features a soaking tub carved into the bathroom floor. A sister B&B, the equally creative, five-room **Secret Garden Inn,** is at 1140 Camino del Mar.

944 Camino del Mar (btw. 9th and 10th sts.), Del Mar, CA 92014. www.lesartistesinn.com. © **858/755-4646.** 12 units. $105–$250 double. DISC, MC, V. Free parking. From I-5, go west on Del Mar Heights Rd. and then left onto Camino Del Mar Rd. Pets accepted with $50 cash deposit plus $30 cleaning fee. *In room:* A/C, TV, fireplace, fridge.

Solana Beach, Encinitas & Carlsbad ★

North of Del Mar about a 45-minute drive from downtown San Diego, the pretty communities of Solana Beach, Encinitas, and Carlsbad provide many reasons to linger: good swimming and surfing beaches, small-town atmosphere, an abundance of charming shops, and a seasonal display of the region's most beautiful flowers. It's also the location of kid-centric **LEGOLAND** theme park.

Carlsbad was named after Karlsbad, Czech Republic, because of the similar mineral (some say curative) waters each produced. Carlsbad's once-famous artesian well was capped in the 1930s, but was redrilled in 1994—and the healthful water is flowing once more. Along with its neighbor Encinitas, Carlsbad is a noted commercial flower-growing region. A colorful display can be seen at **Carlsbad Ranch** (p. 229) each spring when 50 acres of solid ranunculus fields bloom into a breathtaking rainbow; in December, the nurseries are alive with holiday poinsettias. Year-round, the **San Diego Botanic Garden** (p. 230) delights enthusiasts, families, and nature lovers of all stripes with its amazing collection.

VISITOR INFORMATION

The **Solana Beach Visitors Center** is near the train station at 103 N. Cedros (www.solanabeachchamber.com; ✆ 858/350-6006). The **Encinitas Visitors Center** is at 859 Second St. (corner of H St.) in downtown Encinitas (www.gonorthcounty.com; ✆ 760/753-6041); the **Downtown Encinitas Merchants Association** also maintains a handy site: www.encinitas101.com. The **Carlsbad Visitor Information Center,** 400 Carlsbad Village Dr. (in the old Santa Fe Depot; www.visitcarlsbad.com; ✆ 800/227-5722 or 760/434-6093), has information on the flower fields, nursery touring, and attractions.

EXPLORING SOLANA BEACH, ENCINITAS & CARLSBAD

The hub of activity for Solana Beach is South Cedros Avenue, 1 block east of and parallel to Pacific Coast Highway. The **Cedros Design District** (www.cedros avenue.com) is a 2-block stretch (from the train station south) that's the setting for many of San Diego's best furniture and home-design shops, antiques stores, art dealers, and boutiques selling imported goods. You'll also find the **Belly Up Tavern,** one of San Diego's most appealing concert venues (p. 171).

If you've ever wanted to get a glimpse into the artistic process, get yourself to the **Lux Art Institute** in Encinitas, 1550 S. El Camino Real (✆ 760/436-6611; www.luxartinstitute.com). This unique facility, a work of art in itself, allows visitors to watch as an artist-in-residence paints, sculpts, or draws in a studio environment. It's open to the public Thursday and Friday 1 to 5pm, and Saturday from 11am to 5pm ($5, ticket good for two visits; free for those 20 and under). Every third Wednesday of the month is Lux@Night, a wine-and-cheese reception from 7 to 9pm ($5). Lux also has a retail component that features local artists and products.

The **San Elijo Lagoon Ecological Reserve ★★** encompasses coastal wetlands that were nearly lost to development. This 1,000-acre preserve features 7.5 miles of hiking trails and is home to some 700 species of plants and animals; the **San Elijo Nature Center,** 2710 Manchester Ave., Cardiff by the Sea (www.sanelijo.org; ✆ 760/634-3026), interprets the flora and fauna. Free, naturalist-led walks are offered Saturday at 10am.

Everyone flocks to **Moonlight Beach** for good reason—it offers plenty of facilities, including free parking, free Wi-Fi, a children's playground, volleyball nets, restrooms, showers, picnic tables, and fire rings. The beach entrance is at the end of B Street (at Encinitas Blvd.). Also in Encinitas is the appropriately serene **Swami's Beach.** It's named for the adjacent Self-Realization Fellowship complex (see below), whose lotus-shaped towers are emulated in the pointed wooden stairway leading to the sand from First Street. This lovely little beach is surfer central; it adjoins little-known **Boneyard Beach,** directly to the north. Here, low-tide coves provide shelter for romantics and nudists; this isolated stretch can be reached only from Swami's Beach. There's a free parking lot at Swami's, plus restrooms and a picnic area.

The **Self-Realization Fellowship Retreat and Hermitage** (www.yogananda-srf.org; ✆ **760/753-2888**) was founded in 1920 by Paramahansa Yogananda, a guru born and educated in India. The exotic-looking domes are what remain of the retreat originally built in 1937 (the rest was built too close to the cliff edge and tumbled to the beach); today the site serves as a spiritual sanctuary for holistic healers and their followers. Serene meditation gardens line a cliff; they're a terrific place to cool off on a hot day, and no disciples will give you a sales pitch. Enter the gardens at 215 W. K St.; they are open Tuesday through Saturday 9am to 5pm, and Sundays 11am to 5pm. Admission is free. The **Hermitage,** where Yogananda lived and worked for many years, is also on site and usually open Sundays from 2 to 5pm. A stylish bookstore and gift shop that sells distinctive arts, crafts, and musical instruments from India is nearby at 1150 S. Coast Hwy.

Carlsbad is a great place for antiquing and boutique shopping. Whether you're a serious shopper or seriously window-shopping, park the car and stroll the 3 blocks of **State Street** between Oak and Beech streets; there's a welcoming village atmosphere here.

What about those therapeutic waters that put Carlsbad on the map? They're still bubbling at the **Carlsbad Mineral Water Spa,** 2802 Carlsbad Blvd. (www.carlsbadmineralspa.com; ✆ **760/434-1887**), an ornate European-style building on the site of the original well. Step inside for mineral baths ($65 for 30 min.), massages, or body treatments in the spa's exotic theme rooms—or just pick up a refreshing bottle of this "Most Healthful Water" to drink on the go.

Carlsbad State Beach (aka Tamarack Surf Beach) parallels downtown and has a wide concrete walkway that's a fine place to take a stroll. It attracts outdoor types for walking, jogging, and in-line skating even at night (thanks to good lighting). Although the sandy strand is narrow, the beach is popular with bodysurfers, boogie boarders, and fishermen; surfers tend to stay away. Enter on Ocean Boulevard at Tamarack Avenue; parking is $2 per hour or $10 for the day. About 4 miles south of town is **South Carlsbad State Beach** (www.parks.ca.gov; ✆ **760/438-3143**), with almost 3 miles of cobblestone-strewn sand. A state-run campground at the north end is immensely popular year-round; and if you're within 150 feet or so of the lifeguard headquarters, you'll be able to pick up the free Wi-Fi. There's a $12 per vehicle fee at the beach entrance, along Carlsbad Boulevard at Poinsettia Lane (make a U-turn at Breakwater Rd.); surfers favor the southern portion of the beach.

Just a stone's throw from LEGOLAND is a diversion for music lovers, the **Museum of Making Music,** 5790 Armada Dr. (www.museumofmakingmusic.org; ✆ **877/551-9976** or 760/438-5996). Visitors go on a journey from Tin Pan Alley to MTV, stopping along the way to learn historic anecdotes about the American music industry; or try your hand at playing drums, guitars, or a digital keyboard. It's open Tuesday through Sunday from 10am to 5pm. Admission is $8 for adults; $5 for seniors, military, and children ages 6 to 18; free for children 5 and under.

Opened in 2007, the **Crossings at Carlsbad,** 5800 The Crossings Dr. thecrossingsatcarlsbad.com; ✆ **760/444-1800**), is a view-enhanced public course located about 1 mile inland. This $70-million, 18-hole championship cour. features a handsome 28,000-square-foot clubhouse, restaurant, and bar.

Carlsbad and its neighbor Encinitas make up a noted commercial flower-growing region. The most colorful display can be seen each spring (Mar through early May) at the **Flower Fields at Carlsbad Ranch,** 5704 Paseo del Norte (www.theflower fields.com; ✆ **760/431-0352**), just east of I-5 on Palomar Airport Road; see p. 21 for additional information on this seasonal event. Also popular is **Weidners' Gardens,** 695 Normandy Rd., Encinitas (www.weidners.com; ✆ **760/436-2194**). Its field of 25,000 tuberous begonias blooms from mid-May to August; fuchsias and impatiens show their true colors between March and September; and the holiday season brings an explosion of pansies and poinsettias, as well as the opportunity to dig your own pansies. Touring the grounds is free; Weidners' is open to the public November 1 to December 22, and March 1 through Labor Day, 9am to 5pm (4:30pm in winter), and closed Tuesdays. In January and February, it's open Friday through Sunday, 9am to 4:30pm.

LEGOLAND California ★ ☺ Opened in 1999, this 128-acre theme park is the ultimate monument to the world's most famous plastic building block. This was the third LEGOLAND to open, following branches in Denmark and Britain (and now Germany and Florida). Forty minutes north of downtown San Diego, the Carlsbad park offers a full day of entertainment for families. **Note:** LEGOLAND is geared toward children ages 2 to 12, and there's just enough of a thrill-ride component to amuse preteens, but teenagers will find it a snooze. There are more than 50 rides, shows, and attractions, including hands-on interactive displays; a life-size menagerie of tigers, giraffes, and other animals; and scale models of international landmarks (the Eiffel Tower, Sydney Opera House), all constructed of LEGO bricks. **Star Wars Miniland** re-creates scenes from the beloved film series, while in the Egyptian-themed **Land of Adventure,** the signature ride takes you on a search for stolen treasure and tests your laser-shooting skills. **Pirate Shores** features buccaneer-themed, water-based attractions—all designed to get you good and wet; and the **Wild Woods** miniature golf course plays through more than 40 LEGO forest animals. In 2008, a sister attraction opened just outside the LEGOLAND gates—**Sea Life Aquarium,** focusing on the creatures (real ones, not LEGO facsimiles) found in regional waters from the Sierra Mountains to the Pacific Ocean. The highlight of this interactive, educational aquarium experience is a 200,000-gallon tank with sharks, rays, and colorful tropical fish; a 35-foot acrylic tunnel takes you right into the depths of it. Separate admission is required; discounted two-park tickets are available. The 5½-acre **LEGOLAND Water Park,** where kids can splash down water slides, float along a lazy river, or wade at a sandy beach, opened in 2010; ticket upgrades including the Water Park are $15. An on-site LEGOLAND resort hotel opens in 2013.

1 Legoland Dr. www.legoland.com, www.visitsealife.com. ✆ **877/534-6526** or 760/918-5346. LEGOLAND $72 ages 13 and up, $62 children 3–12, free for children 2 and under; Sea Life $20 adults, $15 seniors and children 3–12; discounted 1- or 2-day park-hopper tickets available. AE, DISC, MC, V. June daily 10am–5 or 6pm; July–Aug daily 10am–8pm; off season Thurs–Mon 10am–5 or 6pm. Parking $12. Closed Tues–Wed Sept–May, but open daily during winter and spring holiday periods. Water Park closed Nov–Mar, weekends only early Sept–Oct and Apr–May. From I-5, take the Cannon Rd. exit east ½ mile, following the signs toward Legoland Dr.

SIDE TRIPS FROM SAN DIEGO

North County Beach Towns

...Juicy, Bose to ...of the biggest names ...tail are elbow to elbow ...**mium Outlets,** Paseo del Norte, via Palomar Airport Road (www.premiumoutlets.; ☎ **888/790-7467** or 760/804-9000). This smart,

upscale outlet mall features some 90 stores, including Crate & Barrel, Barney's New York, Nine West, and Harry & David. It even has a fine-dining component: **Bellefleur Winery & Restaurant** (p. 231).

San Diego Botanic Garden ★ You don't have to possess a green thumb to appreciate an afternoon at this wonderful botanical facility, formerly known as the Quail Botanical Gardens. It has the country's largest bamboo collection, plus more than 35 acres of California natives, exotic tropical species, and cacti, as well as Mediterranean, Australian, and other unusual collections. Four miles of scenic walkways and trails crisscross the compound, which is home to more than 3,300 varieties of plants and trees. There's also a Children's Garden, featuring a treehouse built into a 20-foot, climbable tree. Guided tours are given Saturdays at 10:30am, and there's a gift shop and nursery; a variety of special events and classes (including bird-watching, children's activities, and floral design) are scheduled throughout the year. The gardens are free to everyone on the first Tuesday of the month.

230 Quail Gardens Dr., Encinitas. www.sdbgarden.org. ☎ **760/436-3036.** Admission $12 adults; $8 seniors, students, and military; $6 children 3–12; free for children 2 and under. AE, MC, V. Daily 9am–5pm (till 8pm Thurs in summer). Parking $2. From San Diego take I-5 N. to Encinitas Blvd.; go ½ mile east, left on Quail Gardens Dr.

WHERE TO EAT

Always crowded, **Fidel's Little Mexico ★** is reliable for tasty Mexican food and kickin' margaritas; it's in Solana Beach at 607 Valley Ave. (www.fidelslittlemexico. com; ☎ **858/755-5292**). **Claire's on Cedros ★★**, 246 N. Cedros Ave. (www. clairesoncedros.com; ☎ **858/259-8597**), is another Solana Beach crowd pleaser, serving breakfast and lunch; it's also LEED-certifiably green. In Encinitas, pizza lovers can't go wrong with **Blue Ribbon Artisan Pizzeria ★★**, at the Lumberyard shopping center, 897 S. Coast Hwy. 101 (www.blueribbonpizzeria; ☎ **760/634-7671**), where you can even get a gluten-free crust; beers and burgers are on tap at the **Encinitas Ale House ★**, 1044 S. Coast Hwy. 101 (www.encinitasalehouse. com; ☎ **760/943-7180**). Other local Encinitas hangouts include the **Potato Shack Cafe ★**, 120 W. I St. (www.potatoshackcafe.com; ☎ **760/436-1282**), good for breakfast carbo-loading; and casual **Swami's Cafe ★**, 1163 S. Coast Hwy. 101 (☎ **760/944-0612**), for sandwiches, wraps, and smoothies.

For dining with a little more international flair, Encinitas is also home to **Siamese Basil ★**, 527 S. Coast Hwy. 101 (☎ **760/753-3940**), featuring zesty Thai food; and **Yu Me Ya Sake House ★★**, 1246 N. Coast Hwy. 101 (www.sakehouseyumeya. com; ☎ **760/633-4288**), which skillfully prepares Japanese delicacies. Chocoholics should not miss Venezuelan **Chuao Chocolatier ★★**, which has several North County locations, including the Lumberyard mall, 937 S. Coast Hwy. (www.chuao chocolatier.com; ☎ **760/635-1444**), and the Del Mar Heights shopping center, 3485 Del Mar Heights Rd., Del Mar (☎ **858/755-0770**).

10

SIDE TRIPS FROM SAN DIEGO | North County Beach Towns

In Carlsbad, dining highlights include **Paon Restaurant and Wine Bar ★★**, 2975 Roosevelt St. (www.paoncarlsbad.com; © 760/729-7377), serving Franco-Californian food; and **West Steak and Seafood ★** at the West Inn & Suites (see below), 4980 Ave. Encinas (www.weststeakandseafood.com; © 760/930-9100), featuring a contemporary American menu.

Bellefleur Restaurant ★ CALIFORNIAN/MEDITERRANEAN This busy restaurant boasts a "California winery" experience, although no wine country is evident among the surrounding outlet retailers and car dealerships. But its cavernous, semi-industrial dining room, coupled with the wood-fired and wine-enhanced aromas emanating from a clanging open kitchen, do somehow evoke the ambience of California wine-producing regions. In addition to the main seating area, there are an open-air dining patio, a tasting bar, and a glassed-in barrel aging room. The place can be noisy, drawing exhausted shoppers for cuisine that incorporates North County's abundant produce with fresh fish and meats. It adds up to an experience that surpasses the shopping-mall standard. Sunday champagne brunch is served from 10am to 2pm.

5610 Paseo del Norte, Carlsbad. www.bellefleur.com. ©760/603-1919. Reservations suggested. Lunch $9–$16; dinner $17–$35; brunch $22 adults, $10 children 2–11. AE, DC, DISC, MC, V. Mon–Thurs 11am–9pm; Fri–Sat 11am–10pm; Sun 10am–9pm.

Q'ero ★★ LATIN AMERICAN 📖 The Q'ero are the isolated people of the Peruvian Andes who believe themselves to be the last descendants of the Inca, and the guardians of ancient knowledge. So thank your lucky mountain spirits that this tiny Encinitas restaurant has decided to share their food with us. Of course this is no ethnographical culinary survey; there's plenty of recognizable Latin American fare, from ceviche and *papa relleno* (mashed potatoes stuffed with savory beef and raisins), to cheese-filled cornmeal-cake *arepas* and the melt-in-your mouth *tres leches* sponge cake. There are lots of exotic ingredients, too, from sweet *chancaca* glazes to the minty herb *huacatay*, so there's more than enough to keep adventurous eaters happy, as well. **Note:** This is a very small space; dinner reservations are a must. Also, if you nab one of the sidewalk tables, you will not be able to drink alcohol.

564 S. Coast Hwy. 101 (btw. D and E sts.), Encinitas. www.qerorestaurant.com. ©760/753-9050. Reservations recommended. Lunch $9–$20, dinner $21–$30. AE, DISC, MC, V. Lunch Tues–Sat 11:30am–3pm; dinner Mon–Thurs 5–9pm, Fri–Sat 5–10pm. Bus: 101.

Solace & The Moonlight Lounge ★★ AMERICAN Opened in 2011, this sister restaurant to North Park's **Urban Solace** (p. 130) brings design sizzle and upscale American fare to a neighborhood in want of both. Set in an eco-friendly, LEED-certified bi-level space, the restaurant has a modern vibe that's warmed with wooden accents. The downstairs dining room feels more formal, while the airy upstairs lounge offers a bar and communal table; both have outdoor seating areas. Environmental consciousness extends to the menu as well, which features grass-fed, hormone-free beef, sustainable fish, and local produce; even high fructose corn syrup has been banned from the premises (the sodas are all-natural and cocktail mixes are house-made). It's not all high-minded seriousness here, though—the friendly service and portrait of the Dude (aka Jeff Bridges in *The Big Lebowski*) hanging over the small raw bar dispel any notion of that.

25 E. E St., Encinitas. www.eatatsolace.com. ©760/753-2433. Main courses $10–$32 lunch and dinner, $8–$17 weekend brunch. AE, DISC, MC, V. Mon–Thurs 11:30am–10pm; Fri 11:30am–11pm; Sat 10:30am–11pm; Sun 9:30am–9pm; lounge stays open 1 hr. after dinner. Bus: 101.

Vivace ★★★ ITALIAN Romantically lit, plushly upholstered, and adorned with decorative glassware and elegant floral displays, Vivace is as striking a dining destination as San Diego has to offer. Located at the Park Hyatt Aviara (formerly the Four Seasons Aviara, see below) in Carlsbad, Vivace serves a seasonal, sophisticated menu of Italian fare, including pastas, seafood, and prime beef; the lobster risotto is a house specialty. Vegetarian and gluten-free menus are also available. If the weather is nice, request a table out on the terrace, which features ocean, lagoon, and golf course views; on a chilly evening, cozy up next to the fireplace. The Vivace experience is all about class and elegance.

7100 Aviara Resort Dr., Carlsbad. www.vivace-restaurant.com. © **760/448-1234.** Reservations required. Main courses $23–$38. AE, DC, DISC, MC, V. Mon–Thurs 6–9:30pm; Fri–Sat 6–10pm. Free validated valet parking.

WHERE TO STAY
Very Expensive
Park Hyatt Aviara Resort ★★★ ☺ A nasty management dispute prompted this former Four Seasons property to change over to the Park Hyatt flag in 2010. The high standards (and AAA Five-Diamond ranking) that longtime guests—and locals who come for special events and to dine at the exceptional signature restaurant, **Vivace** (see above)—have come to expect, are maintained though. When not wielding club or racquet, you can lie by the dramatically perched pool, relax in a series of carefully landscaped gardens, or luxuriate in the award-winning spa. A recreation center also offers everything from sand volleyball to bocce ball; there's even a surf concierge who can give lessons, and a beach butler who will arrange a perfect day at the shore for you. The resort also includes an Arnold Palmer–designed golf course that maintains harmony with the surrounding Batiquitos wetlands; a walking/jogging trail also skirts the lagoon.

7100 Aviara Resort Dr., Carlsbad, CA 92009. www.parkaviara.hyatt.com. © **800/633-7313** or 760/448-1234. Fax 760/603-6801. 329 units. From $300 double; from $400 suite. Children 17 and under stay free in parent's room. $25/day resort fee. AE, DC, DISC, MC, V. Valet parking $30. From I-5, take Poinsettia Lane east to Aviara Pkwy. S. **Amenities:** 4 restaurants; 2 bars; babysitting; bike rental; children's center and programs (age 4–12); concierge; golf course; health club; Jacuzzi; 2 outdoor pools; room service; spa; 6 lighted tennis courts; watersports equipment/rentals. *In room:* A/C, TV/DVD, CD player, fridge, hair dryer, minibar, MP3 docking station, free Wi-Fi.

Expensive
Beach Terrace Inn ★ At Carlsbad's only beachside hostelry (others are across the road or a little farther away), almost all the rooms—as well as the pool and Jacuzzi—have ocean views. This downtown property, which was given a clean and contemporary makeover in 2009, is tucked between rows of high-rent beach cottages and touts its scenic location as its best quality. The rooms are extra-large (some with balconies) and feature fridges, wet bars, and work spaces, making this a good choice for business or pleasure. Plus you can walk everywhere from here—except LEGO-LAND, which is a 5-minute drive away.

2775 Ocean St. (at Christensen Way), Carlsbad, CA 92008. www.beachterraceinn.com.© **800/433-5415** or 760/729-5951. Fax 760/729-1078. 48 units. From $246 double (nonsummer rates considerably lower). Extra person $20. Rates include continental breakfast. AE, DC, DISC, MC, V. Free parking. **Amenities:** Jacuzzi; outdoor pool. *In room:* A/C, TV, fridge, hair dryer, MP3 docking station, free Wi-Fi.

La Costa Resort and Spa ★★ ☺ Families and golf and tennis enthusiasts come to this campuslike setting with its mission-style motif for some pampering and time on the links and courts; those in search of mind/body health and wellness flock to the acclaimed spa and the (Dr. Deepak) **Chopra Center for Well-Being.** The huge spa features 42 treatment rooms, a sprawling gym, and gorgeously landscaped outdoor sunning areas; the Chopra Center offers special programs, workshops, and spa services (which are also available to nonguests). **BlueFire Grill,** the stylish bar and signature restaurant, faces out onto a lovely plaza and has three distinctly different, chic spaces. Following a $50-million renovation completed in 2011, this 400-acre property has refreshed its guest rooms, overhauled its golf course, created a new spa menu, and opened a new sports-themed lounge. Dedicated areas for kids feature high- and low-tech entertainments, and several pools even have theme park–style water slides. The resort has 149 privately owned luxury villas (some with kitchens) available as well.

2100 Costa del Mar Rd. (at El Camino Real), Carlsbad, CA 92009. www.lacosta.com. © **800/854-5000** or 760/438-9111. Fax 760/931-7585. 611 units. From $279 double; from $489 suite; from $489 villa with kitchen. Children 17 and under stay free in parent's room. $24/day resort fee. Golf, spa, and tennis packages available. AE, DC, DISC, MC, V. Valet parking $25 overnight; self-parking $12. From I-5 take La Costa Ave. east; left on El Camino Real. **Amenities:** 5 restaurants; 4 bars; bike rentals; children's center and programs (age 6 months–16 years); concierge; 2 golf courses; health club; 5 Jacuzzis; 8 outdoor pools; room service; spa; 17 tennis courts (7 lighted). *In room:* A/C, TV, hair dryer, minibar, free Wi-Fi.

West Inn & Suites ★★ ☺ Opened in 2006, this family-owned, nonsmoking property charms with its friendly service, thoughtful touches, and plentiful freebies. Located about 2 miles from downtown Carlsbad, you're about a 10-minute walk from the nearest coastal access. Any thoughts of being isolated from the action, though, are assuaged by amenities like courtesy shuttle service (within a 5-mile radius, which includes LEGOLAND), full complimentary breakfast, and free parking. Kids (and adults) will love the library—with its fireplace, comfy chairs, and communal tables—stocked with games and books, as well as the evening spread of milk and cookies. The hotel's **West Steak and Seafood** is a popular spot for guests and locals alike, serving sustainable fish as well as produce from its own farm.

4970 Avenida Encinas, Carlsbad, CA 92008. www.westinnandsuites.com. © **866/431-9378** or 760/448-4500. Fax 760/448-4545. 86 units. $219–$259 (2-night minimum stay summer weekends). Rates include full breakfast. AE, DISC, MC, V. Free parking. From I-5, exit west on Cannon Rd., turn right on Avenida Encinas. Pets accepted. **Amenities:** 2 restaurants; 2 bars; concierge; dog park; exercise room; Jacuzzi; outdoor pool; room service. *In room:* A/C, TV/DVD, CD player, fridge, hair dryer, microwave, MP3 docking station, free Wi-Fi.

Moderate

Pelican Cove Inn ★ Two blocks from the beach, this Cape Cod–style bed-and-breakfast hideaway combines romance with luxury. Your hosts see to your every need, from furnishing guest rooms with feather beds and down comforters to providing beach chairs and towels or preparing a picnic basket (with 24 hr. notice). Each room features a gas fireplace and private entrance and bathroom; some have spa tubs. The Pacific Room is most spacious, while the airy La Jolla Room has bay windows and a cupola ceiling. Courtesy transportation from the Carlsbad or Oceanside train stations is available.

320 Walnut Ave., Carlsbad, CA 92008. www.pelican-cove.com. © **888/735-2683** or 760/434-5995. 10 units. $95–$215 double. Rates include full breakfast. Extra person $15. AE, MC, V. Free parking. From downtown Carlsbad, follow Carlsbad Blvd. south to Walnut Ave.; turn left and drive 2½ blocks. *In room:* TV, no phone, free Wi-Fi.

Tamarack Beach Resort Located in Carlsbad village across the street from the beach, this resort property is outfitted with standard-issue floral pastel furnishings—some rooms offer full ocean views with private patios. Individually owned 1- and 2-bedroom condos are also available on the second and third floors, featuring stereos, full kitchens, washers, and dryers. The nonsmoking Tamarack has a pleasant lobby and a sunny pool courtyard with barbecue grills; there's also a recreation room with pool, table tennis, and board games. The on-site restaurant, **Dini's by the Sea,** has an ocean-view patio and is a good bet for steak and seafood and drinking with the locals.

3200 Carlsbad Blvd., Carlsbad, CA 92008. www.tamarackresort.com. ©**800/334-2199** or 760/729-3500. Fax 760/434-5942. 77 units. $149–$169 double; from $230 1-bedroom condo. Children 12 and under stay free in parent's room. Rates include continental breakfast. AE, MC, V. Free underground parking. **Amenities:** Restaurant; bar; concierge; exercise room; 2 Jacuzzis; outdoor pool; recreation room. *In room:* A/C, TV/DVD, fridge, hair dryer, free Wi-Fi.

Oceanside

For decades, Camp Pendleton, the huge Marine base established in 1942, defined this northernmost community in San Diego County. Now a city of 170,000, Oceanside is forging an identity beyond the military, even to the point of nurturing a nascent artists' scene, anchored by the **Oceanside Museum of Art** (see below). Yes, this place still has an inordinate number of barbershops with Marines spilling out onto the sidewalk waiting to get their buzz cuts, but appealingly low-rise Oceanside is a blue-collar surf town with a welcoming, Middle America feel. And it's caught the attention of restaurateurs and artists trying to find a place in the sun.

Oceanside claims almost 4 miles of beaches and has the West Coast's longest wooden pier, measuring 1,942 feet. The beach, pier (and its adjacent outdoor amphitheater), and downtown attractions are all within easy walking distance of the train station.

VISITOR INFORMATION

Just north of downtown is the **California Welcome Center,** 928 N. Coast Hwy. (www.visitoceanside.org; © **800/350-7873** or 760/721-1101). It provides information on local attractions, dining, and accommodations; it also has a gift shop.

EXPLORING OCEANSIDE

One of the nicest things to do in Oceanside is to stroll around the city's **harbor.** Surrounded by apartment complexes of unfortunate architecture, the harbor has a Cape Cod–themed shopping village with a rustic, if faux, charm; the marina bustles with pleasure craft, fishing boat charters, and sightseeing excursions. The **Harbor Days Festival,** held the third weekend in September, typically attracts 100,000 visitors for a crafts fair, entertainment, and food booths; check www.oceansideharbordays.com or call © **760/722-1534** for more details.

Probably the area's most important attraction is **Mission San Luis Rey de Francia ★**, 4050 Mission Ave. (www.sanluisrey.org; © **760/757-3651**), located a few miles inland. Founded in 1798, it's known as the "King of the Missions," and is the largest of California's 21 missions. You can take a self-guided tour of the impressive church, exhibits, and grounds; in the cemetery you'll find the names of some of California's most important early families (Pico, Alvarado, Bandini). The cost is $5 for adults; $4 seniors, $3 ages 6 to 18; free for kids 5 and under and for active-duty military and their dependents. Hours are Monday through Friday 9:30am to 5pm, and weekends 10am to 5pm; a gift shop and small bookstore are also on site.

For a wide selection of rental watercraft, head to **Boat Rentals of America,** 256 Harbor Dr. S. (www.boats4rent.com; © **760/722-0028**). It rents everything from kayaks, personal watercraft, and electric boats for relaxed harbor touring to power-boats and 14- and 23-foot sailboats. Sample rates: single kayak, $15 per hour; power-boat, from $65 per hour; and personal watercraft, $105 per hour. This operation keeps seasonal hours, so call for specific information.

The **California Surf Museum ★** (www.surfmuseum.org; © **760/721-6876**) has a slick, facility located at 312 Pier View Way. Founded in 1985, the museum has an extensive collection that includes surfboards (everything from a 155-lb. redwood board to the motorized "Jet Board"), photos documenting surfing's early days, and other relics that chronicle the development of the sport. There's also a gift shop sell-ing surf-themed music, T-shirts, and other items. The museum is open daily from 10am to 4pm (Thurs till 8pm); admission is $3 adults, $1 seniors, students and mili-tary, and ages 11 and under are free. The museum is free to all on Tuesdays.

The **Oceanside Museum of Art ★**, 704 Pier View Way (www.oma-online.org; © **760/435-3720**), presents contemporary artwork by both regional and interna-tional artists; past exhibits have included everything from pop surrealism to quilts. OMA's Central Pavilion, opened in 2008, is a cutting-edge glass-and-steel box space that links the museum complex's two other structures—Oceanside's old city hall, designed by Irving Gill in 1934, and a Gill-designed firehouse built in 1929. The museum also presents concerts, lectures, and films. OMA is open Tuesday through Saturday 10am to 4pm, Sunday 1 to 4pm; admission is $8 adults, $5 seniors, free for students and military.

Oceanside's string of beaches starts just outside Oceanside Harbor, and runs south to the border of Carlsbad. Along the way you can enjoy the **Strand,** a sand-hugging walk-way that begins just south of the jetty where the San Luis Rey River meets the ocean, and ends at **Wisconsin Street Beach.** The sandbar formed by the confluence of river and ocean makes **Breakwater Way** beach a popular spot for surfers. The beaches north of the pier are wide, sandy, and generally less crowded; **Pier View South** beach and **Tyson Street Park** are where you should go if you want to be in the thick of things. Between them, these two adjacent beaches offer restrooms, showers, picnic areas, fire rings, vendors, playgrounds, and surf lessons. Oceanside's world-famous surfing spots also attract competitions, including the **World Bodysurfing Championships** and **Longboard Surf Contest** (both on p. 23), both held in August. Parking is at metered street spaces or in pay lots ($5 per day), which can fill up on nice summer days. The most southern beaches have some free parking in lots or on the street.

WHERE TO EAT & STAY

Livening up the dining scene is **333 Pacific ★★**, 333 N. Pacific St. (www.cohn restaurants.com; © **760/433-3333**), a spendy steak and seafood spot with a deep vodka selection and ocean views. Hipster sushi is available at **Harney Sushi ★**, 301 Mission Ave. (www.harneysushi.com; © **760/967-1820**), the sister restaurant of the Old Town favorite; it features cool design, mood lighting, and DJs adding some grooves to go along with the rolls. At the end of the long pier you'll find the 1950s-style diner **Ruby's** (www.rubys.com; © **760/433-7829**). This place can get crazy busy, but it's a great spot for burgers and fountain drinks, especially in the Tiki-inspired upstairs dining room and patio.

You can wait in line with the locals for breakfast or lunch at **Beach Break Cafe ★★**, 1802 S. Coast Hwy. (http://beachbreakcafe.menutoeat.com; © **760/439-6355**), or pull a pint of house-brewed beer at **Breakwater Brewing Co.,** 101 N.

Disneyland and its sister park, **California Adventure,** are less than a 2-hour drive away up I-5 in Anaheim. It's an exhaustingly long excursion, but you can make it up and back in a day. Transportation choices include taking Amtrak train service (www.amtrak.com; ℭ **800/872-7245**) to the Anaheim station, then catching the Anaheim Resort Transit route 15 bus right to the park; or leave the driving to a bus tour like Gray Line (www.sandiegograyline.com; ℭ **800/331-5077**).

If a day trip seems a bit overwhelming, there's no shortage of places to lay your head, including the sprawling **Disneyland Hotel** and **Disney's Grand Californian Hotel & Spa;** they are almost as much an attraction as the parks themselves. You can get info for both at www.disneyland.com or ℭ **714/956-6425**.

A single-day, single-park ticket costs $80, and $74 for ages 3 to 9; park-hopper and multiday discounts are available. For park info, call ℭ **714/781-4565,** or go to www.disneyland.com. For details on accommodations, dining, and shopping in the area, contact the **Anaheim/Orange County Visitor & Convention Bureau** at www.anaheimoc.org or ℭ **714/765-8888.**

Coast Hwy (www.breakwaterbrewingcompany.com; ℭ **760/433-6064**). Along the harbor, you'll also find a cluster of view-endowed surf-and-turf stalwarts, as well as a second Beach Break Cafe location.

Elsewhere in Oceanside, you can get a side helping of history with your burger and fries at the original **101 Cafe,** 631 S. Coast Hwy. (www.101cafe.net; ℭ **760/722-5220**). This humble diner dates from the earliest days of the old coast highway, the only route between Los Angeles and San Diego until 1953 brought the interstate. Slow food specialist **Flying Pig Pub & Kitchen ★★**, 626 S. Tremont St. (www.flyingpigpubkithen.com; ℭ **760/453-2940**), serves rustic American cuisine; while **Hill Street Cafe ★**, 524 S. Coast Hwy. (www.hillst.org; ℭ **760/966-0985**), set in a landmark Victorian home, offers an eclectic menu of Mexican, American, vegetarian, and vegan fare for breakfast, lunch, and dinner. Across the garden courtyard is its sister restaurant, a sushi eatery called the **Fish Joint ★** (www.thefishjoint.com; ℭ **760/450-0646**).

Book early for a summertime stay at the **Wyndham Oceanside Pier Resort ★★** ☺, 333 N. Myers St. (www.wyndhamvacationresorts.com; ℭ **800/251-8736** or 760/901-1200). The privately owned one- and two-bedroom suites at this property feature lots of amenities, look out over the pier, and have kitchens and sleeper sofas—and they book up fast. Beware of studio rooms with no view and train tracks for a neighbor. Rates vary by season and day of the week, ranging from moderate to expensive. The **Oceanside Marina Suites,** 2008 Harbor Dr. N. (www.omihotel.com; ℭ **800/252-2033** or 760/722-1561), also has a scenic location, surrounded by water on three sides at the mouth of the harbor. The moderate-to-expensive rates will get you an exceptional view, but accommodations that are a bit on the dingy side. The moderately priced **Holiday Inn Oceanside Marina ★**, 1401 Carmelo Dr. (www.holidayinn.com; ℭ **888/465-4329** or 760/231-7000), opened in 2009 and is clean and contemporary. For a seaside home away from home, check in with **Beachfront Only Vacation Rentals** (www.beachfrontonly.com; ℭ **888/338-0061** or 858/759-0381).

NORTH COUNTY INLAND

The coastal and inland sections of North County are as different as night and day. Inland you'll find beautiful scrub hills, citrus groves, and conservative ranching communities where agriculture plays an important role.

Rancho Santa Fe is about 27 miles north of downtown San Diego; from there the scenic Del Dios Highway (S6) leads to Escondido, 32 miles north of San Diego. Nearly 70 miles from the city is Palomar Mountain in the Cleveland National Forest, which spills over the border into Riverside County.

Rancho Santa Fe

Exclusive Rancho Santa Fe was once the property of the Santa Fe Railroad, but the area was "discovered" in the early 1900s by movie director Theodore Reed, who encouraged his friends Douglas Fairbanks and Mary Pickford to purchase property as an investment; they bought 800 acres in 1924. After just a few minutes in town today, you'll notice that Rancho Santa Fe is a playground for the über-wealthy, though not in the usual pretentious sense—this upscale slice of North County is a sweet little town that's enjoyed by everyone. Primarily residential, Rancho Santa Fe has just two hotels that blend into the stately eucalyptus groves surrounding the town. Shopping and dining—both refined and quite limited—revolve around a couple of understated blocks known locally as "the Village." There are more real estate businesses here than anything else, and the homes advertised all list for well into the seven digits. This is one of the most affluent communities in the United States.

ESSENTIALS

GETTING THERE   From San Diego, take I-5 N. to Lomas Santa Fe (County Hwy. S8) east; it turns into Linea del Cielo and leads directly into the Village. If you continue through town on Paseo Delicias, you'll pick up the Del Dios Highway (County Hwy. S6), the scenic route via Lake Hodges to Escondido and the **Zoo Safari Park.**

WHERE TO EAT

If you're looking for a casual lunch, breakfast, or snack, seek out **Thyme in the Ranch ★★**, 16905 Av. de Acacias (www.thymeintheranch.com; ℂ **858/759-0747**), a bakery/cafe that's open Tuesday through Saturday from 7am to 3pm. Hidden on a small plaza behind chic Mille Fleurs, this tiny treasure is well known (as evidenced by constant lines at the counter). Salads, sandwiches, soup, and quiche are the menu mainstays—all delicious—but the baked treats are extra-special.

Delicias ★★ CALIFORNIAN   Refined but relaxed, with a welcoming, comfortable interior featuring a stone fireplace as its centerpiece, this cozy restaurant also has outdoor dining available on its patio and fireplace-warmed courtyard. Delicias is equally appropriate for a casual meal or special occasion; service is attentive and personable, and the food is delicious. The California cuisine menu may include appetizers such as oven roasted Carlsbad mussels or organic beet salad with caramelized yogurt. Classic comfort foods are also served, such as excellent burgers, wood-fire pizzas, and mac-and-cheese (albeit primped with herbs and pancetta). Dinner features creative takes on meat and seafood, abetted by an excellent wine list. Happy hour is scheduled Monday through Friday from 4 to 6pm.

6106 Paseo Delicias. www.deliciasrestaurant.com. ℂ **858/756-8000.** Reservations recommended on weekends. Main courses $12–$20 lunch, $13–$42 dinner. AE, DC, MC, V. Mon–Fri 11:30am–2:30pm; Mon–Thurs 5:30–9pm; Fri–Sat 5:30–10pm.

Mille Fleurs ★★★ CALIFORNIAN/FRENCH   Chef Martin Woesle has been wowing critics and patrons for years at this landmark restaurant, owned by the same restaurateur who operates **Bertrand at Mister A's** (p. 127). Although Mille Fleurs has a French name and a Gallic country-cottage atmosphere, Woesle mixes in elements of American and Californian cuisine, along with tastes from his native Germany. The menu changes daily, highlighted by whatever Woesle has found during his morning sojourn to nearby Chino Farm. Expect something along the lines of venison rib chop with dried blueberries and cacao-juniper berry sauce, accompanied by one of the best wine lists in San Diego; there's always a healthy list of vegetarian appetizers and entrees as well. The piano lounge features nightly entertainment and a bistro menu, offering more casual service and prices ($12–$20); you can also take advantage of 5- and 7-course prix-fixe meals ($75 and $95, respectively). If you want to have a really private dinner, ask for the "Booth," a very intimate space that seats up to eight.

6009 Paseo Delicias. www.millefleurs.com. © **858/756-3085.** Reservations recommended. Main courses $13–$26 lunch, $21–$41 dinner. AE, DC, MC, V. Tues–Fri 11:30am–1:45pm; nightly 6–10pm (from 5:30pm Sat); happy hour Mon–Fri 2–6:30pm.

WHERE TO STAY

The Inn at Rancho Santa Fe ★★   This 23-acre resort features an idyllic, community-like setting with chirping birds, flowering plants, and towering eucalyptus trees; and the Village is directly accessed from the inn's front door via a pathway surrounded by a manicured lawn and colorful garden. There are a variety of room styles (as well as 1-, 2-, and 3-bedroom suites), ranging from rather austere digs with tile floors and vaulted ceilings to ones with a warmer, English-country flavor; there are also generously sized rooms in the original 1920s lodge building. Some rooms have kitchenettes, modern marble bathrooms with tricked-out showers, and wood-burning fireplaces; others have secluded patios with outdoor fireplaces. The **Inn Fusion** restaurant serves classic steak and seafood fare, as well as Asian-inspired dishes; the lounge features a roaring fireplace and live piano music.

5951 Linea del Cielo (P.O. Box 869), Rancho Santa Fe, CA 92067. www.theinnatrsf.com. © **800/ 843-4661** or 858/756-1131. Fax 858/759-1604. 87 units. From $259 double; from $525 suite. Extra person $25. AE, DC, MC, V. Free parking. From I-5, take the Lomas Santa Fe exit, following signs to Rancho Santa Fe. The Inn is in the center of town. Pets accepted. **Amenities:** Restaurant; bar; babysitting; exercise room; nearby golf course; Jacuzzi; outdoor pool; room service; 3 tennis courts. *In room:* A/C, TV/DVD, CD player, hair dryer, spa services, free Wi-Fi.

Rancho Valencia Resort & Spa ★★★ 🖭   This luxurious tennis-resort hideaway is set on 45 beautifully landscaped acres. It features 49 stand-alone, hacienda-style accommodations, all with fireplaces, colorful tilework, and private garden terraces. A $20-million renovation completed in 2012 has refreshed the casitas and added a stand-alone bar with expanded outdoor seating; a new yoga pavilion and Pilates studio have also been created. The impressive spa facility encompasses 2½ acres; it has five pools (including a designated Watsu pool for floating massages), indoor/outdoor treatment rooms, and treatment rooms for couples, with fireplaces and private outdoor showers and tubs. Rancho Valencia's main dining room, with its oak-beamed ceilings, fireplace, and large picture windows, is at once rustic and sophisticated; outdoor dining is available on the patio overlooking the tennis courts and the valley beyond, providing sunset vistas accented with drifting hot-air balloons.

5921 Valencia Circle (P.O. Box 9126), Rancho Santa Fe, CA 92067. www.ranchovalencia.com. © **800/548-3664** or 858/756-1123. Fax 858/756-0165. 49 units. $700 double; from $1,000 suite. AE, DC, MC, V. Free parking. From I-5, take the Del Mar Heights exit heading east, go left on El

Camino Real, right on San Dieguito Rd., right on Rancho Digueño Rd., and make an immediate left onto Rancho Valencia Dr. Pets $75/day. **Amenities:** Restaurant; bar; bike rentals; concierge; croquet; exercise room; playing privileges at 3 nearby golf courses; 2 Jacuzzis; 2 outdoor pools; pro shop; room service; spa; 18 tennis courts; car transportation (free use of a Mercedes-Benz; restrictions apply). *In room:* A/C, TV/DVD, CD player, CD/DVD library, fridge, hair dryer, free Internet, minibar, MP3 docking station.

Escondido

Best known as the home of the San Diego Zoo Safari Park (p. 38), Escondido is a city of 138,000, founded near the site of a historic battlefield where U.S. forces tangled with *Californios* during the Mexican-American War. Escondido is surrounded by agriculture, particularly citrus and avocado (neighboring Fallbrook is known as the avocado capital of the world). Grand Avenue, old Escondido's main drag, is experiencing a well-conceived renewal, with historic storefronts filled by restaurants and antiques stores, including the **Escondido Antique Mall,** 135 W. Grand (✆ **760/743-3210**), holding dozens of individual dealers. For more information on events and offerings, check www.downtownescondido.com.

The **California Center for the Arts ★**, 340 N. Escondido Blvd., is an attractive 12-acre campus with postmodern architecture and two theaters, an art museum, and a conference center. Renowned symphonies, eclectic musical artists, Broadway roadshows, and national dance companies are regularly scheduled here, often making the 45-minute drive from downtown to Escondido (along I-15 N. to the Valley Pkwy. exit) worth the effort. To find out what's playing and to get tickets, visit www.artcenter.org or call ✆ **800/988-4253.**

Kids and their art-loving chaperones will want to check out the amazing **Queen Califia's Magical Circle ★★** (www.queencalifia.org; ✆ **760/839-4691**) at Kit Carson Park, 3333 Bear Valley Parkway; the entrance to the park is at the corner of Bear Valley Parkway and Mary Lane. This wildly fanciful creation is the only American sculpture garden by acclaimed artist Niki de Saint Phalle, who in the years before her death in 2002 called San Diego her home. This brilliantly imaginative work features 10 sculptures and totems—the tallest standing 24 feet—encircled by an undulating, 400-foot-long wall of mosaic snakes. Composed of glass, stone, and tile, it's a riot of color and shape. The installation is open Tuesday through Sunday from 8:30am to 3:30pm (closed on Mon and rainy days); entrance is free.

As this is a major agricultural area, the **farmers' market** (www.sdfarmbureau.org; ✆ **760/745-8877**), on Tuesday afternoons, is unsurprisingly one of the county's best. It's held on Grand Avenue, between Juniper and Kalmia streets, from 3:30 to 7pm (2:30–6pm Oct–Apr). Another attraction is **Orfila Vineyards** on the way to the Wild Animal Park (see "Special-Interest Sightseeing," in chapter 4).

Two miles east of the Zoo Safari Park is the **San Pasqual Battlefield State Historic Park,** 15808 San Pasqual Valley Rd. (www.parks.ca.gov; ✆ **760/737-2201**). There's a picnic area, a .5-mile loop trail, and a small museum that details the bloody clash of 1846 in which *Californios* loyal to Mexico, armed only with lances, skirmished with invading U.S. troops. It's open weekends only, 10am to 5pm.

WHERE TO EAT & STAY

Leading the way for fine dining in Escondido is **Vincent's ★★**, 113 W. Grand Ave. (www.vincentsongrand.com; ✆ **760/745-3835**), a refined French bistro. Accommodations, meanwhile, are pretty much limited to economy chains, and on-again, off-again plans for a seven-story Marriott appear to be iffy once more. The **Welk**

Resorts San Diego, 8860 Lawrence Welk Dr. (www.welksandiego.com; ✆ **800/932-9355** or 760/749-3000), is an expensive-to-very-expensive, 600-room resort about 10 miles north of town. Lodging is in one- and two-bedroom condo-style "villas," and the 600-acre property offers golf, tennis, and live theatrical entertainment.

Hacienda de Vega ★★ 🍴 MEXICAN   San Diego County has an abundance of Mexican restaurants but a shortage of places that specialize in *Mexican* Mexican—food one would encounter in an upscale Mexico City venue. Hacienda de Vega is a 1930s adobe home whose grounds spread over 1½ acres and feature a lovely garden with a large pond and waterfall. This oasislike escape is located just south of downtown Escondido. You can start with one of several margarita options—the tamarind-flavored variety offers a vibrant twist on this classic—and move on to an appetizer sampler that will prime your taste buds with potato/chorizo quesadillas, *sopes*, and ceviche. Entrees include robust dishes such as chicken in mole sauce, seared pork loin lathered in a beer-and-potato sauce, and zesty pork *carnitas* wrapped up like an enchilada.

2608 S. Escondido Blvd. www.haciendadevega.com. ✆ **760/738-9805.** Reservations recommended for dinner. Main courses $7–$12 lunch (until 3:30pm), $14–$22 dinner. AE, DC, MC, V. Mon–Thurs 11:30am–10pm (kitchen closes at 9pm); Fri–Sat 11:30am–midnight; Sun 10am–8pm. Free parking. From San Diego and I-15 N., take the Centre City Pkwy. exit; after 1 mile, turn right onto Citracado Pkwy. and take an immediate right onto the frontage road, S. Escondido Blvd.

Stone Brewing World Bistro & Gardens ★★★ 🍴 INTERNATIONAL   Service can sometimes be off, and some dishes seem like they should be better than they are, but this place is one of San Diego County's gems. With a super-cool, Asian-influenced modern design and 1-acre garden with lovely landscaping, this huge complex features international cuisine that ranges from chicken *tikka masala* to *yakisoba*, duck tacos to penne pasta. Beer finds its way onto the menu, naturally, with dishes like cheddar and garlic soup with a dash of IPA, or the mac 'n' beer cheese. Stone is one of the nation's great microbreweries, but it's not afraid of a little friendly competition when it comes to what's on tap; you'll find more than 30 draft beers, plus a huge bottle list, from an international roster of craft brewers. You can combine a free brewery tour and tasting with a meal or a leisurely stroll through the gardens, pint in hand; it doesn't get any better than that.

1999 Citracado Pkwy. www.stoneworldbistro.com. ✆ **760/294-7866.** Reservations recommended for weekends. Main courses $11–$19 lunch, $15–$33 dinner. AE, DISC, MC, V. Sun–Thurs 11am–11pm; Fri–Sat 11am–midnight (kitchen closes nightly at 10pm). From San Diego, take I-15 N. to 9th Ave. exit and Auto Park Way; turn left on Citracado Pkwy. from Auto Park Way.

Palomar Mountain

At an elevation of 5,600 feet, **Palomar** is a tiny mountain community 70 miles north of downtown San Diego. The village probably wouldn't be here today but for its famous observatory, which escaped unscathed from the severe scorching the mountain took from wildfires in 2007. From San Diego, take I-15 North to Highway 76 East and turn left onto County Highway S6—a serpentine road climbs to the summit. Even if you don't want to inch your way to the top, drive the 3 miles to the lookout or just beyond it to the campground, grocery store, restaurant, and post office.

    Palomar Observatory ★ (www.astro.caltech.edu/palomar; ✆ **760/742-2119**) has kept silent watch over the heavens since 1949. The telescope project was proposed and funded with $6 million from the Rockefeller Foundation in 1928, but it took another 2 decades to find a suitable site, build the 135-foot-high dome, perfect the massive mirror (made from the then-new glass blend Pyrex), and build a road to

Over the line in Riverside County, 60 miles north of San Diego via I-15, **Temecula** is known for its 30-plus wineries and the increasingly noteworthy vintages they produce. The town's very name (pronounced "ta-*meck*-you-la") provides the first clue to this valley's success in the volatile wine-making business/art. It translates (from a Native American language) as "where the sun shines through the mist," identifying two climatological factors necessary for viticulture. A third component is Rainbow Gap, an opening to the south through the Agua Tibia Mountains that funnels cool afternoon sea breezes to the valley, which sits at an elevation of 1,500 feet. Some believe Franciscan friars from Mission San Luis Rey planted the first grapevines here in the early 1800s, but this was cattle country—the 87,000-acre Vail Ranch operated from 1904 until it was sold in 1964. Orange groves followed, but they gave way to grapevines; the first commercial vineyard was planted in 1968.

Most of the wineries are strung along Rancho California Road, and harvest time is generally from mid-August to September. But visitors are welcome year-round to tour, taste, and stock up. Among the more notable are **Callaway Vineyard & Winery** (www.callawaywinery.com; ✆ **800/472-2377** or 951/676-4001), the biggest winery in the region and also the best known. In-depth tours are offered at 11am, 1pm, and 3pm (hourly 11am–4pm weekends), and they have a casual bistro. Across the street from Callaway stands another old-timer, **Thornton Winery** (www.thorntonwine.com; ✆ **951/699-0099**), which makes a good choice if you visit only one location—Thornton provides an all-in-one overview of Temecula's wine country. It has a striking setting, fragrant herb garden, extensive gift shop, and award-winning restaurant, and tours are offered on weekends, between 11am and 4pm. Jazz concerts are also presented from April to October.

Mount Palomar Winery palomar.com; ✆ 800/854-5 951/676-5047) specializes in style blends, as well as port and sherry; the tasting room and bistro are open daily. Perhaps the most welcoming tasting room is the yellow farmhouse of the **Maurice Car'rie Winery** (www.maurice carriewinery.com; ✆ **800/716-1711** or 951/676-1711), famous for its baked brie and sourdough bread (made Fri–Sun only). A $18 passport will get you 10 tastings and a logo glass here and at Maurice Car'rie's sister winery, **Van Roekel** (✆ **951/699-6961**); both wineries are open daily from 10am to 5pm, and each has gourmet deli items for composing a picnic to enjoy in Maurice Car'rie's rose-filled front garden and patio.

You can make a night of it at **South Coast Winery Resort & Spa,** 34843 Rancho California Rd. (www.wineresort. com; ✆ **866/994-6379** or 951/581-9463). This is Temecula wine country's ultimate destination, featuring luxury accommodations, full-service spa, tasting room (daily 10am–6pm), indoor/outdoor fine dining, gardens, and gift shop.

For more on Temecula wine touring, contact the **Temecula Valley Winegrowers Association** (www.temeculawines. org; ✆ **800/801-9463** or 951/699-3626); the website has details about individual wineries, offers discount coupons, and has lots of logistical info. The **Temecula Valley Convention & Visitors Bureau,** 28690 Mercedes St. (www.temeculacvb. com; ✆ **888/363-2852** or 951/491-6085), can fill you in on accommodations, recreation (golf, fishing), and the region's famous **Temecula Balloon & Wine Festival,** held in June (p. 77). Your best call, though, might be to **Grapeline** (✆ **888/894-6379** or 951/693-5755; www.gogrape.com), which can pick you up from your hotel and shuttle you on a wine country tour.

10

SIDE TRIPS FROM SAN DIEGO | North County Inland

mmit. Owned by the California Institute of Technology, the Hale telescope's 0-inch mirror weighs 530 tons—it took 2 days to haul it up the Palomar road. The Hale was for many years the world's largest telescope; now completely computerized, it is still actively searching the skies.

The visitor center is open daily, 9am to 3pm, from early November through mid-March, till 4pm mid-March through October. The gift shop is open daily in summer, weekends only the rest of the year. Palomar is primarily a research facility, and you'll only be able to look at (not through) the mammoth telescope. Behind-the-scenes tours are offered Saturday and Sunday, April through October, at 11am, 1pm, and 2:30pm; tickets ($8) are available at the gift shop. Tour capacity is limited, and tickets are sold on a first-come, first-served basis; self-guided tour podcasts can be downloaded from the website. Evening tours are offered through the Reuben H. Fleet Science Center (p. 51). **Note:** The interior of the dome is kept at nighttime temperature (as low as 30°F to 40°F)—dress accordingly. The tour is also not recommended for children 5 and under.

JULIAN: GOLD, FIRES, APPLES & MORE

60 miles NE of San Diego; 31 miles W of Anza-Borrego Desert State Park

A trip to Julian (pop. 3,000) is a trip back in time. The old gold-mining town, now best known for its apples, has a handful of cute B&Bs; its popularity is based on the fact that it gives city-weary folks a chance to get away from it all, especially on weekdays, when things are a little quieter here.

Prospectors first ventured into these fertile hills—elevation 4,225 feet—in the late 1860s. They struck gold in 1870 near where the **Julian Gold Rush Hotel** (p. 248) stands today, and 18 mines sprang up like mushrooms. The mines produced up to an estimated $13-million worth of gold in their day. During all the excitement, four cousins—all former Confederate soldiers from Georgia, two with the last name Julian—founded the town. Ironically, African-American roots run deep in Julian, too—it was a black settler who originally found gold here in 1869, and the Julian Gold Rush Hotel was opened by a freed slave in 1897.

In October 2003, Julian was nearly engulfed by the devastating Cedar Fire, and firefighters made a valiant stand to protect the town against what seemed insurmountable odds. For several days, it was touch-and-go, and some 800 homes in the surrounding hillsides were lost. The central historic part of Julian was saved, though, along with all of the town's famed apple orchards. Today, you can stand on Main Street again without knowing a catastrophe visited just a few hundred yards away. Most of Julian's residents do live on the outskirts of town, though, and more than a third lost their homes and livelihoods; many left and never returned. A 15-mile stretch of State Route 79 is known as the Steven Rucker Memorial Highway in honor of a firefighter who died battling the blaze—one of the inferno's 15 victims.

Essentials

GETTING THERE   You can make the 90-minute trip on Highway 78 or I-8 to Highway 79. You can take one route going and the other on the way back. Highway 79 winds through Rancho Cuyamaca State Park. Highway 78 traverses countryside and farmland severely burned by the Witch Fire, one of Southern California's epic

Eastern San Diego County

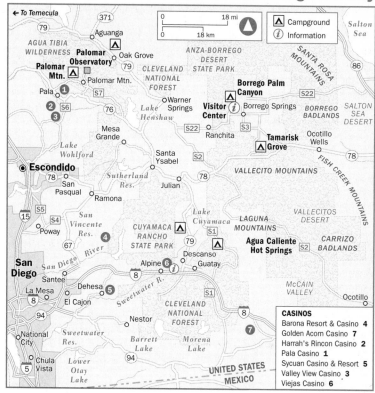

← To Temecula

0 — 18 mi	▲ Campground
0 — 18 km	ⓘ Information

371
79
Aguanga
AGUA TIBIA
WILDERNESS   **Palomar** ▲
Observatory
Palomar ▲
Mtn.
Palomar Mtn.
Oak Grove   79
CLEVELAND
NATIONAL
FOREST
S7
Pala ❶
❷ S6
❸
76
Mesa
Grande
Lake
Henshaw
Warner
Springs
S22
Ranchita
Santa
Ysabel
S2
Julian
78
ANZA-BORREGO
DESERT
STATE PARK
SANTA ROSA
MOUNTAINS
86
Borrego Palm
Canyon
Visitor ⓘ   Borrego Springs
Center
S22
S3
Tamarisk ▲
Grove
Ocotillo
Wells
VALLECITO MOUNTAINS
BORREGO
BADLANDS
SALTON
SEA
DESERT
FISH CREEK MOUNTAINS
78
Salton
Sea

Lake
Wohlford
● **Escondido**
78
San
Pasqual
Ramona
15   S5
S4
San
Vincente
Res.
Poway
67
❹
CUYAMACA
RANCHO
STATE PARK
79
Descanso ▲
Alpine ❻ ⓘ
8
Guatay
Lake
Cuyamaca
S1
LAGUNA
MOUNTAINS
Agua Caliente
Hot Springs
S2
VALLECITOS
DESERT
CARRIZO
BADLANDS
McCAIN
VALLEY
Ocotillo

Sutherland
Res.

San
Diego
Santee
La Mesa
8
Dehesa ❺
El Cajon
San Diego River
Sweetwater R.
S1
CLEVELAND
NATIONAL
FOREST
8

94
National
City
Chula
5   Vista
Sweetwater
Res.
Nestor
Barrett
Lake
Morena
Lake
94
Lower
Otay
Lake
❼
UNITED STATES
MEXICO

CASINOS
Barona Resort & Casino **4**
Golden Acorn Casino **7**
Harrah's Rincon Casino **2**
Pala Casino **1**
Sycuan Casino & Resort **5**
Valley View Casino **3**
Viejas Casino **6**

wildfires in 2007. If you come via Cuyamaca, you'll still see residual damage from the 2003 fire.

VISITOR INFORMATION The **Julian Chamber of Commerce** is at 2129 Main St. (www.julianca.com; ☏ **760/765-1857**); staffers always have enthusiastic suggestions for local activities. The office is open daily from 10am to 4pm. Main Street in Julian is only 6 blocks long, and shops, cafes, and some lodgings are on it or a block away. Town maps and accommodations fliers are available from Town Hall; public restrooms are located here as well. There's no self-service laundry (so come prepared), but you'll find a post office, a liquor store, and a few grocery stores.

The Save Our Heritage Organisation (www.sohosandiego.org) has also purchased the historic **Santa Ysabel General Store,** built in 1884, and plans to convert into a nature interpretive center, visitor information outpost, and gift shop. It's located at 30275 Hwy. 78, at the junction of Highway 79.

SPECIAL EVENTS **Apple Harvest Days** take place mid-September through October and include lots of special events, including **arts and crafts shows,** the **Grape Stomp Festa, Back Country Music Jamboree & Banjo, Fiddle Contest,** and even an **old-time melodrama.** There's also plenty of cider and apple pie, plus brilliant fall foliage. And year-round (weather permitting), **Doves & Desperados**—performers in Old West costume—present skits and stroll the streets on Sunday from noon to 4pm.

Exploring Julian

Radiating the aura of the Old West, Julian offers an abundance of early California history, quaint Victorian streets filled with apple-pie shops and antiques stores, fresh air, and friendly people. While Walmart and McDonald's have invaded formerly unspoiled mountain resorts such as Big Bear and Mammoth, this 1880s gold-mining town has managed to retain a rustic, woodsy sense of its historic origins, despite the arrival of a Subway sandwich shop.

Be forewarned, however, that downtown Julian can be exceedingly crowded during the fall harvest season. Consider making your trip during another season (or midweek) to enjoy this unspoiled relic with a little privacy. Rest assured, apple pies are baking around town year-round. But autumn is perfect; the air is crisp and bracing. Julian gets dusted (sometimes buried) by snow during the winter; spring prods patches of daffodils into bloom.

The best way to experience Julian is on foot. Two or three blocks of Main Street offer plenty of diversions for an afternoon or longer, depending on how much pie you stop to eat. And don't worry, you'll grow accustomed to constant apple references very quickly here—the fruit has proven to be more of an economic boon than gold ever was.

After stopping in at the chamber of commerce in the old Town Hall—don't miss the vintage photos in the auditorium—cross the street to the **Julian Drug Store & Miner's Diner,** 2130 Main St. (✆ **760/765-3753**). This old-style soda fountain serves sparkling sarsaparilla, burgers, and sandwiches, and conjures images of guys in buckskin and gals in bonnets. Built in 1886, the brick structure is one of the many well-preserved buildings in town on the National Historic Register; it's jampacked with local memorabilia.

The **Eagle and High Peak Mine,** built around 1870, at the end of C Street (✆ **760/765-0036**), may seem to be a tourist trap, but it offers an interesting and educational look at the town's one-time economic mainstay. Tours take you underground to the 1,000-foot hard-rock tunnel to see the mining and milling process; antique engines and authentic tools are on display. Tours are usually given beginning at 10am, but hours vary, so it's best to call ahead. Admission is $10 for adults, $5 for children under 12, $1 for children 5 and under. At the **Smith Ranch,** 2353 Ethelwyn Lane (www.pioneerways.com; ✆ **760/765-2288**), you can ride on a narrow-gauge railroad, explore a gold mine (then pan for gold), and get a general immersion in the old-time ways. A variety of kid-friendly tours are offered; the 1½ hour train-and-gold mine excursion is scheduled Monday through Saturday (reservations are required). The cost is $15 adults, $12 ages 3 to 12, and free for children 2 and under.

There's more local history on view at the **Julian Pioneer Museum,** 2811 Washington St. (✆ **760/765-0227**). It's open April through December, Thursday through Sunday 10am to 4pm; weekends only 10am to 4pm the rest of the year. And no historic survey of Julian is complete without a visit to **Pioneer Cemetery** (www.juliancemetery.org), a hilltop graveyard straight out of *Our Town* or *Spoon River Anthology.* It can be accessed by a stairway on Main Street (which becomes Farmer Rd.), just past A Street; at one time, this steep climb was the only entrance, but now you can also get there by car via A Street.

A ride with **Main Street Carriage Company** (② 760/765-0438) is a quintessential Julian experience. You can clip-clop through the heart of town in a horse-drawn carriage, getting a 15-minute narrated historical tour along the way; tickets are $7 adults, $3 children 10 and under (up to 6 or 7 people can be accommodated at a time). Your carriage awaits at the corner of Washington and Main streets; hours are usually Friday noon to 4:30pm, Saturday and Sunday from noon to 5:30pm.

Animal lovers might also want to look into the **California Wolf Center** ★ (www.californiawolfcenter.org; ② 760/765-0030 or 619/234-9653), located about 4 miles from town. This educational and conservation facility offers public programs on Saturday at 2 and 4:30pm (10am and 2pm in fall and winter), and Sunday at 10am (reservations required; $10–$20 adults, $5–$10 children); tours include a visit with the resident wolf pack. Private tours can be arranged Monday through Friday ($50 per person). There's more animal attraction at **Lions, Tigers & Bears,** south of Julian in Alpine, 24402 Martin Way (www.lionstigersandbears.org; ② 619/659-8078). This exotic-animal rescue facility is open by appointment only; it also offers luxury overnight accommodations (www.whiteoakwildnights.com; ② 619/445-0997).

Within 10 miles of Julian are numerous hiking trails that traverse rolling meadows, high chaparral, and oak and pine forests. Fire damage is visible—oaks have recovered, but pine trees have not; hiking here makes for a fascinating look at how Mother Nature works, and the additional good news is that you can actually see more of the vistas than you could before. The most spectacular hike is at **Volcan Mountain Preserve,** an area not affected by the 2003 or 2007 fires. It's located north of town along Farmers Road; the trail to the top is a moderately challenging hike of about 5 miles round-trip, with a 1,400-foot elevation gain. From the top, hikers have a panoramic view of the desert, mountains, and sea. Free ranger-led hikes are offered monthly, spring through fall; for a schedule, check www.volcanmt.org or call ② 760/765-4098.

The 26,000-acre **Cuyamaca Rancho State Park,** along Highway 79 between Julian and I-8, was badly burned during the October 2003 forest fires. It is regenerating nicely, but if you're looking for a conifer forest here, you may be disappointed. There are creeks and wildflower-enhanced meadows, and more than 100 miles of trails for hikers, bikers, and horseback riders. For a map and further information about park status, stop in at the **park headquarters** (www.parks.ca.gov; ② 760/765-3020), or check in with the **Cuyamaca Rancho State Park Interpretive Association** (www.cuyamacasp.org; ② 619/756-5354). Outside of Pine Hills is 929-acre **William Heise County Park** (www.co.san-diego.ca.us/parks; ② 760/765-0650), which has an easy .5-mile loop trail.

Eight miles south of Julian (and not part of the state park), **Lake Cuyamaca** has a tiny community at the 4,600-foot elevation that centers on lake activities—primarily boating and fishing for trout (stocked year-round), plus bass, catfish, bluegill, and sturgeon. There's a general store and restaurant at the lake's edge. The fishing fee is $6 per day, $3.50 per day for kids 8 to 15, free for children 7 and under; rods and reels are also available ($10). A California state fishing license is required for those over 16 ($14 for the day). Rowboats are $15 per day, motorboat rentals run $45 for the day ($35 after 1pm), and pontoon boats are $150. In the summer, canoes and paddle-boats can be rented by the hour for $15. For boat rental, fishing information, and RV or tent sites, see www.lakecuyamaca.org or call ② 877/581-9904 or 760/765-0515.

For a different way to tour, try **Llama Treks** (www.wikiupbnb.com; ② 800/694-5487). You'll lead the llama, which carries packs, for a variety of hikes that include a visit to a winery or a historic gold mine. Rates for a 4- to 5-hour trip run $95 per person ($75 for children 10 and under) and include a picnic lunch.

WHERE TO EAT

Before you leave, you must try Julian's apple pies. You'll need to sample them all to judge whether the best pies come from **Mom's Pie House ★**, 2119 Main St. (www.momspiesjulian.com; *℀* **760/765-2472**); the **Julian Pie Company ★**, 2225 Main St. (www.julianpie.com; *℀* **760/765-2449**); **Apple Alley Bakery ★**, a nook on Main Street between Washington and B streets (*℀* **760/765-2532**); or the **Julian Café & Bakery ★**, 2112 Main St. (*℀* **760/765-2712**).

The special attraction at Mom's Pies is a sidewalk plate-glass window through which you can observe the mom-on-duty rolling crust, filling pies, and crimping edges. The shop routinely bakes several varieties of apple pie and will, with advance notice, whip up apple-rhubarb, peach-apple crumb, or any one of a number of specialties. There's a country cafe in the store serving soups and sandwiches (11am–3pm), as well as confections such as fudge and saltwater taffy. Mom's is open Monday through Friday from 8am to 5pm, 8am to 7pm on weekends.

The Julian Pie Company's blue-and-white cottage boasts a small front patio with umbrella tables, a no-frills indoor parlor, and a large patio deck in back where overhanging apples are literally up for grabs. The shop serves original-style, Dutch, apple-mountain berry, and no-sugar-added pies as well as walnut-apple muffins and cinnamon cookies made from pie-crust dough. Light lunches of soup and sandwiches are offered weekdays from 11am to 2pm; it's open daily from 9am to 5pm.

Julian Grille ★ AMERICAN Set in a cozy cottage festooned with lacy draperies, flickering candles, and a warm hearth, the Grille is the nicest eatery in town. Lunch here is an anything-goes affair, ranging from soups, sandwiches, and large salads to charbroiled burgers and hearty omelets. There are delectable appetizers such as baked brie with apples and pecans, and the "Prime Tickler" (chunks of prime rib served cocktail-style au jus with horseradish sauce). Dinner features grilled and broiled meats, seafood, and prime rib. If it's a nice day, enjoy your meal out on the shady patio.

2224 Main St. (at A St.). *℀* **760/765-0173.** Reservations recommended Fri–Sun. Main courses $8–$13 lunch, $15–$28 dinner. AE, DISC, MC, V. Lunch Mon 11am–3pm, Tues–Sat 11am–4pm, Sun 10:30am–4pm; dinner Tues–Thurs 4:30–8pm, Fri–Sun 4:30–9pm, no dinner on Mon.

Romano's Dodge House ★ ITALIAN Occupying a historic home just off Main Street (vintage photos illustrate the little farmhouse's past), Romano's is proud to be the only restaurant in town *not* serving apple pie. It's a home-style Italian spot, with red-checked tablecloths and straw-clad chianti bottles. Romano's offers pizzas and calzones, as well as more creative fare like spicy apple-cider sausage, and pork loin in cinnamon, garlic, and whiskey sauce; the wine list features local vintages from nearby Menghini, Jenkins, and Orfila wineries. Seating is on a narrow shaded porch, in the wood-plank dining room, and in a little lounge in back (which sometimes stays open late, particularly on Sat).

2718 B St. (just off Main St.). *℀* **760/765-1003.** Reservations recommended. Main courses $8–$19. DISC, MC, V. Wed–Mon 11:30am–8:30pm.

SHOPPING

One of the simple pleasures of any weekend getaway is window- or souvenir-shopping in unfamiliar little stores like those lining both sides of Main Street (most merchants are open daily 10am–5pm). Rickety old structures are filled with antiques and collectibles—including places such as **Antique Boutique**, 2626 Main St. (✆ 760/765-0541), and **A Rose Path,** 2229 Main St. (www.arosepath.net; ✆ 760/765-1551), a rustic hideaway with two small art galleries and a retail area selling antiques and scented candles made on-site. **The Warm Hearth,** 2125 Main St. (✆ 760/765-1022), is a vintage barn housing country crafts, candles, and woven throws among the woodstoves, fireplaces, and barbecue grills that make up the shop's main business.

Nearby is the **Julian Cider Mill,** 2103 Main St. (✆ 760/765-1430), where you can see cider presses at work October through March. It offers free tastes of the fresh nectar, and jugs to take home. Throughout the year, the mill also carries the area's widest selection of food products, from apple butters and jams to berry preserves, several varieties of local honey, candies, and other goodies.

You'll have to step uphill 1 block to find the charming **Julian Tea & Cottage Arts,** 2124 Third St. (www.juliantea.com; ✆ 866/765-0832), for afternoon tea served amid a treasure-trove of tea-brewing tools and other tea-themed paraphernalia; the kettle is boiling Thursday through Monday, with several seatings between 10:30am and 4pm, (reservations required for weekends). If that sounds too frilly, head upstairs to the **Culinary Cottage,** home to stylish housewares, fine cookbooks, and gourmet foods (some of which are often available for tastings). Book lovers will enjoy stopping into the **Old Julian Book House,** 2230 Main St. (✆ 760/765-1989), purveyor of new and antiquarian volumes alike; it also carries a smattering of maps, sheet music, CDs, and ephemera.

Wineries have a presence in the area, too, including rustic **Menghini Winery,** 1150 Julian Orchards Dr. (www.menghiniwinery.com; ✆ 760/765-2072), which has a small tasting area and gift shop, and rolling picnic grounds that host special events throughout the year. Right in town are tasting rooms for **Blue Door Winery,** 2608 B St. (www.thebluedoorwinery.com; ✆ 760/765-0361), set in Julian's historic livery stables, and **Witch Creek Winery,** 2000 Main St. (www.witchcreekwinery.com; ✆ 760/765-2023).

A number of **roadside fruit stands and orchards** dot the Julian hills; during autumn they're open all day, every day; in the off season, some might open only on weekends or close entirely. Depending on the season, most stands sell apples, pears, peaches, cider, jams, jellies, and other homemade foodstuffs. Many are along Highway 78 between Julian and Wynola, 3 miles away; there are also stands along Farmers Road, a scenic country lane leading north from downtown Julian.

Ask San Diegans who regularly make excursions to Julian, and they'll concur: No trip would be complete without stopping for a loaf (or three) of bread from **Dudley's Bakery,** 30218 Hwy. 78, Santa Ysabel (www.dudleysbakery.com; ✆ 760/765-0488). Loaves are stacked high, and folks are often lined up at the counter clamoring for the nearly 20 varieties of bread baked fresh daily since 1963. Choices range from raisin-date-nut to jalapeño, with some garden-variety sourdough and wheat grain in between. There's also a deli and gift shop stocking jewelry, books, and crafts. Dudley's is open Thursday through Sunday from 9am to 5pm, and on Monday from 9am to 1pm. If it's closed, never fear—**Don's Market** (✆ 760/765-3272) next door stocks a good selection, as well as sweet treats from Mom's Pies. There's also a Julian Pie Company outpost here.

WHERE TO STAY

Julian is B&B country, and they fill up months in advance for the fall apple-harvest season. The **Julian Bed & Breakfast Guild** (www.julianbnbguild.com; ✆ 760/765-1555) has about 10 members and is a terrific resource for locating accommodations that suit your taste. **Pine Hills Lodge,** 2960 La Posada Way (www.pinehillslodge.com; *©* **760/765-1100**), is a rustic getaway about 2 miles from town that serves a Sunday brunch (9am–noon) in a wonderfully knotty dining room; there's also a small pub (Fri–Sat from 5pm) and a great deck area.

Julian Gold Rush Hotel ★   Built in 1897 by freed slave Albert Robinson, this frontier-style hotel is a living monument to Julian's boomtown days—and it's one of the oldest continually operating hotels in Southern California. Centrally located downtown, the hotel isn't as secluded or plush as some of the B&Bs in the area, but if you seek historically accurate lodgings in Queen Anne style to complete your weekend time warp, this is the place. The 14 rooms and two cottages have been authentically restored (with nicely designed private bathrooms added where necessary) and feature antique furnishings; some rooms are also authentically tiny, so claustrophobes should inquire when reserving. Upstairs rooms are engulfed by a mélange of colorful wallpapers; downstairs, an inviting private lobby is stocked with books, games, literature on local activities, and a wood-burning stove.

2032 Main St., at B St. (P.O. Box 1856), Julian, CA 92036. www.julianhotel.com. *©* **800/734-5854** or 760/765-0201. Fax 760/765-0327. 16 units. $135–$165 double; $170–$210 cottages. Rates include full breakfast and afternoon tea. AE, MC, V. Take I-8 E. to Hwy. 79. *In room:* A/C, no phone, free Wi-Fi.

Orchard Hill Country Inn ★★★ 📷   This AAA Four-Diamond inn is the most upscale lodging in Julian—a surprisingly posh, two-story Craftsman lodge and 12 cottages on a hill overlooking the town. Ten guest rooms, a lovely dining room (serving a guests-only gourmet dinner 4 nights a week, reservations required), and a great room with a massive stone fireplace are in the lodge; the cottages are spread over 3 acres and offer romantic hideaways. All units feature contemporary, nonfrilly country furnishings and snacks. While rooms in the main lodge feel somewhat hotel-ish, the cottage suites are secluded and luxurious, with private porches, fireplaces, wet bars, and whirlpool tubs in most. Several hiking trails lead from the lodge into adjacent woods. Check for specials and packages on the website.

2502 Washington St., at Second St. (P.O. Box 2410), Julian, CA 92036. www.orchardhill.com. *©* **800/716-7242** or 760/765-1700. Fax 760/765-0290. 22 units. $195–$275 double; from $295 for cottages. 2-night minimum stay some weekends. Rates include breakfast and afternoon hors d'oeuvres. AE, MC, V. From Calif. 79, turn left on Main St., and then right on Washington St. **Amenities:** Restaurant; bar; bikes. *In room:* A/C, TV/DVD w/movie library, CD player, hair dryer.

ANZA-BORREGO DESERT STATE PARK ★★★

90 miles NE of San Diego; 31 miles E of Julian

The sweeping 650,000-acre Anza-Borrego Desert State Park, the largest state park in California, lies mostly within San Diego County (in fact it makes up more than 20% of the county). A sense of timelessness pervades this landscape—the desert is home to fossils and rocks dating from 540 million years ago; human beings arrived about 12,000 years ago. The terrain ranges in elevation from 15 to 6,100 feet above sea level. It incorporates dry lake beds, sandstone canyons, granite mountains, palm groves fed by year-round springs, and more than 600 kinds of desert plants. After the winter rains, thousands of wildflowers burst into bloom, transforming the desert into a brilliant palette of pink, lavender, red, orange, and yellow. The giant ocotillo bushes flower extravagantly, hummingbirds fill the air, and an occasional migratory bird stops off en route to the Salton Sea. The park got its name from the rare bighorn sheep, or *borrego,* which can sometimes be spotted navigating rocky hillsides. The other half of the name comes from Spanish army officer Juan Bautista de Anza, who, from 1774 to 1775, led back-to-back expeditions (including one with more than 200 men, women, and children, plus livestock), through the desert from the Gulf of Mexico to the California coast. Following his second journey to the ocean, he made his way north, laying the groundwork for the presidio and mission that would become the city of San Francisco.

Many people visit the area with little interest in the flora and fauna—they're here to relax and sun themselves in tiny Borrego Springs, a town surrounded by the state park. It is, however, somewhat remote, and its supporters proudly proclaim that Borrego Springs is and will remain what Palm Springs used to be: a small, charming resort community with more empty lots than built ones. Yes, there is a golf resort, some chic fairway-view homes, and a regular influx of vacationers, but it's still plenty funky. One of the valley's unusual sights is scattered patches of tall, lush palm tree groves, perfectly square in shape: Borrego Springs's tree farms are a major source of landscaping trees for San Diego and surrounding counties.

When planning a trip here, keep in mind that temperatures rise to as high as 125°F (52°C) in July and August. Winter days are very comfortable, with temperatures averaging around 70°F (21°C) December through January, but nighttime temps can drop to freezing. Hypothermia is as big a killer out here as the heat.

Essentials

GETTING THERE   The drive to Anza-Borrego Desert State Park is spectacular; the scenery ranges from rolling, pastoral landscapes to endless bird's-eye vistas from precarious dead-man's curves. It's about a 2-hour drive from San Diego; the fastest route is I-15 North to the Poway (S4) exit to its end, left on 67 north to Ramona, which turns into 78 East, to Santa Ysabel. From here, go left on 79, right on S2, and left on S22. Alternatively, follow I-8 East past Alpine to Highway 79. Follow 79 North for 23 miles to Julian; take a right on 78, and then a left on S3 to Borrego Springs. Another (longer) option is to take I-8 to Ocotillo, and then San Diego's loneliest highway, Highway S2, north. Along this 40-mile stretch, you'll follow the Southern Overland Stage Route of 1849 (be sure to stop and notice the view at the Carrizo Badlands Overlook) to 78 East into Borrego Springs. The closest airport with scheduled service is Palm Springs, 75 minutes away by car.

GETTING AROUND   You don't need a four-wheel-drive vehicle to tour the desert, but you'll probably want to get off the main highways and onto the jeep trails. The Anza-Borrego Desert State Park Visitor Center staff (see below) can tell you which jeep trails are in condition for two-wheel-drive vehicles. The Ocotillo Wells area of the park has been set aside for off-road vehicles such as dune buggies and dirt bikes. To use the jeep trails, a vehicle has to be licensed for highway use.

ORIENTATION & VISITOR INFORMATION   In Borrego Springs, a town completely surrounded by the state park, Palm Canyon Drive is the main drag. Christmas Circle surrounds a grassy park at the entry to town; the "mall" is just west and contains many of the town's businesses. The architecturally striking **Anza-Borrego Desert State Park Visitor Center** (www.parks.ca.gov; *C* **760/767-4205** or

10

SIDE TRIPS FROM SAN DIEGO

Anza-Borrego Desert State Park

Desert Blooms in Anza-Borrego

The natural beauty of the Anza-Borrego Desert State Park is enhanced by the almost magical appearance of **desert wildflowers ★★** in the spring: blazing star, wild heliotrope, prickly poppy, Spanish needles, scarlet bugler, desert lily (the holy grail for aficionados), and more. The full bloom is only for 2 to 6 weeks—usually from late February through March, depending on winter rainfall. The park provides a 24-hour **wildflower hotline (© 760/767-4684)** as well as a postcard notification program that will alert you about 2 weeks prior to optimum bloom. To be contacted by mail, send a stamped, self-addressed postcard in an envelope to: Wildflowers, 200 Palm Canyon Dr., Borrego Springs, CA 92004. Or check www.parks.ca.gov for the latest information.

760/767-5311) lies 2 miles west of Borrego Springs; it's cut into the side of a hill and is totally invisible from the road. In addition to a small museum with interactive exhibits, it supplies information, maps, and two 15-minute audiovisual presentations, one on the bighorn sheep and the other on wildflowers; an interpreted loop trail is also on site. The visitor center is open October through May daily from 9am to 5pm, June through September weekends and holidays from 9am to 5pm. You should also stop by the **Desert Natural History Association,** 652 Palm Canyon Dr. (www.abdnha.org; © 760/767-3098), whose Borrego Desert Nature Center and Bookstore is open daily, 9am to 5pm. It features an impressive selection of guidebooks, educational materials for kids, native plants, regional crafts, and a minimuseum display that includes a pair of frighteningly real taxidermied bobcats. This is also your best source for information on the nearby Salton Sea.

For recorded wildflower updates, call © **760/767-4684;** for more details on the park, check in with the **Anza-Borrego Foundation Institute** (www.theabf.org; © **760/767-0446**). For information on lodging, dining, and activities, contact the **Borrego Springs Chamber of Commerce,** 786 Palm Canyon Dr. (www.borregospringschamber.com; © **800/559-5524** or 760/767-5555); it's open Monday through Saturday, 9am to 5pm.

Exploring the Desert

Remember when you're touring in this area, hydration is of paramount importance. Whether you're walking, cycling, or driving, always have a bottle of water at your side (not to mention a hat and sunscreen). The temperatures in the desert vary like the winds; do yourself a favor and dress in layers to protect yourself from the elements. If you will be out after dusk, or anytime during January and February, warm clothing is also essential.

You can explore the desert's stark terrain on one of its many trails or on a self-guided driving tour; the visitor center can supply maps. For starters, the **Borrego Palm Canyon self-guided hike ★** starts at the campground near the visitor center, and is 1.5 miles each way. It's a beautiful, easy-to-moderately difficult hike (depending on what Mother Nature has been up to) winding around boulders and through dry washes to a waterfall and a native grove of massive fan palms. Keep an eye out for the rare bighorn sheep on the canyon walls above. If you've got some time and crave solitude, try **Hellhole Canyon** trail ★.

The **Borrego Springs Resort,** 1112 Tilting T Dr. (www.borregospringsresort.com; ✆ **888/826-7734** or 760/767-3330), has three 9-hole courses—you'll play more than 6,700 yards over any 18 holes. There are four sets of tees to accommodate all levels of play, five lakes, a driving range, clubhouse, and pro shop; **The Arches Restaurant** and **Fireside Lounge and Bar** are in the clubhouse. The greens fee for 18 holes (cart included) is never more than $65 during high season (Oct–May); prices drop from there in the off season (June–Sept). The resort also offers stay-and-play packages.

You can also take a guided off-road tour of the desert with **California Overland ★** (www.californiaoverland.com; ✆ **866/639-7567** or 760/767-1232). Visit spectacular canyons, fossil beds, ancient Native American sites, caves, and more in military-style vehicles; you'll learn about the history and geology of the area along the way. There are 2-, 4-, 5-, 8-, and 10-hour (as well as overnight) excursions; you can also arrange for a private guided jeep tour. Tours include drinks and snacks (or box lunch on longer treks); prices start at $55 for the standard 2-hour adventure, $35 for children age 3 to 12.

Whether you tour with California Overland or on your own, don't miss the sunset view of the Borrego Badlands from **Font's Point.** Savvy travelers plan ahead and bring champagne and beach chairs for the nightly ritual. *Note:* The road to Font's Point—just past mile marker 29 on Palm Canyon Drive—is suitable only for four-wheel-drive vehicles; it is possible to walk to from the road though.

You'll find some of Borrego Springs' original inhabitants—including saber-toothed cats and mammoths—hanging around the **Galleta Meadows Estate** (www.galletameadows.com). There are more than 125 life-sized sculptures sprinkled around the area; check the website for a map of their locations. The collection—the result of a collaboration between a wealthy local landowner and a Mexican metal artist—also includes raptors, miners, an homage to migrant farm workers, and a 350-foot serpent.

If you have only 1 day to spend here, a good day trip from San Diego would include driving over on one route, taking in a few sculptures, then heading to the visitor center, hiking to Palm Canyon, having a picnic, and driving back to San Diego using another route.

Where to Eat

Pickings are slim in Borrego Springs, but you can follow legions of locals into the downtown mainstay **Carlee's Place,** 660 Palm Canyon Dr. (✆ 760/767-3262), a casual bar and grill with plenty of neon beer signs, a well-worn pool table, and a fine trophy of a jackalope (the mythic creature that's part jack rabbit, part antelope) mounted over the bar. For Mexican food, look to **Carmelita's Mexican Grill & Cantina,** 575 Palm Canyon Dr. (✆ **760/767-5666**); for a diner-esque breakfast there's **Kendall's Cafe,** 587 Palm Canyon Dr., in the mall (✆ 760/767-3491), where steaks, teriyaki, and Mexican combo platters are also available for lunch and dinner. French food has carved a niche here, as well, at the **French Corner,** 721 Av. Sureste (www.thefrenchcorner.biz; ✆ **760/767-5713**), serving seasonally October through May. Hours are Wednesday through Sunday 11am to 2:30pm for lunch, and 5 to 9pm for dinner; antiques and decorative items are for sale here, too.

10

SIDE TRIPS FROM SAN DIEGO

Anza-Borrego Desert State Park

Krazy Coyote Bar & Grille/Red Ocotillo ★ AMERICAN/CALIFORNIAN
Sharing a space overlooking the pool at the retro Palms Hotel, this two-for-one dining spot combines the hotel's seasonal, dinner-only restaurant with the popular comfort-food eatery that was formerly housed in a Quonset hut on the other side of town. Red Ocotillo serves breakfast, plus refreshing salads, creative burgers, and pastas from 7am to 9pm; beginning at 5:30pm, the more upscale Krazy Coyote menu joins the party, featuring prime steaks, fresh fish, and individual gourmet pizzas. The evening ambience is especially welcoming and romantic here, as the sparse lights of tiny Borrego Springs twinkle on the desert floor below; the classy cocktail menu adds to the allure.

In the Palms Hotel, 2220 Hoberg Rd. www.thepalmsatindianhead.com. ℰ **760/767-7788.** Dinner reservations highly recommended. Main courses $7–$15 breakfast and lunch, $10–$40 dinner. AE, DISC, MC, V. Usually daily 7am–9pm (call ahead for seasonal hours); Krazy Coyote offers a limited menu in summer.

Where to Stay

Borrego Springs is small, but there are enough accommodations to suit all travel styles and budgets. Peak season—from November to April—corresponds with the most temperate weather and wildflower viewing. Most hotels also post lower midweek rates; substantially cheaper prices are available in summer. For basic, 1950s-style digs there's the conveniently located **Hacienda del Sol,** 610 Palm Canyon Dr. (www.haciendadelsol-borrego.com; ℰ 760/767-5442); another option is **Palm Canyon Resort,** 221 Palm Canyon Dr. (www.palmcanyonresort.com; ℰ 800/242-0044 or 760/767-5341), a large complex that includes a moderately priced hotel, RV park, restaurant, and recreational facilities.

Borrego Valley Inn ★★   Stepping into the courtyard here—with its adobe casitas, desert landscaping of agave and bougainvillea, clumps of chilies drying in the sun, an aviary of chirping birds—is an evocative experience. Perhaps an Ennio Morricone theme will whistle through your brain, as you study the Hollywood-perfect surroundings that lend the air of a charming Southwestern pueblo. Featuring private patios adorned with fruit trees and Mexican *chiminea* fireplaces, the meticulously maintained accommodations have Saltillo tile floors and a Southwest/Mex decor; larger rooms have kitchenettes. The La Casita suite has a full kitchen and a 500-square-foot patio with a propane barbecue grill. This nonsmoking hotel is close to town and has two pools, one of which—surrounded by a high fence—is clothing optional.

405 Palm Canyon Dr., Borrego Springs, CA 92004. www.borregovalleyinn.com. ℰ **800/333-5810** or 760/767-0311. 15 units. From $215 double; from $280 suite (summer rates considerably less). Rates include continental breakfast. 2-night minimum seasonal weekends. AE, DISC, MC, V. No children 13 or under. **Amenities:** 2 Jacuzzis; 2 pools. *In room:* A/C, TV, CD player, fridge, hair dryer, MP3 docking station, Wi-Fi.

The Palms Hotel ★★ 🛎   This classic retro desert retreat originally opened in 1947, but was rebuilt after a fire in 1958. It was a favorite hideaway for San Diego and Hollywood elite, playing host to movie stars, including Clark Gable and Marilyn Monroe. In 1993, new owners rescued it from extreme disrepair, clearing away the most dilapidated guest bungalows and restoring the resort to its midcentury modern glory. Ten rooms are in the main building, while two casitas close to the pool have a fireplace and wet bar, and offer a little more privacy. Staying here is comfortable and satisfying; the old glamour is tangible, and sweeping views across the undeveloped desert set an easygoing mood. The Palms also has one of the best restaurants in town, the **Krazy Coyote/Red Ocotillo** (see "Where to Eat," above), and a fabulous, completely restored Olympic-length pool.

2220 Hoberg Rd., Borrego Springs, CA 92004. www.thepalmsatindianhead.com. ☏ **800/519-2624** or 760/767-7788. Fax 760/767-9717. 12 units. $159–$229 double (summer rates considerably less). Rates include continental breakfast. 2-night minimum seasonal weekends. Extra person $20. AE, DISC, MC, V. No children 12 or under. **Amenities:** Restaurant; bar; Jacuzzi; pool; room service; free Wi-Fi. *In room:* A/C, TV, fridge, no phone.

CAMPING

The park has two developed campgrounds. **Borrego Palm Canyon,** with 120 sites, is 2½ miles west of Borrego Springs, near the visitor center. **Tamarisk Grove** (closed July–Sept), at Highway 78 and County Road S3, has 25 sites. The overnight rate at both is $20 to $25 without a hookup, or $35 with a hookup (at Palm Canyon only); both have restrooms with pay showers (bring quarters) and a campfire program. Reservations are required in winter/spring high season; contact **Reserve America** (www.reserveamerica.com; ☏ **800/444-7275**). Primitive and backcountry camping are also allowed, making this one of the few parks in the country where you can just pull off the road and find yourself a spot to commune with nature (ground fires are not allowed, though). For more information, check with the visitor center (www.parks.ca.gov; ☏ **760/767-4205** or 767-5311).

TIJUANA: GOING SOUTH OF THE BORDER

17 miles S of San Diego

First things first: The city's name is pronounced—at least in gringoized Spanish—"Tee-*wanna*," not "Tee-*uh*-wanna." And despite her presence in the wax museum (p. 258), there was no kindly rancho matriarch named Tía (aunt) Juana for whom the city was named. Tijuana derives its name from "tycuan," an indigenous word meaning "near the water," a reference to a broad, shallow river that is now little more than a trickle (except during storms) running down a concrete wash.

Vibrant, chaotic, colorful, and confounding, Tijuana has a population of more than two million people, making it Mexico's fifth-largest city (and the second largest on the West Coast—only Los Angeles is bigger). Although the majority of San Diegans are basically estranged from our neighbor to the south, the history of the two cities is inextricably linked—Tijuana exists because of San Diego. T.J., as San Diegans refer to it, was little more than a village at the turn of the 20th century. It grew explosively in response to the needs of San Diego and the rest of California, providing a workforce for factories and fields, especially during World War II. It also offered succor, becoming a decadent playground for Americans deprived of booze and gambling by Prohibition and moral reformers. The city's economic engine is now driven by free-trade policies that gave rise to the *maquiladoras*—foreign-owned factories where appliances, furniture, and other goods are assembled by young, poorly paid workers, with little environmental or labor oversight.

Architecturally, little remains of Tijuana's boomtown days. Most of the city is of a more modern vintage, and some structures are quite striking; but for the most part this is, sorry to say, not an attractive urban landscape. Tijuana's beauty lies within. The city has fabulous restaurants and a burgeoning art and music scene; yet many still visit solely for the two-for-one drink specials or photo ops with a zebra-striped

STAYING SAFE IN TIJUANA

Violence has risen dramatically in Tijuana, mostly due to the presence of organized crime. In 2008, the U.S. State Department heightened its travel alert after the city was rocked by a series of shootouts between drug cartels and the federal police, sent in by President Felipe Calderón. For the latest security advisories, go to http://travel.state.gov; you can also call toll-free © **888/407-4747** Monday through Friday 5am to 5pm. From Mexico, dial 001/202-501-4444 (tolls apply).

Although a few tourists have been caught in the crossfire, they are not the targets—cartels wage turf wars, businessmen are extorted, political scores are settled, and wealthy *Tijuanenses* are kidnapped for ransom. There is petty crime, too, so don't flash a lot of cash and expensive jewelry, and stick to populated areas. *Mordida*, "the bite," is also still known to occur. That's when

uniformed police officers extort money in exchange for letting you off some infraction, like a traffic ticket. If you do find yourself dealing with an official, never offer a bribe—you may find yourself in much more trouble than you bargained for. And if you do meet up with corruption, you have little recourse but to comply, and then report any incident to your consulate in Tijuana (be sure to note the officer's name, as well as badge and patrol car numbers). English-speaking traveler's assistance is available 24/7 by dialing © **078;** you can also file complaints about police or city officials in English at www.consulmexsd.org (scroll down and click on the link "Complaints About Your Trip to Tijuana"). Another option is the city of Tijuana Internal Affairs 24-hour hot line at © **664/688-2810;** the San Diego Police Department will take crime reports and forward them to the proper agency, as well.

burro. If you want to find the real treasures of Tijuana, you'll have to venture out of the main tourist zone of Avenida Revolución.

Essentials

GETTING THERE

BY TROLLEY   The easiest way to get to Tijuana from downtown San Diego is to hop the bright-red **San Diego Trolley.** Take the Blue Line headed for San Ysidro and get off there (it's the last stop). From the trolley, cross the street and head up the ramp that accesses the border-crossing bridge. Tijuana's shopping and nightlife district, Avenida Revolución, is about a $5 taxi ride from the border, or you can walk the mile into the tourist area. The trolley is simple and inexpensive and takes about 50 minutes from downtown San Diego; the one-way fare is $2.50. The last trolley to San Ysidro departs downtown around midnight; the last returning trolley from San Ysidro is at 1am.

In an effort to stem the flow of illegal weapons coming from the United States, Mexican authorities have begun screening pedestrians and vehicles heading south. This, coupled with ongoing construction to expand and update the port of entry (scheduled to be completed in 2016), may result in some delay as you cross into Tijuana. Coming home, the border crossing for pedestrians can require as little as a few minutes midweek, or more than 2 hours on weekend and holiday afternoons. This is, after all, considered the busiest land-border crossing in the world. Travelers going no farther south than Ensenada for less than 72 hours do not need a Mexican

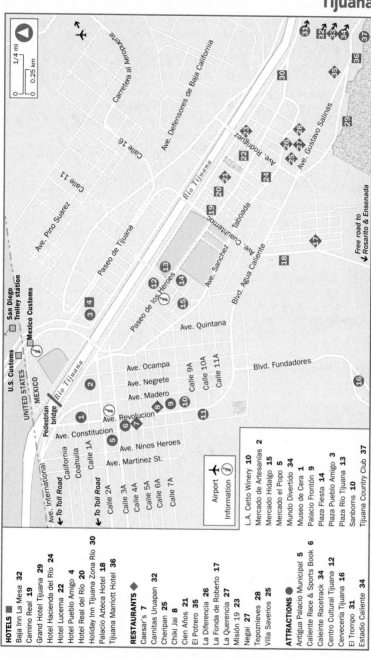

Tijuana

1/4 mi
0.25 km

San Diego
Trolley station

U.S. Customs

Mexico Customs

UNITED STATES
MEXICO

Pedestrian
bridge

Rio Tijuana

Carretera al Aeropuerte

Ave. Defensores de Baja California

Calle 16

Calle 11

Ave. Pino Suarez

Paseo de Tijuana

Rio Tijuana

Ave. Rodriguez

Ave. Gustavo Salinas

Ave. Cuauhtemoc

Ave. Sanchez Taboada

Blvd. Agua Caliente

Paseo de los Heroes

Ave. Quintana

Ave. Ocampa
Ave. Negrete
Ave. Madero

Calle 9A
Calle 10A
Calle 11A

Blvd. Fundadores

Ave. Revolucion

Ave. Constitucion

Ave. Ninos Heroes

Ave. Martinez St.

California
Coahuila
Calle 1A
Calle 2A
Calle 3A
Calle 4A
Calle 5A
Calle 6A
Calle 7A

To Toll Road
Ave. International

Free road to
Rosarito & Ensenada

Airport ✈ ⓘ
Information

HOTELS ■

Baja Inn La Mesa **32**
Camino Real **19**
Grand Hotel Tijuana **29**
Hotel Hacienda del Rio **24**
Hotel Lucerna **22**
Hotel Pueblo Amigo **4**
Hotel Real del Rio **20**
Holiday Inn Tijuana Zona Rio **30**
Palacio Azteca Hotel **18**
Tijuana Marriott Hotel **36**

RESTAURANTS ◆

Caesar's **7**
Carnitas Uruapan **32**
Cheripan **25**
Chiki Jai **8**
Cien Años **21**
El Potrero **35**
La Diferencia **26**
La Fonda de Roberto **17**
La Querencia **27**
Misión 19 **23**
Negai **27**
Tepoznieves **28**
Villa Saverios **25**

ATTRACTIONS ●

Antigua Palacio Municipal **5**
Caliente Race & Sports Book **6**
Caleinte Racetrack **34**
Centro Cultural Tijuana **12**
Cervecería Tijuana **16**
El Trompo **31**
Estadio Caliente **34**
L.A. Cetto Winery **10**
Mercado de Artesanías **2**
Mercado Hidalgo **15**
Mercado el Popo **5**
Mundo Divertido **34**
Museo de Cera **1**
Palacio Frontón **9**
Plaza Fiesta **14**
Plaza Pueblo Amigo **3**
Plaza Rio Tijuana **13**
Sanborns **10**
Tijuana Country Club **37**

tourist card. In order to cross back, U.S. citizens need **a passport,** passport card, or similarly secure document such as a SENTRI card (used by frequent border crossers) or enhanced driver's license (currently issued by Washington, Michigan, Vermont, and New York); those 15 and under must have a birth certificate or naturalization certificate. Non-U.S. citizens will need a passport, an I-94, a multiple-entry visa, or a Resident Alien Card to return to the U.S. Check with the **U.S. Department of State** (www.travel.state.gov; ✆ **877/487-2778**) before your visit, for more information.

BY CAR   Unless you want to explore more of Baja California, leave your car north of the border. If you do drive, take I-5 South to the Mexican border at San Ysidro; the drive takes under a half-hour from downtown San Diego. Returning north, allow at least 1 hour to cross back to the U.S., or a minimum of 2 hours on weekends or holidays. It is hoped that the expansion project will ease the waits eventually, but the impact of construction on day-to-day border operations is another wild card.

An alternative is to drive to the border and park in one of the long-term parking lots on the U.S. side for about $6 to $10 a day; a shuttle can take you to Avenida Revolución for $4 ($6 round-trip). Once you're in Tijuana, it's easier to get around by taxi than to adapt to the local driving standards.

If you do cross with your vehicle, Mexican auto insurance of around $25 to $30 a day (depending on the value of your ride) is highly recommended. It's not compulsory, but if you're involved in an accident and don't have it, you may end up in police custody until the details are sorted out, even if you weren't at fault. Insurance is available at various outlets just north of the border in San Ysidro, from a stateside AAA office (if you're a member), or from online services like **Baja Bound** (www.baja bound.com; ✆ **888/552-2252** or 619/702-4292). Some car-rental companies in San Diego, such as **Avis** (✆ **800/230-4898** or 619/231-7137; www.avis.com), also allow their cars to be driven into Baja California, at least as far as Ensenada.

BUS TOURS   **Gray Line San Diego** (www.sandiegograyline.com; ✆ **800/331-5077** or 619/266-7365) offers tours of Baja, including a Tijuana excursion for $40 per person ($24 for children 3–11, or up to two children 3–11 free with two paying adults); the twice-daily departures are at 8:30am and 1:30pm on Tuesday, Thursday, Friday, and Saturday. Tours to Rosarito and Ensenada are also available. **Five Star Tours** (www.sdsuntours.com; ✆ **877/704-0514** or 619/232-5040) offers a $43 ($23 for children 3–11) tour into Tijuana from 11am to 5pm every Wednesday and Friday; there are excursions to Rosarito, Ensenada, and Puerto Nuevo for a lobster meal, too. Five Star also has a daylong Baja winery tour that leaves downtown on Saturdays at 8:45am ($93 adults, $43 children); you can arrange for pickup from major hotels as well.

Do-it-yourselfers who aren't interested in a narrated tour or rigid time constraints can grab a **Mexicoach** bus (www.mexicoach.com; ✆ **619/428-9517**) for transportation to Tijuana ($6 round-trip) or Rosarito ($20 round-trip; reservations required). You can find them at the Border Station parking lot or adjacent to the San Ysidro trolley stop. Trips to the heart of Avenida Revolución run daily from 8am to 6pm. The company also has a city bus tour with (usually) bilingual guides; the loop tour departs from the CECUT cultural center and stops at 13 sites around Tijuana, allowing on-and-off privileges along the way ($10, $5 for seniors and children); a 14-stop tour operates in Ensenada, as well. For offbeat day outings, contact **Turista Libre** (www. turistalibre.com)—self-dubbed "rad" Tijuana tours that get you to the places locals go (everywhere from a cemetery for *Día de los Muertos* to *lucha libre* wrestling matches).

GETTING AROUND

If you've come to Tijuana on the San Diego Trolley, or if you leave a car on the U.S. side of the border, you will walk across the pedestrian bridge and through a makeshift Customs area. Straight ahead you'll see the **Visitor Information Center** (*C* 664/607-3097), open Monday to Saturday from 9am to 6pm, Sunday till 3pm; it has maps, safety tips, and brochures that cover the city's highlights. From here, you can make the 15-minute walk into the center of town or take a taxi. If you're walking, a good landmark is the tall silver archway known as **Reloj Monumental;** it marks the intersection of Calle 1A (First Street) and Avenida Revolución, the main tourist strip that extends to the south. *Note:* If you head north from the monument, you'll enter the red-light district.

Taxicabs are easy to find; they queue up around most of the visitor hot spots, and drivers often solicit passengers. It's customary to agree upon the rate before stepping into the cab, whether you're going a few blocks or hiring a cab for the afternoon. One-way rides within the city cost $5 to $10, and a trip to Playas de Tijuana might be $10 to $13; tipping is not expected. Some cabs are "local" taxis, frequently stopping to take on or let off other passengers during your ride; they are less expensive than private cabs. Metered taxis *(taxi libre)*—the cars are white with red stripes—are often a little cheaper than cabs with a negotiated rate. As opposed to places like Mexico City, there's no threat of crime from larcenous-minded cabbies.

VISITOR INFORMATION

The **Tijuana Convention & Visitors Bureau** has a website that will get you started: www.seetijuana.com (navigate past the homepage and look for the "English" icon in the upper right-hand corner). You can request a free visitors' guide by mail via the site; in Tijuana, the main office is across the street from the Centro Cultural, Paseo de los Héroes 9365, Ste. 201 (*C* 664/684-0537), and is open Monday through Friday, 9am to 6pm. If you are thinking about a longer trip to Baja, the **Discover Baja Travel Club** (www.discoverbaja.com; *C* 800/727-2252 or 619/275-4225) might be a worthwhile investment. For a $39 membership fee, you can get discounted insurance; special offers from restaurants, hotels, and shops; and deals on an extensive inventory of books, maps, and other Baja-related goods. Nonmembers can purchase items at the normal price, including online insurance. Discover Baja is at 3264 Governor Dr.; it's open Monday through Friday, 9am to 5pm, Saturday from 10am to 1pm.

If you run into problems in Tijuana, you can get English-speaking tourist assistance by dialing *C* 078; it operates 24/7. For information on events or attractions, you can call *C* 664/683-1405. Mexico's "911" is *C* 066. The Convention & Visitors office can also help with legal assistance for visitors who encounter trouble while in Tijuana. The following countries have consulate offices in Tijuana: the **United States,** Av. Tapachula No. 96 (http://tijuana.usconsulate.gov; *C* 664/622-7400); **Canada,** Germán Gedovius 10411-101 (www.mexico.gc.ca; *C* 664/684-0461); and the **United Kingdom,** Blvd. Salinas No. 1500 (www.ukinmexico.fco.gov.uk; *C* 664/681-7323). If you need to find an MD or dentist, contact **MexDoctors** (www.mex doctors.com; *C* 664/634-3744, or 619/378-0104 in San Diego). More than a few San Diegans have medical procedures done in Tijuana to avoid the high cost of U.S. healthcare. *Note:* When calling from the U.S., dial 011-52 then the 10-digit number.

SOME HELPFUL TIPS   The city does not take time for an afternoon siesta; you'll always find shops and restaurants open, as well as people in the streets. Most streets are safe for walking; observe the same precautions you would in any large city. Most people who deal with the traveling public speak English, often very well.

In 2009, the Mexican government quietly decriminalized possession of small amounts of drugs, including marijuana, cocaine, heroin, and LSD. This does not mean that, as a visitor, you can't end up in a world of trouble if you're caught holding drugs; decriminalization is not legalization. Do yourself a favor and stay away from narcotics and those who deal them while in Mexico.

CURRENCY   The Mexican currency is the peso, but you can easily visit Tijuana (and Rosarito and Ensenada) without changing money; dollars are accepted just about everywhere. Many prices are posted in American (indicated with the abbreviation "dlls.") and Mexican ("m.n.," *moneda nacional*) currencies—both use the "$" sign. Bring a supply of smaller-denomination ($1, $5, and $10) bills. Although change is readily given in American dollars, many merchants are reluctant to break a $20 bill for small purchases. Visa and MasterCard are accepted in many places, but never assume they will be; ask before dining or purchasing. When using credit cards at restaurants, it's a nice gesture to leave the tip in cash. As of this writing, the dollar is worth about 12 pesos.

TAXES & TIPPING   A sales tax of 11%, called an IVA, is added to most bills, including those in restaurants. This does not represent the tip; the bill will read *IVA incluído,* but you should add about 10% for the tip if the service warrants. Taxi drivers do not expect a tip.

Exploring Tijuana

For many visitors, Tijuana's main event is bustling **Avenida Revolución,** the street whose reputation precedes it. Beginning in the 1920s, Americans flocked to this street for bawdy, illicit fun (and you can still find a few girlie shows here), but drinking and shopping are the main order of business these days. While young people from across the border knock back tequila shooters and dangle precariously at the upstairs railings of glaring neon discos, bargain-hunters peruse the never-ending array of goods (and not-so-goods) for sale. You'll find the action between *calles* 1 and 9; there's a visitor information booth at Revolución and Third, on the east side of the street.

Among the numerous curio shops, bars, and restaurants are a few attractions, too. If you've made the 15-minute walk from the border, the first one you'll encounter is the **Museo de Cera (Wax Museum),** 8281 Calle 1, between avenidas Revolución and Maderas (© 664/688-2478). It's filled with characters from Mexican history and lore, and includes a few incongruous figures such as Bill Clinton and Whoopi Goldberg. This creepy sideshow is open daily from 10am to 6pm; admission is about $1.50. In an attractive, flagstone-fronted space on Revolución at Calle 4 is the **Caliente Race & Sports Book** (www.caliente.com.mx; © 664/688-3425), which opened in 2006. Here you can bet on international sporting events including NFL, NBA, and soccer games; there's also electronic gaming. Caliente also operates the **Hipódromo Caliente (Caliente Racetrack),** Bulevar Agua Caliente and Tapachula (© 664/633-7300), home of daily greyhound racing and another sports book. It's about a 10-minute cab ride from the tourist drag.

For something decidedly more cultural, head west down Calle 2. Just past Avenida Constitución is the **Palacio de la Cultura** (www.imac.tijuana.gob.mx; © 664/688-1721), a multipurpose complex that opened in 2006. Featuring galleries, a library, and event spaces, it's set in the **Antigua Palacio Municipal,** which served as a seat of government from 1921 to 1986 (it's one of the area's few remaining historical buildings). Within the complex, you'll find the **Museo de Historia de Tijuana,** which offers an overview of the city's cultural, business, and political life; the information is all in Spanish, but the images and artifacts will make their points (admission is about $1.50). Adjacent to the Palacio on Calle 2, kitty-corner from the Cathedral, is **Mercado el Popo,** a quintessentially Mexican marketplace selling nuts, candy, and produce. One of the most ornate buildings in town is the **Palacio Frontón (Jai Lai Palace)**, Revolución and Calle 7, where the fast-paced court game was once played. The facility is now used for concerts and special events.

A short cab ride away in the **Zona Río** is Tijuana's cultural icon, the **Centro Cultural Tijuana (CECUT)** ★, Paseo de los Héroes, at Avenida Independencia (www.cecut.gob.mx; ✆ **664/687-9600**). You'll easily spot the ultramodern complex, which opened in 1982—its centerpiece is a gigantic sand-colored sphere, "La Bola," which houses an IMAX Dome Theater; at least two different 45-minute Spanish-language films are shown daily. Joining La Bola is "El Cubo," a $9-million, state-of-the-art gallery that opened in 2008; it hosts major touring exhibits. There's a cafe and a great museum bookshop, as well. CECUT (pronounced see-*coot*) also has a museum that covers the history of Tijuana and Baja, with a collection of artifacts from pre-Hispanic times through the modern political era (descriptions are in both Spanish and English); music, theater, and dance performances are held in the center's acoustically excellent concert hall. The center is open Tuesday through Sunday from 10am to 7pm (the IMAX theater, garden, and some galleries are open daily); admission to the museum's permanent exhibit is about $2 for adults, $1.30 for children; tickets for the films are about $4 for adults and $2 for children. Prices for special exhibitions and events vary.

CECUT also gets you away from the tourist kitsch and into the more sophisticated Zona Río, where you can admire the wide, European-style **Paseo de los Héroes.** The boulevard's intersections are marked by gigantic traffic circles, at the center of which stand statuesque monuments to leaders ranging from Aztec Emperor Cuauhtémoc to Abraham Lincoln. In the Zona Río, you'll find some classier shopping, a colorful local marketplace, and some of Tijuana's best restaurants.

Mundo Divertido, Vía Rápida Poniente 15035 (www.mundodivertido.com.mx; ✆ **664/701-7133**), is an ultimate destination for kids, featuring roller coasters, batting cages, miniature golf, go-carts, video games, and more. It's open daily from about noon to 9pm. There's also a movie theater at the Plaza Mundo Divertido, and Hollywood films are sometimes presented in English with Spanish subtitles. Young ones might also learn a thing or two at the interactive children's museum **El Trompo,** Vía Rápida Poniente near Parque Morelos (www.eltrompo.org; ✆ **664/634-3476**), a science and technology funhouse with various galleries and a 3-D movie theater. It's open Monday through Friday 9am to 5pm, and weekends 10am to 6pm; a family four-pack ticket is $12.

Adult pleasures await at **L.A. Cetto Winery (Cava de Vinos)** ★, Av. Cañón Johnson 2108, at Avenida Constitución Sur (www.cettowines.com; ✆ **664/685-3031**), where you can get an introduction to the Mexican winemaking industry, the heart of which is based in the Valle de Guadalupe, a fertile region southeast of Tijuana. Many of the local high-quality vintages are exported to Europe; most are unavailable in the United States due to high tariffs. Shaped like a wine barrel, L.A. Cetto's unique facade is made from old oak aging barrels; an impressive visitor center offers an array of treats, including not only the company's award-winning wines, but also its line of tequila, brandy, and olive oil. Admission is $2 for the tour (and tastings, for those 18 and above; kids 17 and under are admitted free with an adult), $5 with souvenir wineglass. It's open Monday through Saturday from 10am to 5pm.

About 6 miles west of the Zona Centro, off the scenic toll road that heads toward Rosarito and Ensenada (but before you reach the first tollbooth), is the beach community of **Playas de Tijuana** ★. The large, sandy beach is popular with families, and a line of ramshackle restaurants and cafes on a bluff overlooking the surf offers great spots for lunch and a cold beer; a stone's throw away is the bullring-by-the-sea known as **Plaza Monumental** (p. 266). Perhaps the most notable feature here, though, is the border fence sporting colorful graffiti and guerilla art. The imposing, rusted girders that disappear into the ocean provide a stark contrast to the laughing children splashing in the surf next to it.

Where to Eat

Although the irresistible aroma of street food—*carne asada* (marinated beef grilled over charcoal) tucked into corn tortillas, for starters—is everywhere, less well known is that Tijuana has restaurants of real quality, despite the presence of touristy joints that lure many of the visitors. The following places are worth the taxi trip. The main meal of the day is *la comida* (lunch); restaurants are busiest around 2:30pm.

Note: Do not drink water unless it comes straight from a bottle (this includes ice, or uncooked vegetables, including lettuce, that have been washed), or you might leave Tijuana with a going-away gift; restaurants listed below generally have sanitary conditions, but it doesn't hurt to be cautious.

For breakfast (or lunch or dinner, for that matter), a local favorite not far from the Grand Hotel is **El Potrero,** Blvd. Salinas 4700 (✆ **664/686-3626**). Like Hollywood's old Brown Derby, this restaurant is shaped like a giant hat—a sombrero, to be exact. The interior is filled with cowboy memorabilia from the owner's days as a *charro* (horseman).

Tijuana is also home to outstanding restaurants representing international cuisines—just because you're in Mexico, doesn't mean you have to eat Mexican. There's award-winning Argentine food at **Cheripan** ★, Escuadrón 201 No. 3151 (www.cheripan.com; ✆ **664/622-9730**); excellent Mediterranean-Baja fusion at **Villa Saverios** ★★, Blvd. Sánchez Taboada at Escuadrón 201 (www.villasaverios.com; ✆ **664/686-6442**); sushi at **Negai** ★, Escuadrón 201 No. 3110-3 (✆ **664/971-0000**); and the flavors of Spain at **Chiki Jai,** Av. Revolución 1388 (✆ **664/685-4955**). Except for Chiki Jai, the preceding eateries are all in the Zona Río's dining district.

For something really unusual, stop by **Tepoznieves** ★, Blvd. Sánchez Taboada 10737, Zona Río (✆ **664/634-6532**), an ice-cream parlor that serves a dizzying array of flavors it dubs the "ice cream of the gods." The treats here include wine- and spirits-infused sorbets (tequila, white wine, gin); poetically named concoctions such as *mil flores*, or "thousand flowers" (cream, almonds, and herbal tea); and traditional ice creams made with everything from rose petals to prunes. This gourmet spot will have you coming back for more, and yes, they do have chocolate, too.

Carnitas Uruapan ★ MEXICAN *"El que no conoce Carnitas Uruapan, no conoce Tijuana."* He who does not know Carnitas Uruapan does not know Tijuana—so goes the boast at this popular locals' spot specializing in *carnitas*, a beloved dish in Mexico, consisting of marinated pork roasted on a spit until it's falling-apart tender, and then served in chunks with tortillas, salsa, cilantro, guacamole, and onions. At Carnitas

Uruapan, the meat is served by the kilo (or portion thereof) at long, communal wooden tables, accompanied by *ranchera* music. A half-kilo of *carnitas* is plenty for two people and costs around $12, including beans and that impressive array of condiments. Other traditional Mexican fare is served, and there is a bar as well.

Blvd. Díaz Ordaz 12650 (across from Plaza Patria), La Mesa. ℰ **664/681-6181.** Menu items under $5. MC, V. Mon–Thurs noon–8pm; Fri–Sat 8am–midnight; Sun 8am–10pm. Follow Blvd. Agua Caliente south toward Tecate. It turns into Blvd. Díaz Ordaz, also known as Carretera Tecate and Hwy. 2.

Cien Años ★★ MEXICAN   One of Tijuana's finest restaurants, this elegant Zona Río eatery offers the artfully blended Mexican flavors you expect (tamarind, poblano chilies, and mole), but with a host of traditional offerings that date back centuries, all stylishly presented. Go ahead and try something exotic such as the stingray tacos or the crocodile (or stick to the basics with a fabulous steak); then top dinner off with a crepe made tableside—though you may not want to see how much butter and sugar actually goes into it. Cien Años also serves breakfast, and the creativity is evident here, too; dishes include omelets stuffed with cactus, mushrooms, and cheese in a mango sauce.

José María Velazco 2578, Zona Río. www.cien.info. ℰ **664/634-3039** or from the U.S. 888/534-6088 or 619/819-5079. Reservations recommended. Main courses $8–$22. AE, MC, V. Mon 8am–8pm; Tues 3–6pm; Wed 11am–1pm and 6–8pm; Thurs 7am–10am and 2–10pm; Fri–Sun 9am–11pm (hours subject to change).

La Diferencia ★★ MEXICAN   This enchanting Zona Río restaurant has a delightful courtyard with a fountain, bird cages, and muraled walls. Even though it's a faux, indoor setting in a modern building, you'll swear you are dining at a rustic hacienda. After the salsa is handmade at your table, the creative appetizers are wheeled out—if you ever wanted to try fried crickets, this is the place. Most of the fare is made with delicate sauces offering a variety of unusual spices and flavors from around Mexico. Entrees include steaks, seafood, duck, and chicken; for breakfast, you can order such classics as a *cazuela* breakfast stew, or *chilaquiles,* a layered tortilla dish said to cure a hangover.

Av. Sanchez Taboada 10521, Zona Río. www.ladiferencia.us. ℰ **664/634-3346.** Reservations recommended. Main courses $9–$22. AE, MC, V. Mon–Sat 8am–10pm; Sun 8am–6pm.

La Fonda de Roberto ★ MEXICAN   A short drive (or taxi ride) from downtown Tijuana, La Fonda's colorful dining room opens onto the courtyard of a kitschy 1960s motel, complete with retro kidney-shaped swimming pool. The festive atmosphere is perfect for enjoying a variety of regional Mexican dishes, including a decent chicken mole and generous portions of *milanesa* (beef, chicken, or pork pounded paper thin, and then breaded and fried). A house specialty is *queso fundido,* deep-fried cheese with chilies, and mushrooms served with freshly made corn tortillas.

In La Sierra Motel, Blvd. Cuauhtémoc Sur Oriente 2800 (on the old road to Ensenada). ℰ **664/686-4687.** Reservations recommended. Most dishes $7–$11. Disc, MC, V. Tues–Sun 9am–10pm.

La Querencia ★★ MEXICAN/MEDITERRANEAN   Chef Miguel Angel Guerrero, a fourth-generation native of Baja, is at the forefront of a cuisine he calls Baja Med. He takes his inspiration from the cooking of Mediterranean cultures (noting that Baja shares a similar climate and also produces wine, dates, and olives), mixes in a hint of Asian flavor, and ties it all together with traditional Mexican style. An incredible range of fresh, local product is incorporated, including lobster, marlin, tuna, oysters, deer, quail, and lamb. Whether it's duck tacos, sashimi scallops, or venison cooked in the wood-burning stove, the results are memorable. The space is casual and modern, with concrete floors, exposed air-ducts, and steel beams, as well as a disconcerting array of stuffed animal trophies. Chef Miguel's latest venture **El Taller,** Av. Río Yaqui 2969B (© **664/686-3383;** www.eltallerbajamed.com), is also making waves with its warehouse style and fresh ingredients.

Escuadrón 201, No. 3110 (btw. Av. Sanchez Taboada and Blvd. Salinas), Zona Río. www.laquerenciatj. com. © **664/972-9935** or 972-9940. Dinner reservations recommended. Menu items $1.50–$26. AE, MC, V. Mon–Thurs 1–11pm; Fri–Sat 1pm–midnight.

Misión 19 ★★ MEXICAN/MEDITERRANEAN Opened in 2011 by one of Tijuana's highest-profile chef/restaurateurs, this glass-and-concrete gastronomical redoubt is the standard-bearer for Tijuana's renaissance. Sexy and sophisticated, it's a gathering place for the city's bold and beautiful, who feast on meticulously crafted fare referred to locally as Baja Med. With almost all product sourced from within a 120-mile radius, where a Mediterranean-like climate prevails, highlights include local wine, cheese, game, and seafood. Ingredients are also organic, and hormone- and antibiotic-free, parlayed into dishes such as short ribs wrapped in fig leafs atop black mole, and skewers of roasted octopus and squid. Misión 19 is part of a family-owned restaurant group that also includes Tijuana's iconic **Caesar's** (Av. Revolución btw. Fourth and Fifth sts.; © **664/885-1927,** www.caesarstijuana.com), where the eponymous salad was created and is still being prepared tableside in the traditional style.

Misión San Javier 10643 (second floor of the VIA office building), Zona Río. www.mision19.com. © **664/634-2493.** Main courses $8–$25. MC, V. Mon–Thurs 1–10pm; Fri–Sat 1–11pm.

Rincón San Román ★★ FRENCH/MEXICAN Along the scenic toll road on the way to Rosarito, at Km 19.5, is the golf resort Real Del Mar. Within this minicommunity (it even has its own church), set in a small plaza, is this world-class restaurant. It's no fluke the cuisine mixes French and Mexican traditions—chef Martín San Román trained at the Academie Culinaire de France and is one of Baja's most acclaimed chefs. Upstairs is a sophisticated, upscale room with fine modern art on the walls and views of the Islas los Coronados; downstairs has a casual European bistro feel. Lunch and dinner are served, and it's worth the drive.

Km 19.5 Ensenada Cuota, Real Del Mar. © **664/631-2241** or 631-2242. Reservations recommended for parties of 3 or more. Menu items $13–$27. MC, V. Mon–Sat 1–10pm.

Shopping

Tijuana's biggest attraction is shopping—you can take advantage of reasonable prices on a variety of merchandise: colorfully glazed pottery, woven blankets and serapes, embroidered dresses and sequined sombreros, onyx chess sets, beaded necklaces and bracelets, silver jewelry (beware of fake gold, though), leather bags and huarache sandals, hammered-tin picture frames, thick drinking glasses, Cuban cigars, and Mexican liquors such as Damiana (native to Baja), Kahlúa, and tequila. You're permitted to bring $800 worth of purchases back across the border duty-free (but none of those Cuban stogies), including 1 liter of alcohol per person (for adults 21 and older).

If your total purchases come anywhere near the $800 per-person limit, it's a good idea to have receipts on hand for the border crossing; customs officers are familiar with the average cost of handcrafted items. Pharmacies in Tijuana also do a brisk business selling "controlled" medicines such as Viagra without a prescription. U.S. law allows for the importation of about 1 month's supply (50 dosages) of any medicine that requires a prescription in the states.

When most people think of Tijuana, they picture **Avenida Revolución,** which appears to exist solely for the extraction of dollars from American visitors. Dedicated shoppers quickly discover most of the curios spilling out onto the sidewalk look alike, despite the determined sellers' assurances that their wares are the best in town. Browse for comparison's sake, and duck into one of the many *pasajes,* or passageway arcades, for more shopping. ***But be forewarned:*** The incessant cajoling and wheedling of the merchant barkers will grow wearisome. They've seen their business plummet over the years and are more determined than ever to make a sale. If you are in the buying mode, your best move is to just walk away—quoted prices will quickly drop. At the visitor center you can pick up a map showing the locations of the Outstanding Host establishments—reputable businesses that carry the highest quality merchandise. Some of these places won't bargain with you, but especially if you're in the market for jewelry, they are smart choices.

Notable shops include **Casa Rodriguez,** 1080 Av. Revolución (✆ **664/685-9960**), which is entered through an easily missed doorway that leads to a huge showroom of wrought-iron and wood furnishings; **Hand Art,** 931-A Av. Revolución (www.handartmx.com; ✆ **664/688-0868**), featuring hand-embroidered tablecloths and dresses, and classic guayabera shirts; and **Sara's London Shop,** 907 Av. Revolución (✆ **664/685-0622**), selling a vast array of perfumes, soaps, and body sprays. Sara's first opened for business in 1944, making it one of the oldest businesses on the street. One of the few places in Tijuana to find better-quality crafts from a variety of Mexican states is **Tolán,** Avenida Revolución between calles 7 and 8 (✆ **664/688-3637**). Look for blue glassware from Guadalajara, glazed pottery from Tlaquepaque, crafts from the Oaxaca countryside, and distinctive tile work from Puebla.

An alternative is to visit **Sanborns,** Avenida Revolución between calles 8 and 9 (✆ **664/688-1462**; www.sanborns.com.mx), a branch of the Mexico City department store. It sells an array of regional folk art and souvenirs, books and CDs, and candies and bakery treats; you can also have breakfast in the sunny cafe. There's another location in Zona Río at Paseo de los Héroes and Boulevard Cuauhtemoc (✆ **664/684-8999**).

If a marketplace atmosphere and spirited bargaining are what you're looking for, head to **Mercado de Artesanías (Crafts Market),** Calle 2 and Avenida Negrete. Vendors of pottery, clayware, clothing, and other crafts fill an entire city block.

Shopping malls are as common in Tijuana as in any big American city. You shouldn't expect to find typical souvenirs, but shopping alongside residents and other intrepid visitors is often more fun than feeling like a sitting-duck tourist. The biggest and most convenient is **Plaza Río Tijuana** (on Paseo de los Héroes at Av. Independencia). It's an outdoor plaza anchored by several department stores, with dozens of shops and casual restaurants; this is the place to buy shoes.

For a taste of everyday Mexico, join the locals at **Mercado Hidalgo** (1 block west at Av. Sánchez Taboada and Av. Independencia), a busy indoor-outdoor marketplace where vendors display fresh flowers and produce, sacks of dried beans and chilies by the kilo, and a few souvenir crafts, including some excellent piñatas. Morning is the best time to visit the farmers' market.

Where to Stay

When calculating room rates, remember that hotel rates in Tijuana are subject to a 13% tax. Also note this guide uses the term "double" when listing rates, referring to the American concept of "double occupancy." However, in Mexico a single room has one bed, a double has two, and you pay accordingly.

Befitting Tijuana's prominence as an international commerce center (companies such as Sony and Sanyo have factories here), a number of hotels cater to business travelers. **Camino Real,** Paseo de los Héroes 10305 (www.caminoreal.com; ℂ 877/215-3051 from the U.S., 800/025-6350, or 664/633-4000), is right in the heart of the Zona Río shopping and dining district; **Tijuana Marriott Hotel,** Blvd. Agua Caliente 11553 (www.marriott.com; ℂ 888/748-8785 from the U.S., or 664/622-6600), is adjacent to the golf course; and **Hotel Pueblo Amigo,** Vía Oriente 9211 (www.hotelpuebloamigo.com; ℂ 800/386-6985 from the U.S., 800/026-6386, or 664/624-2700), is in Zona Río's Plaza Pueblo Amigo, where several popular restaurants and clubs are clustered. The **Holiday Inn Tijuana Zona Río,** Paseo de los Héroes 18818, Zona Río (www.hotelesmilenium.com; ℂ 664/636-0000), has an in-house spa (www.vitaspatijuana.com; ℂ 664/636-0016), where you can soak in the healthful, sulfurous—though disconcertingly brown—thermal waters that are tapped from directly beneath the hotel. The **Hotel Real Del Río,** José María Velasco 1409-A (www.realdelrio.com; ℂ 877/517-6479 from U.S., 800/025-7325, or 664/634-3100), is a stylish, modern accommodation for business and leisure travelers.

If you want to stay at Playas de Tijuana, a solid choice is the **Hacienda del Mar,** Paseo Playas de Tijuana 116 (www.haciendahotel.net; ℂ 664/630-8603).

Grand Hotel Tijuana ★ These 28-story mirrored twin towers are visible from all over the city. Modern and sleek, the hotel opened in 1982 and is popular with business travelers, visiting celebrities, and for society events and live shows. Rooms, though nothing special design-wise, have spectacular views from the top floors; and the fourth-floor pool deck, while concretely austere, offers great open-air perspectives of the city and golf course. The two buildings and the arcade that connects them practically form a minicity unto itself: You'll find doctors offices, a day spa, restaurants, and the popular club **Clásico.** Tours to Ensenada or San Diego, and golf packages with the adjacent Tijuana Country Club are also available; a taxi stand is located out front too.

Agua Caliente 4500, Tijuana, BC 22440, Mexico. www.grandhoteltij.com.mx. ℂ **866/472-6385** from U.S., 800/026-6007, or 664/681-7000. Fax 664/681-7016. 422 units. From $85 double; from $176 suite. AE, MC, V. Covered parking. **Amenities:** 3 restaurants; 2 bars; babysitting; nearby golf course; exercise room; Jacuzzi; outdoor heated pool; room service; sauna; 2 tennis courts. In room: A/C, TV, fridge, hair dryer, free Wi-Fi.

Hotel Hacienda del Río Located in the Zona Río, this reliable hotel is close to Tijuana's fine-dining, commercial, and financial district. It's part of a small chain that includes a property in the heart of Ensenada, the **Hotel Cortez** (ℂ 646/178-2307), as well as the **Baja Inn La Mesa,** Blvd. Díaz Ordaz Esq. con Gardenias 50 (ℂ 664/681-6522), near the Tijuana racetrack (about a $8–$10 cab ride from downtown). Rates are cheaper at the La Mesa property, topping out at about $65 per night for the best room.

Blvd. Sanchez Taboada 10606, Tijuana, BC 22440, Mexico. www.bajainn.com. ℂ **888/226-1033** from the U.S., 800/026-6999, or 664/684-8644. Fax 664/684-8620. 131 units. From $60 double; from $80 suite. Extra person $7. AE, MC, V. Free parking. **Amenities:** Restaurant; bar; exercise room; pool; room service. In room: A/C, TV, free Wi-Fi.

Hotel Lucerna Once the most chic hotel in Tijuana, the neoclassical Lucerna still offers hospitable accommodations with plenty of personality. The hotel is in the Zona Río, away from the noise and congestion of downtown, so a quiet night's sleep is easy. It's kept in great shape for the international visitors who enjoy Lucerna's proximity to the financial district, and the staff's friendly and attentive service reflects this clientele. The five-story hotel's rooms all have balconies or patios but are otherwise unremarkable. Sunday brunch is served outdoors by the swimming pool.

Blvd. Paseo de los Héroes 10902, Zona Río, Tijuana, BC 22320, Mexico. www.hoteleslucerna.com. © **800/026-6300** or 664/633-3900. 168 units. From $85 double; from $120 suite. AE, MC, V. **Amenities:** 2 restaurants; bar; exercise room; outdoor pool; room service. *In room:* A/C, TV, hair dryer, free Wi-Fi.

Palacio Azteca Hotel   Popular with businesspeople and airline flight crews, this seven-story hotel looks rather drab from the outside. The interior is modern and inviting, though, with gleaming marble, honey-blond wood, and a fireplace in the lobby lounge area. Located near where the downtown bullring once stood, it has a small but stylish bar, a pool area shaded by palms, and a restaurant that serves a daily breakfast buffet for $11 ($8 kids; $18 Sun). The rooms are simply and tastefully furnished, and the master suites have long balconies that afford an overview of the city.

Blvd. Cuauhtémoc Sur 213, Tijuana, BC 22400, Mexico. www.hotelpalacioazteca.com. © **888/901-3720** from U.S., 800/026-6660, or 664/681-8100. Fax 664/681-8160. 197 units. From $63 double; from $150 suite. Extra person $10. AE, DISC, MC, V. Free parking. **Amenities:** Restaurant; bar; exercise room; Internet; pool; room service. *In room:* A/C, TV, hair dryer.

Entertainment & Nightlife

It won't be difficult to find the bars offering cheap drinks and loud music, but Tijuana offers much more than that, if you know where to look. Just off Revolución is the all-night joint **Dandy Del Sur,** Calle 6 Flores Magón No. 2030 (© **664/688-0052**); the tiny bar's status was secured when the Nortec Collective, the city's pioneering electronica band, named a song after the place. Across the street, you'll find locals dancing away to salsa and other Latin rhythms at the dance-hall dive **La Estrella;** look for the white star. Also located on Sixth, between Revolución and Madera, is **La Mezcalera** (© 664/634-1980), a hipster mescal bar and music club. In the Zona Río, a smorgasbord of clubs, bars, and restaurants is found in **Plaza Pueblo Amigo,** Vía Oriente and Paseo Tijuana; and **Plaza Fiesta,** Paseo de los Héroes 9415, making it easy to pick and choose the venue that's right for you. In Pueblo Amigo, you'll find an alternative dance party at **Mofo Bar** (www.mofobar. com; © 664/683-5427); there are more than a dozen choices at Plaza Fiesta, where the music ranges from reggae to Norteño and top draws include **Sótano Suizo** (www.sotanosuizo.com; © 664/684-8834), **Monte Picacho** (© 664/684-0705), and **Berlin Bar** (www.myspace.com/berlintijuana). You can also work up a sweat at the dance club **Baby Rock,** Av. Diego Rivera 1482, Zona Río (www.clubbabyrock. com; © 664/634-2404). Tijuana's gay bars can be found along Avenida Constitución, north of Calle 1; west of Avenida Revolución, along Calle Coahuila, you'll find flashy strip clubs like **Hong Kong Gentlemen's Club** (www.hktijuana.com; © 877/497-8747) and **Adelita Bar** (www.adelita.com.mx; © 664/685-3580). Even midweek on a winter night, Coahuila will be jumping.

Brewery, restaurant, and nightclub **Cervecería Tijuana,** Blvd. Fundadores 2951 (www.tjbeer.com; © 664/638-8662), will transport you to the beer halls of Prague, of all places. Everything in this wood-paneled tavern, located a few minutes' drive from the tourist zone, was imported from the Czech Republic. Upstairs is club space presenting a variety of karaoke and live music Thursday through Saturday. For salsa or *trova* (singer/songwriter balladeers), check out **Antigua Bodega de Papel,** Calle

11 No. 2012, Zona Centro (www.myspace.com/laantiguabodegadepapel; © **664/664-8246**); or, for a complete immersion in Tijuana arts and culture, go to **El Lugar del Nopal,** Callejón 5 de Mayo 1328, Zona Centro (www.lugardelnopal.org; © **664/685-1264**), a gallery, cabaret, and restaurant all in one. For something more traditional, you'll find mariachis blasting away at lively **Los Remedios Restaurante Bar & Cantina,** Diego Rivera 2479, Zona Río (www.losremedios.mx; © **664/634-3065**). It has the cure for whatever ails you.

Sports

BULLFIGHTING Tijuana's downtown bullring, the Toreo de Tijuana, fell to the wrecking ball, but the city still has bullfighting. The impressive **Plaza Monumental** (www.plazamonumental.com; © **664/680-1808**), the bullring-by-the-sea in Playas de Tijuana, stages a season from about April to November. Contests are scheduled as often as every other Sunday (at 4pm). Ticket prices range from around $12 to $47 (premium seats are on the shady side of the arena); tickets are for sale at the bullring. If you want to catch the bullfights but don't want to drive, **Five Star Tours** (www.sdsuntours.com; © **877/704-0514** or 619/232-5040) offers bus trips that depart from downtown San Diego; the price is $25 round-trip, plus the cost of your bullfight ticket. Or you can take a taxi from the border (about $12). You can find a nice English-language primer on bullfighting, as well as scheduling info, at www.bullfighting new.com.

GOLF Once the favorite of golfing celebrities and socialites who stayed at the now-defunct Agua Caliente Resort, the **Club Campestre de Tijuana (Tijuana Country Club),** Bulevar Agua Caliente at Avenida Gustavo Salinas (www.tijuanacountryclub.com or www.campestretij.com; © **888/217-1165** from the U.S., or 664/104-7545), is near the Caliente Racetrack and behind the Grand Hotel Tijuana. It's about a 10-minute drive from downtown. The course attracts mostly business travelers staying at nearby hotels, many of which offer golf packages (see Grand Hotel Tijuana, above). This course has quite a pedigree: It was designed by Alister MacKenzie, who, along with Bobby Jones, was the creator of the course at the Augusta National Golf Club. Greens fees are $53 to $64, including cart, and caddies are available. Stop by the pro shop for balls, tees, and a limited number of other accessories; the clubhouse also has two restaurants with cocktail lounges.

Along the toll road to Rosarito, at Km 19.5, is the golf community of **Real Del Mar** (www.realdelmar.com.mx; © **800/662-6180** from the U.S., or 664/631-3406). Open to the public, this course has incredible ocean vistas, as well as plenty of wildlife playing through; stiff breezes, as well as rattlesnakes in the summer, make for some interesting challenges here. Rates are $45 Sunday through Thursday, $55 Friday and Saturday; twilight rates are available. After your game you can repair to the wonderful on-site restaurant **Rincón San Román** (p. 262).

SOCCER Tijuana's beloved professional soccer team is the **Club Tijuana Xoloitzcuintles de Caliente** (www.xolos.com.; © **664/647-4786**). Don't bother trying to pronounce it—just call them the Xolos (Cholos), like everyone else does. The club, founded in 2006, is named for an ancient, hairless breed of Mexican dog that was considered sacred by the Aztecs, who believed the dogs escorted their souls through the underworld. The Xolos play in Mexico's top division, hosting games in the 33,000 seat Estadio Caliente, near the racetrack (tickets, when you can get them, start around $20). **Five Star Tours** (www.sdsuntours.com; © **877/704-0514** or 619/232-5040) offers ticket-and-transportation packages from San Diego.

Exploring Beyond Tijuana

If you have a car, venture into Baja California for a long day trip or an overnight get-away. Beyond the border city of Tijuana are the seaside resort towns of **Rosarito,** just 18 miles south of Tijuana, and **Ensenada,** 42 miles farther south. About 10 miles south of Rosarito you'll find the former fishing hamlet of **Puerto Nuevo,** now a kind of lobster-meal Disneyland, with more than 30 restaurants—all serving the same thing; northeast of Ensenada is the **Valle de Guadalupe,** Mexico's wine country. Discounts on lodging, dining, and shopping are available from both the Rosarito and Ensenada visitor bureaus; contact them at www.rosarito.org (© **800/962-2252**) and www.enjoyensenada.com (© **800/310-9687** from the U.S., 800/025-3991, or 646/178-8578). **Note:** Most U.S. auto insurance policies don't cover drivers or their vehicles south of Tijuana. Mexican auto insurance is advised, and avoid driving the highway at night when animals and other obstacles can't be seen. Also be aware that many businesses are cash only. You can visit Rosarito, Ensenada, and the wine coun-try on a tour, as well (see "Bus Tours," p. 256).

Two well-maintained roads link Tijuana and Puerto Nuevo: the scenic, coast-hugging toll road (marked *cuota* or 1-D; $3 at each of the three tollbooths between Tijuana and Ensenada) and the free but slower public road (marked *libre* or 1). Start out on the toll road, but cut over to the free road at the first Rosarito Beach exit so that you can stop and enjoy the view at a leisurely pace. This coastal area was once sparsely populated, but developers began exploiting the world-class ocean vistas here, and luxury condominiums—mostly snapped up by Americans—cropped up every-where. The ensuing real estate bust has led to a string of unsightly, unfinished proj-ects, the most notable of which was Donald Trump's Ocean Resort Baja that went bankrupt in 2009.

Once a tiny resort town that remained a secret despite its proximity to Tijuana, Rosarito developed explosively in the 1980s; it's now garish and congested beyond recognition. But it remains popular for a couple of reasons: 1) It's the first beach resort town south of the border, and 2) its reputation continues to lure visitors. For years, the **Rosarito Beach Hotel** (www.rosaritobeachhotel.com; © **866/767-2748** from the U.S., or 800/265-2322, 661/612-1111) was a hideaway for Hollywood celebrities, and it remains the most interesting place in town—check out its expert tile and woodwork, as well as the lobby's panoramic murals. The original owner's mansion is now home to a spa and a decadent gourmet restaurant, **Chabert's.** Not to be missed is the amaz-ingly tiled **Salon Quijote,** where you can escape for a quiet drink (the chandelier is rumored to have been a gift from gangster Al Capone). Sadly, the hotel fell victim to the post-millennial building craze, too, and unleashed a 17-story, 271-unit condo hotel that is monstrously out of proportion to its surroundings.

If you don't mind being a little outside of town, **Las Rocas Resort & Spa,** Km 38.5 (www.lasrocas.com; © **866/445-8909** from the U.S., 800/788-5648, or 661/614-9850), is a sweet spot with killer views—minus the crowds. It sits under the watchful gaze of a 70-foot Jesus that was built on a hilltop on the other side of the highway.

Bulevar Benito Juárez is Rosarito's main drag. The southern end is anchored by the Rosarito Beach Hotel; this is where you'll find all things touristic, including the rustic shopping arcade **Pueblo Plaza,** home to one of the city's best restaurants, **Susanna's** (www.susannasinrosarito.com; © **661/613-1187**). Also nearby is **Bazar de las Artesanías,** where you can get lost among the stalls of souvenirs, clothing, and gewgaws. The best shopping, though, is south of town along the free road, where there are several quality art galleries, as well as sellers of ceramics, wood furniture, and wrought-iron goods.

The big draws for young people are the enormous, thumping, beachfront clubs: **Papas & Beer** (www.rosarito.papasandbeer.com; ☏ **661/612-0444**), which also has a branch in Ensenada, and **Iggy's** (☏ **661/612-0537**). For dining, best bets include the very fun **El Nido,** Blvd. Benito Juárez 67 (www.elnidorosarito.net; ☏ **661/612-1430**), and the French **Bistro le Cousteau,** Blvd. Benito Juárez 184 (☏ **661/612-2655**); for a quick taco, head east off Benito Juárez on Calle de la Palma to **Tacos el Yaqui** (☏ **664/158-0537**). A few minutes' drive south of town is the **Hotel Calafia,** Km 35.5 (www.hotel-calafia.com; ☏ **661/614-9815** or 619/739-4343 from the U.S.). You can dine alfresco on tiered tables that overlook the ocean, but the surroundings outshine the food. There's also a chic wine bar, a small exhibit on Baja history, and a scale replica of a Spanish galleon for kids to clamber on.

From Rosarito, drive south and stop at **Puerto Nuevo,** a tiny, portless fishing village with more than 30 restaurants—all serving lobster in the local style: halved, grilled, and slathered in butter. Around 1952, the wives of fishermen started serving local lobsters from the kitchens of their simple shacks; many eventually built small dining rooms onto their homes or constructed restaurants. The result is a crustacean lover's paradise, where a feast of lobster, beans, rice, salsa, limes, and fresh tortillas costs $15 to $25. **Ortega's** is probably the oldest restaurant and has expanded to several locations in the village, including **Villa Ortega's** (☏ **661/614-0706** or 619/632-4875 from the U.S.), the most upscale spot in town, offering ocean views. Puerto Nuevo regulars prefer the smaller, family-run joints, though, such as **Sandra's** (☏ **661/614-1051**), **Puerto Nuevo Numero Uno** and **Dos** (☏ **661/614-1411** and **1454**), and **La Casa de la Langosta** (☏ **661/614-1072**), which also has an outpost in Rosarito. Alas, overfishing means there's now a lobster season, so if you come April through September you'll probably be eating imported crustaceans. The fishing town of **Popotla** also serves lobster and other seafood, in somewhat less commercial trappings; it's located just past the Xploration movie studio (once a tourist attraction, now closed to the public) and through the concrete arch. *Note:* Many small restaurants are closed Tuesdays.

About 10 miles farther south, roughly halfway between Rosarito and Ensenada at Km 59.5, is **La Fonda,** a beloved hotel, restaurant, and spa (www.lafondabaja.com; ☏ **646/155-0308**). The Sunday brunch is an orgy of food, everything from "paella to pancakes," washed down with free-flowing Bloody Marys. You can sit under thatched umbrellas on the tiled terrace overlooking the breaking surf; there's also a bar and easy access to the sandy beach below.

Continue your journey for several more miles to **Ensenada**—the drive is flat-out breathtaking. This port city of 150,000 offers good shopping, a friendly atmosphere, and some of the best fishing around (but no beaches). Deep-sea charters take visitors out on cruises for a chance to catch albacore, barracuda, and bonito. Ensenada also purports to be the birthplace of the fish taco.

The tourist area is compact and walkable; nearby is the harborside *malecón* (sea wall boardwalk), where you can rent fishing or sightseeing boats and grab a fish taco at the open-air fish market. You can put silver jewelry, leather goods, textiles, and folk art on your shopping list, too. The most interesting cultural attraction is the lovely **Riviera del Pacifico,** Boulevard Costero at Avenida Riviera (☏ **646/176-4233**), a former gambling palace that's been converted into a cultural center and museum with beautiful gardens.

When you're ready to take a break from touring, stop by **Bodegas de Santo Tomás,** Av. Miramar 666 (www.santo-tomas.com; ☏ **646/174-0829**), a historic winery open for tours and tastings. If you're in the mood for a beer—and even if you aren't—pay a visit to legendary **Hussong's Cantina,** Av. Ruiz 113 (www.cantina hussongs.com; ☏ **646/178-3210**), which opened for business in 1892, making it one of the oldest bars in the Californias. For the nicest meal in town, **El Rey Sol,** Av. López Mateos 1000 (www.elreysol.com; ☏ **646/178-1733**), has few competitors.

True to its name, **Hotel Misión Santa Isabel,** Blvd. Costero 1119 (www. hotelmisionsantaisabel.com; ☏ **619/825-0139** from the U.S. or 646/178-3616), is an attractive, mission-style lodging at the southern end of the tourist zone. It's affordably priced and within walking distance of all the action, but far away enough to be peaceful. **Las Rosas Hotel & Spa,** Km 105.5 (www.lasrosas.com; ☏ **866/447-6727** or 646/174-4310), offers more luxury, and has an enviable setting on the edge of Ensenada's huge Todos Santos bay. The only drawback is that it's 2 miles north of town.

About 20 miles south of Ensenada is **La Bufadora.** This ocean blowhole sprays a torrent of water high into the air with amazing force, often showering giggling onlookers who watch from observation decks. There are also numerous curios stands, restaurants, and bars here; you can get a taste of rural Mexico, too, as you drive along the highway, where roadside vendors sell nuts, tamales, and olives. To the northeast of Ensenada is the **Valle de Guadalupe,** Mexico's most important wine region, where some 20 wineries are making waves in the oenological world; tours and tastes are offered (see www.wineriesinbaja.com for more information). The valley is also the site of one of the finest restaurants on either side of the border, **Laja** (reservations required; www.lajamexico.com; ☏ **646/155-2556**). It's located at Km 83 along the Tecate-Ensenada highway. For overnight accommodations, contact Grupo Habita (www.grupohabita.mx) about the hotel company's new **Endémico Resguardo Silvestre,** a collection of architecturally dazzling modernist cabanas set on a 99-acre spread overlooking the valley.

PLANNING YOUR TRIP TO SAN DIEGO

This chapter contains all the practical information and logistical advice you need to make your travel arrangements a snap.

GETTING THERE

By Plane

San Diegans have a love-hate relationship with **San Diego International Airport** (www.san.org; © **619/231-2100**), also known as Lindbergh Field. The facility (airport code: SAN) is just 3 miles northwest of downtown, and the landing approach is right at the edge of the central business district. Pilots thread a passage between high-rise buildings and Balboa Park on their final descent to the runway—you'll get a great view on either side of the plane. The best part: We usually count the time from touchdown to gate-park in seconds, not minutes, and departures are rarely delayed for weather problems.

Lindbergh Field is the nation's busiest single-runway commercial airport—all 600 daily arrivals and departures use just one strip of asphalt. And while its dainty size makes it easy for travelers to navigate, its truncated facilities make it virtually unusable for international travel. Most overseas visitors arrive via Los Angeles or points east (**Air Canada, Volaris, Japan Airlines,** and **British Airways** are the only international carriers flying into San Diego). Domestically, the city is served by most national and regional airlines, although none utilize Lindbergh Field as a connecting hub. City officials are well aware of the critical need to enlarge or move the airport. Plans have ranged from a floating airport-at-sea (yes, really) to setting it in the Anza-Borrego Desert to conscripting Miramar Naval Air Station.

The latest plan calls for a build-out of the current site, and a facilities improvement of Terminal 2—dubbed "the Green Build" for its commitment to recycling and energy conservation—is presently underway. This $1-billion project, scheduled to be completed by 2013, includes a two-level roadway to separate traffic coming to pick up or drop off passengers, curbside check-in, 10 new gates, and additional shopping and dining options.

Planes land at Terminal 1 or 2, while the Commuter Terminal, a half-mile from the main terminals, is used by regional carriers **American Eagle** and **United Express,** and for connecting flights to Los Angeles (for flight info, contact the parent carriers). The Airport Loop shuttle provides free, 24-hour service from the main airport to the Commuter Terminal, or there's

LONG-HAUL FLIGHTS: HOW TO STAY
comfortable

o Your choice of airline and airplane will definitely affect your legroom. Find more details about U.S. airlines at www.seatguru.com. For international airlines, the research firm Skytrax has posted a list of average seat pitches at www.airlinequality.com.

o Emergency exit seats and bulkhead seats typically have the most legroom. Emergency exit seats are usually left unassigned until the day of a flight (to ensure that someone able-bodied fills the seats); it's worth checking in online at home (if the airline offers that option) or getting to the ticket counter early to snag one of these spots for a long flight. Many passengers find that bulkhead seating offers more legroom, but keep in mind that bulkhead seats have no storage space on the floor in front of them.

o To have two seats for yourself in a three-seat row, try for an aisle seat in a center section toward the back of the coach. If you're traveling with a companion, book an aisle and a window seat.

Middle seats are usually booked last, so chances are good you'll end up with three seats to yourselves. And in the event that a third passenger is assigned the middle seat, he or she will probably be more than happy to trade for a window or an aisle.

o To sleep, avoid the last row of any section or the row in front of an emergency exit, as these seats are the least likely to recline. Avoid seats near highly trafficked toilet areas. Avoid seats in the back of many jets—these can be narrower than those in the rest of coach. Or reserve a window seat so you can rest your head and avoid being bumped in the aisle.

o Get up, walk around, and stretch every 60 to 90 minutes to keep your blood flowing. This helps avoid **deep-vein thrombosis**, or "economy-class syndrome."

o Drink water before, during, and after your flight to combat the lack of humidity in airplane cabins. Avoid caffeine and alcohol, which will dehydrate you.

a footpath. General **information desks** with visitor materials, maps, and other services are near the baggage claim areas of both terminals 1 and 2. You can exchange foreign currency at **Travelex** (www.travelex.com) in Terminal 1, across from United check-in, and in Terminal 2, beyond security, near the food court. **Hotel reservation** and **car-rental courtesy phones** are in the baggage-claim areas of terminals 1 and 2.

If you are staying at a hotel in Carlsbad, Encinitas, or Rancho Santa Fe, the **McClellan-Palomar Airport** (www.sdcounty.ca.gov; © 877/848-7766 or 760/431-4646) in Carlsbad (CLD) may be a more convenient point of entry. The airport is 42 miles north of downtown San Diego and is served by **United Express** from Los Angeles.

Attention visitors to the U.S. from abroad: Some major airlines offer transatlantic or transpacific passengers special discount tickets under the name Visit USA, which allows mostly one-way travel from one U.S. destination to another at very low prices. Unavailable in the U.S., these discount tickets must be purchased abroad in conjunction with your international fare. This system is the easiest, fastest, cheapest way to see the country. Inquire with your air carrier.

ARRIVING AT THE AIRPORT

IMMIGRATION & CUSTOMS CLEARANCE   International visitors arriving by air, no matter what the port of entry, should cultivate patience and resignation before setting foot on U.S. soil. U.S. airports have considerably beefed up security clearances in the years since the terrorist attacks of September 11, 2001, and clearing Customs and Immigration can take as long as 2 hours.

GETTING INTO TOWN FROM THE AIRPORT

BY BUS   The **Metropolitan Transit System** (**MTS;** www.transit.511sd.com; ✆ **619/233-3004**) operates the San Diego Transit Flyer—bus route no. 992—providing service between the airport and downtown San Diego, running along Broadway. Bus stops are at each of Lindbergh Field's three terminals. The one-way fare is $2.25, and exact change is required. If you're connecting to another bus or the San Diego Trolley, you'll need to purchase a Day Pass; free transfers are no longer given. A 1-day pass is $5 and is available from the driver. The ride takes about 15 minutes, and buses come at 15-minute intervals.

At the **Transit Store,** 102 Broadway, at First Avenue (✆ **619/234-1060**), you can get information about greater San Diego's mass transit system (bus, rail, and ferry) and pick up passes, free brochures, route maps, and timetables. The store is open Monday to Friday, 9am to 5pm.

BY TAXI   Taxis line up outside terminals 1 and 2. The trip to a downtown location, usually a 10-minute ride, is about $15; budget $25 for Coronado or Mission Beach, and about $30 to $35 for La Jolla.

BY SHUTTLE   Several airport shuttles run regularly from the airport to points around the city; you'll see designated pickup areas outside each terminal. The shuttles are a good deal for single travelers; two or more people traveling together might as well take a taxi. The fare is about $8 per person to downtown hotels; Mission Valley and Mission Beach hotels are $12; La Jolla, $20; and Coronado hotels, $16. Rates to a residence are about $3 to $7 more than the above rates for the first person, with discounted rates for additional passengers. One company that serves all of San Diego County is **SuperShuttle** (www.supershuttle.com; ✆ **800/974-8885**).

BY CAR   If you're driving to downtown from the airport, take Harbor Drive south to Broadway, the main east-west thoroughfare, and turn left. To reach Hillcrest or Balboa Park, exit the airport toward I-5, and follow the signs for Laurel Street. To reach Mission Bay, take I-5 N. to I-8 W. To reach La Jolla, take I-5 N. to the La Jolla Parkway exit, bearing left onto Torrey Pines Road. For complete information on rental cars in San Diego, see "Car Rentals" later.

 Need a Lift into Town?

Remember to ask your hotel whether it has an **airport shuttle** from Lindbergh Field. Hotels often offer this service—usually free, sometimes for a nominal charge—and some also provide complimentary shuttles from the hotel to popular shopping and dining areas. Make sure the hotel knows when you're arriving, and get precise directions on where it will pick you up.

By Bus

Greyhound buses serve San Diego from downtown Los Angeles, Phoenix, Las Vegas, and other Southwestern cities, arriving at the downtown terminal, at 120 W. Broadway (www.greyhound.com; ℭ **800/231-2222** or 619/239-3266; 001/214-849-8100 outside the U.S.). A number of hotels, Horton Plaza, and the Gaslamp Quarter are within walking distance, as is the San Diego Trolley line. Buses from Los Angeles are as frequent as every hour, and the ride takes about 2½ hours. One-way fare is $24 and round-trips are $38. You can whittle the price down by purchasing nonrefundable tickets or by getting them in advance online. If you want to pay with cash, you can make an online reservation and pick up your ticket within 48 hours from a participating 7-Eleven convenience store.

Greyhound is the sole nationwide bus line. International visitors can obtain information about the **Greyhound North American Discovery Pass.** The pass can be obtained from foreign travel agents or through www.discoverypass.com for unlimited travel and stopovers in the U.S. and Canada.

By Car

Three main interstates lead into San Diego. **I-5** is the primary route from San Francisco, central California, and Los Angeles; it runs straight through downtown to the Tijuana border crossing. **I-8** cuts across California from points east such as Phoenix, terminating just west of I-5 at Mission Bay. **I-15** leads from the deserts to the north through inland San Diego; as you enter Miramar, take **Highway 163** south to reach the central parts of the city.

If you're planning a road trip, being a member of the **American Automobile Association (AAA)** offers helpful perks. Members who carry their cards with them not only receive free roadside assistance, but also have access to a wealth of free travel information (detailed maps and guidebooks). Also, many hotels and attractions throughout California offer discounts to AAA members—always inquire. Call ℭ **800/922-8228** or your local branch, or visit www.aaa-calif.com, for membership information.

Visitors driving to San Diego from Los Angeles and points north do so via coastal route I-5. From points northeast, take I-15 and link up with Highway 163 South as you enter Miramar (use I-8 W. for the beaches). From the east, use I-8 into the city, connecting to Highway 163 South for Hillcrest and downtown. Entering the downtown area, Highway 163 turns into 10th Avenue. If you are heading to Coronado, take the San Diego–Coronado Bay Bridge from I-5. Maximum speed in the San Diego area is 65 mph, and many areas are limited to 55 mph.

San Diego is 130 miles (2–3 hr.) from **Los Angeles;** 149 miles from **Palm Springs,** a 2½-hour trip; and 532 miles, or 9 to 10 hours, from **San Francisco.**

For information on car rentals and gasoline (petrol), see "By Car," in the "Getting Around" section, to follow.

By Train

Trains from all points in the United States and Canada will take you to Los Angeles, where you'll need to change trains for the journey to San Diego. You'll arrive at San Diego's Santa Fe Station (ℭ **619/239-9021**), downtown at the west end of Broadway, between Pacific Highway and Kettner Boulevard. It's within walking distance to many downtown hotels and the Embarcadero. Taxis line up outside the main door,

TRAVELING WITH pets

Many of us wouldn't dream of going on vacation without our pets. And these days, more and more lodgings and restaurants are going the pet-friendly route. The **Loews Coronado Bay Resort** (p. 215), **W San Diego** (p. 193), **Hotel Indigo** (p. 189), and **Hotel Solamar**, in particular, go out of their way to welcome pets. Many San Diegans congregate with their canine friends at **Dog Beach,** at the north end of Ocean Beach, where dogs can swim, play, and socialize. After your pooch is thoroughly coated in seawater and sand, take him to the do-it-yourself **Dog Beach Dog Wash,** 2 blocks away at 4933 Voltaire St. (www.dogwash.com; 🕿 **619/523-1700**). Nate's Point in Balboa Park is another favored place to let your pooch run loose. It's at the west end of the park, on the south side of Cabrillo Bridge.

Good resources include www.pets welcome.com, which dispenses medical tips, names of animal-friendly lodgings and campgrounds, and lists of kennels and veterinarians; as well as www. pettravel.com and www.travelpets.com.

If you plan to fly with your pet, a list of requirements for transporting live animals is available at **http://airconsumer. ost.dot.gov/publications/animals.htm**. You may be able to carry your pet on board a plane if that pet is small enough to put inside a carrier that can slip under the seat. Pets usually count as one piece of carry-on luggage. The ASPCA discourages travelers from checking pets as luggage at any time, as storage conditions on planes are loosely monitored, and fatal accidents are not unprecedented. Your other option is to ship your pet with a professional carrier, which can be expensive. Ask your vet whether you should sedate your pet on a plane ride or give it anti-nausea medication. Never give your pet sedatives used by humans.

the trolley station is across the street, and a dozen local bus routes stop on Broadway or Pacific Coast Highway, 1 block away.

Amtrak (www.amtrak.com; 🕿 **800/872-7245;** 001/215-856-7953 outside the U.S.) trains run between downtown Los Angeles and San Diego 12 times daily each way. Stops include Anaheim (Disneyland), Santa Ana, San Juan Capistrano, Oceanside, and Solana Beach. Two trains per day also stop in San Clemente. The travel time from Los Angeles to San Diego is about 2 hours and 45 minutes (for comparison, driving time can be as little as 2 hr., or as much as 4 hr. if traffic is snarled). A one-way ticket to San Diego is $36, or $51 for a reserved seat in business class.

International visitors can buy a **USA Rail Pass,** good for 15, 30, or 45 days of unlimited travel on Amtrak. The pass is available online or through many overseas travel agents. See Amtrak's website for the cost of travel within the western, eastern, or northwestern United States. Reservations are generally required and should be made as early as possible. Regional rail passes are also available.

By Boat

San Diego's **B Street Cruise Ship Terminal** is at 1140 N. Harbor Dr., right at the edge of downtown (www.sandiegocruiseport.; 🕿 **800/854-2757** or 619/686-6200). Carnival Cruise Lines (www.carnival.com; 🕿 **800/764-7419**) counts San Diego as a year-round home port, while several others, including Holland America Line (www. hollandamerica.com; 🕿 **877/932-4259**), Royal Caribbean (🕿 **866/562-7625;** www.royalcaribbean.com), and Celebrity (www.celebritycruises.com; 🕿 **800/647-2251**) make seasonal stops here.

SPECIAL-INTEREST TRIPS & TOURS

Adventure & Wellness Trips

Surrounded by ocean, mountains, and desert, San Diego's prime location makes quick getaways to commune with nature a snap. For organized tours of the region, two great resources are the **San Diego Natural History Museum** (p. 53) and the **Birch Aquarium at Scripps** (p. 62). Each offers guided outings, such as day hikes or grunion hunts (p. 180), as well as multiday excursions, including trips to the desert or to the Pacific gray whale breeding lagoons in Baja California.

In the Anza-Borrego Desert, **California Overland** (p. 251) will guide you through otherworldly landscapes on trips lasting anywhere from a few hours to 2 days. They provide all the gear and do all the cooking on the overnight trips—all you have to do is sit back and enjoy the campfire and the spectacular display of stars overhead.

For an unforgettable immersion in Baja wilderness (but with plenty of creature comforts), check out **Baja Airventures** (www.bajaairventures.com; ✆ 800/221-9283), which will fly you in a small plane from San Diego to remote parts of the Baja peninsula for personalized tours that can encompass fishing, surfing, snorkeling, kayaking, or just snoozing in a hammock. For something a little more terrifying, **San Diego Shark Diving Expeditions, Inc.** (www.sdsharkdiving.com; ✆ 619/299-8560) will dangle you in a shark cage in the waters off Mexico's Guadalupe Island as great white sharks circle. These 5-day trips are for certified divers only.

Stateside, **Hike Bike Kayak** (p. 79) is a one-stop shop for outdoor activities in San Diego. You can arrange everything from a surfing lesson to exploring La Jolla's sea caves via kayak (you can even set up a full-day, three-sport combo package).

The region is also home to a number of wellness spas, including **Rancho La Puerta,** which was founded in 1940 just across the border in Tecate, Mexico. This groundbreaking venture pioneered the concept of the destination spa, where feel-good massages take a back seat to mind-and-body workouts.

Holistic guru Deepak Chopra has also set up shop in San Diego with his **Chopra Center for Wellbeing,** located at La Costa Resort and Spa. Here you'll find an array of classes and treatments, as well as a gift shop. At **Warner Springs Ranch** in the Cleveland National Forest, you can soak in the healthful mineral water, and also enjoy horseback riding, golf, and hiking (all at a fraction of the cost of the upscale wellness resorts). For more information on San Diego's healthful havens, see p. 212.

Food & Wine Trips

San Diego is adjacent to two prolific wine regions: Temecula Valley to the north, just across the Riverside County line, and to the south, the Valle de Guadalupe, where you will find Mexico's most important wineries. Either makes for an easy day trip, with plenty of overnight options, as well. For more information on Temecula, see p. 241; for tours to Mexico's wine country, see p. 256. You can also sample some of San Diego's renowned beers without having to worry about a designated driver. **Brew Hop** and **Brewery Tours of San Diego** can guide you to the city's top brewers. See p. 176.

You can combine food, wine, and local history with walking tours from **So Diego Tours** (www.sodiegotours.com; ✆ 619/233-8687) and **Bite San Diego** (www.bitesandiego.com; ✆ 619/634-8476). Each offer nighttime restaurant and bar crawls through neighborhoods such as Old Town, Little Italy, the Gaslamp Quarter, and Hillcrest.

Great News!, 1788 Garnet Ave., Pacific Beach (www.great-news.com; ✆ 888/478-2433 or 858/270-1582), has been a fixture in San Diego since 1977. Cooking classes in the state-of-the-art kitchen run the seasonal and ethnic gamut; plus they sell just about any piece of cookware or food gadget you could ever want. In La Jolla, **Cups,** 7857 Girard Ave. (www.cupslj.com; ✆ 858/459-2877), is a stylish "cupcakery" selling organic, gluten-free treats. It also offers a variety of hands-on classes that cover anything from pickling to preparing a low-fat Passover meal.

Guided Tours

Escorted tours are structured group tours, with a group leader. The price usually includes everything from airfare to hotels, meals, tours, admission costs, and local transportation.

Collette Tours (www.collettevacations.com; ✆ 800/340-5158), **Globus** (www.globusjourneys.com; ✆ 866/755-8581), and **Tauck World Discovery** (www.tauck.com; ✆ 800/788-7885) each offer California coastal tours that hit the state's highlights, from San Francisco to San Diego.

Walking Tours

San Diego's distinct neighborhoods lend themselves to exploration by foot, and there are plenty of options for guided walking tours, many of them free.

You can learn the history of the vibrant Gaslamp Quarter with a Saturday morning tour from the **Gaslamp Quarter Historical Foundation,** while **Walkabout International** offers dozens of free walking tours all across the county, including wilderness hikes. The **San Diego Natural History Museum** is another great resource for free guided nature hikes; and at sublime parks such as Torrey Pines State Reserve, Cabrillo National Monument, and Mission Trails Regional Park, rangers also lead regularly scheduled walks. For more information, see p. 75.

GETTING AROUND

By Car

Traffic woes have increased over the years, but San Diego is still easy to navigate by car. Most downtown streets run one-way, in a grid pattern. However, outside downtown, canyons and bays often make streets indirect. Finding a parking space can be tricky in the Gaslamp Quarter, Old Town, Mission Beach, and La Jolla, but parking lots are often centrally located. Rush hour on the freeways is generally concentrated from 7 to 9am and 4:30 to 6pm.

You won't have any trouble finding a gas station—they are everywhere (and almost all accept credit cards). Be aware that San Diego's gas prices are often among the highest in the country; as of this writing they were topping out at more than $4 per gallon (one U.S. gallon equals 3.8 liters or .85 imperial gallons, and taxes are already included in the printed price).

Also, generally speaking, San Diegans are not the best drivers in the rain—vehicles careening out of control during the rare wet weather keep the Highway Patrol and local news channels very busy. For up-to-the-minute traffic info, dial ✆ 511.

Note on driving to Mexico: If you plan to drive to Mexico, be sure to check with your insurance company at home to verify exactly the limits of your policy. Even if your insurance covers areas south of the border, you may want to purchase Mexican car insurance because of the two countries' different liability standards. Mexican car insurance is available from various agencies (visible to drivers heading into Mexico) on the U.S. side of the border.

MAIN ARTERIES & STREETS

It's not hard to find your way around downtown San Diego. Most streets run one-way, in a grid pattern. First through Eleventh avenues run north and south—odd-number avenues are northbound, even numbers run south; A through K streets alternate running east and west. Broadway (the equivalent of D St.) runs both directions, as do Market Street and Harbor Drive. North of A Street, the east-west streets bear the names of trees, in alphabetical order: Ash, Beech, Cedar, Date, and so on. Harbor Drive runs past the airport and along the waterfront, which is known as the Embarcadero. Ash Street and Broadway are the downtown arteries that connect with Harbor Drive.

The Coronado Bay Bridge leading to Coronado is accessible from I-5, south of downtown, and I-5 North leads to Old Town, Mission Bay, La Jolla, and North County coastal areas. Balboa Park (home of the San Diego Zoo), Hillcrest, and Uptown areas lie north of downtown San Diego. The park and zoo are easily reached by way of Park Boulevard (which would otherwise be 12th Ave.), which leads to the parking lots. Fifth Avenue leads to Hillcrest. Highway 163, which heads north from 11th Avenue, leads into Mission Valley.

CORONADO   The main streets are Orange Avenue, where most of the hotels and restaurants are clustered, and Ocean Drive, which follows Coronado Beach.

DOWNTOWN   The major thoroughfares are Broadway (a major bus artery), Fourth and Fifth avenues (which run south and north, respectively), C Street (the trolley line), and Harbor Drive, which curls along the waterfront and passes the Maritime Museum, Seaport Village, the Convention Center, and PETCO Park.

HILLCREST   The main streets are University Avenue and Washington Street (both two-way, running east and west), and Fourth and Fifth avenues (both one-way, running south and north, respectively).

LA JOLLA   The principal streets are Prospect Street and Girard Avenue, which are perpendicular to each other. The main routes in and out of La Jolla are La Jolla Boulevard (running south to Mission Beach) and Torrey Pines Road (leading to I-5).

MISSION VALLEY   I-8 runs east-west along the valley's southern perimeter; Highway 163, I-805, and I-15 run north-south through the valley. Hotel Circle is an elongated loop road that parallels either side of I-8 to the west of Highway 163; Friars Road is the major artery on the north side of the valley.

PACIFIC BEACH   Mission Boulevard is the main drag, parallel to and 1 block in from the beach, and perpendicular to it are Grand and Garnet avenues. East and West Mission Bay drives encircle most of the bay, and Ingraham Street cuts through the middle of it.

DRIVING RULES

San Diegans are relatively respectful drivers, although admittedly they often speed and sometimes lose patience with those who don't know their way around.

California has a **seat-belt law for both drivers and passengers,** so buckle up before you venture out. State law requires drivers to use **hands-free cellphone technology** (drivers age 17 and under cannot use a cellphone at all); **text messaging while driving** is also illegal. The first-offense fine for both is $20. **Smoking in a car with a child** age 17 and under is punishable by a $100 fine; an officer cannot pull

Street-parking rules are color-coded throughout the city. A **red curb** means no stopping at any time. **Blue curbs** are used to denote parking for people with disabilities—the fine for parking in these spaces without a distinguishing placard or a disabled license plate is $400 (out-of-state disabled plates are okay). A **white-painted curb** signifies a passenger loading zone; the time limit is 3 minutes, or 10 minutes in front of a hotel. A **yellow curb** is a commercial loading zone—which means that between 6am and 6pm Monday through Saturday, trucks and commercial vehicles are allowed 20 minutes to load or unload goods, *and* passenger vehicles can unload passengers for 3 minutes (from 6pm–6am and all day Sun, anyone can park in a yellow curb zone, though some yellow zones are in effect 24 hours—be sure to check any nearby signage). A **green curb** designates short-term parking only—usually 15 or 30 minutes (as posted). Unpainted curbs are subject to parking rules on signs or meters.

you over for this, but can tack it onto another infraction. You may **turn right at a red light after stopping** unless a sign says otherwise; likewise, you can turn left on a red light from a one-way street onto another one-way street after coming to a full stop. **Pedestrians have the right of way at all times,** not just in crosswalks, so stop for pedestrians who have stepped off the curb. Penalties in California for **drunk driving** are among the toughest in the country. Speed limits on freeways, particularly Highway 8 through Mission Valley, are aggressively enforced after dark, partly as a pretext for nabbing drivers who might have imbibed. Also beware of main beach arteries (Grand Ave., Garnet Ave., and Mission Blvd.). Traffic enforcement can be strict—random checkpoints set up to catch drunk drivers are not uncommon.

PARKING

Metered parking spaces are found in downtown, Hillcrest, and the beach communities, but demand outpaces supply. Posted signs indicate operating hours—generally Monday through Saturday from 8am to 6pm. Be prepared with several dollars in quarters—some meters take no other coin, and 25¢ usually buys only 12 minutes, even on a 2-hour meter. In the downtown and Hillcrest areas the city is also experimenting with meters that use wireless technology and will accept credit cards. There is one meter per block, so after you get your receipt, return to your car and place it on the vehicle's dashboard.

Most unmetered areas have signs restricting street parking to 1 or 2 hours; count on vigilant chalking and ticketing during the regulated hours. Three-hour meters line Harbor Drive opposite the ticket offices for harbor tours; even on weekends, you have to feed them. If you can't find a metered space, there are plenty of hourly lots downtown. Parking in Mission Valley is usually within large parking structures and free, though congested on weekends—particularly leading up to the winter holidays.

Downtown parking structures on Sixth Avenue (at Market and K sts.) have helped ease parking issues, but it's still a challenge. Of special concern are game nights—and days—at PETCO Park (Apr–Sept). Unless you're staying downtown or want to attend the game, it's best to avoid the baseball traffic and head elsewhere for dining or nightlife.

STREET MAPS

The Convention & Visitors Bureau's **International Visitor Information Center,** 1140 N. Harbor Dr., along the downtown Embarcadero (www.sandiego.org; © 619/236-1212), provides an illustrated pocket map. Also available are maps of the 59-mile scenic drive around San Diego, the Gaslamp Quarter, Tijuana, San Diego's public transportation, and a "Campgrounds and Recreation" map for the county.

The **Automobile Club of Southern California** has 10 San Diego offices (www. aaa-calif.com; © 619/233-1000). It distributes great maps, which are free to AAA members and to members of many international auto clubs, and it sells auto insurance for those driving within Mexico.

Car-rental outfits usually offer maps of the city that show the freeways and major streets, and hotels often provide complimentary maps of the downtown area. You can buy maps of the city and vicinity at the retail stores listed under "Travel Accessories," in chapter 7. The **Transit Store,** 102 Broadway, at First Avenue (© 619/234-1060), is a storehouse of bus and trolley maps, with a friendly staff on duty to answer specific questions.

If you're moving to San Diego or plan an extended stay, the *Thomas Guide* (www. thomasmaps.com) is all-encompassing, deciphering San Diego County street by street. It's available online for $17; you can also pick it up at bookstores, drugstores, and large supermarkets.

CAR RENTALS

Those staying downtown will find plenty to see and do without having to rent a vehicle; Balboa Park, Old Town, even Tijuana are within easy reach with public transportation. In just about all other parts of San Diego, though, you will probably want your own set of wheels. You *can* reach virtually all sights of interest using public transportation, but the distances between attractions and indirect bus routes usually make it a very time-consuming proposition.

All the major car-rental firms have an office at the airport, and several have them in larger hotels. *Note for Mexico-bound car renters:* Some companies, including Avis, will allow their cars into Mexico as far as Ensenada, but other rental outfits won't allow you to drive south of the border. Drivers between the ages of 21 (the minimum-age requirement for most companies) and 24 will most likely pay an additional surcharge; few companies have upper-age limits.

If you're visiting from abroad and plan to rent a car in the United States, keep in mind that foreign driver's licenses are usually recognized in the U.S., but you may want to get an international one if your home license is not in English. International visitors should also note that insurance and taxes are almost never included in quoted rental-car rates in the U.S. Be sure to ask your rental agency about additional fees for these. They can add a significant cost to your car rental.

Check out **Autoslash.com** or **Breezenet.com,** which can land you car-rental discounts with some of the most competitive rates around. Also worth visiting are **Orbitz.com, Hotwire.com, Travelocity.com,** or **Priceline.com,** all of which offer competitive online car-rental rates.

Saving Money on a Rental Car

Car-rental rates vary even more dramatically than airline fares. Prices depend on the size of the car, where and when you pick it up and drop it off, the length of the rental period, where and how far you drive it, whether you buy insurance, and a host of other factors. A few key questions could save you hundreds of dollars:

- Are weekend rates lower than weekday rates? Ask if the rate is the same for pickup Friday morning, for instance, as it is for Thursday night.
- Does the agency assess a drop-off charge if you don't return the car to the same location where you picked it up?
- Are special promotional rates available? If you see an advertised price in your local newspaper, be sure to ask for that specific rate; otherwise, you may be charged the standard cost.
- Are discounts available for members of AARP, AAA, frequent-flyer programs, or trade unions?
- How much tax will be added to the rental bill? Local tax? State use tax?
- How much does the rental company charge to refill your gas tank if you return with the tank less than full? Though most rental companies claim these prices are competitive, fuel is almost always cheaper in town.

Demystifying Renter's Insurance

Before you drive off in a rental car, be sure you're insured. Hasty assumptions about your personal auto insurance or a rental agency's additional coverage could end up costing you tens of thousands of dollars, even if you're involved in an accident that was clearly the fault of another driver.

If you already hold a **private auto insurance** policy, you're most likely covered in the United States for loss of or damage to a rental car and liability in case of injury to any other party involved in an accident. Be sure to find out whether you're covered in the area you're visiting, whether your policy extends to everyone who will be driving the car, how much liability is covered in case an outside party is injured in an accident, and whether the type of vehicle you are renting is included under your contract. (Rental trucks, SUVs, and luxury vehicles or sports cars may not be covered.)

Most **major credit cards** (especially gold and platinum cards) provide some degree of coverage as well, provided they're used to pay for the rental. Terms vary widely, however, so be sure to call your credit card company directly before you rent.

If you're **uninsured,** your credit card will probably provide primary coverage as long as you decline the rental agency's insurance and as long as you rent with that card. This means that the credit card will cover damage or theft of a rental car for the full cost of the vehicle. (In a few states, however, theft is not covered; ask specifically about state law where you will be renting and driving.) If you already have insurance, your credit card will provide secondary coverage, which basically covers your deductible.

Note: Though they may cover damage to your rental car, *credit cards will not cover liability,* or the cost of injury to an outside party, damage to an outside party's vehicle, or both. If you do not hold an insurance policy, you may seriously want to consider purchasing additional liability insurance from your rental company, even if you decline collision coverage. Be sure to check the terms, however. Some rental agencies cover liability only if the renter is not at fault; even then, the rental company's obligation varies from state to state.

The basic insurance coverage offered by most car-rental companies, known as the **Loss Damage Waiver (LDW)** or **Collision Damage Waiver (CDW),** can cost as much as $20 a day. It usually covers the full value of the vehicle with no deductible if an outside party causes an accident or other damage to the rental car. Liability coverage varies according to the company policy and state law, but the minimum is usually at least $15,000. If you are at fault in an accident, you will be covered for the full replacement value of the car, but not for liability. Some states allow you to buy additional liability coverage for such cases. Most rental companies will require a

Day Passes allow unlimited rides on MTS (bus) and trolley routes. Passes are good for 2, 3, and 4 consecutive days, and cost $9, $12, and $15, respectively. Multiday passes are for sale at the Transit Store and all trolley station automated ticket vending machines (bus drivers sell 1-day passes only). See www.transit.511sd. com or call (✆ **619/234-1060** for more information.

police report to process any claims you file, but your private insurer will not be notified of the accident.

By Train

San Diego's express rail commuter service, the **Coaster**, travels between the downtown Santa Fe Depot station and the Oceanside Transit Center, with stops at Old Town, Sorrento Valley, Solana Beach, Encinitas, and Carlsbad. Fares range from $4 to $5.50 each way, depending on how far you go, and can be paid by cash or credit card at vending machines at each station. Eligible seniors and riders with disabilities pay $2 to $2.75; ages 5 and under are free. The scenic trip between downtown San Diego and Oceanside takes 1 hour. Trains run Monday through Friday from about 6:30am (5:30am heading south from Oceanside) to 7pm, with four trains in each direction on weekends; log on to www.transit.511sd.com, or call (✆ **800/262-7837** or 511 (TTY/TDD 888/722-4889) for the current schedule.

Amtrak (www.amtrak.com; (✆ **800/872-7245**) trains head north to Los Angeles about 12 times daily each way. Stops include Solana Beach, Oceanside, San Juan Capistrano, Santa Ana, and Anaheim (Disneyland). Two trains per day also stop in San Clemente. A one-way ticket from San Diego to Solana Beach is $12; to Oceanside, $17; to San Clemente, $20; to San Juan Capistrano, $21; and to Anaheim, $27.

The **Sprinter** rail service runs west to east alongside Highway 78, from Oceanside to Escondido. The Sprinter operates Monday through Friday from about 4am to 9pm daily, with service every 30 minutes in both directions. On weekends, trains run every half-hour from 10am to 6pm, with hourly service before and after those times. Basic one-way fare is $2; $1 for seniors and travelers with disabilities.

By Public Transportation
BY BUS

The **MTS Transit Store**, 102 Broadway at First Avenue ((✆ **619/234-1060**), dispenses passes, tokens, timetables, maps, brochures, and lost-and-found information. It issues ID cards for seniors 60 and older, as well as for travelers with disabilities—all of whom pay $1.10 per ride. Request a copy of the useful brochure *Fun Places by Bus & Trolley*, which details the city's most popular tourist attractions and the public transportation that will take you to them. The office is open Monday through Friday from 9am to 5pm.

San Diego has an adequate bus system that will get you to where you're going—eventually. Most drivers are friendly and helpful; on local routes, bus stops are marked by rectangular red, white, and black signs every other block or so, farther apart on express routes. Most bus **fares** are $2.25. Buses accept dollar bills and coins, but drivers can't give change. Transfers are no longer issued, so if you need to make a connection with another bus or trolley, purchase a $5 day pass from the driver, at the Transit Store, or from the trolley station ticket vending machine. It gives you unlimited use of most bus and trolley routes for the rest of the service day.

For assistance with route information from a living, breathing entity, call MTS at ☎ 619/233-3004. You can also view timetables, maps, and fares online—and learn how the public transit system accommodates travelers with disabilities—at www.transit.511sd.com. If you know your route and just need schedule information—or automated answers to FAQs—call **Info Express** (☎ 619/685-4900) from any touch-tone phone, 24 hours a day.

Some of the most popular tourist attractions served by bus and rail routes are:

- Balboa Park west entrance: Routes 1, 3, and 120
- Balboa Park east entrances and San Diego Zoo: Route 7
- SeaWorld: Route 9
- Cabrillo National Monument: Route 84
- Seaport Village: San Diego Trolley Orange Line
- Qualcomm Stadium: San Diego Trolley Green Line (plus special event Red Line service from downtown)
- Tijuana: San Diego Trolley Blue Line
- San Diego International Airport: Route 992
- Convention Center: San Diego Trolley Orange Line
- PETCO Park: Routes 3, 4, 5, 11, 901, 929; San Diego Trolley Orange and Blue lines (plus special event Red Line service from Qualcomm Stadium)
- Coronado: Route 901 or Bay Ferry
- Gaslamp Quarter and Horton Plaza: most downtown bus routes and San Diego Trolley Blue and Orange lines
- Old Town: Routes 8, 9, 10, 28, 30, 35, 44, 88, 105, 150; San Diego Trolley Blue and Green lines; and the Coaster

The Coronado Shuttle, bus no. 904, runs between the Marriott Coronado Island Resort and the Old Ferry Landing, and then continues along Orange Avenue to the Hotel del Coronado, Glorietta Bay, and back again. No. 901 goes all the way to Coronado from San Diego.

When planning your route, note that schedules vary and most buses do not run all night. Some stop at 6pm, while other lines continue to 9pm, midnight, or 2am; budget cuts have also reduced Sunday service—ask your bus driver for more specific information.

The privately owned bus tours operated by **Old Town Trolley Tours** (p. 75) and **Vizit Tours** (p. 75) are also an excellent way to get around much of the city during a short visit. Both are narrated sightseeing tours, but you can disembark at various points and join up later with the next passing group.

BY TROLLEY

Although the system is too limited for most San Diegans to use for work commutes, the San Diego Trolley is great for visitors, particularly if you're staying downtown or plan to visit Tijuana. There are three routes. The **Blue Line** is the one that is the handiest for most visitors: It travels from the Mexican border (San Ysidro) north through downtown and Old Town. The **Orange Line** runs from downtown east through Lemon Grove and El Cajon. The **Green Line** runs from Old Town through Mission Valley to Qualcomm Stadium, San Diego State University, and on to Santee. The trip to the border crossing takes about 50 minutes from downtown; from downtown to Old Town takes 10 to 15 minutes. For a route map, see the inside front cover of this guide. *Note:* The trolley system is being upgraded with new vehicles that require construction of different platforms; some stations may be closed on weekends (shuttle buses will service shuttered stations). When the upgrades are completed in 2015, the Green Line will be extended to downtown.

Trolleys operate on a self-service fare-collection system; riders buy tickets from machines in stations before boarding (some machines require exact change). It's a flat fare of $2.50 for travel between any two stations; a $5 day pass is also available, good for all trolley trips and most bus routes. Fare inspectors board trains at random to check tickets.

The lines run every 15 minutes during the day and every 30 minutes at night; during peak weekday rush hours the Blue Line runs every 10 minutes. There is also expanded service to accommodate events at PETCO Park and Qualcomm Stadium. Trolleys stop at each station for only 30 seconds. To open the door for boarding, push the lighted green button; to open the door to exit the trolley, push the lighted white button.

For recorded transit information, call ✆ 619/685-4900. To speak with a customer service representative, call ✆ 619/233-3004 (TTY/TDD 619/234-5005) daily from 5:30am to 8:30pm. For wheelchair lift info, call ✆ 619/595-4960. The trolley generally operates daily from 4 or 5am to about midnight; the Blue Line provides service until 1am; check the website at www.transit.511sd.com for details.

BY TAXI

Half a dozen taxi companies serve the area. Rates are based on mileage and can add up quickly in sprawling San Diego—a trip from downtown to La Jolla will cost about $30 to $35. Other than in the Gaslamp Quarter after dark, taxis don't cruise the streets as they do in other cities, so you have to call ahead for quick pickup; there are also cab stands at Horton Plaza (on Broadway Circle, in front of the Lyceum Theatre) and the zoo. If you're at a hotel or restaurant, the front-desk attendant or concierge will call one for you. Among the local companies are **Orange Cab** (✆ 619/291-3333), **San Diego Cab** (✆ 619/226-8294), and **Yellow Cab** (✆ 619/444-4444). The **Coronado Cab Company** (✆ 619/435-6211) serves Coronado. You can also just dial ✆ 511 and say "taxi" and you will be connected to a dispatcher. There is no pickup from Coronado or at the airport with this service (but you can be dropped off at those locations).

BY WATER

BY FERRY   There's regularly scheduled ferry service between San Diego and Coronado (www.flagshipsd.com; ✆ 800/442-7847 or 619/234-4111). Ferries leave from the Broadway Pier (1050 N. Harbor Dr., at the intersection with Broadway) and the Fifth Avenue Landing (600 Convention Way, located behind the Convention Center). Broadway Pier departures are scheduled daily on the hour from 9am to 9pm, and Friday and Saturday until 10pm. They return from the Ferry Landing in Coronado to the Broadway Pier Sunday through Thursday every hour on the half-hour from 9:30am to 9:30pm and Friday and Saturday until 10:30pm. Trips from the Convention Center depart about every 2 hours beginning at 9:25am, with the final departure at 8:25pm (10:25pm Fri and Sat); return trips out of Coronado begin at 9:17am, then run about every 2 hours thereafter until 8:17pm (10:17pm Fri and Sat). Commuter ferries depart from the Broadway Pier hourly from 5:15am to 8:10am. The ride takes 15 minutes. The fare is $4.25 each way; buy tickets at the Flagship (formerly known as San Diego Harbor Excursion) kiosk on Broadway Pier, the Fifth Avenue Landing, or at the Ferry Landing in Coronado (vending machines take cash or credit cards). The ferries do not accommodate cars; bikes are allowed.

BY WATER TAXI   Water taxis (www.flaghsipsd.com; ✆ **619/235-8294**) will pick you up from any dock around San Diego Bay and operate Sunday through Thursday from 9am to 9pm, and Friday and Saturday 9am to 11pm. If you're staying in a downtown hotel, this is a great way to get to Coronado. Boats are sometimes available at the spur of the moment, but reservations are advised. Fares are $7 per person to most locations.

By Bicycle

San Diego is ideal for exploration by bicycle, and many roads have designated bike lanes. Bikes are available for rent in most areas; see "Outdoor Activities," in chapter 4, for suggestions.

San Diego iCommute publishes a comprehensive map of the county detailing bike *paths* (for exclusive use by bicyclists), bike *lanes* (alongside motor vehicle ways), and bike *routes* (shared ways designated only by bike-symbol signs). The free **San Diego Regional Bike Map** is available online at www.511sd.com, or by calling ✆ **511** or 619/699-1900; it can also be found at visitor centers. **The San Diego County Bicycle Coalition** (www.sdcbc.org; ✆ **858/487-6063**) is also a great resource. For more in-depth information, track down *Cycling San Diego* by Nelson Copp and Jerry Schad.

It's possible to take your two-wheeler on the city's **public transportation.** For buses, let the driver know you want to stow your bike on the front of the bus, then board and pay the regular fare. The trolley also lets you bring your bike on the trolley for free. Bikers can board at any entrance *except* the first set of doors behind the driver; the bike-storage area is at the back of each car. The cars carry two bikes except during weekday rush hours, when the limit is one bike per car. For more information, call the **Transit Information Line** (✆ **619/233-3004**). Bikes are also permitted on the ferry connecting San Diego and Coronado, which has 15 miles of dedicated bike paths.

[FastFACTS] SAN DIEGO

Area Codes   San Diego's main area code is **619,** used primarily by downtown, uptown, Mission Valley, Point Loma, Coronado, La Mesa, El Cajon, and Chula Vista. The area code **858** is used for northern and coastal areas, including Mission Beach, Pacific Beach, La Jolla, Del Mar, Rancho Santa Fe, and Rancho Bernardo. Use **760** to reach the remainder of San Diego County, including Encinitas, Carlsbad, Oceanside, Escondido, Ramona, Julian, and Anza-Borrego.

Business Hours   Banks are open weekdays from 9am to 4pm or later, and sometimes Saturday morning. Stores in shopping malls tend to operate from 10 or 11am until about 9pm weekdays and until 6pm weekends, and are open on secondary holidays.

Car Rental   See "By Car," under "Getting There," earlier in this chapter.

Cellphones   See "Mobile Phones," later in this section.

Crime   See "Safety," later in this section.

Customs   Every visitor 21 years of age or older may bring in, free of duty, the following: (1) 1 U.S. quart of alcohol; (2) 200 cigarettes, 50 cigars (but not from Cuba), or 3 pounds of smoking tobacco; and (3) $100 worth of gifts. These exemptions are offered to travelers who spend at least 72 hours in the United States and who have not claimed them within the preceding 6 months. It is forbidden to bring into the country almost any meat products (including canned, fresh, and dried meat products such as bouillon, soup mixes, and so on). Generally, condiments including vinegars, oils, pickled goods, spices, coffee, tea, and some cheeses and baked goods are permitted. Avoid rice products, as rice can often harbor insects. Bringing fruits and vegetables is prohibited since they may harbor pests or disease. International visitors may carry in or out up to $10,000 in U.S. or foreign currency with no formalities; larger sums must be declared to U.S. Customs on entering or leaving, which includes filing form CM 4790. For details regarding U.S. Customs and Border Protection, consult your nearest U.S. embassy or consulate, or U.S. Customs (www.cbp.gov).

For information on what you're allowed to take home, contact one of the following agencies:

Canadian Citizens: Canada Border Services Agency, Ottawa, Ontario, K1A 0L8 (www.cbsa-asfc.gc.ca; ℂ **800/461-9999** in Canada, or 204/983-3500).

U.K. Citizens: HM Customs & Excise, Crownhill Court, Tailyour Road, Plymouth, PL6 5BZ (www.hmce.gov.uk; ℂ **0845/010-9000;** from outside the U.K., 020/8929-0152).

Australian Citizens: Australian Customs Service, Customs House, 5 Constitution Ave., Canberra City, ACT 2601 (www.customs.gov.au; ℂ **1300/363-263;** from outside Australia, 612/6275-6666).

New Zealand Citizens: New Zealand Customs, the Customhouse, 17–21 Whitmore St., P.O. Box 2218, Wellington, 6140 (ℂ **04/473-6099** or 0800/428-786; www.customs.govt.nz).

Disabled Travelers   Most disabilities shouldn't stop anyone from traveling in the United States. There are more options and resources out there than ever before, and San Diego is one of the most accessible cities in the country. Most of the city's major attractions are wheelchair friendly, including the walkways and museums of Balboa Park, the San Diego Zoo (which has bus tours to navigate the steep canyons), SeaWorld, the Zoo Safari Park, and downtown's Gaslamp Quarter. Old Town and the beaches require a little more effort, but are generally accessible.

Manual wheelchairs with balloon tires are available free of charge daily at the main lifeguard stations in Ocean Beach, Mission Beach, Pacific Beach, La Jolla, and Del Mar, among others. Beach conditions permitting, the Mission Beach, Coronado, and Oceanside lifeguard stations have electric wheelchairs available. Mission Beach hours are daily (except Tues) 11:30am to 4:30pm from May through October, and Friday to Sunday, 11:30am to 3:30pm, from November through April (ℂ **619/525-8247** or 619/980-0275). For Coronado information call ℂ **619/435-0126;** for Del Mar, ℂ **858/755-1556;** and for Oceanside, ℂ **760/435-4018.**

Obtain more specific information from **Accessible San Diego** (www.asd.travel; ℂ **619/325-7550**), the nation's oldest center for information for travelers with disabilities. The center has an info line that helps travelers find accessible hotels, tours, attractions, and transportation. The annual *Access in San Diego* pamphlet, a citywide guide with specifics on which establishments are accessible for those with visual, mobility, or hearing disabilities can be ordered online for $5; a downloadable version can be purchased for $3.

On buses and trolleys, riders with disabilities pay a fixed fare of $1.10. Because discounted fares are subsidized, *technically* you must obtain a Transit Travel ID from the **Transit Store** (ℂ **619/234-1060**); the ID card certifies that a rider is eligible for the discount, but most drivers use visual qualifications to establish criteria. All MTS buses and trolleys are equipped with wheelchair lifts; priority seating is available on buses and trolleys. People with visual impairments benefit from the white reflecting ring that circles the bottom of the trolley door to increase its visibility. Airport transportation for travelers with disabilities is available in vans holding one or two wheelchairs from **SuperShuttle** (www.supershuttle.com; ℂ **800/974-8885** or 858/974-8885, TDD 866/472-4497).

The America the Beautiful: National Parks and Federal Recreational Lands Access Pass (formerly the **Golden Access Passport**) gives visually impaired travelers or travelers with permanent disabilities (regardless of age) free lifetime entrance to federal recreation sites administered by the National Park Service, including the Fish and Wildlife Service, the Forest Service, the Bureau of Land Management, and the Bureau of Reclamation. This may include national parks, monuments, historic sites, recreation areas, and national wildlife refuges.

The America the Beautiful Access Pass can be obtained in person at any NPS facility that charges an entrance fee. You need to show proof of a medically determined disability; you can also order the pass online (www.nps.gov/fees_passes.htm) and receive it by mail ($10 processing fee). Besides free entry, the pass also offers a 50% discount on some federal-use fees charged for such facilities as camping, swimming, parking, boat launching, and tours. For more information call the United States Geological Survey (USGS), which issues the passes, at ✆ **888/275-8747.**

Organizations that offer a vast range of resources and assistance to travelers with disabilities include **MossRehab** (www.mossresourcenet.org; ✆ **800/225-5667**), the **American Foundation for the Blind** (www.afb.org; ✆ **800/232-5463**), and the **Society for Accessible Travel & Hospitality** (www.sath.org; ✆ **212/447-7284**). Air Ambulance Card (✆ **877/424-7633** or 205/297-0060; www.airambulancecard.com) will fly you home to the hospital of your choice if you need medical assistance while traveling; plans start at $195 per year.

Many travel agencies offer customized tours and itineraries for travelers with disabilities. Among them are **Flying Wheels Travel** (www.flyingwheelstravel.com; ✆ **877/451-5006** or 507/451-5005) and **Accessible Journeys** (www.disabilitytravel.com; ✆ **800/846-4537** or 610/521-0339).

British travelers should contact **Tourism for All** (www.tourismforall.org.uk; ✆ **0845-124-9971** in the U.K. only) to access a wide range of travel information and resources for seniors and those with disabilities.

Doctors   In a life-threatening situation, dial ✆ **911.** For a doctor referral, contact the **San Diego County Medical Society** (www.sdcms.org; ✆ **858/565-8888**) or **Scripps Health** (www.scripps.org; ✆ **800/727-4777**). For dental referrals, contact the **San Diego County Dental Society** at ✆ **800/201-0244** or 619/275-0244 (www.sdcds.org), or call ✆ **800/DENTIST** (336-8478 or 855/294-9614; www.1800dentist.com). Also see "Hospitals," below.

Drinking Laws   The legal age for purchase and consumption of alcoholic beverages in California is 21. **Proof of age is a necessity**—it's requested at bars, nightclubs, and restaurants, even from those well into their 30s and 40s, so always bring ID when you go out. Beer, wine, and hard liquor are sold daily from 6am to 2am and are available in grocery stores.

Do not carry open containers of alcohol in your car or at any public area not zoned for alcohol consumption—the police can fine you on the spot. **Alcohol is forbidden at all city beaches, boardwalks, and coastal parks.** Pay heed or pay the price: First-time violators face a $250 fine.

Nothing will ruin your trip faster than getting a citation for DUI (driving under the influence), so don't even think about driving while intoxicated.

Driving Rules   See "By Car," in the "Getting Around" section, earlier in this chapter.

Electricity   Like Canada, the United States uses 110 to 120 volts AC (60 cycles), compared to 220 to 240 volts AC (50 cycles) in most of Europe, Australia, and New Zealand. Downward converters that change 220 to 240 volts to 110 to 120 volts are difficult to find in the United States, so bring one with you.

Embassies & Consulates   All embassies are in the nation's capital, Washington, D.C. Some consulates are in major U.S. cities, and most nations have a mission to the United Nations in New York City. If your country isn't listed below, call for directory information in Washington, D.C. (✆ **202/555-1212**) or check www.embassy.org/embassies.

The embassy of **Australia** is at 1601 Massachusetts Ave. NW, Washington, DC 20036 (www.usa.embassy.gov.au; ✆ **202/797-3000**). Consulates are in New York, Honolulu, Houston, Los Angeles, and San Francisco.

The embassy of **Canada** is at 501 Pennsylvania Ave. NW, Washington, DC 20001 (www.canadainternational.gc.ca/washington; ✆ **202/682-1740**). Other Canadian consulates are in Buffalo (New York), Detroit, Los Angeles, New York, and Seattle.

The embassy of **Ireland** is at 2234 Massachusetts Ave. NW, Washington, DC 20008 (www.embassyofireland.org; ✆ **202/462-3939**). Irish consulates are in Boston, Chicago, New York, San Francisco, and other cities. See website for a complete listing.

The embassy of **New Zealand** is at 37 Observatory Circle NW, Washington, DC 20008 (www.nzembassy.com; ✆ **202/328-4800**). New Zealand consulates are in Los Angeles, Salt Lake City, San Francisco, and Seattle.

The embassy of the **United Kingdom** is at 3100 Massachusetts Ave. NW, Washington, DC 20008 (http://ukinusa.fco.gov.uk; ✆ **202/588-6500**). Other British consulates are in Atlanta, Boston, Chicago, Cleveland, Houston, Los Angeles, New York, San Francisco, and Seattle.

Emergencies Call ✆ **911** for fire, police, and ambulance. The TTY/TDD emergency number is ✆ **619/233-3323.** The main police station is at 1401 Broadway, at 14th Street (✆ **619/531-2000;** from North San Diego call ✆ **858/484-3154**).

If you encounter serious problems, contact the San Diego chapter of **Traveler's Aid International** (www.travelersaid.org), which has locations at the airport (✆ **619/295-1277**) and at 110 W. C St., Ste. 1209 (✆ **619/295-8393**). This nationwide, nonprofit, social-service organization geared to helping travelers in difficult straits offers services that might include reuniting families separated while traveling, providing food and/or shelter to people stranded without cash, or even emotional counseling. If you're in trouble, seek them out.

Family Travel With its plethora of theme parks, animal attractions, and beaches and parks, San Diego is an ideal family vacation destination. And, of course, Disneyland is right up the road, too.

To locate accommodations, restaurants, and attractions that are particularly kid-friendly, refer to the "Kids" icon throughout this guide. Also, keep in mind some hotels offer free or discounted lodging for children who share a room with a parent or guardian—be sure to ask.

Recommended family travel websites include **Family Travel Forum** (www.familytravelforum.com), a comprehensive site that offers customized trip planning; **Family Travel Network** (www.familytravelnetwork.com), an online magazine providing travel tips; and **TravelWithYourKids.com** (www.travelwithyourkids.com), a site written by parents for parents offering sound advice for long-distance and international travel with children. You might also consider checking out *The Unofficial Guide to California with Kids* (John Wiley & Sons, Inc.).

For babysitting services look to **Marion's Childcare** (www.hotelchildcare.com; ✆ **888/891-5029** or 619/303-4379) or **Panda's Domestic Service Agency** (www.sandiegobabysitters.com; ✆ **619/295-3800**).

Gasoline (Petrol) See "By Car," in the "Getting Around" section, earlier in this chapter.

Health Contact the **International Association for Medical Assistance to Travellers** (www.iamat.org; ✆ **716/754-4883** or 416/652-0137 in Canada) for tips on travel and health concerns, and for lists of local doctors. The United States **Centers for Disease Control and Prevention** (www.cdc.gov; ✆ **800/232-4636**) provides up-to-date information on health hazards by region or country and offers tips on food safety. The website www.tripprep.com, sponsored by a consortium of travel medicine practitioners, **Travel Health Online,** may also offer helpful advice on traveling abroad. You can find listings of clinics overseas at the **International Society of Travel Medicine** (www.istm.org).

If you suffer from a chronic illness, consult your doctor before your departure. Pack **prescription medications** in your carry-on luggage, and carry them in their original containers, with pharmacy labels—otherwise they won't make it through airport security. Visitors from outside the U.S. should carry generic names of prescription drugs. Medications are readily available throughout San Diego at various chain drugstores such as **Walgreens** (www.walgreens.com), **Rite-Aid** (www.riteaid.com), and **CVS** (www.cvs.com), which sell pharmaceuticals and nonprescription products. If you need a pharmacy after normal business hours, the following branches are open 24 hours: **CVS,** 8831 Villa La Jolla Dr., La Jolla (✆ **858/457-4480**), and 313 E. Washington St., Hillcrest (✆ **619/291-7170**); and **Rite-Aid,** 535 Robinson Ave., Hillcrest (✆ **619/291-3705**). Local hospitals also sell prescription drugs.

For U.S. travelers, most reliable healthcare plans provide coverage if you get sick away from home. Foreign visitors may have to pay all medical costs upfront and be reimbursed later. See "Insurance," below.

Hospitals   Near downtown San Diego, **UCSD Medical Center–Hillcrest,** 200 W. Arbor Dr. (http://health.ucsd.edu; ✆ **619/543-6222**), has the most convenient emergency room. In La Jolla, **UCSD Thornton Hospital,** 9300 Campus Point Dr. (http://health.ucsd.edu; ✆ **858/657-7000**), has a good emergency room, and you'll find another in Coronado, at **Sharp Coronado Hospital,** 250 Prospect Place, opposite the Marriott Resort (www.sharp.com; ✆ **619/522-3600**).

Insurance   Although it's not required of travelers, health insurance is highly recommended. Most health insurance policies cover you if you get sick away from home—but check your coverage before you leave.

International visitors to the U.S. should note that unlike many European countries, the United States does not usually offer free or low-cost medical care to its citizens or visitors. Doctors and hospitals are expensive, and in most cases will require advance payment or proof of coverage before they render their services.

For information on traveler's insurance, trip cancellation insurance, and medical insurance while traveling, please visit www.frommers.com/planning.

Internet & Wi-Fi   More and more hotels, resorts, airports, cafes, and retailers are going Wi-Fi (wireless fidelity), becoming "hotspots" that offer free high-speed Wi-Fi access or charge a small fee for usage. Wi-Fi is found in campgrounds, RV parks, and even entire towns. Downtown's Gaslamp Quarter offers 2 hours of free Wi-Fi from any public space (go to www.freewifisandiego.com for information). To find other public Wi-Fi hotspots, check www.jiwire.com; its Hotspot Finder holds the world's largest directory of public wireless hotspots.

For dial-up access, most business-class hotels in the U.S. offer dataports for laptop modems; bring a **connection kit** of the right power and phone adapters, and an Ethernet network cable—or find out whether your hotel supplies them.

If you don't have a computer with you, try www.cybercaptive.com or www.cybercafe.com to hunt for publicly accessed computers. The best options are business-service shops such as **FedEx Office** (www.fedex.com/office) and **public libraries** (search www.sandiego.gov/public-library to find the nearest location before you leave home).

Legal Aid   While driving, if you are pulled over for a minor infraction (such as speeding), never attempt to pay the fine directly to a police officer; this could be construed as attempted bribery, a serious crime. Pay fines by mail, or directly into the hands of the clerk of the court. If accused of a more serious offense, say and do nothing before consulting a lawyer. Here, the burden is on the state to prove a person's guilt beyond a reasonable doubt, and everyone has the right to remain silent, whether he or she is suspected of a crime or actually arrested. Once arrested, a person can make one telephone call to a party of his or her choice. International visitors should call their embassy or consulate.

LGBT Travelers   Despite its reputation for conservative local politics, San Diego is one of America's gay-friendliest destinations. Over the years, the city has had several openly gay politicians and public officials, including the country's first openly gay district attorney, Bonnie Dumanis. San Diego also has one of the nation's oldest gay and lesbian theater companies, Diversionary Theatre. **Note:** As of this writing, Proposition 8, outlawing same-sex marriage, is still in effect in California.

Gay and lesbian visitors might already know about Hillcrest, near Balboa Park, the city's most prominent "out" community. Many gay-owned restaurants, boutiques, and night-spots cater to both a gay and straight clientele, and the scene is lively most nights of the week. In the 1990s, the community's residential embrace spread west to Mission Hills, and east along Adams Avenue to Kensington.

The **International Gay Rodeo Association** stage rodeos—and even conducts schools on how to ride and rope like a real cowboy or cowgirl—at the rodeo grounds in the East County city of Lakeside; see www.sandiegorodeo.org or call ✆ **619/993-6818** for more info. For information on the **Annual San Diego LGBT Pride Parade, Rally, and Festival,** see "San Diego Calendar of Events," in chapter 2.

The free *San Diego Gay and Lesbian Times* (www.gaylesbiantimes.com), published every Thursday, is the most information-packed of several local out publications, and available at the gay and lesbian **Obelisk** bookstore, 1029 University Ave., Hillcrest (www.obeliskshoppe.com; ✆ **619/297-4171**), along with other businesses in Hillcrest and neighboring communities. And check out the **San Diego Gay & Lesbian Chamber of Commerce** online at www.gsdba.org (✆ **619/296-4543**). You can search the business directory with its 800-plus members and find a variety of restaurants, cafes, hotels, and other establishments that welcome gay and lesbian clients. The **San Diego Convention & Visitors Bureau** also publishes a pamphlet, *San Diego from Gay to Z,* with information on gay accommodations and events. For more information or to order the free pamphlet, go to www.sandiego.org. The CVB also has touring suggestions for gay and lesbian visitors on its cultural website, www.sandiego artandsol.com. For matters of health and wellness, you can contact the **San Diego LGBT Community Center,** 3909 Centre St. (www.thecentersd.; ✆ **619/692-2077**); it's open Monday to Friday 9am to 10pm, Saturday 9am to 7pm.

The **International Gay & Lesbian Travel Association** (www.iglta.com; ✆ **954/630-1637**) is the trade association for the gay and lesbian travel industry, and offers an online directory of gay- and lesbian-friendly travel businesses and tour operators. Other web sources include **OutTraveler.com** (www.outtraveler.com), which features information on worldwide destinations, travel tips, and special deals, and the Canadian website **GayTraveler** (www.gaytraveler.ca), which offers ideas and advice for international gay travel.

Mail   At press time, domestic postage rates were 32¢ for a postcard and 45¢ for a letter. For international mail, a first-class letter of up to 1 ounce costs $1.05 (85¢ to Canada); a first-class postcard costs the same as a letter. For more information, go to www.usps.com and click on "Calculate Postage." Always include zip codes when mailing items in the U.S. If you don't know your zip code, visit www.usps.com/zip4.

If you aren't sure what your address will be in the United States, mail can be sent to you, in your name, c/o General Delivery at the main post office of the city or region where you expect to be. (Call ✆ **800/275-8777** for information on the nearest post office.) The addressee must pick up mail in person and must produce proof of identity (driver's license, passport, and so on). Most post offices will hold mail for up to 1 month.

San Diego's main post office is located in the boondocks, but the former main office, located just west of Old Town at 2535 Midway Dr., is a good alternative; it's open Monday from 7am to 11pm, Tuesday through Friday from 8am to 11pm, and Saturdays from 8am to 4pm. There are also downtown post offices at 815 E St. (Mon–Fri 9am–5pm) and at 51 Horton Plaza, next to the Westin Hotel (Mon–Fri 9:30am–6pm, Sat 10am–5pm). There is a post office in the Mission Valley Shopping Center, next to Macy's (Mon–Fri 9:30am–6pm, Sat 9:30am–4pm).

Medical Requirements   Unless you're arriving from an area known to be suffering from an epidemic (particularly cholera or yellow fever), inoculations or vaccinations are not required for entry into the United States. If you have a medical condition that requires **syringe-administered medications,** carry a valid signed prescription from your physician; syringes in carry-on baggage will be inspected. Insulin in any form should have the proper pharmaceutical documentation. If you have a disease that requires treatment with **narcotics,** you should also carry documented proof with you—smuggling narcotics aboard a plane carries severe penalties in the U.S.

For **HIV-positive visitors,** requirements for entering the United States are somewhat vague and can change. For up-to-the-minute information, contact **AIDSinfo** (www.aidsinfo. nih.gov; ℂ **800/448-0440** or 301/315-2816 outside the U.S., TTY 888/480-3739) or the **Gay Men's Health Crisis** (www.gmhc.org; ℂ **800/243-7692** or 212/367-1000). Also see "Health," above.

Mobile Phones   Just because your cellphone works at home doesn't mean it'll work everywhere in the U.S. It's a good bet your phone will work in major cities, but take a look at your wireless company's coverage map on its website before heading out. If you need to stay in touch at a destination where you know your phone won't work, **rent** a phone that does from **InTouch USA** (www.intouchglobal.com; ℂ **800/872-7626** or 703/222-7161). InTouch offers 99¢ rates for incoming and outgoing calls.

In San Diego, you can rent a phone from **BearCom,** 8290 Vickers St., Ste. D (www. bearcom.; ℂ **877/706-2327** or 858/430-2327); it delivers to hotels within the metro area. And you can purchase relatively inexpensive "pay as you go" phones almost everywhere, if your phone doesn't have coverage or has high roaming charges.

If you're not from the U.S., you'll be appalled at the poor reach of the **GSM (Global System for Mobile Communications) wireless network,** which is used by much of the rest of the world. Your phone will probably work in most major U.S. cities; it definitely won't work in many rural areas. To see where GSM phones work in the U.S., check out www.t-mobile.com/coverage. And you may or may not be able to send SMS (text messaging) home.

If you have Web access while traveling, consider a broadband-based telephone service (in technical terms, **Voice-over Internet Protocol,** or **VoIP**) such as **Skype** (www.skype. com) or **Vonage** (www.vonage.com), which allow you to make free international calls from your laptop. Neither service requires the people you're calling to also have that service (though there are fees if they do not). Check the websites for details.

The Value of the Dollar vs. Other Popular Currencies

US$	Aus$	Can$	Euro €	NZ$	UK £
$1	A$.95	C$.99	0.76€	NZ$1.23	63p

Money & Costs   Frommer's lists exact prices in local currency. The currency conversions quoted above were correct at press time. However, rates fluctuate; before departing, consult a currency exchange website such as www.oanda.com/currency/converter to check up-to-the-minute rates. For help with currency conversions, tip calculations, and more, download Frommer's convenient Travel Tools app for your mobile device; go to www. frommers.com/go/mobile.

The cost of living is not cheap in San Diego, but it's still a moderately priced destination compared with New York, London, or Tokyo. It's always advisable to bring money in a variety of forms on a vacation: a mix of cash, credit cards, and traveler's checks or a prepaid debit card. You should also exchange enough petty cash to cover airport incidentals,

What Things Cost in San Diego	US$
Taxi from the airport to downtown	15.00
Bus from the airport to downtown	2.25
Local telephone call	0.50
Double at the Hotel del Coronado (very expensive)	325.00
Double at the Horton Grand (expensive)	229.00
Double at the Crowne Plaza San Diego (moderate)	179.00
Double at Little Italy Hotel (inexpensive)	99.00
Breakfast or lunch for one at the Mission (inexpensive)	11.00
Lunch for one at Casa de Guadalajara (moderate)	16.00
Two-course dinner for one at Filippi's (inexpensive)	15.00
Two-course dinner for one at Caffé Bella Italia (moderate)	25.00
Two-course dinner for one at El Agave Tequileria (expensive)	36.00
Two-course dinner for one at Baleen (very expensive)	50.00
Pint of beer at Stone Brewing	5.00
Large cappuccino at Lestat's Coffee House	3.60
All-day adult ticket aboard Old Town Trolley Tours	34.00
SeaWorld adult admission	73.00
Top ticket at La Jolla Playhouse	80.00

tipping, and transportation to your hotel before you leave home, or withdraw money upon arrival at an airport ATM.

Nationwide, the easiest and best way to get cash away from home is from an ATM (automated teller machine), sometimes referred to as a "cash machine," or "cashpoint." The **Cirrus** (www.mastercard.com; C **800/424-7787**) and **PLUS** (www.visa.com; C **800/843-7587**) networks span the country; you can find them even in remote regions. Go to your bank card's website to find ATM locations at your destination. Be sure you know your daily withdrawal limit before you depart. **Note:** Many banks impose a fee every time you use a card at another bank's ATM, and that fee is often higher for international transactions (up to $5 or more) than for domestic ones (where they're rarely more than $2). In addition, the bank from which you withdraw cash may charge its own fee. To compare banks' ATM fees within the U.S., use www.bankrate.com. Visitors from outside the U.S. should also find out whether their bank assesses a 1% to 3% fee on charges incurred abroad.

Credit cards are the most widely used form of payment in the United States: **Visa, MasterCard, American Express, Diners Club,** and **Discover.** They also provide a convenient record of all your expenses, and offer relatively good exchange rates. You can withdraw cash advances from your credit cards at banks or ATMs, but high fees make credit card cash advances a pricey way to get cash. It's highly recommended you travel with at least one major credit card. You must have a credit card to rent a car, and hotels and airlines usually require a credit card imprint as a deposit against expenses.

Beware of hidden credit card fees while traveling. Check with your credit or debit card issuer to see what fees, if any, will be charged for overseas transactions. Reform legislation in the U.S., for example, has curbed some exploitative lending practices. But many banks have responded by increasing fees in other areas, including fees for customers who use credit and debit cards while out of the country—even if those charges were made in U.S.

dollars. Fees can amount to 3% or more of the purchase price. Check with your bank before departing to avoid any surprise charges on your statement.

Multicultural San Diego   Although San Diego has a reputation as a predominantly white, middle-class, conservative-leaning metropolis, a closer look reveals a more diverse picture: 32% of the city's inhabitants are Hispanic, 11% are Asian, and 5% are African American. The **San Diego Art + Sol** website (www.sandiegoartandsol.com) is an excellent place to get additional information on the city's contemporary cultural attractions; it also features a variety of touring itineraries.

The **San Diego Museum of Man** covers 4 million years of hominid history, with a particular focus on the native heritage of the Americas (p. 53). The history of San Diego's indigenous peoples is related at **Mission Trails Regional Park** (p. 59) and the **Junípero Serra Museum** (p. 58).

With the Mexican border, just 16 miles from downtown San Diego, Mexico's influence is unmistakable, and Spanish street and place names are prevalent. The **Mission Basilica San Diego de Alcalá** (p. 58), **Junípero Serra Museum,** and **Old Town** (p. 60) showcase Spanish-Mexican history, while contemporary culture is reflected in the murals of **Chicano Park** (www.chicano-park.org; © 619/563-4661) under the San Diego–Coronado Bay Bridge. **Voz Alta,** 1754 National Ave. (www.vozaltaprojectgallery.com), is a gathering spot in Barrio Logan for writers, artists, and musicians with a Chicano bent that hosts concerts, art exhibits, poetry slams, and other events. The **Centro Cultural de la Raza** (p. 49), in Balboa Park, offers classes, live entertainment, and gallery exhibits.

Cinco de Mayo (May 5) is a huge celebration in Old Town, but any day is great for shopping for Latin-American handicrafts at **Bazaar del Mundo** or **Fiesta de Reyes** (p. 155). Americanized Mexican food is ubiquitous, but for a taste of the real Mexico, try **El Agave Tequileria** (p. 131), or head south of the border. While in Tijuana, be sure to visit the excellent **Centro Cultural Tijuana** (p. 259), which covers the history, contemporary art, culture, and performing arts of Baja California and the rest of Mexico.

Initially lured by the California gold rush in the 1850s, a small Chinese community came to live in San Diego and controlled much of the fishing industry until 1890; Chinese also helped build (and later staff) the Hotel del Coronado. Chinatown—downtown, south of Market Street—eventually merged with the rough-and-tumble Stingaree, San Diego's red-light district. At the turn of the last century, the area was a hub of gambling, prostitution, and opium dens, and Chinese families ran notorious saloons such as the Old Tub of Blood and the Seven Buckets of Blood. Today, an **Asian/Pacific Historic District** is beginning to materialize, concentrated between Market and J streets, and between Third and Fifth avenues. Eighteen buildings in this area have strong historical ties to the Asian/Pacific-American community. Also here is the **San Diego Chinese Historical Museum** (p. 56), which offers walking tours of the old Chinatown the second Saturday of the month.

An African presence has also been felt in small but important ways throughout San Diego history. Black slaves were part of Juan Cabrillo's expedition along the California coast in 1542, and Pío Pico, a San Diegan who became the last Mexican governor of California before it was annexed by the United States, was of African descent. The **Clermont Hotel,** 501 Seventh Ave., is nondescript but socially significant—it was built in 1887 and was one of the city's first black-owned businesses. A segregated hotel "for colored people" until 1956, it may be the oldest surviving historically black hotel in the nation and was designated an African-American landmark in 2001.

In Old Town, the ramshackle **Casa del Rey Moro African Museum,** 2471 Congress St. (www.ambers.com; © 619/220-0022), provides a scholarly look at black history, with a special emphasis on how it has played out in San Diego and California. The **WorldBeat Center** (p. 54), in Balboa Park, produces reggae and African music concerts, has a variety of classes, a gift shop, and even runs its own radio station. In the mountains east of San

Diego, you'll find the **Julian Gold Rush Hotel** (p. 248), built in 1897 by freed slave Albert Robinson. The town itself was founded after gold was discovered in 1869 by another freed slave, Frederick Coleman. **Soul of America** (www.soulofamerica.com) is a comprehensive website, with travel tips, event and family-reunion postings, and sections on historically black beach resorts and active vacations. The section on San Diego is fairly detailed and has a calendar of events.

Newspapers & Magazines   The *U-T San Diego* (formerly known as the *San Diego Union-Tribune*) is published daily, and its entertainment section, "Night & Day," is in the Thursday edition; "Night & Day" is also distributed around the city for free. The free *San Diego Reader* is published Thursdays and is available at many shops, restaurants, theaters, and public hot spots; it's the best source for up-to-the-week club and show listings. The free alternative weekly *San Diego CityBeat* is distributed on Wednesdays. It also has listings and can get you up-to-speed on local issues and local music. *San Diego* magazine has covered all aspects of the city since 1948, and is plumped with social news and dining listings. *San Diego Home/Garden Lifestyles* magazine highlights design and art, and also includes articles about Southern California gardening and the local restaurant scene. Both magazines are published monthly and sold at newsstands. The *Los Angeles Times,* the *New York Times,* and *USA Today* are widely available. International publications are available at **Paras Newsstand,** 3911 30th St. (© **619/296-2859**), in North Park.

Packing   There's rarely need for a heavy coat in San Diego, but May Gray and June Gloom (p. 20) make things cooler and damper than many visitors anticipate. Be prepared with a light coat or sweater. San Diego is also very casual, meaning you can show up at a restaurant or theater wearing just about anything you want. The only dress codes you'll really find are at downtown clubs, where people tend to dress to impress.

For more helpful information on packing for your trip, download our convenient Travel Tools app for your mobile device. Go to www.frommers.com/go/mobile and click on the Travel Tools icon.

Passports   Virtually every air traveler entering the U.S. is required to show a passport. All persons, including U.S. citizens, traveling by air between the United States and Canada, Mexico, Central and South America, the Caribbean, and Bermuda are required to present a valid passport. U.S. and Canadian citizens entering the U.S. at land and sea ports of entry from within the Western Hemisphere must now also present a passport or other documents compliant with the Western Hemisphere Travel Initiative (WHTI; see www.getyouhome.gov for details). Children 15 and under may continue entering with only a U.S. birth certificate, or other proof of U.S. citizenship. *Note:* These rules are in effect for U.S. citizens who wish to visit Tijuana for the day, as well.

It is advised to always have at least one or two consecutive blank pages in your passport to allow space for visas and stamps that need to appear together. It is also important to note when your passport expires. In general, your passport should have at least 6 months left before its expiration; the U.S. does have an agreement with many countries (including Australia, Canada, Ireland, New Zealand, and the U.K.) that allows for use of a current passport up to the actual date of expiration. If you are traveling without a visa, though, you will only be admitted until the date of your passport's expiration. See "Embassies & Consulates" on p. 286 for whom to contact if you lose your passport while traveling in the U.S. For other information, contact the following passport offices:

For Residents of Australia   Contact the Australian Passport Information Service at © **131-232,** or visit www.passports.gov.au.

For Residents of Canada   Contact the central Passport Office, Department of Foreign Affairs and International Trade, Ottawa, ON K1A 0G3 (www.ppt.gc.ca; © **800/567-6868**).

For Residents of Ireland   Contact the Passport Office, Setanta Centre, Molesworth Street, Dublin 2 (www.foreignaffairs.gov.ie; ✆ **01/671-1633**).

For Residents of New Zealand   Contact the Passports Office, Department of Internal Affairs, 47 Boulcott St., Wellington, 6011 (www.passports.govt.nz; ✆ **0800/225-050** in New Zealand or 04/474-8100).

For Residents of the United Kingdom   Visit your nearest passport office, major post office, or travel agency or contact the Identity and Passport Service (IPS), 89 Eccleston Sq., London, SW1V 1PN (www.ips.gov.uk; ✆ **0300/222-0000**).

For Residents of the United States   To find your regional passport office, check the U.S. State Department website (travel.state.gov/passport), or call the National Passport Information Center (✆ **877/487-2778**) for automated information.

Petrol   See "By Car," in the "Getting Around" section, earlier in this chapter.

Police   The downtown police station is at 1401 Broadway (✆ **619/531-2000;** from North San Diego call ✆ **858/484-3154** or visit www.sandiego.gov/police. Call ✆ **911** in an emergency; the TTY/TDD emergency number is ✆ **619/233-3323.**

Safety   San Diego is a relatively safe destination, by big-city standards. Of the 10 largest cities in the United States, it historically has had the lowest incidence of violent crime per capita. Tijuana, on the other hand, has seen a dramatic rise in violence (for information on staying safe south of the border, see p. 254).

Virtually all areas of San Diego are safe during the day. In Balboa Park, caution is advised in areas not frequented by regular foot traffic (particularly along the trails and walkways on the Sixth Ave. side of the park). Transients are common in San Diego—especially downtown, in Hillcrest, and in the beach areas. They are rarely a problem but, like anyone, can be unpredictable when under the influence. Downtown areas to the east of PETCO Park are sparsely populated after dusk, and poorly lit.

Parts of the city that are usually safe on foot at night include the Gaslamp Quarter, Hillcrest, Old Town, Mission Valley, Mission Beach, Pacific Beach, La Jolla, and Coronado.

Avoid carrying valuables with you on the street, and keep expensive cameras or electronic equipment bagged or covered when not in use. If you're using a map, try to consult it inconspicuously—or better yet, study it before you leave your room. Hold on to your pocketbook, and place your billfold in an inside pocket. In theaters, restaurants, and other public places, keep your possessions in sight.

Always lock your room door—don't assume that once you're inside the hotel, you are automatically safe and no longer need to be aware of your surroundings. Hotels are open to the public, and security may not be able to screen everyone who enters.

Driving safety is important too, and carjacking is not unprecedented. Question your rental agency about personal safety, and ask for a traveler-safety brochure when you pick up your car. Obtain written directions—or a map with the route clearly marked—from the agency, showing how to get to your destination; a GPS navigation system may be available too. San Diego's airport area, where most car-rental firms are based, is generally safe. If you drive off a highway and end up in a dodgy-looking neighborhood, leave the area as quickly as possible. If you have an accident, even on the highway, stay in your car with the doors locked until you assess the situation or until the police arrive. If you're bumped from behind on the street or are involved in a minor accident with no injuries, and the situation appears to be suspicious, motion to the other driver to follow you. Never get out of your car in such situations. Go to the nearest police precinct, well-lit service station, or 24-hour store.

Whenever possible, always park in well-lit and well-traveled areas. Always keep your car doors locked, whether the vehicle is attended or unattended. Never leave packages or valuables in sight. If someone attempts to rob you or steal your car, don't try to resist the thief/carjacker. Report the incident to the police department immediately by calling ✆ **911.**

Senior Travel   Nearly every attraction in San Diego offers a senior discount; age require-ments vary, and prices are discussed in chapter 4 with each individual listing. Public transpor-tation and movie theaters also have reduced rates. Don't be shy about asking for discounts, but always carry identification, such as a driver's license, that shows your date of birth.

Members of **AARP,** 601 E St. NW, Washington, DC 20049 (www.aarp.org; ✆ **888/687-2277** or 202/434-3525), get discounts on hotels, airfares, and car rentals. AARP offers members a wide range of benefits, including *AARP The Magazine* and a monthly newslet-ter. Anyone 50 or older can join.

The U.S. National Park Service offers an **America the Beautiful: National Parks and Federal Recreational Lands Senior Pass** (formerly the **Golden Age Passport**), which gives seniors 62 years or older lifetime entrance to all properties administered by the National Park Service—national parks, monuments, historic sites, recreation areas, and national wildlife refuges—for a one-time fee of $10. The pass can be purchased in person at any NPS facility that charges an entrance fee, or obtained via the mail; go www.nps. gov/fees_passes.htm to download the form ($20 for pass and processing). Besides free entry, the America the Beautiful Senior Pass also offers a 50% discount on some federal-use fees charged for such facilities as camping, swimming, parking, boat launching, and tours. For more information, call the United States Geological Survey (USGS), which issues the passes, at ✆ **888/275-8747.**

Road Scholar (formerly known as **Elderhostel,** www.roadscholar.org; ✆ **800/454-5768**) arranges worldwide study programs for all ages, but the core demographic is ages 50 and above. **ElderTreks** (www.eldertreks.com; ✆ **800/741-7956,** 0808-234-1714 in the U.K., or 416/588-5000 anywhere else in the world) offers small-group tours to off-the-beaten-path or adventure-travel locations (including Baja); restricted to travelers ages 50 and older.

Single Travelers   On package vacations, single travelers are often hit with a "single supplement" to the base price. To avoid it, you can agree to room with other single travel-ers or find a compatible roommate before you go, from one of the many roommate-loca-tor agencies. **TravelChums** (www.travelchums.com) is an Internet-only travel-companion matching service with elements of an online personals-type site. Many reputable tour com-panies also offer singles-only trips. **Singles Travel International** (www.singlestravelintl.; ✆ **877/765-6874**) offers singles-only escorted tours. **Backroads** (www.backroads.com; ✆ **800/462-2848**) offers "Singles + Solos" active-travel trips to destinations worldwide.

Smoking   Smoking is prohibited in nearly all indoor public places, including theaters, hotel lobbies, and enclosed shopping malls. In 1998, California enacted legislation prohib-iting smoking in all restaurants and bars, except those with outdoor seating. Smoking in a car in which a child under age 17 is riding is illegal, as well. San Diego has also banned smoking from all city beaches, boardwalks, piers, and parks, which includes Mission Bay Park and Balboa Park. *Be forewarned:* Fines start at $250.

Student Travel   Check out the **International Student Travel Confederation** (www.isic. org) website for travel services information and details on how to get an **International Stu-dent Identity Card (ISIC),** which qualifies full-time students (ages "12 to 112") for sub-stantial savings on rail passes, plane tickets, entrance fees, and more. It can also provide students with basic health and life insurance, as well as a 24-hour help line. The card is valid for a maximum of 18 months. You can apply for the card online or in person at **STA Travel** (www.statravel.; ✆ **800/781-4040** in North America, 134-782 in Australia, or 0871/2-300-040 in the U.K.), the biggest student travel agency in the world; check out the website to locate STA Travel offices worldwide. If you're no longer a student but are still under 26, you can get an **International Youth Travel Card (IYTC)** from the same people; it entitles you to some discounts. There's also a card available for full-time teachers. **Travel CUTS** (www.travelcuts.com; ✆ **800/592-2887,** or 866/246-9762 in Canada) offers similar services for Canadians and U.S. residents alike. Irish students may prefer to turn to **USIT**

(www.usit.ie; ☎ **01/602-1906**), an Ireland-based specialist in student, youth, and independent travel.

Taxes   The United States has no value-added tax (VAT) or other indirect tax at the national level. Every state, county, and city may levy its own local tax on all purchases, including hotel and restaurant checks and airline tickets. These taxes will not appear on price tags. In San Diego, sales tax in restaurants and shops is 7.75%. Hotel tax is 10.5%, or 12.5% for lodgings with more than 70 rooms.

Telephones   Generally, hotel surcharges on long-distance and local calls are astronomical, so you're better off using your **cellphone** or a **public pay telephone.** Many convenience groceries and packaging services sell **prepaid calling cards** in denominations up to $50; for international visitors these can be the least expensive way to call home. Many public phones at airports now accept American Express, MasterCard, and Visa credit cards. **Local calls** made from public pay phones in most locales cost either 35¢ or 50¢. Pay phones do not accept pennies, and few will take anything larger than a quarter.

Most long-distance and international calls can be dialed directly from any phone. **For calls within the United States and to Canada,** dial 1 followed by the area code and the seven-digit number. **For other international calls,** dial 011 followed by the country code, city code, and the number you are calling.

Calls to area codes **800, 888, 877,** and **866** are toll-free. However, calls to area codes **700** and **900** (chat lines, bulletin boards, "dating" services, and so on) can be very expensive—usually a charge of 95¢ to $3 or more per minute, and they sometimes have minimum charges that can run as high as $15 or more.

For **reversed-charge** or **collect calls,** and for person-to-person calls, dial the number 0, then the area code and number; an operator will come on the line. Specify whether you are calling collect, person-to-person, or both. If your operator-assisted call is international, ask for the overseas operator.

For **local directory assistance** (information), dial **411;** for long-distance information, dial 1 and then the appropriate area code and **555-1212.**

Most hotels have **fax machines** available for guest use (be sure to ask about the charge to use them). Many hotel rooms are even wired for guests' fax machines. A less expensive way to send and receive faxes may be at places such as **The UPS Store** (www.theupsstore.com).

Time   The continental United States is divided into **four time zones:** Eastern Standard Time (EST), Central Standard Time (CST), Mountain Standard Time (MST), and Pacific Standard Time (PST). Alaska and Hawaii have their own zones. For example, when it's 9am in San Diego (PST), it's 7am in Honolulu (HST), 10am in Denver (MST), 11am in Chicago (CST), noon in New York City (EST), 5pm in London (GMT), and 2am the next day in Sydney.

San Diego, like the rest of the West Coast, is in the Pacific Standard Time zone, which is 8 hours behind Greenwich Mean Time.

Daylight saving time (summer time) is in effect from 1am on the second Sunday in March to 1am on the first Sunday in November, except in Arizona, Hawaii, the U.S. Virgin Islands, and Puerto Rico. Daylight saving time moves the clock 1 hour ahead of standard time.

For help with time translations, and more, download our convenient Travel Tools app for you mobile device. Go to www.frommers.com/go/mobile and click on the Travel Tools icon.

Tipping   Tips are a very important part of many workers' income, and gratuities are the standard way of showing appreciation for services provided. (Tipping is certainly not compulsory if the service is poor.) In hotels, tip **bellhops** at least $1 per bag ($2–$3 if you have a lot of luggage) and tip the **chamber staff** $1 to $2 per day (more if you've left a disaster area for him or her to clean up). Tip the **doorman** or **concierge** only if he or she has provided you with some specific service (for example, calling a cab for you or obtaining difficult-to-get theater tickets). Tip the **valet-parking attendant** $1 every time you get your car.

In restaurants, bars, and nightclubs, tip **service staff and bartenders** 15% to 20% of the check, tip **checkroom attendants** $1 per garment, and tip **valet-parking attendants** $1 per vehicle.

As for other service personnel, tip **cabdrivers** 15% of the fare; tip **skycaps** at airports at least $1 per bag ($2–$3 if you have a lot of luggage); and tip **hairdressers** and **barbers** 15% to 20%.

For help with tip calculations, currency conversions, and more, download our convenient Travel Tools app for your mobile device. Go to www.frommers.com/go/mobile and click on the Travel Tools icon.

Toilets   You won't find public toilets or "restrooms" on the streets in most U.S. cities, but they can be found in hotel lobbies, bars, restaurants, museums, department stores, railway and bus stations, and service stations. Large hotels and fast-food restaurants are often the best bet for clean facilities. Restaurants and bars in resorts or heavily visited areas may reserve their restrooms for patrons.

Horton Plaza and Seaport Village downtown, Balboa Park, Old Town State Historic Park, and the Ferry Landing Marketplace in Coronado all have well-marked public restrooms. In general, you won't have a problem finding one; they are usually clean and accessible.

VAT   See "Taxes," above.

Visas   The U.S. State Department has a **Visa Waiver Program (VWP)** allowing citizens of the following countries to enter the United States without a visa for stays of up to 90 days: Andorra, Australia, Austria, Belgium, Brunei, Czech Republic, Denmark, Estonia, Finland, France, Germany, Greece, Hungary, Iceland, Ireland, Italy, Japan, Latvia, Liechtenstein, Lithuania, Luxembourg, Malta, Monaco, the Netherlands, New Zealand, Norway, Portugal, San Marino, Singapore, Slovakia, Slovenia, South Korea, Spain, Sweden, Switzerland, and the United Kingdom. (**Note:** This list was accurate at press time; for the most up-to-date list of countries in the VWP, consult www.travel.state.gov/visa.)

Even though a visa isn't necessary, in an effort to help U.S. officials check travelers against terror watch lists before they arrive at U.S. borders, visitors from VWP countries must register online through the **Electronic System for Travel Authorization (ESTA)** before boarding a plane or a boat to the U.S. Travelers must complete an electronic application providing basic personal and travel eligibility information. The Department of Homeland Security recommends filling out the form when you begin making your travel plans (at minimum, 3 days before traveling). Authorizations will be valid for up to 2 years or until the traveler's passport expires, whichever comes first. Currently, there is a $14 fee for the online application. **Note:** Any passport issued on or after October 26, 2006, by a VWP country must be an **e-Passport** for VWP travelers to be eligible to enter the U.S. without a visa. Citizens of these nations also need to present a round-trip air or cruise ticket upon arrival. E-Passports contain computer chips capable of storing biometric information, such as the required digital photograph of the holder. If your passport doesn't have this feature, you can still travel without a visa if the valid passport was issued before October 26, 2005, and includes a machine-readable zone; or if the valid passport was issued between October 26, 2005, and October 25, 2006, and includes a digital photograph. For more information, go to www.travel.state.gov/visa. Canadian citizens may enter the United States without visas, but will need to show passports and proof of residence.

Citizens of all other countries must have (1) a valid passport that expires at least 6 months later than the scheduled end of their visit to the U.S.; and (2) a tourist visa.

For information about U.S. visas, go to www.travel.state.gov and click on "Visas." Or go to one of the following websites:

Australian citizens can obtain up-to-date visa information from the **U.S. Embassy Canberra,** Moonah Place, Yarralumla, ACT 2600 (✆ **02/6214-5600**), or by checking the U.S. Diplomatic Mission's website at **http://canberra.usembassy.gov/visas.html**.

British subjects can obtain up-to-date visa information by calling the **U.S. Embassy Visa Information Line** (✆ **09042-450-100** from within the U.K. at £1.20 per minute; or ✆ **866/382-3589** from within the U.S. at a flat rate of $16, payable by credit card only) or by visiting the "Visas to the U.S." section of the American Embassy London's website at **http://london.usembassy.gov/visas.html**.

Irish citizens can obtain up-to-date visa information through the **U.S. Embassy Dublin,** 42 Elgin Rd., Ballsbridge, Dublin 4 (✆ **1580-47-VISA** [8472] from within the Republic of Ireland at €2.40 per minute; **http://dublin.usembassy.gov**).

Citizens of **New Zealand** can obtain up-to-date visa information by contacting the **U.S. Embassy New Zealand,** 29 Fitzherbert Terrace, Thorndon, Wellington (**http://new zealand.usembassy.gov**; ✆ **644/462-6000**).

Visitor Information In downtown San Diego, the **Convention & Visitors Bureau (ConVis;** ✆ **619/236-1212;** www.sandiego.org) has an International Visitor Information Center located on the Embarcadero at 1140 N. Harbor Dr., across from the B Street Cruise Ship Terminal. Daily summer hours are from 9am to 5pm; for the remainder of the year it's open daily from 9am to 4pm. ConVis offers great info and deals on its website, but you can also get your hands on the glossy *Official Visitors Planning Guide* at the information center or by mail. The guide includes information on accommodations, dining, activities, attractions, tours, and transportation. ConVis also features discounts on hotels, restaurants, and attractions online.

In La Jolla, ConVis operates a walk-up-only facility at 7966 Herschel Ave., near the corner of Prospect Street. This office is open daily in summer, from 10am to 6pm (till 5pm Sun); from September to May the center is open daily but with more limited hours.

The **Coronado Visitor Center,** 1100 Orange Ave. (www.coronadovisitorcenter.com; ✆ **866/599-7242** or 619/437-8788), dispenses maps, newsletters, and information-packed brochures. Inside the Coronado Museum, it's open Monday through Friday from 9am to 5pm, Saturday and Sunday from 10am to 5pm.

You can also find staffed information booths at the airport, train station, and cruise terminal.

Browse for online information and discounts in advance of your trip at www.discoversd.com and www.infosandiego.com; for details on La Jolla's offerings check www.lajollabythesea.com. For information on San Diego's North County destinations—including Del Mar, Encinitas, Carlsbad, and Oceanside—go to, respectively, www.delmarmainstreet.com, www.gonorthcounty.com, www.visitcarlsbad.com, and www.visitoceanside.org. For more helpful websites, see "The Best of San Diego Online," on p. 88.

Wi-Fi See "Internet & Wi-Fi," earlier in this section.

Index

See also Accommodations and Restaurant indexes, below.

General Index

A

AAA (American Automobile Association), 273
Access in San Diego, 285
Accommodations, 184–219. *See also* Accommodations Index
  alternative, 218–219
  best, 184–186
  Borrego Springs, 252–253
  Coronado, 213–217
  downtown, Gaslamp Quarter, and Little Italy, 186–195
  fitness spas, 212
  getting the best deal, 218
  high season, 217
  Hillcrest and Uptown, 196–199
  Julian, 247–248
  La Jolla, 206–212
  Mission Bay and the Beaches, 201–206
  North County, 232–234
  Oceanside, 236
  Old Town and Mission Valley, 199–201
  pet-friendly, 274
  price categories, 184
  private homes/rooms, 219
  Rancho Santa Fe, 238
  rates, 185, 217–218
  Tijuana, 260–265
Adams Avenue Unplugged, 22
Adelita Bar (Tijuana), 265
Adventure and wellness trips, 275
Africa & Beyond, 158
Africa Tram Safari, 38
Ah Quin, former home of, 97
Air & Space Museum, San Diego, 7, 51, 72, 112
Airbnb, 219
Air Conditioned (North Park), 33
Airport shuttles, 272
Air travel, 270–272
Alcazar Garden, 110
Alexander Salazar Fine Art, 151
Almost Famous (film), 17
Alternative entertainment, 178–179
Altitude Sky Lounge, 173
American Apparel, 154
American Automobile Association (AAA), 273
The American Comedy Co., 173
American Institute of Architects, 71
America the Beautiful—National Parks and Federal Recreational Lands Access Pass, 286

America the Beautiful—National Parks and Federal Recreational Lands Senior Pass, 295
AMSDconcerts, 171
Amtrak, 220, 274, 281
Anaheim/Orange County Visitor & Convention Bureau, 236
Anchorman (film), 17
Animal attractions, 3–4
Animal rights issues, 26
Anthology, 171
Antigua Bodega de Papel (Tijuana), 265–266
Antigua Palacio Municipal (Tijuana), 258–259
Antique Boutique (Julian), 247
Antiques and collectibles, 159–160
  Escondido, 239
  Julian, 247
Antiques on Kettner, 159–160
Anza-Borrego Desert State Park, 5, 79, 248–253
  Visitor Center, 249
  wildflowers, 21
Anza-Borrego Foundation Institute, 250
Apple Alley Bakery (Julian), 246
Apple Box Toys, 165
Apple Harvest Days (Julian), 243
Architectural highlights, 70–71
Area codes, 284
A Rose Path (Julian), 247
Art and crafts, 160
Art galleries, 160
Art museums and exhibition spaces
  The Greatest Generation Art Collection, 101
  Marston House Museum & Gardens, 50
  Mingei International Museum, 50
  Museum of Contemporary Art San Diego, 67
  Museum of Contemporary Art San Diego Downtown, 56, 68
  Museum of Contemporary Art San Diego La Jolla, 64
  Museum of History and Art, 65
  Museum of Photographic Arts, 50–51
  Oceanside Museum of Art, 234, 235
  San Diego Museum of Art, 52–53, 110
  Sculpture Garden of the Museum of Art, 110
  SDAI Museum of the Living Artist, 51
  Stuart Collection, 64
  Timken Museum of Art, 53–54
ARTS TIX, 168
ArtWalk, 22
Asian/Pacific Historic District, 292
Athenaeum Music & Arts Library, 62, 68, 118

Attractions, 37–118
  Balboa Park, 46–54
  beaches, 42–46
  best ways to see San Diego like a local, 7–8
  Coronado, 65
  downtown and beyond, 54–57
  free, 66–67
  free, 66–68
  for kids, 68–70
  La Jolla, 61–65
  major animal parks, 37–42
  Mission Bay and the Beaches, 60–61
  organized tours, 73–77
  special-interest sightseeing, 70–73
  by theme index, 89–90
  Tijuana, 258–260
  top 15, 37
Auto insurance, 280
Automobile Club of Southern California, 279
Automotive Museum, San Diego, 51–52
Avenida Revolución (Tijuana), 258, 263
Aviara Golf Club (Carlsbad), 82

B

Babette Schwartz, 154
Baby Rock (Tijuana), 265
Babysitting services, 287
Backesto Building, 95
Backstage Passes (San Diego Zoo), 41
Baja Airventures, 275
Baja Betty's, 177
Balboa Park, 2–4, 6, 13, 70
  attractions, 46–54
  free attractions and activities, 67
  guided tours, 49
  money-savers, 48
  special events and festivals, 21–23, 25
  walking tour, 107–114
Balboa Park December Nights, 25
Balboa Park Miniature Railroad and Carousel, 48
Balboa Park Municipal Golf Course, 82
Balboa Park Visitors Center, 48
Balboa Tennis Club, 88
Balboa Theatre, 92, 167
Ballooning, 77
Bankers Hill, 71
Barnes & Noble, 161
Barnes Tennis Center, 88
Barnstorming Adventures, 78
Barona Creek Golf Club, 26, 82
Barona Resort & Casino (Barona Reservation), 179–180
Bar Pink (North Park), 33
Bars and lounges, 173–177
Baseball, 180–181

Baum, L. Frank, 15
Bay Books, 159
Bayshore Bikeway, 78
Bazaar del Mundo, 156
Bazar de las Artesanías (Rosarito), 267
Beaches, 4, 42–46. *See also* specific beaches
　Del Mar, 221
　Northern San Diego County, 46, 220–236
　Solana Beach, Encinitas, and Carlsbad, 227–228
　for walking, 85
Beachfront Only Vacation Rentals, 236
The BeachWood, 175
Bea Evenson Fountain, 113
Bed & breakfasts (B&Bs), 218–219
Beer and breweries, 19, 176
　Festival of Beer, 24
　San Diego Beer Week, 24
Beer Company, 176
The Belly Up Tavern, 171, 227
Belmont Park, 61
Beluga Interaction Programs (SeaWorld), 42
Berkeley (ferry), 56
Berlin Bar (Tijuana), 265
Bernardo Winery, 73
Best Western Seven Seas, 218
Bettie Page, 151
Bike Revolution, 78
Bikes and Beyond, 79, 86
Biking, 7, 78–79, 284
　Gran Fondo San Diego, 22
Birch Aquarium at Scripps, 7, 62, 69, 77
Birch North Park Theatre, 167
Birding Hot Spots of San Diego, 79
Bird-watching, 79
　Chula Vista Nature Center, 66
Bishop's School, 61
Bite San Diego, 76, 120, 275
The Black, 156
Black's Beach, 45
Blind Lady Ale House, 176
Blink-182, 16
Blondstone Jewelry Studio, 158
Bloomingdale's, 161
Blue Door Winery (Julian), 247
Blue Horizons (SeaWorld), 41
Boating and sailing (boat rentals), 79–80, 235
Boating events, 181
　Festival of Sail, 23–24, 181
　Fleet Week, 24, 72
　San Diego Bayfair, 24
　San Diego Crew Classic, 21–22, 181
Boat Rentals of America (Oceanside), 235
Boat travel and cruises, 5, 73–75, 100, 274, 283–284
　evening bay cruises, 178–179
　whale-watching, 76–77

Bodegas de Santo Tomás (Ensenada), 269
Bohemian Market, 151
Boneyard Beach, 46, 228
Bonita Cove, 44
Bookstores, 161
Boomerang for Modern, 152
Borrego Palm Canyon Campground, 253
Borrego Palm Canyon self-guided hike, 250
Borrego Springs Chamber of Commerce, 250
Borrego Springs Resort, 251
Botanical Building (Balboa Park), 13, 48–49, 112
Botanic Garden, San Diego, 71
Bottlecraft, 176
Boudoir, 173–174
Bourbon Street Bar & Grill, 177
The Brass Rail, 177–178
Breakwater Brewing Co. (Oceanside), 235–236
Breakwater Way (Oceanside), 235
Breweries, 7, 19, 176
Brew Hop, 176
Broadway San Diego, 168
Brokers Building, 97–98
B Street Cruise Ship Terminal, 274
Buffalo Exchange, 154
Buick Invitational, 181–182
Bulevar Benito Juárez (Rosarito), 267
Bullfighting (Tijuana), 266
Business hours, 284
Bus tours, 75
　Tijuana, 256
Bus travel, 272, 273, 281–282
BUT's Wild Note Cafe, 171

C

Cabrillo, Juan Rodríguez, 11
　statue of, 54
Cabrillo Bridge, 108
Cabrillo National Monument, 2, 6, 36, 42, 54, 72, 76, 85
Cal-a-Vie (Vista), 212
Calendar of events, 21–25
Caliente Race & Sports Book (Tijuana), 258
Caliente Racetrack (Tijuana), 258
California Adventure (Anaheim), 236
California Ballet, 170
California Center for the Arts (Escondido), 168, 239
California Department of Fish and Game, 81
California Dreamin', 77
California Overland (Anza-Borrego Desert), 251, 275
California Surf Festival, 24
California Surf Museum (Oceanside), 235
California Welcome Center (Oceanside), 234

California Wolf Center (Julian), 245
Callaway Vineyard & Winery (Temecula), 241
Camping, Borrego Springs, 253
Cantina Mayahuel (North Park), 32
Carlsbad, 13, 227–234
Carlsbad Fall Village Faire, 24
Carlsbad Marathon & Half Marathon, 21
Carlsbad Mineral Water Spa, 228
Carlsbad Premium Outlets, 162, 230
Carlsbad Ranch, 227
　flower fields in bloom at, 21
Carlsbad Spring Village Faire, 22
Carlsbad State Beach, 228
Carlsbad Visitor Information Center, 227
Carnival Cruise Lines, 274
Carol Gardyne, 152
Carousel, Seaport Village, 102
Car rentals, 279–281
Carriage Works, 98
Car travel, 272, 273, 276–279
　Tijuana, 256
Cart Safari, 38
Casa Artelexia, 152
Casa de Balboa, 112–113
Casa de Bandini/Cosmopolitan Hotel, 104–105
Casa de Estudillo, 12
Casa del Prado, 113
Casa del Rey Moro African Museum, 292
Casa Rodriguez (Tijuana), 263
The Casbah, 171
Casinos, 179–180
Cathedral, 154
Cave Store, 158
Cedros Design District (Solana Beach), 159, 227
Celebrity Cruises, 274
Cellphones, 290
Centers for Disease Control and Prevention, 287
Centro Cultural de la Raza, 49
Centro Cultural Tijuana (CECUT), 259
Cervecería Tijuana, 265
Chandler, Raymond, 15
Chargers, San Diego, 181
Cheap Rentals, 78, 86
Chicano Park, 66–67
Chicano Park Murals, 4
Children, families with, 287
　best experiences for, 3–4
　Mother Goose Parade (El Cajon), 25
　restaurants, 120
　sights and attractions for, 68–70
Children's Pool, 3, 44–45, 61, 115
Children's Zoo, 40
Chillers Showroom, 156
Chinese Historical Museum, San Diego, 56–57, 97

Chinese Mission, 97
Chopra Center for Wellbeing (Carlsbad), 212, 233, 275
Chuao Chocolatier (North County), 230
Chuck Jones Gallery, 151
Chula Vista Nature Center, 66, 69, 79
Cinco de Mayo (May 5), 292
Cinemas, 179
Cinema Under the Stars, 179
Cirque de la Mer (SeaWorld), 41
City Ballet, 170
Claire de Lune Coffee Lounge, 177
Classical music, 169–170
  Mainly Mozart Festival, 22
Clermont Hotel, 292
Climate, 19–20
Club and music scene, 170–177
Club Campestre de Tijuana (Tijuana), 266
Club Tijuana, 266
Club Tijuana Xoloitzcuintles de Caliente, 183
The Coaster, 281
Coast Walk, 68, 85, 116
Coffeehouses with performances, 177
Co-Habitat, 154
College bowl games, 25
Collette Tours, 276
Colorado House, 105
Comedy clubs, 173
The Comedy Store, 173
Comic-Con International, 23
Command Museum, 72
Committee of 100, 49
Consulates, 286–287
  Tijuana, 257
Controversial Bookstore, 161
Convention & Visitors Bureau, 298
Convention Center/Embarcadero Marina Park South, 102
Cooking classes, 276
Copley Symphony Hall, 172–173
Coronado
  accommodations, 213–217
  brief description of, 30
  farmers' market, 163
  main streets, 277
  restaurants, 143–145
  shopping, 158–159
  sights and attractions, 65
    free, 68
Coronado Beach, 43
Coronado Ferry, 100
Coronado Flower Show weekend, 22
Coronado Municipal Golf Course, 82–83
Coronado Visitor Center, 298
County Administration Center, 70, 100
Craft & Commerce, 174

Craigslist, 219
Credit cards, 291–292
Creek, Nickel, 16
Cremolose, 94
Cricket Wireless Amphitheatre (Chula Vista), 172
Croce's Restaurant & Jazz Bar, 171
Crossings at Carlsbad, 229
Culinary Cottage (Julian), 247
Cups, 276
Curbs, color-coded, 278
Currency, Mexican, 258
Customs regulations, 284–285
Cuyamaca, Lake, 245
Cuyamaca Rancho State Park, 245
Cygnet Theatre, 168

D
Dale's Swim Shop, 159
Dance performances, 170
Dandy Del Sur (Tijuana), 265
Davis, William Heath, 12
Day at the Docks, 22
Daylight saving time, 296
Deep-vein thrombosis, 271
Del Mar, 220–226
Del Mar Beach, 46
Del Mar Fair, 23
Del Mar Library, 221
Del Mar National Horse Show, 22, 182
Del Mar Plaza, 221
Del Mar Racetrack & Fairgrounds, 182, 221
Del Mar State Beach, 221
Department stores, 161–162
Desert Natural History Association (Borrego Springs), 250
D.G. Wills Books, 161
Dining, 21, 24–25, 119–150. See also Restaurant Index
  best, 119–120
  Borrego Springs, 251–252
  Coronado, 143–145
  by cuisine, 147–150
  Del Mar, 221, 223–225
  downtown, Gaslamp Quarter, and Little Italy, 121–127
  Escondido, 239–240
  fish tacos, 134
  hamburger spots, 126
  Hillcrest and Uptown, 127–131
  Julian, 246
  La Jolla, 138–143
  Mission Bay and the Beaches, 133–137
  Oceanside, 235–236
  off the beaten path, 145
  Old Town and Mission Valley, 131–133
  parking, 147
  price categories, 119
  Rancho Santa Fe, 237
  reservations, 146
  special events and tours, 120

  tours, 275
  with a view, 142
Disabled travelers, 285–286
Discount shopping, 162–163
Discover Baja Travel Club, 257
Disneyland (Anaheim), 236
Diversionary Theatre, 168
Dizzy's, 171
DNA European Design Studio, 152
Dog Beach, 43, 274
Dog Beach Dog Wash, 274
Dolphin Interaction Programs (SeaWorld), 42
Don's Market (Julian), 247
Doves & Desperados (Julian), 244
Downtown
  accommodations, 186–195
  brief description of, 30
  main streets, 277
  nightlife, 173–175
  restaurants, 121–127
  shopping, 151–153
  sights and attractions, 54–57
Downtown Encinitas Merchants Association, 227
Downtown Information Center, 66, 71, 73
Drinking laws, 286
Driving rules, 277–278
Dr. Seuss, 16
Dr. Seuss' How the Grinch Stole Christmas!, 25
Drugstores, 288
Dudley's Bakery (Julian), 247

E
Eagle and High Peak Mine (Julian), 244
East Village, 30
East Village Tavern & Bowl, 174
Eating and drinking, 18–19. See also Food stores and markets; Restaurants
  best experiences, 2–3
  Julian Fall Apple Harvest, 24
  San Diego Bay Wine & Food Festival, 24–25
  tours, 76
Economy-class syndrome, 271
El Campo Santo, 58, 107
El Cid Campeador (sculpture), 111
Electricity, 286
Elephant Odyssey (San Diego Zoo), 40
Ellen Browning Scripps Park, 45, 115
El Lugar del Nopal (Tijuana), 266
El Niño weather pattern, 20
El Prado, 70
El Trompo (Tijuana), 259
The Embarcadero, 6
  walking tour, 98–102
Embarcadero Marina Park North, 102
Embassies and consulates, 286–287

Emerald City: The Boarding
  Source, 87
Emergencies, 287
Emilia Castillo, 158
Encinitas, 227–234
Encinitas Fall Festival, 25
Encinitas Visitors Center, 227
Endémico Resguardo Silvestre
  (Valle de Guadalupe), 269
Ensenada (Mexico), 267–269
Entertainment and nightlife,
  167–183
  alternative entertainment,
    178–179
  bars and lounges, 173–177
  casinos, 179–180
  cinemas, 179
  classical music, 169–170
  club and music scene, 170–177
  coffeehouses with
    performances, 177
  comedy clubs, 173
  current listings, 167
  dance, 170
  gay and lesbian nightlife,
    177–178
  getting tickets, 168
  opera, 170
  performing arts, 168–170
  spectator sports, 180–183
  theater, 168–169
  Tijuana, 265–266
Environmental concerns, 26–27
Equestrian events, 182
Escondido, 239–240
Escondido Antique Mall, 239
Evening bay cruises, 178–179
Eveoke Dance Theatre, 170

F
Fallbrook Winery, 73
Falling Sky Pottery, 156
Families with children, 287
  best experiences for, 3–4
  Mother Goose Parade (El
    Cajon), 25
  restaurants, 120
  sights and attractions for, 68–70
Farmers Insurance Open, 21, 182
Farmers' markets, 163
  Escondido, 239
Fashion Valley Center, 164
Ferries, 283–284
Ferry Landing Marketplace, 159
Festival of Beer, 24
Festival of Sail, 23–24, 181
Festivals and special events,
  21–25
Fiesta Cinco de Mayo, 22
Fiesta de Reyes, 104, 155
Fiesta Island, 43
52-mile San Diego Scenic
  Drive, 66
Film Festival
  San Diego, 24
  San Diego Latino, 21
Films, 16

Firehouse Museum, 55
First Church of Christ Scientist, 70
Fishing, 80–81
  Day at the Docks, 22
Fish tacos, 3, 18, 134
Fitness spas, 212
Five Star Tours, 256, 266
Flagship, 73, 77, 178
The Flame, 178
Flashbacks Recycled Fashions,
  154
Fleet Week, 24, 72
Flicks, 178
Flightline (zipline ride), 38
FlowBarrel, 61
Flower Fields at Carlsbad Ranch,
  229
FlowRider, 61
Folk Arts Rare Records, 165
Font's Point, 251
Food and wine trips, 275–276
Food stores and markets,
  163–164
  Julian, 247
  Tijuana, 259, 263
Football, 181
Fort Rosecrans National
  Cemetery, 72
4th & B, 172
Four Winds Trading Company,
  156, 160
Franciscans, 11
Free and dirt cheap activities,
  66–68
  best, 4
Frey Block Building, 97
Furniture and Treasures, 154
F. W. Woolworth Building, 94

G
Galleries, 160
Galleta Meadows Estate (Borrego
  Springs), 251
Gardens, 71–72
  Alcazar Garden, 110
  Balboa Park, 113
  Japanese Friendship Garden,
    50, 112
  Marston House Museum &
    Gardens, 50
  San Diego Botanic Garden
    (Encinitas), 230
Gaslamp Quarter, 2, 6, 54, 66,
  70, 71
  accommodations, 186–195
  brief description of, 30
  Mardi Gras in, 21
  restaurants, 121–127
  shopping, 151–153
  walking tour, 91–98
Gaslamp Quarter Historical
  Foundation, 76, 91, 276
Gator by the Bay, 22
Gays and lesbians, 288–289
  nightlife, 177–178
  San Diego LGBT Pride Parade,
    Rally, and Festival, 23

Geisel Library, 61, 71
Giant Dipper roller coaster, 44, 61
Glider flights, 77–78
Gliderport, 68, 69
Globus, 276
GoCar Tours, 74
GOGA by Gordana, 151
The Golden Door (Escondido),
  212
Golf, 81–84
  Borrego Springs, 251
  environmental concerns, 26
  Farmers Insurance Open, 21
  Tijuana, 266
  tournaments, 181–182
Golf Guide, 81
The Gondola Company, 73–74
Go San Diego Card, 41
Gossip Grill, 177
Grand Del Mar Golf Club, 82
Gran Fondo San Diego, 22
Grapeline, 241
Gray Line San Diego, 75, 256
The Greatest Generation Art
  Collection, 101
Great News!, 276
Greyhound, 273
Grunion Run, 180
G-Star, 151
Guadalupe Valley, 19
Gwynn, Tony, 17

H
Hall of Champions Sports
  Museum, San Diego, 52
Hamels, Cole, 17
Hamilton's Tavern, 33
Hand Art (Tijuana), 263
H&M Landing (Point Loma),
  77, 81
Hang gliding, 84–85
Harbor cruises, 5, 73–75, 100,
  274, 283–284
Harbor Days Festival (Oceanside),
  234
Harbor seals, 44
HatWorks, 151
Health concerns, 287–288
Health insurance, 288
Hellhole Canyon, 250
Heritage Park, 58, 107
The Hermitage (Encinitas), 228
Hike Bike Kayak San Diego,
  79, 275
Hiking, 5, 85
  Anza-Borrego Desert, 250
Hillcrest and Uptown
  accommodations, 196–199
  brief description of, 30–31
  farmers' market, 163
  main streets, 277
  restaurants, 127–131
  shopping, 154–155
Hillcrest Cinema, 179
Hipódromo Caliente (Tijuana), 258
Historic experiences, best, 5–6
History of San Diego, 10–15

HIV-positive visitors, 290
Holiday Bowl, 25
Holidays, 20–21
Holland America Line, 274
Holland's Bicycles, 79
HomeExchange.com, 219
HomeLink International, 219
Hong Kong Gentlemen's Club (Tijuana), 265
Hornblower Cruises, 74, 77, 178–179
Horse racing, Thoroughbred Racing Season, 23
Horse racing and equestrian events, 182
Horse Show, Del Mar National, 22
Horton Grand Hotel, 96
Horton Plaza, 54, 92, 152
Horton Plaza Park, 92
Hospitals, 288
Hostels, 219
Hot-air ballooning, 5
    Del Mar, 221
Hotel del Coronado, 4, 13, 30, 65
    history of, 214
Hotel Discounts, 218
Hotel Lester, 97
Hotels, 184–219. See also Accommodations Index
    alternative, 218–219
    best, 184–186
    Borrego Springs, 252–253
    Coronado, 213–217
    downtown, Gaslamp Quarter, and Little Italy, 186–195
    fitness spas, 212
    getting the best deal, 218
    high season, 217
    Hillcrest and Uptown, 196–199
    Julian, 247–248
    La Jolla, 206–212
    Mission Bay and the Beaches, 201–206
    North County, 232–234
    Oceanside, 236
    Old Town and Mission Valley, 199–201
    pet-friendly, 274
    price categories, 184
    private homes/rooms, 219
    Rancho Santa Fe, 238
    rates, 185, 217–218
    Tijuana, 260–265
House of Blues, 172
House of Charm, 110
House of Pacific Relations International Cottages, 49, 111
Humphrey's, 172
Humphrey's Backstage, 172
Hussong's Cantina (Ensenada), 269

I

Ice Town, 86–87
Iggy's (Rosarito), 268
IMAX Dome Theater, 51, 179
Immaculate Conception Catholic Church, 106
Immigration and customs clearance, 272
Imperial Beach, 43
Industry Showroom, 151
Influx Cafe, 33
Info Express, 282
Ingle Building, 98
In Good Taste, 159
In-line skating, 86–87
Insurance, 288
    renter's, 280
International Gay & Lesbian Travel Association, 289
International Visitor Information Center, 68, 279
Internet and Wi-Fi, 288
InterVac.com, 219
I.O.O.F. Building, 95
Irish Festival, 21
Iron Butterfly, 16
Itineraries, suggested, 33–36
Ivan Stewart's Electric Bike Center, 78
Ivy Nightclub/Ivy Rooftop, 174

J

Jack in the Box, 18
Jackson, Helen Hunt, 15
Japanese Friendship Garden, 50, 112
Jean Isaacs San Diego Dance Theater, 170
Jessop Street Clock, 92
Jesuits, 11
Jewel, 16
Jogging, 85
John's Fifth Avenue Luggage, 165
Joseph Bellows Gallery, 158, 160
Julian, 6, 12, 242–248
Julian Bed & Breakfast Guild, 247
Julian Chamber of Commerce, 243
Julian Cider Mill, 247
Julian Drug Store & Miner's Diner, 244
Julian Fall Apple Harvest, 24
Julian Gold Rush Hotel, 242
Julian Pie Company, 246
Julian Pioneer Museum, 244
Julian Tea & Cottage Arts, 247
June Gloom, 20, 42
Junípero Serra Museum, 58, 70

K

Kahuna Bob's Surf School, 87
Karl Strauss Brewery & Grill, 176
Kayaking, 86
Kearns Memorial Swimming Pool, 87
Keating Building, 94
Ken Cinema, 179
Kendall-Frost Reserve, 79
Kettner Art & Design District, 152
Kids, 287
    best experiences for, 3–4
    Mother Goose Parade (El Cajon), 25
restaurants, 120
sights and attractions for, 68–70
Kita Ceramics & Glassware, 151
Kite flying, Kiwanis Ocean Beach Kite Festival, 21
Kiwanis Ocean Beach Kite Festival, 21
Knott's Soak City U.S.A. (Chula Vista), 66
Kobey's Swap Meet, 162

L

Labor Temple Building, 98
La Bufadora (Mexico), 269
La Casa de Estudillo, 104
L.A. Cetto Winery (Tijuana), 259–260
La Costa Resort and Spa, 82
La Estrella (Tijuana), 265
La Jolla, 13, 71
    accommodations, 206–212
    brief description of, 31
    farmers' market, 163
    main streets, 277
    restaurants, 138–143
    shopping, 156–158
    sights and attractions, 61–65
        free, 68
    walking tour, 114–118
La Jolla Cove, 45, 116
La Jolla Cove Bridge Club, 116
La Jolla Kayak, 86
La Jolla Music Society, 169
La Jolla Playhouse, 168
La Jolla Recreation Center, 61
La Jolla Rough Water Swim, 24
La Jolla Shores, 45
La Jolla SummerFest, 23
La Jolla Surf Systems, 87
La Jolla Tennis Club, 87–88
La Jolla Village, 179
La Jolla Woman's Club, 61
Lake Cuyamaca, 81, 245
Lake Miramar Reservoir, 85
Lake Murray, 85
Lakes Line, 81
La Maisonnette, 158
Lambert, Adam, 16
Lamb's Players Theatre, 168–169
La Mezcalera (Tijuana), 265
Large Rock Monument, 104
Las Americas Premium Outlets, 162
Las Rocas Resort & Spa (Rosarito), 267
Laura Gambucci, 158
La Valencia Hotel, 61, 116
Lawrence Family Jewish Community Center, 87
Layout of San Diego, 28, 30
Lee Palm Sportfishers, 81
Legal aid, 288
LEGOLAND California (Carlsbad), 3, 69, 229
LEGOLAND Water Park (Carlsbad), 229

Lestat's Coffee House, 177
Le Travel Store, 166
Level 9 Rooftop Bar, 190
LGBT travelers, 288–289
    nightlife, 177–178
    San Diego LGBT Pride Parade,
        Rally, and Festival, 23
Ligne Roset, 158
Lily Pond (Balboa Park), 48–49, 112
Lincoln Hotel, 96
Lindbergh, Charles, 14
Lindbergh Field, 14
Lions, Tigers & Bears (Alpine),
    245
Lips, 175–176
Liquid Foundation Surf Shop, 156
Literature, San Diego in, 15–16
Little Italy, 30, 71
    accommodations, 186
    restaurants, 121–127
    shopping, 151–153
Little Italy Festa, 24
Live music, 170–173
Live Wire (North Park), 33
Llama Treks (Julian), 245–246
Llewelyn Building, 95
Lodge at Torrey Pines, 62
Lois Ann Dive Charters, 86
Longboard Surf Club
    Competition, 23
Longboard Surf Contest
    (Oceanside), 235
Los Remedios Restaurante Bar &
    Cantina (Tijuana), 266
Lost Forest zone (San Diego
    Zoo), 40
Louganis, Greg, 17
Louis Bank of Commerce, 92, 94
LOUNGEsix, 174
Lou's Records, 165
Lowery's Hot Glass, 156
Lux Art Institute (Encinitas), 227

M
McClellan-Palomar Airport
    (Carlsbad), 220, 271
McCoy House, 103
Macy's, 162
Maderas Golf Club, 82
Mail, 289
Main arteries and streets, 277
Mainly Mozart Festival, 22
Main Street Carriage Company
    (Julian), 245
Make Good, 33
Malashock Dance, 170
Malls, 164–165
Maps
    bike, 284
    street, 279
Mardi Gras in the Gaslamp
    Quarter, 21
Marian Bear Memorial Park (San
    Clemente Canyon), 85
Marie Hitchcock Puppet
    Theater, 70

Marine Corps Recruit Depot,
    recruit graduation at, 72
Mariner's Point, 44
Maritime Museum of San Diego,
    4, 6–7, 55–56, 69, 100, 181
    sailing adventures, 80
Marston Building, 94
Marston House, 70
Marston House Museum &
    Gardens, 50
Mary, Star of the Sea, 61, 115
Mason Street School, 106
Maurice Car'rie Winery
    (Temecula), 241
May Gray, 20, 42
Medea (yacht), 56
Medical insurance, 288
Medical requirements for entry,
    290
Menghini Winery (Julian), 247
Mercado de Artesanías (Tijuana),
    263
Mercado el Popo (Tijuana), 259
Mercado Hidalgo (Tijuana), 263
The Metropolitan, 95–96
Metropolitan Transit System
    (MTS), 272
Mexican-American War, 12
Mexican Department of
    Fisheries, 81
Mexicoach, 256
Mickelson, Phil, 17
Midway, USS, 14, 101
Mimi & Red, 154
Mingei International Museum,
    6, 50
Miniature Railroad and Carousel,
    Balboa Park, 48, 114
Mint, 154
Miranda's Courtyard, 156
Mission Basilica San Diego de
    Alcalá, 57–59, 70
Mission Bay and the Beaches
    accommodations, 201–206
    brief description of, 31
    restaurants, 133–137
    shopping, 156
    sights and attractions, 60–61
    free, 67
Mission Bay Boat Parade of
    Lights, 25
Mission Bay Park, 43, 60–61
Mission Bay Sportcenter, boating
    and sailing, 80
Mission Beach, 44
Mission Beach/Pacific Beach
    boardwalk, 4, 7
Mission Beach Surf & Skate,
    78–79
Mission Brewery, 176
Mission Hills, 71
Mission Hills Nursery, 71
Mission Point, 44
Missions, 6
Mission San Antonio de Pala (near
    Mount Palomar), 58–59

Mission San Luis Rey de Francia
    (Oceanside), 58, 234
Mission Santa Ysabel (near
    Julian), 59
Mission Trails Regional Park, 58,
    59–60, 67, 76, 79, 85
Mission Valley
    brief description of, 31
    main streets, 277
    sights and attractions, 57–60
Mission Valley Center, 164
Mission Valley Travelodge, 218
Mixture, 152
Mobile phones, 290
Model Railroad Museum, San
    Diego, 52
Modern San Diego (website), 71
Mofo Bar (Tijuana), 265
Money and costs, 290–292
Monte Picacho (Tijuana), 265
Moonlight Beach, 46, 227–228
Mormon Battalion Historic Site, 67
Morton, Jelly Roll, 16
Mother Goose Parade
    (El Cajon), 25
Mount Palomar Winery, 241
Mount Soledad, 62
Mt. Woodson Golf Club, 83
Moxie Theatre, 168
Mraz, Jason, 16
M-Theory Music, 165
MTS Transit Store, 272, 279,
    281, 285
Multicultural travelers, 292
Mundo Divertido (Tijuana), 259
Museo de Cera (Wax Museum;
    Tijuana), 258
Museo de Historia de Tijuana, 259
Museum of Contemporary Art San
    Diego, 6, 67, 101, 179
Museum of Contemporary Art San
    Diego Downtown, 56, 68
Museum of Contemporary Art San
    Diego La Jolla, 61, 64, 115
Museum of History and Art, 65
Museum of Making Music
    (Carlsbad), 228
Museum of Photographic Arts,
    6, 50–51, 179
Museums, best, 6–7
Music, 7, 16
    live, 170–173
    special events and festivals
        Adams Avenue
            Unplugged, 22
        Gator by the Bay, 22
        La Jolla SummerFest, 23
        Mainly Mozart Festival, 22
        Ocean Beach Music & Art
            Festival, 24
        San Diego Symphony
            Summer Pops, 23
        San Diego Thanksgiving
            Dixieland Jazz Festival, 25
    WorldBeat Center, 54

Music stores, 165
My Own Space, 158

N

National Comedy Theatre, 173
Nativa, 154
Native Americans, 11
Natural History Museum, San Diego, 53, 76, 77, 85, 113, 276
Naval Base Coronado (U.S. Naval Air Station, North Island), 30
Neighborhood (restaurant), 174
Neighborhoods in brief, 30–31
Neurosciences Institute, 71
The New Children's Museum, 56, 69
Newport Avenue Antique Center & Coffee House, 160
Newspapers and magazines, 293
New Town, 12–13
Next Level Sailing, 80
Nightlife and entertainment, 167–183
    alternative entertainment, 178–179
    bars and lounges, 173–177
    casinos, 179–180
    cinemas, 179
    classical music, 169–170
    club and music scene, 170–177
    coffeehouses with performances, 177
    comedy clubs, 173
    current listings, 167
    dance, 170
    gay and lesbian nightlife, 177–178
    getting tickets, 168
    opera, 170
    performing arts, 168–170
    spectator sports, 180–183
    theater, 168–169
    Tijuana, 265–266
Noble Experiment, 174
Noel-Baza Fine Art, 152
Nordstrom, 162
North Coast Repertory Theatre, 168
Northern San Diego County (North County), 220
    beaches, 46
    beach towns, 220–236
    getting there, 220
    inland, 237–242
North Island, 14
North Park, 32
NTC at Liberty Station, 167
Numbers, 178
Nunu's Cocktail Lounge, 176

O

Obelisk Bookstore, 161
Ocean Beach, 13, 43
    farmers' market, 163
Ocean Beach Antique District, 156
Ocean Beach Holiday Parade, 25

Ocean Beach Music & Art Festival, 24
Ocean Beach Surf & Skate, 87
Ocean Enterprises, 86
Ocean Front Walk (Pacific Beach), 44
Oceanside, 46, 234–236
Oceanside Museum of Art, 234, 235
OEX Dive & Kayak Centers, 77, 86
Off the Record, 165
Old City Hall, 95
Old Globe Summer Shakespeare Festival, 23
Old Globe Theatre, 69, 110, 169
Old Globe Theatre Tour, 49
Old Julian Book House, 247
Old Town and Mission Valley
    accommodations, 199–201
    brief description of, 31
    restaurants, 131–133
    shopping, 155–156
    sights and attractions, 57–60
        free, 67
    walking tour, 103–107
Old Town's Most Haunted, 76
Old Town State Historic Park, 4, 5–6, 12, 60, 69, 155
Old Town Trolley Tours, 72, 75, 282
    Sea and Land Adventures, 74
One Ocean (SeaWorld), 41
The Onyx Room/Thin, 174
Open Air Theatre, 172
Opera, 170
Orchid Odyssey, 49
Orfila Vineyards (Escondido), 72–73, 239
Organ Festival, Summer, 23
Outdoor activities, 77–88
    ballooning and scenic flights, 77–78
    best, 5
    biking, 78–79
    bird-watching, 79
    boating, 79–80
    fishing, 80–81
    special events
        Carlsbad Marathon & Half Marathon, 21
        Rock 'n' Roll Marathon and Half Marathon, 22
        World Championship Over-the-Line Tournament, 23

P

Pacific Beach, 13, 44
    farmers' market, 163
    main streets, 177
Pacific Beach AleHouse, 176
Pacific Beach Surf Shop, 87
Packing tips, 293
Palacio de la Cultura (Tijuana), 258
Palacio Frontón (Tijuana), 259
Palm Canyon, 111
Palomar, 240, 242

Palomar Observatory, 240, 242
Panama-California Exposition of 1915, 13, 70
Panda Trek (San Diego Zoo), 40
Pangaea Outpost, 156
Papas & Beer (Rosarito), 268
Paragliding, 84–85
Paras Newsstand (North Park), 33
Parking, 278
Park View Little League All-Stars, 17–18
Paseo de los Héroes (Tijuana), 259
Passports, 293–294
Passport to Balboa Park, 48
Passport/Zoo Combo, 48
Pecoff Gallery, 152
Pedroreña House, 106
Pennyfarthing's Bicycle Store, 78
Performing arts, 168–170
PETCO Park, 54, 180–181
Peter Lik Gallery, 158
Pets, traveling with, 274
Pets Rule! (SeaWorld), 41
Pier View South (Oceanside), 235
Pigment, 154
Pilar's, 156
Pilot (boat), 56
Pioneer Cemetery (Julian), 244
Pizza Port Brewing Company, 176
Planning your trip, 270–298
    area codes, 284
    business hours, 284
    customs regulations, 284–285
    disabled travelers, 285–286
    drinking laws, 286
    electricity, 286
    embassies and consulates, 286–287
    family travel, 287
    getting around, 276–284
    getting there, 270
    health concerns, 287–288
    Internet and Wi-Fi, 288
    legal aid, 288
    LGBT travelers, 288–289
    mail, 289
    medical requirements, 290
    mobile phones, 290
    money and costs, 290–292
    multicultural travelers, 292
    newspapers and magazines, 293
    packing tips, 293
    passports, 293–294
    safety, 294
    senior travel, 295
    single travelers, 295
    smoking, 295
    special-interest trips and tours, 275–276
    student travel, 295–296
    taxes, 296
    telephones, 296
    time zones, 296
    tipping, 296–297
    toilets, 297
    visas, 297–298
    visitor information, 298

305

Plant Day, 49
Playas de Tijuana, 260
Plaza Fiesta (Tijuana), 265
Plaza Monumental (Tijuana), 260, 266
Plaza Pueblo Amigo (Tijuana), 265
Plaza Río Tijuana, 263
The Plunge, 61
Poinsettia Bowl, 25
Point Loma farmers' market, 163
Point Loma Sportfishing, 81
Police, 294
Popotla, 268
Port of San Diego Day at the Docks, 80
Port Pavilion, 100–101
Post offices, 289
Powerhouse Park, 221
Private homes/rooms, 219
Progress, 33
Puerto Nuevo (Mexico), 267, 268
Puppet Theater, Marie Hitchcock, 70

Q

Qualcomm Stadium, 172, 181
Queen Califia's Magical Circle (Escondido), 239
Quick Queue (SeaWorld), 42
Quikbook, 218
Quiksilver, 151
Quint Contemporary Art, 158

R

Rainfall, 19–20
Ramada Plaza, 218
Rancho Bernardo Inn, 83
Rancho La Puerta (Tecate, Mexico), 212, 275
Rancho Santa Fe, 237–239
Ray at Night gallery crawl, 160
Real Del Mar (near Tijuana), 266
Reloj Monumental (Tijuana), 257
Reserve America, 253
Responsible tourism, 26–27
Restaurants, 21, 24–25, 119–150.
    See also Restaurant Index
    best, 119
    Borrego Springs, 251–252
    Coronado, 143–145
    by cuisine, 147–150
    Del Mar, 221, 223–225
    downtown, Gaslamp Quarter, and Little Italy, 121–127
    Escondido, 239–240
    fish tacos, 134
    hamburger spots, 126
    Hillcrest and Uptown, 127–131
    Julian, 246
    La Jolla, 138–143
    Mission Bay and the Beaches, 133–137
    Oceanside, 235–236
    off the beaten path, 145
    Old Town and Mission Valley, 131–133

parking, 147
price categories, 119
Rancho Santa Fe, 237
reservations, 146
special events and tours, 120
tours, 275
with a view, 142
Reuben H. Fleet Science Center, 7, 51, 113
Rich's, 178
Riverwalk Golf Club, 83
Riviera del Pacifico (Ensenada), 268
Roar & Snore sleepover programs (San Diego Zoo Safari Park), 40
Robinson-Rose House, 103
Rock 'n' Roll Marathon and Half Marathon, 22
Rodeos, Lakeside Rodeo, 22
Roller derby, 182–183
Rosamariposa, 152
Rosarito (Mexico), 267
Rosarito Beach Hotel (Mexico), 267
Royal Caribbean, 274
Royal Pie Bakery Building, 97
Ruderman Antique Maps, 158
Ruocco Park, 102

S

Safari Caravans, 38
Safety, 294
    Tijuana, 254
Sail Jada Charters, 80
St. Patrick's Day Parade, 21
Sales tax, 166
Salk Institute for Biological Studies, 62, 71
Salon Quijote (Rosarito), 267
Salt Creek Golf Club, 82
Sanborns (Tijuana), 263
San Diego Air & Space Museum, 7, 51, 72, 112
San Diego Asian Film Festival, 179
San Diego Audubon Society, 79
San Diego Automotive Museum, 51–52, 112
San Diego Ballet, 170
San Diego Bayfair, 24
San Diego Bay Wine & Food Festival, 24–25, 120
San Diego Bed & Breakfast Guild, 219
San Diego Beer Week, 24
San Diego Bike Shop, 78
San Diego Black Film Festival, 179
San Diego Boat Parade of Lights, 25
San Diego Botanic Garden (Encinitas), 71, 230
San Diego Chargers, 181
San Diego Chinese Historical Museum, 56–57, 97
San Diego CityBeat, 167
San Diego Convention Center, 70

San Diego-Coronado Bay Bridge, 65
San Diego County Bicycle Coalition, 78, 284
San Diego County Fair, 23, 221
San Diego Crew Classic, 21–22, 181
San Diego Derby Dolls, 182–183
San Diego Film Festival, 24, 179
San Diego Floral Association, 72
San Diego Gay and Lesbian Times, 289
San Diego Golf, 82
San Diego Hall of Champions Sports Museum, 52
San Diego History Center, 52
San Diego International Airport, 270
San Diego Jewish Film Festival, 179
San Diego Junior Theatre, 69–70
San Diego-La Jolla Underwater Park, 5, 61
San Diego Latino Film Festival, 21, 179
San Diego LGBT Pride Parade, Rally, and Festival, 23
San Diego Magazine, 88
San Diego Model Railroad Museum, 52
San Diego Museum of Art, 7, 52–53, 110
San Diego Museum of Man, 53, 108, 110
San Diego Natural History Museum, 53, 76, 77, 113, 276
San Diego Oceans Foundation, 86
San Diego Open, 182
San Diego Opera, 170
San Diego Padres, 180–181
San Diego Polo Club, 182
San Diego Reader, 88, 167
San Diego Regional Bike Map, 284
San Diego Repertory Theatre, 169
San Diego Restaurant Week, 21, 120
San Diego Shark Diving Expeditions, 275
San Diego Sockers, 17
San Diego Surfing Academy, 87
San Diego Symphony, 169–170
San Diego Symphony Summer Pops, 23
San Diego Thanksgiving Dixieland Jazz Festival, 25
San Diego Trolley, 254, 282–283
San Diego *Union* Printing Office, 106
San Diego Zoo, 13, 40–41, 69, 114
San Diego Zoo Safari Park, 38
San Dieguito Lagoon, 221
San Elijo Lagoon Ecological Reserve (Cardiff by the Sea), 227
San Elijo Nature Center, 227

San Pasqual Battlefield State Historic Park, 239
Santa Anas, 20
Santa Fe Depot, 101
Santana, Carlos, 16
Santa Ysabel General Store (Julian), 243
Sara's London Shop (Tijuana), 263
Sauvage, 158
Scenic flights, 77–78
Scott White Contemporary Art, 158
Scuba diving, 86
Scuba San Diego, 86
Sculpture Garden of the Museum of Art, 110
SDAI Museum of the Living Artist, 51
Seafood, 18
Seaforth Boat Rental, 80
Seaforth Sportfishing, 81
Seagrove Park, 221
Sea Life Aquarium (Carlsbad), 229
Sea Lions Live (SeaWorld), 41
Seaport Village, 54, 69, 102, 152–153
Seaside Papery, 159
SeaWorld San Diego, 41–42, 69
Sefton Plaza, 108
Self-Realization Fellowship Retreat and Hermitage (Encinitas), 4, 228
Senior travel, 295
Shakespeare Pub & Grille, 176
Shamu Rocks (SeaWorld), 41
Sheriff's Museum, William B. Kolender San Diego County, 67
Shopping, 151–166
  antiques and collectibles, 159–160
  by area, 151–159
    Coronado, 158–159
    downtown, the Gaslamp Quarter, and Little Italy, 151–153
    Hillcrest and Uptown, 154–155
    Julian, 246–247
    La Jolla, 156–158
    Mission Bay and the Beaches, 156
    Old Town and Mission Valley, 155–156
    Tijuana, 262–263
  art and crafts, 160
  bookstores, 161
  department stores, 161–162
  discount shopping, 162–163
  farmers' markets, 163
  malls, 164–165
  music stores, 165
  practical matters, 166
  toys and games, 165
  travel accessories, 165–166
Sierra Club, 85
Sights and attractions, 37–118
  Balboa Park, 46–54
  beaches, 42–46

best ways to see San Diego like a local, 7–8
  Coronado, 65
  downtown and beyond, 54–57
    free, 66–67
  free, 66–68
  for kids, 68–70
  La Jolla, 61–65
  major animal parks, 37–42
  Mission Bay and the Beaches, 60–61
  organized tours, 73–77
  special-interest sightseeing, 70–73
  by theme index, 89–90
  Tijuana, 258–260
  top 15, 37
Silver Strand, 30, 43
Single travelers, 295
Skating, 86–87
Skechers USA, 156
Skyfari aerial tram (San Diego Zoo), 40
Sky Sailing, 77
Skysurfer Balloon Company, 77
Smith Ranch (Julian), 244
Smoking, 295
Snorkeling, 86
Soccer, 183
  Tijuana, 266
Sockers, 183
So Diego Tours, 76, 120, 275
Solana Beach, 227–234
Solana Beach Visitors Center, 227
Some Like It Hot (film), 16
Sótano Suizo (Tijuana), 265
South Carlsbad State Beach, 228
South Coast Winery Resort & Spa (Temecula), 241
Southern California CityPass, 41
South Park, 33
Spanish Village Art Center, 114, 160
Special events and festivals, 21–25
Spectator sports, 8, 17–18, 180–183
  Tijuana, 266
Spencer-Ogden Building, 94
Sports Fan Shuttle, 181
Spreckels Building, 169
Spreckels Organ Pavilion, 23, 53, 111
Spreckels Theatre, 172–173
The Sprinter, 281
Stadium Golf Center & Batting Cages, 82
Starlite, 177
Star of India, 55–56
Stay-for-the-Day pass, 48
Steele Canyon Golf Club, 26, 82
Stingaree, 175
Stingaree district, 13, 95
Stone Brewing World Bistro and Gardens, 176
The Strand (Oceanside), 235
Street maps, 279
Stuart Collection, 61, 64, 68

Student travel, 295–296
Subtext Gallery, 152
SummerFest, 169
Summer Organ Festival, 23
Sunny Jim Cave, 116, 158
SuperShuttle, 272
Surf Diva, 87
Surfing, 5, 10, 87
  California Surf Festival, 24
  competitions, 23
  Tourmaline Surfing Park, 44
Surfside Race Place, 182
Swami's Beach, 46, 228
Swimming, 87
Switchfoot, 16
Sycuan Resort & Casino (near El Cajon), 83–84, 180
Symphonic Carillon, 108

T
Taboo Studio, 160
Tamarisk Grove Campground (near Borrego Springs), 253
Tasende Gallery, 158, 160
Tauck World Discovery, 276
Taxes, 296
  Mexican, 258
Taxis, 272, 283
Telephones, 296
Temecula, 73, 241
Temecula Balloon & Wine Festival, 77, 241
Temecula Valley, 19
Temperatures, average monthly, 20
Tennis, 87–88
Theater, 7, 17, 168–169
  Old Globe Summer Shakespeare Festival, 23
The 3rd Corner, 163–164
Thomas Guide, 279
Thornton Winery (Temecula), 241
Thoroughbred Racing Season, 23
Tide pools, 42
Tijuana, 253–269
  entertainment and nightlife, 265–266
  exploring, 258–260
  getting there, 254, 256
  safety, 254
Tijuana Convention & Visitors Bureau, 257
Time zones, 296
Timken Museum of Art, 53–54
Tipping, 296–297
  Tijuana, 258
The Tipsy Crow, 175
Tobey's 19th Hole, 82
Toilets, 297
Tolán (Tijuana), 263
Top Gun (film), 16
Top of the Hyatt, 102, 175
Top of the Park, 178
Toronado (North Park), 33
Torrey Pines Beach, 45
Torrey Pines Gliderport, 84–85

ACCOMMODATIONS INDEX

Torrey Pines Golf Course,
5, 62, 84
Torrey Pines State Beach, 221
Torrey Pines State Reserve, 2, 36,
64–65, 76, 79, 85
Torrey Pines Visitors Center, 70
Tourism, 13–14
Tourist information, 298
Borrego Springs, 249
Del Mar, 221
Julian, 243
Oceanside, 234
Solana Beach, Encinitas, and
Carlsbad, 227
Tijuana, 257
Tourmaline Surfing Park, 44
Tours
Balboa Park, 49
organized, 73–77
Toys and games, 165
Traffic (film), 17
Train travel, 273–274, 281
Transit Information Line, 284
Transit Store, 272, 279, 281, 285
Travel accessories, 165–166
Traveler's Aid International, 287
Traveler's Depot, 166
Trolley, 282–283
Tuna Harbor, 101
Tuna Harbor Park, 101
Turf Supper Club, 177
Turista Libre, 256
Turtle Lagoon, 66
Tyson Street Park (Oceanside),
235

U

United Nations Building, 49, 111
University of California, San
Diego (UCSD), 31, 61
University Towne Center (UTC),
164–165
Urban Mo's Bar & Grill, 177
Urban Outfitters, 151, 154
Urban Safaris, 75
USA Rail Pass, 274
U.S. Naval Air Station, North
Island (Naval Base
Coronado), 30
U.S. Olympic Training Center
(Chula Vista), 4, 68
USS Midway, 14, 101
USS Midway Museum, 57
U-T San Diego, 88, 167

V

Vagabond Inn—Hotel Circle, 218
Valle de Guadalupe (Mexico), 267,
269
Valley View Casino (Valley
Center), 179
Valley View Casino Center, 172
Vancouver, George, 12
Van Roekel (Temecula), 241
Vedder, Eddie, 16
Veterans Museum & Memorial
Center, 72

Viejas Arena, 172
Viejas Casino (Alpine), 179
Viejas Outlet Center, 162–163
The Village, 31
Village Hat Shop, 154
Villa Montezuma, 70
Vin de Syrah Spirit & Wine Parlor,
175
Vintage Religion, 154
Visas, 297–298
Visitor Center (Balboa Park), 111
Visitor information, 298
Borrego Springs, 249
Del Mar, 221
Julian, 243
Oceanside, 234
Solana Beach, Encinitas, and
Carlsbad, 227
Tijuana, 257
Vitreum, 152
Vizcaíno, Sebastián, 11
Vizit Tours, 75, 282
Volcan Mountain Preserve, 245
Volunteer travel, 26
Voyeur, 175

W

Waits, Tom, 16
Walkabout International, 66, 75,
276
Walking tours
guided, 75–76, 276
self-guided, 91–118
Balboa Park, 107–114
The Embarcadero, 98–102
Gaslamp Quarter, 91–98
La Jolla, 114–118
Old Town, 103–107
Walter Andersen Nursery, 71
Walton, Bill, 17
Wambaugh, Joseph, 15
The Warm Hearth (Julian), 247
Warner Springs Ranch (Cleveland
National Forest), 275
Warwick's, 161
Water taxis, 284
Watts-Robinson Building, 92
Wave House, 61
Wax Museum (Museo de Cera;
Tijuana), 258
Weather, 19–20
Websites, 88
Weeds (TV series), 17
Weidners' Gardens (Encinitas),
229
West Gate (Balboa Park), 108
West Sea Company, 156
Whakapono Sailing Charters, 77
Whale and Dolphin Conservation
Society, 42
Whale-watching, 25, 54, 69,
76–77
Whaley House, 12, 60, 106
Whaling Bar, 116
Wheelchair accessibility, 285–286
Where You Want to Be Tours,
75–76

Whistle Stop Bar, 33
White Box Contemporary, 151
Wild Animal Park. See San Diego
Zoo Safari Park
Wildflowers, 21
Anza-Borrego, 250
William B. Kolender San Diego
County Sheriff's Museum, 67
William Heath Davis House
Museum, 57, 96
William Heise County Park, 245
William Penn Hotel, 94
Williams, Ted, 17
Windansea Beach, 44
The Wine Bank, 164
Wines and vineyards, 19
attractions for wine lovers,
72–73
Ensenada, 269
Escondido, 239, 241
Julian, 247
San Diego Bay Wine & Food
Festival, 24–25
shops, 164
Tijuana, 259–260
tours, 275–276
WineSellar & Brasserie, 164
Winslow, Don, 15
Wisconsin Street Beach
(Oceanside), 235
Witch Creek Winery (Julian), 247
Wolfe, Tom, 16
Wooden Boat Festival, 181
Woolworth Building, 94
WorldBeat Center, 54, 292–293
World Bodysurfing
Championships, 23, 235
World Championship Over-the-
Line Tournament, 23, 43, 181
Wreck Alley, 86

X

Xplore Offshore, 74–75

Y

YMCA, 87
Yuma Building, 95

Z

Zappa, Frank, 16
Zazen, 159
Zoo Safari Park, 69

Accommodations

Andaz Hotel, 184, 186–188
Balboa Park Inn, 198–199
Banana Bungalow, 219
The Beach Cottages, 205
Beach Terrace Inn (Carlsbad), 232
The Bed & Breakfast Inn at La
Jolla, 209
Best Western Blue Sea Lodge,
204

Best Western Plus Inn by the Sea, 211–212
Borrego Valley Inn (Borrego Springs), 252
Britt Scripps Inn, 185, 196
Camino Real (Tijuana), 264
Catamaran Resort Hotel, 201–202
Coronado Inn, 216
Cosmopolitan Hotel and Restaurant, 199
The Cottage, 196
Crone's Cobblestone Cottage Bed & Breakfast, 196–197
Crowne Plaza San Diego, 199–200
Crystal Pier Hotel, 205
The Dana on Mission Bay, 204
Disneyland Hotel (Anaheim), 236
Disney's Grand Californian Hotel & Spa (Anaheim), 236
El Cordova Hotel, 213–214
Elsbree House, 205–206
Embassy Suites Hotel San Diego Bay-Downtown, 188
Empress Hotel of La Jolla, 209
Estancia La Jolla Hotel & Spa, 210
500 West, 218
Gaslamp Plaza Suites, 185
Glorietta Bay Inn, 214–215
Grand Del Mar, 184, 225
The Grande Colonial, 210
Grand Hotel Tijuana, 264
Hacienda del Mar (Tijuana), 264
Hacienda del Sol (Borrego Springs), 252
Harbor View Days Inn Suites, 218
Hard Rock Hotel San Diego, 188
Hilton San Diego Bayfront, 188–189
Hilton San Diego Gaslamp Quarter, 189
Holiday Inn Express-Old Town, 200–201
Holiday Inn Oceanside Marina, 236
Holiday Inn Tijuana Zona Río, 264
Horton Grand, 189
Hostelling International—SD Downtown, 219
Hostelling International—SD Point Loma, 219
Hotel del Coronado, 185, 213
Hotel Hacienda del Río (Tijuana), 264
Hotel Indigo, 26, 189–190
Hotel Lucerna (Tijuana), 264–265
Hotel Misión Santa Isabel (Ensenada), 269
Hotel Palomar, 190
Hotel Parisi, 184–185, 210–211
Hotel Pueblo Amigo (Tijuana), 264
Hotel Real Del Río (Tijuana), 264
The Inn at Rancho Santa Fe, 238
Inn at the Park, 197–198
Julian Gold Rush Hotel, 248
Keating Hotel, 190
Keating House, 198

Krazy Coyote/Red Ocotillo (Borrego Springs), 253
La Costa Resort and Spa (Carlsbad), 232–233
La Fonda (between Rosarito and Ensenada), 268
La Jolla Beach & Tennis Club, 211
La Jolla Cove Suites, 211
La Jolla Shores Hotel, 206, 208
La Jolla Village Lodge, 218
La Pensione Hotel, 185
Las Rosas Hotel & Spa (Ensenada), 269
La Valencia Hotel, 186, 208
Little Italy Hotel, 195
The Lodge at Torrey Pines, 184, 208
Loews Coronado Bay Resort, 184, 215–216
Manchester Grand Hyatt San Diego, 190–191
Marriott Coronado Island Resort, 216
Marriott San Diego Gaslamp Quarter, 191
Marriott San Diego Hotel & Marina, 191
Motel 6 Hotel Circle, 201
1906 Lodge, 216–217
Ocean Beach International Hostel, 219
Ocean Park Inn, 204–205
Oceanside Marina Suites, 236
Omni San Diego Hotel, 186
Orchard Hill Country Inn (Julian), 248
Pacific Terrace Hotel, 202
Palacio Azteca Hotel (Tijuana), 265
Palm Canyon Resort (Borrego Springs), 252
The Palms Hotel (Borrego Springs), 252
Paradise Point Resort & Spa, 184, 202
Park Hyatt Aviara Resort (Carlsbad), 185, 232
The Pearl Hotel, 206
Pelican Cove Inn (Carlsbad), 233
Pine Hills Lodge, 248
Rancho Valencia Resort & Spa (Rancho Santa Fe), 238–239
Scripps Inn, 209
The Sofia Hotel, 191–192
Sommerset Suites Hotel, 198
Tamarack Beach Resort (Carlsbad), 234
Tijuana Marriott Hotel, 264
Tower 23, 185, 203–204
USAHostels, 219
THE US GRANT, 192
The Village Inn, 217
Welk Resorts San Diego, 239–240
The Westgate Hotel, 192
West Inn & Suites, 233
W San Diego, 193
Wyndham Oceanside Pier Resort, 236

Restaurants

Addison (Del Mar), 223
Alchemy, 33
Analog, 94
Anthology, 122
Anthony's Fishette, 100
Baleen, 120, 134
Bali Hai, 142
Bandar, 121
Bankers Hill Bar + Restaurant, 128
Barra Barra Old Town Saloon, 104
Bay Park Fish Co., 134
Beach Break Cafe (Oceanside), 235
Bellefleur Restaurant (Carlsbad), 230, 231
Bencotto Italian Kitchen, 121
Berta's Latin American Restaurant, 107, 132
Bertrand at Mister A's, 119, 127, 142
Best Western Bayside Inn, 193
Big Kitchen, 33
Bistro le Cousteau (Rosarito), 268
Bleu Bohème, 146
Blue Ribbon Artisan Pizzeria (Encinitas), 230
Blue Water Seafood Market and Grill, 134
BO-beau, 136
Bread & Cie., 130
Brian's 24 Restaurant Bar & Grill, 120, 124
The Brigantine, 134, 143–144
Brockton Villa, 119, 141, 142
Bronx Pizza, 130
Bully's Restaurant (Del Mar), 223
Buon Appetito, 121
Burger Lounge, 126
Burlap (Del Mar), 223
Caesar's (Tijuana), 262
Cafe Chloe, 124–125
Cafe 222, 121
Caffé Bella Italia, 136
Candelas, 120, 122, 142, 143
Carlee's Place (Borrego Springs), 251
Carmelita's Mexican Grill & Cantina (Borrego Springs), 251
Carnitas Uruapan (Tijuana), 260–261
Casa Guadalajara, 104, 132
The Cheese Shop, 96
Cheripan (Tijuana), 260
Chez Loma, 144
Chiki Jai (Tijuana), 260
China Max, 145
Cien Años (Tijuana), 261
Claire's on Cedros (Solana Beach), 230
Clayton's Coffee Shop, 145
C Level Lounge, 123
Coffee Cup, 138
Corvette Diner, 120, 137

Cosmopolitan Hotel and Restaurant, 104
Costa Brava, 134
The Cottage, 142–143
County Administration Center cafeteria, 100
Cowboy Star, 122
Cucina Urbana, 128–129, 146
Danny's Palm Bar & Grill, 126
Delicias (Rancho Santa Fe), 237
Del Mar Motel on the Beach, 226
Dumpling Inn, 145
El Agave Tequileria, 120, 131–132
El Bizcocho, 146
El Camino, 125
El Nido (Rosarito), 268
El Potrero (Tijuana), 260
El Rey Sol (Ensenada), 269
El Take It Easy (North Park), 32
El Taller (Tijuana), 262
El Zarape, 134
Encinitas Ale House, 230
Extraordinary Desserts, 125–126
Farm House Café (North Park), 32–33
Fidel's Little Mexico (Solana Beach), 230
1500 Ocean, 143
Filippi's Pizza Grotto, 120, 126
The Fishery, 134, 136
Fish Joint (Oceanside), 236
Fish Market, 101–102, 142
Fish Market (Del Mar), 223
The Fish Market/Top of the Market, 125
Flavor Del Mar, 223
Flying Pig Pub & Kitchen (Oceanside), 236
French Corner (Borrego Springs), 251
Gaslamp Plaza Suites, 193–194
George's at the Cove, 119, 140, 142
Grant Grill, 121
Green Flash, 142
Hacienda de Vega (Escondido), 240
Harney Sushi, 107, 131
Harney Sushi (Oceanside), 235
Hash House a Go Go, 127
Heaven Sent Desserts (North Park), 32
Hill Street Cafe (Oceanside), 236
Hob Nob Hill, 127
Hodad's, 126
Holiday Inn on the Bay, 194
Hotel Calafia (near Rosarito), 268
Hotel del Coronado, 143
Il Fornaio, 142
Il Fornaio Cucina Italiana (Del Mar), 221, 223
Indigo Grill, 123
Isabel's Cantina, 133
Island Prime, 122–123, 142
Jake's Del Mar, 224
Jasmine Seafood Restaurant, 145

Jayne's Gastropub, 146
JRDN, 133, 142
Julian Café & Bakery, 246
Julian Drug Store & Miner's Diner, 244
Julian Grille, 246
Jyoti Bihanga, 146
Kendall's Cafe (Borrego Springs), 251
Kensington Grill, 145
Kono's Surf Club Cafe, 133–134
Krazy Coyote Bar & Grille/Red Ocotillo (Borrego Springs), 252
La Diferencia (Tijuana), 261
La Fonda de Roberto (Tijuana), 261
Laja (Valle de Guadalupe), 269
La Pensione Hotel, 195
La Querencia (Tijuana), 261–262
L'Auberge Del Mar Resort & Spa, 225
Les Artistes (Del Mar), 226
The Linkery, 26, 120, 129–130
Loews Coronado Bay Resort, 143
Lucha Libre Gourmet Taco Shop, 134
Mamá Testa Taqueria, 130–131, 134
The Marine Room, 119, 138, 142
Market, 26
Market Restaurant + Bar (Del Mar), 120, 224
Mexican Take Out, 145
Michele Coulon Dessertier, 138
Miguel's Cocina, 143
Mille Fleurs (Rancho Santa Fe), 128, 238
Misión 19 (Tijuana), 262
The Mission, 137
Mistral, 142, 143
Mom's Pie House (Julian), 246
Mudville Flats, 194
Negai (Tijuana), 260
Neighborhood, 126
Nick's at the Pier, 142
Nine-Ten, 138
Nobu, 121
The Oceanaire Seafood Room, 124
Old Town Mexican Cafe, 131
101 Cafe (Oceanside), 236
Ortega's (Puerto Nuevo, Mexico), 268
Pacifica Del Mar, 223
Palace Bar, 96
Pamplemousse Grille (Del Mar), 224
Paon Restaurant and Wine Bar (Carlsbad), 231
Paradise Grille (Del Mar), 223
Peohe's, 142
Point Loma Seafoods, 134
Pokez Mexican Restaurant, 121
Po Pazzo, 121
Porto Vista Hotel & Suites, 194
Poseidon on the Beach (Del Mar), 223

Potato Shack Cafe (Encinitas), 230
Prado Restaurant, 114
Prepkitchen (Del Mar), 223
Prepkitchen (San Diego), 118, 141
Q'ero (Encinitas), 231
Rama, 121
Ranchos Cocina, 146
Red Fox Steak House (North Park), 33
Red Pearl Kitchen, 125
The Restaurant at the W, 121
Rhinoceros Cafe & Grille, 145
Richard Walker's Pancake House, 121
Rincón San Román (Tijuana), 262
Rocky's Crown Pub, 126
Rodeway Inn & Suites Downtown, 195
Romano's Dodge House (Julian), 246
Roppongi, 140
Roy's, 102
Rubio's Fresh Mexican Grill, 134
Ruby's (Oceanside), 235
Saffron, 127
Sally's, 121
Sbicca (Del Mar), 223
Sculpture Court Café, 53
Sea Rocket Bistro (North Park), 32
Searsucker, 124
Shimbashi Izakaya (Del Mar), 224–225
Siamese Basil (Encinitas), 230
Sky Room, 138, 142
The Smoking Goat (North Park), 32
Snooze, 131
Sogno DiVino, 121
Solace & The Moonlight Lounge (Encinitas), 231
Solare, 136
South Beach Bar & Grill, 134
Spice & Rice Thai Kitchen, 141
Spicy City, 145
Spread, 146
Stingaree, 121
Stone Brewing World Bistro & Gardens (Escondido), 240
Su Casa, 138
Susanna's (Rosarito), 267
Sushi Ota, 136–137
Swami's Cafe (Encinitas), 230
Tacos el Yaqui (Rosarito), 268
Tapenade, 140
Tea Pavilion, 112
Tepoznieves (Tijuana), 260
The 3rd Corner, 137
333 Pacific (Oceanside), 235
Thyme in the Ranch (Rancho Santa Fe), 237
Tioli's Crazee Burger, 126
Top of the Market, 125, 142
The Tractor Room, 128
Turf Supper Club, 33
25 Forty Bistro & Bakehouse, 132–133

Underbelly, 127
Urban Solace, 130
URBN Coal Fired Pizza/Bar (North Park), 32
Vagabond, 33
Villa Ortega's (Puerto Nuevo), 268
Villa Saverios (Tijuana), 260

Vincent's (Escondido), 239
Vivace, 119, 232
Wa Dining Okan, 145
Wahoo's Fish Taco, 134
Wave Crest (Del Mar), 226
Westgate Room, 121
West Steak and Seafood (Carlsbad), 231

Whisknladle, 141
Whole Foods, 127
World Famous, 142
Yu Me Ya Sake House (Encinitas), 230
Zel's Del Mar, 223
Zenbu, 26, 120, 140–141
Zenbu Lounge, 141